A VOLUME IN THE SERIES

Culture, Politics, and the Cold War

EDITED BY

Christian G. Appy and Edwin A. Martini

OTHER TITLES IN THE SERIES

KENT STATE

KENT STATE

DEATH AND DISSENT IN THE LONG SIXTIES

THOMAS M. GRACE

University of Massachusetts Press

AMHERST AND BOSTON

Printed in the United States of America

ISBN 978-1-62534-111-2 (paper); 110-5 (hardcover)

Designed by Dennis Anderson
Set in Adobe Garamond Pro by House of Equations, Inc.
Printed and bound by Sheridan Books, Inc.

Library of Congress Cataloging-in-Publication Data

Names: Grace, Thomas M , 1950– author.
Title: Kent State : death and dissent in the long sixties / Thomas M. Grace.
Description: Amherst : University of Massachusetts Press, [2016] |
Includes bibliographical references and index.
Identifiers: LCCN 2015040303 | ISBN 9781625341112 (pbk. : alk. paper) |
ISBN 9781625341105 (hardcover : alk. paper)
Subjects: LCSH: Kent State Shootings, Kent, Ohio, 1970. |
Kent State University—History.
Classification: LCC LD4191.072 G7 2016 | DDC 378.771/37—dc23
LC record available at http://lccn.loc.gov/2015040303

British Library Cataloguing-in-Publication Data
A catalogue record for this book is available from the British Library.

In memory of

PFC Donald Angerman, USMC
June 21, 1947–April 27, 1968

Mike Brock, the bravest person I have known
February 14, 1951–November 5, 2001

Thomas V. Grace, who "bled in anguish for the wrongs of the poor"
July 24, 1924–August 29, 2011

Contents

KENT STATE

PROLOGUE

May 4, 1970

IN THE spring of 1970 I was a third-quarter sophomore at Kent State University, majoring in history and political science. During the previous two years I had become increasingly involved in the antiwar movement and had attended rallies sponsored by the SDS, participated in organized demonstrations in nearby Cleveland, and marched against the war in Washington, DC. I also joined in the spontaneous protests that erupted on campus in the wake of the US invasion of Cambodia on April 30. Yet for all my political activism, I was still a conscientious student. Thus, on Sunday evening, May 3, a day after the Ohio National Guard rumbled into Kent on orders from the state's governor, James Rhodes, while some of my roommates confronted the soldiers on campus and as military helicopters hovered above, I sat with a friend in my apartment studying for a history test scheduled for the following morning.

There were subjects I struggled with in college, but history was not one of them. On Monday, May 4, I walked to class, arriving early for a 10 o'clock exam. Before handing out the questions and blue books, the professor invited any student who had had difficulty preparing for the exam to take it another time. I elected to stay.

The test went smoothly. My next class—political science—met in the same spacious room. With National Guardsmen stationed just outside the building, the professor had a made-to-order subject to discuss. As was customary at Kent, many students had left campus for the weekend and missed the three days of turmoil that followed President Nixon's announcement of the Cambodian invasion: the window-breaking in downtown Kent on Friday, the ensuing occupation of the campus and town by over one thousand guardsmen, the mass protest that culminated in the burning of the ROTC headquarters on Saturday night, and the failed sit-in of a city street that ended with students suffering bayonet wounds inflicted by uniformed troops.

At the close of the period, a classmate I recognized from the Student Mobilization Committee stood and announced a noon rally on the Commons, an arena-like expanse in the center of campus, only a short walk from my class. I decided there was no harm in heading over to see what was going on. When I arrived, the tension was palpable. To my left, in the distance, I could see a large contingent of guardsmen standing in a battle line in front of the burned-out ROTC building. This marked the third time in recent days that I had seen sizable numbers of troops and, as before, I stayed clear of them. I later learned that many students had fraternized with guardsmen over the weekend.

To my right, substantial numbers of students—far more than had been in the same location for the initial rally three days earlier—gathered in ever-larger groups. Black flags stood out. Drawing closer, I realized they were held aloft by two of my roommates, Alan Canfora and Jim Riggs. Soon the air filled with loud, angry chants directed at guardsmen a hundred yards away: "One, two, three, four, we don't want your fucking war!" and "Pigs off campus!" A photograph taken at the time shows me chanting along with the rest, raising my right fist for emphasis. Though fervently opposed to the war and outraged by the presence of the National Guard on campus, that was as demonstrative as I sought to be that day. Too many cameras, too much daylight, and above all too many armed troops.

From my low vantage point at the base of a hill that rose steeply behind us, I could see thousands of students surrounding the natural amphitheater that bordered two sides of the Commons. Even though the guardsmen were more than a hundred yards away, I could see that they were focusing on the loudest, flag-waving students grouped near the Victory Bell casement where I stood. Around noon, a campus policeman riding shotgun in a National Guard jeep ordered the crowd through a bullhorn to disperse. "All you bystanders and innocent people," he commanded, "leave this area immediately and go to your homes for your own safety." But his words only whipped the crowd into further frenzy. We felt that this was our campus, that we were doing nothing wrong, and that he had no right to order us to leave.

Soon the jeep returned to the National Guard lines on the other side of the Commons in front of the charred ruins of the ROTC building. Within minutes approximately a hundred guardsmen arrayed in a battle line leveled their bayonets and started to advance in our direction, firing tear gas as they approached. Though not as noxious as the tear gas I had experienced in Washington, DC, the previous fall, its effects were strong enough to drive me and other protestors away from the Commons. Unlike some others, I knew what to do. Cover your nose and mouth with a handkerchief. Don't wipe your eyes, and wash them out as soon as possible. A photo taken by a *Daily Kent Stater* photographer shows me yelling to a fellow student. I was urging her not to rub her eyes.

Losing track of my roommates and retreating around the northeast side of Taylor Hall, I saw students gasping on a patch of lawn that fronted Prentice Hall, a women's dormitory. From inside, students had cranked open the frosted windows of the lavatories and were passing out moistened paper towels so people could relieve their eyes from the effects of the tear gas. I gladly took some, cleansing my eyes and then assisting others who seemed to have been gassed more severely.

I was unaware that a group of National Guardsmen—Company C of the 145th Infantry—had followed the path of our retreat, though they had refrained from pursuing us all the way to Prentice Hall. A second, larger contingent of guardsmen had swept over and past the brow on the other side of Taylor Hall and downhill to a practice football field that lay just beyond. There on the field stood at least seventy guardsmen, isolated from the other troops, milling around, seemingly uncertain what to do next. With Memorial Gym on one side of the practice field, a chain-link fence on another, and irregular lines of students to their front and in a parking lot separating them from Prentice Hall, these two units of guardsmen were hemmed in by people or obstacles in every direction.

I cautiously moved a little closer, to the grassy area in front of Taylor Hall, and watched. Above me, scores of students had gathered near or behind a railing in front of Taylor and were looking down at the troops on the practice field below. To my left and rear, some students in the parking lot were throwing rocks at the National Guard, and some of the guardsmen were picking up the rocks and throwing them back at the students. I didn't see any troops hit by rocks, which seemed to fall short of their intended targets. At one point six or seven guardsmen knelt and assumed firing positions, ominously fixing their weapons on the students in the parking lot. I saw Alan Canfora, alone on the edge of the practice field, defiantly waving his black flag at the troops. I considered going down the incline to urge him to leave. Instead, I stayed with the group closer to Taylor Hall, where I felt more secure.

The impasse on the practice field ended when the guardsmen decided to vacate their exposed position. They reformed their lines and proceeded back toward the top of the hill at the far corner of Taylor Hall where the Pagoda, an umbrella-like structure of wood and concrete, stands. The maneuver took them closer to where I was positioned, on the lower slope of the hill up from the western edge of the parking lot. As the guardsmen retreated, I thought of the biblical parting of the Red Sea. The students moved to one side or the other to let the guardsmen and their bayonets pass.

Throughout the midday struggle, the noise, if not deafening, was extremely loud and raucous. It only seemed to increase as guardsmen reached the high point of the incline that would take them beyond Taylor Hall. I remember yelling, adding my voice to hundreds of others, shouting at a distance of any-where from 225 to 200 feet away.

When the guardsmen reached the summit they turned in unison in the direc-tion of the parking lot—a full 130 degrees, according to later estimates. Then one or two cracks of unmistakable rifle fire. Instinct took over. I turned to run. A step or two later I was on the ground, struck by what felt like a body blow. A bullet had entered my left heel and literally knocked me off my feet. I raised myself to a sitting position to examine my lower leg and I heard someone yell-ing, "Stay down! Stay down! It's buckshot!" I looked up, and about twenty feet away from me, behind a tree, was my roommate Alan Canfora.

His warning may have saved my life, though it soon became apparent that it wasn't buckshot or birdshot. I slumped back to the ground to shield as much of my body as possible. I was caught in the open without cover, and it seemed like the bullets were going by within inches of my head. I can recall seeing people behind me, farther down the hill in the parking lot, dropping. It was impos-sible to tell whether they were being felled by bullets or diving for cover. The worst part was having no means of protection, as if we were soldiers ourselves, trapped in a killing zone, wishing we could disappear into the ground beneath us. I remember thinking *When is this going to stop?*

From Syracuse to Kent

I first heard about Kent State University during summer of 1967, while working in my hometown of Syracuse, New York. I became acquainted with a recent Kent graduate whose description of the school made it sound very appealing, at least appealing enough to prompt me to send away for a catalog. As the oldest child of parents whose college degrees had lifted them a rung or two up the American social ladder, I had always assumed I would follow their example. At my father's insistence, I had applied to a Catholic college in Maryland. But I had little interest in spending another four years at an all-male school with the same number of students as the Catholic high school I attended. All three of the other schools I was considering were coeducational state universities. Kent was the closest, six hours west on the interstate. In the end, it got the nod.

Even though my parents held nominally white-collar jobs—my father was a social worker for the Veteran's Administration and later an administrator for a state agency, my mother a school nurse—we seemed working-class, like the rest of the people in our neighborhood. Just about everybody was Catholic and mostly Italian American, with the remainder of German, Irish, or eastern European descent. Politically, both my fourth-generation Irish American father and my Slovak American mother had come from New Deal Democratic fami-lies, although my mother had a brief period of apostasy during the Eisenhower years. The prospect of a Catholic president in 1960 forever ended her attraction to the GOP.

Life during the Depression on Syracuse's south side had been grim for my father; less so for my mother in Binghamton—a city eighty miles south—where a legacy of Endicott Johnson and IBM company-style paternalism cushioned some of the worst economic scarcity. Certainly conditions in Binghamton were better than in Scranton, Pennsylvania, where my mother's much older siblings had been raised and taught to walk the tracks and return home with metal pails full of black lumps that had fallen from passing coal cars.

Foreign policy seemed to matter little to my father, whose family loyalties to the Democrats extended back to the preceding century. Knowledge that his disabled father—a onetime miner and later railroad worker—could collect Social Security after 1940, that his older brothers had worked in Roosevelt's National Youth Agency and the CCC, and that his family qualified for relief and surplus food, put his political devotion on par with his religious one. With regard to civil rights, he had worked with African Americans on the railroad while attending college and saw them as sharing common, GOP-supported, big-business adversaries. They were all on the same side.

The occupation of Czechoslovakia by the Soviet Union caused Cold War issues to loom larger for my mother. Anticommunism was reinforced by relatives I often visited in Binghamton as well as by some teachers at my high school, where David Miller, who in 1965 became the first person in the country to burn his draft card, had also been a student. Those of my teachers who discussed Miller's action encouraged our disapproval. As far as I could determine, the Democratic Party, with an assist from the church, protected us from all enemies and demons, domestic and foreign.

Shortly after arriving in Ohio to begin college, I sensed that the state, or at least Portage County, where the city of Kent is located, had more Republicans than what I had been accustomed to in New York. I found some comfort in discovering that there was a sizable contingent of out-of-staters on campus. My roommate during summer orientation roommate was from Buffalo, and another, during the fall quarter, from Rochester. We were among the better than 15 percent of students enrolled at Kent from outside Ohio, chiefly western Pennsylvania and New York, along with many from New Jersey.

My inherited New Deal politics seemed under siege when I started college in mid-September 1968. Attending a meeting of the Students for a Democratic Society in late September did little to clarify New Left politics, which seemed to me rather opaque. I had a much better impression of SDS after witnessing first-hand their anti-Nixon zeal when hundreds of its members confronted the GOP candidate at an October campaign appearance in Akron. Shifting to SDS's antiwar stance proved more difficult. The gradual transition was facilitated by

Hubert Humphrey's defeat. Once it became an inherited Republican war, particularly a Nixon war, moving left from the partisan perspective of the Young Democrats, with whom I had been associated that fall, became easier for an unreflective freshman to manage. I retained my allegiance to the principles of domestic New Deal liberalism but soon lost my faith that the United States acted as a force for good in its foreign policy. My critique of the Vietnam War and US imperialism developed from a wide variety of experiences shared with classmates. I engaged in hothouse dorm-room debates, participated in countless meetings and protests, witnessed and received serious threats and attacks from administrators, police, and National Guardsmen, and immersed myself in life-changing books, manifestos, and music.

Participant to Observer

This book reconstructs the complex social and political milieu in which home-grown dissent at Kent State developed. Although the final chapter concerns the subject of memory—now an established concern of the historical craft—the story of the university's student movement is told here by way of a traditional chronological narrative that begins with a 1958 campaign waged by Ohio labor against a right-to-work amendment and ends with the 1973 Paris Peace accords that produced a temporary armistice in Vietnam.

When I first envisioned this book, my thought was to begin the account in 1965. But as I dug deeper into the story, it became clear that I would need to go back further in time to elucidate both the roots of Vietnam-era dissent and the underlying conservatism of the state and region. While fundamentally conservative, neither Ohio nor the city of Kent has exhibited a one-dimensional political character. From time to time, class, racial, and social tensions have erupted and challenged the conservative status quo. My aim is to help readers understand Kent's student movement in that larger historical and political context.

My use of the term "student movement" is also deliberate, for the activist story told here of Kent State is not simply about growing opposition to the Vietnam War but also includes the history of labor and civil rights activism, how the Old Left turned into the New Left, and the rise of Black Power. None can be fully understood apart from the other. Put another way, it is a bottom-up history of dissident political activity over fifteen years, a period many historians now refer to as the "long Sixties." Those who shaped Kent's long Sixties were themselves formed by a variety of familial influences: unionism and a loyalty to New Deal politics, economic populism, Catholic social gospel, Christian existentialism, secular Jewish radicalism, the Old Left, a commitment to racial equality, and Cold War liberalism. Whatever their personal values or traditions, Kent's activists questioned the limits of liberalism and, in doing so, grew increasingly estranged from the dominant social and political order.

To date, no historian has undertaken the task of tracing the beginnings of Kent State's social movement, how and why it originated, expanded, and ultimately clashed with the military arm of state authority. Moreover, no account of the movement's important aftermath has been written, which has allowed otherwise observant historians and writers to breezily assume that Kent State's student movement died along with four young people on May 4.

In this study I stress a number of subthemes, the first being the importance of economic class background. Located almost in the geographic center of Ohio's Western Reserve—so called because Connecticut once claimed this area far to its west—Portage County was small-town and rural in the late 1950s. The larger area surrounding it, however, had by then become one of the most industrialized in the nation. One of Kent State's early presidents called it the "American Ruhr." By 1955–56, the university drew half its students from the area's industrial centers—Cleveland-Lorain, Akron-Barberton, Canton-Massillon-Alliance, and Youngstown-Warren; in the mid-1950s out-of-state students constituted only about 3 percent of Kent's students. Even as the region and nation began to deindustrialize, a third of Kent's students in the late 1960s continued to hail from these manufacturing urban areas, giving the university an increasingly working-class student population. My emphasis will be on those activists who came from urban areas, because such an approach reveals a measure of political continuity between the New Deal and baby boom generations and allows for an exploration of how a culture of unionism and enduring New Deal beliefs helped mold the embryonic politics of young people raised in blue-collar households. Class background often informs how people think and act as well as influencing and often defining their life choices and opportunities. Through the prism of economic class, Kent's activist students can be understood as political and cultural agents, rather than as victims or lawbreakers.[1]

I am not the first to follow the contour of economic class at Kent State. Ken Heineman has published a well-received comparative history of campus activism that addresses the social backgrounds of students. I have also benefited from a collection of essays about Kent—the town and university—skillfully edited by Scott Bills. What has yet to be undertaken is a detailed examination of the origins of Kent State's student movement and how such beginnings contributed to a certain staying power by the students in the challenging months and years following the fatal shootings. Thus this study adds another dimension to our understanding of the complicated political terrain of postwar America.[2]

Related to the incipient politicalization Kent's students received in blue-collar and middle-income homes is the proximity of the campus to Cleveland, thirty miles to the north. I will show how the labor, civil rights, peace, and antiwar struggles in Cleveland, and the presence of Old Left groups there, all served to influence the emergence of a movement on the Kent campus. Not only were students from Cleveland affected by political developments in their hometown, but many of the early speakers at campus meetings visited Kent from the city. Indeed, Kent's first left-wing group, the Young Socialist Alliance, was organized, in part, because of the sponsorship of the Socialist Workers Party and the proximity of a party branch in Cleveland.

These factors alone, however, do not explain why a more vibrant movement expanded at Kent than, say, in Akron or Youngstown. Here, Kent's geographic position and the development of the nation's interstate highway system also affected the growth of the campus movement, especially after 1965, when out-of-state students began to make up an increasing percentage of the student body. Kent had a void to fill when it began to lose students to universities in Cleveland, Akron, and Youngstown that had been added to the state system. The shortfall was increasingly made up by out-of-staters, some of whom added even more of a metropolitan dimension to the ranks of Kent's student activists. As one example of this trend, even though most of the leading activists profiled here were native Ohioans, two of the four students killed on May 4 were from out of the state. By 1970, nearly one of every five Kent students came from states other than Ohio.[3]

Throughout, I have made an effort to chronicle *all* of those—African American and white—who participated in Kent State's student movement. During certain periods, African American and white students went their own ways politically. As the story of sixties activism is usually told, the role of African American students is treated separately or simply ignored. This of course is not how history was experienced. During important periods at Kent, race was the leading factor dominating campus dissent: demonstrations demanding integration or the recognition of the Congress of Racial Equality, or protesting against the Oakland police. While racial suspicion between members of Kent's Black United Students and white radicals was real enough, never was it static. Their story then is told together, rather than discretely.

Still another purpose of this study is to undo the belief that Kent State was an activist backwater before 1970. Even after the passage of decades and numerous books on the shootings, this view of Kent State persists. At the thirtieth anniversary of the shootings, it remained possible for otherwise well-informed writers like David Halberstam to declare that Kent was "in a relatively conservative part of the heartland" and "among the least likely places to find a shrine commemorating civilian victims of a bad war," on a campus "so distanced physically and emotionally from the center of the antiwar movement."[4]

Writers, journalists, and even some of the nation's leading historians regarded the campus in 1970 as though its students were no more than a generation removed from the bucolic imagery of a Grant Wood painting. The assumption was that activism began on the two coasts and by 1970 had spread inward to Middle America. The reality was rather different. Focusing on industrial northeast Ohio, where most of the students originated, and small-town Kent and rural Portage County, where they went to school, I examine the ways in which class and racial tensions and the concomitant urban/small-town strains influenced the growth and development of the campus struggle.

Most of what has been written about Kent State concerns the most infamous date in the school's hundred-year history. Only in the aftermath of the May 4 killings did pre-1970 activism at the university receive much national attention. With most events on the Kent campus failing to capture headlines outside Ohio until 1968, it is understandable that so little of the history and memory of earlier protest would be remembered. Even when the fatal shootings brought the campus unwanted national prominence, Kent State's prior activism remained largely overlooked and the killings became simply one more, albeit enduring, flashpoint of a turbulent time.

Still, the question remains: Why has Kent's activist history before 1970 been overlooked? Some of it no doubt has to do with the university's geographical location. The Midwest is a region, one writer noted, that too readily "slips from view." Ohio, at its gateway, is not New York, Los Angeles, or Chicago. For many, it is part of an indistinct area of the country often referred to as the Heartland. The second and third factors, Kent State's educational rank in the 1960s and the social and economic status of its students, are related, though not identical. Despite achieving an enrollment of about twenty thousand by the end of the 1960s, Kent State had grown so rapidly during the decade that it had yet to establish much of an identity on the nation's educational radar screen. Unlike Big Ten schools, it enjoyed little scholastic or athletic reputation, making it easy to look past the university. Until 1970, Kent's out-of-state students often took pains to explain to people back home that they went to college at Kent State, not the similar-sounding Penn State. Under such circumstances, the modest level of dissent at the school was hardly a good scoop for national reporters searching for a protest story line.[5]

Finally, there was the issue of the class character of the student body. Whether or not Kent State undergraduates deserved being dismissed as the "insurance salesmen of tomorrow," as one faculty member put it, many of the working-class students were the first in their families to enter college. As one labor historian rightly argues, the pervasive use of the three-class schema—upper, middle, and lower—tends to make blue-collar Americans, be they students or wage earners, "nearly invisible." The city of Kent and Portage County represented something of a small-town and rural oasis, but the university drew large numbers of working-class students from nearby industrial cities.[6]

Hence a series of different but related factors made Kent State, before 1970, largely a site unseen. Until cast into the national limelight, the small Ohio city was in a forgettable midwestern place, its university relegated an unremarkable spot in academia and its students consigned to a veiled position in America's class structure. Events on May 4, 1970, changed some of that and brought the university historic notice as a protest symbol. Yet subsequent books about the killings did little to uncover the existence of an earlier movement for social change that had emerged slowly and, to some, even imperceptibly.

Just as the events of May 4 eclipsed much of the vital prelude at Kent State, what followed on the campus has been not so much overlooked as ignored. "The Movement that the young radicals had worked so hard to build fell apart in the wake of the killings at Kent State," one leading historian has written. Another was equally firm: "The collective judgment of ex-activists, journalists, government officials, and historians has been remarkably consistent: the deaths at Kent State marked the end of the mass youth protest." Such opinions, widely shared, are not borne out by the evidence I present in chapters 13 and 14.[7]

THIS CHRONICLE draws on newspaper accounts, oral interviews, archival evidence, unpublished memoirs, and secondary sources, and it is organized into a linear narrative focusing on the role of student protest in the small city of Kent. The conservative interests that dominated the city and the political machinery of Portage County also controlled Kent State University. As the class character of the university's undergraduate population began to change after World War II, and when, in the late 1950s, the small number of African American students reached a critical mass, a movement started to take shape that challenged Kent's small-town values and way of life. The movement grew slowly in the inhospitable milieu of Cold War–era Kent, but a small nucleus of activists persisted in their efforts to fashion a culture of opposition.

An appendix, "After the War—The Fates of Kent's Activist Generation," follows the main text. It is designed with a twofold purpose: in a crowded narrative, the reader may find it a useful way to keep track of the people appearing in the account; and there may well be some interest in learning what these student activists, who helped bend the arc of justice, did with the remainder of their lives.

Although I do not use the first person in the narrative, where necessary or when useful to the chronicle, readers will find some firsthand observations in the endnotes or, in some of the later chapters, a number of sidebars. Years after I was wounded in May 1970, I told a reporter interviewing me that I had gone to Kent State to study history, not to be part of it. Thus a final word is in order on objectivity in historical writing. Doing a history on an experience in which the author figures should give one some pause, as indeed it did for me. Yet I soon discovered that my "insider" credentials gave me access to people who would have not spoken with another historian or writer. What is more, in writing about the campus movement during and after 1968, experience told me where to look for the story. Certainly, as Peter Novick has argued, there is no bias-free history. Good history, however, is fair-minded and faithful to the factual record. Readers will judge whether that goal has been attained.[8]

CHAPTER 1

The Working Class Goes to College

WHEN EIGHTEEN-YEAR-OLD Akron, Ohio, native Carl Oglesby set foot on the grounds of Kent State University in the fall of 1953, he stepped onto a campus that had changed a lot in recent years. Founded in 1910 as an institution for training public school teachers, the college, once known as Kent State Normal School, had evolved over the past four decades into a university offering a full range of undergraduate and graduate programs in the arts and sciences. By midcentury, in the wake of World War II, the student population had grown to 4,800. Seventy percent of the students were veterans taking advantage of benefits offered under the Servicemen's Readjustment Act, better known as the GI Bill. Enrollment dipped in the early 1950s, as the influx of vets subsided and draft calls for the Korean War spiked. But the growth of Kent State soon resumed, fueled by the demands of an increasingly complex postwar society for highly skilled and better educated workers. Across the thousand-acre campus, new buildings sprang up and old ones were adapted to new uses to accommodate the school's expansion. During Oglesby's freshman year, the largest dormitory to date was constructed, while the former student union, a reassembled military barracks, became home to the Reserve Officers' Training Corps (ROTC) program.[1]

Although not a veteran, Oglesby was part of an ongoing wave of working-class college students who would contribute to the transformation of the nation's system of higher education and challenge its Cold War political culture. In time, Oglesby would go on to become both president of the Students for a Democratic Society (SDS) and a major figure in the New Left, but in the early 1950s his politics were still rooted in the mainstream of the unionized American working class. He embraced his mother's progressive attitudes on issues of race and his father's mistrust of Akron's rubber company bosses, counted the liberal anticommunist senator Hubert Humphrey among his heroes, and won a high school competition sponsored by the National Forensic League for a speech, "Peace or Freedom," that argued for a more confrontational approach to the Soviet Union.[2]

At Kent, Oglesby's political views and cultural values began to evolve in a new direction, one that remained faithful to his roots but was decidedly non-conformist, as was reflected in his interest in jazz, literature and poetry, and especially theater. His friends (among them his future wife, Cleveland native Beth Rimanoczy) playfully dubbed themselves the Macedonians, a reference to the ancient enemies of Greece, because they opposed the racially discriminatory policies of the Greek fraternities and sororities. These incipient radicals, whose political activities were barely visible, included veterans—and fellow Ohioans—Don Thomson from Cleveland, William Thomas Metts from Youngstown, Alex Fraser from Geneva near the Lake Erie shore, and Paul Zimmer, a poet from Canton. There were African Americans in the circle as well, such as Don Henderson from Youngstown, and Ed Gray, a native of Newport, Rhode Island. Along with Oglesby's fellow Akronite Gabriel Kolko, who tried and failed to organize a chapter of the Student League for Industrial Democracy (the predecessor of SDS), these undergraduates were part of the generation born before the war and not far removed from the working-class struggles of the 1930s that swept Ohio's industrial heartland cities and even convulsed the small city of Kent.[3]

Scholars of 1960s America know the names of SDS leaders like Oglesby and New Left historians like Kolko, yet most of those who formed Kent's activist cohort from 1958 to 1973 were relatively anonymous and decidedly ordinary. What distinguished them was a resolve to face the issues of their time: old issues of class and power, unresolved issues of racial segregation, and the new concerns generated by the crosscurrents of the Cold War.

Some of the students who came to Kent during this period carried with them family legacies of strikes and sit-downs, as well as participation in Old Left parties and hard-fought political campaigns. A much larger number retained less stirring, but no less important, working-class allegiances and identities. By the mid-1950s, close to 95 percent of Kent State's students came from the northeast Ohio counties of Cuyahoga, Summit, Stark, Trumbull, and Mahoning, all areas with sizable urban centers dominated by the manufacture of steel, rubber, chemicals, or automobiles: Cleveland, Akron, Youngstown, Canton, Lorain, Warren, Massillon, Barberton, and Alliance. Nearly 57 percent came from the region's larger industrial cities, chiefly Cleveland, Akron, and Canton. The urban, working-class backgrounds of these students set them apart socially as well as ethnically, religiously and, increasingly, racially from the small-town and rural culture of Kent and Portage County. Their presence also reinforced in microcosm the sharp political divide between the New Deal Democrats who ruled Ohio's industrial cities and the conservative Republicans who dominated much of the rest of the state.[4]

Battling Right-to-Work

Although a much-ballyhooed entente between capital and labor helped forge an ideology of "consensus" during the early years of the Cold War, deep-seated class antagonisms resurfaced with the onset of a nationwide recession in 1957. A year later, as unemployment spiked to the highest levels in seventeen years, Ohio's workers were confronted with an additional test in the form of a so-called right-to-work amendment to the state constitution. Grounded in a provision of the Taft-Hartley Act of 1947, which had gutted national labor law by ceding jurisdiction over union security clauses to the states, the amendment would prohibit agreements between workers and management that made union membership a condition of employment. Supporters of the amendment termed this business-friendly section of the Taft-Hartley law a guarantee of the "right to work" without being compelled to join a labor union.[5]

Encouraged by the success of a similar measure in neighboring Indiana the previous year, Ohio businessmen saw a golden opportunity in 1958 to bring a right-to-work law to their own state. Although the man most responsible for enacting the original federal law, Ohio senator Robert A. Taft, had died in July 1953, his long-standing opposition to organized labor continued to influence state politics. Not only did a group called Ohioans for Right-to-Work receive the commitment of Republican governor William O'Neill, but they drew added support from conservative Democrats, such as Frank Lausche, a former governor then serving as a US senator, who termed the right to work "sacred." Newspapers large and small backed passage of the amendment; the *Cleveland Plain Dealer* declared, "If you believe every Ohio worker . . . should not be forced to join or remain a member of any union against his will, vote 'Yes' on Issue No. 2." Robert C. Dix, publisher of Portage County's *Record-Courier,* agreed, calling it "a check (which we badly need) . . . on the absolute power of some labor leaders."[6]

Confronted by widespread support for the amendment and believing their very survival to be at sake, Ohio unionists mounted a major counteroffensive. In the heavily industrialized northeast quadrant of the state, the campaign against the amendment proved an easy sell, despite a heavily financed pro-business campaign on behalf of the measure. Larry Lamovsky, then a young Cleveland Heights resident and later a supporter of SDS at Kent State in the late 1960s, remembered watching the ads on television and thinking that "it was unfair that people who didn't want to join a union were being forced to join." His father, who had worked at a Fisher Body plant during World War II, "straightened me out pretty quick," he recalled, explaining how the term "right to work" was misleading and that "the only way unions could do their job was to have 100 percent of the workers belong and have the strength of all the workers behind them." The same argument was heard in most blue-collar households and many middle-class homes as well. Rubber workers Rocco Modugno and his wife, Irma, whose son Vince was to become a leader in the Kent Committee to End the War in Vietnam as well as SDS, both vocally opposed the initiative, drawing their experiences as shop floor organizers and memories of family participation in a sit-down strike at the Goodrich Tire plant during the Akron Rubber Strike in 1936. James Dyer, a former miner who had gone to jail in the early 1950s for defying an injunction to end a United Mine Workers strike, and whose son David later became a Democratic Party activist at Kent State, put an anti-right-to-work sticker on his car to ensure that his coal-country neighbors knew his position. Albert Canfora, a United Auto Workers vice president in Akron, whose children Alan and Roseann both became leading antiwar activists at Kent State, drove a sound truck through the streets of his Barberton, Ohio, hometown to turn out the vote against the anti-union measure.[7]

Debating Right-to-Work on Campus

At Kent State, the right-to-work campaign ended a decade-long dearth of public political activity. By 1958 enrollment had reached 6,700, spurred in part by the depressed job market, and political sentiment among the students was divided. One Akron-area student argued in the pages of the campus newspaper, the *Daily Kent Stater,* that ratification of the ballot issue would "put an end to collective bargaining as we know it today." Another from the steel city of Lorain argued on behalf of the union position in a campus debate a week before the vote. Yet others agreed with Governor O'Neill, who publicly declared that "the real issue" of the campaign was "Shall the corrupt labor bosses be permitted to take over Ohio?" Supporters on campus complained that opponents of the measure were taking direction from their unionist fathers and echoing the same pro-labor positions "we've been hearing day after day on the radio." They weren't altogether wrong. Millions of Ohioans heard and heeded labor's message on the radio, studied it in the few newspaper editorials that were sympathetic to their cause, listened to it in union halls, or read it in flyers like those passed out in Cleveland, where members of the Young Socialist Alliance assisted with voter mobilization. "There were union people giving out literature at just about every polling place. People greeted each other as 'brother' and 'sister,'" a hopeful young socialist recalled.[8]

Albert Canfora was jubilant when the November 1958 totals came in, remembering it years later as "the biggest battle since the thirties." He saw the vote as a multiple victory, "for not only did we beat the issue more than 2 to 1, we also elected a Democratic governor, [Michael] DiSalle—and the senator [Stephen M. Young] too." The outpouring of unionists and African Americans not only crushed the amendment by nearly a million votes out of some three million cast, but also swept Governor O'Neill and Republican senator John Bricker from office. Like Canfora, DiSalle was the son of a union member and the child of Italian immigrants. Raised in Toledo, he became mayor of that city and later headed the Office of Price Stabilization during President Truman's administration. He had lost a number of earlier bids for office, including an ill-timed run for governor in the Republican landslide of 1956. DiSalle's opposition to the right-to-work amendment finally made the difference in securing his election to statewide office. The sixty-nine-year-old Young, who had battled conservative Martin Davey Sr., a former mayor of Kent, for the Democratic gubernatorial nomination in 1936, also won a stunning victory over Bricker, a fixture in Ohio politics since 1938. One political reporter described Young's win as being "in line with the leftward drift of his party." The defeated O'Neill had warned that DiSalle and Young were "obligated" to the powerful labor leader Walter Reuther and aimed "to build [Ohio] in the image of Michigan where the labor bosses dominate the state."9

The 1958 vote heralded the promise of a social breakthrough in a state where traditionalists had held a grip on power for over half a century. DiSalle's administration would introduce a series of legislative changes benefiting education, racial minorities, and the aged, as well as labor. While Ohio, like other states, had benefited from national New Deal legislation, the fight against the right-to-work amendment installed a state government willing to defend labor and allowed union members to maintain and improve their standard of living, which enabled many blue-collar parents to afford college tuition for their children. The battle also underscored a point once made about Walter Reuther's beliefs that social boundaries could be extended if unions tied "civil rights . . . to the fortunes of the labor movement."10

While they could not have known it then, fathers such as James Dyer and Albert Canfora and mothers like Alma Oglesby and Irma Modugno were serving as political models whom their children would both consciously imitate and unconsciously follow as activists at Kent State. "Just as the twig is bent, the tree's inclin'd" observed Alexander Pope long ago. Sometimes the progeny of these working-class parents would be inclined in political and, more often, cultural directions that their parents neither approved nor comprehended. Even so, class loyalties remained a part of the makeup of Kent's budding activists. These working-class parents who had helped defend Ohio's unions and bring to office a New Deal–style governor were, in a way, responsible for spawning the Sixties as well, with their offspring, in the years to come, confronting the persistence of conservative strains: McCarthyism, racial inequality, and third-world military intervention.

A Regroupment of the Left

The defeat of the right-to-work amendment energized unionists, New Deal Democrats, African Americans, and committed leftists. During the anti-amendment campaign, a pair of such leftists, Richard and Jean Tussey, also worked to organize a "National Conference of American Socialists" to be held in Cleveland. Veteran Cleveland radicals associated with the Socialist Workers Party's paper and causes, the couple aimed to revive the local fortunes of America's left. Buoyed by the campaign against the amendment, the Trotskyist Socialist Workers Party and independent socialists began publicizing the late November conference in October 1958. Although the Socialist Workers disdained the Democratic Party, they did see in the fall elections the promise of "new opportunities for promoting socialist unity and revitalization."[11]

The conference drew one hundred leftists, with the Socialist Workers Party represented by the Tusseys, Jerry Gordon from Cleveland, who later headed the National Peace Action Coalition, and Sam Pollock, of the Meat Cutters union in Cleveland and a veteran of the 1934 Toledo Auto-Lite strike. Ideological rivals from the Communist Party attended, as did independently minded radicals from the *National Guardian* and labor leader Jack Spiegel. Like Gordon, Spiegel would play a prominent role in the movement against the Vietnam War, as the codirector of the Chicago Peace Union. Members of Norman Thomas's Socialist Party also participated.[12]

Although falling well short of a desired left-wing "regroupment," the conference did succeed in making socialists visible again in Cold War America. Saul Landau, the future filmmaker and journalist, was one of a dozen student registrants; he called for "effective opposition to the dynamic ideology of the American ruling class." Gordon, who later would politically counsel student activists at Kent State, addressed the importance of holding more "forums, [and pursuing] cultural activity creating a new democratic image of what socialists stand for which will . . . attract youth." Within a few years, the first of many Kent political activists would begin confronting the ills they perceived in Cold War America.[13]

Class, Race, and Hierarchy in Small-Town Kent

By the time Kent State approached its semicentennial in 1960, the town of Kent had grown into a small city of about seventeen thousand people. Settled in the early 1800s by Congregationalist migrants from Connecticut, the town, initially known as Franklin Mills, steadily grew as westward expansion and industrialization brought German American migrants from Pennsylvania, Irish canal workers, southern European immigrants, and African American railroad workers to northeast Ohio. In the early decades of the twentieth century, after the founding of Kent State Normal, it began to take on an additional personality as a college town. In 1936, in the midst of the Great Depression, a violent confrontation between strikers and strikebreakers convulsed the town, but afterward city fathers moved quickly to restore the image of Kent as a bastion of tidy provincial order rather than labor-inspired chaos. At the center of much of the labor strife was Ohio governor Martin L. Davey Sr., scion of Kent's most prominent family. In addition to owning the prosperous Davey Tree Company, the Daveys had acquired the local newspaper, the *Courier,* from the heirs of the Kent family for whom the town had been renamed. They later bought the rival *Tribune* and merged the two papers in 1929 before selling them to another member of the local elite, Robert C. Dix.[14]

Governor Davey was one those conservative Ohio Democrats who embraced many core Republican principles, particularly in the realm of economic policy. When he died, in 1946, his son and namesake inherited his father's ideology as well as the family business. The younger Davey became president of Kent's largest company and guided it through a period of record growth. He also circulated the McCarthyite magazine *Counterattack* to those he believed would benefit from its insights. Launched by three former FBI agents, *Counterattack* promised to provide its readers with the "Facts to Combat Communism," stressing that the "way to treat Communists is to ostracize them." For a fee, the three former agents promised to investigate any employee a company thought suspect. Weeks after the outbreak of the Korean War in 1950, Martin Davey Jr. forwarded a complimentary subscription to Kent State's president, George Bowman. Well enough acquainted with Davey to address him by his boyhood nickname, "Brub," Bowman wrote to thank him, adding, "There is a great need for dissemination of facts about communism."[15]

Editors of the *Record-Courier,* the newly renamed local paper, were likewise vigilant about the dangers of communist subversion at the local university. Using his column "The Roasting Pan" to alert the paper's readers, Loris Troyer reported in March 1950 that an anonymous donor had attempted to present a subscription of *Soviet Russia Today* to Kent State's library. Not tempted by the offer, the librarian unsuccessfully sought the sponsor's identity and, along with Troyer, concluded that Soviet sympathizers were using literature to further "communistic activities." Nor was the problem at the university confined to magazines. Shortly before Troyer's column appeared, the paper reported that Senator McCarthy had accused Esther Brunauer, a State Department representative and speaker at a conference at Kent State in 1948, of being a communist sympathizer. Despite her vehement denials, Brunauer was dismissed from her government position. During Kent's Flag Day ceremonies a year earlier, an army general told a huge campus rally that "communism attains its ends by infiltration, threats, intimidation and disruption of [the] national economy." Kent's local elites, in common with the state's conservative leadership, found that anticommunism provided an opportunity to shape the future with the politics of the past. As one observer noted after the war, in states "that have many prosperous farms and a disproportionately large number of small towns—Ohio, Indiana, and Wisconsin," GOP conservatism became "more of an agricultural and small-town faith, as it was in the beginning."[16]

John Carson, a local pharmacist who would serve as Kent's mayor in the mid- to late 1960s, remembered the late 1950s and early '60s as a time of "tremendous growth . . . in the city and the university." Yet amid all the change Kent remained, according to Carson, a town riven by deep fissures of class, race, and ethnicity. A keen observer of social change who came into daily contact with a wide cross-section of residents, he saw "a segmented community" divided between the "old townies and the university," a "small industrial labor group," and "the bedroom community," which included both blue-collar and white-collar workers with out-of-town jobs. Of those who comprised the "labor group," many initially lived in the town's south end, a section called the flats. The area housed many Erie and B&O railroad workers who serviced train cars in the nearby roundhouse, along with others employed in the town's machine shops. One resident of the flats remembers this section of town as a place where his father operated a grocery that served fellow Italian Americans for over a quarter century. Back then, Albert Ciccone recalled, "the Italians went to the Italian store, the Germans went to the German stores, and that was it." Housing followed a similar pattern: "each [ethnic group] had their own [streets]." After serving in World War II, Ciccone inherited the corner store. With the moderate income from the store and the availability of a VA loan he could afford to marry and, by the late 1950s, buy a home in Kent's more middle-class West Side area.[17]

Kent's flats section was also home to a small number of African Americans that included the Brown family. Josh Brown, like Albert Ciccone, had served in the military. Yet unlike Ciccone, he found conditions distressingly similar to what he had known before his segregated service in World War II, as he tried and failed to land a position at a local factory. The incident that wounded Brown most deeply occurred at the university, where he worked as a custodian in the 1950s. He had learned about a swimming safety program being offered and, believing it would be open to all, Brown and his wife agreed that lessons would be valuable for their children. "My wife had called and they must have thought she was white," he remembered, "because they agreed to take [our] three children. Then they saw who she was, [and] they said 'We're not having a swimming program.' [Looking at a pool full of white children,] she said 'I see all the rest of them.' They said, 'Well, I'm sorry.'" This incident, coupled with problems he encountered securing employment and a mortgage from Kent's Home Savings and Loan Bank for a house in a white area, convinced Brown to work for racial change. "That's when I started fighting," he said. He joined an NAACP branch that had been in decline and soon became its president. Yet even with a revitalized organization and the support of some local whites, Brown and his allies were unable to make much headway against discriminatory practices that remained commonplace in Kent.[18]

Among the first to publicize the issue of racial discrimination were the students who produced the campus literary magazine, the *Kent Quarterly*. In 1957, its writers criticized the exclusionary policies of the Greek fraternities, the administration's tolerance of bigotry, and the more ubiquitous prejudice found in the town. One black student offered readers of the *Quarterly* an unflinching picture of problems all too familiar to Kent's African Americans, describing restaurant signs in town announcing "We reserve the right to refuse to serve Anyone." Kenneth Cooley also recounted an unsuccessful effort by one veteran, just home from Korea, to receive service in four different restaurants in Kent: "It was my first day in Kent, and I was ready to go home. I know now, as any Kent resident knows, the dirtiest, freight-yard tramp can wander into any eating establishment in Kent and will be served as long as he has money . . . to pay his bill. I was refused because my skin is black."[19]

The civil rights movement was still in its infancy and largely confined to the South, yet already students at Kent and other northern universities had begun questioning long-standing racial codes and mores. Carl Oglesby and his fellow Macedonians followed the Montgomery bus boycott in 1955 and the school integration crisis in Little Rock, Arkansas, two years later. Others at Kent took notice in February 1960 when four African American students staged the first "sit-in" at a segregated lunch counter in Greensboro, North Carolina. In mid-April 1960, the Kent Council on Human Affairs (CHA), organized in October 1959 and composed of a few faculty and nearly fifty black and white university students, along with a small number of Kent residents, secured support from KSU's Student Council for the southern sit-ins. John Sinnott, a student from New York State, who composed the solidarity statement adopted by the Student Council, charged that segregation ran "contrary to the ideals upon which this nation was founded." Led by a group of KSU students from neighboring urban areas like Cleveland, Akron, and East Liverpool, as well as western Pennsylvania, the CHA later that month defied threats of an injunction and conducted several sizeable sympathy pickets of Kent's Woolworth store. In the coming months, thousands of university students across the country imitated the tactics in Greensboro of nonviolent direct action and joined the struggle for racial equality, while at the same time launching a movement of their own.[20]

"Students in Kent Stage Bar Sit-In"

In Kent, as in Greensboro, the first direct-action protest against racial discrimination was aimed at an establishment that refused to serve African Americans. In the fall of 1960, the newly formed Council on Human Affairs decided to organize its own sit-in after one of its members, Clarence Rogers Jr., was unable to buy a drink at an off-campus bar. The incident had taken place during "Greek Week" the previous spring, when an interracial group of fraternity students that included Rogers had entered the Corner Bar on Main Street and ordered drinks, but only the white students had been served. Although no confrontation occurred at the time, when classes resumed after the summer break Rogers and the CHA decided to take action.[21]

Like most of the 140 or so African Americans enrolled at Kent in 1960, and unlike a growing number of white students, "Tirney" Rogers, as he was generally known, came from a comfortably middle-class family. His father had worked for the *Pittsburgh Courier,* a leading African American newspaper, before moving to Cleveland in the late 1950s to try to establish his own paper. Rogers's good friend and roommate, Paul Cheeks, also a member of the CHA, came from a similar social background; his mother was a Fisk College graduate and he was himself an Army veteran. Class status, of course, had not shielded either young man from the sting of racism; on the contrary, by bringing them into more frequent contact with whites it made them even more aware of the many forms racial bigotry could take. Cheeks's experience in the recently integrated American military had been particularly instructive in this respect, offering both an opportunity for personal advancement and a reminder of how little prevailing attitudes toward race had actually changed.[22]

At the beginning of the 1960 spring quarter, Rogers was named vice president and Lance Buhl, a white history and political science major from the Cleveland area, president of the CHA for the upcoming school year. A self-described "democratic liberal," Buhl had traveled to the University of Michigan during the spring to attend the "Human Rights in the North" conference in late April 1960, which served as his introduction to the national civil rights movement. There he and two other students from Kent State were among the 150 registrants who had listened to featured speakers such as Michael Harrington and former SLID (Student League for Industrial Democracy) organizer James Farmer and met members of the Student Nonviolent Coordinating Committee (SNCC), newly formed in the wake of the Greensboro sit-ins. Inspired by the commitment of these activists to the cause of racial justice, Buhl returned to Kent intent on following their example. In planning the sit-in at the Corner Bar, Buhl emphasized the need to adhere to the principles of nonviolent direct action. If attacked by anyone during the confrontation, CHA members, white or black, were not to strike back under any circumstances. "A lot of time was spent making sure that people understood that they couldn't get angry," Paul Cheeks recalled years later.[23]

On October 28, 1960, shortly before the presidential election and just two days after civil rights leader Martin Luther King Jr. had been freed from a Georgia jail, a determined if apprehensive group of eleven African American students entered Kent's Corner Bar intent on being served. Much of the decision-making impetus came from Buhl, who, Cheeks later observed, was somebody who got "this person to do this and that person to do that." Despite being new to campus and on the fringes of CHA, John McCann also played an instrumental role, as he would for the next five years at Kent. The son of a Cleveland-area skilled tradesman, McCann was an air force veteran who came to be known for his physical courage. He went ahead of the larger sit-in team to gauge the situation at the Corner Bar, and he found the popular nightspot beginning to fill with students. Around nine o'clock, Rogers, Cheeks, Billy Bass (later Cleveland's best known FM disk jockey), Odessa Penny, and seven other black students quietly entered and took seats (apparently procured in advance by McCann) at the bar. Most of the other patrons obtained drinks within minutes. Not so the African American students, whose efforts over the next hour to win attention of the bartenders were to no avail.[24]

The crowd of students who had gathered for a Friday night of fun seemed divided in their reaction to the sit-in. Some were quietly sympathetic to the protestors, with one remarking to a reporter on the scene how "ashamed [he was] that this should happen." But others voiced racial catcalls and taunts that created what Paul Cheeks remembered as a "scary" atmosphere that was enhanced by the female proprietor's icy hostility. The situation became so tense that Cheeks worried about keeping his pledge of nonviolence in the face of "being verbally abused." After an hour-long stalemate the proprietor called the police. Sergeant Roy Thompson entered with two city patrolmen to investigate reports of a "disturbance" in the bar. The arrival of the officers coincided with the addition of another bartender. Thompson instructed the proprietor to have the students served, then ordered Cheeks and the others to leave after finishing their drinks.[25]

On Saturday morning, area residents awoke to the newspaper headline "Students in Kent Stage Bar Sit-In Demonstration: No Violence Is Reported." The paper reported that "some Negroes [had] been refused service in public places" in town and conceded that this was "unfortunate." But the editors of the *Record-Courier* offered a more equivocal assessment of the incident. "Kent is a long way from having the prejudices of some areas," they wrote, "but we still have to go a little farther." Endorsing the notion of a natural self-separation of the races, the editors insisted that "people will always want to select their own groups for various reasons," while at the same time urging readers to "try to rule out any arbitrary selection because of pigmentation." Days later, in his "Along the Way" column, publisher Robert C. Dix sought to put an end to the affair by complimenting police at the scene for "suggest[ing] . . . that it would be a good idea to serve the group and then the trouble would be over."[26]

The "trouble" may have ended, but the issue of racial discrimination remained. Laying out the aims of the CHA, president Lance Buhl wrote that it was their intent to seek enforcement of state laws that had recently been strengthened by Governor DiSalle, and declared that the CHA "pledges itself to do whatever it can" to work toward the opening of public accommodations to all races. Cheeks summed up the sit-in: "We had gotten through it without injury or a breaking of our spirit. We felt then that we could do more." Still a tiny minority, African Americans in Kent had created an interracial alliance that had put on a public display of solidarity. The sit-in furthered political and personal relationships among the protestors and forged lasting bonds that served as a foundation for years of activism still ahead.[27]

Civil Rights Move North

The success of the Corner Bar sit-in emboldened activists at Kent. Weeks later, on the first anniversary of the Greensboro sit-ins, the Council on Human Affairs organized a discussion on campus devoted to the issue of civil rights. With the aid of Oscar Ritchie, Kent's first African American professor, they brought the Reverend James Lawson Jr., a thirty-three-year-old Nashville-based minister, to talk with students about the growing national movement. A member of the pacifist Fellowship of Reconciliation and a resident of Massillon, Ohio, Lawson had pioneered the philosophy of nonviolent direct action that the SNCC made its own. "Brutality," Lawson told Kent students, resulted from "white thugs" determined to maintain a system of racial supremacy and therefore had to be confronted with its opposite. "This problem cannot only be resolved in the South. It is nationwide and must be treated as thus," he declared. Although CHA members listened attentively to Lawson's words, only Daniel Thompson, a KSU student from Cleveland, would go to Nashville, where Lawson and others were training recruits for the Freedom Rides. Thompson served time in Mississippi's notorious Parchman Farm Prison and was later roughed up during a violence-filled week in Monroe, North Carolina, where he had gone to aid the black activists Robert F. Williams and Willie Mae Mallory, who soon thereafter were being sought on a false kidnapping charge. With the assistance of celebrated attorney William Kunstler, he eventually made his way back to Ohio, more determined than ever to carry on the fight for racial equality.[28]

After Lawson's visit, campus civil rights activists prepared for a new campaign against housing discrimination. Housing bias on campus and in town dated back to at least the 1930s, when black female students were quartered separately in what the local NAACP chapter derided as Jim Crow housing. Although by 1961 dorms were no longer segregated, mortgage redlining and widespread rental practices in Kent continued to confine minorities seeking off-campus accommodations to apartments several streets away from the campus. As the number of minority and international students attending Kent State grew, incidents of discrimination multiplied, even in apartments sanctioned by the university. Throughout February and March 1961, the CHA conducted an investigation of racial bias in university-approved housing and soon documented numerous instances of discrimination. In all but three of twenty-five cases, white landlords advertising housing vacancies turned away minority CHA members who approached them, while white activists speaking with the same proprietors were offered the available apartments. When the CHA went public with its findings, their charges of racial bias ignited a controversy that caught the university's president, George Bowman, off guard.[29]

Bowman had come to Kent State in 1944 and had presided over its rapid growth in the years following World War II. In addition to increases in student enrollment and the physical size of the main campus, he had overseen the establishment of the university's first regional campus in Canton in 1946. The following year he had appointed Oscar Ritchie as the first full-time African American faculty member of any university in Ohio. Yet if Bowman's politics could be considered liberal, it was a liberalism of the Cold War variety, in which principles of freedom and democracy were perpetually in tension with a commitment to consensus, order, and conformity. In this respect he was not unlike many American university administrators at the beginning of the 1960s: men (and they were almost always men) who found it difficult to reconcile their professed political beliefs with the policies they implemented and were obliged to enforce.[30]

The campus culture at Kent State, as at most other colleges in the early 1960s, reflected the nation's Cold War politics. Bowman in particular discouraged not only protests against administration policy but public controversy of any sort. University officials insisted on conventional dress for dormitory meals, and classes in "Clothing Appreciation" were offered to home economics majors. Freshmen wore "beanies" on their heads and carried the undergraduate handbook, which specified rules of conduct. Residence hall sentries guarded female dormitories and rigidly enforced curfews. Students receiving federal scholarship aid were expected to take loyalty oaths as a precaution against "anti-Ameri-canism." Despite some evidence of growing interest in political affairs, most students lived in a world limited to bars, pranks, and social activities such as the Rowboat Regatta, Little Sister Weekend, and February's "Sweetie Week." Female students focused on who was being "pinned" in which fraternity, while male students often directed their attention to the school's struggling sports teams.[31]

As in the earlier action at the Corner Bar, Buhl and McCann each took leading roles. The students who joined the CHA dissented from this domi-nant culture, and they did not shy away from acting on their nonconformist beliefs. When the CHA's housing survey revealed a systematic prejudice against African American students, John McCann publicized the findings in an April 1961 issue of the *Daily Kent Stater,* whose editors demonstrated a consistent support for civil rights. Quoting President Bowman as saying the university would act "when the time was right," McCann argued that since KSU utilized state funds, the institution needed to divorce itself from landlords practicing racial discrimination. University officials initially dismissed the charge on the grounds that the CHA survey "was based on insufficient evidence." Bowman then elaborated on the university's position in a meeting with *Stater* reporters. Defending the practice of maintaining separate housing lists for white and black students, he argued that KSU had no control over the town's landlords and affirmed a proprietor's "traditional American right . . . to determine . . . who he admits as a paying resident." He also defended the incendiary comments of Oscar Ibele, a political science professor who had entered the housing debate on behalf of the university after announcing his affiliation with the far-right John Birch Society.[32]

Members of the campus community reacted strongly both to Bowman's de-fense of landlords' rights and to Ibele's proclamation of his Birch Society mem-bership. The *Stater* implicitly criticized Bowman's indifference to the housing issue, questioning how the United States could claim to be the champion of freedom when minorities and international students were "shunned by Kent residents." Mocking Bowman's statements, the editor wrote, "We have 'freedom of choice' all right—freedom to win or lose the Cold War right here in Kent." Similarly, James Olsen, another political science professor, censured Ibele for be-longing to a "dogmatic" organization and for using the classroom as his pulpit.[33]

Yet what provoked the most significant response was Olsen's collaboration, with seven other faculty members, on a letter that appeared in the *Stater* on April 28, which supported John McCann's efforts to root out what they called Kent's "discriminatory practices." Among the signatories were Olsen's depart-mental colleague Louis Harris, English professor Charles Felver, who served as adviser to the *Kent Quarterly,* and Oscar Ritchie from the sociology department. Ritchie had long been grateful to Bowman for appointing him to a teaching post, but when faced with the choice of jeopardizing a cordial relationship with Kent State's president or honoring his commitment to the CHA and to racial justice, Ritchie opted for the latter.[34]

In a memo dated May 2, 1961, Bowman promptly rebuked Ritchie and the other faculty who had signed the letter for a "performance . . . [that] is something less than loyal." His sense of umbrage was personal as well as political. Upset that they had seen fit "to air [their criticisms] in a newspaper," he further questioned their ethics and professionalism. Sensing they needed a lesson about the perilous times in which they lived, Bowman went on: "There is not one of you who is not aware of the delicate and explosive situation which seems to exist among undergraduates throughout the world. Our campus is no exception. I am grateful for the fact that there has been, and I am confident will continue to be, a stability in our student body which will save this University from some of the grievous demonstrations which have broken out in this country and even worse abroad." On May 4, Ralph Smith, a professor in the art department, became the first of four faculty members to resign over this chilling administrative reproach. The following day the faculty adviser to the *Kent Quarterly* also gave notice, likening Bowman's behavior to "the tyranny of an undemocratic department head."[35]

News of the faculty resignations broke on May 9. Although Bowman's memo may have intimidated some faculty members, it only further propelled the CHA. They wrapped up a petition drive that called on the university "to deny placement on the approved housing list to all persons not submitting a statement of willingness to rent . . . regardless of race, religion, or nationality." Organizers gathered twelve hundred supportive signatures, and added a cover letter signed by Lance Buhl and African American student Oscar Hearn, president and president-elect of the CHA, respectively. The activists personally delivered the petitions to Bowman's office.[36]

Despite the administration's hopes of containing the furor, the petition drive garnered support from 12 percent of the student body and compelled a meeting with Buhl and Hearn. In advance of the meeting, John McCann wrote a letter to the *Stater* reinforcing the CHA's call for an end to "racial discriminatory practices." Dissecting Bowman's earlier comments, he accused the president of "condoning Jim Crow policies" by directing minority students seeking housing to "the Negro ghetto a mile from campus." McCann declared, "If President Bowman thinks this call for action will die by ignoring it, he is mistaken."[37]

When Bowman met with CHA leaders in his office on May 10, they received the same treatment he had accorded the faculty who had questioned him. In a thinly veiled reference to the percentage of students who had signed the anti-discrimination petition, he promised a forthcoming statement that would please "90 per cent of the better element of the student body." Bowman conceded that some town residents refused to rent to African Americans but asked, "Why make a study about it?" He further questioned Oscar Hearn's reasons for transferring to Kent. Why wasn't Hearn "at home in Chicago with his mother," Bowman asked. For good measure, the president voiced renewed suspicions about John McCann, saying publicly what he had expressed privately to the professors: that the sophomore was "a student who is hanging on academic ropes." With the meeting ending unproductively, McCann warned Bowman that the threat of a campus demonstration hung in the air, and McCann soon found himself being followed by campus and city police.[38]

If Bowman had little tolerance for dissent, he had even less for public protest. After his tempestuous meeting with CHA leaders, Bowman told the city and campus press that any public demonstrations "would be extremely harmful to the university." His statement was made with the knowledge that the university would soon be receiving a group of Russian educators, the second time in weeks that the campus had hosted officials from the USSR. During the first week of April, an envoy from the Soviet Union's Washington embassy spoke at Kent State's Little United Nations Assembly, which provoked unfavorable mention in William Buckley's *National Review*. Bowman thus found himself in the middle of a thorny ideological and political conflict. On the one hand, he was being criticized for receiving Soviet educators and for coddling dissident students; on the other hand, civil rights proponents disapproved of his failure to do more to challenge discrimination at a time when the country was becoming increasingly concerned with its racial image abroad.[39]

Kent State's First Demonstration

On May 11, 1961—the day before the Russian educators were scheduled to arrive, and George Bowman's sixty-eighth birthday—the CHA mobilized forty student pickets in front of the main administrative offices. The first campus protest in Bowman's eighteen-year tenure as Kent's president, the picket marked the beginning of a pattern of student activism in the face of administrative hostility that would continue through the 1960s and beyond.[40]

Bowman and security officer Don Schwartzmiller confronted the picketers, first asking the identity of their leaders and then demanding everyone's name. Some, like Paul Cheeks, refused to comply. The dean of men, Ronald Roskins, told reporters on the scene that he "did not know what would happen" to the pickets, but suggested they could face expulsion. A large group of counterdemonstrators also arrived on the scene. Student members of Oscar Ibele's Conservative Club waved signs of their own proclaiming "A Man's Home Is His Castle," a favorite slogan of open housing opponents. Jane Evans, treasurer of the student body and a senior from rural Wayne County, reflected the sentiments of many campus conservatives when she declared that rights activists "had hurt the university's reputation" and that the demonstration "would hurt even more."[41]

Supportive notes and calls trickled in to Bowman's office. William Fisher, a journalism professor who served as adviser to the *Stater,* assured the president that he was "sickened by the activity in front of the Administration Building," as were "all responsible people." The director of physical education enlisted department members to write their own notes, with one expressing her "whole-hearted support . . . in this current fracas revolving around supposed segregation." Off campus it was much the same. Following the lead of a *Record-Courier* editorial, Kent's mayor, Redmond Greer, voiced his backing of Bowman. Greer, who had mustered support for Nixon's presidential campaign in 1960, endorsed the circulation of a petition that sanctioned the "legal rights of home-owners."[42]

Fortified by these expressions of support, Bowman became impatient to bring the protest to a close. At the end of the day, CHA leader Lance Buhl struck a compromise. In exchange for a promise from KSU authorities not to discipline picketers, students agreed not to renew the protests on Friday. Believing they had made their point, and under intense pressure from authorities to put off further protests in the presence of the Russian visitors, Buhl announced that "it would be a mistake to say a demonstration is the best way to proceed in this matter." But realizing, too, the need to negotiate with the less compromising McCann, and knowing that Cheeks remained defiant, Buhl affirmed the organization's right to undertake further action.[43]

The days following the picket were a time of political reassessment. On campus, the first demonstration in decades had met with considerable opposition from the administration and sharp criticism from undergraduates organized by the Young Conservative Club. The first letters to appear in the *Stater* following the picket were critical of the CHA; community opposition also persisted, as evidenced by threats that "further demonstrations might . . . cause the Negroes' position in the University and city community to become more serious." One Kent resident wondered whether the protest had been a "Demonstration Staged for Russians." Another put the question more bluntly: "Have the Communists taken over Kent University?"[44]

Anticommunism remained a potent weapon against dissent, even against democratically inspired protest of the kind conducted on the campus in May 1961. The motivation of the participants mattered little to those who felt that a communist lurked inside every demonstrator and that every protest represented an "un-American" act. Although McCann had radical views, there is no evidence at this point of his later association with leftist groups. Buhl, the self-described "democratic liberal," never strayed from that framework. Dedicated to equal rights, Paul Cheeks supported any friend of that cause and had little interest in the brand of Marxism that McCann later embraced. While less is known about Hearn's politics, he was certainly adept at critiquing America's racial ills. "Who am I?" Hearn asked in a letter published in the *Stater* in April 1961. "I am the factory worker, not the engineer. . . . I am the farm animal, . . . the Negro." Explaining their purposes, the CHA stated, "We . . . cannot understand fully the motives of those who are quick to call us 'Communist-inspired' or 'Communists.'"[45]

A general lack of ideological enthusiasm seemed to extend to the larger student body as well. Louis Harris, one of the signers of the faculty letter supporting the CHA, arranged a showing of *Operation Abolition,* a film about the disruption of the House Un-American Activities Committee hearings. It failed to generate any discussion, whereas on other campuses the movie triggered both debate and derision. At Kent, an administrative insider observed that while the "room was filled with students," a scheduled forum following the movie fizzled when most of them left the hall.[46]

By May 20, three weeks after eight faculty members had signed a letter in support of CHA's open housing campaign, just two were present to meet with the university's vice president, Robert I. White. Four had resigned from the university and another had been critically injured in an auto accident. The sixth signer, Oscar Ritchie, had made a separate peace with the president. In a report to Bowman—the lone account of the meeting known to exist—White indicated that Olsen and Harris were in "firm agreement that . . . a letter to the *Stater* was incorrect." He quoted Harris as saying it had been "an honest mistake and not an effort to hurt anyone," but had "done more harm than good." As a final guarantee of good faith, White said the two political scientists believed that Bowman's "record in race relations is enlightened."[47]

Despite the acquiescence of the CHA's faculty supporters, advocates of racial equality at Kent retained allies and won new support. The *Stater*'s editor, whose first editorial about the protest had been equivocal, wrote a subsequent commentary on Bowman's gradualist policy in which she concluded that the time for waiting for racial progress was over and insisted that "the time [for change] is now." Several Akron-area citizens expressed similar sentiments, with one citing the important international context and the need to recognize that "America's effort to lead the free world will succeed only in proportion to the success with which we resolve our racial problems at home."[48]

Just a Start

Not long after the *Stater* voiced its support for the off-campus open housing campaign, Leroy Peoples, the new head of Kent's NAACP chapter, accompanied by the organization's field secretary and its state president, gained an audience with Bowman. Who arranged for the meeting remains unclear. Possibly Oscar Ritchie, who had been appointed by Governor DiSalle in 1959 to an advisory committee to the Ohio Civil Rights Commission, quietly used his influence in Columbus and with Bowman. Or perhaps the NAACP threatened to sue the university and make KSU a target of a campaign against racial bias. However it happened, the involvement of the NAACP in the housing controversy had an immediate and decisive impact, prompting Bowman to reverse course. The statewide president of the NAACP indicated to reporters that he told Bowman and another university administrator that Kent State's responsibility was "to the students and not the landlords." On May 23 the *Stater* and other nearby dailies learned that Bowman declared that he saw "no reason" why he should not remove the names of landlords who refused to abstain from housing discrimination.[49]

The promised policy shift came even sooner than that. Later that same week Bowman announced that Kent's board of trustees had authorized a policy barring discrimination in university-approved commercial housing. Just two weeks after his paper had sided with Kent's landlords, *Record-Courier* publisher Robert C. Dix, who was on KSU's board, also made public his switch of positions in a front-page headline. Spinning a defeat into a community victory, an accompanying editorial lauded Bowman and the trustees, contrasting the board's decision with news "out of the Deep South," where white segregationists had repeatedly assaulted Freedom Riders in Alabama. The *Stater* welcomed the university's change of heart, but credited instead the CHA and its "mature leaders, Oscar Hearn and Lance Buhl," rather than the university's president and trustees. An editorial in the paper echoed the prevailing CHA view that the new policy was "Just a Start," though at least one prominent member of the organization, John McCann, wasn't convinced it was even that. "Things are no better than before," he declared.[50]

Two years after passage of a stronger state civil rights law and the creation of an enforcement commission, and just seven months after the Corner Bar sit-in, activists had toppled racial practices entrenched in Kent for decades. Although some critics continued to question the activists' methods, the protest had thawed some of the icy chill of Cold War orthodoxy and provided an opening for those who would challenge its precepts in the years to come. A strong current of anticommunism would continue to flow and inhibit dissent. But by linking the cause of civil rights in a small northeast Ohio city to the Cold War rhetoric of "freedom" at home and abroad, the CHA and its allies had managed to expose a contradiction at the heart of the established order. In doing so, they inaugurated Kent's decade of dissent.[51]

Cold War Kent

If the cultural assumptions and values of the Cold War shaped domestic politics in the postwar era, they had an equally profound influence on popular perceptions of international affairs. Framed as a Manichean struggle between the "Free World" and the "Communist Bloc," the ongoing efforts of the United States and the Soviet Union to win the allegiance of the emerging nations of the third world dominated discussion of foreign relations throughout the 1950s and early 1960s. It was a paradigm that allowed no place for nations newly independent of European colonial control that sought to align with neither superpower. Cambodia in Southeast Asia, which obtained independence from France in the early 1950s, was one such country. In the fall of 1960, with the nation's attention fastened on presidential debates over Cold War politics, and CHA activists mapping plans for the Corner Bar sit-in, the campus of Kent State provided a platform on which the leader of Cambodia would declare a middle way for his country, one independent of the East–West conflict. By chance, the appearance of the Cambodian head of state nearly coincided with an area campaign stop by Vice President Richard Nixon the first day of October.

Seven years earlier Prince Norodom Sihanouk had hosted Nixon, then in the first year of his vice presidency, in Cambodia, and then later met him briefly in Washington, DC. Now, in the autumn of 1960, the two leaders whose fates would be forever linked almost crossed paths again, one campaigning in Akron in pursuit of the presidency, the other seeking a neutral place for Cambodia in the Cold War world. The first Saturday night in October found Nixon "in good fighting form" in the opinion of the *Akron Beacon Journal*'s political reporter. A "roaring ovation" from a packed hall included three busloads of supporters from Portage County, brought in by Kent's Republican mayor. They applauded Nixon when he called America "a guardian of world peace" that would "extend freedom throughout the world." As he spoke, Sihanouk was already en route to Ohio in a car convoy. Arriving in Kent two days later, on October 3, he made it clear to a large audience of Kent State students that his country needed no guardian; rather, Cambodia could "only hope to remain at peace by staying outside of the ideological struggle."[52]

Speaking in English, Sihanouk delivered a sharp attack on *Time* magazine's coverage of Asian affairs. Calling Henry Luce's publication an example of Western distortion, he complained that whenever he criticized America's pressure on his country's neutralist path, he was characterized as "a wretched Communist [who] must be thrown into the stocks and pointed out as a criminal by the decent folk who read *Time*." Sihanouk later avowed that he was "deeply moved" by the reception he received from the students, and the *Record-Courier* managed balanced coverage of the prince's address. But the paper would continue to run shrill editorials warning against "The Communist Peril" and advise its readers "How to Win the Cold War." Their opinion of Sihanouk's backing for China's admission to the UN was later expressed through an editorial cartoon depicting the Cambodian leader walking into the toothy jaws of a dragon marked "China." Little did they understand that Sihanouk's chief worry was not his giant neighbor to the north, but the threat of an American-backed war to the east in Vietnam.[53]

A decade later, in early 1969, President Nixon ordered the secret bombing of the North Vietnamese targets in Sihanouk's Cambodia. Nixon's motive was to demonstrate to Hanoi his unflagging commitment to a noncommunist South Vietnam. The massive bombings destabilized Cambodia, however, and drew it into a downward spiral of war that culminated in genocide. A year later, with Sihanouk ousted in a military coup, Nixon ordered a ground invasion of Cambodia, causing a storm of nationwide protests, including those at KSU that led governor James Rhodes to order National Guardsmen to campus in May 1970. Thus Cambodia's little known connection to Kent State was established a decade before the events of 1970 forever associated them in the public mind.[54]

National and State Politics

After Sihanouk's departure, the attention of Kent returned to the presidential campaign stirring the nation. Nixon's visit to the area had been preceded by a campaign stop in Akron by Democratic candidate John F. Kennedy on September 27. The vast throng must have encouraged his most important backer in the state, Governor DiSalle, for he, too, had much at stake. Kennedy considered Ohio essential to his election hopes, while DiSalle struggled with raising revenue for a legislative program in the face of a political culture inhospitable to his agenda. His triumph in 1958 had owed much to an enormous turnout of minority voters, who were rewarded with a new civil rights law and the establishment of a state commission to execute its implementation. With a push from activists such as those at Kent State, some of the most blatant examples of discrimination in public accommodations were eliminated during DiSalle's tenure. He also tried to mollify organized labor, as unions placed their own agenda before the governor. Aided by new Democratic majorities in both the Ohio Senate and House, DiSalle succeeded in passing legislation that legalized supplemental unemployment payments, improved workmen's compensation benefits, and enacted a Fair Employment Practices Law.[55]

In Kent, some members of the Council on Human Affairs, like Paul Cheeks, found time to devote to the election campaign. The KSU Young Democrats did their part, publishing a monthly newsletter that extolled the party's stand on education and promoted Kennedy's "Forceful Leadership . . . [on] Civil Rights." Campus elders were less enthusiastic, with a straw poll taken the week before the election showing that 48 percent of the faculty backed Nixon while 42 percent supported Kennedy.[56]

In the end, with the support of every major newspaper save one, and what one partisan called a "sweep of Protestant small-town and rural voters," Nixon carried Portage County and the state as a whole, winning Ohio by 273,000 votes. Running ahead of Nixon and leading the ticket in Portage's towns and hamlets was the incumbent state auditor from Jackson County, James Rhodes. Vanquished in virtually every rural area, Kennedy claimed only three nonurban counties. A few years after the 1960 election, one political scientist observed that "the Democratic Party in Ohio was largely composed of foreign-born and their sons and daughters, Catholics, and Negroes."[57]

Nationally, the 1960 election revived liberal spirits. Not in Ohio. There the experiment with liberalism came to an abrupt end. Republican-won control of the state legislature guaranteed that the second half of DiSalle's four-year term would be a political deadlock. The Democrats' sagging fortunes provided an opening to James Rhodes, the only candidate whose statewide office had not been up for election in 1958, when the GOP suffered sweeping losses. Having avoided defeat in 1958, and by leading the ticket in 1960, Rhodes set his own gubernatorial candidacy in motion.[58]

Nixon's national prospects must have appeared distressingly similar to what DiSalle faced at the state level. Although victorious in Ohio, Nixon's agonizing loss in the presidential contest, coupled with an inglorious defeat two years later in the California gubernatorial race, seemed to end his political career. While out of office for most of the 1960s, the resilient Nixon was seldom out of the foreign policy arena. Riding the currents of political reaction that ran deep during much of the post–World War II era, Nixon exerted a major influence on the course of America's involvement in Vietnam, Cambodia, and Laos. Presidents Kennedy and Johnson could not ignore Nixon's capacity for labeling opponents as "soft on communism" as they fashioned their Southeast Asian policies. Having seen the Republicans capitalize on the "fall of China" in the late 1940s, they knew all too well the dire political consequences of "losing" Asian countries to communist revolutions.[59]

Sihanouk might have had his own favorite in the 1960 American presidential contest. Although he could not have realized it at the time, the outcome of the campaign brought him some respite from the war that enveloped neighboring Vietnam. By way of later contrast, Kennedy better tolerated his neutralism than Nixon would when he took over the war. Had the United States embraced neutralism, a disastrous war might have been averted. A decade later, the stubborn commitment to a failed policy of counterrevolution in Vietnam, and the extension of that policy into Cambodia and Laos, had already killed forty thousand Americans and as many as two million Southeast Asians. And, on May 4, 1970, two months after Sihanouk was forced into exile, the bloodshed would even extend back to a campus in Ohio he had once visited.[60]

CHAPTER 2

Democracy and Free Speech

To ANYONE who grew up in 1950s America, the threat of nuclear war was an inescapable and unsettling omnipresence. "Duck and cover" air raid drills at school, the proliferation of public and private fallout shelters, and the installation of Nike missile batteries in major urban areas all served as reminders that the Cold War could at any moment turn hot, that nuclear Armageddon loomed just beyond the horizon. In the early 1960s, tensions between the United States and the USSR steadily mounted over the failed Bay of Pigs invasion, the construction of the Berlin Wall, and the spread of "wars of national liberation" throughout the third world, including Vietnam. Then, in late October 1962, the placement of Soviet missiles in Cuba provoked a stand-off between the world's two superpowers that came within a hair's breadth of igniting the long-feared nuclear holocaust.

In the long wake of the Cuban missile crisis, organizations that had long been advocating the abolition of nuclear weapons, such as the Committee for a Sane Nuclear Policy (SANE), gained fresh momentum in their campaign to "ban the bomb." In Kent, members of the Student Peace Union, including Marty Pahls, Barbara Brock, and Danny Thompson, joined with local residents to form a new branch of SANE and invited the organization's executive director to the city for a talk at the local Unitarian Universalist Church. Kent SANE soon won the endorsement of the *Daily Kent Stater*, whose editors called on President Bowman to reconsider the administration's denial of official campus standing to student disarmament groups. Though Bowman refused, support for peace advocacy increasingly took hold. In the spring of 1963, a coalition of student and community activists that included Dave Edwards—whose father, George, was a Cleveland steelworker and Communist Party member—organized an Easter/Passover "Peace Walk." The *Stater* sympathetically interviewed students about SANE's call for a treaty banning all nuclear testing.[1]

Although polls showed that a majority of Americans favored some effort to control the spread of nuclear weapons, the local newspaper, the *Record-Courier*, continued to favor a peace-through-strength approach. The editors viewed an "expanding free world market" as the best means of prevailing in the Cold War struggle, and warned that those who advocated disarmament threatened to create a false sense of security, thereby increasing the possibility of war. "Their argument would lead to an acceptance of what has been summarized in the phrase, 'Better Red than dead,'" the editors contended. Despite majority sentiment in favor of nuclear control, Cold War orthodoxies remained firmly in place.[2]

The Ohio Free Speech Movement

In April 1962, Philip A. Luce, an Ohio State University alumnus, was prevented from speaking on the OSU campus because of his ties to the Communist Party's Emergency Civil Liberties Committee. OSU's president, Novice G. Fawcett, declared that Luce was "not qualified to contribute to the intellectual growth of this university" and invoked a 1951 rule requiring nonstudents to have administrative sanction to speak on campus. Hundreds protested the ban. John Bricker, a university trustee and former senator who had suffered defeat in Ohio's right-to-work landslide in 1958, led those coming to Fawcett's defense.[3]

Several months later the House Committee on Un-American Activities (HUAC) turned its attention to Marxists living in northeast Ohio. In early June 1962, the committee summoned fifteen witnesses from the Cleveland area. Unlike Cleveland's Socialist Workers Party members active in the Fair Play for Cuba Committee, who had been targeted in 1961 by the Senate Internal Security subcommittee, the suspected communists summoned by HUAC had not been particularly visible. None, however, had renounced their political convictions. The witnesses, including Abe and Sylvia Strauss and Ruth Emmer, invoked their Fifth Amendment rights when asked about membership in the Communist Party and their current and past political involvement. Cleveland newspapers printed the names, addresses, and telephone numbers of the witnesses; as might be expected, there were employment repercussions for Ruth and Jack Emmer, both of whom lost jobs. Ruth Emmer recalls that her son Howard, then fifteen, had expressed little interest in politics before that summer; the unwelcome publicity in June 1962 cost him most of his friends, and put him on a new trajectory that also led to his later involvement with the Kent chapter of Students for a Democratic Society (SDS). Similarly, the Strausses' son David returned to Cleveland two years later from the University of Michigan as a member of SDS to work in the organization's new Economic Research and Action Project, and found his parents willing to provide the young activists with a supportive set of contacts. HUAC's tactics and those of the Cleveland newspapers may have chilled dissent, yet they radicalized some of the younger generation by exposing the disparity between professed democratic ideals and the repressive exercise of state power.[4]

The issue of campus radicalism resumed with the start of a new academic year. On October 3, 1962, the *Stater* ran a story titled "Communists Aim at Campus," which mentioned the barring of speakers at Ohio State earlier in the year. In the article, a professor of philosophy advocated a policy of tolerance toward speakers with dissenting points of view. Much earlier in the year, KSU's president, George Bowman, had cautiously supported the same approach, noting that "we are not helping the cause of democracy by trying to subdue voices." Circumstances changed radically when news broke of the Cuban missile crisis on Monday, October 22, forcing cancellation of a planned visit to the campus by Vice President Lyndon Johnson. That day Bowman declared communism to be "a wicked conspiracy whose avowed purpose is to overthrow our government" and further asserted that any organization embracing its ideology had no "claim to a platform on any college or university campus, and least of all, on that of a government-supported institution." Bowman's statement reflected a combination of his most deep-seated convictions, the grave state of world tensions, and the political reality that the state's upcoming elections would surely bring to office a governor far more conservative than the incumbent, Michael DiSalle.[5]

In the November election, state auditor James Rhodes soundly defeated DiSalle to become Ohio's new governor, winning nearly 60 percent of the vote. Not an Old Right ideologue in the mold of John Bricker, Rhodes had cast himself during the campaign as a "modern" Republican. What that meant in practical terms became clear as Rhodes avoided new taxes and instead floated bonds to fund education and state services, abandoning the old Republican policy of "pay-as-you-go" in favor of a "borrow-and-spend" approach. Yet in other ways he remained very much a Cold War conservative, including his attitude toward political dissent.[6]

The new governor had ideological company. In April 1963, Republican state representative Chalmers Wylie introduced legislation in the Ohio House of Representatives that would ban a variety of lecturers from speaking at state universities. Perhaps with an eye toward people like Ruth Emmer, who had taken shelter under the Bill of Rights, Wylie's measure outlawed the appearance of any speaker who had "pleaded the fifth amendment." The proposed legislation applied the same restrictions to anyone with communist affiliations, as well as those "convicted of a felony."[7]

College students throughout Ohio greeted Wylie's initiative as a threat to their civil liberties. During the 1963 spring quarter, Kent students from Cleveland and Barberton, following the lead of their counterparts at Ohio State and Miami University, circulated petitions opposing the bill. KSU's newly emboldened student council, backed by the editors of the *Stater*, also joined the campaign, while Lawrence Kaplan, a professor of history and president of the Kent State chapter of the American Association of University Professors, added his organization's opposition.[8]

Despite what the *Stater* termed "a storm of protest" on Ohio campuses, Wylie told a reporter for the paper that he was "more convinced than ever" of the need for his anticommunist legislation. In late May, the Ohio house, dominated by rural interests, passed the bill by better than a four-to-one margin. Afterward, Wylie said the new law would prevent "every screwball beatnik and rabble rouser [from] seeking public attention." Another Columbus-area Republican added that the bill would derail what he alleged was a communist plan to subvert students through repeated "saturation" levels of communist propaganda. Urban Democrats like Cleveland's Carl Stokes—who would later become the first African American mayor of a major city—voted against the bill, but GOP control of the state's bicameral General Assembly ensured passage of the measure. When signed into law, after a compromise measure passed the state senate, authority to control campus speakers continued to rest with university trustees. In putting his signature to the legislation, Governor Rhodes declared that "it makes explicit what I have always assumed to be the law." The senate version served to blunt the most restrictive feature of the original bill, although the principle that state authorities had the right to limit free speech was affirmed by the law.[9]

New President on Campus

As Ohio debated whether to allow communists to appear as speakers at its publicly funded universities, a group of trustees, headed by *Record-Courier* publisher Robert C. Dix, deliberated about who would replace George Bowman at the helm of Kent State. In mid-January 1962, Bowman announced his intention to retire. He had already effectively handpicked his replacement, however: Robert I. White, who later acknowledged that he "had been groomed for the job." As Dix noted in an April 1964 letter to Bowman, "You practically picked White. . . . My job there [as trustee] was merely to keep the board from acting too quickly until the evidence piled up [for White]. That I did."[10]

Bowman had previously appointed White to the newly created position of vice president of academic affairs in 1958, and had entrusted him with the task of meeting with dissident faculty members during the height of the off-campus housing controversy in 1961. In a January 18, 1963, issue of the *Stater*, Bowman said of the president-select, "I know of no one on campus in whom I have greater confidence or who has shared in as many top level decisions as

Dr. White." The following week, the campus paper offered a lukewarm endorsement: "Even for a man who has been close to Kent State, its problems, needs and goals, the job will be difficult."[11]

Like Bowman, White had started his career in a small-town school system in the Midwest. Hailing from Illinois, White earned all of his degrees from the University of Chicago and worked his way from secondary school classrooms to the presidency of a junior college in Iowa. When the opportunity arose he took a faculty position in the School of Education at his alma mater. There he could renew acquaintances and develop peer relationships with those who had once instructed him, like the Civil War historian Avery Craven and playwright Thornton Wilder. The chance to head Kent State's School of Education during a time of exploding postwar enrollment was enough to entice White to relocate to northeast Ohio in 1946. Just three years later, peers selected him the "most distinguished" member of the faculty.[12]

Bowman remained active during the final months of his twenty-year tenure. Along with his counterparts at Ohio's other state universities, he fought a proposal by the newly inaugurated Governor Rhodes to establish a board of regents to oversee the state and municipal universities, which challenged their longtime autonomy. In addition, the six university presidents took sharp issue with spending reductions proposed in the Rhodes budget for their respective campuses. Enlisting the aid of their students, the presidents, in a bid to retain their autonomy, dueled with the governor throughout the year. Ultimately the two sides compromised. In exchange for their acquiescence to Rhodes's insistence on a board of regents, the university presidents received a guarantee that the bulk of a $250 million bond issue would go to a capital improvement fund reserved for the state universities. Thus, for the remainder of the decade, these schools experienced a massive building program and an explosive growth in student population. Although rankled by the manner in which the governor planned to raise the funds, Bowman helped achieve the revenue foundation that enabled his successor to preside over the expansion of what became—until May 1970—the largest obscure university in the country.[13]

Old Left and New

The expansion of Kent State, along with the extension of the nation's interstate highway system, made it possible for the school to attract more out-of-state students. During 1963, a number of students enrolled who were soon to give the campus leftist movement a more durable presence, including Roy Inglee, Ron Wittmaack, Dave Edwards, and Student Peace Union member Barbara Brock. With John McCann, who had been active in the 1960–61 desegregation protests, they formed the nucleus of what would become the Kent chapter of the Young Socialist Alliance (YSA), a national organization that did much to implant an ascetic and strict Trotskyist form of radicalism on the Kent State campus. YSA had been founded as an associated student group in 1958 by Socialist Workers Party (SWP) leadership and Trotskyist-leaning members of the Young Socialist League. The origins of the SWP in the United States dated to the late 1920s, when Leon Trotsky and his supporters lost a power struggle with Soviet leader Joseph Stalin. From then on opponents of the Soviet Union, American followers of Trotsky styled themselves more revolutionary than the Communist Party. In point of fact, while practicing a tactically cautious form of radicalism, during the 1950s and 1960s the SWP and YSA took positions to the left of the more orthodox communists, especially in espousing support for proponents of Black Nationalism like Robert F. Williams and later Malcolm X, as well as for revolutionary states such as Cuba. When the SWP and YSA turned their attention to Vietnam in 1965, they insisted that the US government immediately withdraw its forces from the country. By the middle of the decade the YSA had established small chapters at several dozen universities throughout the country, including a number in the Midwest.[14]

Not yet acquainted, two future members of the YSA, Inglee and Wittmaack, had been among the huge throng of marchers in Washington, DC, on August 28, the day Martin Luther King Jr. called for racial and social justice in his now famous "I Have a Dream" speech. Inglee, who had grown up in a small paper-mill town north of Albany, New York, learned leftist views at home from his unionist father and from stories about his paternal uncle, who had died fighting for the Republic in the Spanish Civil War. During the March on Washington, he was favorably impressed by having to pay for his copy of *The Militant*, the newspaper of the SWP, taking this as one indication that the Trotskyists were a serious organization. Loaded down with socialist literature he had obtained in Washington, Inglee reached Kent ready to start graduate school in English and to look for like-minded activists. He first met Dave Edwards at the Unitarian Universalist Church in Kent, which was draped in black in memory of the deaths of four young girls killed in the Birmingham church bombing in mid-September.[15]

Coincidentally, the rooming house that Inglee initially called home when he arrived in Kent also housed Wittmaack, and the two young men quickly discovered that both had been at the Washington march weeks earlier. The son of a machinist and Henry Wallace progressive, young Wittmaack saw four years of army duty in Korea, where he became disillusioned with American foreign policy during the Laotian crisis in 1961. That year, US forces overseas were placed on alert by the Joint Chiefs of Staff and readied for air strikes against North Vietnam. Instead, the Kennedy White House moved diplomatically, with an ostensibly neutral Laos evolving from an international conference. Fresh from

the service, Wittmaack, an architecture student, found that Inglee's loquacious-
ness prevented him from doing much studying. Soon Wittmaack found himself
paying more attention to the views of his boarding house companion than to
his architectural drawings.[16]

Twenty-seven years old in the fall of 1963, John McCann had been a periodic student at Kent since the late 1950s. As we have seen, he had been notable
in the planning of the Corner Bar sit-in and a central figure in the drive to
force the university to adopt a nondiscriminatory off-campus housing policy in
1961. While living in Cleveland, McCann had met Danny Thompson, a fellow
Clevelander and Kent student jailed while participating in the Freedom Rides
in Mississippi. Along with Thompson, McCann became involved in the defense
of the civil rights activist Willie Mae Mallory, who sought asylum in Ohio after
charges were levied against her in North Carolina. In that effort McCann also
came into contact with other activists from the SWP. According to Don Smith,
who recruited McCann into the YSA, McCann excelled at "putting [political
ideas] into practice," a sentiment others shared. When Cleveland SWP veteran
Herman Kirsch first came to Kent and McCann returned, this time as an YSA
member, Roy Inglee looked to Kirsch, a participant permanently injured in the
bloody 1934 Toledo Auto-Lite strike, for "strategic insight" and to McCann to
learn public speaking.[17]

Joined by Barbara Brock and Dave Edwards, the new group of friends took
steps to gain campus recognition for the national Student Peace Union (SPU).
Progress came in halting steps. At the first organizational meeting on October
29, 1963, activists heard a talk by one of the Bloomington 3, a trio of YSA
supporters who had been indicted for allegedly advocating the overthrow of
Indiana state government. The following week a KSU security officer openly
tape-recorded another SPU meeting at which a student from Hunter College
delivered a speech critical of the anticommunist McCarran Act. The incident,
for which university officials apologized, must have reinforced the beliefs of YSA
members about the use of state power.[18]

Early Kent activists drew on many national and international links. Brock,
despite her youth, was one of the more veteran members of Kent's SPU. Introduced to socialist ideas by Clevelander and KSU student Marty Pahls (future
brother-in-law of the underground cartoonist Robert Crumb), her "starting
point" came in northern Alabama, where she witnessed the injustice of Jim
Crow segregation while visiting her father's hometown. Dave Edwards, despite
exposure to his father's Communist Party ties, gravitated to the party's doctrinal
foe, the SWP. Kent had but one known party member, library science professor
Sidney Jackson, and virtually no open party presence.[19]

Kent's links to the hereditary left and Cleveland's working class were among
the reasons a movement developed on the Portage County campus. "Part of

the reason the YSA could thrive there," Roy Inglee later recalled, "were these old connections." Tony Walsh had a related set of leftist associations. He spent much of his early life in a Catholic orphanage in Cleveland following the death of his Irish immigrant mother. His uncle, who took him in during his teenage years, had soldiered in the Irish Republican Army and saw service with the Steel Workers Organizing Committee. Drawing on his familial ties, Walsh described Kent as a place that "was big for the sons and daughters of the working class, the sons of steelworkers who couldn't afford to go to [Case] Western Reserve [University]."[20]

These personal "hereditary" foundations enabled a small cohort of Kent students to begin forming a coherent leftist ideology that provided a means for seeing the world differently. Linking up with African American students who were seeking to complete the unfinished business of Reconstruction, and developing what they saw as a sensible critique of Cold War liberalism, these leftists crafted an appeal that would, in time, offer an alternative, and increasingly compelling, perspective on issues of social justice and American foreign policy to a much larger number of their less ideological, working-class fellow students from nearby industrial cities and more distant mining communities.

By the fall of 1963, the necessary elements for a potent social movement were in place at Kent State. Every year brought record levels of growth to a campus increasingly populated by students from working-class families and out-of-state urban centers. A group of energetic activists was developing personal ties based on an inherited belief system. To a considerable extent, the activists, a mix of mature young adults and more typical college-age youth, enjoyed the backing of their families. Moreover, in the Cleveland SWP branch they had an organization to which they could turn for ideological support, advice, and political guidance from veterans of the Ohio labor wars who had been subsequently toughened further by their trials with McCarthyism.

Just as all sustained movements have vanguards, flourishing ones require faithful followers. Dave Dyer never spoke at a campus rally, nor did he ever author or distribute a radical leaflet. During the six or so years he attended Kent State, however, he listened to a multitude of speakers and read many a radical circular. Students such as Dyer were, in some ways, prototypical of and indispensable to the long-term success of the campus movement at Kent State.[21]

One of a handful of students from Coshocton County (a coal-mining area seventy miles to the south), Dyer had spent his first years living on the edge of Appalachia. Born in 1946, he became part of the first wave of the postwar baby boom. At the age of four, he saw his father and grandfather led from the house in handcuffs on their way to jail for defying a back-to-work order that crushed a United Mine Workers recognition strike the two had helped organize. Later, both men were active in the campaign to defeat the 1958 right-to-work amendment. Like Barbara Brock and other Kent students, Dyer saw examples of raw prejudice during a trip with his grandfather to Charleston, South Carolina, in 1958.[22]

Soon after Dyer arrived in Kent in September 1964 he began to realize the socially insular nature of his upbringing. Of the ninety-six students who attended his high school in West Lafayette, Ohio, only one was Catholic; none were Jews or people of color. With an absence of religious and racial distinctions, at least until John F. Kennedy's faith became an issue in Coshocton County during the 1960 presidential election, it was class and partisan differences that seemed paramount to him. Just as was true for a number of other activists from working-class stock, the experiences and values of Dyer's extended family rooted him politically, while also making him aware, at times acutely so, of the sometimes distinctive comportment of students who came from more affluent families, especially those who joined Kent State's elite fraternities. (Instead of identifying themselves by Greek fraternity letters, students like Dyer labeled themselves "I," for Independent.) In short, coming to the university and being exposed to the material advantages enjoyed by others reinforced the concealed injuries of class. At the same time, however, the sense of being an outsider caused Dyer to relish the opportunities college provided to explore books that provoked thinking through issues of class and race. Hence the majority of such supporters of activism were not exclusively, as the historian Milton Cantor points out, "radicalized in the home, but by society at large and specifically on the campus." With the possible exception of those from left-wing families, most students who later formed the concentric circle of campus militants would probably have agreed with Dyer when he said, "Coming to Kent made me a lot more political."[23]

The battle over free speech and the interracial campaigns for civil rights gave the YSA the political space and opportunity to develop, providing the campus with an able and determined group possessing great energy and a core of students eager to provide the university community with a comprehensive political view of national and international events. In time, the YSA influenced others who shared some of their critique, if not their rules and sense of convention. More dynamic, but less ideologically consistent than the YSA, was SDS. Another version of the still developing New Left, SDS would contribute experimentation, impatience, and volatility to the political mix.

Battling for CORE

In 1964, as President Johnson pushed a major new civil rights bill through Congress, activists at Kent State renewed their own civil rights efforts, spurred by events in nearby Cleveland, home to many of the university's black students. In the two decades since the end of World War II, Cleveland's African American population had increased by more than 100,000—from under 150,000 to nearly 280,000—as a second wave of southern blacks migrated to the urban centers of the North. Most settled on the city's East Side, leading to white flight to the suburbs and de facto segregation throughout much of the city. New arrivals put enormous pressure on the city's public education system; by the early 1960s, East Side schools had become so overcrowded that many libraries, gyms, storerooms, and basements were converted into classrooms, while some schools were forced to institute morning/afternoon split sessions.[24]

Frustrated by the Cleveland school board's failure to deal with the over-crowding even though many schools in white neighborhoods were under-utilized, African American parents took action, forming the United Freedom Movement (UFM), a clearinghouse for civil rights activities. This new cohort of African American activists, southern migrants inspired by the civil rights movement, adopted direct-action tactics aimed at attracting media attention to the discriminatory policies of the school board. Beginning in the fall of 1961, they demanded an end to half-day schooling, staged protest marches to fill empty classrooms, and picketed the school board offices calling for an end to segregation.[25]

The Congress of Racial Equality (CORE) chapter, operating within the broader UFM, served as a channel for the involvement of working class and poor Cleveland blacks. Through direct-action tactics, CORE sought, according to one study, "housing, jobs, and schools," which were in short supply for the city's black population. Using confrontative tactics that had achieved success in the South, CORE captured the imagination and backing of African Americans in Cleveland as well as support from radicals in the city and on the Kent State campus who saw the campaign as Black Nationalism in action.[26]

Entering the fourth calendar year of protest, in late January 1964 CORE renewed the picketing campaign against overcrowding in the city classrooms and encountered duplicitous school board officials and hostile white ethnics. The African American newspaper *Call and Post* characterized the opposition as "a race hating mob" and noted the indifference of the police when counter-protestors encouraged their snarling dogs to threaten CORE's pickets. In the second week of protests that winter, a group of CORE activists (including future SDS Economic Research and Action Project organizers Ollie Fein and Charlotte Phillips) staged a sit-in at the school board's offices. According to one account, police "dragged [protestors] down three flights of concrete stairs" and arrested twenty demonstrators, including Ollie Fein.[27]

Seeking to defuse tensions, the school board proposed the construction of new schools for African Americans that would, however, remain segregated. Dissatisfied, UFM moved to stop school construction, and during a protest at a construction site the Reverend Bruce Klunder, vice president of Cleveland's

CORE chapter, was crushed and killed when he attempted to block a bulldozer. Enraged by what they had seen, one protestor went after the bulldozer operator while another commandeered the vehicle. Police moved in on horseback, rescued the driver, secured the bulldozer, and dispersed the crowd. Riots followed in the black community, along with a school boycott. Malcolm X traveled to Cleveland to support the school actions, and in his April 3 "Ballot or Bullet" speech declared, "We will work with anybody, . . . nonviolently as long as the enemy is nonviolent, but violent when the enemy gets violent." Absorbing the message, activist Lewis G. Robinson announced the formation of a rifle club "for the protection of civil rights demonstrators in Cleveland." The *Call and Post* wrote that Klunder's death had smeared his "blood upon the Cleveland Board of Education," while James Farmer, the national director of CORE, called Klunder a casualty of the "bulldozer of Jim Crow."[28]

Angered by Klunder's death and with his faith in CORE undiminished, John McCann used his experience in the Cleveland school campaign to organize a student branch of CORE at Kent. McCann remained a troublesome figure to the administration, but he had behind him YSA members and a network of independent supporters such as Paul Cheeks, who had worked with him since the 1960 Corner Bar sit-in. The socialist circle, which included Brock, Inglee, and Wittmaack, stepped up their organizing pace and soon attained a level of political activity previously unseen on the Kent State campus.[29]

When McCann declared his intention to establish a CORE chapter, political conditions on campus were more hospitable than they had been under the Bowman presidency. In his inaugural address as KSU's president, Robert I. White spoke of the need for "institutional autonomy," adding, in a veiled reference to intrusive state officials seeking to impose regents' control on the university system, that "those who do not know the campus" should refrain from interference in its affairs. Although White had his predecessor's cautious qualities, his administration initially proved more open to left-of-center groups on the campus. Bowman, for instance, had refused recognition to the SPU, but the peace group had gained a measure of acceptance under White. The new president had also given the student senate a role in the approval process for campus groups, and that boded well for McCann. Despite his past notoriety, it was not a foregone conclusion that he would automatically meet resistance to his plans to charter a CORE chapter at Kent State.[30]

Early signs looked promising for the two dozen students and faculty members interested in bringing CORE to Kent. The day after McCann stated their intentions on January 22, 1964, the *Daily Kent Stater* urged that "prompt and positive action" be given to both CORE and the NAACP in their recognition bids. Alluding to a pro–civil rights statement by President Kennedy, the *Stater* wrote that "the battle for full citizenship . . . is not over; it has barely begun."

Still, as would be the case throughout the decade, those struggling for progressive social change encountered determined opposition.[31]

YSA members were also interested in supporting anticolonial revolutions, and they tried to arrange for two pro-Cuban lecturers to speak on campus in early February under SPU sponsorship. Since the pair had traveled to Cuba in defiance of the US State Department, the university prevented the program by citing an "equal opportunity" rule—on the books but never before invoked—and insisting that the meeting be run by a tenured member of the faculty. The KSU administration was criticized by the *Stater* for preventing the SPU-sponsored talk while at the same time allowing the university's Student Activities Board to fund an appearance by a religious anticommunist radio personality not long after. Still, that McCann was associated with the attempt to bring the controversial speakers to campus made his bid to establish CORE more difficult.[32]

YSA dropped the attempt to bring the pro-Cuban radicals to Kent, and White, after taking criticism for preventing them from speaking, announced the formation of a student–faculty committee to interpret guidelines for lecturers under the state's speaker-ban law, which established the authority of state university trustees to ban those with communist affiliations from speaking on Ohio campuses. The student body president, Terry Moran, was one of three students White named to the committee.[33]

Blocked on one front (of speaker choice), YSA moved to another. Working again under the SPU aegis, the left-wingers brought a member of the Bloomington 3 back to campus. The appearance earned front-page coverage in the *Stater* and showed the KSU administration that the campus left would remain assertive. In mid-February, the *Stater* ran an interview with McCann in which he charged that the administration feared "any group which might seriously disturb the status quo." While waiting for permanent approval for the CORE chapter, activist students must have received temporary authorization to conduct meetings, because Cleveland CORE president Ruth Turner spoke on campus about the organization's ongoing struggle to integrate the city's school system—describing the arrests of CORE members by Cleveland police as "one of the most brutal things I've ever seen North or South."[34]

The day after the interview with McCann appeared, Eric Rackham, KSU's dean for educational and student services, gave the administrative go-ahead for recognition of the CORE chapter, announcing that he was sending the request to student body president Terry Moran and the student senate, whose members comprised a student council, for final approval. Knowing that the last stage of the recognition process might prove more difficult, supporters of CORE sought to influence members of the student senate in preparation for the February 19 vote, and organized attendance at the student government meeting, which was presided over by Moran. Only weeks before, Moran's father, a Cleveland police lieutenant, had apparently been involved with the arrests of Ruth Turner and other CORE protestors who had sat in at the school board meeting. The session was heated. Inglee recalled that "Moran pulled out this file from his brief case. He's reading [from the file] all this shit and he's pointing at Dave Edwards [and making him out to be] this master puppeteer that's running [the CORE campaign] from Moscow by [orders of] the KGB." McCann experienced similar treatment. Asked if he was a communist, he replied to Moran, "I'm not on trial here." Through his father, Moran may have had access to an Ohio Highway Patrol description of McCann as having a "communistic background."[35]

Moran persuaded many of his fellow senators to reject CORE's bid for recognition, including conservative students from rural Wayne County who remained bitter over McCann's involvement in the campaign against housing discrimination.[36] Describing CORE as an "extremist" group, Moran, reading from file notes and using a flow chart, presented a forceful case. He knew he could count on his officers during the tense roll-call balloting, but not on former student body president Craig Stephens, who supported recognition of the CORE chapter. The matter appeared headed for a deadlock when one of the thirty-eight members of the student senate abstained, allowing pro-CORE senators to prevail in a 19–18 vote, thereby recognizing the civil rights organization as an official student group.[37]

Both sides were stunned. Before the vote, Roy Inglee could think only of defeat. In retrospect, he believed they prevailed because Moran's anticommunism had gone too far: "There was a political milieu [on campus ranging] from radical to liberal, a couple of hundred who [were] committed to civil rights and people that rejected the witch hunt propaganda utterly. People that otherwise would be wishy-washy on the question [of anticommunism] got a little spine when they saw [Moran's tactics]. 'I know Dave Edwards, this [CORE] is not the KGB.'" Paul Cheeks, who became treasurer of the CORE chapter, recalled the red-baiting atmosphere of the meeting: "I didn't know whether he [McCann] was involved in those things [socialist activities] and didn't care. My concern became what John was doing [for civil rights], . . . a cause that I [was] involved with. . . . Knowing him [McCann] was a very good experience for me."[38]

Moments after the vote, a furious Moran announced his resignation as president and slammed the senate's decision, accusing CORE of using "violence [as] . . . one of their standard operating procedures." The *Stater* reflected the same divisions. Ron Clark, the managing editor, who was from a small Wayne County town, proposed a student body referendum, hoping that the decision to approve the "controversial" CORE chapter might be reversed and that Moran might be enticed back to the presidency. Amid the controversy, however, the *Stater*'s editorial board condemned Moran for his "shameful inability to grasp the importance of the country's foremost domestic problem," and a columnist for the *Call and Post* wrote that Lieutenant Moran had passed on "the virus of race prejudice" to his son. The Portage County Labor Council weighed in obliquely on the side of CORE by hailing passage of the Civil Rights bill in the House of Representatives and by announcing the formation of a Committee for Progress—a biracial organization spun off from the United Auto Workers that supported civil rights legislation.[39]

It is not known what role the administration played in the behind-the-scenes decision making, although it appears that it counseled student conservatives to accept the senate's one-vote margin. Having seen the important role of the *Stater* in influencing political debate on the campus, however, White took steps to ensure that by the time CORE was ready to launch its first campaign, administration-friendly editors would be reporting and commenting on the news.

After the vote, McCann and Cheeks faced questions from campus conservatives over CORE's use of direct-action tactics and the hot-button issue of communism. In a letter to the *Stater,* a rural ally of Moran derided CORE for what he termed its "direct militant Action." The head of the right-wing Council on Freedom took the *Stater* to task for its coverage of an SPU meeting and soon thereafter, in late February, verbally assailed the Kentucky activist Carl Braden, a crusading white supporter of civil rights who was giving a lecture on campus, and forced him to defend himself from charges of communist associations.[40]

In this feverish atmosphere the *Stater* devoted an editorial to Cold War red-baiting. "It's a curious fact indeed that Communists seem to be behind all the worthwhile movements in this country," the editor wrote. Defending those who challenged inequality, the paper heralded the civil rights activists for "making this country's democracy live." Tony Walsh of Cleveland, who would soon take McCann's place as the most prominent campus activist, sarcastically attacked Moran for his behavior at the student council meeting, calling his "defense of Cleveland police brutality . . . deeply moving." Seemingly untroubled by the difficulties involved in the effort to charter CORE, hard-boiled YSA members took stock of their success. Likewise tested by the furor, White had acquitted himself well in his first major encounter with Kent's student movement.[41]

University Moves

As CORE laid plans for its first campaign—which called for the removal of discriminatory clauses from the bylaws of Greek fraternities and sororities—most students were immersed in final exam preparations or making arrangements for spring break. President White made plans of his own: to move against an uncooperative newspaper. Apparently he did so with the support of the newly named director of the School of Journalism, Murv Perry. Mindful of the

Stater's editorial support for chartering CORE, and convinced that the paper lay, as Perry said later, "in the hands of an early group of student radicals," Perry discarded the established method of naming a new editor who had been groomed by the incumbent. Instead, Perry intervened and as chair of the Student Publications Policy Committee—a body composed of an equal number of faculty and students—made certain that his choice prevailed. When White announced Marie Slivka as the paper's editor for the 1964 spring quarter, the winter quarter editor and two former editors publicly objected, charging that Slivka had been selected for her conservative beliefs rather than on the strength of her qualifications. Despite their protests to White over Slivka's inexperience, the selection stuck. Slivka, in turn, named fraternity member Ron Clark, who tried to organize a campus referendum against CORE, as managing editor.[42]

The university also began heeding signals from the community about the need to inhibit CORE and other leftist groups. A *Record-Courier* columnist asserted that "the university has the right to deny the 'constitutional rights' of students," adding, "The university has a responsibility to maintain its good name throughout the state and nation. . . . [Otherwise] it becomes a haven and platform for every radical in town." Days later, White's administration promulgated six rules governing demonstrations, the most important of which mandated specific approval by the university for any campus protest. Hence, as CORE prepared for the campaign against the fraternity and sorority discrimination clauses, the civil rights group faced a civil liberties battle as well.[43]

John McCann again provided adroit leadership. Advising the administration of a planned picket but not requesting approval for it, he mustered a small group of students to protest the policy on demonstrations. Pickets distributed handbills on April 7 that read in part: "The constitution of the United States guarantees you the right to free speech and free assembly. It does not say everyone has these rights except students." Ohio Highway Patrol monitored the event, but did not interfere—perhaps the first instance of police on campus for political reasons at KSU. As they had done during the May 1961 protest over bias in off-campus housing, university officials deliberated about what to do with recalcitrant students. Police shadowed the dissidents. Slivka, the new *Stater* editor, dueled with CORE in her editorials and lectured them about their responsibilities. Former president George Bowman weighed in with praise for the editor's stand. Assured of *Stater* support, White placed McCann on conduct probation for having failed to obtain advance permission for a picket. Undeterred, McCann and his growing circle brought SWP presidential candidate Clifton DeBarry to campus (after wisely backing away from plans to invite Cleveland's Lewis Robinson, head of that city's Medgar Evers Rifle Club). DeBerry addressed an auditorium of 150 students, while CORE sought to paint Slivka and Clark as "pawns of the university." McCann received the editorial support of the *Akron Beacon Journal* and, two weeks later, the backing of the Kent State's Association of American University Professors chapter, which took issue with the regulations governing campus protests.[44]

Having to contend with wider faculty opposition to his administrative governance than did Bowman, White reversed himself. He issued a revised policy that required only advance notice, rather than administration permission, for demonstrations. An unhappy *Stater* editor termed the modified policy as "ultra-liberal" and bemoaned the demise of the original "strong, sturdy policy."[45]

Vietnam

The YSA political line held that American involvement "against the people of South Vietnam must be opposed and stopped, and U.S. troops withdrawn." On May Day 1964, members of Kent's YSA and SPU transferred their attention for the first time to the unfolding war in Southeast Asia. After complying with the requirements of the amended demonstration policy, the socialist students picketed in front of the campus administration building carrying signs that read "War on Poverty, Not on Vietnam," and denounced what they called "slaughter" in that country. Inspiration for the small picket—among the first protests against the Vietnam War in Ohio—had originated in a conference in Connecticut weeks earlier that resulted from cooperation between the YSA and the Progressive Labor Movement. Factional differences soon precluded further collaboration between the groups, but the organizations' temporary alliance as the "May 2nd Movement" sponsored a few regional demonstrations against US policy in Southeast Asia, including one in New York City that drew one thousand antiwar marchers.[46]

ERAP and Students for a Democratic Society

A development that would ultimately have a major effect on the Kent antiwar movement was the establishment in Cleveland of an SDS program called the Economic Research and Action Project (ERAP). Even though no Kent students participated in the creation of ERAP, the campus was, later in the decade, heavily influenced by a pair of the project's key participants, Terry Robbins and Charlie Tabasko. Robbins, a Kenyon College student, and Tabasko, a Cleveland native attending Bowling Green University, were SDS leaders on their respective campuses. Both later served as traveling organizers for SDS in northeast Ohio.[47]

Charlotte Phillips and Ollie Fein, medical students at Cleveland's Case Western Reserve University, had met at Swarthmore College, where they came to know Carl Wittman. Furthering their activism as medical students, they responded first to the CORE campaign and later to Wittman and Tom Hayden's formative SDS document "An Interracial Movement of the Poor?" by putting together an ERAP organization in Cleveland. The Cleveland Community Project, as it was known, placed SDS/ERAP members in low-income communities to organize around the needs of the city's impoverished residents; they included Kathy Boudin, Carol McEldowney (who would travel to Cambodia in 1967), and University of Michigan student and Cleveland native Dave Strauss, whose parents had been compelled to appear before a HUAC panel two years before. Through Strauss the organizers were able to make contact with activists from the older cohort of left-wing radicals; they also received help from the Meat Packers Union, and with such assistance were able to concentrate their work among the most disenfranchised of the urban poor.[48]

Having this familial link may well have helped radicals like Strauss sustain their commitment to ERAP. Strauss himself remained with the Cleveland Community Project for three years, and his efforts enabled project organizers to expand their work to one of the mostly black East Side neighborhoods, where Charlie Tabasko had been raised. Born in 1947, Tabasko grew up in a duplex on 124th Street. His father, a furnace repairman, came "home dirty everyday," Tabasko later said. As a youngster, Tabasko attended Hazeldell Elementary School with Arvo Hall, who lived on the next block. The two remained friends until Hall's family moved away in the late 1950s. When Arvo's father, Gus Hall, completed an eight-year prison sentence in Leavenworth during 1959, the reunited family soon relocated to New York, where the elder Hall assumed the duties of general secretary of the Communist Party.[49]

Though his friendship with young Arvo Hall served to blunt any anticommunism feelings Tabasko might have otherwise experienced in his early years, the spark for his radicalism was provided by a teacher at his junior high school who enabled the teenager to make sense of the overcrowded classrooms and cope with the teeming racial tensions at the overwhelming African American school. Had Tabasko remained in Cleveland he would have been a student at Glenville High School and experienced firsthand the desegregation battles waged by CORE. Instead, and following a migratory pattern of many urban whites, Tabasko's father moved the family to an apartment in an adjacent suburb, Cleveland Heights.[50]

After graduation Tabasko chose Bowling Green State University. Like Kent, the university had its share, Tabasko recalled, "of working-class kids." By his sophomore year the campus also had an SDS chapter, which Tabasko helped to organize. Like Robbins, Tabasko left school in 1966, and he began working with ERAP in his old Cleveland neighborhood. He came to be impressed by the activists. "They were pooling their incomes, . . . putting it into a common pot and then taking money according to your needs, sort [of] Marxist." One who came to stand out was, like him, new to the Cleveland project: Terry Robbins.[51]

Born in the Bronx, Robbins spent his first years there until his father, a salesman, moved the family to a suburb near Queens. An intellectual youth with a well-developed sense of social justice, he spent his years at Lawrence High School immersed in history and literature. He had a particular fascination with the novels of Herman Melville and Howard Fast. As was once said of Melville, Robbins seemed to "never rest until he gets hold of a definite belief." Describing the influence that Howard Fast's novel *Spartacus* had on him, the sixteen-year-old wrote: "Man cannot long endure the pain and the agony of his own enslavement. He must . . . rebel and through [*sic*] off the shackles that bind him. This insight, so important to the understanding of the human spirit, can guide our dealings with all the tyrannies of the world. It seems all the greater shame, therefore, that the dream of Spartacus, the dream of freedom for all men, has not yet even been realized in our own country today."[52]

Robbins gained admission to Kenyon College in 1964, and one of his first experiences there was a chance to see and hear Bob Dylan, with whom Robbins would later be forever linked through the song "The Subterranean Homesick Blues." Described as an "intense, driven . . . Dylan freak," and interested more in activism than scholastics, Robbins landed in Cleveland the following summer, where, according to a former SDS leader, "he was drawn to the [ERAP] community organizing model." Eventually dropping out of Kenyon, Robbins turned to student organizing work with Tabasko. By 1968, Kent State numbered among the northeast Ohio colleges with an SDS chapter. "The Cleveland ERAP project," Tabasko wrote four decades later, "rolled into the summer organizing . . . for the Democratic convention. . . . Had Terry not already been there who knows [how all this may have been]."[53]

Election 1964

Throughout 1964 Kent State's YSA, together with nonsocialist radicals, continued to advance a civil rights agenda. At the same time, the Young Socialists paid increased attention to the war escalating on the other side of the world. More from staying power than genuine academic ambition, that spring John McCann obtained his diploma from Kent State. That his focus remained on activism became apparent when he and his associates—who, by mid-1964, included Youngstown area senior Barbara Gregorich—advanced the cause of SWP presidential candidate Clifton DeBerry. On a return visit to the Kent State campus in October, DeBarry condemned America's "dirty war" in Vietnam. He got a hearing from hundreds of student listeners, but few votes.[54]

Attention understandably fixed on the presidential campaign's major candidates. Barry Goldwater, the Arizona senator and GOP presidential contestant, had his son stump the Kent campus and call the crusade against communism "a policy of natural survival." The senior Goldwater spoke in such apocalyptic terms that Lyndon Johnson could campaign as the moderate. Johnson covered his right flank with the Gulf of Tonkin incident and its aftermath, which enabled him to campaign later in the fall as the peace candidate. The show of force in August 1964 may have helped in Ohio and elsewhere, for his approval ratings skyrocketed after the Gulf of Tonkin Resolution, and he won the support of most of the nation and an astonishing percentage of traditionally Republican Ohio. When his vice-presidential running mate, Hubert Humphrey, campaigned in Ashtabula, seventy-five miles from Kent, during early October, sixty KSU students traveled there to welcome and support the Democratic ticket. KSU's Young Democrats were part of an audience in Akron on October 21, when the president assured thousands of loyalists with his now legendary remark that he was "not about to send American boys 9 or 10,000 miles away from home to do what Asian boys ought to be doing for themselves." His declarations were both comforting and deceiving. LBJ couched his message in terms that compared favorably to Goldwater's loose talk about the use of atomic weapons during a fall whistle-stop tour through Ohio and Indiana.[55]

Beyond the Republican Party's steadfast base, support for Goldwater in the usually reliable GOP state seemed hard to find. Despairingly, state Republican Party chairman Ray Bliss, who had experienced the right-to-work debacle of 1958, thought back to another disastrous campaign: "We face another 1936 and any goddamn fool that doesn't believe it had better." Johnson won nearly 63 percent of Ohio's 4 million votes. Robert Taft Jr., whose father's constituency Goldwater had inherited, also lost his bid to topple incumbent Democratic senator Stephen Young. Still, conservative stalwarts at Kent State gave it their all, applauding a Goldwater statement about Vietnam one of them cited at campus debate, which concluded, "If it means war, it means war." In the aftermath of the election, one Council on Freedom member saw "victory" amid the ashes of defeat. Writing a week after the election, a frequent conservative critic and KSU student called on supporters "to rally around the flag and to achieve a real and complete victory for America in 1968." One battle had ended and another had begun.[56]

The war Goldwater was prepared to conduct was instead waged by his victorious opponent. In the fall of 1964, the escalation of the Vietnam conflict and the later confrontation at Kent State between the militant antiwar left that SDS brought into being and the veteran Ohio National Guard units Governor James Rhodes deployed was off on an unseen horizon. Surely, the lethal outcome of the protest six years later was scarcely imaginable, but by "reading backward" one can identify the elements that led to the May 1970 implosion. From the very beginning, dissenters at Kent State, many from Cleveland and other urban areas of Ohio, who were attracted by proximity and cheap tuition, boldly challenged a small-town elite whose traditional racial, political, and social mores had been fixed firmly in place by a decade of Cold War anticommunism. From the very beginning, those questioning the Cold War consensus met with scorn, red-baiting, and bureaucratic opposition.

CHAPTER 3

The Beginning of Wartime Dissent

IT IS ALWAYS easier to read to read history backward, to see signs of where things were headed when you know where they ended up. Thus, revisiting Kent State in the mid-1960s, it comes as no surprise that tickets for an upcoming Peter, Paul & Mary concert in late September 1964 sold "better than expected," while a year later an appearance by Broadway singer Robert Goulet generated only tepid interest. Goulet's music had hardly sunk like a stone, but he could not quite bring back the old times of popular entertainment. In Kent, off-campus hangouts, too, like the Blind Owl and the Needle's Eye, were attracting cultural rebels looking for an alternative to Goulet's musical style and the corsage-era Greek social scene. Yet for every hint of the new there was as much evidence that little had changed. The question of whether to allow female "coeds" to wear slacks to class during the winter months resurfaced on campus, and fraternities and sororities continued to draw many new pledges.[1]

As we saw in chapter 2, the presence of Trotskyist-style socialists on campus was not new; the political leanings of John McCann, Dave Edwards, and others had been an issue during the debate over the establishment of CORE almost a year earlier. Against this larger cultural backdrop, members of the tiny Young Socialist Alliance (YSA), having addressed themselves largely to civil rights issues through involvement in organizations like CORE, decided in January 1965 to seek recognition as a student group at Kent State. Despite its small size, YSA received a disproportionate amount of attention from local law enforcement and the KSU administration. After its members submitted the necessary applications to the student senate's committee on organizations, the question of establishing a YSA chapter on campus became controversial when area newspapers mistakenly reported that approval had already been granted.[2]

Area residents began writing to either KSU's president, Robert I. White, or directly to the governor to condemn university complicity with the group.

One called on White to ban YSA and to "promote the study of truth about communism and what Americans stand to lose if the predicted revolution . . . is brought about." Another, obliquely referring to the recent campus appearance of Senator Eugene McCarthy, urged similar action by White in order to keep "known subversives . . . off the Kent State campus, whether they be students, educators, or United States Senators." The same writer recommended the creation of a club to study "the evils of this atheistic cancer," suggesting that materials could be obtained from J. Edgar Hoover. Another complainant wrote directly to Governor James Rhodes demanding action against YSA.[3]

Even with the opposition of community and student conservatives, the campaign to prevent the recognition of the YSA gained little traction on the campus. The new *Daily Kent Stater* editor for the winter term reminded her readers that YSA, like CORE the previous year, should be judged no differently than any other student group. Allowing that the views of YSA enjoyed little currency, the editor warned against the danger of "unlimited authority of the majority."[4]

There is evidence that White and his administrators, with the example of Berkeley's Free Speech Movement still fresh, were also heeding the plea for toleration as they sought a way of dealing with the dilemma of allowing students with controversial views a place within the university community. In the fall of 1964, the University of California at Berkeley had been the scene of a sustained and successful student campaign that overturned a ban on campus political activity. The predicament then facing university presidents, almost all of whom were Cold War liberals of one sort or another, was how to "contain" student dissent without appearing soft on communism or weak generally. Since repression seemed counterproductive—in fact, it seemed only to feed dissent—the strategy adopted by many, including White, was some form of toleration. The logic behind White's approach was the assumption that in the democratic marketplace of ideas, the "truth" will prevail and the extremes will be discredited or absorbed.[5]

The YSA's bid for official recognition began to move through student government channels before going to the Student Affairs Council and to President White for ultimate approval. A clearly worried KSU administration struggled to adopt a policy that would satisfy liberal principle, yet pacify anticommunists. The Committee on Organizations, chaired by a conservative student, asked YSA members Roy Inglee, Dave Edwards, and Barbara Brock to answer questions about potential conflicts between the declared aims of the YSA and the Ohio and US constitutions, a tactic favored by Senator Joseph McCarthy in the 1950s. All parties agreed to a taping of the session.[6]

Inglee did not pull his punches, yet the answers given by the YSA apparently satisfied White regarding the organization's intention to work within the guidelines prescribed by the US Constitution. Dr. James W. Fox, director of student activities and the first administrator to read the transcript, framed the matter for Eric Rackham, the executive dean for educational and student services: "The question for us," he wrote, is "what is the most effective method of handling these 'fringe' groups?" Marking out three choices—prohibition, acceptance like "any other group" (the free speech position of the *Stater*), and "cautious acceptance"—Fox recommended the third option. Remembering the chill of 1950s political orthodoxy and thus mindful of the dangers of being seen as coddling Marxists, Fox expressed the hope that he could "move one or two members [of YSA] away from communism" and asked Rackham for a "statement of . . . confidence in writing." Rackham provided him with a letter expressing his "complete confidence" in Fox's "undivided loyalty to your university and to your country." Rackham noted that YSA was not on any subversive list and that the student senate was likely to recommend approval, adding that the university administration could provoke the campus community by overruling the student senate. In a memo to White that accompanied a copy of his letter to Fox, Rackham affirmed that the question was "serious business," but declared, "If Jim [Fox] goes 'on record' I think I ought to also. My neck isn't worth any more than his."[7]

White's reply acknowledged the "awkward predicament" the issue created. As administrators struggled with their position on recognition, Rackham, who had the unenviable job of replying to anti-YSA letters sent to White, continued having to mollify anticommunists in the Kent community. On the day the *Stater* announced that the YSA recognition question would be taken up by the student senate, Rackham met with a representative of Kent's American Legion, who supplied him with copies of YSA literature to make his case against the group. Rackham apparently sought to downplay the group's significance and convince the self-appointed guardian of the Kent community of his "tremendous confidence in the vast majority of our young people on this campus."[8]

As the YSA issue simmered, the war in Vietnam suddenly intensified. Concerned with charges from Richard Nixon and the GOP right that he was soft on communism, and tormented by the question of withdrawal or escalation, President Johnson launched a series of US bombing strikes over North Vietnam after an assault in early February by National Liberation Front guerrillas on the Pleiku airbase in South Vietnam killed eight US servicemen. Sorties over North Vietnam involving 150 US jet aircraft hit four targets. Within a week of the reprisal raids, the Joint Chiefs of Staff offered Johnson a more ambitious plan that launched what would become the lengthiest and most sustained bombing campaign in US history.[9]

In Cleveland, the renowned pediatrician Benjamin Spock, who was a professor in the medical school at Case Western Reserve University, was "hopping mad" when informed of the air attacks and sent a series of critical letters to the president he had just helped to elect. Unlike most Americans, including most Kent State students, the members of the YSA had no illusions about Johnson and embarked immediately on a direct protest of their own. Roy Inglee recalled, "When the bombing happened, . . . we hit the streets of Kent with a big bundle of *Militants* . . . and passed out maybe a thousand leaflets in opposition to the war. . . . We were trailed around by a large posse of armed cops. . . . It was reasonably intimidating."[10]

Conditions soon became more daunting for the antiwar dissidents. On February 9 a *Stater* headline announced, "Socialists [to] Protest over US Vietnam Retaliation." The six protesters—the entire YSA membership at the time—began their action by walking in a tight circle atop the steps of the newly constructed Bowman Hall. Counterdemonstrators, including Dennis Durand, later known for his ties to the campus police, numbered between a hundred and two hundred students. As would become their custom, boisterous male residents of adjacent Stopher Hall hung an American flag from a window and broadcast abuse, threats, and patriotic music from their dorm. Gerald Graham, recently involved in the Goldwater campaign and active in the Young Americans for Freedom, supplied flyers to counter the YSA's claim that the bombing campaign was but one more "step in the relentless march of imperialism." Others in the crowd of counterdemonstrators intended to prevent the establishment of the YSA as a recognized student group. The only reinforcement for YSA that day was fellow student activist Tony Walsh, an unaffiliated radical who hailed from Cleveland.[11]

After one of the counterprotestors climbed piggyback on the shoulders of another and kicked (perhaps accidentally) Barbara Brock in the head, the leftists gave ground, forced into the sunken entranceway to Bowman Hall. There they were pelted with pieces of fruit, but sustained no real injuries. Brock recalled being struck: "I guess I was angry enough that it didn't hurt." Speaking for herself and her companions, Brock displayed an outlook that came to characterize these activists, saying years later that the opposition "wasn't that hard to take," and adding. "People should not be scared off. . . . Nobody broke up our demonstration."[12]

YSA received encouragement but also forthright criticism from elders in the Cleveland Socialist Workers Party (SWP) for their failure to anticipate and plan for the intensity of the counterprotest. The growth of the antiwar movement was a complex phenomenon, and at Kent State its development owed much to Old Left connections. Indeed, Sidney Jackson, a transplanted New Yorker who taught library science at KSU and was a member of the Communist Party, had been the first person in Kent to question publicly American involvement in Vietnam. His letters in opposition to US support of the Diem regime, which appeared in the *Record-Courier* in September and early November 1963, came months before the tiny protest that YSA members, demonstrating through the aegis of the Student Peace Union (SPU), held in May 1964.[13]

Support came, too, from the editor of the *Stater,* who ridiculed the jeering students. Aside from the letters written by pro- and antiwar participants, all the others that appeared in the *Stater* were critical of the behavior of the prowar opponents. As Brock later told it: "We were isolated in a way, but there was a big community that was sympathetic. They didn't want to stick their necks out. But they would sit around and talk about ideas. It's not like everybody hated us." The YSA protest and the opposition it engendered marked the real beginning of a rancorous campus debate over the Vietnam War that lasted as long as the war itself. No longer feeling it necessary to invoke its affiliation with the more serene-sounding Student Peace Union, Kent's Young Socialist Alliance now stood on its own as the leading antiwar group on campus, one indication that as Vietnam became a hot war, Cold War fears were beginning to dissipate.[14]

Elsewhere in the country, antiwar activists did protest as SPU members and, depending on the place, they were joined by other groups including SDS, the Catholic Worker movement, Women Strike for Peace, and the War Resisters League. At the University of Kansas in Lawrence, where a movement in favor of civil rights and in opposition to the war maintained a trajectory remarkably similar to the one at Kent, a small SPU protest in February 1965 also stimulated a modest prowar demonstration of equal size. There, vocal opponents serenaded the peace activists with the Marines' Hymn.[15]

Knowing that opposition to the war had spread to other universities and that some on the Kent State campus shared their opinion of the Vietnam conflict, YSA held fast to its purpose, and to an ideological perspective that was reinforced by more politically seasoned veterans of the Cleveland SWP, including Herman Kirsch, who was the party organizer in Cleveland. Roy Inglee saw determination in Kirsch's every step: "Herman walked with a limp because he was run down by a truckload of scabs during the Auto-Lite strike in Toledo in '34." Inglee stressed that Kirsch and others "who were of the generation of the '30s and '40s . . . gave political advice because they'd been through these struggles. . . . [They] strengthened [us] emotionally and intellectually."[16]

An Appeal to the FBI

The YSA protest gave new prominence to the issue of its recognition. When the *Cleveland Press* ran a premature headline on February 25 announcing "Socialist Group Recognized at Kent State," the news generated a new round of letters to the office of President White. Dean Rackham dutifully replied to them all, explaining in one that " 'recognition' means just that, and that [it] neither [implies] 'endorsement' nor 'rejection' of principles." In addition to the anticommunist sentiments expressed by area residents, White also had to contend with the declared alarm of Republican lieutenant governor John W. Brown. Upon learning that the Kent State's Student Affairs Council had recommended recognition for the YSA, Brown wrote immediately to White informing him of his letter of that same day to J. Edgar Hoover about "the status of the Young Socialist Alliance relative to Communist-front activities in the United States." Brown asked White to defer a final decision until Hoover replied. "I trust you will consider this as a personal request rather than as a directive from this office," Brown wrote. White asked Rackham and George Betts, his director of university relations, to prepare a tentative statement he could distribute to the state legislature's Finance Committee. Labeling his request "urgent," White directed that it include the sentiment that "if it is desired [by the Ohio Legislature] to make these extreme viewpoints popular and to attract thousands of sympathizers, then try to suppress them." White's shrewd forewarning implicitly recognized the inherent dialectic between radicalization and repression that would characterize much of the turmoil of the 1960s, on campus and off. His logic seemed to reflect the belief of his advisers James Fox and Eric Rackham that YSA would shrivel over time.[17]

With no direct response from White, the lieutenant governor wrote him a second time, enclosing the reply he had received from Hoover. The longtime FBI director assured Brown of the uniformity of their views and charged that the SWP represented "a dangerous menace to our freedom." When White finally responded to Brown on March 18, he cited a series of personal and administrative matters that had prevented him from answering the lieutenant governor. He then got to the heart of the matter.

> We have a problem. Some of my friends know me as a stuffy reactionary. At the same time, I know some of the facts of life so far as college students are concerned. I am quite sure I can do America and the State of Ohio more good by a procedure which, I am sure, will outrage many good people. If I can have maneuvering room, these youngsters will have a brief day and then . . . will be quietly gone with no ruckus or statewide uproar endangering all of us. All I need is some . . . space and the understanding of people such as you.
>
> White's letter included statements by both the Ohio and US attorney generals' offices supporting his position.[18]

Although White had asked for Brown's patience, the lieutenant governor's reply to Betts (filling in during White's absence) indicated "great concern, for [your statements] . . . are in direct contradiction to what I have received from the Attorney General of the State of Ohio." In his final letter to Betts, Brown concluded that "if you have decided to recognize them, it would be my suggestion that you omit any reference to the Attorney General's Office, State of Ohio." The day before Brown wrote his letter, however, the administration had issued a release notifying the press that YSA had been recognized as a student organization at the university.[19]

Area papers and the *Stater* carried the news. White's announcement in the *Stater* described the YSA as being "distasteful to the overwhelming majority of us," though it observed that the group was on no official list of subversive organizations. After reading the *Stater* story, one department head wrote to White commending his handling of the affair and predicting that "once permitted to appear on the campus [the YSA] will merely wither on the vine."[20]

Easter in Washington

Although not much of an organizational presence at Kent State until 1968, the quintessential New Left group, SDS, had earlier established itself in northeast Ohio. In Cleveland, SDS organized an Economic Research and Action Project program among public assistance recipients. Across town at Case Western Reserve campus, where Dr. Spock taught, SDS appealed to that campus's more traditional student base. Southwest of Cleveland, at Oberlin College, Paul Potter and Rennie Davis provided leadership for the new SDS chapter that formed there in 1962. Both were working with ERAP—Potter in Cleveland and Davis as the project's national director—in December 1964 when, weeks before the Johnson administration intensified the Vietnam conflict, SDS issued a call for an antiwar march in Washington on Easter Saturday, April 17, 1965.[21]

Thirteen days before the scheduled march, the *Akron Beacon Journal's* editor, John S. Knight, strongly condemned the American build-up in Vietnam. Despite, or perhaps because of, his military service in World War I and his time in London during World War II as director of the US Office of Censorship, Knight had developed a suspicious attitude toward governments' use of the press to further foreign policy goals. Knight, a Pulitzer Prize–winning journalist whose oldest son had been killed in action during the last months of World War II, believed that his newspaper chain had an obligation to question what he regarded as government misinformation. Knight used his Sunday column to insist that the United States was "embarked upon a disastrous course." He dismissed Richard Nixon's arguments for even stronger military action and lamented the absence of congressional dissent, which, he asserted, had placed the nation "on the verge of a major war."[22]

Tony Walsh, the nephew of a Cleveland Steel Workers Organizing Committee member, seconded these concerns in a letter to the *Stater* on April 6, but shifted the focus to the Kent campus, taking direct aim at the US Army's Reserve Officers' Training Corps (ROTC) as evidence of the university's complicity in the war. In seeking to drum up support for the Washington antiwar march, Walsh, an army veteran disdainful of military authority, cited historical reasons to buttress his position against ROTC and employed his characteristic sarcasm to express disagreement with the war. Walsh became the first of many to link the presence of ROTC on the Kent State campus with the Vietnam War. On campuses nationwide, ROTC would become the most hated symbol of the war, rousing more ire than even the military draft itself.[23]

Walsh organized an ad hoc committee for the march on Washington that called for the withdrawal of all US forces from Vietnam, and he distributed thousands of flyers to publicize the protest and arranged for an SDS representative to speak at a campus teach-in about the Washington rally. Teach-ins, begun shortly before at the University of Michigan, were freewheeling discussions that had been generated by the escalation of the war. Modest in importance compared to the well-attended events held at Michigan, Kent State's teach-in failed to attract much of a crowd. Undeterred, Walsh mustered the YSA, Bob Ehrlich, an instructor in the English department, and a half dozen English department faculty to parade in a tight circle to promote the upcoming march. Although a small crowd of counterprotestors heckled the pickets in front of Bowman Hall, the vast majority of students seemed unwilling to get involved either way. Interviews conducted by the *Stater* showed that some undergraduates were indifferent, others believed it misguided, and still others thought that the picket "wasn't large enough. It just didn't seem like a demonstration."[24]

On April 17, twenty thousand antiwar partisans gathered in Washington, DC. The march attracted contingents from some fifty campuses, including Kenyon College and approximately two dozen students from Kent State. The majority, like Tony Walsh, traveled first to Cleveland, where they boarded buses for the trip to the capital. Roy Inglee and Ron Wittmaack had participated in the huge civil rights march in August 1963, and Barbara Brock had been among the five thousand demonstrators who had circled the White House in February 1962 to press the case for nuclear disarmament, but most from KSU were first-time participants. Whatever their experience level, they tried to stay within sight of the protestor who held high a sign that read simply KENT STATE.[25]

The April 1965 protest was small compared to the massive demonstrations that would follow, but it was, at the time, "the largest peace march in American history." Those in attendance on that warm spring day remember being stirred by the lacerating lyrics of Ohio State's passionate troubadour Phil Ochs and by SDS president Paul Potter's concluding speech, which the journalist Milton Viorst later described as "among classic statements of the radicalism of the 1960s." Potter's address embraced New Left philosophy and eschewed Old Left class-laden ideology, as he insisted that the war in Vietnam "provided the razor, the terrifying sharp cutting edge that has finally severed the last vestige of illusion that morality and democracy are the guiding principles of American foreign policy."[26]

The antiwar activity in Kent before the march gave dissidents more of a toehold on campus, while the Washington rally confirmed for them that the movement was national. Yet the political calculus at KSU among students, faculty, and administration seemed to favor the Johnson White House and Congress. Counterprotestors remained visible and boisterous. Board of trustees member Robert C. Dix advanced a "stay the course" position on Vietnam in his newspaper column. The university's president disliked the protests on his campus, but could take satisfaction from the knowledge that prowar students and faculty heavily outnumbered antiwar activists. White and the administration never found fault with the recognition and presence of the ultra-right Council on Freedom, but agonized over approving the YSA. Still, recognition of the YSA represented an upholding of liberal principle and a significant step away from Cold War orthodoxy of the 1950s. Most of all, though, White did not like outside meddling, either from state government or by local residents. Believing the best way to avoid it was to contain problematic leftist students, White's administration tolerated occasional ungentle treatment of radical activists by prowar conservatives, athletes, and fraternity members.[27]

President Lyndon B. Johnson and his advisers likewise sought to impede antiwar opposition, but without unleashing the McCarthy-style demons of the political right. Campus forums conducted by the State Department—the administration's answer to the antiwar teach-ins—became Johnson's moderate vehicle of choice. A four-person group, one of several dubbed "truth teams" by *Time* magazine, toured a half dozen midwestern universities in May. It is unclear whether Kent State made the official tour list, but a State Department representative, William Stearman, addressed the subject of Vietnam there on May 12, the day after prowar students rallied on the campus. KSU's Young Democrats and Young Republicans—bitter rivals just months before—had come together in support of Johnson's Vietnam policy as Democrat Matt Bufwack, a student from Warren, Ohio, and Young Republican leader Arnold Topp brought out two hundred people to back the war effort. The featured speaker, political science professor Robert S. Getz, stressed the importance of averting a US defeat in Vietnam and "making [the Communists] pay."[28]

Inspired by the bipartisan rally and the authority of a State Department speaker, the student senate joined the fray, passing a nearly unanimous resolution in support of Johnson's course of action in Vietnam. The newly conservative student senate also defeated a motion to give Bob Ehrlich university authorization to continue raising funds for civil rights activists in Selma, Alabama, where civil rights marchers had been brutally beaten by police and state troopers in March. One representative denounced Ehrlich as a communist for endorsing what became known as the "Selma bill." The charge stung Ehrlich, and for Dave Edwards the smear evoked memories of the treatment he received from other student senators during the CORE recognition dispute a year earlier. Conservatism would, for a time, slowly lose its vigor. But its roots were deep.[29]

Main Street in Middle America

In the spring of 1965, the Ohio Board of Regents announced a plan for the continued growth of higher education in the state, noting that the "greatest expansion requirements would be in northeastern Ohio." The regents anticipated that by the end of the next decade the state would need to support another 140,000 students, products of both the post–World War II baby boom and the increased affluence of American society. Fully a third of those students, they estimated, would come from cities in the densely populated northeast quadrant of Ohio. They expected Kent State, the largest public university in the region, to help accommodate the spike in enrollments by absorbing 7,000 to 8,000 new students into a number of branch campuses, such as those at Ashtabula, East Liverpool, and New Philadelphia, after capping registration on the main campus at 20,000.[30]

For President White and Robert C. Dix, the sudden sprouting of the campus represented an opportunity. More students meant more recognition and resources for both the university and the town. The growth of Kent State's doctoral programs would enable White to be the first KSU president to confer a PhD, and funding for research would increase 65 percent. Beyond being a source of local pride, the enlarged student body presented a range of business opportunities. Students needed off-campus housing, visiting parents required hotel rooms, and a wide variety of stores, restaurants, and bars desired customers and an inexpensive pool of labor. A bigger school required additional faculty, whose demand for housing would help raise local property values. Thus there were many advantages that town fathers, such as Robert Dix, hoped would come Kent's way as a result of the growth.[31]

At the same time, expansion of the campus that borders Kent's Main Street presented the prospect of less welcome change. Certainly, another five to ten thousand students, many from the cities, with their curiosity about the developing counterculture and different political orientations, were bound to put a strain on the more conservative culture of the Kent community. Most residents of Kent knew what they liked and liked what they knew. Thus, as one KSU faculty member observed, "[some] people resent the university." A town resident since 1950, this professor was convinced that, reasonably enough, the more established inhabitants "would prefer to keep Kent a quiet, small town." Even with the importance many attached to conformity, Kent had known labor strife in the 1930s and, beginning in the 1960s, racial friction when African Americans demanded more citizenship rights. Compared to a place like Lawrence, Kansas, at least Kent had a competitive, albeit conservative, two-party system. But all in all, in the mid-1960s Kent's surface politics lay between moderate conservative and conservative on the political spectrum, and beneath that surface lay a volatile, acidic subsoil of reaction.[32]

Robert C. Dix, one of the chief leaders of opinion in the city, came from a line of Ohioans. Although he and his twin brother, Raymond, also a newspaper publisher, were born in Wayne County in 1908, Dix lived most of his adult life in Portage County, where both his father and grandfather had originated. His twin brother chose to remain in his hometown of Wooster, where he operated the *Daily Record* in one of Ohio's most Republican counties. Portage County, on the other hand, had viable Democratic and Republican parties. Thus Robert Dix kept a lower profile in the Republican Party than did his brother. Still, besides the *Record-Courier*, his holdings included a television station and several radio stations that ensured he had much to say about local affairs. Some in the county may have had more money, but it is doubtful that any had more influence. Possessing a sometimes quick temper, Dix, as president of the KSU board of trustees, kept a close watch on the university and its faculty. When he learned that a political scientist who was a specialist on the Soviet Union was being considered for a teaching position, he asked the KSU president to look into his background. Monthly meetings of the board ensured that White and Dix were in regular contact.[33]

Robert White also had midwestern sensibilities, but his politics were not as conservative as Dix's. Whether he was a staunchly anticommunist Cold War liberal, a classical liberal in the John Stuart Mill tradition, or "the last of the Jeffersonian liberals," as one faculty member described him, is hard to say with certainty. In any case, there is no doubt that during his years at Kent State White's political skills were severely tested.[34]

"He was kind of the old-style college president," an education department professor recalled. Assuming the position in the fall of 1963, White faced challenges that rivaled any encountered by his five predecessors. According to his longtime secretary, "President White worked harder than anybody else, and put in longer hours. He was a very kind person and [was] highly respected by others, [by his] peers."[35]

By 1965, Dix and White had known each other for twenty years. Almost the same age, they favored gray suits, liked foreign travel, maintained memberships in the Rotary Club, held varying degrees of commitment to the GOP, and shared a mutual aversion to left-wing radicalism. James Michener, in his book on the Kent State shootings, observes: "The two Bobs, as they were called, had much in common. Both were retiring, both were soft-spoken . . . both dedicated to the building of a greater Kent. Neither was flamboyant, neither charismatic, neither bold in appearance. . . . They were low-key, stubborn men who believed in the virtues of Middle America."[36]

Escalation and the Draft

Tony Walsh, who bore a striking physical resemblance to the folksinger Dave Van Ronk, also stubbornly adhered to his beliefs, but his ideological roots lay in urban, ethnic America, where increasing numbers of Kent students originated. Yet Walsh, Ehrlich, and others opposed to American intervention were making little headway in the battle between antiwar and prowar students. The ranks of those supporting the war included KSU's Young Democrats, an organization that also attracted many ethnic, blue-collar students. The vast majority of working-class college kids, at least those in northeast Ohio, had yet to reject the Cold War liberalism that had formed out of the New Deal and World War II and to embrace antiwar, activist politics. Most continued to back the Johnson administration's Vietnam policies. At the end of summer quarter, campus reporters randomly interviewed several dozen students, questioning them about Johnson's recently announced deployment of another fifty thousand troops and an increase in draft calls. Two-thirds expressed varying degrees of support for the escalation, several citing the need to resist aggression and the spread of communism. This was consistent with a national Gallup Poll showing that 70 percent of the public—and an even larger majority of young people—backed the war effort. At Michigan State, where many undergraduates came from working-class homes, sixteen thousand students signed petitions circulated by conservatives in support of Johnson's policies. For most it came down to how the war affected them personally. In the *Stater* poll, the few who questioned the war cited a number of reasons, including skepticism about the military and a belief in Vietnam's right of self-determination. But the biggest concern was the draft. Even a young woman who backed the war made it clear that she favored Johnson's actions only "because my husband won't have to go."[37]

For the movement at Kent to widen beyond the radical core of socialist and independent leftists, the war had to begin intruding directly on students' lives. Concern over the draft grew as troop deployment increased and deaths in Vietnam mounted, and President White had to answer inquiries from US senators, such as Wisconsin's Gaylord Nelson, about the effect of the draft on KSU students. Hoping, however unrealistically, to compel his opposition to the military draft, Barbara Brock pressed White to make clear the university's position on conscription, but without success. The only known instance of White using his influence with the Selective Service System came when an Illinois draft board endangered his senior administrative assistant. White intervened and managed to assure an occupational deferment.[38]

White's situation was made easier by a conscription system that deferred or exempted thousands of draft-age men for a variety of reasons, from student status to employment in a growing number of occupational categories. In addition, many young men failed induction tests for physical, developmental, or psychological reasons; some worked at failure and received help from draft counselors and physicians. Married men were deferred from 1963 through 1966, though later the deferment applied only to married fathers. College undergraduates were eligible for 2-S deferments, while medical and dental students received automatic exemptions, as did those in divinity schools. Those morally opposed to war could apply to local draft boards for the often unattainable Conscientious Objector status, which, if granted, meant that their service requirement could be satisfied by work in hospitals or mental health facilities.[39]

After July 1965 the typical eligible male was, according to White House press secretary George Reedy, "planning draft avoidance as carefully as he is planning his career." An expanding network of physicians, clergy, and lawyers opposed to the war helped many well-to-do young men avoid conscription by taking advantage of the complicated rules and technicalities of the Selective Service System. But for working-class draftees who lacked access to such support, the options were more limited unless they had the resources and qualifications to attend college. As Christian Appy has shown in his careful study, *Working-Class War*, "Class . . . was the crucial factor in determining which Americans fought in Vietnam." Such was certainly the case in ethnically diverse working-class Barberton, a city that in 1960 had a whopping 63 percent of its workforce engaged in manufacturing. Alan Canfora graduated from Barberton High School in 1967 and went on to attend one of Kent State's branch campuses, but most of his classmates went into the service. Young blue-collar men in rural areas faced the same issue. Larry Mowrer, twenty-four years old in the summer of 1965, had dropped out of Kent State after attending intermittently for several years. Single and working construction jobs in Wayne County, he enlisted in the Ohio National Guard in December of that year, thereby obtaining a deferment from full-time military service.[40]

Part-time National Guard duty provided one alternative to being drafted, while also supplying a supplemental income. It also virtually guaranteed that the enlistees would not be sent to Vietnam. James Farriss and Roger Maas, from conservative Wayne County, joined the Ohio National Guard in 1964. Richard D. Lutey enlisted in January 1965, a month before the war escalated with the bombing of North Vietnam and the subsequent introduction of US ground forces. Robert James, a twenty-one-year-old also from Wayne County, signed up in May 1965, a few months before the first large call-up. For these men, who later saw duty at Kent State, the incentive may have been economic. William Herschler, of the same age and from the same area, a scheduler for Pittsburgh Plate and Glass, enlisted after the major call-ups began. Like the others, Herschler served in the 145th Infantry. So did Ronnie Myers, an aide at the Ohio Agricultural and Research Center in Wayne County, who joined around the same time. James Pierce, a graduate of the class of 1962 at Kent-Roosevelt High School, attended college on and off, including, for a time, the University of Hawaii; he enlisted the Guard as soon as President Johnson's draft call-ups were announced. Pierce's unit, Troop G of the 107th Armored Cavalry, drew its recruits primarily from Portage and Summit counties. With 170,000 men drafted between September 1965 and January 1966, National Guard service became an attractive alternative.[41]

The antiwar movement remained small over the summer of 1965. Kent State's Carl Oglesby won election as SDS president, the first product of a second-tier university to do so; his selection came at a time when the organization had just three thousand members on approximately eighty campuses, including Michigan, where he was then based, along with Kenyon, Western Reserve, and Oberlin. Oglesby was the first SDS president raised in a working-class home, but, as of yet, the organization had no chapters in Ohio on campuses with significant populations of working-class students. This would begin to change during Oglesby's term, as the war demanded more and more working-class youth. In the meantime, Committees to End the War in Vietnam were emerging in midwestern cities and on state college campuses, such as Kent's, with the aim of extending the movement to include nonsocialists and moderate students. These efforts against the Vietnam War would shape Kent State University for the remainder of the decade.[42]

CHAPTER 4

The Kent Committee to End the War in Vietnam

FALL QUARTER 1965 brought another record level of students to Kent State, with enrollment reaching nearly fifteen thousand. Thanks in large part to the expansion of the interstate highway system and state toll roads that shortened travel times, an increasing number of new students were out-of-staters from Pittsburgh, western New York, and as far away as Long Island and New Jersey. As in the past, however, the vast majority—more than 85 percent—were residents of Ohio, and a substantial proportion were from places close enough to permit daily commutes or weekend visits back home.[1]

Wherever they came from, undergraduates busied themselves with issues that typically concern students—roommate problems, homesickness, learning to navigate an often unfamiliar environment, acquiring course books, adding and dropping classes, and exploring the campus and off-campus social scene. For many of these students, the war in Vietnam remained a distant abstraction. Though draft calls had spiked since the introduction of American ground troops the previous spring, 2-S deferments continued to insulate college students from military service in a war most assumed would be over by the time they graduated.

Yet for a small but growing core of political activists at Kent, the problem was not the draft but the war in Vietnam it fed. For them, the beginning of the new academic year signaled the resumption of efforts to bring the war to end. It was now clear to protesters like Barbara Brock, Tony Walsh, Bob Ehrlich, and Barbara Gregorich—the last of whom had just returned to campus as an English instructor after earning a master's degree at the University of Wisconsin—that in order to magnify their impact they needed to increase their ranks. They knew they would have to create a broad-based organization that encouraged students of all political persuasions to participate, even as the more ideologically minded continued to educate the campus community about what they perceived to be the underlying causes of the war.[2]

This tactical shift reflected a larger debate beginning to churn in the peace movement. After the campus teach-ins and Washington protest in April 1965, SDS pulled back from becoming a national center for the antiwar movement, as many in the organization were hesitant to become a "single issue" group. These members gave priority to working among the poor in the urban ghettoes of northern cities like Cleveland. Ironically, SDS had elected a new president, Carl Oglesby, who was drawn to the organization because of its antiwar stance at the very moment the group relinquished the opportunity, as former president Todd Gitlin later lamented, to fashion "an anti-imperialist peace movement." Partly to fill this void, the National Coordinating Committee to End the War in Vietnam (NCC), came together as an ad hoc body that would serve as a clearinghouse to organize marches and educational programs. This should have been an agreeable enough undertaking given the ecumenical aims of the radical pacifists, civil rights veterans, and members of the Committee for a Sane Nuclear Policy who founded NCC, but the selection of a Communist Party member to head the group immediately raised the suspicions of the party's ideological rivals in the Socialist Workers Party. Moderates in the newly formed NCC, understanding little of the quarrel, were bewildered. But over time such tensions, which filtered down to local levels, would help shape, educate, and eventually divide members of the soon-to-be organized Kent Committee to End the War in Vietnam and the campus antiwar community generally.[3]

A dozen or so activists at Kent State responded to the call to participate in the first of what the NCC called "International Days of Protest." Marching in Cleveland on Saturday, October 16, 1965, Bob Ehrlich and Barbara Gregorich were among those from Kent who helped make the demonstration one in which opponents of the war outnumbered counterprotestors. Still, jeering right-wingers and self-styled patriots waded into the crowd of marchers, provoking fights, tearing down antiwar banners, and using a bullhorn to shout down speakers. Ehrlich was shoved and had a sign torn from his hands by a war supporter; a Cleveland policeman refused to intervene.[4]

Bob Ehrlich may have lacked combative qualities, but not political commitment, as he had proven by going to Alabama in the late winter of 1965 for the Selma-to-Montgomery march. Though he could be guarded, and "very much a loner" in the estimate of one activist, he was reliable, intelligent, and imaginative. He also had a base in the English department, where most of the professors and an even larger number of the instructors opposed the war. When he returned to Kent after the confrontation in Cleveland, Ehrlich joined with Tony Walsh to launch the Kent Committee to End the War in Vietnam (KCEWV).[5]

As Fred Halstead noted in his memoir of the antiwar movement, on many campuses the Young Socialist Alliance (YSA) "threw itself into building independent committees and fought within them to maintain their focus on antiwar activity and their nonexclusive character." To reassure prospective recruits that the KCEWV would not be dominated by the YSA, Ehrlich (who sympathized with the group but was not evidently a member) and Walsh (an independent) agreed to rotate responsibility for chairing the new organization with Barbara Gregorich, who did belong to the YSA. Looking to mobilize students for the next Washington march in late November, the KCEWV scheduled its first meeting for October 27, 1965, in the Student Union. The day before, they were confronted by Gerald Graham's conservatives, affiliated with the Young Americans for Freedom, who promised to oppose any antiwar pickets that the new committee might organize.[6]

The activists intended, their flyer announced, to form "a permanent committee to end the United States' war against Vietnam" that would include "people from all walks of life and from a wide variety of organizations." Sidney Jackson, the library science professor mentioned earlier as the first at KSU to criticize the Vietnam War, agreed to serve as faculty adviser to the KCEWV, and the group experienced no difficulty in eventually obtaining university recognition; the administration, fatigued perhaps after the CORE and YSA battles, voiced no evident opposition. At the first organizational meeting, several speakers took turns explaining the committee's purpose. That seventeen people present volunteered for the group's steering committee suggests several things—a high degree of enthusiasm, that there were more leaders than followers, and that control of the committee may have been an issue from the start.[7]

The new academic year also saw the establishment of other groups. Vince Modugno, the son of an Akron rubber worker, helped organize the Student Religious Liberals (SRL). Bob Bresnahan, a senior English major from Akron, and Harold Rogers, a former Peace Corps volunteer, announced plans for the formation of a campus chapter of the Student Nonviolent Coordinating Committee (SNCC). In publicizing the SNCC meeting, Bresnahan insisted that "every student has a stake in civil rights," and added that "every man's freedom is threatened by segregation." Unlike many of Kent's activists, Bresnahan and Rogers came from well-to-do families; Bresnahan's father was a prominent trucking executive, and Rogers, an African American, hailed from the affluent Cleveland suburb of Shaker Heights. A year later, after briefly considering affiliating with the W. E. B. Du Bois Clubs, a national youth organization sponsored by the Communist Party USA, Bresnahan and Rogers left SNCC and moved into the orbit of the YSA.[8]

SNCC had been like a battering ram against Jim Crow segregation in the deep South, but at Kent State the group made little impression. The SRL proved far more enduring but did not attract large numbers of students. That distinction belonged more to the KCEWV, whose membership grew steadily in the weeks leading up to the planned antiwar march in Washington. On November 2, the group drew some three hundred people to a talk by Sidney Peck, a sociology professor at Case Western Reserve University with a background in both the union movement and electoral politics. Peck, whose activism stretched back to the 1948 Progressive Party, had helped ignite the campus teach-ins in early 1965, drawing three thousand people to the one organized at Western Reserve. Believing that the war wasted the nation's economic resources, diverted attention from civil rights, and violated self-determination for Southeast Asian countries, Peck told those assembled in the Bowman Hall lecture room that the war was not "in the interest of the American people, or the Vietnamese people or the people of the world."[9]

Just weeks later the KCEWV hosted another Western Reserve professor, the famous Dr. Benjamin Spock. An early proponent of nuclear disarmament, Spock, like his colleague Sid Peck, argued that US military policies had thwarted democratic elections in Vietnam and had "alienated even our allies." He urged his audience of over two hundred to attend the Washington rally, where he and Carl Oglesby would be among the principal speakers.[10]

Joe Jackson was among those who heeded the call to go to Washington. The son of KCEWV faculty adviser Sidney Jackson, he was born in the Bronx but had moved to Kent at the age of thirteen when his father accepted an appointment in the library department in 1959. Though the elder Jackson became well known for his commitment to liberal causes, working with the Kent NAACP to promote civil rights and frequently writing letters to the *Record-Courier* on topics ranging from racial discrimination to foreign affairs, his son had avoided politics and focused on his studies after enrolling at the university in 1964. But by his sophomore year, as both the war in Southeast Asia and the controversy surrounding it heated up, young Jackson decided he had to get involved. After a bouncer threw him out of a downtown bar in the fall of 1965 for making antiwar comments, he decided "I needed to do more than I'd done to explain the issue of the war."[11]

Police

Throughout the fall, members of the Socialist Workers Party (SWP) had been actively involved in the Cleveland mayoral campaign of Carl Stokes, an African American state senator. Although the SWP normally avoided partisan electoral politics, the organization made an exception in the case of Stokes, whose independent campaign they saw as advancing a black liberation agenda. In a disputed four-way election on November 2, Stokes finished a very close second in a contest he believed he was winning until the city's conservative afternoon newspaper, the *Cleveland Press,* warned that "black voters were turning out in unprecedented numbers," which Stokes believed "scared out the whites [to vote] in the [late] afternoon." Despite the narrow loss, the campaign had won the SWP a measure of respect among some in Cleveland's black community and further enmity from the city's police, whose overwhelmingly white members solidly opposed Stokes's election.[12]

Tensions between police and Stokes supporters in the SWP remained high eleven days later, at a fundraiser held at Debs Hall, the party's headquarters in Cleveland. A racially mixed and well-dressed crowd attended the event, which was arranged by Richard B. Tussey, a principal organizer of the 1958 Conference of American Socialists. Near midnight, a group of plainclothes police raided the meeting, and a frightening commotion ensued. Police accounts of what happened next differed sharply from those offered by the attendees, but what ultimately mattered for Kent State activists John McCann, Barbara Brock, and especially Bob Ehrlich and Barbara Gregorich, was the treatment their arrests received in the Cleveland papers and, thereafter, in the *Daily Kent Stater.* In the newspaper coverage, police and state liquor authority agents claimed that they were attacked, with one asserting that "we fought for our lives until enough detectives arrived to quiet the mob." The breathless liquor authority agent said that "my men looked . . . as if they had just come out of a Viet Nam battle." The *Stater* account made no mention of police gunfire, but Gregorich recalled it vividly:

> Out of the blue [with] no warning, seven or eight cops burst through the door, guns drawn. They began yelling something at us and several of the black men and John [McCann] got really angry. John charged at them and I thought he was going to be shot. The cops [fired] seven or eight times into the ceiling. All of us ducked, hid, or reached for someone. After they shot, they handcuffed John, two black guys, and another white guy, Herman Kirsch. They dragged them down the stairs and arrested thirty-one of us. It made the newspapers the next day.
>
> When I showed up at Kent on Monday . . . [I told] my brother [Mark Gregorich, a KSU student at the time] . . . I didn't do anything wrong and that the fault was with the cops. The head of the English department [Kenneth R. Pringle] asked me to explain. I sat down and explained it. I never heard a bad word [from him].[13]

Meanwhile, the fighting in Vietnam intensified. From mid-October until late November, American troops operating in the western part of Vietnam, along the Cambodian border, engaged regular units of the North Vietnamese

Army for the first time. Over three hundred American soldiers died in the Ia Drang Valley during the fighting in Pleiku Province, nearly half of them in a single deadly ambush during the process of withdrawal. Although the North Vietnamese reportedly suffered more than ten times the US losses, the Battle of Ia Drang Valley, as it came to be called, sent shock waves through official Washington, making it clear to American political and military leaders that it was going to be a long and bloody war. Nor were mounting battlefield losses the only measure of the war's escalating costs. In early November 1965, while fighting still raged in the Ia Drang, two committed pacifists—one a Quaker, Norman Morrison, the other a Catholic, Roger LaPorte—burned themselves to death in separate incidents in protest over the widening war. Morrison did so outside the Pentagon office window of defense secretary Robert McNamara, who witnessed emergency medical personnel covering the body.[14]

Dramatic as these horrifying incidents were, antiwar leaders remained convinced that the tactic of mass marches held the greatest promise of bringing the war to an end. As they prepared for the upcoming antiwar march in Washington, members of the KCEWV ran into many of the same obstacles they had encountered the previous spring. A picket organized in front of Bowman Hall to generate publicity for the march again attracted derisive heckling from male students living in nearby Stopher Hall, and again Kent city police were on hand to monitor the event. Over the objections of an English professor, the police forced demonstrators whom "they could not identify readily" to reveal their names, something authorities had done in 1961 when students on campus had picketed against racial discrimination in area housing. A KCEWV meeting the following evening went off without incident, save for the usual police presence, but the day after that Gregorich and Ehrlich were ordered by campus police to discontinue distribution of *The Drummer,* a newsletter that publicized the YSA/SWP version of the arrests and shooting incident in Cleveland two weeks earlier.[15]

Washington Again

Concurrent with the November 27 antiwar rally, organizers met in Washington for the first convention of the National Coordinating Committee to End the War in Vietnam, where the cadres of the left, old and new, once again locked horns in their ongoing ideological struggle. In a renewal of long-standing unsolved tensions, the SWP filled the convention room with its members and youthful supporters, to the consternation of veteran peace activist Dave Dellinger, who feared the outbreak of bare-knuckle brawls. Many of the fifteen hundred who came to the conference believing they would be helping to end the war instead saw in-fighting over organizational position and advantage.[16]

Although delegates not linked to the Communist Party and SWP may not have understood the quarrel, those who persevered had little trouble remembering their purpose in coming to Washington—to protest the war. "The crowd was huge," Joe Jackson recalled; the turnout numbered some forty thousand demonstrators. Though large in contrast to the minimal expressions of dissent seen during the McCarthyite 1950s, the march and rally were small compared to what came later. Jackson, who was participating in his first such rally, remembered that "we had a busload of people—Kent was one of the bigger groups."[17]

Jackson listened again to Dr. Spock and to an array of prominent personalities, but it was Carl Oglesby whose speech earned, according to SDS historian Kirkpatrick Sale, "the only standing ovation of the afternoon." Oglesby—trained in theater at Kent State—was a spellbinding extemporaneous orator, but this time he had prepared his talk. Censuring the country's racial policies in the wake of the 1964 Freedom Summer campaign in Mississippi and the recent 1965 Watts uprising in Los Angles, Oglesby argued that the same rebellious spirit animated the struggle of the Vietnamese against widening US involvement. Expanding his wide-ranging condemnation, he dissected America's role abroad, ranging from the Central Intelligence Agency's involvement in Iran in 1953 through the subsequent covert and overt interventions in Guatemala, Cuba, and the Dominican Republic, denouncing it all as a means to enrich "our American corporate system." For SDS's newest leader, America's big-business-backed foreign policy amounted to and resulted in nothing less than "a crime that so few should have so much at the expense of so many." The address made him famous in movement circles, and his critique set the tone for the remainder of SDS's existence; reprints of the speech became part of the organizations must-read program of study. Oglesby also told his listeners that the task of dealing with the "colossus" would not be easy.[18]

Tony Walsh and other KCEWV activists knew the truth of Oglesby's remarks. When they returned to Kent State they learned that hundreds of students had signed petitions supporting the war, and numerous others had submitted letters to the *Stater* condemning Walsh's sarcastic Veterans Day comments against the ROTC program (composed, he wrote, of "incompetent schoolboy gladiators") of the kind he had been making for months. A sailor aboard a naval vessel who had appealed for letters from young women at Kent State thanked them for the correspondence he had received and informed them that he had inscribed their "names on some of the bombs that have gone to North Viet Nam." More in keeping with the spirit of the approaching Christmas holiday, President White had the *Stater* photograph him sending the first of thousands of holiday cards to troops who had just fought in the Ia Drang Valley.[19]

New Draft Scare

Returning to campus after the holidays, students were greeted with news that got everybody's attention: the Selective Service System was considering ending deferments for full-time college students. The first *Stater* issue of the quarter announced "College Men Face Prospect of Draft—Hershey." Selective Service director Lieutenant General Lewis B. Hershey named two proposals: continue exempting those men pursuing certain courses of study, especially science and math; or requiring male students to remain in the upper three-fourths of their respective classes in order to maintain eligibility for the 2-S student deferment.[20]

In March, Hershey decided instead to revive an aptitude test known as the Selective Service College Qualification Test (SSCQT) as an additional method for preserving 2-S status. With a score of seventy or better, students would be able to keep their student deferments, continuing the policy of favoring those who pursued "socially useful" careers. Kent State served as one of twelve hundred sites for students to take the examination, administered three times that spring. The SSCQT was voluntary, but failure to take it put students at further risk if their class standing dropped into the lowest quartile. A *Stater* editorial urged students to sign up for the test. English department faculty, including Barbara Gregorich, offered guidance to students with suspicions about the exam. On another front, Barbara Brock of the KCEWV unsuccessfully pressed the university president to make a public statement against the draft. All students facing the draft did receive an unexpected favor from the KSU administration when a bureaucratic glitch prevented grade reports from being processed in a timely fashion. The error resulted in an academic first for the university: for the winter 1966 quarter there were no dismissals for poor grades.[21]

The record is unclear as to the number of students at Kent State who lost their 2-S status as a result of either poor grades or a low score on the SSCQT. Of the 1.8 million students holding a 2-S in January 1966, less than half took the Selective Service examination. Led by its president, Carl Oglesby, who vigorously advanced antiwar, antidraft work in the organization, SDS used the scheduled SSCQT to circulate their own, which they labeled a counter-draft exam, to educate students politically about the history of the war. Concern about the draft was widespread, although the anxiety did not immediately lead to a significant increase in antiwar participation on campus.[22]

SDS largely failed to generate much interest in their alternative test about the war. None of those interviewed for this book who took the SSCQT remembers the SDS effort, but some lost or surrendered their 2-S deferment. These included blue-collar students like Mark Lencl, a student at Cuyahoga Community College in Cleveland in 1966, who dropped below the required number of credit hours because of his work schedule and was drafted in April, and John Conklin, from an industrial city in northeast Ohio, who left KSU as a result of low grades and found himself drafted into the army. Another, twenty-year-old Ken Johnson, a student at KSU's Ashtabula branch, quit school in 1965 and enlisted in the US Army, despite being at low risk because he was married. Like Lencl and Conklin, Johnson was the son of union members, and like them he immersed himself in Kent's antiwar movement following his discharge. Still later he became president of the campus Vietnam Veterans Against the War chapter. Whatever fate awaited young men, Chris Butler, a Kent State student and a musician, spoke for them all when he said of the draft, "When you hit eighteen, it was crunch time." Indeed, beyond high school, military conscription lay in the future for virtually every able-bodied male unable to obtain a prized exemption. Draft opponents, at least the majority, disliked the war and its rationale on a variety of moral and political grounds. Whatever the nature of the objections, the draft posed wrenching dilemmas for those affected.[23]

In addition to broadening the base of the antiwar movement at Kent, the KCEWV also succeeded in linking the war to the issue of civil rights. After a campus meeting that featured a civil rights worker who spoke on "The Vietnamese People and the Negro Revolt," the KCEWV hosted a program with the same theme at Kent's Union Baptist Church, in the city's tiny African American neighborhood, on February 12. The program featured several African American speakers from Cleveland and was followed by a march into town.[24]

A Desire for Creativity

As far back as the 1950s, countercultural currents were evident in Kent: Carl Oglesby's Macedonians, a poetry circle run by Paul Zimmer, Danny Thompson's civil rights participation, the incipient collaboration of Kent's Marty Pahls with underground cartoonists Robert Crumb and, later, Harvey Pekar in Cleveland; the alternative scene nourished in KSU's art school and theater department, as well as among English faculty, the originators of the *Kent Quarterly*. By the 1960s the corridors of the art department had become a breeding ground for a new politics as well as a new lifestyle.[25]

In an environment where many more students still joined fraternities and sororities, these students were seeking a social life with others who felt alienated from mainstream culture. Off-campus hangouts such as the Erie Café, the Blind Owl, and the Needle's Eye coffeehouse became gathering places for "people who liked Ferlinghetti [and] Kafka, who liked Bob Dylan and were hated by everybody else in town," as Carolyn Knox, an art student at the time, recalled. In her words, KSU had a "fairly hip reputation. There was a filmmaking department, a good art department, a lot of music there." Like many young women at

Kent, Knox chafed under dormitory curfews and dress codes that included high heels for Sunday dinner. To students there and elsewhere, such rules increasingly seemed outdated and unnecessary—"irrelevant" in what soon became the catchword of the day. Chris Butler, who would play in the Numbers Band with Terry Hynde, recalled that during this time "things opened up," as "kids coming out of working-class backgrounds" began to feel "a desire for creativity, to do art." Butler, who later became active in antiwar politics, believed that the tension between class roots and traditional college culture made such students "a little more extreme in their self-expression." Observing the same developments from different perspective, President White told the members of Kent's Lions Club that "these fringed persons have withdrawn into a cloister under which they have adopted a uniform and a ritual enslaving them far more than the so-called conformity they sought to escape."[26]

Another enclave of dissent not quite in keeping with the image President White presented to the Lions Club was the Unitarian Universalist Church on Gougler Street, where the Reverend Peter Richardson had helped Vince Modugno and his friend George Hoffman organize the Student Religious Liberals. Though one historian has noted that the SRL "was, despite its name, highly secularized and radical," it is clear that many antiwar activists were influenced by their religious values. Mainline Protestant denominations like the Methodist Church embraced not only a set of spiritual and ethical principles, but also an explicit antiwar politics. Ministers like Richardson provided a place for Kent's small politicized counterculture to meet and grow. Later, a Catholic priest at Kent's St. Patrick's Church also spoke out against the Vietnam War.[27]

Hoffman and Modugno had both grown up in Akron in ethnic working-class families. Hoffman's German American father had been employed in the rubber industry until wounds suffered during his service in World War II forced him to take work in the family's tin shop. His mother, a Slovak American, had come from Kipling, a southeastern Ohio mining town where, in addition to a commitment to unions, she cultivated a faith in what her son called "the trinity—Jesus, Mary, and FDR, and not necessarily in that order." Over time, George shed much of his own religiosity, but not the class-based politics he learned from his parents. Modugno's Italian American parents, both rubber workers, also exerted influence on his politics, with his father, Rocco, being the first in the household to express opposition to the war. In the late 1950s, the Hoffman and Modugno families both moved to Cuyahoga Falls, where the two future activists became high school friends. There a teacher influenced their views on the war and helped a graduating classmate obtain Conscientious Objector status. Primed politically, the mild-mannered Hoffman and more demonstrative Modugno enrolled at Kent State in the fall of 1965. A year later, after founding the SRL, they set up their coffee house, the Yellow Unicorn, in the basement of the Unitarian Church. Within a few years, the place became known for black flags, black lights, and acid rock music. Attracting their biggest gathering when future James Gang and Eagles guitarist Joe Walsh played there, the club influenced the town's incipient counterculture. Modugno recalled, "The Unicorn was viewed as a radical alternative and attracted large numbers of college and high school students."[28]

The Tide Begins to Turn

As young people with alternative cultural and intellectual interests, longer hair, and rumpled and changing modes of dress became more numerous and more evident in Kent, opposition to their appearance and politics grew. George Hoffman remembers the hostility engendered by the antiwar bumper sticker on his car, and he had objects thrown at him from passing automobiles because of the length of his hair. Yet the blend of New Left politics and youth culture mores also provided activists a kind of shelter for their increasingly familiar activities—meetings, pickets in front of Bowman Hall, and lecture programs. Seeing themselves as "outsiders," they identified with other marginalized groups and learned to link racism and the war in Vietnam. Thus after the Selma march one KCEWV member carried a sign during a police-monitored picket that read "Cattle Prods in Alabama, Napalm in Vietnam."[29]

While the connection between the civil rights struggle and the war in Southeast Asia may have been evident to some young activists, to others it was not clear at all. This was particularly true of Democratic loyalists like Dave Dyer, a coal miner's son from south-central Ohio who saw Lyndon Johnson as the heir of Franklin Roosevelt and the party as the champion of the common man and the underprivileged. Even as the war in Vietnam escalated, they pointed to such landmark domestic legislation as the Civil Rights Act of 1964 and Voting Rights Act of 1965 as evidence of Johnson's commitment to racial justice and progressive policies in general. Only gradually did Dyer and others like him break with the Johnson over his Vietnam policy, and even then they were often reluctant to participate in antiwar protests that were to some extent more unpopular than the war itself. Vince Modugno later recalled the "massive negative crowd" that greeted a small band of antiwar pickets in front of Bowman Hall. The little circular protest was his "first vision of a demonstration at Kent State"—the "fraternity guys" heckling and taunting the protesters while the police "turned a blind eye and sort of patted these guys on the back."[30]

On May 19, 1966, the historian Herbert Aptheker, a Communist Party member, gave a talk at Kent State. Months before, Aptheker had visited Hanoi with fellow historian Staughton Lynd and SDS founder Tom Hayden. Before his trip Aptheker had been barred from appearing at Ohio State, and after it at the

University of North Carolina under a speaker-ban law similar to the one that had been enacted in Ohio. Thus his appearance caused potential problems for President White. Carefully coordinating the university's response with trustee Robert C. Dix, White decided not to interfere with Aptheker's talk, prompting Aptheker to call his address the first "really free" speech at a state university in Ohio. Introduced on the night of his talk by Tony Walsh, Aptheker argued that the war harmed the United States diplomatically and contributed to inflationary pressures that harmed the American economy. Drawing on recent history, Aptheker recommended that the United States do what the French had done a decade earlier: get out of Southeast Asia. There were, as might be expected, detractors; a handful of Young Republican students applauded when Aptheker described the deaths of Vietnamese civilians in the aerial bombings, while another smashed a glass collection jar the KCEWV had been circulating. Most in the crowd of five hundred, though, were supportive.[31]

More than any analysis or ideological critique, however, it was the course of the war itself that influenced the spread of antiwar sentiment at Kent State and on other campuses. Throughout the first half of 1966, as the fighting intensified, US casualties continued to mount. During the first three weeks of March alone, 228 Americans were killed; by the end of the year, total KIAs would exceed 6,000. Months earlier, draft calls reached beyond 40,000 a month, a number matched by enlistments often induced by the threat of conscription. With the conflict showing no signs of ending, many who had been content to ignore the war or support it uncritically were forced to evaluate not only its costs but also its implications—personal, political, and moral. Was the war necessary and just? Was the draft fair? Was the death of a high school classmate or neighbor worth it? What would you do if you were drafted? By the end of spring quarter the KCEWV had added several dozen new members, while its critics had become noticeably less visible and vociferous. The tide had begun to turn, it seemed, though its effects were not yet fully felt. Many students were still reluctant to give public voice to the doubts and criticisms they increasingly shared privately with others. For the leaders of Kent State's small but expanding cohort of antiwar activists, much work remained to be done.[32]

CHAPTER 5

Fire in the City, Vigils on the Campus

IN THE summer of 1966, living conditions for African Americans in Cleveland had hardly changed since the death of Bruce Klunder and the school boycott two years before. Squeezed between "urban renewal" projects that had eliminated large swaths of working-class housing and unwelcoming white suburbs that ringed the city, the most blacks lived in overcrowded neighborhoods with substandard housing stock, segregated schools, limited job opportunities, and sporadic public services. On the night of July 18, 1966, the accumulated tensions fueled by these conditions erupted after an altercation between a white bar owner and a black patron in the heavily segregated Hough area on the city's East Side. As crowds gathered at the scene and the Cleveland police arrived in force, anger escalated into violence. Where the death of Rev. Klunder had triggered rock throwing and vandalism in parts of the city, now there was arson and gunfire. Snipers took shots at police. Others hurled Molotov cocktails and smashed police car windows. "This is just like Vietnam," one officer radioed headquarters.[1]

Unable to contain the disorders with his police force, Ralph Locher, a lackluster second-term mayor who had narrowly defeated Carl Stokes in the racially hued election eight months earlier, appealed to Governor James Rhodes for the Ohio National Guard. On the night of July 20, units of the 107th Armored Cavalry and 145th Infantry—seventeen hundred troops in all—rumbled into the city. Among those assigned to the 107th were a foursome of friends, including Ed Grant and Mike Hill, both of whom held the rank of Specialist 4. The two later recalled that as their convoy set out for Hough from a National Guard armory in the suburb of Shaker Heights, they heard shouts of support from onlookers: " 'Yea! Here come the guard! Go get 'em, shoot those bastards, kill 'em all.' Women held up their kids to get a look at us; crowds lined the curbs, clapping and cheering. These people were all from the white areas bordering the black areas. The four of us were typical of the majority of the Guardsmen, in that we were white and shared the same basic attitude toward the black movement at the time. We felt threatened by it, and rightly so." It took nearly a week for the guardsmen to restore order. By then four people had been killed, thirty critically injured, and three hundred arrested, and more than 240 fires had been reported. The fatalities were all African Americans.[2]

Over dinner at their home not far from the epicenter of the uprising, Tony Walsh and his wife met with SDS members Terry Robbins and Corky Benedict and took stock of what had occurred. All were members of the Cleveland Community Project, where Robbins worked with his roommates, SDSer Bill Ayers and SNCC member Alex Witherspoon. Although their efforts to address the twin issues of economic inequality and racial injustice had met with some success, change had been slow. The events of July 1966 in Cleveland, including a confrontation between Ayers and Witherspoon and some heavily armed guardsmen, accelerated the radical trajectory of these young activists. Within a few years, all of them would embrace the rhetoric of revolution and become advocates of "black liberation."[3]

The Hough rebellion had a similar radicalizing impact, not surprisingly, on many of Cleveland's young blacks, including future Kent State student Erwind Blount, who could see the city burning from his family home on the outer edge of Hough, and Larry Simpson, a KSU-bound transfer from Cleveland State. Simpson later recalled the summer of 1966 as the time when "it all hit home." Having already immersed himself in the writings of W. E. B. Dubois, and deeply troubled by what had taken place, Simpson would eventually connect with other African American undergraduates at Kent State to organize a vehicle for their frustrations: the Black United Students (BUS).[4]

On August 6, shortly after the National Guard left the city, five hundred peace activists gathered in Cleveland for an "International Day of Protest" marking the anniversary of the bombing of Hiroshima, part of a national campaign to raise awareness of the Vietnam War through local protests. Among the speakers that day was Stokely Carmichael of SNCC, who condemned the war for claiming African American lives at a rate twice that of whites while draining resources from social programs. Six weeks earlier, he had been in Mississippi leading thousands of people (including Kent's Freedom Rider, Danny Thompson, and his African American girlfriend, Clevelander Emity Campbell), in the March Against Fear. During the dangerous trek south to Jackson, Carmichael had argued with Martin Luther King Jr. over the war, which both SNCC and CORE had formally denounced.[5]

Even as the escalation of war in Vietnam and spread of urban unrest at home radicalized growing numbers of Americans, these developments also contributed to a deepening polarization and conservative drift in Ohio and elsewhere.

On the eve of the 1966 midterm elections, polls revealed that over half of the white US population believed the pace of racial change to be too rapid; in 1962, only a third had felt that way. Opinion on the war continued to be volatile, and this was reflected in the election results. In Ohio, congressional Democrats, blamed for both racial dissension and the failure to resolve the conflict in Vietnam, lost gains made in the 1964 landside. Their delegation returned to a 19–5 minority, losing incumbent seats in suburban Cincinnati, Dayton, and Columbus as well as in southeastern Ohio, where a four-term congressman suffered a narrow defeat. Governor Rhodes, running for a second term, won an astonishing 62 percent of the popular vote and captured all but one of the state's 88 counties.[6]

The Hough riots, and the authorities' response to them, had been a hot issue throughout the election campaign. Many civic leaders in Cleveland were convinced that a cadre of communist-inspired black nationalists had instigated the violence. Among those they held responsible was Lewis Robinson, who, as we saw in chapter 2, was the founder of the Medgar Evers Rifle Club. Although a federal investigation later found no evidence of communist involvement, the suspicion remained that such influences, rather than the deplorable living conditions in the Hough ghetto, were to blame. The increasingly militant rhetoric of Robinson and other black nationalists only heightened white fears, while at the same time making them more appealing champions of black liberation in the eyes of the Socialist Workers Party (SWP) in Cleveland. On October 26, weeks before Ohio voters went to the polls, Robinson appeared in Kent at the invitation of campus activists and delivered a speech defending the use of force as an expression of black political power. "Another two or three years of violent demonstrations and the American people will be ready to accept Negroes as individuals," he insisted. Though he correctly forecast the duration of the urban rebellions, he seriously misread their long-term political impact.[7]

In early November, just days before the election, peace activists in Cleveland began putting put into operation the plans they had formulated in August for a coordinated set of protests against the Vietnam War. Now calling themselves the November 5–8 Mobilization Committee, they were part of a nationwide campaign to bring the war to the forefront of American politics and link it to the cause of civil rights. A protest in Cleveland sponsored by the group drew twelve hundred marchers; the featured speaker was the brother of an African American GI resister, one of the so-called Fort Hood Three, whose refusal of orders for Vietnam had been highly publicized by the SWP. Although the antiwar movement at Kent had always included a number of veterans—John McCann, Paul Cheeks, Ron Wittmaack, and Tony Walsh—the testimony of the resister's brother underlined for those in attendance the connection between racism and the war.[8]

In the wake of the November protest, the Cleveland branch of MOBE (as it was coming to be known), like its counterparts elsewhere, began planning for major demonstrations in San Francisco and New York the following spring. Mass protests of the sort scheduled for April 15, 1967, were important to building the movement as well as to sustaining morale. But at places like Kent State, such actions did little to solve the problem faced by local antiwar activists: how, in the words of Bob Ehrlich, "to stir up more opposition to the war" on campus. Ever since the lonesome protest in February 1965, the Kent Committee to End the War in Vietnam had organized meetings, forums, teach-ins, pickets, and several local "speak outs" as part of the mobilization effort for the Cleveland protest and, on one occasion, entered a float in the campus homecoming parade. They had even gone on an Akron television show. Still, for all the work involved, the committee had little to show for its labors, especially in mounting significant outdoor protests that would be attract the notice of the thousands of students attending the university.[9]

Silence Is Golden

No one interviewed for this book could recall who conceived of the idea for silent vigils, and the Kent Committee to End the War in Vietnam (KCEWV) kept no minutes. But at the beginning of the winter term in early January 1967, a dozen or so committee members made antiwar signs and stood silently along a pedestrian walkway connecting Bowman Hall and the Commons, the large expanse of ground in the center of campus then best known as the site of the Victory Bell rung after each triumph by a university sports team. Predictably, prowar students disrupted the first vigil. Vince Modugno, new to nonviolent protest, was struck in the head by a rock. Enraged, he had to be restrained by others intent on maintaining the peaceful observance. Otherwise weekly vigils attracted much the same response as the early picket protests—jeers and abusive taunts. In terms of publicity, the *Daily Kent Stater* gave the Wednesday vigils no coverage until a lone counterprotestor, recently returned from Vietnam, made his own sign to register disgust with the KCEWV. Pointing out the imbalance in coverage, militant Dave Edwards quickly damned the *Stater* for disregarding the KCEWV's efforts.[10]

The prowar picket may have spurred the counterprotestors. A "Back Our Boys" group formed soon afterward. Aiding the effort, twenty-two faculty members joined others from northeast Ohio schools in signing a statement supporting US policy in Vietnam, while a campus poll revealed that prowar students outnumbered antiwar opponents nearly four to one. One sophomore later active in SDS remembered the patriotic music blaring from a women's dormitory near the Student Union and tomatoes being thrown at those standing vigil. Yet KCEWV members continued to bear witness every Wednesday during the lunch hour, letting their signs speak for them.[11]

Trying to measure the impact many years later, several members of the committee felt that the vigil may have helped turn campus opinion against the war, as the quasi-religious watch may well have been less threatening to more moderate students. George Hoffman recalled: "We were trying to figure out what to do. There weren't enough of us to have a real demonstration. It was a really heavy thing to be against the war. We kept trying to think of things to do that would get people involved without having to go through that heavy of a commitment. The vigils seemed to be the way to do that."[12] Joe Jackson added:

> My concern was that we weren't reaching enough students and that the committee was becoming too cliquish. We still had faculty that were afraid of being seen at the literature table. To me, the breakthrough came when we decided to hold the peace vigil. It started as a very small group and became so large that we almost ran out of space. . . . One of the things that happened was we started to have faculty join us. They felt safe doing that. The vigils helped legitimize protest on the campus. The group doubled or tripled in size.[13]

Examining his own conversion process and his attitude toward the peace vigils, Bill Whitaker was uncertain whether "we should be there [Vietnam] or shouldn't." He had grown up in the East and spent his early adolescent years in Philadelphia and then in western Pennsylvania. Solidly middle class, he listened to the views of both parents—his father a Protestant businessman and unwavering Republican, his mother just as devout a Catholic and a JFK Democrat. Whitaker, who had a Kennedy-style head of hair and an interest in politics, admitted that at first he wasn't "well versed" and "supported Johnson and the Democratic candidates." Recalling his first reaction to the vigils, he added, "I looked upon the people who were demonstrating as . . . different. I didn't know them."[14]

What Whitaker had in common with the unfamiliar protesters was his opposition to the draft. Although he had moved with his family and was in and out of school for a time, the temporary loss of his 2-S deferment proved not to be a problem, as his frequent address changes created unintentional difficulties for his Philadelphia draft board in trying to locate him. He made sure, however, to take the SSCQT. As the war dragged on, he began to give the people he regarded as "different" a second look: "One day a week there was a vigil. Ten or twelve people. They would just stand there with placards that said 'End The War in Vietnam.' I thought, 'How could these people have any effect?' They would get jeered. The jocks, the guys in the frats made fun of them. I really thought it was courageous. Before the end of the school year I was joining them."[15]

Although hardly typical, Whitaker's experience was not unique. Edward O. Erickson, who went by Ric, had once identified with athletes, having played football at Buchtel High School in Akron. And like Whitaker, with whom he took philosophy classes, he knew something about politics, as his father served as the Democratic mayor of Akron from 1962 to 1965. Still, by the time he got to Kent State in 1964, the twenty-four-year-old Erickson's interests were more focused on the cultural avant-garde than on politics. Yet the war could not easily be avoided. A sensitive and dynamic personality, Erickson became upset one day when he saw former high school teammates threatening peace activists at the vigil. Later he joined the silent protest.[16]

A growing number of faculty members were also joining the ranks of the antiwar opposition. In response to the twenty-two professors who had signed a public endorsement of US policy in Vietnam, Bob Ehrlich organized the English department to draft a letter in support of the Teachers' Committee for Peace in Vietnam. Within three months, more than eighty members of the KSU faculty publicly made known their opposition to the war by listing their names, along with those of almost 250 students, on a statement that ran as a full-page ad in the *Stater*. Some faculty also began showing up at the vigils.[17]

At the UN

Preparing for the April 15 rally in New York City, the KCEWV hosted a fund-raising concert that featured Akron native and KSU student Terry Hynde on alto sax. The donations helped KCEWV finance the transportation of 150 participants, who boarded buses and trains in Cleveland for the rally at the United Nations building. Bill Whitaker and his roommate went after they hooked up with members of the Abraham Lincoln Brigade from Akron. Formed by Communist Party members and sympathizers in the 1930s, the Brigade fought for the Republic in the Spanish Civil War; those who survived kept the organization intact and continued to support left-wing causes. When they arrived in New York, KCEWV activists joined the Midwest contingent, marching with veterans of Depression-era struggles, unionized Meat Cutters, members of the Cleveland CORE chapter, and at least one active-duty GI. KCEWV member Judy Gollust, whose next-door neighbor in Painesville, Ohio, had been killed in Vietnam, recalled the "vast numbers of people"—a throng of 300,000 and the largest protest to date in American history. The speakers included Dr. Spock and Martin Luther King Jr.[18]

Both the size of the crowd and the personalities on the rostrum were of concern to the White House, as President Johnson privately spurned calls from the military and from within his administration to invade North Vietnam and commit an additional 200,000 troops to the fighting. In coming out forcefully against the war, King signaled his break with an administration that had supported civil rights with vital legislation. Most significant for foes of the war, King's stance brought more attention to the intersection of foreign conflict and domestic need, especially with African Americans bearing a disproportionate burden of the fighting. Angered by the high casualty rates of minorities, increasing numbers of African Americans, especially those to the left of King in groups like SNCC, focused on such racial disparities and emphasized the parallel between racial oppression at home and imperial oppression abroad, in both cases against people of color. This very concern led secretary of defense Robert McNamara and his chief deputy to warn the president just weeks after the huge protest that "there may be a limit beyond which many Americans . . . will not permit the United States to go. The picture of the world's greatest superpower killing or seriously injuring 1000 non-combatants a week . . . is not a pretty one."[19]

Whether working locally through the KCEWV or nationally through the MOBE, campus activists still faced a hard road. Most Kent State students, like most Americans, kept apart from both anti- and prowar demonstrations. Whatever the level of political involvement by Kent's student population in mid-1967, opponents of the KCEWV did not fade away after the UN rally. If anything, they became more strident, shocked as some were by the attention given to the march. One detractor of the KCEWV referred to the marchers as part of an "unspeakable malignance which has crept among us." An appearance on the campus in May by Democratic senator Wayne Morse of Oregon—one of only two members of his chamber to vote against the 1964 Gulf of Tonkin resolution—further aroused conservatives, even as others came to his defense.[20]

But if conservatives were taken aback by the size of the New York rally, KCEWV drew strength from it. Always seeking to make clear their position on the war, committee members succeeded in getting a long letter published in the *Stater* on May 25. In their statement, the organization explained that they sought to bring "peace to Vietnam" and that their "view is based on the right of self-determination for all nations." In early June the committee placed the full-page ad in the *Stater* mentioned earlier, which opposed US policy in Southeast Asia and "the extensive suffering the war has brought upon Vietnamese civilians."[21]

Cultural Change

In March 1966, *Stater* editors had raised the possibility that because of its stand on free speech issues, Kent might someday be thought of as the "Little Berkeley of the East." Berkeley activist Michael Rossman, one of the principal leaders of Berkeley's Free Speech Movement, no doubt would have scoffed at the idea. On a journalistic assignment a year later, and fresh out of jail for his activism, Rossman came to Ohio to investigate Kent's antiwar movement. He spent several days in town and came away unimpressed, dismissing the university as "some dreary large public campus to play off against Antioch and Oberlin." Referring to the students as being of "lower-class blood," he added a description of their organizing efforts: "Some months earlier . . .[an] antiwar protest had turned out a hundred for a lonely march. Now I found all told maybe a dozen committed to keeping active, trying to find a way to move it on. . . . They lived in what would become a commune. . . . Over late coffee we talked about organizing, about guerrilla theater, about holding together for warmth. Hang on, brothers and sisters, I said to them, some Spring is coming."[22]

Even if the level of antiwar activism fell short of his standards, Rossman could not help but notice signs of the burgeoning counterculture that had taken root in Kent. Antiwar radicalism and cultural rebellion may not always have inhabited the same person or occupied the same political space. Still, a shift in the politics and culture of the campus had become evident enough for the *Stater* to devote weeks of research to the topic. Quaint-sounding after the passage of many years, the series reads like a digest for the uninitiated. Relying on anecdotal and impressionistic evidence, two investigative reporters found that while marijuana and LSD were not plentiful at Kent State, they were available. They further described how those sharing the same interests and musical tastes found one another, following cues signaled by, say, the style of their clothes or the length of their hair: "People meet each other because they look the same," they revealed. "One person may walk up to a total stranger . . . and a relationship is generally established."[23]

As marijuana became more commonplace on campus and off, Kent attracted increasing numbers of young people throughout northeast Ohio. They came not only to score pot and other drugs, but to check out the thriving music scene and drink in the local bars, where eighteen-year-olds could legally buy 3.2 percent beer. The city's North Water Street, where many of the bars were located, became the place, according to a *Stater* headline, "Where the Action Is!" Students from many other colleges traveled to Kent regularly on weekends. So did young workers, high school students, and those who drifted between the worlds of work and school. The easy mixture of student and nonstudent allowed for the expansion of a critical mass of young people, and out of it Kent's oppositional culture slowly grew. Here committed antiwar radicals and less politically minded cultural rebels came to recognize that they shared many common interests and values as well as a common adversary: the local police.[24]

New Faces, New Energy

The mid-1960s saw much new construction on campus, including the completion of science buildings where Robert E. Franklin (always known as Bobby), a newly arrived doctoral student in chemistry, soon would be teaching. Franklin's arrival on campus contributed to a larger transformation, as the influx of new instructors and faculty accelerated the growth of activism. Exemplifying this change was the turnout for a presentation by *New York Times* correspondent Harrison Salisbury just before the end of the year's last summer session. Salisbury had visited North Vietnam in January, and in his remarks he urged Washington and Hanoi to negotiate a peaceful settlement to the conflict raging in Vietnam. Robert S. Getz, a balding and bespectacled political scientist who two years earlier had been hawkish on the war, told those assembled for Salisbury's talk that in his four years at Kent "this is the biggest turnout I've seen for a guest speaker."[25]

While Getz had yet to join the ranks of the vocal dissenters, eleven other members of his department submitted an open letter to President Johnson that called on him to "de-escalate the war." Dozens of faculty members, many of them new, organized themselves into the Ad-hoc Committee for De-escalation of the War in Vietnam. In an opinion column, Peter Crossland of the political science department advocated greater engagement by the university community, writing that aside from "the activities of the Kent Committee to End the War in Vietnam almost nothing has been done on this campus." His remarks struck a responsive chord. Soon, dissenting faculty set up a week-long "Vietnam School" under KCEWV sponsorship. The educational sessions featured newly appointed faculty members Jerry Lewis and Thomas Lough, tenured professors such as Sidney Jackson, and graduate students Ron Weisberger, Tom Dubis, and Roy Inglee.[26]

In November, when Gabriel Kolko—a New Left historian, Akron native, and Kent State alum—revisited the campus for the first time in a decade to speak at the invitation of the history department, he found the university altered physically. Lecturing in one of the many buildings constructed since his graduation in 1954, he must have marveled, too, at the attitudinal sea change on campus. As a KSU student during the Korean War, Kolko had failed to enroll a single person in the Student League for Industrial Democracy, the predecessor organization to SDS. Since their years at Kent did not overlap, Kolko had not known fellow Akron native Carl Oglesby when they were students, but he had come to know him since. By the time of his lecture, Kolko and activist-minded students at Kent knew of Oglesby's recent book, *Containment and Change,* called by one friendly critic "a bitter condemnation of colonialism, cold war anti-Communism, and corporate liberalism."[27]

Oglesby's book and Kolko's growing body of revisionist scholarship on Cold War history influenced some of Kent State's new and returning graduate students and professors, especially Bobby Franklin, who became one of the best-known figures on campus. He had thought of himself as a leftist since childhood, and with his full beard and army fatigues he resembled Fidel Castro. Franklin's parents, both office workers, had sent him to New York City public schools, and his exceptional academic performance had later enabled him to attend Cornell. Through the Vietnam School during fall quarter, he met veteran activist Ron Wittmaack, who, in turn, introduced him to other members of the KCEWV.[28]

Of the new faculty members, Kenneth Calkins, a historian with a doctorate from the University of Chicago, arrived at Kent State with the most impressive activist credentials. Once the national secretary for the defunct Student Peace Union, Calkins had nearly been killed in a peace protest in the late 1950s. During an attempt to impede the movement of ICBMs from an Air Force base in Wyoming, a truck carrying missiles had struck Calkins and fractured his pelvis. Later, he served as an adviser to SDS at Lake Forest, a small college in the Chicago area, before accepting an appointment at Kent. Modest and earnest, Calkins also joined KCEWV picket lines and gained respect within Kent's emergent activist community.[29]

Tensions in the KCEWV

If the influx of new students and sympathetic faculty broadened the base of Kent's antiwar movement, the day-to-day work remained in the hands of experienced campus activists. Given political training by the SWP after leaving Kent in 1965, Roy Inglee did party work in Boston for several years before returning there. Within the growing activist ranks, those who worked most closely with the KCEWV had not missed Roy Inglee as much as did the Young Socialist Alliance (YSA). Along with John McCann, he had been the engine of the Trotskyist group. Reenrolled in graduate school, he was chiefly interested in socialist education and political organization. He saw to the revival of the YSA, which had lapsed as a recognized student group because the required annual paperwork had been neglected. Soon the organization had visibility once more. This proved something of a mixed blessing, for many in the now broader ranks of the KCEWV disdained the YSA's prominence and political style. Still, regaining independent organizational standing enabled the YSA to sponsor activities in its own name. One such program in late 1967 eventually launched an organization that became vital to the radicalization of the Kent campus: the Black United Students.[30]

The YSA and its parent organization had long advocated what they and other radicals called the "black liberation struggle." For years the SWP supported proponents of armed self-defense, such as Robert F. Williams. An NAACP branch leader in Monroe, North Carolina, in the late 1950s and early 1960s, Williams had attempted to protect local blacks from appalling racial persecution. At the end of a week-long picket and a confrontation with angry whites in August 1961, he had fled Monroe in the face of charges that his group had kidnapped a local white couple. Eventually Williams went to Cuba, where in 1967 he was still living in exile. His influence, however, continued to be manifest, in the growth of the Black Panther Party in places like Oakland, California, and also in Louisiana, where the Deacons for Defense and Justice had armed and organized themselves. One Deacons member, Henry Austin, became both celebrated and notorious for seriously wounding a white man who had been menacing African Americans in Louisiana. In November, the YSA brought Austin to speak on the Kent campus, the first of many visits. He must have made quite an impression on the black undergraduates who attended, for after his speech a number of them initiated discussions that led to the formation of Black United Students. BUS soon made its presence felt at Kent State, as would another student group, SDS.[31]

Since 1965, the implementation of YSA's political program of opposition to the Vietnam War and its vigorous promotion of black self-defense advocates like Lewis Robinson and Henry Austin had either directly or indirectly set in motion the formation Kent State's leading activist organizations, the KCEWV and BUS. Yet the socialist group's narrow theoretical outlook, with its own particular brand of ideological exultation, along with its adherence to conventional manners of dress and personal conduct at a time when the New Left was becoming more culturally permissive, restricted YSA's organizational appeal. Yet the revival of the YSA was greeted positively by some in the burgeoning Kent antiwar community, including newcomers to campus like students Carolyn Carson and Ruth Gibson, who were attracted by the group's energy, ideological clarity, and resolve. Carson recalled that when Roy Inglee "said something," everybody lined up with him." That discipline and determination had helped YSA, in concert with a handful of independent activists, build the KCEWV from its earliest days. But now those same attributes were causing problems. Under Bob Ehrlich's leadership, the KCEWV had focused more on antiwar activities than on advancing the overall YSA program. This united-front approach had succeeded in broadening the antiwar movement on campus by attracting independent activists less inclined to follow the YSA's lead. When Inglee and his allies tried to reassert their own agenda within the KCEWV, many members raised objections, some describing the YSA's role in the committee as "manipulative." Defenders, such as Ron Wittmaack, saw it otherwise: "The YSA participated in the KCEWV the same way we in the SWP participated in all sorts of movements. . . . The point was to achieve the goals of the organization, . . . to educate people and have them join us."[32]

There were other strains. While vigils had clearly enlarged the ranks of the campus protest movement, some within the KCEWV—for example, the combative Dave Edwards and recent arrival Bobby Franklin—either had never been comfortable with the weekly routine of bearing silent witness or found little utility in it. The vigils brought in new converts to the antiwar cause, but to critics they seemed an ineffectual tactic for bringing a halt to the steadily escalating American war in Southeast Asia.[33]

Also factoring into the internal tensions within the KCEWV was a deep-seated mistrust on the part of the more doctrinaire political radicals toward the emerging counterculture. YSA members saw themselves as serious revolutionaries, intent on building an organization committed to a clear ideological agenda, with opposition to the Vietnam War part of a larger struggle to end American imperialism abroad and transform power relations at home. For them, the counterculture, with its free-form oppositional stance toward an amorphous Establishment, represented a distraction that alienated antiwar activists from the exploited working class. YSA/SWP members believed the antiwar movement failed to connect with working-class Americans because many activists were more committed to personal liberation than collective justice.[34]

Overall, by the spring of 1967 the KCEWV had grown significantly. Prowar critics had not gone away, yet no organization could match the KCEWV's influence in shaping campus opinion. Vigils played a vital role in helping people overcome their misgivings about joining the antiwar movement and gave faculty members confidence that they could participate without sacrificing their careers. Faculty involvement, in turn, bestowed on the activists a measure of validity.

Even as the antiwar movement augmented its ranks at Kent State and elsewhere, the war in Vietnam continued with no end in sight. The number of Americans killed in action was averaging nearly a thousand per month, and enemy "body counts" were estimated at ten times that figure. The mounting total of Vietnamese civilian casualties, on both sides, could only be guessed. Some members of Congress, including Senate Armed Services Committee chairman William Fulbright, were openly critical of the war, while others complained about its cost and called for an income tax surcharge to pay for it. Nevertheless, there were no signs that Congress was prepared to force the issue, or that the Johnson administration had any intention of changing course in Vietnam. Meanwhile, the black struggle for social and political equality also escalated, particularly in the major cities of the North, where patterns of racial discrimination proved just as deeply entrenched as in the Jim Crow South. As one historian observed, racial protest in these years would be marked by an "erosion of restraint" and a "sharp rise in black expectations." As antiwar activists faced the future, these two strains—frustration over a seemingly unending war and impatience with the pace of social change—were preparing to converge and shape the future of the movement, at Kent State and across the country.[35]

CHAPTER 6

Moving toward Resistance

BY THE summer and fall of 1967, US forces had been heavily engaged with main units of the North Vietnamese Army for two years. As much as the Johnson administration hoped to have the US military commander, General William C. Westmoreland, continue to report progress from the battlefront, just months earlier an otherwise publicly optimistic Westmoreland painted a inchoate picture of bitter fighting with "no end in sight." Unhappily for official Washington, DC, in August the nation's leading newspaper, the *New York Times,* judged it similarly. The paper's bureau chief in Saigon, R. W. Apple, after conferring with many military officers in Vietnam, described the conflict as a "stalemate," adding, "It is the word used by almost all Americans here, except the top officials, to characterize what is happening." Understanding that "stalemate" itself constituted a "fighting word in Washington," Apple and other Vietnam War skeptics could not have been surprised when the administration directed that a "success offensive" be undertaken in a bid to win the war for public opinion. Vice President Humphrey (despite a private belief that "America is throwing lives and money down a corrupt rat hole"), members of the cabinet, and Ellsworth Bunker, US ambassador to South Vietnam, were all dispatched to convey the view that the United States was achieving its mission. Westmoreland, too, returned to his customary optimism, insisting that "the enemy . . . is certainly losing."[1]

Westmoreland's battlefield assessment coincided with the political needs of the president, as did his opinion of home-front dissent. Speaking before Congress on April 28, 1967, in the wake of the huge antiwar rally in New York weeks before, the commanding general insisted that opposition to the war was America's "Achilles' heel." Yet disagreement over the war could not be contained. By speaking at the April rally, civil rights leader Martin Luther King Jr. broke with the administration in the spring of 1967. Months later, R. W. Apple opined that

"Victory [in Vietnam] is not close at hand. It may be beyond reach." Then, in late November, Minnesota's junior senator, Eugene McCarthy, declared his intention to challenge President Johnson in the 1968 Democratic primaries.[2]

McCarthy's announcement, in turn, had been influenced, at least in part, by the nearly simultaneous protests held on America's coasts in October 1967. Obstructive "Stop the Draft Week" demonstrations in Oakland, California, left some militants bloodied and resulted in hundreds of arrests. In the East, another protest planned for Washington, DC, combined some of this same spirit of resistance to the war with the more traditional tactic of the mass march. Although organizers had expected the October 21 march and planned confrontation at the Pentagon to attract as many, if not more, protestors than had rallied at the United Nations in April, perhaps fewer than a hundred thousand, including several hundred students from Kent State, came to the capital to denounce the war. They listened to a parade of speakers, including an affecting talk by SDSer and former Oberlin student Rennie Davis. Mixed in were songs by Phil Ochs, a friend of Howie Emmer's sister Toby from the years when the singer had been a student at Ohio State. Following the long rally, anywhere from a third to as many as half the demonstrators, led by such figures as Dr. Benjamin Spock and the Depression-era labor priest Monsignor Charles Rice, crossed the Potomac River into Virginia to take their protest directly to the Pentagon. Parallel with the planned Stop the Draft Week protest and the unexpected turmoil that broke out that same week at the University of Wisconsin, the clash at the Pentagon would mark the first large-scale confrontation between antiwar activists and federal authorities.[3]

Members of the Young Socialist Alliance and the growing ranks of independently minded New Left radicals were well represented in the Kent contingent that crossed the bridge under the warm October sky. Young Socialist Alliance (YSA) activists Ron Wittmaack and Barbara Brock felt exhilarated as they proceeded toward the Virginia side of the river and the Pentagon. Kent Committee to End the War in Vietnam members Howie Emmer and Candy Erickson also joined the march, as did George Hoffman and Vince Modugno. Another was Jim Powrie, who grew up in the same working-class/middle-income suburb of Cuyahoga Falls as Hoffman and Modugno. Destined to be one of SDS's most important leaders at Kent State, Powrie had only recently warmed to protest. He was raised in a household he described as financially "poor" but "not poor in education"; his father, a meter reader, made sure their home was stocked with books and classical music records. As Powrie matured, so did his curiosity. He expanded his reading to include a wide variety of utopian literature, including *Walden* and *The Communist Manifesto*. He listened to his parents "argue at the table about Cuba," with his mother taking Castro's side. She insisted that Powrie and his brother Charles (known as Speed) refrain from using racial insults they picked up from other youths in the all-white neighborhood many called "Caucasian Falls."[4]

College would have been financially out of reach for the brothers had it not been for the football scholarships they won. In 1966 Speed went on to the State University of New York at Buffalo, where he ultimately found himself more attuned to the school's radicals, especially SDS, than to the gridiron players, and Jim played at Kent State. With political radicalism developing at a slower pace at Kent than at SUNY Buffalo, Powrie managed to avoid the issue of the war until an acquaintance serving in Vietnam sent home pictures showing him posed with the severed heads of Vietnamese killed by his unit. After that Powrie could no longer ignore the war. His involvement, like that of current and former athletes Bill Whitaker and Ric Erickson, signaled that change was on the way. All the same, Powrie represented something of a vanguard among working-class students, for the large-scale involvement of blue-collar youth in the antiwar movement was still a year or two away.[5]

Despite mounting disagreements in the MOBE—the National Mobilization to End the War in Vietnam—between and among militants, pacifists advocating disciplined civil disobedience, and those wishing to avoid militant confrontation altogether, such as the Socialist Workers Party (SWP), the antiwar coalition that organized the Pentagon march settled on holding a mass rally at the Lincoln Memorial. As we have seen, some of these tactical differences among the MOBE leadership were in evidence at Kent State within the Kent Committee to End the War in Vietnam (KCEWV); nevertheless, both YSA members and the growing ranks of independently minded radicals in the KCEWV were part of the contingent from Kent as they made their way toward the inevitable confrontation of troops and federal marshals protecting the Pentagon. As they neared the massive Pentagon, a small number of militants carrying protest flags charged unsuccessfully toward the building's service ramps and, when met by tear gas, quickly retreated. Meanwhile, luminaries in the front rank of the march who wished to disassociate themselves from such tactics were among the first taken into custody. The author Norman Mailer, the pacifist leader Dave Dellinger, and the renowned linguist Noam Chomsky were arrested by Army MPs, as were some militants, like Walter Teague, head of the Committee to Aid the National Liberation Front. Kent's Howie Emmer, still wrestling with the efficacy and morality of political militancy, evaded arrest even while briefly piercing the lines of the troops guarding the Pentagon.[6]

By late afternoon, tens of thousands had massed on the Virginia side of the river, many in the Pentagon's parking area, where authorities had banned any encroachment. Appeals to the soldiers guarding the Pentagon to leave their ranks went on for hours, as did periodic clashes between SDS radicals and federal marshals. Nightfall thinned the activist ranks as most marchers trekked

back to Washington. But several thousand others, including Emmer and Powrie, stayed. "It was remarkably dramatic," Powrie later recalled. "I haven't seen
anything like it since. A line of soldiers [MPs], protestors, and it was all back-lit
like a Hollywood set. When the [federal] marshals started attacking people, it
was horrible, [and] frightening." Knowing the risks, Powrie and Emmer avoided
the clubs and arrests that hundreds of other protestors experienced. Emmer
recalled that en route to Washington he "was still somewhat moderate" but that
the demonstration had "a *profound* effect" on him.[7]

While troubled by the ferocity of the experience, Emmer overcame his apprehension and used the *Daily Kent Stater* to proclaim to the university community what the confrontation had meant to him and a growing number of
militants at Kent:

> The anti-war movement is entering a phase of resistance. We are willing to
> bodily disrupt and be arrested and maybe beaten because the war is escalating so
> rapidly and viciously. . . .
>
> A folk singer named Phil Ochs sang a song at the rally at the Lincoln Memo-
> rial called "I Declare the War Is Over." On the other hand, I declare the war has
> just begun. The Pentagon action was an early clue in the new direction. Some-
> thing is happening. Resistance will be happening.[8]

Dow Protest

Emmer's words could have come straight from the title of SDS's latest position
paper, "Toward Institutional Resistance," authored by one of the group's leaders, Carl Davidson. Reflecting the same spirit, in the week before the Pentagon
march, SDS members at the University of Wisconsin had declared that they
would "block Dow [Chemical] from recruiting." Dow was the maker of napalm, a flammable gel used extensively and with deadly effect in Vietnam by
the US military, and the company's recruiters had already begun to encounter
SDS protests. The conflict on the Wisconsin campus over Dow recruiting led
to hundreds of arrests, and injuries to a few police and dozens of students. The
actions there and elsewhere, involving tens of thousands of protestors, answered
the national SDS call for "resistance" to the draft, the war, and the police.[9]

On Wednesday, November 1, in a move that marked the first tentative step
toward such resistance at Kent State, Emmer and his compatriots assembled to
protest the presence of Dow recruiters on campus. Ordinarily this was a day for
a silent vigil, but seventy-five activists participated, including Tom Lough of the
sociology department, who carried a placard. Lough carried on the practice, begun by other faculty in the English department, of being among the professors

willing to openly demonstrate with antiwar students. The activists shifted their customary protest site to the Student Activities Center, where the Dow representatives had arranged meetings. Being closer to Stopher Hall meant exposure to stock abuse: right-wing hecklers destroyed antiwar posters, threw mud at dissidents, and displayed taunting signs from windows that read NAPALM DOES THE JOB! On this occasion, campus police intervened, preventing trouble from spreading further. In the lobby of the activities center a university representative accepted Emmer's statement addressed to Dow: "This company manufactures napalm, which . . . is used as an anti-personnel weapon. . . . We cannot stand by and let these atrocities be carried out in our name."[10]

Protests such as the one against Dow, while more direct than silent vigils, did not rise to the level of resistance Howie Emmer might have envisioned, for the campus community was as yet unprepared for such disruption and Kent activists lacked consensus about the use of such tactics. Certainly the director of the Student Activities Center, Betty Hovencamp, perceived the differences, noting that "there has been a rift . . . [between a] group that felt matters should be carried further . . . and the 'old guard' of the Kent Committee." And indeed the emergent emphasis in the KCEWV came from those who insisted on seeing the war as interconnected to urban and racial ills at home, thus requiring stronger protest action. Moreover, they began to adopt SDS's broader analysis and more confrontational approach, especially on the draft. The "old guard," as it were, grouped mostly around the YSA, theoretically understood as much as did their more discontented compatriots, but insisted on a single-issue approach to the war. Trotskyite youth in the YSA favored tactics on campuses that emphasized educational work: staffing literature tables and setting up meetings with antiwar speakers. Those brought into its political orbit would, in turn, help mobilize other students to participate in mass marches in the nation's cities behind the anti–Vietnam War slogan "Out Now!" The SWP youth arm had difficulty working with groups to their political left, especially those like SDS, the very organization whose influence was beginning to appeal to many of the unaffiliated members of the KCEWV. After three years of slowly building their ranks, Kent's blue-collar and middle-class activists had at last assembled in sufficient numbers for an actual, if still peaceful, demonstration. But the building tensions between students associated with SDS resistance and the single-issue approach favored by YSA was undermining the hard-won unity within the KCEWV.[11]

Even with the political strains, the activist ranks grew bit by bit. Sophomore Peggy Atkinson, the daughter of a union worker in Cleveland, joined some of the protests, as did Bill Taylor, one of Hoffman and Modugno's roommates from the Akron area. So did Steve and Rick Lieber, cousins from a Pittsburgh-area steel town. One of the most important recruits, Ken Hammond of Cleveland, focused initially on the mayoral campaign of Carl Stokes. Hammond had taken an interest in civil rights as an adolescent; working with the campus chapter of the Young Democrats, he helped coordinate volunteers to work in Cleveland on the approaching mayoral election, and he took enormous satisfaction in helping Stokes win election as the first African American mayor to head a major US city. Like many Democrats influenced by the pull of Cold War political gravity, his father's service in World War II and his brother's naval assignment on an aircraft carrier off the coast of Vietnam gave him some initial hesitancy about appearing to be antimilitary and antiwar. In time, though, the intellectually inquisitive Hammond saw antiwar involvement differently—as a means to aid his brother and perhaps, with the threat of conscription as looming after college, himself. With this realization, he took an interest in draft counseling and participated in a number of the silent vigils against the war.[12]

With the support for direct-action tactics rising in the KCEWV, activists prepared to send a busload of dissidents to Cleveland for a protest at the city's induction center. No doubt some were further encouraged by a *Stater* poll showing that just 22 percent of the students living on campus supported current US policy in Vietnam. Still, having an opinion and acting on it were different things. Most students were not yet prepared to literally and figuratively step out into the public arena of protest, much less engage in disruptive tactics. Many in the nation, especially among the white majority, frowned on protest as the culture of the Cold War continued to inhibit students and affect an even larger number of older Americans, those whose lives had been shaped directly by the Great Depression and World War II. This latter group, while containing tens of millions still loyal to the New Deal order, could not help but measure their own lives at eighteen or twenty compared to those of young people attending college in the mid- to late 1960s. Even as opinion about the conflict vacillated, opposition meant different things to different people. If military progress seemed to be made, support for the war increased; if setbacks occurred, support eroded. For antiwar activists the war was a matter of both morality and self-interest. For the nonactivist majority, opinion was shaped more by military results than morality. Accordingly, the conflict remained a highly volatile issue with the electorate.[13]

At Kent State, the administration's efforts to stifle dissent continued as students turned increasingly against the war. President White and the newly appointed dean of students, Robert Matson, were bolstered by any sign of undergraduate support for the status quo. And despite the growing turmoil, White still held out hope that by the end of spring quarter 1968 everyone on campus would "feel it has been a good year." Those hopes would soon be dashed.[14]

The Tet Offensive

In late November 1967, General Westmoreland spoke confidently about American progress in the Vietnam War. "With 1968 a new phase is starting," he told members of the National Press Club. "We have reached an important point where the end begins to come into view." At the beginning of the new year, disregarding evidence of a huge buildup by South Vietnamese guerrillas in the National Liberation Front (NLF), military and political deputy Robert Komer similarly insisted that the United States was "in a better position than we have ever been." Even as the sanguine Komer spoke, North Vietnamese units began shelling a Marine base at Khe Sanh in the northwest corner of South Vietnam. The attack was but a prelude to a coordinated and massive offensive launched by the North Vietnamese and their allied local fighters in the NLF throughout the length and breadth of South Vietnam. Over a hundred cities and provincial or district capitals were attacked. NLF combatants penetrated the US embassy in Saigon, and street fighting raged in the old imperial capital of Hue.[15]

Although the Vietnamese communists sustained horrific losses that nearly crippled the NLF fighting strength, the Tet Offensive also shattered the illusion among many Americans that the war was nearing an end. Consequently, the presidential campaign of Minnesota senator Eugene McCarthy, a dissident antiwar Democrat, gained considerable momentum, with McCarthy nearly winning the party's New Hampshire primary over President Johnson. A few weeks later another Democratic senator, Robert F. Kennedy of New York, announced his own plan to challenge Johnson in the party primaries. During the six weeks between the start of the Tet Offensive and the beginning of Kennedy's presidential campaign on March 16, LBJ's presidency was wrecked. The *New York Times* had already voiced grave doubts about the war, and on February 23 a *Wall Street Journal* editorial suggested that "the whole Vietnam effort may be doomed." CBS News dispatched its respected anchor, Walter Cronkite, to Vietnam to make his own assessment. Millions watched on February 27 as the dean of broadcast journalism told his audience that "we are mired in stalemate" and that the United States had no choice but "to negotiate, not as victors but as an honorable people who . . . did the best they could."[16]

In the face of the enormous offensive and despite such broad opposition to the war and its course, General Westmoreland decided to seek the deployment of an additional 200,000 US soldiers to South Vietnam. While his request won the support of the Joint Chiefs of Staff, Johnson's doubts were rising. Special adviser Clark Clifford's advice confirmed them. Closely echoing Vice President Humphrey's earlier assessment, Clifford stated in a high-level meeting that such an escalation would be nothing more than "pouring troops down a rat hole."

When the press revealed Westmoreland's bid for additional troops, opposition in Congress swelled and Democratic primary hopefuls were emboldened, forcing an even more widespread reassessment of the war. While millions of Americans hoped to elect a true antiwar candidate who would end the war, some on the left had already concluded that mainstream politics was hopelessly linked to the prerogatives of the military-industrial complex and could not be trusted to make fundamental changes in American imperial policies. YSA leader Roy Inglee, for example, had warned activists months earlier that "the primary motives of the 'doves' is to emasculate the anti-war movement . . . by coopting all dissenters."[17]

SDS and BUS

The day before Cronkite's report aired, independent-minded New Leftists George Hoffman and Ron Weisberger, a history graduate student, entered the Student Activities Center, where Hoffman completed the paperwork to form yet another campus organization, one that would represent a new phase in the New Left antiwar struggle of resistance: the Kent Students for a Democratic Society. Weisberger, who was working as a teaching assistant and thus had reason to fear reprisals from the university administration, nevertheless agreed to serve as the group's adviser. Hoffman, on the other hand, had been ready for the move for some time, having taken out an individual membership in SDS two years earlier. With rumors circulating of an even larger troop buildup in Vietnam, Hoffman and his friend Vince Modugno were motivated by SDS positions expressed in its weekly tabloid, *New Left Notes,* against the Selective Service System, as well as by the recent defiance of Benjamin Spock and other prominent resisters to the draft. Since the start of the winter quarter, Hoffman and Modugno had been conferring with other disaffected members of the KCEWV, among them Howie Emmer and Jim Powrie, about the concept of political resistance—obstructive tactics to interfere with the war effort. Frustrated with the unending war, many in the New Left believed that symbols of it, such as draft boards, ROTC programs, and military recruiters, should be disrupted and confronted. Two weeks before the opening of the Tet Offensive, Hoffman told a *Stater* reporter that "SDS is basically anarchist, anti-establishment, anti-draft and action-oriented." Explaining the impending split from the KCEWV and reflecting dissatisfaction not only with the Old Left but with liberals supporting antiwar Democrats, Hoffman said disdainfully, "That committee is moderate." While those aligned with the SWP/YSA feared that the antiwar movement might fall under the sway of liberal Democrats and sacrifice its autonomy, those to its left in SDS had a different, but related concern: that the peace movement was too cautious in its tactics and hence ineffective and unable to stop the war. Indeed, the strategic thinking of some in SDS, as reflected in *New Left Notes,* was increasingly apocalyptic; their belief was that the political and economic system that promoted and profited from the Vietnam conflict had to be challenged directly, with drastic measures taken to stop the disastrous war.[18]

As SDS activists took the first steps to forge their chapter, African American students on the Kent campus vigorously debated the formation of their own organization. Challenged by a militant advocate of black self-defense in November 1967 to look at "America [as] a hypocritical, imperialistic country," African American students such as nineteen-year-old Dwayne White (known as Brother Fargo), Robert Pickett, Larry Simpson, Larry Ghe, Donald Thigpen, and Lafayette Tolliver began to thrash out the structure of the new organization, deciding on leadership positions and, according to one leery African American faculty member, engaging in "compulsive 'blacker than thou' confrontations." Larry Simpson remembered the initial sessions differently, recalling them as "highly energizing and exciting," but both recollections are probably to some degree accurate. History lived in these students. Virtually all of the Black United Students (BUS) members from Cleveland had participated in the school boycott organized by the United Freedom Movement in 1964. Prior to the mid-1960s, most of Kent State's small African American student population had been part of the black middle class. While by no means immune from racial discrimination, many of these earlier students were better shielded from its worst effects than were the poorer and less prosperous African Americans who began to enter Kent State in larger numbers in the late 1960s. Whatever their position in the African American class structure—mid-level professional or working-class—many scores of them shared James Baldwin's feeling of "rage in his blood" and likewise agreed with him that "one has the choice, merely, of living with it consciously or surrendering to it."[19]

Being monitored by student informants for the administration, as was the KCEWV (and later SDS), served only to further strengthen the political will of African Americans who formed the BUS. In electing Larry Simpson and later Bob Pickett as presidents of BUS, the organization, unlike the increasingly ideological SDS, managed to be at once militantly principled and politically pragmatic. This was so even as BUS was being influenced by rhetoric associated with Malcolm X and the Black Panther Party. Many of its members, especially by early 1970, were inclined to copy their militant style as well as to help collegians of color negotiate the largely white world of Kent, Ohio.

The militant who had first exhorted Kent's African American students to form their own racial organization was Henry Austin, the former Deacons for Defense member who had spoken on campus in November 1967. A New Orleans native and service veteran, Austin at some point had taken college classes, though his connection with the Kent campus is unclear. Given the YSA's sponsorship of his first talk at Kent, most likely he came to know an assortment of radicals in Cleveland, including SWP members as well as fellow black nationalists. After his November talk, presumably Austin began forging social and political ties with Kent State's African American students. Having relocated to Cleveland from Louisiana, he came to influence the eventual formation of BUS. His part in doing so was not unlike the role played by members of the Old Left in Cleveland who encouraged and supported YSA activists on the Kent campus in 1964 and 1965.[20]

Owing to his experiences in Bogalusa, a city in central Louisiana where he and other members of the Deacons for Defense stoutly defended local African Americans and northern white volunteers from Ku Klux Klan terror, Austin attracted the interest of Cleveland's FBI, along with Cleveland's and Kent State University's police forces. Agents traced his movements to Kent and his activities in and out of JFK House (a community center on Cleveland's East Side founded by the African American civil rights advocate Lewis G. Robinson in 1966), and they made note of militant speeches he made at SWP forums in the city's Debs Hall as well as in Kent. Austin and Harllel Robert Jones (who had been tied by some to the Hough disorders) tried and failed to organize a Deacons chapter in Cleveland. Along with David Tuck, a prominent African American antiwar activist in that city, Austin (like the SNCC) opposed the participation of blacks in the Vietnam War. In March 1967 he had enlisted Cleveland youth to distribute sarcastic antiwar posters, one of which read "Support White Power—Travel to Vietnam, You Might Get a Medal!"[21]

In advance of another series of speeches he gave in Kent at the Christian Fellowship House and on the Kent State campus in the third week of January 1968, Austin released a prepared announcement that stated, "If violence can be used to murder defenseless women and children in Vietnam, then certainly it can be used in Louisiana to defend Negroes' lives and property." During the third week of February, Austin and Tuck, a Vietnam veteran who testified with Carl Oglesby at the Stockholm War Crimes Tribunal, spoke at another campus rally against Dow Chemical, organized by the KCEWV and SDS. There, for the first time on the Kent campus, the taunting cry was heard: *Hey, hey, LBJ, how many kids did you kill today?* The resistance strategy advocated by an increasing number in the leadership ranks of the SDS national office, coupled with Austin's appeals for self-defense and energetic opposition to the war, served to further a rising tide of militant talk within both the Kent SDS and BUS. Eager, perhaps, to promote their agenda and regain their slipping organizational authority in the splintering KCEWV, that same evening the YSA sponsored a talk by SWP notable and antiwar coalition leader Fred Halstead, who condemned

Johnson for placing US Marines in the besieged Vietnamese outpost of Khe Sanh, where hundreds of them had died.[22]

Looking for a Critical Mass

Moving from a picket against Dow Chemical to a demonstration against CIA recruitment on March 1, KCEWV members and the budding SDS chapter might have congratulated themselves for their persistence. They might a found comfort, too, in the national survey polls that showed public opinion continuing to turn against American involvement in Vietnam. Support for the war had fallen to 40 percent. But divisions within the KCEWV over the role of YSA proved discouraging to some members, while new activists had yet to emerge in large numbers. Even after the establishment of the SDS chapter and BUS, the number of committed political activists at Kent was still relatively small. There, as elsewhere throughout the country, most mainstream Democrats were still reluctant to break with a president widely seen as a direct heir to FDR and as a reformer who had championed civil rights and pushed through sweeping social reforms.[23]

First-year student Carole Teminsky might have been a natural fit for the antiwar cause. The daughter of a Youngstown steelworker, she became attuned to racial justice in high school by reading John Howard Griffin's influential book, *Black Like Me.* Like many Cold War Democrats, Teminsky's views slowly evolved out of an anticommunist framework, especially with regard to Vietnam, a conflict that many Catholic ethnics supported initially. She was solidly Democratic on a wide range of domestic issues, including civil rights, and a supporter of Robert F. Kennedy's presidential bid. Though she came to see Vietnam as detrimental to American soldiers and working-class people, like many first-generation working-class students she remained hesitant to participate in public protest.[24]

A critical mass of antiwar students still seemed out of reach. Faculty support surely helped, but many—perhaps most—of Kent's professors remained behind the war effort. Comparing the participation of Kent State students in national protest marches to the turnout for silent vigils at the university, it would seem that the KCEWV often had more success getting students to demonstrate off campus than on. It is certainly possible that the hostile local response to the campus antiwar protests in 1965 and 1966 was difficult to overcome. Some may have found it easier to demonstrate in Washington, DC, or at the UN building, out of the view of unsympathetic classmates and faculty. Others, like Dave Dyer, the coalminer's son from Coshocton County, had different concerns, but not unrelated to Teminsky's. Despite serious misgivings about the war, Dyer found it difficult to break from his Democratic Party roots and support for the Johnson administration. The two were among many working-class students not prepared to abandon the Democratic Party for radical alternatives. Rather, each, to varying degrees, looked for change within the party.[25]

The Presidential Race

For most students, electoral politics was a more comfortable option than walking a picket line, much less embracing the ethos of resistance. The announcement by Eugene McCarthy that he would seek the Democratic presidential nomination, coupled with disillusionment and utter revulsion at the Tet Offensive, motivated dozens at Kent State to participate in McCarthy's and later Kennedy's campaigns. Even before fighting intensified in Vietnam in late January, student body president Bob Hill announced his support for the Minnesota senator, explaining that "even if McCarthy doesn't win he may be able to insert part of a peace platform into the election." McCarthy's unexpectedly strong showing on March 12 in the New Hampshire primary, where he finished a strong second, served up a shock to the political system. Four days later the presidential race was thrown wide open when New York's junior senator, Robert F. Kennedy, feeling the political wind at his back, also declared his intention to challenge Johnson in the Democratic primaries.[26]

On March 31, shortly after the start of the spring quarter at Kent, Johnson delivered yet another shock that astonished Democratic Party regulars and delighted legions of antiwar students, stunning a nationwide audience by announcing that he would not seek reelection. From northeast Ohio to far-off Berkeley, where former Kent State student David King and other expatriates had migrated, the night was remembered as one of celebration. What led to jubilation at Kent State and elsewhere was the series of peace initiatives Johnson proposed in the same speech, and his announcement of the curtailment, and the possibility of a total cessation, of air raids over North Vietnam. Energized by the announcement, days later McCarthy's campus coordinators at Kent State set a goal of recruiting five hundred students to canvass Ohio congressional districts for the peace candidate. Unlike a good number of the legendary army of "Clean for Gene" students who worked on the campaign, most of Kent's McCarthy volunteers were not previously part of the antiwar movement. Campus opinion supported the peace initiatives, although many Kent students who backed dissident Democrats like McCarthy and Kennedy lacked the resources to devote weeks to campaigning at the expense of schoolwork. Such was the concern of Joe Sima, a blue-collar student and Kennedy enthusiast from Cleveland. While campaign fever seized the imaginations of many collegians nationwide, the fervor was dampened by the power of Democratic Party regulars. Harriet Begala, wife of Kent State's renowned wrestling coach, Peter Begala, together with a half dozen others, gathered thousands of signatures for McCarthy. Despite her efforts, the head of the local Portage County party, Roger Di Paolo, refused to accept them, and Begala would watch the convention not as a delegate but as a television viewer.[27]

Death in Memphis

On the night President Johnson made his announcement from the White House, civil rights leader Martin Luther King Jr., despondent over a recent flare-up of violence in Memphis, was preparing to head back there to aid a strike by the city's unionized sanitation workers. Four days later, on April 4, King, Jesse Jackson, and Ralph Abernathy were about to leave their motel in the city for an evening meal when a white sniper put King in his rifle sight. A head shot felled America's leading civil rights leader.

Uproar over the assassination eventually engulfed over 150 cities, including the nation's capital, where disturbances began after news of King's murder reached the predominantly black city. Strife renewed the next day, with government employees leaving work early. Fears rose when smoke from the fires of burning commercial buildings appeared on an otherwise clear afternoon. Before the angry mayhem subsided, eight were dead. Rioting spread to nearby Baltimore, where four more were killed and Republican governor Spiro Agnew called out two thousand National Guardsmen. Cleveland, with a newly elected African American mayor, remained calm, but in Cincinnati, Governor James Rhodes mobilized the state's Guard when turmoil followed a deadly shooting. The nationwide disorders claimed forty-three lives; thirty-nine of those killed were African American.[28]

Not all of the response triggered by King's death came from black America. Thousands of longshoremen—an interracial mix of unionized workers—shut down ports on the east and west coasts. From North Vietnam, where Hanoi's leaders were well aware of King's activities against the war, came words of sympathy to the Southern Christian Leadership Conference, which King had headed. Many whites shared the grief of black America, but fear, and unyielding racial resentment, reigned as well. Countless African America soldiers fighting the war were incensed by the murder, with one calling King a "liberator" and expressing a resolve to return stateside to "help liberate my own people." Yet the same reporter who interviewed black soldiers also surveyed white troops and generally found "a surprising lack of sympathy." Back in the United States, in King's hometown of Atlanta, Georgia, the state's pro-segregationist governor, Lester G. Maddox, skipped the funeral services while making known his unhappiness over the flag being flown at half-staff as King was buried in the city. Mining the same racial vein, George Wallace, the governor of neighboring Alabama, sought to take full advantage of white racial antipathies in a third-party campaign for the presidency that he had launched three days prior to the murder.[29]

Kent Responds

As word spread on the Kent campus the day following the killing in Memphis, elected student leaders organized a memorial service with administrative representatives. One thousand anguished students assembled in the University Auditorium that Friday. Not unlike tens of thousands elsewhere, some called for vengeance. BUS leader Brother Fargo declared that "militancy is the only way now." YSA members agreed, and in contrast to their more muted tactical stance on antiwar protest advocated a combative response as the only road to African American political power. Student body vice president and BUS leader Robert Pickett told listeners they had lost "a great man" and "a black brother who tried to help us." Mindful of his overlapping constituencies, Pickett read aloud statements from such diverse figures as Robert Kennedy, President Johnson, and Stokely Carmichael, who had charged earlier that day that "white America killed Dr. King," leaving blacks "no alternative to retribution."[30]

The following week, marchers, whose numbers grew to over a thousand, gathered to deal collectively with their sorrow. Years of patient organizing had never produced such a response at Kent, but the killing of the nation's leading dissident galvanized the campus. Students were joined by people from the community at Kent's Union Baptist church in the tiny African American section of the town. Among them was Henry Tompkins, a high school student and member of one of Kent's oldest African American families; he would later become a fixture in the campus antiwar movement. For him, King's murder was the second of two violent deaths, as a cousin from a neighboring town had died in Vietnam in late March. The Reverend Fred D. Thomas, pastor of the Union Baptist Church, called King one of the "the martyrs of our time," who had "given us a torch to carry on so that he shall not have died in vain." On campus, the university provost ordered US flag flown at half-mast. For a brief moment students, administrators, and town residents were united in grief.[31]

For increasing numbers of African American and white students, King's murder furthered calls for Black Power that fused with hatred of the war. Together these elements propelled more extreme thinking and activity on both sides of the racial divide. Reflecting this new political mood, Kent SDS members rallied for what the national organization billed as the "Days of Resistance." SDS brought in Kathy Boudin, recently of the Cleveland ERAP collective, to speak, along with Kenneth Calkins of the KSU faculty and draft resister and KSU student Pat Cullie. KCEWV announced plans for a week of teach-ins, many with a focus on the military draft, to prepare for a one-day student strike and rally on April 26. Not to be outdone, and eager to promote its agenda, YSA added a program titled "Black Nationalism and Socialism." Henry Austin made one of his many trips from Cleveland to speak at the newly created Faculty Forum. Robert V. Watson, an antiwar veteran and KSU student, spoke on April 19 at the Needle's Eye on "Being Black in America," and Mark Real, a former seminarian and future SDS leader, arranged for the appearance of draft resister Tom Cornell. Together, these efforts, along with the participation by Kent State antiwar activists in a rally in Cleveland on April 27, represented the most ambitious local and regional antiwar mobilization since Vietnam Week the previous fall.[32]

Rainy weather was not the least of the difficulties encountered by Kent's activists when the day of the strike arrived on April 26. The Student Activities office refused permission for the rally because the activists had billed the protest as a "strike." The organizers went ahead with their plans and, with neither side willing to back down, the administration threatened them with disciplinary action and refused them meeting space and sound equipment.[33] That the university refused to sanction the rally was cited as the reason for the presence during the event of campus police. They were ordered to stay back on the periphery of the Commons, however, which left the four hundred participants unprotected from the potentially troublesome students in Stopher Hall. Pellets or BBs came from the dorm, striking Father Jan Zima, assistant pastor of Kent's St. Patrick's Church, who was there to speak against the war. After hearing feverish complaints from Vince Modugno, campus police entered the dorm, discovering BBs and slingshots but apparently no rifles. The only person charged, however, was rally organizer Ruth Gibson, whom police arrested for using chalk to scrawl notices on a campus building publicizing the rally. For veteran protestors, the uneven response provided more evidence that top administrators were, in the words of one activist, "prejudiced and intolerant." Unease with university conduct by some faculty was such that President White felt compelled to issue a lengthy memo defending his administration's role in the controversy over the rally's planning as well as in the response to the shooting incident.[34]

Humphrey at Kent

In the midst of the "Days of Resistance," the *Daily Kent Stater* informed its readers on April 24 that Vice President Humphrey would be visiting campus on May 3. The announcement, coming just days before Humphrey had declared his candidacy for the Democratic presidential nomination, meant that one of his first appearances as an official candidate would be at Kent State.[35] Dissenters needed little incentive to protest Johnson's Vietnam policies, although few realized that Humphrey had initially cautioned the president against escalating the bombing campaign over North Vietnam. After mid-1966 he was, as he later wrote, "the Administration's primary defender." When a headline in the *Stater* alerted readers that the vice president's visit would receive nationwide coverage, Humphrey became an even more appealing target of protest. Some SDS members, committed to expressing dissent and eager to move beyond the rhetoric of resistance, organized supporters to attend. In the same spirit, BUS huddled with Robert Pitts, an African American instructor intent on establishing a minority affairs office, to determine how they might make use of Humphrey's visit.[36]

Awaiting this first visit by a US vice president to the university, President White understandably hoped for an event that would reflect well on the school. Returning from a trip to South Korea, he took stock of events on campus: the large-scale but peaceful march after the assassination of Dr. King, the growing restlessness of African American students, the controversy over the planning of the April 26 antiwar protest, the charges by dissidents arising out of the shooting incident, and the impending departure of several of his top aides. In this unsettled situation White had to prepare to "welcome and present" the vice president of the United States to Kent State. To maximize student turnout for Humphrey's talk, he ordered classes cancelled for two hours; he may have been worried about protests, but he must also have known that much of Humphrey's audience would consist of friendly students from urban areas that were mainly Democratic.[37]

The twenty-minute address Humphrey delivered to a packed house got off to a promising enough start. Enjoying the presence of Kent's popular mayor (and fellow pharmacist), John Carson, Humphrey ignored the antiwar banner and basked in the mostly positive reception his remarks received, especially when he mentioned the impending start of peace talks with representatives of the Democratic Republic of Vietnam. Before moving to questions from a selected panel that included Bob Pickett, dozens of BUS members staged a highly visible walkout, led by Pitts and Larry Simpson. Whether carried away by spontaneity of the moment or following a prearranged plan, scores of SDS, YSA, and KCEWV members did likewise amid a cacophony of booing. Outside, they rallied with signs, drawing strength from each other as they carried on what they understood then as resistance. Inside, the vice president, clearly annoyed, recalled the Dixiecrat walkout from the 1948 Democratic convention during his stirring address in defense of the party's minority civil rights plank.[38]

Humphrey supporters, as well as those who simply wanted to hear the vice president of the United States, smarted from a mixture of embarrassment and anger. Bob Pickett, a New Jersey native who became one of the most skillful student leaders at Kent State, found a way to tap the protestors' anger without personal affront by challenging the vice president with a direct, heartfelt question. Pickett told Humphrey that "the American Dream for the black man is nothing more than a nightmare," and asked him what he would do "to restore my and my people's faith in the American Dream." Humphrey's answer, spoken with the conviction for which he had been known in previous decades, must have satisfied Pickett, because he later accepted a paid position in Humphrey's presidential campaign.[39]

As shown in campus polls and in the grief over King's assassination, at least some of the public outcry against those who walked out was expressed by students who shared many of the same reservations about the war and beliefs about racial justice. The uproar over the Humphrey affair spilled over into the pages of the *Stater*, with plenty of back-and-forth opinions expressed. Henry Austin, an increasingly prominent figure in Kent, defended BUS and the antiwar activists, and regretted the "intense hatred for the KCEWV, the only people willing to speak out against the war," adding, "They can't end the war themselves and the Negroes can't solve the race problem by themselves."[40]

With his adept handling of the walkout, Humphrey earned the respect of most of the ten thousand people who stayed. Even some of those prominently associated with the walkout—Larry Simpson and Jim Powrie—either knew of and respected Humphrey's civil rights record or took pains to explain many years later that the actions were simply "an act of conscience" against the war. Lost in the acrimony, too, was the fact that not all members of the KCEWV agreed with the walkout. Joe Jackson, representative of those concerned with harming the chances of Democratic control of the presidency, stayed in his seat and disapproved of those students, including his younger sister, who departed the huge gymnasium. Kent's first steps on the road to resistance were hesitant ones. Newspaper coverage tended to downplay the more contentious aspects of the event, but the national television networks, perhaps taken by the theater of it all, focused on the walkout rather than the strength of Humphrey's showing, especially given that the protest occurred not at a prominent coastal or Big Ten school, but a little-known state university. "It was national news because it happened at a place like Kent," said Powrie.[41]

"Nineteen sixty-eight was the pivotal year of the sixties" the historian and journalist Charles Kaiser argued just twenty years later, and many have since agreed. At Kent State, this assessment was more or less true, but the May 3 controversy over the Humphrey walkout represented a footnote in the dispute over the war and within the increasingly bitter Democratic campaign to find a replacement for Johnson. Ohio's May 7 Democratic primary proved anticlimactic for McCarthy and Kennedy, for under the rules in effect at that time, the 241 elected delegates would be attending the upcoming Chicago convention uncommitted to any candidate. Humphrey, confident of winning the nomination with the support of delegates among the party's elected officials, did not bother entering the primary. Nor could the clamor over the walkout compare to what was taking place at New York's Columbia University, where disorder erupted when SDS and the Student Afro-American Society organized protests to stop the construction of a gymnasium on land that encroached on Black Harlem. Three weeks of demonstrations and building takeovers resulted in close to nine hundred arrests, while injuries to Columbia students and New York City police totaled almost two hundred. Although it paled in contrast to the student-sparked protests and general strike that would sweep through Paris, and then all of France, that same spring, the Columbia revolt was unprecedented.[42]

As for Vietnam, Johnson had reassessed the war. Up until then he had allowed the US commanding general wide latitude in determining battlefield tactics, and Westmoreland favored large-scale operations focusing on kill ratios. That changed after Westmoreland was replaced by General Creighton Abrams. Under Abrams the emphasis of the ground war slowly began to shift, as he stressed population control along with combined operations of US and Army of the Republic of South Vietnam (ARVN) forces.[43]

Thus when Kent State experienced its final protest of the academic year in late May—a peaceful sit-in by BUS in support of the Robert Pitts, an instructor in Spanish who had resigned the week before, and the creation of a minority affairs office—most of the press ignored it. However significant locally, protest at Kent State seemed subdued compared to the series of terrible calamities the nation had experienced from January to early June. When the school paper titled an editorial "Wash-Out '68," some may have taken it as a figurative expression about rinsing away the chaos of the year. But for Kent State University, now able to claim status as the nation's "twenty-sixth largest," the hardest rain had yet to fall.[44]

CHAPTER 7

Election 1968

ON THE morning of June 6, 1968, Kent State freshman Joe Sima awoke to the awful news of Robert F. Kennedy's assassination. Kennedy had been shot in Los Angeles the night before, only moments after winning the California primary. "Not again," Sima thought. Two months earlier, while campaigning in the midwestern presidential primaries, Kennedy had spoken in Cleveland about the murder of Martin Luther King Jr., resolutely saying to an audience at the City Club that "no martyr's cause has ever been stilled by his assassin's bullet." Sima found it hard to believe that Kennedy had now been gunned down, too. The son of poor first- and second-generation eastern Europeans, Sima shared the grief felt by many Americans. During his brief campaign to succeed Lyndon Johnson, Kennedy's appeal seemed to transcend the generational, religious, class, racial, and regional divisions that were tearing the nation apart. His murder came as a devastating blow to the aspirations of Catholic ethnics like the Simas, as well as to the urban black and white population and to many poor and working-class citizens of all races. Tens of thousands of these Americans lined the tracks from New Jersey to Washington, DC, to watch the passage of the funeral train carrying his body to Arlington National Cemetery.[1]

Kennedy's death removed from the presidential race the candidate widely viewed as the most electable advocate of peace in Vietnam. In the summer of 1968, as the two major political parties prepared for their nominating conventions, the prominent journalist James Kilpatrick observed that "the Vietnam war lay like a curse on the future" which neither party knew how to lift. Democrats had been openly split between hawks and doves since Eugene McCarthy's presidential bid took hold the previous fall. The leading GOP presidential contender, Richard Nixon, kept open every possibility but withdrawal. Former Alabama governor George Wallace, running as a third-party candidate, proposed his own solution, telling a columnist, "We've got to win this war," and insisting that more military force was needed: "We've got to pour it on."[2]

In addition to his hard line on Vietnam, Wallace also called for "law and order" at home. Wallace had been thwarted twice by civil rights protesters backed by federal power, at the University of Alabama and at the Selma-to-Montgomery march. He moved north in this second presidential campaign determined to uphold segregation and white supremacy and reclaim the white racial constituency captured by Republican candidate Barry Goldwater in 1964. Wallace also employed "law and order" as a code for cracking down on African Americans, and used it to challenge both pro–civil rights and antiwar factions of the Democratic Party. Up until late 1967, Nixon had carefully run to the right of Lyndon Johnson on the war. As the summer conventions approached, Nixon became more circumspect about Vietnam. He left it to the hawkish Wallace to promote a military solution while simultaneously stirring the racial and economic fears of many whites. Both Nixon and Wallace, one inside the Republican Party and the other outside of it, conjured a pre-1964 vision of America before the escalation of the war and the advent of civil rights legislation. Hubert Humphrey, tied to an unpopular war and president, had to contend with a fraying and divided Democratic party. The outcome of the contest would reshape American political landscape for the remainder of the century.[3]

Akron and Cleveland Erupt

Many in northeast Ohio were relieved that they had avoided the urban unrest that rocked nearly a hundred American cities in the wake of Martin Luther King Jr.'s murder in early April 1968. Akron had been among the fortunate. Yet the city's minority population still suffered what a commission later described as "discrimination towards blacks in all areas of community life," and starting on July 17, the morning after police broke up some gang fighting among African American youths, Akron experienced a week of shootings and racial unrest that once again prompted Governor James Rhodes to mobilize the Ohio National Guard. By the time a curfew was imposed days later, gunfire had wounded three city residents, including two black teenagers who were shot by a fifty-four-year-old white man. The turmoil plunged the community into a state of fear. One newspaper reported that "many Negroes in the area have barricaded their doors."[4]

In keeping with his pattern, the governor moved quickly in deploying the National Guard; the call-up came just a day after the disturbances began, and just a few months after Guard troops had been called in to control rioting prisoners at several of the state's penitentiaries. Guardsmen Ed Grant and Mike

Hill, who had experienced riot duty in Hough two years earlier, were in a platoon in the 145th Infantry regiment. During the early stages of the Akron operation they had to confront a mass of angry demonstrators, with the grenadiers among the troops firing tear gas. When tear gas failed to fully disperse the crowd, Grant and Hill recalled being given orders to place their M-1 rifles at the ready and "to take firing positions and aim at the attackers": "When they thought we might shoot, they began diving in doorways and windows to get out of our path. Our action stopped the attack immediately, but how close we had come to opening fire on the large crowd was terrifying."[5]

Over a thousand guardsmen remained on duty in Akron until July 25th. African Americans, organized by the United Black Front, turned to picketing and boycotts. John Ballard, the city's white Republican mayor, focused on preserving order. He extolled "General Sylvester Del Corso and all of the officers and men of the Ohio National Guard" for what the mayor proclaimed as "a most excellent piece of work here in Akron." Nine months later, a mayoral commission charged with investigating the causes of the unrest found that several city services, including refuse collection, street cleaning, the provision of sanitary sewers, street lighting, and recreational programs were substandard in the African American sections of Akron. As to work opportunities, which had been the focus of the United Black Front, the commission concluded that companies had failed to implement nondiscrimination in employment and that the city government lagged in black hiring, especially in the fire and police departments. Maintaining that the Akron police department was "more effective in its law enforcement than . . . public relations," the commission determined that the department was "least effective in its relations with blacks." Further, the commission found "numerous instances of rude, belligerent, and discriminatory actions on the part of individual officers."[6]

Cleveland had remained calm throughout the week of turmoil in Akron. Many attributed the lack of violence to Carl Stokes, the newly elected African American mayor. But racial tensions soared on "Wallace Day," July 20, when white supporters of the candidate collected presidential petition signatures at suburban shopping centers. Then, on July 23, came an incident that is little remembered outside of northeast Ohio, but was one of the deadliest encounters of the 1960s.[7]

In the aftermath of the King assassination, the Cleveland business community launched "Cleveland Now!," a privately funded multimillion-dollar program that sought to address the city's urban woes and high rates of unemployment, especially among youth, by providing opportunities similar to those that would later be recommended in Akron, including job development, recreational opportunities, more housing units, and better provision of health services. In a bid to generate black businesses, Fred "Ahmed" Evans, a racial separatist and decorated Korean War veteran, received a $10,300 grant from the program to fund his popular Afro Culture shop. The grant had unintended consequences. While in the army, Evans was diagnosed with a "paranoid-type personality." Police efforts to close down his shop for code violations fueled his suspicions, and he used some of the grant money to purchase weapons. An African American city councilman learned that police surveillance had set Evans on edge, and he visited him on the evening of July 23, leaving only when satisfied that he had calmed the belligerent shop owner.[8]

What happened later that evening remains in dispute. According to one newspaper report, a tow truck entered the Glenville neighborhood where Evans lived and came under fire. During the next ninety minutes, seven people were slain: three members of Evans's New Libya group, three police officers, and one civilian. Eleven police officers and three civilians were wounded.[9]

The presence of the police and the sight of several of the dead militants lying in the street provoked area residents. "The crowd was berserk," said one observer. They set police cars on fire, pulled white drivers from their vehicles and beat them, and looted and burned stores. Following a pattern seen during the Hough uprising two years earlier, white vigilantes cruised the Glenville area and fired on young blacks at a bus stop. In the ensuing violence, an African American marine on leave was shot and killed. Blocks away, another African American lay dead, the victim of unknown assailants.[10]

Mayor Stokes feared that police and National Guardsmen might further inflame the situation, and deployed only African American police and unarmed community activists, such as Harllel Jones and Baxter Hill, to curb the bloodshed. Some city police were infuriated by Stokes's decision to ban white law enforcement from Glenville, but the tactic proved effective. Although additional property was destroyed, it prevented further loss of life. Polls supported the mayor, yet Major General Del Corso of the National Guard denounced Stokes and later accused him of "surrender[ing] to black revolutionaries."[11]

Many current and future Kent State students, including Erwind Blount of the Glenville neighborhood, witnessed these events in Akron and Cleveland firsthand. The largest number of Kent's African American students came from the two cities, and fully half of all of minority undergraduates were from Cleveland. These experiences certainly encouraged some students to follow a militant trajectory, with Blount explaining, "I've seen the riots. Those cats [Ohio National Guardsmen] move in with rifles, man, they blow your head right off." Within a year and a half of the shoot-out, the eighteen-year-old Blount became the president of the Black United Students at Kent State. By the fall quarter in 1968, most African Americans at KSU either belonged to or readily identified with Black United Students (BUS).[12]

Why Go to Chicago?

African Americans were united by their experiences of racism, even as the events of July 1968 propelled many young blacks to relate more easily to militant organizations. White Americans, in contrast, were increasingly divided along generational lines. Many older whites believed that civil rights advances were compromising their own interests. At the same time, some younger whites questioned what they saw as societal hypocrisy in the United States: the nation was ostensibly committed to racial equality but allowed discrimination in every area of its citizens' lives.

The generational divide was often less evident between left-leaning youth and their parents. Jeff Powell grew up in Stow, a working-class suburb of Akron. He was influenced by his parents' open-minded racial views, family traditions of labor radicalism and Catholic moralism, and the political activism of Mark Real, a fellow Stow High School graduate and former seminarian. Powell typified the trend of youthful radicalism. Writing for an underground school newsletter brought him into contact with Catholic clergymen committed to civil rights work. In the aftermath of the King assassination, Powell and Real traveled to Washington, DC, to participate in the Poor People's Campaign, which Martin Luther King had been planning at the time of his death. King had envisioned assembling an interracial coalition that would camp in the parks and from such bases engage in disruptive, but not destructive, tactics to pressure the government to create public-service employment modeled on the Depression-era Works Progress Administration programs. Powell, Real, and other Ohioans joined fifty thousand marchers, but the campaign largely fizzled in the wake of King's death and literally became bogged down in the muddy encampment known as Resurrection City.[13]

Part of the same breed that began asserting itself after the Pentagon March in the fall of 1967, Kent State activists both current and future (like Powell) increasingly abandoned liberal reformism and embraced New Left radicalism. Whether they entered politics through civil rights activism or through opposition to the Vietnam War, they were all fueled by a fierce urgency to act in response to conditions in the nation and the world. SDS adherents were increasingly action-oriented, and became more radical when they encountered other like-minded young people. Jane Boram, a transfer student from East Liverpool, Ohio, was molded by both her steelworker father's union background and Democratic Party politics and her mother's devout Methodism. Inquisitiveness led her to books such as John Howard Griffin's *Black Like Me*. With this foundation, she became involved in political activism after meeting dedicated Quaker pacifists at a college in Indiana. Relocating back to Ohio and enrolling at Kent State, she met dozens, and later hundreds, of students who were willing to confront what they saw as racist or warlike.[14]

Ohio SDS members, like antiwar activists everywhere, were increasingly frustrated by their inability to influence Washington's foreign policy makers. Spurred on by the growing militancy of African American nationalists, they made plans to go to Chicago and confront the Democratic National Convention—run by those seen as the architects of the Vietnam War. On August 16 and 17, SDS hosted meetings in the Kent–Akron area and in Cleveland; among the featuring discussions were "Why Go to Chicago?" and "Why the Democratic Convention Must Be Stopped." Many potential demonstrators were frightened away by the "shoot to kill" orders and violent rhetoric that Chicago mayor Richard Daley used during the strife in his city after the King assassination. Others were wary of the confrontational tone embraced by SDS and some leaders of the New Mobilization to End the War in Vietnam (New MOBE).[15]

Even so, SDS succeeded in mobilizing dozens of protestors in Akron and Kent. Participants had a variety of motivations for their activism. Ric Erickson was new to SDS if not to politics, having grown up as the son of Akron's liberal Democratic mayor. Though not yet an activist, young Erickson objected when he witnessed athletes harassing peace protestors at silent vigils conducted by the Kent Committee to End the War in Vietnam. He was fundamentally changed by a trip to the South with his wife, Carolyn (Knox) Erickson (known as Candy), in the early spring of 1968. The couple encountered enough raw bigotry to convince Ric to join the activist effort. He went to the convention, he said later, to "confront institutions in Chicago that support racism and the war in Vietnam." Other participants were stirred to action by the news reports from Chicago. Tom Zamaria, a Kent student, Vietnam veteran, and native of blue-collar Warren, Ohio, departed for the city only after the start of the convention when he saw "my people getting beat on the head by cops."[16]

Howie Emmer made the trip from Cleveland to Chicago with a diverse delegation organized by MOBE leader Sid Peck and the Peace Council. Participants included members of the Cleveland Draft Union, African American militants, high school and college students, urban youth from the city's west side, and older, middle-class doves. Many in the last group had jobs and family responsibilities, and made the journey to Chicago and back in one day.[17]

Once in Chicago, protesters discovered what had kept so many people away. Mayor Richard Daley felt that his political prestige depended on hosting a successful Democratic convention for his ally Hubert Humphrey. To ensure order, Daley transformed Chicago into an armed camp. George Hoffman recalled that on his way to an initial protest police accosted him verbally because he was carrying a black flag—the same banner he had carried at the Pentagon and that had hung at the Yellow Unicorn coffee house in Kent. Wishing to avoid further harassment, he tore the flag from its pole and stuffed it in his checkered flannel shirt. Many of the estimated three hundred protestors from Ohio gathered in Lincoln Park, near Lake Michigan, well north of the site of the Democratic convention at the International Amphitheatre. There they spent the weekend of August 25 and 26 and the early part of convention week sparring with police over a city-imposed curfew. On Sunday evening, undercover and uniformed police drove the militants from the park. They arrested dozens of protestors, including Jeff Powell, whose incarceration was just a few hours long but nonetheless terrifying.[18]

On Monday afternoon in Lincoln Park, officers apprehended protest leader Tom Hayden. Word of the arrest spread, and Rennie Davis, a former Oberlin student and another key protest leader, organized a thousand militants to march to the police station adjacent to the Hilton Hotel. An undercover agent radioed that the activists had vowed to storm police headquarters to win Hayden's release. On the way, Jeff Powell and hundreds of others detoured through Grant Park (across the street from the Hilton) and massed around the huge monument of Civil War general John Logan. Powell and dozens of others climbed the equestrian statue waving protest flags and shouting for Hayden's release. Police scattered the demonstrators and broke the arm of a protestor left atop the Logan memorial.[19]

The Ohio contingent experienced another night of rough-and-tumble combat with the police. Powell recalled that growing numbers "were actively battling the cops." Three hundred police clashed with three thousand protestors; one, a minister, suffered a fractured skull. Nearby, officers smashed the windows of dozens of cars bearing McCarthy bumper stickers in the lot at Lincoln Park. The Reverend Charles Rawlings, formerly of Cleveland's Council of Churches, told his hometown paper that "guys with clerical collars really got worked over."[20]

Grant Park

Although the week was a blur to many participants, the events of Wednesday, August 28, stood out. Convention delegates who were critical of the war argued in favor of adopting the minority peace plank, which called for a "swift conclusion" to the war. Meanwhile, thousands of protesters gathered for a daytime rally at the bandshell in Grant Park, followed by an evening march to the convention site that would coincide with Humphrey's nomination. The apprehension among protestors in Grant Park was heightened by the presence of National Guardsmen deployed to supplement a heavy police presence. Powell, benefiting from the previous night's experience, began moistening bandanas as protection from tear gas. When former Kent State student and SDS president Carl Oglesby stood to speak from the bandshell stage, a teenager tried to lower the American flag from a nearby pole. After he was taken away by police, others, accompanied by at least one undercover agent, continued to lower the flag. Kent's Jim Powrie, who knew that agents were serving as provocateurs, disarmed a suspicious man of his Molotov cocktail. Despite such precautions, police and guardsmen surrounding the park began clubbing participants, including Rennie Davis.[21]

Speaking from the microphone on the bandshell stage, Cleveland's Sid Peck restored some order. Hayden, now released from jail, was enraged by Davis's beating and feared protestors would be trapped in the park. He urged the rally-goers to make their way to the streets. Chaos reigned as the avenues in the vicinity of Grant Park and the nearby Hilton Hotel (headquarters for Humphrey's Minnesota delegation) filled with police, guardsmen, and protesters. Peck was beaten and arrested by officers, and he described the police conduct as "the most vicious thing I've ever seen." Just outside the hotel, Charlie Tabasko remembered being "grabbed by a cop, but a kid from Cleveland's West Side saved me." Both escaped "by running over the hoods of cars." Hoffman recalled that in a moment of supreme confusion, Ric Erickson literally drove to the rescue, and they escaped the turmoil in his car.[22]

Powell fled into the Loop, followed by police, who, he said, "seemed to have gone berserk." Having run track in school, Powell dodged National Guard jeeps and made his way back to the Ohio movement's center in the church near Lincoln Park. Exhausted, he and other dissidents recouped while watching television coverage of events inside the International Amphitheatre—just as some convention delegates were watching TV to learn what was going on outside. As the clock reached midnight, Powell returned to the streets outside the Hilton. He became so agitated while in front of the National Guard lines that Powrie had to restrain him. Early the next morning, while it was still dark, police entered the Hilton, contending that objects had been thrown at them from the fifteenth story. They took elevators to that floor and proceeded to beat McCarthy's convention delegates. The mayhem continued down in the lobby, where some of the younger delegates had been taken by the police. A Humphrey legal adviser protested a senseless police assault on a youth in the Hilton's foyer to no avail. The beatings of protestors, convention delegates, campaign volunteers, and even reporters revealed just how porous were the lines between and among those not in uniform. Yet if the brutality pushed those who had been on the receiving end of billy clubs in the direction of political radicalism, for millions of others watching on television the events pushed them in the opposite direction, for even in their distant living rooms many no longer felt safe from the poorly understood violence. Many Americans sided with the authorities, even as many of the same people were turning against war. This same phenomenon recurred in the spring of 1970.[23]

The Cost of Chicago

Humphrey's aide had seen the cost of violence up close, yet nobody knew the price paid better than the nominee. On the night of his nomination, TV networks pulled the coverage of the seconding speech by Cleveland mayor Carl Stokes to show the clashes in the streets. Daley's police had prevented protestors from sleeping in the parks, triggering days of street battles. This action by Daley and his police did tremendous political damage to Humphrey, who later lamented, "I could have beaten the Republicans . . . but it's difficult to take on the Republicans and fight a guerrilla war in your party at the same time." Whether Humphrey was referring to Chicago's mayor or the antiwar protestors remains unclear, but his verdict on the convention was undisputed: "Chicago was a catastrophe." Prior to the party conventions, Gallup polling showed Nixon ahead of Humphrey by just 2 percent nationally. The brutality and anarchy of the events in Chicago left the Democratic nominee with a much steeper hill to climb.[24]

Back in Portage County, many were initially more interested in the Randolph Fair, as thousands turned out to show their livestock and crown the annual king and queen. When attention turned to the political race after Labor Day, polling revealed the damage done by the turmoil in Chicago. Among those in Portage County's "villages and rural areas," where half of those surveyed lived, the results were gloomy for Democrats and perhaps for the Republicans as well. Forty-two percent of respondents backed Wallace and 32 percent supported Nixon. Humphrey managed just 27 percent.[25]

During the convention, police in Chicago clubbed several reporters for the Dix newspaper chain, including Dix's own son David. *Record-Courier* editorial writers wisely sought a middle ground and urged its readers to eschew hatred of those with differing beliefs and instead embrace "respect . . . founded on tolerance." Roger DiPaolo, the conservative head of Portage County's Democratic party, would hear none of it and embraced Mayor Daley for a photo in the local paper. Interviewed at the convention by young David Dix, DiPaolo compared the actions of demonstrators to the "kind of tactics that the Communists and Nazis use." Local opinion seemed to be on DiPaolo's side. One area man called the Chicago protestors "an uncontrolled mob," and a woman attributed the "heartbreaking events" to the work of "paid Communists."[26]

A Sea Change and Second Wave

The events in Chicago created an opportunity for the Kent State SDS to spread student radicalism. Politically and organizationally, SDS soured on elections after Johnson followed his 1964 peace talk with an escalation of the war. The events of 1968—the tangled primaries, the assassinations, the defeat of the peace plank at the Democratic convention, and the experience in Chicago—convinced untold numbers of young people that, as Bill Whitaker noted, "change [would] not come through electoral politics." The Democratic convention had been televised in prime time by all three major networks, and millions of Americans, including many college students preparing to return to school and veterans returning from Vietnam, had been shocked and appalled by graphic footage of Chicago police bludgeoning protestors. The whole world *was* watching. Whitaker recalled that the violence did succeed in "galvanizing young people": "When school convened in the fall of 1968, there was a lot more support for SDS. It was a sea change." Charlie Tabasko concurred, saying that the experience was "very radicalizing." Chicago also changed Jim Powrie, who now saw police as "agents of the politicians who were agents of the wealthy." "The war had come home to us," he said.[27]

SDS's first meeting of the 1968–69 school year drew 250 students, including not only those from urban working-class families, among them veterans returning from the war, but many freshman and sophomores from suburban and eastern metropolitan locales. Although the diverse group largely built on an existing activist foundation, they also further energized the antiwar movement and supplied it with additional daring. Alan Canfora, Matthew Flanagan, and Paul "Roby" Bukosky were all new to the Kent campus and yet part of the same class cohort that had long comprised much of the university's activist core. Hailing from urban Summit and Cuyahoga counties, the sons of industrial and service workers, they were part of what the historian Terry Anderson calls the "second wave" of Sixties protestors and had already been exposed to politics.[28]

Among the same blue-collar contingent of newly arriving students were military service veterans, including Mark Lencl, Ken Johnson, Ray Hudson, and Mike Gorup. Veterans had numbered among Kent's activist students since the 1950s, but these were the first to participate in protests against a war in which many had fought. They were older than many other undergraduates, and their experience carried an authority that other activists lacked; thus they were an important addition to the movement. Lencl, a Cleveland native who had served with the airborne forces in Vietnam before enrolling at Kent, bitterly hated the war. Ken Johnson, who hailed from Ashtabula, drew some of his influences from his working-class family with European socialist roots. In Vietnam, he saw heavy fighting as a sergeant in the 1st Infantry Division. Soured by the war,

Johnson joined SDS before being discharged in mid-1968. Twenty-six-year-old Ray Hudson, a transfer student from Western Michigan University, had served in military intelligence. Akron's Mike Gorup obtained an honorable discharge despite an accusation that he had promoted anti-American views while stationed in Japan.[29]

Others came from northeast Ohio suburbs or eastern cities. Many were from Jewish families. Jerry Persky and Richie Hess initially forged friendships as members of a Jewish fraternity. Persky, whose father had been a member of the left-wing John Reed Club at Ohio State, graduated from the same high school as Howie Emmer. Hess grew up in New York City and was the son of a union printer. He became more radicalized at Kent after meeting Vince Modugno and the "Elm Street Radicals," who took their name from the site of their off-campus residence. Mike Alewitz, another graduate of Cleveland Heights High School, spent his childhood in an ethnic working-class neighborhood in Wilmington, Delaware, in a secular, strongly left-leaning Jewish family. Persky, Hess, and Alewitz all became leaders and mainstays of Kent's antiwar movement.[30]

The top leaders of SDS were preponderantly male, but the group also had a significant number of female members. Their importance to the organization grew over time, especially after the chapter's leadership was decimated by arrests in the spring of 1969. Candy Knox Erickson came from a family of means and attended Vassar until her parents' separation, when she relocated to Ohio with her father. At Kent, she gravitated to the Kent Committee to End the War in Vietnam, and she and her husband, Ric, played a key role in the chapter from its very beginnings. Abby Schindler, another member of the KCEWV, also came to Kent State from a prosperous family, in her case from a New York City suburb. Others, like Jane Boram, were similar in class background to many of their activist and blue-collar male counterparts, as well as some of the other women activists.[31]

Accompanying the spread of political activism was a noticeable shift in the cultural life of the campus. For men this meant longer hair, and for women a reduced concern with makeup. Male and female activists alike increasingly abandoned traditional styles of college dress, although such cultural forms of the flowering rebellion would not become truly significant until the fall of 1969, following the Woodstock festival, and not predominant until the fall of 1970. Music was absolutely central to this New Left culture. A month before to the start of the school year, a new FM radio station, WMMS in Cleveland, began catering to rock music aficionados. Featuring the soothing radio voice of Billy Bass, an African American former KSU student, the station became a sensation and quickly supplanted all others. The new station helped promote the mobilization of young people to go to Chicago. Just as long hair did not necessarily make one an antiwar activist, however, most listeners tuned in for the largely commercial-free music that included Cream, Jimi Hendrix, the Doors, Bob Dylan, and Jefferson Airplane, as well as newer artists such as former Buffalo Springfield guitarist Neil Young.[32]

Larger numbers of young people turned the radio dial to WMMS and read the newly launched *Rolling Stone* magazine, while more and more Kent State freshmen unloaded crates of rock records into their living quarters. Buyers of the latest Janis Joplin album could not have missed the eye-popping cover—the work of former Cleveland resident Robert Crumb. Kent students also frequented the North Water Street bars, especially JB's. For 75 cents, they could hear the James Gang, Pacific Gas and Electric, and later Terry Hynde's band, 15-60-75. And, of course, marijuana began to become a prominent part of the nascent counterculture scene.[33]

While impossible to categorize as a percentage, innumerable devotees of the counterculture were not necessarily political radicals, although many did believe that they were separate from and sometimes opposed to the mainstream society. They saw themselves as a vanguard of something new and different, and if many in the generational cohort were not eager to challenge the Vietnam War and the existing political order that gave rise to it, untold numbers were at least willing to rethink or reimagine the social reality.

The ongoing war and the presidential election dominated that reality in the fall of 1968. The *Daily Kent Stater* reported on the campaigns of Humphrey, Nixon, and Wallace, and Young Democrats and their GOP counterparts looked for students to volunteer in the campaigns. Although SDS members increasingly rejected electoral politics, Humphrey continued to enjoy the support of many at KSU. A busload of students met him at the Cleveland airport on the third weekend of September. He told them that "young people can be the difference in this campaign." Humphrey was mindful of the need to try to erase the memory of events in Chicago and emphasized, "We are united to see that peace and justice prevail in this land of ours." When he proceeded downtown, however, he encountered protestors. The *Stater* reported that "some of them were shouting unprintable anti-Humphrey slogans." The president of the KSU Young Democrats, recognizing that the stakes were high and Humphrey's poll numbers were low, tried to educate students about the party's core values. Supporters sent letters to the *Stater* or took advantage of talks on campus by Carey McWilliams, editor of *The Nation,* and former Kennedy speechwriter Ted Sorensen.[34]

Even then, New Deal intellectuals stumping for Humphrey could not escape the stain of Chicago. McWilliams had to contend with a persistent activist who wanted the small audience to know what he had seen in the streets of Chicago. Weeks later, Sorensen experienced similar treatment from Ric Erickson. The SDS leader firmly asserted that "social change . . . won't come from the top down," insisting that "it won't be decided on election day." The sure-footed Sorensen firmly handled the challenge, informing the large crowd that he had "more reason to be bitter about politics than most," but he still believed that rejecting electoral participation was "bad politics."[35]

SDS members believed that their politics were different and new. The fall of 1968 represented the apogee of the chapter's brief New Left phase, before the embrace of Marxism and third-world revolution. Many members became involved with the "Free University," organized by chemistry professor Arif Kazmi and history graduate student and SDS adviser Ron Weisberger. Seen and intended as a cultural alternative to mainstream academic life, the Free University attracted more than three hundred students to noncredit classes on Zen Buddhism, folk guitar, the US labor movement, Afro-American culture, and above all, Herbert Marcuse's *One-Dimensional Man.* Before SDS had a chance to organize a single protest on campus that fall, however, critics were complaining about the organization's influence within the Free University. In a lengthy article in the *Stater,* one detractor asked, "Could it be that the Free University is only a tool of the campus radicals . . . to generate enthusiasm among potential and proto-activists for the dogma of the New Left?" SDS answered for itself, but many of the credit-free courses offered by the Free University can be found in college catalogs today.[36]

Confronting Wallace and Nixon

Supporters of the Free University argued that it addressed the real issues of the day, such as the nation's racial divide, that were largely ignored in standard classes. SDS believed in mixing educational thought with social practice, and helped organize demonstrations against the campaign of George Wallace in Canton, Akron, and Cleveland, where interracial crowds of demonstrators were confronted by Wallace supporters. Scuffles broke out in Canton on October 3 when a devotee described as "a Wallace strongman" punched a female reporter for the *Stater* as she tried to cover a story about the harassment of an African American student. Portage County residents were among the Wallace faithful in Canton; the voices of three hundred mostly African American protestors competed against ten times as many Wallace supporters. A reporter for the *Record-Courier* described the scene in Canton as "explosive . . . but nobody lit the match that could have touched off a riot."[37]

Closer to Kent in Akron, Wallace and his followers were confronted by SDS members dressed as hooded Klansmen. Mark Real, wearing his customary coat and tie, explained to a reporter SDS's opposition to all three candidates, but added that "Wallace is the worst of them." An unrobed, authentic Klansman at the rally told a reporter that "civil rights is the big domestic issue . . . [and]

Wallace will do something about it." A reporter described the dissenting taunts as "the worst since Wallace hit the [campaign] trail." In response to the demonstration, Akron police arrested several African Americans and ignored Wallace supporters who tore signs from the hands of protesters.[38]

Akron police loyalties lay solidly with the former Alabama governor, who shared their "law and order" sentiments. An Akron officer told a reporter that "80% of the men in his department . . . [were] voting for Wallace." Akron's large, transplanted white Appalachian population also supported Wallace in substantial numbers. One man showed his solidarity by arriving at the rally dressed in a Confederate uniform. Fundamentalist leaders such as the television evangelist Rex Humbard also turned out. Rev. Humbard had given Lurleen Wallace a bible for her inauguration when she succeeded her husband as governor of Alabama. Now the head of Akron's Cathedral of Tomorrow bestowed a bible on the presidential aspirant, in the hope that it would be needed for the inaugural ceremony.[39]

Wallace was attaining high poll numbers a month before the election. His angry pitch to the forgotten "common man" had succeeded in reaching beyond the Goldwater constituency and the area's concentration of transplanted upper-South whites. His blue-collar populism appealed to organized and nonunion white workers alike, through a perfect mixture of race polarization, anti-elitist economic resentment, and alarm over civil disorder. Wallace hit these themes repeatedly, and denounced racial busing and "the blackmail . . . of anarchists." And without explaining how, he promised that if the United States failed to win in Vietnam "diplomatically . . . [at the peace talks] in Paris, I'm going to . . . end the war militarily."[40]

When Wallace's entourage reached Cleveland, the situation became volatile. Wallace and his newly named running mate, retired air force general Curtis LeMay (who hailed from Mount Vernon in central Ohio), appeared before 4,500 supporters and 800 protestors who had gained access to the Public Auditorium by posing as "Whippies for Wallace." The Whippies confused Wallace partisans with a series of pro- and anti-Wallace chants as they divided into groups of fake supporters and genuine adversaries. As the candidate team arrived, Wallace partisans caught on to the ruse when protestors directed their chants at the presidential hopeful: "Politicians lie, GI's Die!" Wallace received thunderous cheers from supporters when he responded, "You are the folks this country is tired of."[41]

Satisfied that they had made the speeches inaudible, SDS and Youth Against War and Fascism (YAWF, the student arm of the Trotskyist Workers World Party) members moved outside en masse. As they did so, a reporter observed the approach of "a group of about 40 Negroes" led by the well-known Cleveland militant Harllel Jones. The African American protestors "chanted 'Chicago,

Chicago' as one of their members played bongo drums and another held a tricolor black nationalist flag." The diverse group of demonstrators soon found themselves under police attack. The officers were egged on by Wallace's hard-ened followers, some of whom fell victim to the very police violence they had encouraged. At least half a dozen people received injuries requiring treatment, including an anti-Wallace demonstrator with a fractured skull. Ted Dostal, a sixty-two-year old radical steelworker, numbered among those arrested, charged with assaulting a police officer. Dostal and a YAWF codefendant were the first of many activists to face trials in northeast Ohio in the coming months and years.[42]

The Kent SDS had experimented with a walkout against Humphrey and creative theater against Wallace. They saved the tactic of noisy confrontation for the Republican candidate, Richard Nixon. On October 10, during a speech in Akron, the former vice president encountered what *Time* magazine described as "serious heckling for the first time [in his campaign]." Dave Dyer gave Nixon the two-middle-finger salute as the candidate entered the hall. Inside, over one hundred SDS members and a few young Democrats incessantly interrupted him with derisive chanting, successfully reducing Nixon's rally to a "shambles." The war of words ended when another Kent student, Tim DeFrange, stood and hurled an ear-piercing invective at Nixon. When authorities threw DeFrange out of the arena, the rest of SDS marched out with him.[43]

Two days before Nixon's stop in Akron, an official representing Governor James Rhodes announced that the state's National Guard would be placed on stand-by for election day, November 5. Knowing the political gains Wallace made from his tough "law and order" talk, General Del Corso promised a call-up "if we have any indication of disturbances." There had not yet been any major demonstrations in Kent, but officials identified Portage County as one of the state's "potential trouble spots." Rhodes's unnamed official noted, "It's a hell of a way to have a free election, . . . but if we pick up any rumblings that anyone is going to disrupt, intimidate or heckle voters, the troops will be called."[44]

The Stand of Labor

At the beginning of October, a national Gallup poll showed how badly is-sues of war, race, and domestic disorder had frayed the New Deal coalition. The coalition once comprised white southerners, urban dwellers, blue-collar workers, Catholic ethnics, Jews, women, and African Americans. Of these di-verse groups, only the last held completely firm. Much of the white South had deserted the Democratic Party four years earlier following the passage of the Civil Rights Act. Racial division and raw fears of busing and housing integra-tion among blue-collar whites threatened to overwhelm economic solidarity and further erode the party's base. The combustible issue of Vietnam caused working-class whites to be of two minds: they were simultaneously weary of the war's cost and supportive of patriotic imagery, concerned about the fate of their army and draft-age sons yet proud of their own service and sacrifices during World War II. Ohio labor leaders, a decade removed from the unified fight against the right-to-work bill and with the UAW split from the rest of the AFL-CIO over the war, launched a determined campaign in Ohio to win back members who had defected to Wallace. UAW leader Albert Canfora Sr. worked nonstop in his hometown of Barberton and in his workplace at Goodyear Aerospace. He put up yard signs and spoke at meetings to undercut those in labor "who would be pushing Wallace." Humphrey knew the problem full well. He later wrote that by Labor Day, "in precinct after precinct, . . . in Cleveland . . . in Akron, . . . Wallace gained support that belonged, by habit and tradition if not ideology, to the Democrats."[45]

John Nardella, president of Local 2 of the United Rubber Workers in Akron, remembered that "what hurt Hubert was the damn war and it was tough for him to overcome the evils of that." Nardella felt he needed someone to catch his members' attention, so he invited actor Lorne Greene, who played patriarch Ben Cartwright on the hugely popular TV western *Bonanza*, to speak to the union. Peppering his talk with four-letter words, Greene brought the message to rubber workers at a labor breakfast and at plant gates throughout the Akron area: *Stand with Humphrey.*[46]

Democratic operatives believed that the battleground state of Ohio was within Humphrey's reach. The UAW and the AFL-CIO hammered away at Wallace's counterfeit economic populism. Union volunteers distributed a handbill prepared by the AFL-CIO's Committee on Political Education that featured an outline of Wallace's home state. They effectively reminded their fellow members of Alabama's dismal record on everything from per capita income to illiteracy. "The unions entirely out-performed the middle-class liberals," the authors of one campaign study noted. Humphrey agreed: "My trade union friends stood firm when a lot of my liberal, former ADA [Americans for Democratic Action] colleagues and some Democratic politicians ran for cover."[47]

The Democratic Party contended with divisions on both its right and left, just as it had in the presidential election twenty years earlier. Problems on the right had been evident with Wallace in the 1964 primaries and again with the enormous mid-term election losses in 1966. On the left, Vietnam had split the party. For all their effort, some labor allies had contributed to the vice president's problems because of their harsh words for the demonstrators in Chicago. In their zeal to sustain Johnson and later Humphrey, the unyielding support for the war by many mainstream labor leaders made deep wounds deeper.[48]

The Last Days

Despite these difficulties, Humphrey pulled closer in Ohio as the race neared the end. Sensing the shifting fortunes, KSU political science professor Kenneth Colton mustered students to canvass in Akron neighborhoods the weekend before the election. The *Stater* endorsed Humphrey on October 22, citing the possibility of a bombing halt. On the last day of the month, Johnson further boosted Humphrey's slim chances by announcing the bombing halt for which many had hoped. The race had become so close that the *Record-Courier* ran competing editorials for Nixon and Humphrey. Publisher Robert C. Dix wrote in his regular column, "Along the Way," "Our editors are stalled on Nixon-Humphrey. I am too, in a way, but my background makes me lean to the former."[49]

During the last full week of the campaign Humphrey was in Akron, where three thousand people assembled on short notice for a rally. Sensing momentum, Humphrey continued to focus on the state, attracting a crowd of six thousand in Youngstown on November 1. In a speech to a Chicago audience, Humphrey had credited antiwar liberals for the bombing halt: "Those brave men who led the dissent last spring have made their mark on policy." Soon afterward McCarthy extended his support to the candidate. One final poll showed that Humphrey had moved ahead of Nixon in Ohio, even as an *Akron Beacon Journal* survey indicated the opposite.[50]

The day before the vote, Kent SDSers carried a mock coffin representing "the politics of death" into a crowded campus lecture hall. The four "pallbearers" briefly disrupted a political science class as they proceeded silently down one aisle and back out the next. Students who were not befuddled booed. On election day, as voters made their way to the polls, 150 SDS members marched around the campus with the same symbolic coffin.[51]

Overwhelming numbers of citizens rejected SDS's nonvoting stance, and more than 90 percent of eligible voters cast their ballots in Summit County on November 5th. Wallace had generated indisputable fervor, but that passion fed off anger and racial resentment, not hope. Voters had twice rejected Nixon, and Humphrey's support remained thin even in his own party. Voters seemed motivated to stop the candidates they most feared.[52]

As the clock reached midnight on the East Coast, NBC television broadcast that Humphrey had a 1 percentage point lead in the national popular vote. The election still hung in the balance as Cleveland's large African American population delivered what a research team deemed "an enormous vote to Humphrey." Ultimately, it proved too little. Nixon took Ohio by 91,000 votes, making it the closest presidential race in the state since Harry Truman's victory twenty years before. The *Beacon Journal* had predicted in its final pre-election poll that Nixon would win Ohio by 14 percent; in the end, he prevailed by just over 2 percent. Humphrey carried Portage along with the urban counties of Summit, Cuyahoga, Trumbull, and Mahoning. Labor succeeded in whittling Wallace's showing to fewer than 12 percent of the total, making the race competitive and enabling Humphrey to run closer to Nixon than Kennedy had in his 1960 win. The near comeback, however, provided little consolation to Humphrey and those who sought to maintain the New Deal order. They had suffered a momentous defeat.[53]

The frayed Roosevelt coalition had not been the only loser, for the peace movement had lost as well. While most in the antiwar community saw Humphrey as nothing more than Johnson's minion, the vice president, in victory, would have headed a divided party with the peace wing in ascendance. Having had the negative example of a president who failed to heed the voice of that movement, it is unlikely that Humphrey would have ignored the growing strength of the antiwar forces inside and outside the party. Now, with Nixon as president-elect in the fall of 1968, the political culture at KSU would shift rapidly to the left.

The Cambodian head of state, Prince Norodom Sihanouk, and his wife, Monique, arrive at Kent State on October 3, 1960. At his next campus appearance twenty years later at Cornell University, he said that the students at Kent "lost their lives for the cause of the Indochinese people." Courtesy Special Collections and Archives, Kent State University Libraries.

Students raise placards for John F. Kennedy at a mock political convention at Kent State, circa March 1960. Courtesy Special Collections and Archives, Kent State University Libraries.

George Bowman (photo on left, hand on chin), president at the dawn of Kent State's protest era, took a dim view of the civil rights movement. Vice president Robert I. White (pictured in both photos) had the backing of board of trustees member Robert C. Dix (in ceremonial robe) in becoming Kent's sixth president in 1963. While less resistant to change than his predecessor, White failed to manage dissent at crucial moments of his presidency. Courtesy Special Collections and Archives, Kent State University Libraries.

Lance Buhl and Oscar Hearn confer during Kent State's first protest of the era on May 11, 1961. Pickets pressed the university to end racially discriminatory policies regarding off-campus housing. *Cleveland Press* photo by Jerry Horton, courtesy Special Collections and Archives, Kent State University Libraries.

Socialist John McCann in 1971. While Lance Buhl may well have been Kent's most effective student leader in the early 1960s, McCann was the most radical. Courtesy of Barbara Gregorich.

Diminutive Barbara Brock, carrying an antiwar sign, with Tony Walsh (bearded man holding sign) in the background at one of the first antiwar pickets. Circa February–March 1965. Photo by Gerry Simon.

Tony Walsh serving as emcee for Herbert Aptheker's talk, May 19, 1966. Photo by Gerry Simon.

Kent Committee to End the War in Vietnam float in the fall 1966 homecoming parade, with Tony Walsh at the wheel. Photo by Gerry Simon.

One of the first campus peace vigils, circa January–March 1967. Photo by Gerry Simon.

This peace vigil in front of Student Union in the spring or fall of 1967 reflects the growth of the campus antiwar movement. The banner reads "Vigil for Peace in Viet Nam." Photo by Gerry Simon.

On April 15, 1967, Martin Luther King Jr. spoke to an estimated crowd of 300,000 antiwar demonstrators at the United Nations in New York City, including hundreds from Kent State. Pictured here are Judy Gollust and Bob Ehrlich (in white raincoat). Photo by David King.

George Hoffman, both arms raised and giving the peace sign, following the walkout of Hubert Humphrey's appearance at Kent State, May 3, 1968. To Hoffman's left are Abby Schindler (wearing dress under white coat) and Larry Lamovsky (holding banner and wearing sunglasses). Behind the large banner, also wearing sunglasses, is Curt Resnick. The student in jacket and tie is George Gibeaut. Photo by Gerry Simon.

Mark Rudd speaking to a capacity crowd in the University Auditorium on October 24, 1968. Marilyn Hammond is in the front row (on left with black glasses and long hair). Photo by Gerry Simon.

On November 18, 1968, black students leave campus in a mass exodus in response to the collapse of negotiations over their demand for amnesty from the Oakland Police sit-in days earlier. The walkout succeeded and led to a Black Studies program and other reforms. Courtesy Special Collections and Archives, Kent State University Libraries.

Ric Erickson speaking to supporters at the Administration Building, April 8, 1969. Jeff "Donovan" Powell on left; Terry Robbins on right. Photo by David King.

SDS protestors being arrested by plainclothes campus police on April 9, 1969. Pictured with their arms raised in defiance are, from left to right, Jeff Powell, Colin Neiburger, and Howie Emmer. Reporters from the *Daily Kent Stater,* shown at left, race to keep up. SDSer Larry Finn is immediately behind the trio as other supporters of the radicals follow. Photo by David King.

Counterprotestors in the portico
of the Music and Speech Building
before the melee between them and
SDS breaks out on April 16, 1969.
SDS supporters gained access to the
building through another entrance.
The protest resulted in nearly sixty
arrests. Photo by David King.

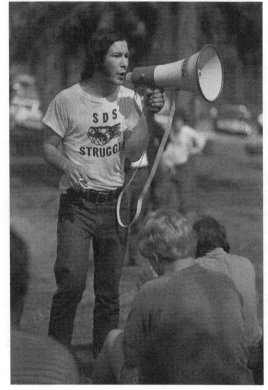

Howie Emmer speaking at an
SDS rally in a town park on April
17, 1969, the day after the arrests at
the Music and Speech Building.
The rally drew 250 participants.
Photo by David King.

Students voting in a referendum on 3-C proposals in April 1969, following the university's banning of SDS and the arrests in Music and Speech. Over 8,600 students participated in the voting, the largest turnout of any during the Vietnam era. Photo by David King.

Ruth Gibson speaking with Black United Students president Bob Pickett on the KSU Commons, circa 1968–69. Photo by David King.

CHAPTER 8

Black and White (Alone) Together

As members of the Kent State SDS trudged their way into the Akron auditorium on October 10 to confront a man who would become their nemesis, others from the campus headed west. Bound for distant Boulder, Colorado, they traveled in a borrowed Rambler in order to take part in what SDS called its National Council meeting. There, five members of Kent's newly organized chapter would, for the first time, represent the school at a conference of the national organization, which by the fall of 1968 had approximately four hundred chapters.[1]

Until the founding of SDS at Kent, the dissident movement on the campus had a largely homespun feel. True, the Kent Committee to End the War in Vietnam had been strongly influenced by the dedicated members of the nationally active Young Socialist Alliance, but the KCEWV contained enough independently minded activists to enable it to develop mostly of its own accord. After nearly three years of existence, the bulk of them decided that YSA had too much to say about the direction of the KCEWV. The majority drifted away and, rather than rely on solely their own efforts, looked for another organization that might be better suited to the political and cultural mood of the times.

The Kent SDS members who arrived in Boulder quickly found themselves immersed in a dense ideological debate between cultural and political radicals such as themselves and another disciplined group that operated within the national SDS—the Progressive Labor Party—whose politics, if not its style, bore some similarity to the YSA and the Socialist Workers Party, whose beliefs and positions the Kent radicals found equally turgid. Formed in 1962 by a coterie of pro-Maoist Marxists, the Progressive Labor Party (PLP, or simply PL) initially bemused and fascinated some SDSers. Whatever mild interest the group may have had for freewheeling SDSers in the beginning, by 1968 PL—seeing SDS as a recruiting ground—behaved like haughty and unwelcome house guests. What was most disturbing for those who opposed the intruders was PL's ideological antagonism toward the Black Panther Party and the Vietnamese National Liberation Front, with whom SDS sought to ally and, in the case of the Vietnamese, whose cause they wanted to promote. The time was fast approaching when SDS would show the self-styled ideological mavens the door.[2]

Kent's interracial contingent included the young Chicago protest veteran Jeff Powell (known among fellow SDSers as "Donovan" for his resemblance to the popular Scottish-born folksinger), his friend and sometime roommate, West Virginian George Gibeaut, and Ken Hammond, the former Young Democrat whose investigative efforts would soon help to produce the Kent SDS's most impressive research document.[3]

Powell sensed the "crisis atmosphere" that pervaded the SDS sessions. The 450 delegates felt not only the urgency of Vietnam and the need to counter the approaching elections, but also, in the wake of the brutality at the Chicago Democratic Convention, the fear that Boulder police were preparing to attack the assembly. As the meeting unfolded, words were the only means of attack— and quite a few of these were exchanged between different factions of SDS who struggled over supremacy in the organization. John Jacobs and several others in the larger anti-PL grouping introduced a resolution that, in the aftermath of Chicago, advocated more direct action as opposed to electoral participation, a position that in retrospect set the stage for the "Days of Rage" a year later. Believing, too, in the need to mobilize ever younger people, like Powell, into the movement against what the resolution called "the political parties of racism and imperialism," a second resolution aimed at organizing high school students passed handily. Meanwhile, delegates from Progressive Labor had their proposal for a Student Labor Action Project defeated by a two-to-one margin.[4]

Powell, who encountered SDS during his senior year at Stow High School, gravitated naturally to the workshop on high school organizing. Such radical outreach among adolescents was in bloom at many northeast Ohio high schools by that fall. In Cleveland, SDS had developed contacts in a half dozen area schools, including Shaw High in East Cleveland, where Ike Coleman and Hunter Havens were among the students attracted to SDS. A month before leaving for Boulder, Powell had been ordered out of his alma mater for distributing literature there. Recalling his own students' rights issues in high school, Powell and other SDSers urged students to form a union in order to overturn dress codes, end corporal punishment, and obtain editorial autonomy for the student paper. Such organizing even reached Kent's Theodore Roosevelt High School and earned representatives of the budding union an audience with the city's tolerant mayor, John Carson. Inquiries about the union from a *Record-Courier* reporter and a subsequent editorial titled "Preserve Authority" put an end to any plans for an organization of high school students in Kent. Still, the paper's editorial writers realized that such efforts by the students reflected the state of "the current American social revolution."[5]

Less than three months removed from his years at Stow and having gained valuable experience during his participation in protests in Washington, DC, and Chicago, Powell possessed sufficient authority to volunteer his own experiences during the workshop on high school organizing. His remarks caught the attention of the SDS's newly elected interorganizational secretary, Bernardine Dohrn, who asked Powell to stay behind for additional discussion. They both liked what they saw. Powell drew inspiration not only from Dohrn but from other well-known SDSers. Meeting "other long-haired freaks and radicals" reinforced his growing devotion to action-oriented politics and the growing cultural polarization he was feeling. His experiences in high school, and certainly in Chicago, confirmed the animosity he felt from "older America," while his contacts with other young people also validated "that we were a numerous and growing tribe." Powell and his four friends received further confirmation of the enmity some older Americans held for them while they were on their way back to Ohio: on a mountainous interstate highway, the drivers of several semi trucks hurled firecrackers at their lumbering automobile. Finding temporary refuge at an all-night gas station, they waited until the trucks were safely past.[6]

Columbia Is Coming

Mark Rudd, who numbered among the SDS delegates in Boulder on the weekend of October 11–13, was on the Kent campus two weeks later for a talk on the state of the student movement. Rudd, who was the chairman of the Columbia University chapter of SDS, had appeared on the cover of *Newsweek* on September 30, the central figure in a photo of an altercation with police during the Columbia revolt of the previous May. His leadership of the confrontation there led to his dismissal from Columbia, as SDS tactics proved controversial even among many liberals. Yet SDS most assuredly knew what they were protesting—a decision by Columbia to demolish neighborhood housing for thousands of poor African Americans in order to make way for a gymnasium for affluent college students. With the protests against the gym starting within weeks of Martin Luther King's assassination, militants like Rudd could rightly assert that destroying the homes of impoverished African Americans added further injury to the already irreparable harm done by King's murder. Moreover, police had initiated the violence at Columbia, beating African American students and Rudd's fellow SDSers as they cleared the seized university buildings.[7]

Rudd's first full day in Kent did not begin well. Local SDS members arranged for him to be interviewed at Ric Erickson's apartment by reporters from the campus radio station, WKSU. Unbeknown to SDS, one of them, Margaret Ann

Murvay, was passing along information about the campus radicals to KSU's police department. Predictably enough, the interview turned into a debate, and a profanity-laden one at that. With no common ground, and with Rudd's comments violating FCC decency standards, both sides agreed that the tape could not be used. An argument then ensued over ownership of the tape, which SDS—after offering to pay for the reel—insisted belonged to them.[8]

That Rudd possessed great certitude surprised no one, but the splenetic manner he exhibited during the aborted interview, and later in his speech to a crowd of no less than twelve hundred Kent State students, certainly did. Many in his huge audience quickly found Rudd's temperament offensive, although his explanations of SDS activity during the Columbia strike and at the Chicago Democratic Convention nevertheless resonated with those who had been shaken by the one-sided violence at both events. Rudd denounced an assortment of wrongs that, had he cared to notice, also troubled many in his audience. He criticized the war and social ills in a way that one critic described as "abusive, obscene, biased, and boring." Another termed his performance "disgraceful and revolting," noting that Rudd "completely defeated his purpose in coming here." Later in the night, at an otherwise fun-filled gathering back at the rented home of Ric and Candy Erickson where his day began, Rudd topped everything off by getting into a scuffle with one of his hosts over how to divide the $130 collected during his talk. Such belligerence by an SDS leader cast the venerable KCEWV in a new, seemingly more moderate light. Little wonder that Chuck Ayers, the editorial cartoonist for the *Daily Kent Stater,* depicted an SDS leader being asked by a student longing for the old days, "Whatever happened to the KCEWV?"[9]

Between the troubled interview and the bombastic presentation, Rudd at least brought attention to SDS, an organization that was new to most Kent State students. Many did not like what they had seen, and tensions heightened the following evening when Bob Carpenter, the host of WKSU's "Talk Back," opined on his program that "there was a cancer on the campus and that the malignity was SDS." It is unclear whether Carpenter knew of Margaret Ann Murvay's relationship with the KSU police, but he invited her to call in with a comment about her failed interview with SDS. With Carpenter still on the air, six SDS members—angry about the lack of balance in his program—arrived at the station demanding equal time on the show. Radio station staff called the campus police, who promptly marshaled the militants out.[10]

The following week, Kent's SDS managed to restore some good will with an appearance by the earnest and courteous Rennie Davis. The Oberlin graduate and SDS alumnus had been pummeled by police clubs in Chicago, and after the election he would be indicted for his role in organizing the convention protests. Just a month before speaking at Kent, Davis predicted that "enormous energy will be released on the campus to confront universities connected with the U.S. military effort." As if to prove his point, the next day twenty members of SDS, in protest over the presence of the military at Kent State, did mock calisthenics in front of ROTC cadets as they drilled on the campus Commons.[11]

Furthering Student Dissent

Whatever the blunders of a youthful Kent SDS, an increasing number of people in the university community found that the war loomed larger and more murderous than anything the student militants did or did not do. Nationally, a plurality of voters had hoped, in supporting the GOP candidate, that he would find a way to end the war, but Nixon's victory on November 5 convinced others, including many at Kent State, that conditions in the country and world would only worsen as a result. *Newsweek* predicted as much. "No one can forecast what will happen on campus this year," the magazine noted five weeks before the November vote, adding, "One scenario is that if Nixon is elected President, the public mood will favor repressing student dissent . . . and more students will become further alienated and join SDS."[12]

Looking to take advantage of such alienation, Mark Rudd asked Lewis Cole, a confidant at Columbia, to represent SDS at a symposium in June 1968 with New Left counterparts in Europe. Traveling in Germany that summer gave Cole exposure to a radical theory he and other militants found instructive in understanding their methods at Columbia. Termed "exemplary action," the notion was predicated on the assumption that audacious tactics employed by small groups—such as those utilized by the Argentinean revolutionary Che Guevara—would, in turn, be emulated by others, thereby producing mass change.[13]

Curbing Student Dissent

That same month, KSU president Robert I. White also traveled to Germany. There he visited several universities, including one in the Ruhr, home to the country's industrial heartland whose counterpart was America's Great Lakes region. White was doubtless unfamiliar with the concept of exemplary action, but he witnessed it in practice in Berlin, where he saw students display a banner proclaiming an occupied building to be the "Che Guevara Institute." Writing to the president of the American Council on Education after his return, White expressed amazement at the reforms undertaken by German universities, hastening to add that many European educators "deplore[d] the students' methods." As Lewis Cole and especially Mark Rudd tried to spread dissent among SDS, including their fellows at Kent, White would seek new means to curb it.[14]

Before departing for Germany, White issued instructions for the university's summer retreat in July, asking administrators to formulate plans to contain expected protest during the coming academic year. White later cryptically noted in a letter to dean of students Robert Matson and other officials that the outcome of the retreat was "quite useful," even with the failure to answer "a number of Dean Matson's particular questions." With a foundation laid, by the end of August the university's board of trustees adopted new regulations designed to curb student dissent.[15]

In preparation for the many challenges White expected to face, he needed to find replacements for departing administrators on whom he had relied since assuming the presidency, including the positions of vice president and provost. Among the candidates was Matson; an Ohio native who had been with KSU since 1965, he came to the university from a small college in Wisconsin and had served as dean of students since 1968. A former college quarterback, Matson struck some as obdurate and insensitive. On some level, his unyielding methods appealed to White, who had witnessed disorders abroad and feared more at home. To retain the steadfast Matson, White expanded his authority with the tacit understanding that he might soon fill one of the vacant vice president positions.[16]

Showing that he could be a man of two minds on the methods of curbing campus dissent, White also courted the liberal-minded, Harvard-educated lawyer Barclay D. McMillen. The two first met in 1967, and White persuaded the Cleveland native to forsake his prominent corporate-law practice in Washington, DC, and join the KSU faculty and teach constitutional law. White came to appreciate McMillen's views on student dissent and believed that he could serve as a counterpoint to the more unyielding Matson. White expected McMillen and Matson to stay informed about campus developments and to keep him up to date even if their differences ensured that they would be offering conflicting advice.[17]

Before classes resumed in September, rumors reached White's office about a potential boycott of downtown businesses, as students were thought to be upset with the pricing of textbooks. Like his predecessor, George Bowman, White maintained close contact with the president of the board of trustees. Accordingly, Robert C. Dix, wearing his third hat as president of Kent's Chamber of Commerce, placed a front-page article in his paper welcoming students to the city. Doing the same on campus, White tried to personally greet every freshman as thousands shook his hand in long receiving lines at orientation sessions.[18]

With the events at the Democratic convention in Chicago and the May 1968 sit-in by the Black United Students (BUS) still fresh in their minds, the KSU trustees issued a new eleven-point resolution explicitly aimed at "maintaining law and order on the Kent State University campus." Dix and his fellow trustees prohibited students from engaging in any number of activities, including disruptive behaviors or lewd and disorderly conduct, physical abuse of persons, unauthorized entry, use or possession of illegal drugs, and possession of explosives. The penalties for violation included suspension or expulsion. At the same time White, remembering the BUS sit-in and perhaps heeding some of the reforms he noted in Germany, asked Matson to consider a role for a student and BUS member, Donald Thigpen, as the university's Minority Affairs representative.[19]

The Oakland Police

KSU's freshman class of 7,500 included barely 200 African American students, bringing the total number of minority undergraduates to about 400. Small in number, African American students felt they had recently suffered large losses: the killing of Martin Luther King Jr., the rejection of BUS's demands for the hiring of Robert Pitts, and the violent disturbances in Akron and Cleveland that brought home the issue of National Guard and police conduct. African American campus leaders included Robert Pickett, who had worked during the summer as a staffer in the Humphrey campaign and expected to complete his term as student body vice president that fall, and Larry Simpson, who served in the student senate and shared the task of chairing BUS. Dwayne White, aka Brother Fargo, remained a widely recognized figure on the campus. Like most of the BUS leadership, Fargo believed that, in overcoming racial issues, whites should "work on the whites and we blacks will work on the blacks." Still, Fargo reached out to whites more than most; for example, he represented BUS when the Methodist Wesley Foundation asked the group to supply a speaker to discuss problems encountered by Kent's African American students. Fargo addressed concerns ranging from student housing to relations with the area police.[20]

BUS, like SDS, readily made connections between national and local events. As both were coming to terms with the looming Nixon presidency, word reached the two organizations that officers from the Oakland Police Department would be coming to the campus. In a major miscalculation, the head of Kent State's law enforcement school had invited recruiters from the controversial police department to interview any students interested in careers in police work. Oakland, California, home to the Black Panther Party, had been the scene of a shoot-out with city police just after the King assassination, which left seventeen-year-old Bobby Hutton dead from a gunshot wound to the back. Then, two months before the Kent State visit, Oakland law enforcement officers shot up Black Panther headquarters on the very day party leader Huey Newton was convicted of manslaughter in the death of a policeman. Temporarily overcoming their wariness of working with radical whites, BUS decided to act in concert with SDS in order to stop the recruiting. Exactly a week after the November election, members of BUS attended an SDS meeting where a short film titled *Panther*, produced by the Newsreel Films collective, was shown; it depicted the price being paid by the party in defending themselves and the African American community against the Oakland Police Department. Thus university officials had unwittingly brought African American and white students together in common cause.[21]

BUS and SDS—Alone Together

BUS joined SDS in audaciously vowing to stop the interviews by the Oakland police. In the early afternoon of November 13, no fewer than 150 African American students—a significant percentage of those on campus—occupied the corridor of the Student Activities Center in an effort to block the recruiting scheduled in placement offices that lined both sides of the narrow hallway. BUS members were the first to enter the building, which also served as a covered walkway between two dormitories, Johnson and Stopher Halls. Marching from the Administration Building at the front of the sprawling campus where they had rallied, reinforcements from SDS, between 150 and 200 in all, carrying banners that read "End K.S.U. Complicity with Racism" and "Oakland Cops Must Go," entered the Student Activities Center from the opposite direction and effectively blocked the other doorway. Unlike the largely unsuccessful sit-in by BUS the previous spring, but similar to the walkout against Humphrey, this interracial protest united virtually all of Kent's radicals in opposition to the Oakland police, prefiguring the much larger opposition faced by the National Guard in 1970.[22]

Led by Bob Pickett, Larry Simpson, Nelson Stevens, and Larry Ghe, BUS occupied one end of the center's constricted space, while SDS, with most of its membership present, occupied the crowded remainder. Those inside, including Jane Boram—participating in her first protest—expected a police assault, as SDS leader Mark Real told the protestors to prepare for one. Mincing no words, Real, attired in a tie and trench coat and speaking through an amplified microphone, told the apprehensive crowd of seated protestors to remove all jewelry including watches and earrings. At first the only scuffle involved a white student who tried unsuccessfully to force his way through to visit a police recruiter. Within an hour of the takeover, however, Dean Matson—representing the administration since President White had left the campus for the day—entered the center and, along with several campus policemen, ordered the occupants to leave or face arrest. To reinforce their seriousness, one campus policeman kicked SDS founder George Hoffman in the head. Despite the threats of arrest, nobody left. Protestors insisted they would remain until the Oakland police recruiters departed from the campus. As the afternoon faded into dusk, the interracial protestors held firm until BUS decided the matter. At around 7 p.m., satisfied they had made their point, African American students made their way out, followed by SDS. Marching around campus, BUS and SDS chanted in unison, "Pigs Off Campus! Pigs Off Campus!"[23]

Throughout the sit-in, conservative white students from Stopher and Johnson Halls gathered outside the Student Activities Center, shouting insults. One, Nick Haskasis, whose massive physique and large head made him seem older than most students, donned a black glove and raised his fist in a mock Panther-style salute. During the interracial march that followed the exit from the center, racial epithets were yelled from the safety of dorm rooms and skirmishing broke out between the two factions. The fighting marked the first time during the 1960s that campus radicals actively defended themselves from the provocations of right-wing students. Still enraged by the experience of Chicago, feeling their growing strength, and with an anger fed more recently by police violence against the Panthers in Oakland, neither BUS nor SDS cared to turn the cheek any longer. Although SDS had lost some potential supporters as a result of Mark Rudd's harangue, the organization geared up well for the Oakland police confrontation, with educational programs about the Panthers and a final preparatory session with BUS before the sit-in. In advance of the takeover, Mark Real confidently predicted to his fellow SDSers that many campus liberals would rally to the side of BUS in the event of arrests and a subsequent campus walkout by African American students.[24]

For several days after Tuesday's sit-in, the threat of university sanctions hung over all participants, with KSU vice president Ronald Roskens, a tall, nearly bald man whose glasses gave him an owlish appearance, along with the resolute Matson, arguing for no compromises. One graduate student, BUS member Nelson Stevens, reportedly faced charges, while actions against eight others were pending. On November 15, aided by new leaders like army veteran Ray Hudson, SDS leader Ric Erickson spoke to a packed meeting of students about the joint BUS/SDS demands. During the week of crisis, Matson, meeting separately no less than four times with SDS and BUS, rejected amnesty demands while making it clear that the university would apply any punitive action equally. One meeting involved Matson and BUS members and some of their families; BUS had already promised to leave the campus en masse unless the university administration backed away from charging sit-in participants. Rather than calming the situation, Matson—a man whose appearance, one faculty member noted, was characterized by a "hardness to his face"—waved his finger "in a gesture of self-righteousness" and, according to several witnesses, began employing "the words 'you people' as if he were saying 'boy' or 'nigger.'" In McMillen's judgment, Matson "turned off the parents and turned on the impetus to extend the confrontation."[25]

It is doubtful that Matson intentionally sought to alienate his listeners. Yet he had unconsciously disaffected virtually his entire audience of African American students and their families. African American parents, who had grown up in a segregated world less hospitable than the one being inherited by their progeny, better understood, after listening to Matson, why their sons and daughters felt the need to leave the campus. His words and manner had cast the die, and White, now back on campus, backed the unyielding stance of Matson and Roskens. Rejecting the demand for what SDS and BUS called amnesty, White declared it to be "an impossible alternative."[26]

BUS Walks Out

With the campus and surrounding area increasingly divided on one side by conservative students, hard-line administrators, a chorus of newspaper editors, and everyday citizens calling for a get-tough approach, and on the other by SDS militants and mainstream civil rights groups, as well as liberal professors like Jerry Lewis of the sociology department, who said he would not teach on an all-white campus, Kent State teetered, Matson said later, "on the fringe of large-scale disorder." In this environment, BUS leader Larry Simpson told his members that they needed to leave campus in a demonstration of solidarity. Doubters were advised that white hostility on campus was such that they were safer leaving than staying behind. By Monday, November 18, an overwhelming number of African Americans left campus, carrying their belongings in a solemn procession that literally and symbolically passed through the university gate and over its seal. Many departed for nearby Akron where, in several churches, and near where National Guardsmen had clashed with Akron's African American community the previous July, BUS members established a kind of university in exile. Others returned to their homes in Cleveland. Wherever they went, BUS promised to stay away until the university granted "amnesty." Watching the somber march by BUS as they quit the campus, Kenneth Colton, a political science professor who had backed Humphrey's presidential bid, told the *Stater* he had "never seen a quieter demonstration." Cleveland's Jerry Persky, who had worked to elect Carl Stokes a year earlier, said it was, up until then, the "most dramatic event I witnessed on the campus."[27]

Adhering to a stern line, White may well have been surprised by the widespread support the walkout enjoyed among Kent's African American students. Worse yet for the administration, sympathy for it spread, even as many conservatives adopted a "good riddance" attitude. African American university students in Akron maintained close contact with those they hosted from Kent State, while students at Wooster College and Central State staged sympathy protests. At Kent, SDS held teach-ins and picketed classroom buildings on a campus made nearly all white by the walkout. Dozens of broadminded KSU professors—many of whom were untenured and thus may have feared reprisals—lobbied bravely, in the words of one, "to move the administration off dead center." Within a day of the walkout, the same spokesmen for the faculty, sociologist Paul Sites, told the *Beacon Journal* that "none of the administrators were willing to think in terms of human justice."[28]

Narrowly interpreted, Sites had it right, for McMillen served as a faculty member, not an administrator. In whatever terms McMillen thought, politically and legally he recognized a losing hand when he saw one, and he had questioned Matson's inflexible stance from the outset. Indeed, he sensed that BUS might be willing to enter into negotiations and that the bargaining position of the African American students grew stronger while the university's diminished every day the walkout lasted. Seeing a need for both a way out and an ally in pursuit of a parlay with BUS, White gave McMillen the title Special Counsel for the university. McMillen urged the president to seek a route out of the crisis by citing a lack of sufficient evidence to win "a conviction under a charge of disorderly conduct." In advocating a policy of flexibility, McMillen encountered indignant opposition from Roskens and Matson, who together, as McMillen recalled, "fought any form of capitulation." White had made up his mind. Calling his team together, and using McMillen's rationale about faulty evidence, the president read a prepared statement that would be released to the media: "Dean Matson, therefore, has decided not to place individual charges of disorderly conduct [against the protestors]." McMillen, silent on any reaction Matson may have expressed, did later recall the KSU vice president's own ability to pivot and cede ground: "When President White read this to us and thus undercut Matson's and Roskens's position, Vice President Roskens said, 'That was a fine statement, President White.'"[29]

The BUS Trip Ends

For the remainder of the crisis, White gave McMillen a prominent role in the final negotiations with BUS, while excluding Matson from any further bargaining sessions. Once it became clear from meetings with the exiled BUS leadership that terms for their return could be brokered, White decided to settle more than the issue of clemency The KSU administration wanted no more of the powerful BUS/SDS alliance, and to ensure an end to the pairing decided to address a number of festering issues that concerned BUS: the tiny number of African American faculty, the underrepresentation of minority students relative to their percentage numbers in northeast Ohio cities, and the lack of specialized offices to assist students of color at the university. Although no document has surfaced that enumerates the terms under which BUS members agreed to return, it is clear they did so with more than just the assurance that charges against them would be dropped.[30]

Assembling on the steps of the administration building on November 21, the same edifice they had filled the previous spring in a largely unsuccessful occupation, BUS leaders, rightfully proud of their accomplishment, listened to Milton Wilson, the newly appointed dean of the Human Relations Center, read their organization's carefully worded statement. Quoting a declaration issued by African Americans in 1831—the year of Nat Turner's bloody slave revolt—Wilson read the historic words: "We do not believe that things will always continue the same. . . . [T]he rights of all shall be properly acknowledged and appreciated. This is our home, and this is our country." Building on these hopeful expressions, the BUS statement offered to work with the administration in order "to test the viability of the system."[31]

The decision, of course, also eliminated any possible charges against members of SDS. Speaking for SDS at an organizational meeting on November 20, Mark Real said: "The Oakland confrontation proved decisively the exciting possibility of creating a movement for fundamental social change in KSU. We welcome the opportunity to be reunited with our black brothers and to continue with them to raise the moral issue of the Oakland confrontation." The differing tones of the respective statements reflected the growing distance between the BUS and SDS leadership, a characteristic of the different kinds of groups they were. Defined by race, the BUS membership contained people with a variety of viewpoints, whereas SDS, a self-selected political organization, was ideologically far more cohesive. They were less interested in testing the viability of the system than in transforming it altogether.[32]

Reforms and Revolution

If differences in strategic goals—one nationalist and radical/reformist, the other increasingly defining itself as revolutionary—were not immediately apparent to SDS, they were by the end of the fall quarter. As SDS had already learned at Columbia, and as pointed out by one author, "1968 was not a year for 'black and white together.'" The bright and always well-dressed Mark Real fell sick for several months after the sit-in, but being homebound gave him time to prepare an insightful and surprisingly candid review of the state of the BUS/SDS alliance. Real's article, which appeared in sixth issue of the Cleveland SDS newsletter, *The Big Us*, read more like an internal document than anything intended for wider circulation. He wrote that BUS represented an "example of collegiate cultural nationalism." Distinguishing them from SDS, with its forceful anti-imperialist views, he further described BUS as an organization "hampered by a lack of political perspective," yet one that "was nevertheless willing to initiate a joint action." Given that the third week of November 1968 represented the high point of militant, interracial unity on the campus, its decline, and Real's analysis of the decline, deserves a longer look.[33]

> Though contact may be continued, the pressures . . . within both groups will probably prevent joint action in the future. For the campus, the confrontation revealed the inadequacy, stupidity, dishonesty, and disorganization of the administration. The exposure of police infiltration of SDS . . . further desanctified the mythology of administration neutrality. . . .
>
> The BUS decision to remain apolitical . . . may open them to cooptation with more black culture and scholarships and the addition of human relationship staff . . . with no real discussion of racism or [of the role of] the university.[34]

SDS's view of BUS, while not without merit, reflected only one side of the matter. For BUS, a working relationship with a chastened administration promised more than any alliance SDS could deliver. Minority students were able to expand their numbers through additional scholarship assistance, gain support to increase their low graduation rates, receive more cultural funding, and win the hiring of additional African American faculty, such as Paul Cheeks (one of the participants in the October 1960 Corner Bar sit-in). Moreover, BUS members had not forsaken radical politics. Speaking with a reporter from the *Cleveland Press,* a student who identified himself simply as No. 6 (believed to be Julius Suber) explained his participation in the sit-in against the Oakland police: "They shoot and kill black people. They put Huey Newton (a Black Panther party leader) in jail. This was our way of fighting back." Other BUS members felt that the political differences were over means and not ends. Finally, while there may have been no clear trajectory toward revolutionary politics, the BUS leadership would, by the early spring of 1969, reacquire the language of revolutionary nationalism.[35]

Real's article also revealed an inclination by SDS to see itself as being all-knowing. BUS was not hampered by a lack of political perspective; rather, they maintained a political perspective different than that of SDS. Such inclinations to ideological purity had already deprived the Kent SDS of allies and would eventually split the chapter into factions. These problems were still latent, however, and the organization continued to enjoy a high degree of internal cohesion in late 1968. Moreover, the ephemeral coalition with BUS gained the mostly white SDS a significant degree of political currency on the campus. Whatever the state of the alliance, SDS, despite a number of political miscalculations, ended the academic quarter in a strong position.

Who Rules Kent?

Reform versus revolution: the posing of such stark and difficult alternatives became ever more commonplace among young radicals as they grappled with the ongoing war, the struggle for racial equality, and the prospect of a Nixon presidency. It was apparent enough who was paying the price for the ills. Increasingly, radicals asked themselves *Who is benefiting?*

The campaign against the Oakland police generated a series of SDS educational flyers. With BUS finalizing its plans to leave campus, SDSers distributed a handbill that asked "What Are the Issues?" This represented the first effort by SDS to lay bare the link between and among area businessmen and the university. To find the perfect exemplar of the local ruling class, SDS examined the role of Robert C. Dix. As the president of KSU's board of trustees, the owner and publisher of the *Record-Courier,* and the head of Kent's Chamber of Commerce, Dix and his family had dominated the town like no other since the death of former governor Martin L. Davey.[36]

An expanded version of the circular soon appeared as a twenty-page mimeographed pamphlet titled "Who Rules Kent?" Inspired by the instant classic *Who Rules America?,* the booklet was the most sophisticated research document published by the Kent SDS. Authored by Ken and Marilyn (Davis) Hammond, with help from others including Jim Powrie, the exposé revealed a number of things. First and foremost, by undertaking a detailed accounting of the business backgrounds of the various members of the KSU trustees—a figurative banker's dozen that included rubber company magnates and regional publishing and television executives—SDS argued that the nexus of such interests proved that the university functioned to benefit what they later called "the global profit-making machine of the American ruling class." The class analysis "Who Rules Kent?" contained made clear the authors' debt to Marxism and marked the activists' transition from a single-issue antiwar stance to being critics of an entire economic system. Besides the ties SDS drew between area business figures and their control over the university, the pamphlet contained an implicit question: "Who *should* rule Kent?" The question in the pamphlet's title, and the inherent answer it provided, revealed an interest in careful organizing to accrue power through research, education, and base building, followed by protest. Such an approach contrasted sharply with the notion of "exemplary action," the name given it by European radicals and practiced by the martyred revolutionary Che Guevara. Mark Rudd had his own disdainful way of viewing systematic organizing of the kind favored by the Hammonds and Jim Powrie. "Organizing," he once declared, "is just another word for going slow." Like regional organizer Terry Robbins, Rudd was a man in a hurry.[37]

Yet the question of whether to use patient methods to amass political power or to pursue revolutionary means as a shortcut was no sterile debate in 1968. However much talk of revolution involved a fundamental disconnect between the consciousness of a relative handful and the actual circumstances of the vast majority of people in the country, SDS, the Panthers, and other such organizations knew conditions were deteriorating for many. Underscoring the tensions being played out over the propriety of the Oakland police being at Kent State, Black Panther Party members were involved in a another shoot-out with the Oakland police on the last full day of the November campus standoff. In contrast to April 1968, when the young Panther party member Bobby Hutton died in a hail of shooting, on this occasion policemen were the only casualties, as the exchange of fire left three officers wounded and eight militants in custody.[38]

SDS: "The ones with whom real battle will have to be had"

SDS and BUS were not alone in trying to determine where to go politically after the sit-in. President White had political fences to mend with forces outside the university who believed he had capitulated to the student radicals. White wrote to Colonel Robert Chiaramonte, superintendent of the Ohio Highway Patrol, just days after settling the crisis, and sent a copy to Governor Rhodes. Equal parts explanation and sparing apology, White's letter gave his account of the dilemma, claiming that "200 . . . black students . . . had been 'suckered' in by the SDS." White noted that Matson, reluctant to arrest them en masse, "proposed instead to charge them under University discipline," but conceded, "I did concur." He offered his assurances that such indecision would not be repeated and promised future "arrests at the first sign of disruption."[39]

The most prescient section of the letter came when White expressed the conviction that "we have now separated them [BUS] from the S.D.S. group who, privately, I believe to be the ones with whom real battle will have to be had." In addition to clearing up matters with the Highway Patrol, White also owed a reply to Ohio congressman John Ashbrook about the recent events on the Kent campus. Ashbrook, one of the nation's most conservative representatives, had been a pioneer of the Goldwater campaign and had done as much as any operative to restore the far right to its place in national and state politics.[40]

White certainly took more satisfaction staying in touch with former colleagues than he did in apologizing to Chiaramonte or in answering Ashbrook. Wishing to keep old friends in the loop, in early December White wrote back to former KSU provost John Kamerick. Months beforehand, in White's absence,

Kamerick handled the difficult days on campus during the King assassination; soon after he left Kent to assume the presidency of North Texas State University, where SDS had established a chapter in 1964. Thus Kamerick read White's account of the BUS/SDS crisis with particular interest. Displaying the same confidence evident in his letter to Chiaramonte, White told Kamerick that "we have separated them [BUS] from the S.D.S. if we play our cards properly," adding that it was "no mean achievement if we can hold it." Adducing the age-old stratagem of divide and rule, White further addressed "the danger of allowing interests or groups to become merged."[41]

Few outside of White's administrative circle knew of the president's conviction, as expressed to the Highway Patrol superintendent and the governor, of the looming "battle . . . to be had" with SDS, just as militants, especially Terry Robbins, advocated "the use of confrontation and aggressive politics in building revolutionary consciousness." Barclay McMillen numbered among those on the inside who likewise knew his enemy in the impending conflict. A week after final exams, McMillen and Matson debated the subject of which organization, BUS or SDS, presented the most significant danger to the administration. The exchange between them threatened the bounds of collegiality. A recent promotion to vice president had not fully assuaged Matson. Perhaps showing the influence of his southern Ohio roots, for Matson it was race that mattered. He also insisted that BUS remained KSU's principal adversary because the administration had "caved in" to them. The Washington lawyer (as one contemptuous faculty critic called McMillen during the crisis) felt otherwise. In his exchange with Matson, McMillen backed White, maintaining that "S.D.S. was our threat."[42]

Many among the urban, working-class, and increasingly interracial student population reached a different conclusion about Kent State's greatest crisis of 1968—recognizing the value of unity and believing that the war and what SDS called the "repression of black people" were the paramount issues facing and threatening them. Solutions to these issues required their utmost dedication. Many more shared these concerns, but were not convinced that SDS yet merited their trust. Still, among those fearing the presidency of Richard Nixon, scheduled to assume power on January 20, there was an even stronger antipathy toward the national government, as it soon would be in the hands of a lifelong anticommunist.[43]

Looking forward to the New Year with a mixture of youthful ardor and concern over the survival of SDS at Kent State—as he also thought about Nixon's inauguration—Mark Real closed his article for *The Big Us* with a warning and a clarion call: "A strong movement is essential to defeat efforts to deny campus recognition to SDS. On to Washington!" For SDS, at both Kent and elsewhere, internal strength would prove as necessary as it was fleeting. And, in looking back at the tumultuous year that had produced so much violence, death, and bitterness, those in the radical orbit had little reason to expect less of it in the future. Some on the left had succumbed to the mystique of violence; others knew all too well of a historical toleration for its use. Whatever the past portended for the future, the election of Richard Nixon did not augur well for stopping a war that increasing numbers of Americans were desperate to end.[44]

CHAPTER 9

SDS Spring Offensive

IN JANUARY 1969, Bill Whitaker earned the dubious distinction of being the first Kent SDS member to be arrested. He was apprehended by campus police after being involved in an alleged shoving fracas with two conservative students who took down a satiric poster Whitaker had put up on a crowded message board in the Student Union. The poster, like many others on the board, was unapproved by the Student Activities Center. It publicized plans for a counter-inaugural demonstration in Washington, DC, on January 19 and 20 to protest Richard Nixon's inauguration and the new Nixon administration. Whitaker's poster showed a skull superimposed on the US Capitol and a passage attributed to Adolph Hitler: "The streets of our country are in turmoil. The universities are filled with students rebelling and rioting. Communists are seeking to destroy our country. Russia is threatening us with her might. And the republic is in danger. Yes! danger from within and without. We need law and order! Without law and order our nation cannot survive."[1]

At its National Council meeting in Ann Arbor, Michigan, in December 1968, SDS, now divided by Progressive Labor factionalism, had declined to sanction the counter-inaugural demonstration. Some leaders of the sponsoring National Mobilization Committee (the MOBE) had different grounds for opposing the protest. Fearing an anemic turnout and another Chicago-style battle with authorities, a number of MOBE's longtime organizers refused to endorse the protest, which was being promoted by Rennie Davis and veteran pacifist David Dellinger.[2]

Individual SDS chapters, including Kent's and others in Ohio and Michigan, as well as Columbia University's, joined the protest. About fifty Kent SDSers participated; the contingent comprised a diverse group, and not all were politically on the same page. Leading the way were the most recognized leaders in the chapter, Ric Erickson and Howie Emmer. Erickson—impetuous in manner and physically imposing, with a lanky frame and full mustache—had fully embraced political radicalism by the summer of Chicago. Many found him dynamic, even charismatic. As his father did during his mayoral campaigns in Akron, Erickson took time to cultivate people and win them to his point of view. Emmer, more deliberate in approach and shorter in stature, had been on a radical trajectory ever since his mother had been made to appear before the House Un-American Activities Committee in 1962. Raised in a home where suspicion of federal and state authority was part of political survival, Emmer also knew how to prevail in organizational infighting. Having acquired similar, although not identical, political skill sets in their respective boyhood homes, they also shared the quality of fluent self-expression. If Erickson's magnetic and forceful personality failed to sway opponents, Emmer's logic and knowledge of history provided the final spell. Finally, there was the experience of the Chicago convention, which further bonded the men together and reinforced their credibility and authority.[3]

Along with Terry Robbins, Colin Neiburger, and Jeff Powell (who, despite having just turned eighteen, had quickly become a significant member of the chapter), they collectively represented the more action-oriented element in the Kent SDS. Other participants in the protest—Whitaker, Ken and Marilyn Hammond, and Jim Powrie—continued to advocate for broadening the ranks of SDS through education and recruitment. Besides Marilyn Hammond, a number of other women SDSers participated in the protest, including Jane Boram, Sharon Post, Joyce Cecora, and Mary Ann Jackson, as did high school students Hunter Havens and Larry Finn. Regardless of experience, age, gender, or radical proclivity, they all managed to mix well, at least initially. Differences in the Kent SDS were not yet paramount, although they would become so in the spring, when militant confrontations on the campus threatened the very existence of the chapter.[4]

The students who planned to attend the counter-inaugural were united in their concern about the use or misuse of presidential power. To bolster their numbers for the protest, Ken Hammond used his column in the *Daily Kent Stater* to criticize "Nixon's corporate cabinet," explaining how the SDS analysis had "changed from 'America has a problem' to 'America is the problem.'" Jim Powrie had learned to operate an offset press from Terry Robbins, giving SDS another means to disseminate its anti-imperialist message. Preparing for their second confrontation in three months with the incoming president, the SDSers gathered ranks and used the press to make signs reading "You Can Win but You Can't Govern." Their concerns about presidential power were not unfounded, for although the president-elect had recast his public image during the campaign and presented himself as the "new" Nixon, he remained essentially unchanged. A shrewd master of pragmatic realpolitik in both foreign and domestic affairs, Nixon continued to be driven by an anticommunist ideology and a personality that were mutually reinforcing. Whereas LBJ actually agonized over the moral implications of his failed policies, Nixon had no such compunctions. He was obsessed with using the power of the presidency to achieve his domestic and foreign policy objectives. "I'll put it this way," he said to a sympathetic reporter, "one achieves his ambition when he *becomes* president. But that is only the beginning. Not *getting* the office, but *using* it, is the main thing."[5]

How Nixon would use the presidency was very much on the mind of Jeff Powell, who rented three heatless vans to take the group to DC in late January. Traveling through the snowy mountains of western Pennsylvania, the protestors saw themselves as left-wingers for all seasons, patriots setting out to restore the nation's honor when so many others were willing to ignore the immoral war being waged in Vietnam. Writers for a law enforcement commission investigating the protest later noted that the "bitter cold" held down participation in the counter-inaugural protest, leaving roughly ten thousand activists, whom the *New York Times* characterized as the "small, hard core of the country's disaffected youth."[6]

Inauguration and Counter-Inauguration

The counter-inaugural protestors were sheltered in several "movement centers" throughout Washington, DC. Protestors from Ohio, including the Kent contingent, were housed in the Brightwood Methodist Church. Situated in the heart of the largely African American city, the church stood far from the Ellipse and the federal buildings downtown. Starting on Saturday, January 18, and throughout the weekend, participants covered miles of urban terrain to join in the protests.[7]

Protestors disrupted inaugural receptions, such as the one at the Washington Hilton Hotel. Jeff Powell and another SDSer slyly gained entry to the event, where they saw a score of invited dignitaries looking outside at the assembled demonstrators. Initially going unnoticed, they paused long enough to hear disparaging comments about the protestors below. "At least . . . there's no blood on their hands," Powell said aloud to the group, at which point one well-dressed inaugural guest began swinging wildly at him. Insults were exchanged, but no punches landed, as Powell and the other SDSer managed to exit the scene unhurt. Powell's defiant behavior in the midst of a larger group of official luminaries typified the audacity of the counter-inaugural. Although several hundred thousand visitors came from out of town to witness and celebrate the official events, a tiny fraction of that number sought to actively disrupt the celebration.[8]

On Sunday, January 19, thousands of protestors massed for the counter-inaugural parade down Pennsylvania Avenue. Although the march went off largely without incident, Kent SDSers Sharon Post, Mary Ann Jackson, and George Gibeaut were arrested, as one of their number was snatched by police and several others sought unsuccessfully to rescue her. Later, Powell joined five thousand demonstrators who endured frigid temperatures to confront attendees at a reception for Vice President Spiro Agnew at the Smithsonian Institution. Police on horseback clubbed protestors in an attempt to disperse the jeering crowd. Jane Boram, Powell, and Paul Bukosky outmaneuvered police as they darted across the grassy expanse of the National Mall, using war whoops and firecrackers to frighten the horses.[9]

Later, while many endured the "boot-sucking mud" at a counter-inaugural ball to hear Phil Ochs entertain on the Washington Monument grounds, Columbia SDSer Mark Rudd debated MOBE leader and longtime pacifist Dave Dellinger over the wisdom of a final protest—and possible confrontation with police—at Monday's inaugural parade. Reflecting some of the political unease that had kept other MOBE leaders from going to the counter-inauguration, Dellinger believed it unwise to protest at the inaugural parade route, where police and the Secret Service were certain to be hypervigilant. Never before in the nation's history had protesters had the impertinence to demonstrate along the parade route on inauguration day. Meeting at one of the SDS movement centers, Rudd—unhappy with the low level of militancy at the march—pressed Dellinger to seek a permit for a demonstration in Franklin Square Park (an urban park just blocks from Pennsylvania Avenue) on January 20. Sympathetic MOBE attorneys reached an understanding with both SDS and the authorities, and successfully obtained sanction for Monday's inaugural day protest in Franklin Square Park.[10]

On the morning of the inauguration, the heated debate renewed at Brightwood Methodist Church. Erickson, Emmer, and Robbins convincingly argued that the Ohio delegation should participate in the Franklin Square Park rally, where (as everyone seemed to know) they would march a few short blocks to the parade route on Pennsylvania Avenue to witness the passage of the presidential entourage. While two hundred protestors congregated in the park, a separate group led by Mark Rudd gathered a few blocks away, positioned to make the short trek down to the inaugural route and thus extend the frontage of the protest on the sidewalk facing Pennsylvania Avenue. With the separate parts of the cohort under the watchful eyes of city police, the dissidents pressed on five blocks south to Pennsylvania Avenue, where the presidential motorcade would pass. When they reached the intersection of 15th Street and Pennsylvania Avenue, the two converging groups of chanting protestors crowded out GOP supporters. As the presidential car finally approached, protestors hurled mud and an empty whiskey bottle in the direction of the limousine. The police took immediate action: using their cruiser-blaring sirens and three-wheel motorcycles, they beat and scattered protestors and took nearly one hundred into custody. Although the out-of-town protestors were mostly white, south of the parade route near the Washington Monument an estimated two hundred black youths, "hearing the sirens and commotion, . . . ran and joined the demonstrators."[11]

Though the widespread Chicago-style violence some feared did not materialize, Powell reflected afterward that the antiwar movement had "upped the level of risks" at the counter-inaugural in preparation for more intense protest. Barberton, Ohio, native Alan Canfora, who was new to the Kent SDS, was also emboldened; the protest made him realize that there were people willing to "shake the system to its foundations to get some changes." Although a student reporter with the *Kent Stater* traveling with the Kent contingent also saw the inaugural protest as a harbinger, national antiwar leaders were less sanguine. The MOBE, despondent that the efforts in Chicago had failed to attract greater numbers and that the counter-inaugural had split their leadership ranks, suspended operation. Whether the protest represented, as one writer later mused, "voices from another era—disgruntled remnants out to ruin the new atmosphere of peace and conciliation," or showed that hardened opposition to the war was growing despite fissures within the left, could not yet be known. Protestors returning to Kent State felt encouraged, while the new president, wrongly believing that no arrests had been made at the inaugural parade site, wondered why an opportunity to "score political points against war opponents" had been lost. He would see to it that such opportunities would not be missed again.[12]

Cambodia and the "Dormant Beast"

President Nixon recognized that the protests would continue under his administration, but he had no intention of halting the US war in Vietnam. In his view, and that of national security adviser Henry Kissinger, the war on some level remained winnable. In their view, America's problem in Vietnam was neutral Cambodia, which provided a conduit for supplying North Vietnamese and National Liberation Forces in South Vietnam. Nixon and his advisers therefore sought a means of simultaneously checking the Vietnamese liberation movement while keeping quiet what Kissinger called "the dormant beast of public protest." The solution to these twin dilemmas became known initially as "Operation Breakfast," a plan hatched in relative secrecy by Nixon and Kissinger. The operation, which the military was ordered to conceal by having pilots report false targets within South Vietnam, involved a campaign of saturation bombing raids over eastern Cambodia beginning on March 17. Over the next thirteen months, in a series of raids eventually termed Operation Menu, waves of B-52s pounded Cambodia with 100,000 tons of explosives, destroying vast tracts of land and killing tens of thousands of Cambodians. The press reported the B-52 air strikes only in passing, ensuring that they remained largely unknown to the public. As a result, the heavy bombing of Cambodia failed to provoke much public protest or debate on the nation's campuses. This was also true at Kent State; Cambodia did not appear on Kent SDSers' list of countries that exemplified the United States' unequal relationship with poorer countries of the underdeveloped world. How successful the bombing campaign was from a military standpoint is still a matter of debate, but because it went on in secrecy it did not become a domestic distraction.[13]

For the remainder of winter quarter, SDS at Kent hosted programs about the organization's counter-inaugural activities in Washington, the war in Vietnam, US military domination of the Dominican Republic, and the United Fruit Company's decades-long exploitation of Guatemala. In loose coordination with BUS, SDS also mounted a guerrilla theater–style performance at KSU's first annual President's Ball on February 1, to protest student government leaders' failure to invite the heads of the leftist and African American organizations. One critic wryly termed the episode part of "SDS's new image-building program."[14]

Factions in Kent SDS

Kent SDS leaders like Ken Hammond realized that patient organizing was necessary to reach a broad mass of Kent's working-class students. The Hammonds, Jim Powrie, Bill Whitaker and his wife, Melissa, and roughly a dozen other members tried to preserve SDS as George Hoffman had envisioned it—a mass-based group that organized students against the war, the draft, racism, and economic inequality. Doug Vaughan, who hailed from Erie, Pennsylvania, and had first learned politics from his "bank-hating," populist father, had the distinction of being the lone member of the Kent chapter who identified, however quietly, with the notion of PL's worker–student alliance. Collectively, with Vaughan on the edges, they were a small circle of budding or quasi-Marxists composed mostly of blue-collar and a few middle-class students. They believed that SDS could not succeed without broadening its support, first with students and later among multiracial working people. Implicit in this view was an understanding of power: who possessed it, the means to acquire it, and how it might be used to foster change. They saw antiwar youth, African Americans, and working people of all colors as the potential beneficiaries of exercise of a "people's power." By 1969, however, advocates for a long view of such movement-building were losing authority in SDS.[15]

Bernardine Dohrn's election to the post of interorganizational secretary in the national organization confirmed the change of direction within SDS. Dohrn was a leading promoter of the "action faction" within SDS. Terry Robbins was her leading disciple in northeast Ohio, ensuring that the faction would have a strong advocate at Kent State. Those associated with this budding faction, soon to be called Weatherman or the Weather Underground, understood their role differently than those in SDS who hoped to broaden the organization's base among blue-collar citizens. The latter faction, which came to be identified with a group within SDS called Revolutionary Youth Movement II, saw themselves operating on behalf of those Americans affected by the Vietnam War, while the action faction believed that they were fighting on behalf of disadvantaged African Americans and impoverished Vietnamese peasants. Many drawn to the action faction were relatively new to the Kent SDS. Like those advocating more patient and broader organizing, they included working-class students, but also a larger number of economically better-off students, at least by Kent's modest standards. Thus, while activists such as Hammond and Powrie aimed to broaden their ranks on campus through appeals to the still dormant bulk of blue-collar and middle-income students, Kent's principal SDS leaders, especially Erickson and Emmer, sought to consolidate existing members of the chapter around a program of action. By the spring, the action proponents were committed to "stopping the country, not changing it."[16]

In February, SDS sustained another arrest—similar to Whitaker's, but more controversial. Despite his nickname, Matt "Rebel" Flanagan did not look all that rebellious. Still, a university policeman arrested the blue-collar youth in late February for posting and distributing literature that, despite having the required Student Activities approval stamp, was deemed "indecent and immoral" by the county prosecutor. The offending flyer depicted a gang of police sexually violating Lady Liberty, and included the provocative name of the SDS chapter in New York City, the Motherfuckers. The administration's legal adviser, Barclay McMillen, considered the arrest a mistake that was certain to antagonize others beyond SDS. And indeed it did. Graduate student Roman Tymchyshyn, whose connections to Kent's culture of dissent went back more than a decade, protested on behalf of the Graduate Art Association. KSU's Lutheran campus minister called on President White to criticize the action of the police. A number of student government representatives also condemned the arrest, while others supported Flanagan's free speech rights by distributing the very same flyer inside the campus police station. Even dorm councils criticized the arrest. McMillen worried that "the incident [would] lead to another disturbance."[17]

A disturbance came soon enough. Graduate art students led several hundred students in a protest aimed at the university's failure to build a promised art building. The rickety building that housed the art department, West Hall, had been a World War II military barracks. Activists denounced the building's "ghetto-like conditions" and had no trouble collecting thousands of signatures in support of erecting a new structure. Then, in an effort to speed up the process, somebody set West Hall afire on the evening of March 7—the last day of classes before finals week. Firemen quickly contained the blaze, but not before the flames could be seen across the expansive campus. The damage left the building unusable.[18]

The SDS Spring Offensive and the Four Demands

The torching of West Hall provided an illuminating portent for SDS's "Spring Offensive." This campaign was inspired by an SDS regional conference in Columbus in January 1969, where leaders of the still-developing action faction resolved to "Smash the Military in the schools." SDS quoted the Cuban revolutionary José Martí in the title of a document outlining the campaign: "Now is the time of the furnaces, and only light should be seen."[19]

The document listed SDS's four "non-negotiable" demands—demands that the radicals believed could be used to build a movement that paid renewed attention to opposing the Vietnam War and "hurt[ing] imperialism" by forcing programs connected to the military and law enforcement off the campus. The first demand was that the university disassociate itself from ROTC. For the campus left, ROTC's inescapable presence of military-style barracks and uniformed cadets was a daily reminder of the university's complicity with the Vietnam War. SDS also wanted an end to the Law Enforcement School (which had brought the Oakland police recruiters to the campus), the Northeast Ohio Crime Lab, and the Liquid Crystals Institute, which many radicals believed to be connected with counterinsurgency research. These three demands focused on university programs that SDS saw as tools used by law enforcement and the military against minorities and third-world revolutionaries.[20]

Although the SDS members in the still-emerging action faction saw the demands as a potential basis for rallying shock troops for a frontal assault against the university, they failed to capture the attention of most students. The only one to gain considerable currency beyond SDS ranks was against ROTC. It was also the one that most worried the KSU administration. Indeed, the university gave some consideration to dropping academic credit for ROTC. The *Record-Courier* immediately called that into question and gave front-page attention to the local American Legion's opposition. The spokesman for the Summit County Young Republicans wrote directly to the governor, asking him to protect Kent's ROTC program and indirectly questioning President White's resolve.[21]

White needed no prodding to take SDS seriously. Just after the January counter-inauguration, he asked his public safety director for confirmation of "an F.B.I. prophecy of sharply accentuated demonstration activity this Spring." The director's reply cited FBI information that Kent State had "a very active [SDS] group." On April 2, the Committee on Internal Security of the US

House of Representatives announced that it was launching an investigation of the Kent SDS. Publicly, at least, the university wished to distance itself from intelligence agencies; articles in the city and campus newspapers maintained that "the university had no advance information of . . . plans [by the committee] to come to Kent." The SDS's spring offensive later became a central part of the committee's investigation.[22]

SDS members made little effort to conceal their growing militancy. They educated the campus community about the importance of ROTC in training students to be combat officers who would help sustain the military effort in Vietnam. Months earlier the administration had been caught off guard by the swiftness of the Oakland police sit-in and the powerful, if ephemeral, SDS/BUS alliance. Now, however, SDS was going up against a prepared adversary. The organization overstated its intentions and underestimated its foe, violating the centuries-old wisdom that "to announce too much of what one means to do is the way not to do it at all." Even had the emerging Kent SDS "action faction" been aware of this adage, however, it is doubtful they would have paid it heed. A commitment to sweeping change, not concessions, propelled the activities of these proto-Weatherman SDSers. They believed that dramatic deeds won attention and forced others to take sides.[23]

SDS launched its spring campaign at noon on April 8. In what became their fashion, the organization first rallied on the front part of campus outside the Student Union, bolstering themselves with chants delivered melodically in Black Panther style (such as "No more brothers in jail, Pigs are gonna catch hell") and, on this occasion, a series of speeches by Howie Emmer, Colin Neiburger, Joyce Cecora, and George Gibeaut. Gibeaut made clear SDS's support of third-world revolutions, telling a mixed crowd of as many as five hundred cheering adherents, cautious supporters, and jeering opponents that "there's a war going on and it's . . . not just . . . in Vietnam, or the black community, . . . [but] in Guatemala, . . . South Africa, . . . and right here on this campus."[24]

After a short march, Emmer spoke again and then urged the reassembled crowd to return to the front part of campus, where SDS would present its four demands to the administration. When the vanguard of fifty SDSers arrived at the administration building, they found all of the entrances blocked. Campus police guarded the large doors of the neoclassical-style building, and a furious tug of war broke out between SDSers seeking to pry open the thick, mostly glass doors, and police equally determined to keep them closed. The authorities prevailed in the ten-minute struggle, and SDS was left on the outside looking in. The police later alleged that they were assaulted by SDSers trying to enter the building, and warrants were prepared against Emmer, Gibeaut, Neiburger, Ric Erickson, Jeff Powell, and Alan DiMarco. An African American student ally involved in the skirmish could easily have been charged as well, but the administration and police did not want to take any action that might renew the BUS/SDS alliance.[25]

The six SDS members were charged with assault and, at Barclay McMillen's urging, further enjoined by the county court from returning to campus. Breaches of the injunction would be considered contempt of court, and violators would be subject to immediate jail sentences. Months earlier, after selling the idea to the administration and clearing it with the Ohio attorney general, McMillen and KSU vice president Robert Matson had visited seventy-nine-year-old county judge Albert Caris to win court sanction for the use of injunctions. "Boys, when you go after them, go with both guns blazing," Caris urged.[26]

In addition to the double-barreled threat of arrests and injunctions, the administration had other weapons. SDS had been operating with a temporary recognition charter since George Hoffman had first filed the necessary paperwork more than a year earlier. Over McMillen's objections, Matson ordered that the charter be revoked and that those SDS members who were students be suspended from the university. Negating the charter did not prevent the Kent SDS—one of a half dozen chapters nationwide to be banned from operating on a particular campus—from simply using another organizational designation. And since court injunctions trumped student suspensions, the arrested militants were already effectively banned from campus.[27]

Powell and Emmer reasoned that they would be arrested when they saw footage of themselves on the national *CBS Evening News* on the night of the April 8 protest. And the pair, along with Colin Neiburger, expected a public arrest when they appeared at an SDS rally in front of the Student Union the next day. They were noisily taken into custody by campus police supported by city police and Portage County sheriff's deputies. Their seizure at the rally provoked cries of protest from fellow SDSers and induced outrage from other students, who were shocked by the sight of dozens of helmeted police ushering the threesome to awaiting law enforcement vehicles. Erickson and the others were quietly arrested elsewhere.[28]

Despite the setback of the April 9 arrests, SDS pressed its demands that same evening at the Asian Affairs Conference, a gathering organized by the university's political science department. By apparent coincidence, the spring offensive coincided with the opening of the symposium, which drew nationally renowned academics, including John K. Fairbank of Harvard University, a historian specializing in China. Kent radicals targeted Fairbank specifically because of an article he had written criticizing the Chinese Communist Party and its leader, Mao Tse Tung, and they denounced the entire conference as "a farce and a lie . . . meant to convince people that they should be willing to be cannon fodder in imperialist wars." Terry Robbins, who wrote many of the chapter's flyers, was likely the author of a leaflet condemning the gathering, titled "You Don't Need a Weatherman to Know Which Way the Wind Blows." Although no one recognized at the time, the line taken from a 1965 Bob Dylan song would prove a portent of things to come.[29]

SDS, depleted by arrests, still mustered fifty members to protest outside the Music and Speech Building, where the conference was held, that evening. Some of the radicals, including Ken Hammond, went inside to make statements critical of the proceedings. Although there were ample numbers of KSU police present to prevent the SDSers from entering en masse, Robb Ross, a business administration major, gathered 350 fraternity members to reinforce security forces. Campus police lent them a bullhorn to amplify their message. After making what the *Stater* termed a "show of strength," the frat men marched away in triumph. They had stood up to an SDS that, according to Ross, seemed "scared and tired." Fuming, SDS saw the fraternity presence as proof positive of collaboration with the administration. If fear existed, SDS claimed, the dread was felt by the "ruling class," which was "scared of our demands." Maintaining their bravado, they added ominously, "We intend to scare them a lot more."[30]

Open It Up or Shut It Down!

The suspension of the six SDSers led to a series of appeals. The administration held the hearings on campus but closed them to all except witnesses testifying for the suspended students. The first appeals were those of Colin Neiburger and Alan DiMarco, on April 16; since they were banned from campus, KSU police transported them to the hearing site along with the arrested militants testifying on their behalf. The decision to shut the hearings and keep the location secret made it appear to many that the university intended to conceal the process. The stage was set for Kent's gravest political crisis to date.[31]

SDS had been meeting off campus since the suspension of its charter a week earlier, but the loss of access to the university grounds did not stop the campaign. If anything, the arrests, suspensions, and organizational ban aroused new sympathy for the group. Heartened in the face of adversity, SDS distributed flyers into the eighth day of its spring offensive. On the day of the suspension hearings, SDS issued a leaflet calling on supporters to attend, in order to "Open It Up, or Shut It Down!" Several hundred people mobilized and rallied in support of an open hearing process.[32]

Neiburger's and DiMarco's hearings were scheduled for late afternoon at an undisclosed campus site, so SDS rallied at their customary location in front of the Student Union. Athletes and fraternity members again turned out to confront them. SDS representatives struggled to be heard above hecklers. After a speech by the Reverend Bob Begin, a radical priest from Cleveland, Jim Mellen, a national SDS leader associated with the Michigan–Ohio action faction, raised a bullhorn. "The young people in this country are fighting," Mellen declared, ". . . at San Francisco State, and they are fighting at Kent State. We are fighting the battle of Vietnam. We are fighting the battle of black people of this country." He continued:

> The one thing you people better understand and learn quickly [is] that we are [no] longer asking you to . . . help make revolution, we are telling you that the revolution is on— And you better make a choice because the revolution is going to roll right over you if you get in the way. . . . [Y]our racism and your ideas that you can dominate people like the Vietnamese is going to come to an end. . . . I know there are pigs out there who think you can go into the black ghettos and push people around, but the thing is you can't do it anymore.[33]

Mellen's intensity temporarily quieted opponents and steeled radicals for a difficult march. SDSers had learned that the hearings were being held in the Music and Speech Building on the far side of the campus, and Mark Lencl, the airborne veteran of the Vietnam War, led hundreds there. On the way, Lencl fought off a succession of attackers. Dave Dyer, who up until then had avoided antiwar protest, aided a female demonstrator being roughed up by fraternity men. SDSers and independents, like Dyer, found more opposition at the hearing site, where the partially enclosed portico of the Music and Speech Building had been blocked by many of the same people they had confronted at the Student Union.[34]

Separated under the portico by a few yards, the two sides exchanged threats that quickly escalated into a fierce, if short-lived, melee—the worst fighting, perhaps, between left- and right-wing students at Kent State in a decade. Shaken by the combativeness of the SDSers (including former KSU football player Jim Powrie), one counterprotestor temporarily calmed the situation by standing between the enraged groups. Just as he did so, the standoff ended when a cry went up among the radicals that a way into the building had been found through another entrance. Moving quickly, Lencl, Powrie, and Paul Bukosky led the radicals up a stairwell to the third floor of Music and Speech. There, despite the presence of campus police defending the hall entryway, the trio wedged open the door with a bar from a metal coat rack. Lencl, who had experienced hand-to-hand fighting in Vietnam, impulsively charged toward the police, who had retreated from the doorway. Ric Erickson (who left a nearby room where the hearing was being conducted) shouted at Lencl to drop the six-foot-long bar. Jolted by Erickson's unexpected scream, Lencl sensibly did so. A policeman later said that if Lencl had not dropped the bar, they would have shot him at point-blank range, and Kent's first fatality in a confrontation over the war might well have been a Vietnam veteran who had earned a Combat Infantry Badge.[35]

After the vanguard cleared the doorway, the mass of the student protestors (most of whom knew nothing of the commotion at the top of the stairway) made their way to the third floor, believing that they would at last witness the suspension hearings. All of the suspended SDSers were already there, prepared to testify. Loudly welcoming the reinforcing throng, SDS leaders altered the mood, temporarily creating a celebratory atmosphere. This soon changed. Within ten minutes dozens of riot-clad police reinforcements from the State Highway Patrol had sealed off both stairways, effectively trapping 175 SDS members and supporters inside. Although the incident was portrayed by local media as a militant takeover, those ensnared in the police vise had come to observe a hearing, not to occupy a building. With thousands massing outside, and with tension building, the affair dragged on for hours. Unknown to police, however, two KSU professors, Carl Moore and Ken Calkins, used a key to an unwatched freight elevator to slip as many as 120 protestors out of the building.[36]

The configuration of the third-floor hallway initially prevented police from noticing the ever-shrinking crowd, but they eventually detected and sealed the route of escape. The only militants allowed to leave were those KSU detective Tom Kelley called "the colored kids." As with the April 8 scuffle at the Administration Building, the university, wanting to stay away from a renewal of the SDS/BUS alliance, avoided arresting any African American students; police allowed the few who were present to be escorted out by members of BUS. In all, fifty-eight students and nonstudents were taken into custody, including twenty women. Those arrested on April 8 and out on bail, including Erickson, Emmer, Gibeaut, and Powell, were again jailed for contempt of court—even though they had been given permission to be on campus for the hearing. The four of them and a number of others, including Candy Erickson, Jim Powrie, Terry Robbins, Paul Bukosky, and Mike Gorup, also faced various felony charges, including malicious destruction of property. The arrests snared additional activists, among them Jane Boram and Vince Modugno, who were charged with trespassing. Four-fifths of those arrested were students, and they were suspended immediately.[37]

President White again handed control of the events to Vice President Matson, who made decisions in tandem with McMillen as he had during the BUS walkout following the Oakland police sit-in. During the height of the April 16 protest, White went to his on-campus home, where he took calls. Neither Matson nor McMillen bothered to go to the scene of the aborted hearing. McMillen, ignorant of the fact that many students wanted to leave Music and Speech, gave the order to seal off the building and let no one out. He later regretted this decision but also criticized White's detached management style. McMillen later described how the president would leave his office when the threat of a confrontation loomed, preferring to keep abreast of events by telephone from his home. With the flood of events that month, "there was not time to consult him," McMillen recalled.[38]

Students knew nothing of this disconnected managerial style and believed the president to be actively engaged in decision making. White reinforced this image, using the *Stater* and the *Record-Courier,* as well as memos and announcements bearing the imprimatur of his office, to make statements justifying the arrests and suspensions. White initially received considerable support; most KSU faculty united behind him, as did Kent citizens, who submitted supportive petitions bearing over a thousand signatures. For its part, SDS managed to rally 250 people at the city's Fred Fuller Park the day after the arrests, the largest gathering since the start of the campaign. Although Howie Emmer and others tried to keep the focus on the organization's four demands, it was the university's handling of the arrests, rather than the demands, that generated controversy among the students and sympathetic faculty.[39]

The Concerned Citizens Community

While SDS remained tied to its demands, liberals, student government leaders, members of the Young Socialist Alliance (YSA), and SDS leader George Hoffman turned their attention to the threat to students' civil liberties. Hoffman had founded the chapter believing in the need to fuse student rights with antiwar activism. He continued to participate in the protests, but, like Vince Modugno, he felt estranged from the action faction of SDS. While dozens of the most militant members of the SDS chapter shifted their attention to a region-wide organizational meeting in Akron, those concerned with the rights of the students formed the Concerned Citizens of the Kent State University Community, known as the 3-C. With the national eye on Cornell University, where well-armed African American students had barricaded themselves in the Student Union after being attacked by white fraternity members, five thousand people at KSU—a quarter of the students—marched around the campus to protest the arrests and suspensions. It had taken a decade to reach a critical mass, but students protested the administration's actions in surprising numbers when the constitutional rights of some were thought to have been seriously violated.[40]

Seeking to prevent an explosion of opposition, Matson and McMillen set out to divide their adversaries. Administrators launched an effort to discredit those who had emerged as the leaders of the 3-C, using reports from the Highway Patrol, whose intelligence agents were monitoring the regional SDS conference in Akron. Steve Sharoff, a history graduate student new to the campus, became a center of the controversy. The son of a small-town police chief in New York's Catskill Mountains, the charismatic Sharoff quickly emerged as the 3-C's principal spokesman. Politically more liberal than leftist, he found himself distrusted by both the radicals and university authorities. Though Sharoff was much less radical than his SDS counterparts, Matson seemed especially eager to undermine him. Sharoff blamed Matson for circulating a rumor that he had been at the SDS regional conference, when he had actually been meeting with the KSU provost in an apparent good-faith effort to soften the university's actions against SDS.[41]

Just as the administration earlier worried about a BUS/SDS alliance, they likewise feared a broad-based coalition of disaffected mainstream liberals and leftists. They therefore reacted strongly to the creation of 3-C and sought to undermine Sharoff. SDS alone they could deal with, but a BUS/SDS alliance or a left–liberal coalition with thousands of supporters was something else altogether.

A wide political coalition was taking shape in 3-C. Veteran activist Ruth Gibson and the self-assured YSA leader Mike Alewitz threw themselves into coalition work. Even a few SDS members were involved—Nelson Riddle, Judy Gollust, and George Hoffman—but they, like the YSAers, favored a civil liberties approach. Others in 3-C were independent radicals such as Sue Ink and Bobby Franklin, an antiwar science instructor. Still others, like Joe Cullum— the Teamster's son from Canton whose older brother was serving with the US Marines in Vietnam—straddled the fence between political restraint and forceful radicalism. Most 3-C supporters were political liberals or moderates, like Carole Teminsky, who participated in her first protest believing that the university had abrogated the rights of the SDS radicals, thereby diminishing all students' civil liberties.[42]

New Dealers and the New Left

Students like Carole Teminsky and Joe Cullum came from New Deal Democratic families that harbored varying degrees of suspicion toward ruling elites, but also tended to have a positive view of government. They saw themselves as loyal, patriotic Americans. Their attitudes and aspirations had been influenced by their parents' experience of the Great Depression and the sacrifices of World War II, in which many of their fathers had served. These countervailing pushes and pulls may explain why many working-class Americans had ambivalent feelings about both the war and student unrest, and why it was hard for students like Teminsky to actively participate in the antiwar movement. It may also explain why student dissent did not spread as quickly at Kent as it did at more privileged schools. At Kent State, many antiwar students, especially non-

SDSers, sought to balance activism, academics, and after-school jobs with an eye toward their future livelihoods.[43]

Why did some working-class students become radical activists while others sat on the sidelines until opposition to the war became a mass movement? The most committed working-class activists tended to come from families that supported their views. The parents of Howie Emmer, Mark Lencl, and Mike Alewitz had varying ties to the political parties of the Old Left, and those of Alan Canfora and Vince Modugno had been union activists. Canfora's father had been involved in labor confrontations as a teenager and as an adult had led dangerous wildcat strikes that easily could have cost him his job. Modugno's grandfather had been a member of the Industrial Workers of the World, and his father opposed the war even before Vince. Jerry Persky's father had been in the leftist John Reed Club at Ohio State. Others, like Jim Powrie and George Hoffman, initially enjoyed just their mothers' tacit support; Hoffman's father—a disabled World War II veteran—came to his side only after May 1970. These student activists formed the vanguard of the New Left at Kent.[44]

Peripheral involvement or sympathetic noninvolvement became an easier option for students who were risk-averse or non-joiners, or who lacked personal connections to more activist-minded students. Speaking for the many antiwar sympathizers reluctant to actively support the confrontational SDS, Carole Teminsky explained, "It was hard for me to understand how some people could push the boundaries." Whether Kent's working-class students were on the frontlines or sidelines, the increasingly ideological New Left provided them with a framework for understanding the Vietnam War as part of a larger imperialist project, and for linking it to issues of racial justice at home.[45]

Discrediting the Concerned Citizens Community

A final piece of the Kent administration's divisive strategy remained. Matson argued that a dark conspiracy threatened the existence of Kent State. He pointed to an SDS brochure from 1968 that he claimed was a kind of "how-to manual" for radical action, as well as to the presence of some SDSers who had come from the regional conference in nearby Akron to help leaflet the campus. He succeeded in peeling away support for the 3-C by some student government leaders, such as student body president Bill VanderWyden, and getting others, such as Frank Frisina, a pliant student senator and presidential candidate, to denounce the 3-C.[46]

The biggest coup came when the administration gained the cooperation of the *Stater*. Publishing only its second extra in school history, the paper urged readers to boycott a 3-C rally planned for Monday, April 21. Editors ran a front-page opinion piece by Bill Armstrong, a McMillen ally who contended that the coalition was nothing more than an SDS front group. For emphasis, the special issue ran an editorial about the midday rally titled "Don't Go!" along with articles such as "[Ohio] 'Legislature Could Step In,'" "Ohio Region of SDS Moves Forces to Kent," "SDS Strategy vs. Occurrences," and "VanderWyden Renounces 3-C Steering Committee Actions," the last of which condemned Sharoff. Effective in the short term, the special issue infuriated many students. Unwittingly, it also turned the 3-C into something other than it had been initially, driving moderates within it further left, to radicalism. The administration / student government / *Kent Stater* nexus proved to growing numbers of students that SDS was right: those running the university could not be trusted. It also gave SDS material for one of its most cogent pieces of agitation, a poster-sized satirical collage titled "*Record Beacon Stater:* All the Stuff We Choose to Print."[47]

White was satisfied that he had weakened the new group, and even with the support of former BUS president Bob Pickett, who condemned the administration's behavior, turnout at the protest rally was down from expected numbers. Soon thereafter, White denied 3-C's requests to drop all charges against the students and to reinstate the SDS charter. In view of the hardening of White's position, Sharoff and some faculty proposed a nonbinding student referendum asking whether to support the position of the administration on the arrests and suspensions, or register opposition in one of three ways: through a boycott, a teach-in, or a strike. Fearing the outcome of the referendum and perhaps the influence of BUS, KSU's administrative troika opposed the idea. Still, the vote went forward and almost nine thousand students participated, the largest voting turnout in school history. Results were mixed: the vote essentially supported the administration's position on the arrests and suspensions, but a slight majority of students backed one of the three other options of a boycott of classes, a teach-in, or a strike. Both sides drew positive conclusions from the plebiscite: 3-C pointed to the size of the vote and the interest in educational teach-ins, while White's administration took solace from the backing their decisions received from 62 percent of the voting students.[48]

Meanwhile, SDS struggled with the arrests and court injunctions against its leading members, along with bail bonds in excess of $100,000. In the short term, the vote proved most important to those who had opposed it, as the KSU administration interpreted the outcome as an endorsement of its hard line. The 3-C might have better anticipated the division of opinion on the alternatives it offered to the administration's uncompromising position, because, despite the vote, the meaning of it seemed in some doubt. Even with the KSU administration declaring its satisfaction with the results, the fact that thousands of students had opposed their actions and that hundreds were left embittered seems not to have entered their political calculus. The size of the turnout demonstrated that students had been activated by the university's forceful response. Even if many initially supported the administration, thousands did not, and many of those became further radicalized.[49]

Bloody Forecasts and a Bitter End

Kent SDS got support from civil rights veterans Mae Mallory and Julian May-field, who appeared in Cleveland to demand freedom for political prisoners including "the Kent 4" (Powell, Emmer, Neiburger, and Erickson). Corky Benedict of the Cleveland SDS brought Bernardine Dohrn to Kent to con-demn the university's actions against the chapter. As some predicted, SDS cir-cumvented the organizational ban by calling campus meetings under different group names. Benedict, a combative member of the action faction, spoke of the coming battle with the ruling system. Dohrn's speech alluded to both the con-frontation at Cornell between African American students and white fraternity members, and the shooting deaths of three African Americans in Orangeburg, South Carolina, a year earlier. She told a crowd of 125 people that "blacks had been killed on campuses" and that "while no whites had been . . . they eventu-ally would be." Robert Dix offered his own comment about Cornell, urging the campus to avoid armed extremes: "Carried to the limit one way and you have anarchy; to the . . . other way and you have over-reaction and something else that is ugly."[50]

Many were unhappy with SDS's tirades, identification with third-world movements, and sneering attitude toward those unable to accept the entirety of its positions. In an article titled "The War at Kent State," Terry Robbins described the would-be defenders in the 3-C as "a liberal . . . coalition" that "viciously red-baited us," while the Cleveland SDS newsletter, *The Big Us,* dis-missed them as a "liberal group [that] didn't actually give a damn about SDS." Chapter meetings became scenes of factional acrimony. Many SDS members, like Ray Hudson, drifted away. Mike Gorup, out on bail and evicted from the apartment he shared with Boram (because of police pressure on the cou-ple's landlord), went to Detroit to work for SDS's Radical Education Project. Others, like Jim Powrie, who had been in the forefront of the fighting at Music and Speech, were accused of having "a non-struggle attitude" by some proto-Weatherman SDSers. Powrie and others concerned with the drift of the chapter argued against Terry Robbins's advocacy of extremism. Carl Oglesby, the one-time Kent State student who had risen to the presidency of SDS, was losing the same battle with the national office. Increasingly, like many at Kent, he felt lost within an organization he had done so much to build.[51]

The spring offensive that opened with considerable bluster in early April ended in late May with a small, dispiriting anti-ROTC protest, where a dozen

SDS members were arrested. Some students who joined the protest were unaware that they had been participants in an SDS maneuver. Unknown to many, perhaps most, of those participating in the anti-ROTC protest, the demonstration was intended to draw police attention to the campus and away from the off-campus Liquid Crystals Institute, enabling other SDSers to shackle its unguarded doors. Apparently willing to trade more arrests for a symbolic, if hollow, victory, what was left of SDS exulted in the outcome, headlining their leaflet "Liquid Crystals Chained Shut!" *Stater* editors saw little point in arresting more students, whose protest caused no real harm to either ROTC or the Liquid Crystals Institute. The only real harm had been done to SDS, and that was self-inflicted.[52]

A mixture of external forces and internal pressures destroyed the Kent SDS chapter after fifteen feverish months, paralleling the ideological trajectory in national SDS. Most of its leaders were never again active at Kent State. At least a dozen members received jail sentences, with one student who was convicted of malicious destruction at the Music and Speech protest incarcerated for more than a year. Many of the Kent SDS leaders were ostracized on campus. Although SDS alienated many potential supporters, in the long run the Vietnam War and the US government's persisting racial injustice proved far more unpopular with young people than did SDS's immoderation. Allen Richardson, the son of a Lorain steelworker, found the core of the organization's critique of US policy persuasive yet held back from active involvement in SDS rallies. He recalled years later: "I remember thinking that some of them (not all) were more into melodrama and self-aggrandizement than solid strategy and tactics. I was convinced they had not thought out what they were doing, what they really hoped to accomplish, or made a convincing case why anyone should put themselves on the line in support of them." Richardson and many other undergraduates at Kent carried with them a class consciousness they learned at home, yet they also bore the weight of their parents' aspirations. They wanted to do well at college, get a degree and "good job," and achieve a level of economic security beyond what their parents had known. Students such as Richardson did absorb SDS's hatred of the war and embraced some of its identification with liberation movements.[53]

In the end, it may have been the administration's unforgiving response that left people most embittered. The campus religious coordinator resigned her position, apparently under administrative duress, after it was revealed that her office photocopy machine had been used by SDS. At a 3-C meeting on May 7, her husband proclaimed, "SDS doesn't radicalize people, the administration does. Matson is our best organizer." Youthful opponents of the administration agreed, and carried their anger and resentment with them when they responded furiously to the Cambodian invasion the following spring.[54]

Fallout

There were electoral consequences of the SDS meltdown. The new KSU student body president, Frank Frisina, won approval from the *Stater* and the administration. A hometown boy, aspiring lawyer, fraternity member, and admirer of Richard Nixon, Frisina would play a part in aiding the KSU administration in the events of the following May. LeRoy Satrom, a traditionalist Democrat who had served as both a city councilman and the city engineer, was elected mayor of Kent in November 1969, gaining favor with many voters who were unhappy with news from the university campus. A transplant from North Dakota, Satrom would have a far more central role in May 1970 than Frisina. Compared to his predecessor, the moderately liberal John Carson, Satrom held strongly negative views of radical students. When the next surge of protest came in Kent, it would encounter a solid wall of opposition at every level of government: from the head of the student body to the university president, from the mayor's office to the Statehouse in Columbus, and from the Ohio governor to the president of the United States.[55]

In his regular column, Robert C. Dix often took the pulse of local, state, and national events. In the spring of 1969 he worried aloud about the strain of radical politics on his friend Bob White and about the reputation of Kent State. Weeks earlier, White had privately expressed a similar anxiety about making "headlines in the wrong way . . . too many times." Dix lamented, "When . . . traveling about these days, you don't have to tell anybody where Kent is. Everybody knows; it's one of the country's chief trouble spots." He may have slightly overstated the case. Although it was big news in Ohio, the upheaval at Kent State was part of a national pattern affecting three hundred campuses across the country, including not only Cornell but North Carolina Agricultural and Technical State University and the University of California at Berkeley, where one protester was killed and thirty-two were injured by National Guardsmen in a violent clash over the fate of "People's Park." Although Kent State had developed a regional reputation as a center of protest, and even with the looming investigation by the House Internal Security Committee, the university had yet to enter into the national consciousness as a major focal point of dissent.[56]

CHAPTER 10

Months of Protest, Days of Rage

OVER THE course of the summer of 1969, the counterculture of
America came together as SDS came apart. For years the two had evolved along
parallel paths: the left-wing student organization sharpened its rhetoric and
commitment to direct action, while the burgeoning youth culture broadened its
freeform assault on the edifice of Cold War conventions and mores. At the end
of the decade the two movements finally began to converge. Political activists
and youthful nonconformists found common cause in opposing an Establishment that hypocritically preached "law and order" at home while perpetuating
a bloody and costly war abroad. Ironically, just as the expanding counterculture
began to throw its weight into politics, the SDS politicos of the New Left
narrowed their ideological course and split their ranks, dividing first into two
factions and then into three.

In June 1969, the wrangling disciples of the New Left met in Chicago for the
annual SDS convention. At some point in the seven years since the publication
of its defining manifesto, the Port Huron Statement, the SDS had been actively
involved in the struggle for civil rights and economic justice, the student "free
speech" movement, and the ballooning antiwar movement. But over time the
idealism and commitment to "participatory democracy" that had fueled the
growth of the New Left had been steadily undermined by disputes over ideology and political tactics.[1]

The drift toward factionalism had been exacerbated by the entry into SDS
of the Progressive Labor Party (PLP) in early 1966. PLP had broken from the
Old Left Communist Party in 1962 (coincidentally, the same year as the issuance
of the Port Huron Statement), and had aligned itself with the People's Republic
of China in the wake of the Sino-Soviet split. Concentrated in Boston and New
York City, and eventually spreading to the West Coast, PLP initially operated

among minority communities and in industry. In New York, audacious and sometimes dangerous work in combating police violence in Harlem was combined with more conventional, if still difficult, organizing in New York City's garment industry. As became typical of the long Sixties era, PL's modest successes led its leaders to immodestly see themselves as both the theoretical and actual leaders of the working class, even as its ranks grew much faster on college campuses than in factories and workshops. Within a few years of proclaiming themselves a party, PLP leaders issued policy statements rejecting the growing Black Power movement and denouncing the struggles of the Vietnamese nationalists as lacking sufficient revolutionary purity.[2]

At first, most SDSers paid little mind to PLP, but that changed as its influence and authority in the organization grew. To compete with the well-read, if dogmatic, PL faction, a core of SDS leaders began studying Marxism and third-world liberation theory and, by late 1968, reorganized themselves as the Revolutionary Youth Movement (RYM). While leaders of the RYM rejected PL's criticism of the Black Panther Party and the Vietnamese National Liberation Front (NLF), the anti-PLers were themselves increasingly at odds and estranged from rank-and-file SDS activists. To some extent, these divisions could also be seen at Kent State, where chapter members divided between those favoring patient organizing in order to build a broader radical movement and the "action faction" soon to become Weatherman. Losing faith in the revolutionary potential of white workers, Weathermen narrowed their list of allies and came to believe largely in their own power to bring about change through revolutionary violence.[3]

In contrast to the rapidly expanding youth culture, PLers and many leaders of the RYM caucus favored what they understood to be a more conventional working-class appearance. As shorter hair for young men became less common, PLP encouraged its male members to keep their hair tidy and well groomed and to wear blue-collar clothing, thinking it would allow for better integration with the American proletariat. With the same end in view, some male SDS members adopted a 1950s "greaser" look, complete with slicked-back hair. These makeovers came at a time when many blue-collar youth were growing their hair long and dressing in bell-bottom jeans and other styles of clothing newly popular on college campuses. Even though Weatherman took its name from a line in a Dylan song, suggesting a modicum of countercultural hipness, the vanguard element of SDS was out of step politically and culturally from its student base.[4]

All of the Kent delegates at the 1969 convention, including Jeff Powell, Howie Emmer, Ric Erickson, Matt "Rebel" Flanagan, Jane Boram, and Jim Powrie, sided with the RYM faction and opposed the PLP, whose dedicated cadre probably made up at least a third of the fifteen hundred delegates. RYM adherents likely matched PLP in numbers, but not in organizational discipline. The remainder of the delegates, unaligned with either faction, would vote by issue rather than by caucus affiliation.[5]

The tensions within the New Left that had been growing over the past year came to the forefront in mid-June, with as many as five hundred additional nonvoting supporters of the different factions gathering in the cavernous and dilapidated Chicago Coliseum. The factions all came armed with position papers. RYM's outlook was outlined in a lengthy statement written in part by a New York SDSer, Terry Robbins, who was part of a committee to draft the anti-PLP position paper. A Dylan devotee since his days at Kenyon College, Robbins mined a leaflet he had written months earlier for the Kent SDS and gave the interminably long statement its name: "You don't need a weatherman to know which way the wind blows."[6]

At the outset of the convention, a series of preliminary motions made it clear to SDS/RYM delegates that they could not outvote the disciplined PLP. After days and nights of what Jane Boram termed tumultuous debate, SDS/RYM, backed by Fred Hampton and the authority of Black Panthers in Chicago, insisted that SDS could not continue to exist in alliance with the Panthers with a PLP presence. Lacking the votes to expel PLP before the full convention, some six hundred SDS/RYM delegates and supporters met separately from the other delegates in the Coliseum and voted by a margin of five to one to oust PLP; they then returned en masse to the main convention. Without bothering to take a second vote of the full delegate body, Bernardine Dohrn, perhaps the most dynamic of the RYM leaders, announced that PLP was expelled from SDS and then proceeded to lead all those who cared to depart out of the convention hall. Jim Powrie, the former high school football player who had temporarily subordinated his differences with the Weathermen in order to deal with the more vexing PLP (and who, because of his physical size, guarded SDS's cash box), numbered among the many hundreds who joined the exodus. Years later he recalled the collective departure: "The Chicago Coliseum was a dark hall with bits of light streaming in, and there was a romantic feeling. We all walked out through several thousand people. At the time we saw it as the beginning of something. But it was the end of SDS."[7]

Powrie's assessment captures the meaning of the moment. The walkout had split SDS, and while nationwide the RYM adherents could claim the broader following, PLP, having remained in the Coliseum, claimed control of the organization. From that point on, two groups, and soon three, insisted that they legitimately represented SDS. When word reached the SDS rank and file, most of them at home from college for the summer, as many as a hundred thousand members and supporters were left bewildered by what had occurred.

With Progressive Labor still inside the Coliseum, SDS/RYM members regrouped next door in a smaller sports center and turned their attention to settling their own significant differences, which had already become apparent at Kent State and elsewhere. More traditional Marxists in SDS, such as Mike Klonsky, who favored patient base-building among the working class, began calling themselves RYM II. They distanced themselves from RYM I / Weatherman adherents, who saw little revolutionary potential in older or middle-aged white workers employed in Ohio's mills and factories. Painting with the broadest brush, Weathermen believed that such workers were complicit with the ruling order. Equally, Weathermen saw their role as the leading element of the international struggle against imperial rule inside the United States. While representing a tiny minority within SDS nationally, Weatherman had a majority of the non-PL delegates at the convention. This fact was borne out by the eventual adoption of a turgid position paper arguing that white workers were beneficiaries of the prevailing economic system and that, apart from a tiny minority of whites, only racial minorities had revolutionary potential.[8]

Before the rump convention ended, the Weatherman faction adopted a program they called "Hot Town." Similar in some ways to the Economic Research and Action Project (ERAP) that SDS established in Cleveland and other midwestern locales in the mid-1960s, the plan called for the creation of urban-based collectives through which working-class youths, as distinguished from their parents, might be won to revolutionary politics. Seeking to shift their base from college students to blue-collar youth, action-faction members of the Kent SDS and from chapters elsewhere in Ohio formed collectives in Cleveland, Akron, and Columbus. Unlike activists in ERAP, however, who sought to blend in with the surroundings of the urban poor and work patiently with their neighbors on homegrown issues, Hot Town participants were often polarizing. Typifying their extreme behavior, on July 4 a small group of Weathermen ran through a Columbus city park "with an NLF flag, leafleting and rapping." Later that month, following some unrest in the city's black community, one of the female members of the collective was jailed for inciting to riot. In advance of setting up the summer collectives, the Weathermen, at that point still based among college students, had announced their intention, when working in the urban neighborhoods, to "retain a sense of struggle from the campus." In the narrowest of ways, they had succeeded.[9]

Nationwide, a preponderance of Weatherman leaders attended prestigious schools and were often from affluent families. This was less true of the Weatherman cohort from Kent State and Cleveland, yet even those from middle-income and blue-collar homes, such as Jeff Powell, Mark Lencl, Matt Flanagan, and Corky Benedict, found organizing among other white working-class youth difficult and often dangerous. They knew from experience to expect police surveillance, but the physical harassment from neighborhood residents exceeded anything they experienced on campus. Although claiming some progress, Powell learned the larger realities of trying to recruit young Appalachian whites—many of them recent arrivals to Akron who had backed the Wallace presidency—to a radical program that included solidarity with blacks. Powell became caught up in brutal street fights with young toughs who felt they were protecting neighborhood turf. If anything, conditions were more hazardous in Cleveland. There Ric Erickson, Corky Benedict, and others tried to reach out to young Puerto Ricans who had been warring with a white gang. When asked to help, none of the SDSers relished the invitation to join the battle, but neither did they shirk from the fight. During one encounter, several Puerto Ricans were knifed before the rival white gang could be driven off and the wounded transported to a hospital. Weathermen received criticism throughout the larger SDS orbit, as most radicals condemned their politics and style of work. Few, however, doubted their daring and commitment.[10]

Internally, the damage was more self-inflicted. One historian described the collectives as "harsh environments" for radicals, who had had little money to sustain them and huge demands made on their time. Organizing produced few gains. Hard circumstances and unsparing political criticism began to drive some away. On top of police scrutiny and fights with hostile neighbors, the Akron collective endured threats from right-wing groups, including the Minutemen and the Ku Klux Klan. To face such challenges, they armed themselves, a move that proved too much for some activists, while more toughened radicals like Emmer, Lencl, and Powell stayed. When Hot Town militants went to the adjacent industrial city of Barberton to recruit reinforcements, they found themselves unwelcome. "They . . . talked about karate and self-defense," said former SDSer Alan Canfora, a Barberton resident. "And they passed out leaflets . . . calling for youth to fight for communism. The kids of Barberton didn't know where these people were coming from." The Weatherman appeal remained decidedly narrow and, for all but a few, their approach was repellent.[11]

As he would that summer and fall, Canfora could and did influence the kind of kids who rejected Weatherman, bringing them around to his radical analysis of the war and police repression. His methods were much different than the Weathermen's, however. Although he could certainly be combative about his beliefs, Canfora knew enough not to write leaflets that the uninitiated could not comprehend, or expect people to adopt a sweeping critique of societal ills on the basis of a five-to-fifteen-minute harangue from a complete stranger. A number of Canfora's friends in Barberton were returning from military service in 1969, and several others were preparing to leave for Vietnam. Many returning vets had come to question the war or even to openly oppose it. Some now chose to enlist in the antiwar movement, while others drifted into the mushrooming counterculture. All this together made for complicated politics within the working class, particularly with respect to issues of race and the war. What became clear, however, was that growing numbers of noncollege urban youth were open to new ways of thinking when the messenger knew how to speak and behave in ways they could understand.[12]

The Summer of Peace and Music

That same summer, Alan Canfora, like many readers of the new rock periodical *Rolling Stone,* learned about a major music festival scheduled to take place in mid-August near White Lake in southeastern New York State. Billed as an "Aquarian Exposition—3 Days of Peace and Music," the Woodstock Music and Art Fair drew nearly half a million young people, including Canfora and a number of other KSU students, to a farm in the town of Bethel to listen to live music by many of the rock stars of the day, including Janis Joplin, Crosby, Stills, and Nash, Jimi Hendrix, and Santana.[13]

Ultimately, the word "Woodstock" would come to be associated with an entire generation, or at least the part of it that embraced the "sex, drugs, and rock 'n' roll" ethos of the Sixties counterculture. But it also signaled something more. As the last summer of the decade neared its close, the counterculture and antiwar movement were beginning to converge. Although many hardcore political activists eschewed drugs on principle, by the late 1960s and into the 1970s marijuana had become commonplace; surveys showed that 60 percent of college students had used it. Bob Pardun, an SDSer who also embraced the cultural rebellion, wrote that he "liked the way [marijuana] brought everyone together as we sat in a circle and passed the pipe around." Grass became part of an expanding youth culture whose devotees listened to the same music, wore the same type of clothes, and opposed the Vietnam War and the "establishment" responsible for it. SDS activist Paul Krehbiel, who set aside plans to organize an antiwar demonstration in Buffalo to attend the Woodstock festival, remembered relishing the antiwar message of Jefferson Airplane's "Uncle Sam's Blues," as well as the moment when Berkeley activist, naval veteran, and songwriter Country Joe McDonald led hundreds of thousands in singing "I-Feel-Like-I'm-Fixin'-to-Die Rag," with its mordant refrain "And it's one, two, three, / What are we fighting for? / Don't ask me, I don't give a damn, / Next stop is Vietnam."[14]

Yet what made the experience unique for Krehbiel and many others was not so much what the festival offered as what it didn't: "no rules, no authorities, no hierarchy, no police." From the natural hillside amphitheater where the enormous throng could set their eyes on the stage and observe a crowd four times as large as those that filled the country's largest outdoor stadiums, Woodstock, and the rock and folk music played there, offered a glimpse of an alternative world, an imagined future. The historian Michael Frisch noted that in the absence of authority, a more "inclusive youth culture" stressing "mutuality" began to take shape at Woodstock. Festival-goers demonstrated the "capacity to solve problems . . . in ways that advanced a broader vision of change." And after Woodstock boundaries between cultural and political radicalism became even more porous, as skepticism of authority and experiments in communal living became widespread. As the underground newspaper editor Abe Peck observed, "Many Woodstockers carried away tastes of egalitarianism and authenticity, a real triumph of peace-and-love values." One journalist, Jacob Brackman, recognized the seeds of this change; several months earlier, assessing the political impact of America's youth on a society that had given them the Vietnam War, he noted that among them "great numbers could begin to conceive of something more decent than submitting to the culture."[15]

The same spirit flowed when school resumed at Kent State in September 1969. Just before the start of classes, rock groups, including northeast Ohio's premier group, Joe Walsh's James Gang, staged their own festival. Fans and antiwar activists bearing NLF flags listened to bands in Fred Fuller Park, and they could also hear Walsh's band at JB's on Kent's North Water Street strip. Storefronts bearing exotic names like Hallelujah Leathers, Inside Out, Halcyon Days, and Quite Rightly attracted self-proclaimed "freaks" and stylish imitators. As Inside Out proprietor Daniel Thompson explained, "We started with the idea of supplying hipper things to college students at good prices." Hundreds of KSU men grew beards, and thousands let their hair grow long; woman also adopted the natural look in hairstyles. Young men and women alike favored bell-bottom jeans; the better-off patronized avant-garde boutiques sprouting up in Cleveland and Kent, while others favored less expensive blue work shirts and army surplus wear. Kent now seemed culturally to be a different place, an expanding enclave of radical expression and utopian experimentation where a new order might be imagined and sustained. However poorly defined the boundaries were between political radicalism and cultural utopianism, one drew and gained strength from the other, at Kent and across the country. In a way it had to: the war and its effect on American youth, particularly those of working-class origin, knew few limits. Nineteen sixty-nine would be the second bloodiest year of the war, with almost twelve thousand American dead.[16]

The End of SDS at Kent

For all the visible change at Kent, politically things were at once the same and different. In June, Kent State president Robert White appeared as a witness before the House Internal Security Committee to testify about the Kent SDS and its expulsion from the campus. Questioned by Ohio congressman John Ashbrook, an intractable conservative who would challenge Richard Nixon for the Republican nomination in 1972, White explained his hard line, asserting that "without the arrests [of SDS members], events would have proceeded in a much different manner, which would have led to turmoil and chaos with rather serious implications." White may have taken quiet satisfaction when several congratulatory letters he received from Governor Rhodes and the American Legion were read into the record.[17]

The SDSers charged in the events White described faced trials in the fall. Given the conservative jury pool in the nearby Portage County seat of Ravenna, no one was surprised by the conviction of the first defendant, Jeff Powell. But the proceedings did convince county authorities that additional trials involving seventy other defendants would be expensive. SDS lawyers reached an understanding with the court: Powell, Ric Erickson, Howie Emmer, and Colin Neiburger would receive six-month sentences in exchange for guilty pleas. Mike Gorup and a dozen or so others would serve sentences ranging from fifteen to forty-five days. Scores of remaining SDSers accused of trespassing at the Music and Speech Building disturbance were given fines and suspended sentences.[18]

The KSU administration had delivered a serious blow to Kent's antiwar movement. The movement had enjoyed an unusual degree of stability and leadership continuity since its beginnings in February 1965. Now SDS leaders were facing the start of their jail terms and the organization was banished from campus. The chain of continuity had been broken, shattered by the organizational bans, mass arrests, suspensions, and injunctions. At the same time, the movement's antiwar message, now fused with counterculture radicalism, seemed broader than before, as the thousands who had marched in defense of SDS rights were now willing to do so against the war.

In this time of flux, a few SDS leaders and influential members had managed to avoid arrest, among them the Hammonds, George Hoffman, and Mark Real. Others charged with simple misdemeanors, including Bill Whitaker, Vince Modugno, and recent graduate Jane Boram, evaded jail through the plea deals. But the absence of a bona fide SDS created a void, as the militants not in jail or on probation lacked an organization. Others were forced, for a variety of reasons, to give up on Kent. Jim Powrie, who faced years of probation, relocated to Buffalo, New York, where his brother lived. Judy Gollust would opt to forsake teaching after the big Moratorium demonstrations in the fall and stay on in Washington, DC, to organize high schoolers against the war. Her future husband, David King, decided not to wait for Kent to become the little Berkeley some had predicted and moved to the West Coast university city itself. Most of the largely defunct Young Socialist Alliance (YSA) left as well. Ron Wittmaack and Barbara Brock also moved to the Bay area, where they became involved in a strike at

San Francisco State. John McCann and Barbara Gregorich remained politically active, but they were now in Cleveland. Bob Bresnahan and the tireless Roy Inglee transferred to the Socialist Workers Party (SWP) branch in Boston.[19]

Although these seasoned organizers were not easily replaced, newer and younger activists stepped into the leadership vacuum. Mike Alewitz, the eighteen-year-old from Cleveland Heights who had helped the 3-C defend student rights in April 1969, was one of a tiny handful of YSA members still enrolled at Kent. Alewitz learned of plans for a nationwide antiwar moratorium while attending the YSA-affiliated Student Mobilization Committee (SMC) conference in Cleveland in early July. Unlike SDS, which was composed of ideologically devoted youth who committed themselves to long meetings and frequent leafleting, the YSA/SWP saw its SMC creation as a looser, single-issue antiwar organization that would ask much less of its members. If SMC members showed interest in issues beyond the war, YSA, and eventually the SWP, had a ready-made political home for them within their ranks.[20]

The more broadly based moratorium was the design of the newly organized Vietnam Moratorium Committee (VMC) and was backed by a reorganized and renamed New Mobilization Committee to End the War in Vietnam (New MOBE). The VMC was in part the brainchild of Sam Brown, a former youth director for presidential candidate Eugene McCarthy in 1968, and it favored a different approach to opposing the war. Its leadership included small businessmen as well as antiwar students with marginal, if still evolving, ties to Washington insiders. Brown and others like him sought to bring mainstream Americans into the movement against the war. Rather than focus on large-scale protests in Washington, the VMC leadership envisioned local protests that would take place throughout the nation on the same day. Building on the promise of success, VMC organizers hoped to expand the length of the protests every month. While initially hesitant to cooperate, the VMC later agreed to help promote a massive demonstration in Washington—with the result being the most effective sustained two months of protest ever mounted by peace advocates. The SMC threw its support to the VMC proposal for local protests in October 1969, and Alewitz found himself at the organizing center of what became Kent's largest antiwar demonstration of the decade.[21]

In his new column for the *Daily Kent Stater,* Alewitz envisaged a massive march. If the SDS trials kept alive lingering animosities toward the KSU administration, the Moratorium provided evidence that antiwar work would flourish despite the trials and punishments. Former SDSers now affiliated with RYM II who had spent the summer aiding strikers at Akron General Hospital returned to antiwar activity on the campus still intent on doing the broader political work they had advocated the previous spring. These ex-SDSers, together with new antiwar recruits and pro-peace professors and graduate assistants, as well as individual supporters like Black United Students (BUS) leader Larry Simpson, developed a broad coalition against the US role in Vietnam.[22]

Alewitz's prediction about the size of the antiwar protests proved prescient. He and other members of the coalition saw the changing milieu and knew that many fraternity men, who months earlier were fighting SDS, were now growing their hair longer and lending their names to the protest. Football players, like freshman Mike Brock, were also taking an interest in the protests. The *Daily Kent Stater* had a checkered record on supporting student dissent, but it also had a new editor every academic quarter. During the fall quarter, under the leadership of editor Stu Feldstein and managing editor Saul Daniels, the *Stater* gave its strongest endorsement yet to an antiwar protest. Students, whose numbers included more than a thousand military veterans by the fall of 1969, were further motivated by the lengthening casualty lists of American soldiers. A former infantry sergeant who had lost dozens of friends told the paper that the bombing of Vietnam had to stop and that the US should get out. Tim DeFrange joined the protests while mourning the recent death of his brother, killed near Pleiku in June 1969. Alan Canfora, cognizant of the frightful toll the conflict had already taken on his community, worried about friends who were still fighting there. Still others, like Greg Hawthorne, a sophomore from Ohio's coal country, participated in his first protest. Hawthorne had grown resentful that Belmont County had already lost too many of its young people in Vietnam. The war's ongoing death toll on working-class youth, the threat of the draft, the appeal of broad peace coalitions, and the juncture of radical and counterculture politics combined to produce what organizers had sought since 1965—a critical mass for Kent's antiwar movement.[23]

On October 15, 1969, the first stage of a planned series of Moratorium protests was held nationwide, and in Kent nearly four thousand students marched through the streets behind the SMC banner "Bring the Troops Home Now." It was the largest protest to occur within the city since a violent labor strike during the Great Depression. On the whole the march was peaceful. The changed appearances of students did not go unnoticed, however. According to the local paper, many marchers were "hippie-type students with customary long hair and casual clothes." But sophomore Allen Richardson, who himself had grown long hair and a mustache, saw enough conventionally dressed adults in the streets to believe that the marchers represented "a real cross-section of America." Reflecting the fusion of counterculture spirit and antiwar politics, an even larger crowd later jammed the college gymnasium to hear the James Gang. Speeches were delivered by future governor John Gilligan, who had championed the Democrats' antiwar plank in Chicago, Cleveland UAW leader Leo Fenster, Bill Whitaker of RYM II and SDS, Father Bernard Meyer of the DC 9 (a group of Cleveland Catholics who threw blood inside Dow Chemical offices in Washington), and an active-duty soldier on leave from Fort Bragg.[24]

Never before had an antiwar protest at Kent State been so well received. Although the march and rally had been organized by radicals, the approach was broad-based. Years of American involvement and nearly forty thousand combat deaths had convinced most of those on campus that the Vietnam War had to end. Opinion in the community proved harder to measure, however. Increasingly liberal KSU faculty members and their families, as well as former students who remained in town, were becoming integrated into the community, making Kent a more diverse place. Eugene McCarthy canvasser Harriet Begala, the wife of a faculty member, mustered her network of family, friends, and political supporters to march in the protest. Weeks in advance of Kent's November municipal election, mayoral candidate and city council head George Pierson hoped that voters like Begala would justify his cautious approval of the local antiwar protest.[25]

Yet even as opposition to the war reached new heights, it generated growing political polarization. As the antiwar movement swelled, opposition, aided in no small part by the Nixon administration, also grew, in Kent and throughout the nation. The city's service director, Bill Roberts, surveying the October 15 protest, asked rhetorically, "How many clean-cut kids did we see?" If Kent's mayoral election served as an antiwar barometer, the results were not encouraging. Pierson, a moderate candidate in the John Carson mold, lost two-to-one to conservative LeRoy Satrom. Satrom argued that the university was expanding too rapidly and stressed the need to halt further growth. Reflecting the views of most voters, he held that the university had passed the point of being a community asset. Not only had Kent State become too big, but its long-haired antiwar students numbered too many.[26]

Days of Rage

While thousands marched in Kent, as millions did elsewhere, the Nixon administration focused its attention on the antiwar leadership as part of a strategy to undercut their political impact. FBI agents tapped phones and infiltrated the meetings of the VMC as well as the more left-wing New MOBE. In Chicago, RYM I / SDS / Weatherman prepared to protest the trials of those indicted back in March by the Justice Department for their roles in organizing the 1968 Democratic convention demonstrations. Weathermen planned to demonstrate their fury over the trial of the defendants known collectively as the Chicago 8, promising to "Bring the war home" to America's Second City. The eight defendants were indicted and charged with having crossed state lines with the intent to participate "in a riot" at the Chicago Democratic Convention a year earlier. A week before the national Moratorium on October 15, hundreds of Weatherman militants, including about twenty from Kent, launched a series of aggressive demonstrations that the Chicago press dubbed the "Days of Rage." Thousands of National Guardsmen and law enforcement personnel were mobilized to stop them.[27]

On Monday, October 6, prior to the three days of protest scheduled to begin on October 8, a Weatherman bomb destroyed a statue honoring policemen who had been killed in the Haymarket strike a century earlier. Immediately after the bombing, the president of the city's Police Sergeants Association stated, "We now feel that it is kill or be killed." With that incident and statement setting the tone, on the evening of the first day of protests hundreds of radicals smashed windows and fought police with makeshift 2 x 2 clubs in a wealthy section of Chicago that included the area where the judge presiding over the Chicago 8 trial resided. Jeff Powell, one of the participants in the fighting, later recounted the experience of police gunfire directed against the Weathermen. "I saw his [arm] come up, gun in hand," he wrote, "[and] knew he was going to fire." When he heard the shots crack behind him he yelled " 'Go, go!' " Running for his life, the former track team member slowed to let others in his group catch up. "We looked at each other" and said " 'Damn! Those fuckers were shooting.' " Police wounded six Weathermen with shotgun and small-arms fire that night, including one left for dead in the street. Friends took the partially paralyzed man, John Van Veenendaal, to the hospital for treatment.[28]

During one of the last "actions" of the three-day protest, Powell was beaten ferociously by several police officers. He was taken to the hospital emergency room by police, who told the staff there, "Look at this scum so we can lock him up. He's one of those tearing up the Loop." They then transported the bandaged Powell to a Chicago precinct station, the second time in fourteen months the activist found himself within one. He was taken downstairs to the station house basement alone, where he was threatened by the arresting patrolmen, who told him of their intention to "break [him] . . . into little pieces." Having every reason to expect the worst after three days of street fighting, Powell next heard the voice of an officer from outside the cellar room: "These cruds have to go to the lockup." Powell was relieved to be taken to the crowded booking desk, where he would face nothing more than an arrest. Upstairs he saw dozens of other Weathermen who were familiar to him. Approximately three hundred were taken into custody, including Howie Emmer, Matt Flanagan, Mark Lencl, and Corky Benedict. The shrunken SDS/Weatherman faction had predicted that thousands would rally for their protest in Chicago, but most radicals wisely boycotted that dangerous confrontation, aware that it was tactically desperate and doomed to fail.[29]

Days of mayhem added to the legal complications already facing Kent's Weathermen in Ohio. Powell was indicted for assault, and Emmer, Benedict, and former KSU English department member Bobbi Smith were all named as co-conspirators in the "Days of Rage" protest. At the end of that same month, the Kent 4 began their terms in the Portage County Jail. The local paper opined that the sentences were "stiff enough penalties to make them think twice about ever becoming involved . . . again." Mark Real offered some proof that such hopes were misplaced when he organized remaining SDS/Weatherman members to protest the jailing and sentences. Days later, a dozen or so protestors, including Mark Rudd, marched around the ROTC building. Putting up a brave front and trying to ignore jeers, one Weatherman said, "Don't be discouraged. Che and Fidel started with twelve people." In contrast to Rudd's earlier appearance at Kent State, no crowds turned out to see him; he was gone before most on the campus knew he was there. That same night, however, nearly seven hundred students assembled in a campus building to hear Dr. Benjamin Spock condemn what many believed were repressive trials in both Chicago and Kent. The large gathering for Spock's appearance confirmed once again that it mattered who delivered the antiwar message.[30]

Even with SDS banned from campus and most of its leadership jailed or on probation, the antiwar movement persisted. On October 29, the day Real and Rudd faced down hecklers, the pair promised that SDS/Weatherman would be in Washington, DC, for the second national Moratorium on November 15, "where the ruling class will be attacked." Elsewhere on campus that day, Mike Alewitz rallied the SMC against Dow Chemical's role in manufacturing napalm. Finally getting the message, this time Dow recruiters stayed away. *Stater* editorials had been right about protest at Kent: students had concluded that those complicit with the war had no business on the campus.[31]

The Washington Moratorium

Despite the breakup of SDS into competing factions, the political base of the antiwar movement had never been broader. Hundreds of thousands of peace protestors went to Washington, DC, for the largest antiwar demonstration to date. Those attending from northeast Ohio included left-wing teaching assistants Arif Kazmi, Roman Tymchyshyn, and Bobby Franklin, who had been active in Kent's Free University, as well as former SDSers Ken Hammond, George Hoffman, and Jane Boram, and former rubber worker and Akron University transfer student Rick Felber. Another onetime SDSer, Alan Canfora, made his way to the Moratorium march with a Barberton neighbor as well as his roommate Jim Riggs. The Friday night before the march they encountered RYM II members circulating flyers announcing an antiwar protest later that evening at the nearby South Vietnamese embassy, with a march to begin a few blocks away at DuPont Circle. The three were among thousands of protestors at DuPont Circle who were turned back from the embassy by blinding clouds of noxious tear gas unleashed by city police, which sickened as many as six hundred demonstrators. Flag-carrying militants in the crowd, including some Weathermen, responded by shattering windows, breaking windshields of police cars and motorcycles, and battling law enforcement personnel. The historian Jeremy Varon notes that "something of the fighting spirit that Weatherman had quickly come to symbolize surfaced within the crowd." The same combative attitude was on display the next day, when a still larger crowd of militants protested the Chicago 8 trials at the headquarters of the Justice Department.[32]

Among the protestors from throughout the East, Midwest and upper South were no less than six hundred from Kent State, as well as significant numbers of GIs and veterans. The mid-morning march attracted Americans from all walks of life and was led by drummers beating a funeral cadence for twelve coffins bearing the names of close to forty thousand Americans who had died in Vietnam. Unlike the mood the previous evening at the DuPont Circle protest, a sense of calm and fellowship prevailed, and the marchers encountered no tear gas there or at the subsequent rally on the grounds of the Washington Monument. New MOBE protest organizer Fred Halstead best captured the feel of the multitude: "more serious, . . . but not a generally angry tone. . . . [T]hey had not come in a violent mood. Indeed, if they had, . . . their numbers were such that the police could not have stopped them."[33]

Even so, some could not avoid hostility. During the march, not far from the White House (which was surrounded by a barrier of parked buses), a middle-aged man burst from a crowd of observers swinging a long pole, as thick as a baseball bat and bearing an American flag, at Canfora and other protesters. Canfora quickly subdued the man until peace marshals intervened. At the rally following the march, longtime pacifist and Chicago 8 defendant David Dellinger put both the Vietnam War and the previous evening's disorders in perspective: "The greatest question is whether we can stop the violence of the status quo, not stop violence at the demonstration." Most marchers agreed, but a small percentage, about five thousand militants, including Kent student Jim Riggs, broke away and raced to the Justice Department, several blocks away, to protest the trial against Dellinger and his fellow defendants. Police drove them back from the building with clouds of tear gas, and they responded with a cascade of rocks.[34]

Many marchers' initial feelings of exhilaration were deflated when President Nixon made clear that the protests would not affect his policies in Vietnam. Nixon declared that he held a lock on the loyalties of America's "silent majority," while Vice President Agnew referred to militants as something "rancid."

Left-leaning editors of the *Stater*, however, choose to emphasize the well-behaved dissenters. Although the paper carried news stories covering the disorders at the South Vietnamese embassy and the Justice Department, an editorial in the same issue, citing the orderly Moratorium march, noted: "Their protest was a peaceful one. Other incidents may have marred the quiet of the weekend, but the march itself showed that the people involved wanted to avert violence this time." A warning followed, however: "If they are ignored, . . . idealists will become more frustrated. It may seem to some that violence is the only way to accomplish anything. Mr. President, we don't want that to have to happen."[35]

A Winter of Deadly Repression and Hardened Resolve

After months of large-scale protests, a downturn in mass antiwar activity was virtually inevitable. The SMC and VMC had proved they could turn out collegians for mass protests, but unlike SDS, the Old Left SWP that exercised considerable influence in the SMC and the liberals who dominated the VMC failed to inculcate an organizing mentality in most antiwar students. After the heady actions of the fall, the SMC reentered their familiar cycle of conferences and demonstration planning, while the top-down VMC learned that its broad base of antiwar marchers "had not accepted the fact that ending the war would take a long time and a great deal of dirty work." Planned work by the VMC beyond the October and November protests faltered. The collapse and repression of SDS also played a role in the seeming quietude of the late fall. Those militants not in jail or otherwise constrained either waited for opportunities to resume collective action or found other ways to resist the war. Fires set at draft boards in Akron and three other northern Ohio cities supplied proof of that.[36]

On December 1, 1969, the Selective Service System conducted the first draft lottery at its headquarters in Washington, DC. Conceived by the Nixon administration and authorized by Congress—and watched by millions on national television—the lottery was ostensibly intended to make conscription more equitable by assigning every draft-age male an eligibility number based on a random selection of birth dates, represented as the numbers 1 through 366 inscribed on slips of paper enclosed in capsules and drawn from a glass jar. With the draft call for 1970 set at a quarter million, those with birth dates in the first 120 capsules selected could expect military induction within the next twelve months or when they left college; those with the next 80 numbers might or might not be drafted (although, as it turned out, numbers as high as 195 were called). But those with numbers above 200 could reasonably anticipate being left alone. Since the draft had long been a major target of the antiwar movement, the Nixon administration believed the lottery would undermine antiwar dissent by removing the element of self-interest for many young men. "This will take care of a lot of draft dodgers," he promised.[37]

Lorain, Ohio, native Allen Richardson had number 43 in the draft lottery, making him highly vulnerable upon leaving school, but a student who lived on the same floor in his dorm came up 364. Richardson later recalled that the student, safe in the knowledge that he was immune from the draft, "packed his bags and left school that night, though not before throwing himself a big party." The occurrence was not unique. Greg Hawthorne remembered that some of his friends who were working on the railroad while in school did likewise. Alan Canfora had a high number; his roommate Jim Riggs did not. Soon after, Riggs visited Toronto to look into the city's community of antidraft exiles. Coupled with Nixon continuing his predecessor's policy of Vietnamization—the replacement of American forces by South Vietnamese soldiers, which allowed the beginning of US troop withdrawal—the draft lottery gave a welcome reprieve to millions of lucky young men. KSU administrators puzzled over the unexpected enrollment decline in January 1970, but part of the reason may have been students forsaking college deferments they no longer needed. Those with low draft numbers, of course, had added reason for staying in school, as well as for opposing the war.[38]

If dissent could be absorbed, it could also be repressed. During the late 1960s federal and local authorities had become increasingly concerned about the spread of militant radicalism with the nation's black communities, especially where chapters of the Black Panther Party had taken root. On December 4, three days after the draft lottery, Chicago Black Panther leader Fred Hampton was killed in his bed by police in a raid on his apartment. African American students at Illinois State reacted by ransacking a campus building. The Reverend Ralph Abernathy, heir to Martin Luther King's Southern Christian Leadership Conference, compared the December 4 killing to the actions of "Nazi Germany." BUS leader Bob Pickett predicted that the violence would result "in the birth of 100 Hamptons across the nation." Radicals who regarded Hampton as a role model could not contain their fury. One Ohio pacifist, Donna Willmott, abandoned nonviolence and joined the Weathermen, who moved closer to the guerilla edge of left-wing politics. A leader of that faction, Cathy Wilkerson, identified Hampton's slaying as the "moment that the [Weather Underground] was born." Hearing the news in jail, Jeff Powell and his cellmates saw the murder as proof that "the U.S. was becoming a police state."[39]

By early 1970, many veterans of the antiwar movement were discouraged. Only a few months after the largest rally to date against the Vietnam War, leaders of some of the most prominent antiwar organizations were at a loss as to what to do next. One VMC leader, Ken Hurwitz, described the cause as "an all-but-forgotten movement," while another, Sam Brown, felt exhausted. The prevailing feeling was that "you just couldn't do any more," he recalled years later. SDS members doing time in Portage County Jail were also demoralized. Jane Boram, who had taken a position as a caseworker in Cleveland, found her imprisoned husband, Mike Gorup, to be quite depressed during her regular visits. Those serving longer sentences, like Powell and Flanagan, could not make their next move until their scheduled release date in late April. Until then, boredom ruled the small cell the two inmates shared, subsisting for months on bad food and weak tea. Along with Erickson, Emmer, Neiburger, and those serving shorter sentences, like Mark Lencl and Terry Robbins, they came to know other prisoners, some of them Vietnam veterans, many of them African American, and all of them poor. The experience served only to reinforce their certainty that they lived in a grossly unequal society that needed to be overthrown and replaced.[40]

The incarceration of the core SDS leadership did not, however, bring an end to student activism at Kent in the early 1970s. Since the KSU administration's successful outreach to the BUS following the November 1968 walkout, the group's leaders had mostly worked quietly with the university administration. The election of Erwind Blount as BUS president in January 1970 ended the cooperation. As editor of the organization's nationalist paper, the *Black Watch*, Blount had already signaled that his presidency would place BUS at odds with the administration. The first issue following Hampton's killing featured graphics from the Panther newspaper and named Chicago 8 defendant and party member Bobby Seale "Hero of the Month." Blount, who typified the growing number of working-class black students at Kent, promised a revolutionary new era for BUS and operated with Panther-style officers, including a position for defense institute chairman. Denouncing the fatal shootings of Hampton and his associate, Mark Clark, Blount sent representatives to Chicago to show solidarity with the besieged party.[41]

However disturbing the leadership change in BUS may have been for the university, President White might have been thankful that Blount had not been at the helm of the student organization a year earlier. Had his administration been confronted simultaneously by the twin militancy of BUS and SDS in the spring of 1969, certainly student protest would have been more difficult to contain. Although BUS leaders such as Larry Simpson and Bob Pickett criticized the administration's tactics against SDS and spoke against the war, they did not mobilize their members but remained committed to practicing the time-honored politics of negotiation.[42]

By the time African American militancy reasserted itself with Blount's election, SDS—the organization most likely to support such a posture—had already collapsed. The single-issue SMC, for all Alewitz's work, was simply too small and respectful of norms to offer the level of assistance SDS provided during the Oakland police crisis. Initially, Blount favored a nationalist approach and was wary of close cooperation with most radical whites. Still, as the year unfolded, Blount and BUS members, like Brother Fargo and future historian Darlene Clark (later Hine), realized that BUS shared some of the same concerns, as both black and white radicals worried about the fate of Bobby Seale and the rest of the Chicago 8.[43]

By simultaneously indicting Black Panther chieftain Bobby Seale and antiwar leaders, Nixon's Justice Department broadened dissident ranks and raised the level of resistance to the trial of the Chicago 8 defendants. Activists realized that guilty verdicts were almost inevitable. They planned "The Day After" rallies to protest what they saw as the legal railroading of the Chicago defendants, who were reduced to seven when Bobby Seale's case was severed from the rest. When mixed verdicts were rendered in February, family and friends of the defendants exchanged menacing threats with police outside the courtroom in Chicago's Federal Building. Demonstrations somehow remained peaceful in Chicago, but rallies elsewhere became unruly, resulting in injuries and hundreds of arrests. Less effectively, and as would become their practice, members of the Weather Underground firebombed the home of the presiding judge of yet another trial of political radicals, this one of the Black Panther 21 in New York.[44]

According to SDS historian Kirkpatrick Sale, "the hard core became harder" in the wake of the Hampton killing and the convictions of some of the Chicago defendants. Just prior to his release from Portage County Jail in late January or early February 1970, Terry Robbins led a jail strike in order to obtain badly needed medical attention for an elderly and acutely ill African American prisoner. If jail strikes can be counted as mass organizing, it proved to be Robbins's last such effort. Despite his role in the jail protest, he was released on schedule. Prior to leaving, he confided to one of his cellmates that he would head to his hometown of New York City. As part of his plea bargain he agreed to the same condition as all those who received forty-five-day sentences for their roles in the April 1969 Kent protests: "Defendant shall not be a member of . . . any organization that advocates unlawful violence or is involved in unlawful violence or any other unlawful activity or means to attain its purposes or objectives."[45]

Robbins soon headed for New York City and dropped from sight. But he had no intention of abiding by the court's mandate. Instead, he took up residence with several other members of the Weather Underground in Greenwich Village, where together they began plotting their next actions, aimed not only at ending the war but furthering the revolution they were certain was coming.

As WE have seen, during the previous year the leadership of the antiwar movement had been undermined by the collapse of the New Left, partly as a result of its own internal ideological disputes and partly as a result of governmental and institutional clampdown on student radicalism during the Nixon administration. The new draft lottery system reduced the number of young men who had a personal stake in the war. At the same time, Nixon had tried to shore up popular support by gradually withdrawing American troops and replacing them with South Vietnamese forces, and by appealing to the reflexive patriotism of the so-called "silent majority."

From one perspective, the Nixon strategy seemed to work. By early 1970 many antiwar activists were discouraged, uncertain about what further steps they might take to bring the hated war to an end. The nationwide moratoriums of the previous fall had been largest antiwar demonstrations in US history, but the promise to continue and build upon them had dissipated by the early months of the new year.

And yet, paradoxically, throughout 1969 the ranks of the antiwar movement had steadily grown. More and more Vietnam veterans were joining the movement, and the antiestablishment posture of the expanding youth counterculture had become increasingly politicized. Nixon's claims to represent the "silent majority" notwithstanding, polls showed that a clear and growing majority of Americans believed the war was "a mistake" and favored bringing it to an end. More telling still, antiwar sentiment ran particularly high within the working class, whose sons were doing the lion's share of fighting and dying in Vietnam, and whose opposition was thus more practical than ideological.[46]

How this would unfold, no one knew. But the ingredients for a confrontation between the forces of order and the forces of change were all there. All that was needed was a spark.

CHAPTER 11

Cambodia—A Match to the Last Straw

FOR ALL the mobilizing work done for the Vietnam Moratoriums, in 1970 the war went on unabated. A growing number of Americans were convinced that Richard Nixon had no "secret plan" for ending the war, as he implied during the 1968 campaign. In reality, he still believed that the war could be won—or if not won, fought to a stalemate that would allow the United States to avoid defeat. After the 1968 Tet Offensive, Hanoi had shifted its strategic attention to the area northwest of Saigon in an effort to put more pressure on the South Vietnamese government. Beginning in January 1969, US forces had countered with a secret bombing campaign against North Vietnamese Army (NVA) supply lines in eastern Cambodia (dubbed Operation Menu), and by developing a network of interlocking combat and fire support bases along the Vietnamese–Cambodian border with the aim of limiting NVA infiltration into South Vietnam. The raids caused heavy casualties but failed to destroy an elusive Vietnamese communist command center that the Cambodian head of state, Prince Sihanouk, had little choice but to tolerate. And the North Vietnamese still benefited from an arrangement with Sihanouk's government that allowed them to ship supplies through the Cambodian port of Sihanoukville. In the ten years since the prince spoke at Kent State, he had been increasingly preoccupied with maintaining his fragile control. On March 18, 1969, while Sihanouk was in Moscow, he was deposed by a military coup that placed Lon Nol in power.[1]

The coup gave the White House a new opportunity to take stronger action against enemy sanctuaries in the country's borderlands. Just after Sihanouk's ouster, Nixon scribbled a note on an official memo that read, "Let's get a plan to aid the new government. . . . Handle [it] like our air strike." Before the end of March, Nixon's presidential press secretary, in either a slip or a test of public opinion, told reporters (in words paraphrased by the *New York Times*) that "American troops . . . were permitted to cross the Cambodian border in response to enemy threats."[2]

On the home front, the president sought to mollify public dissatisfaction with the war by stepping up the policy of Vietnamization, the phased withdrawal of US forces and their replacement by South Vietnamese troops. In June 1969 he announced the withdrawal of the first contingent of 25,000 troops, coupled with a reduction in draft calls. Nevertheless, opposition to the war continued to grow, within the establishment—in Congress, in the mainstream media, among the nation's clergy—as well as in the streets. The spread of antiwar sentiment had infuriated Nixon and convinced him, as he confided to aides John Ehrlichman and H. R. Haldeman, that 1970 was likely to be "the worst year" of his presidency.[3]

Yet if Nixon was apprehensive about the road ahead, so, too, were the leaders of the antiwar movement, who seemed to have no clear plan for following up on the previous fall's Moratoriums. Scores of its organizers, along with countless thousands of marchers, felt a deep pessimism that their efforts had not done more to change Nixon's Vietnam policies. The demise of SDS, meanwhile, propelled what remained of the New Left on an increasingly revolutionary trajectory, as they became convinced that the end of the war required the overthrow of the established order itself.[4]

Few embodied this radical turn more than Terry Robbins, the longtime SDS organizer. After his release in late January from the Portage County Jail, he followed his plan of returning to his native New York City. There he connected with several Weathermen and began recruiting others to join him in the formation of a revolutionary cell. Like many others in the Weather Underground, now shrunk to about a hundred members, Cathy Wilkerson had been prepared since the police killing of Fred Hampton to meet "violence with violence, as the Vietnamese had been forced to do." After getting a call from Robbins in early February, Wilkerson caught a flight from Seattle to New York, where she joined Kathy Boudin, Ted Gold, and a woman identified simply as Martine as members of Robbins's new cell. They took up temporary residence at a Manhattan townhouse on West 11th Street owned by Wilkerson's father, who was vacationing out of the country at the time.[5]

On March 4, a decision was made by the secretive Weatherman leadership to transfer Martine and replace her with Diana Oughton, just arrived from Michigan. It was then that Robbins first informed the group of the target he had chosen, a dance at an officers club at Fort Dix, New Jersey, scheduled for Friday, March 6. Exploding an antipersonnel bomb at a military base, he believed, would drive home opposition to US policy in Vietnam and inflict punishment on those waging the war. Robbins decided they would use a dynamite-packed pipe bomb, despite his complete lack of experience with such devices. According to the only insider account ever written, Cathy Wilkerson's *Flying Close to the Sun,* considerable thought was given to the symbolism and little to the consequences. Robbins did require that they all adopt aliases, though, choosing for himself the nom de guerre of Adam.[6]

On Friday morning Robbins assembled the foot-long pipe bomb in the basement of the townhouse, where Wilkerson's father had a workbench. Next to him were several crates of dynamite, which he accidentally ignited, most likely by crossing some wires. The huge explosion reduced the elegant four-story structure to a pile of smoking rubble and killed Robbins, Oughton, and Gold. Wilkerson and Boudin miraculously made it out of the building alive; one of them, probably Wilkerson, was overheard asking, "Where's Adam?"[7]

Although virtually no one who read the *Newsweek* account of the townhouse blast knew what to make of the single reference to "Adam," Jeff Powell did. Along with his companions in the Portage County Jail, Powell got much of his news from magazines smuggled in by friends. Reading about the explosion, Powell knew the unidentified third fatality had to be Robbins. Eventually, he summoned up the will to tell cellmate Howie Emmer what the madness had yielded.[8]

Bill Ayers, who had a brotherlike radical partnership with Robbins, now reconnected with his own brother, Rick Ayers, as the Weathermen scrambled to make sense of what had happened. Although they grieved for their friends, as Rick's former wife, Melody, later recalled: "It had always been a question of who would die first. We didn't say it aloud, but we all understood quite well. If we hadn't killed ourselves, we would have killed others. Deep down, we knew that the townhouse saved us."[9]

Few militants dared to approach the dangerous edge where the Weathermen and the once peaceful Student Nonviolent Coordinating Committee (SNCC) now operated. Within days of the townhouse blast, two members of SNCC perished near Bel Air, Maryland, in an explosion that destroyed their automobile. SNCC blamed their deaths on government agents, while the FBI charged that the pair was planning to plant a time bomb at a courthouse where an SNCC leader was to face trial.[10]

Yet if few were ready to use bombs, tens of thousands of militants were willing to engage in direct and sometimes destructive confrontation with the forces of "law and order." The violent deaths of the Weatherman trio and the two members of SNCC followed in the wake of the burning of a Bank of America branch by a crowd of angry students in Isla Vista, California, in response to the Chicago 7 convictions. Such incidents of collective action, often spontaneous and almost always directed at property rather than people, came to characterize the popular upheaval of the era.[11]

Public officials responded to these disorders with a fury that more than matched their opponents' in rhetoric as well as action. Bank of America officials compared the rioters in Isla Vista—students from the nearby University of California at Santa Barbara—to Hitler's Brown Shirts, while California governor Ronald Reagan blamed the turmoil on "outside agitators." Speaking before an agribusiness group in early April 1970, he also outlined his solution to the trouble: "If it's to be a blood-bath, let it be now." Reagan stated publicly what many in the political establishment believed to be necessary. Using generally more muted terms, Richard Nixon did likewise. In his case, though, one of his aides kept a diary of the president's private fulminations. Just as Nixon's antipathy toward the left had been well established since the 1940s, his belief in the use of harsh methods extended beyond his ideological foes. The dialectic of radicalization and repression had intensified throughout the 1960s. By early 1970 further escalation of violence on both sides seemed inevitable.[12]

Ohio Labor Resurgent

By early 1970 the long-term impact of the Vietnam War was also stirring discontent within the ranks of labor. Although opinion surveys had long shown widespread opposition to the war within the working class, most labor leaders in the AFL-CIO had been outspoken in support of President Johnson's policies. In 1965, shortly after the first American combat troops arrived in Vietnam, AFL-CIO president George Meany declared that organized labor would support the war "no matter what the academic do-gooders and apostles of appeasement may say." Critics of the war, he claimed, were "victims of Communist propaganda."[13]

Although workers affiliated with the Socialist Workers Party and a few small labor groups opposed the war almost from the outset in places like Cleveland, the first major change in the position of organized labor occurred in November 1967 with the formation of the Labor Leadership Assembly for Peace. In June 1969 the United Auto Workers and the International Brotherhood of Teamsters formed the Alliance for Labor Action and called for an immediate end to the war. In part, that political shift reflected the impact of an overheated economy. Although the economy of the early 1960s boomed and defense spending created many jobs, as the Vietnam War escalated and dragged on the burdens imposed on working-class Americans began to outstrip the benefits. Not only were their sons doing most the fighting and dying in Southeast Asia, but rising taxes and a spike in inflation were "wiping out all gains made at the bargaining table."[14]

In the early spring of 1970, a series of strikes signaled an end to labor's tacit support for the status quo. Shortly after midnight on March 18, US postal workers in Manhattan went on strike after Congress voted itself a 41 percent pay increase at a time when some postal employees earned so little they qualified for welfare. The unprecedented wildcat strike, one widely supported on the left, quickly spread to Akron, Cleveland, and a hundred other cities across the country, involving 200,000 postal workers. In response President Nixon took the extraordinary step of mobilizing the National Guard to deliver the stalled mail. A few days later the air traffic controllers' union staged a nationwide "sick out" that disrupted air travel for over two weeks.[15]

Then, on April 1, the day their national contract expired, the rank and file Teamsters launched their own wildcat strike to protest the meager pay raise the union's leadership had accepted. Teamsters president Frank Fitzsimmons, filling in for the imprisoned James Hoffa, quickly ordered drivers to return to the job. But many in Ohio refused. Confrontations ensued with the union hierarchy as well as the police, as some members used their guns to enforce solidarity in their ranks and prevent anyone else from driving their rigs.[16]

Though usually quick to deploy the state's National Guard to quell prison riots, urban unrest, or campus disturbances, Ohio's Republican governor, James Rhodes, hesitated this time, for reasons that remain unclear. Barred by the state constitution from a third consecutive term, Rhodes was running for a US Senate seat that year and was anticipating a tough battle in the primary; he may have been worried about alienating members of a powerful union that, despite its recent decision to oppose the Vietnam War, historically had been friendlier to the GOP than most. He may also have recalled the political price his party had paid when it took on Ohio labor in the 1958 battle over the Republican-sponsored right-to-work bill. Whatever the reason, Rhodes let the volatile strike go into its fourth week before mobilizing the state's militia.[17]

That spring Bill Whitaker, late of the Kent SDS, had a night job as a warehouse worker—and Teamsters member—to support his family and to pay for his education at Akron University's law school. Despite his educational pedigree and long hair, he had eventually gained acceptance from other Yellow Freight warehousemen in the traditional working-class way—by standing up to the foremen who ruled their workday lives. On April 29, Whitaker rose early to meet fellow strikers at an Akron-area bar, the Clearview Inn; from there they intended to block truck shipments moving out of a nearby Consolidated Freight terminal. The action was planned in defiance of a proclamation issued by Governor Rhodes accusing the strikers of organizing "unlawful assemblies" composed of "roving bodies of men acting with intent to . . . do violence to persons or property." The decree ordered the Guard "to take action necessary to the restoration of order."[18]

Whitaker remembered that the Clearview Inn was "jammed—wall-to-wall Teamsters." Though unaware that a detachment of the 145th Infantry was already rolling toward them on Cleveland-Massillon Road, the strikers were angry over the governor's decision to call out the Guard. When a television broad-caster erroneously reported that a National Guard helicopter had been shot down during a student demonstration at Ohio State University, "the Teamsters cheered in unison," Whitaker recalled. "Some, who knew that I had been an SDS activist at Kent State, said, 'My God, maybe we can learn some things from you guys.'"[19]

Yet as the Teamsters left the bar and prepared to march en masse toward the Consolidated Freight terminal, they got no farther than the parking lot before the guardsmen arrived, jumped out of their trucks, and surrounded the strikers with fixed bayonets. "No one moved," Whitaker remembered. "There was a lot of yelling and screaming at the Guard. Some of the Teamsters had rocks in their hands. We were livid that they were serving as the storm troopers for management."[20]

Having hemmed in the strikers, the guardsmen allowed truck traffic to move out of the terminal without any interference. Among the armed troops stand-ing watch were Ed Grant, Richard Love, and Richard Lutey, all members of Company C of the 145th. The trio to some extent typified the social class of many northeast Ohio guardsmen: almost entirely white; more likely small-town or suburban than urban in background; neither of the industrial working class nor solidly middle class; perhaps some higher education, but probably not a four-year degree. Grant, a native of Canton, operated a cleaning business and spent his free time hunting. Love, twenty-four, who grew up in the Cleveland suburb of Mayfield Heights, had two years of college at Akron University and worked as an account clerk. Lutey, a rifle team leader in the Guard, lived in the small community of Mogadore in Portage County. Twenty-six years old, he had joined the guard in January 1965 before the Vietnam buildup and worked for the Postal Service. Within days of being ordered to the Clearview, C Company, commanded by Captain James Ronald Snyder, who was also a detective in the Portage County sheriff's office, would be dispatched to Kent State University.[21]

Just miles down the Cleveland-Massillon Road from where Teamsters faced down guardsmen, tire builders at Akron's Goodyear plants had walked off the job demanding higher pay as well. If the work stoppage at Goodyear failed to win their demands, United Rubber Workers leaders threatened to take out five thousand more unionists and shut down Akron's B. F. Goodrich operation. On May Day, thousands of construction tradesmen in northeast Ohio also put down their tools in a demand for higher wages. As antiwar activity was be-ing renewed on many Ohio campuses, strikers like Teamster Leo Cullum and United Rubber Workers member John Felber knew to expect that their sons would be joining the protests. Concerned enough about their families' eroding living standards to join strikes on the job, these workers supported their activist sons even while worrying about other sons still serving in Vietnam. Workers such as Cullum and Felber strongly identified with their unions and the urban blue-collar working-class and had instilled such values in their offspring. Their own strikes were defensive battles aimed at securing more take-home pay from industrialists trying to slow wage growth, but were also influenced by the militancy of the Vietnam era, as workers faced the beginning of the end of what had been a long period of postwar wage increases.[22]

April Protests

On April 14, antiwar students at Kent State gathered in the rain for a protest march organized by Mike Alewitz, chair of the Student Mobilization Committee (SMC), who hoped the march would demonstrate the spread of antiwar sentiment on campus. A few days earlier, on April 10, a rally organized by veteran activists Vince Modugno and George Hoffman, which featured a rock band and the recently convicted Chicago 7 defendant Jerry Rubin, drew two thousand students. The sizable gathering provided more evidence for the accuracy of an SMC straw poll showing that Kent students favored immediate withdrawal from Vietnam by a seven-to-one margin. The *Daily Kent Stater* corroborated this sense of the campus mood, noting that " 'supporters' of the war . . . have diminished to a fraction of their former strength." In the end, perhaps because of the weather, perhaps owing to the failure to develop a broader coalition to support the SMC protest, the turnout for the April 14 march was disappointingly small, about two hundred.[23]

Still, there were clear signs, for those who cared to look closely, that the ranks of the antiwar movement at Kent were in fact growing. The day after the Kent march, Alan Canfora, and his roommates, along with two of Canfora's Barberton, Ohio, friends—Frank Zadell, recently returned from Vietnam, and George Caldwell—headed to Cleveland for yet another antiwar protest. A recently discharged marine himself, Caldwell carried with him his grief; he had just learned that his younger brother Bill had been killed near the Cambodian border—one of more than five hundred Americans killed in action since March 1. It was Caldwell's first public protest of the war.[24]

This group of a dozen or so students and veterans joined with other campus activists for a mass protest at the site of AT&T's annual stockholders' meeting. Organized by the Socialist Workers Party (SWP) and the radically minded New Mobilization Committee, the rally had targeted AT&T because of its involvement in military defense work, and a crowd of thousands showed up. Although SWP leaders and SMC marshals, including Kent's Mike Alewitz, tried to maintain order, the protest soon devolved into what one local underground paper called "by far the most militant and . . . large-scale demonstration Cleveland has seen," featuring "spontaneous, vital, and militant actions by large numbers of freaks." When protestors tore down a large AT&T welcome sign and tossed it onto the Convention Center's entrance ramp, police swarmed in to disperse the crowd. Six people from Kent State were arrested, including Jerry Persky and KSU science instructor Bobby Franklin. Alewitz, who was trying to calm the situation, recalled being "clubbed by the cops" anyway.[25]

In seeking to avoid a confrontation with the police, Alewitz was acting in accordance with YSA/SWP policy. Yet even most of those who reveled in the growing militancy of the antiwar movement recognized that such direct-action tactics came at a price. Fighting with mounted police may have "turned on" lots of kids, an underground journalist observed, but "unfortunately . . . it turned off a lot of older people." Unfortunate or not, increasing numbers of antiwar activists had already come to the conclusion that the trade-off was worth it, that only heightened struggle could stop the war, and that regardless of the personal costs involved, the movement need to be prepared "to take a lot more risks." As the historian Thomas Powers observed a few years later, "The violence in Vietnam seemed to elicit a similar air of violence in the United States, an appetite for extremes: people felt that history was accelerating, time was running out, great issues were reaching a point of final decision."[26]

In early April, before the SMC-sponsored march and before the confrontation at the AT&T convention in Cleveland, a dozen KSU undergraduates living in Tri-Towers, a dorm complex well known for its countercultural free spirits, began planning their own demonstration against the war. Though the Tri-Towers residents had not played much of a part in the campus political scene, in many respects they typified those who would be in the ranks of protestors in the events that were to come. Robby Stamps, a Cleveland-area student who was an occasional supporter of Alewitz's SMC and had a flair for the dramatic, described the composition of the plotters: "black, white, girl, boy, eastern seaboard liberal and home-grown Cleveland working-class radical. . . . Still, we were a brigade of nonconformists, and no one flashed an SDS card or the Chairman's [i.e., Mao's] little red book." Their effort represented at least the third attempt by campus activists to awaken the university community to the horrors of napalm.[27]

In mid-April, Stamps decided to publicize the group's intentions in his Social Problems class, announcing that at noon on Tuesday, April 22, in front of the Student Union, "a group of concerned students will napalm a dog to demonstrate scientifically the effects of this incendiary on a living organism." Members of the class gasped or denounced Stamps, and the professor later admonished him. Reports of the announcement spread around the campus, assisted by leaflets about the napalming circulated by the activists themselves. When the appointed day arrived, Stamps, Steve Buck, Bill Arthrell (a native of nearby Oberlin), and the others who had participated in the plan found that hundreds of students—including members of the golf team armed with their irons—had gathered to stop them. So had Portage County prosecutor Ron Kane, the campus police, and representatives of the ASPCA. The provocateurs failed to produce the dog they had threatened to immolate, but Arthrell did address the crowd. "Napalm is a . . . jelly that once ignited may reach 2,000 degrees centigrade," he said. "The flaming gel . . . adheres quite well to human or animal flesh." He then quoted Dow Chemical's stated motivation for manu-facturing napalm: "good, simple citizenship"[28]

Surveying the crowd, Arthrell asked how many were prepared to stop them. Most indicated they would. He then disclosed their true purpose: to make the point that students were more exercised about cruelty to animals than to people. Contending that "halfway around the world, napalm falls daily," he urged the crowd, whose threats had changed to cheers, to hear the "screams" of the Viet-namese. Arthrell thanked the now united crowd for their support and ended with the hope that "We [will] . . . see you at other rallies on the campus."[29]

Black Power on Campus

The spring of 1970 also brought an end to the entente that had existed between Black United Students and the administration since the Oakland police crisis. Throughout much of 1969, BUS welcomed the administration's willingness to expand African American enrollment, which rose, according to one esti-mate, to 660 by spring quarter. This was, however, only a 10 percent increase from approximately 600 in the fall of 1968 and still represented just 3.3 percent of the 20,000 students attending school on the main campus. BUS had also pressed President White to provide support for academically challenged stu-dents from inner-city Cleveland and Akron, to increase, however modestly, the number of black faculty, and to establish the Institute for African American Affairs, founded in 1969. An increase in African American enrollments brought to schools such as Kent and Ohio State students who had seen urban rioting in their neighborhoods and who increasingly identified with the Black Power movement.[30]

The election of twenty-year-old Erwind Blount to the presidency of BUS in January 1970 signaled the ascendancy of this new cohort of black students, and a return to the militancy that had characterized the organization during the Oakland police sit-in and the de facto alliance with SDS. As we have seen, Blount was from the poor Glenville section of Cleveland, the same area where, in July 1968, a shoot-out between police and militants left seven dead and fourteen wounded. Along with other officers, such as fellow Clevelander E. Timothy Moore (BUS's Minister of Culture), Akronite Byron Jones (Minister of Defense), and Columbus native Curtis Pittman (Minister of Education),

Blount promised "a new era for BUS." Collectively, they all embraced the Black Nationalist perspective that had already been articulated by Brother Fargo, who sometime after 1971 adopted the Muslim name Ibrahim al-Khafiz.[31]

As the new BUS set out on a more militant path in the spring of 1970, Kent's black students tested the university administration with a series of demands nearly as challenging as those presented by SDS during its abortive spring offensive. Erwind Blount made it known through the organization's newspaper, *The Black Watch,* that BUS expected the administration to address a list of racial grievances: the underrepresentation and inadequate financial support of African Americans at KSU, the paucity of black faculty, and the lack of sufficient space for the Black Cultural Center. Later, he added a demand for disarming the university police.[32]

BUS's demands came at a time when the campus was already preoccupied by a raging controversy over the number of African American athletes on the university's basketball team. The team of fifteen had only three black players, none of them starters, and their lack of playing time became an issue. So, too, did the insistence of the basketball coach that the three players trim their mustaches and Afro hairstyles, which black students saw as a racist effort to regulate their appearance. Tensions rose after BUS's Bob Pickett and a student sportswriter exchanged opposing points of view in the *Daily Kent Stater* in January 1970. The situation then became red-hot when the sportswriter, Richard Zitrin, complained about some black KSU students cheering for the highly ranked Florida State team during an unexpectedly close home game in early February. Zitrin's critique appeared under a provocative headline, likely crafted by an editor but based loosely on Zitrin's own words: "Blacks Are 'Sickening' in KSU Loss."[33]

Amid the acrimony, BUS's negotiations with the university over the issues of black student and faculty representation rapidly deteriorated, with Blount insisting on a commitment by the administration to enroll five thousand black students and demanding White's resignation. In response, White issued a public letter to Blount expressing sympathy for the reforms being demanded but explaining that change would be gradual, through the use of "established channels." He called on BUS to exercise "wise and responsible leadership . . . during these turbulent days." BUS leaders shot back with a condemnation of both the administration's 1969 "policies of repression" and more recent threats allegedly made against them in private. Questioning White's good will, they asked, "Does the university see open warfare and mass repression as the only answer?"[34]

BUS wanted to show that they meant business. When Roger Cloud, a candidate in the upcoming Republican gubernatorial primary, arrived on campus looking for votes, he was met by a group of twenty African American students standing in silent formation. Led by Blount and Brother Fargo, they wore black berets, black jackets, and dark slacks, and carried black liberation flags in the trademark style of the Black Panthers. After spoiling Cloud's arrival, they broke into a fiery, cadenced chant and marched away. The confrontation occurred at a time when similar demands for more black faculty, students, and programs had been made at Ohio State University. After six antiwar activists were arrested on April 21 for trespassing at a military recruitment session on the Ohio State campus, demands for equal representation for blacks and dismissal of the charges against the antiwar protestors merged and resulted in a unified Ad-Hoc Committee for Student Rights. On April 24 the Ohio State group issued a call for a boycott of classes to begin four days later. Aided, to a greater or lesser extent, by their white student allies, the demonstrations in April 1970 at Ohio State and Kent State epitomized the struggle of black students for a greater say in how their communities would be served by the state's university system. On a wider level, the protests were part of demands for grassroots racial change that accelerated after the King assassination and had earlier rocked campuses from San Francisco State to Cornell University.[35]

When the Kent 4 SDS leaders were released from the Portage County Jail on Wednesday, April 29, they were given an assessment of Kent's political situation. Jeff Powell, Ric Erickson, and the others learned from Steve Drucker, who had been a peripheral member of SDS, that the campus was quiet and would likely remain so. Yet Powell noticed at once that a "lot more people [were] wearing longer hair and hip clothes. It seemed . . . that there had been vast changes in six months." Drucker's friend Jeff Miller—a recent transfer student from Michigan State—was one of many who seemed to embody the change. Miller handed Powell his first marijuana joint in six months and said, "Welcome back."[36]

Kent's momentary calm following the large rallies and smaller marches proved deceptive. Events happening elsewhere would transform the campus and, for the first time in ten years, reconnect Cambodia and the university. A still developing story ran alongside the April 30 *Record-Courier* article announcing the release of Powell, Erickson, Emmer, and Neiburger: "Nixon Talks on Cambodia Tonight," while the banner headline read "Battle Resumed at Ohio State—7 Wounded in War Protest." Nixon had hoped to weaken the antiwar movement with troop withdrawals and the draft lottery. Instead, his Cambodian decision produced something else altogether.

The Last Straw

If some in the antiwar movement were pessimistic after the seeming letdown following the massive protests in the fall, President Nixon was clearly frustrated as well in the spring of 1970, but his frustration owed more to the failure of his various efforts to bring the war to an acceptable conclusion. The replacement of Sihanouk with Lon Nol had not had any noticeable impact on communist military operations along the Cambodian border northwest of Saigon, while the continuing saturation bombing of the Cambodian countryside had, if anything, only made things worse, driving displaced peasants into the ranks of the Khmer Rouge and NVA regulars deeper into the country's interior. Negotiations with Hanoi (secret as well as public) were stalled, and his various gambits aimed at undermining the antiwar movement, including instituting the draft lottery and attempting to isolate and repress the most radical factions, were having little measurable effect; in fact, the ranks of the self-styled revolutionary left and cultural opposition were steadily growing.[37]

Nixon's anger over the Senate's rejection of two of his Supreme Court nominees may have played a role in his foreign policy decisions; as national security adviser Henry Kissinger later implied, no amount of documentation "could reveal . . . the accumulated impact of accident, intangibles [and] fears" motivating the president to send ground forces into Cambodia. Yet there was also a strategic logic to Nixon's thinking about Cambodia, even if that logic rested on faulty assumptions, such as a belief in the existence of a fixed and attackable NVA/NLF "Pentagon"—COSVN—just beyond the Cambodian border and the false hope that the war could still in some way be "won" through bold, aggressive decision making. In Nixon's judgment, the situation in Cambodia offered an opportunity to assert what he believed was his uncontested authority and to elevate his presidency with a "great decision." In a televised address on April 30, the president insisted that his order sending tens of thousands of American and South Vietnamese troops into the country did not represent "an invasion of Cambodia," but rather a grand move that would bring the war to a close. Cloaking himself in the prestige of his predecessors, Nixon reminded his audience that his decision to enter Cambodia was made and was being broadcast from the same Oval Office where "Woodrow Wilson made the great decisions which led to victory in World War I; Franklin Roosevelt made the decisions which led to our victory in World War II; Dwight D. Eisenhower made the decisions which ended the war in Korea."[38]

In retrospect, the White House announcement should not have come as much of a surprise. Throughout the month of April newspapers had carried articles about US operations near the Cambodian border. Still, the news shocked people like George Hoffman, who huddled with his roommates in front of a television in their rented Elm Street house. Like countless others who tuned in on the evening of April 30, Hoffman felt a rising anger: "We had just had enough. After all the anti-war speeches, all the days spent at literature tables, all the demonstrations and now the war was getting bigger." For him, the announced movement of US forces into Cambodia "was the last straw." On his second night of freedom, Jeff Powell sat in a friend's apartment in Kent feeling much the same. They all "watched in horror," Powell recalled. "We could hear someone shouting at the TV next door. I felt like someone had jammed my fingers into an electric socket." Trying to listen in a packed television lounge in the Tri-Towers dorm complex, Larry Raines heard shouting, too. He had to repeatedly hush his dorm mates' loud jeering in order to hear Nixon's speech.[39]

All over Kent, anger spread. Some did not wait for morning light to answer the president. A former KCEWV leader went down to Water Street and spray-painted "US out of Cambodia" on a fence next to a popular bar. Chased away by the owner, she found other unguarded targets. The next day her work, and that of others, could be seen all over town and on campus. Not satisfied with the covert artistry, four antiwar graduate students got together to plan a public protest against the Cambodian invasion. One member of the group, Steve Sharoff, was an easily recognized figure, while Tom Dubis, Jim Geary, and Chris Plant were lesser known. Wickedly dubbing themselves the World Historians Opposed to Racism and Exploitation (WHORE), they issued a leaflet urging students to meet at the Victory Bell on the central Commons at noon on May 1 to bury the US Constitution in symbolic protest of President Nixon's usurpation of congressional authority to declare war. Three hundred students showed up for the event. Chris Plant, who had suggested the name for the ad hoc group, began by expressing his sympathy for the Cambodian people, and then buried a copy of the Constitution that he had torn from a history survey text. Geary—a highly decorated Vietnam veteran—then burned his discharge papers, as did veteran Tim Butz. Before breaking ranks, the aspiring historians allowed another future historian—former SDSer Ken Hammond—to ask the remaining protestors to reassemble on Monday to resume the protest.[40]

BUS held a second rally hours later. They managed to bring out Mike Brock, Tim Butz, Bob Pickett, and three hundred other students, matching the number who joined the first gathering on the Commons. Through the efforts of BUS president Blount and Rudy Perry, the rally was the largest racially mixed demonstration since the Oakland police sit-in. The protest was in support of the BUS demands and in solidarity with African American and antiwar students striking at Ohio State.[41]

There were those at one or both rallies who wanted to do more than attend passive protests. They approached the most militant-minded dissidents present at the noon and three o'clock rallies, saying cryptically, "downtown tonight"—an indication that the outrage over Cambodia would be renewed in the streets of Kent. Before dark, Hoffman and Modugno saw Ric Erickson, fresh out of jail, on a street in Kent's small downtown. The two had not forgiven Erickson for his role in the breakup of the SDS chapter, but they knew that nighttime disturbances were likely and that the Kent 4 would probably be held responsible. Because they did not want to see Erickson blamed and returned to jail, they gave him the same stern warning being delivered elsewhere to Powell, Neiburger, and Emmer: *You need to get out of here.* The former SDS leaders, more accustomed to giving advice than taking it, departed Kent grateful for the words of caution.[42]

That evening, crowds gathered outside the North Water Street bars, where beer and music were available, but the political radicals who lingered on Water Street that night paid little attention to either. George Hoffman recalled that "all these people were there and they were pissed off [about Cambodia]." Soon, he said, the chaos "mushroomed": "No organization, just people on their own, moving." Roman Tymchyshyn was a graduate assistant who had been part of Kent's cultural and political scene since the late 1950s. He saw and heard "people spilling into the street" and shouting "1–2–3–4, We don't want your fucking war.'" As the chants filled the air, others painted antiwar slogans on the outside walls of the bars. Members of an area motorcycle gang, the Chosen Few, began to ride their big bikes in the street. The roar of engines contributed to the mounting excitement.[43]

Emboldened by the lack of police presence, some in the crowd dragged rubbish from an adjacent alley into the center of the street and set the debris on fire. John Hartzler, who had been at Woodstock and the Washington Moratorium, saw that the boisterous scene would prevent him from being able to drive his car down Water Street to deliver pizzas. He told his boss that he had delivered his last pizza of the evening and joined the crowd of onlookers. Mike Brock watched from a barstool inside Orville's, where he worked as a bouncer. He saw police cars arrive at the scene and become targets of bottles thrown by the gathering crowd. Other cruisers got the same reception. Later in the evening, an elderly motorist determined to drive through the unruly crowd bumped or nearly hit a person. What really happened is still unclear, though the effect was not: it further riled the growing ranks of protestors.[44]

Around midnight, the most daring members of the crowd dashed south on Water Street, smashing the windowpanes of banks and loan companies along with the windows of a corner hardware store—the latter hardly a symbol of capitalism. Kent's small police force arrived and, aided by deputy sheriffs and a few members of the Highway Patrol, began firing tear gas haphazardly and closing and emptying the bars. That decision was one of a number of critical miscalculations made by authorities. Instead of confronting several hundred protestors, undermanned police now faced thousands of bewildered and inebriated people who had been treating the evening as an ordinary Friday night in Kent. Liberal use of tear gas compounded the problem. It seeped into fraternity houses as authorities drove crowds of students and nonstudents away from downtown and toward the nearby campus. Officers using indiscriminate methods had confronted activists employing equally arbitrary tactics. The end result was that a small, improvised disorder became a mob. The home-front battle over the Cambodian invasion had arrived.[45]

The conflict first erupted on North Water Street near where it crosses Main Street—the figurative and literal intersection of Kent's political and cultural radicalism. The activists involved were mostly students or former students, such as coal-county native Dave Dyer. A political science graduate, Dyer had gone on to study law at Akron University. On May 1—May Day to some protestors, Law Day to Mayor LeRoy Satrom—Dyer was focused more on the war than on his future profession. Forced from downtown to campus that night, Dyer threw rocks at police for the first and only time in his life. Large numbers of cultural radicals, such as former Firestone worker Rick Felber, had enrolled at Kent more for the draft deferment than the degree. He and his roommate, James Harrington, made Water Street something of a second home. Another of his roommates, Jerry Rupe, worked in one of the town's countercultural leather shops while also plying the pot trade. Still others were frequent visitors who came to Water Street from towns as much as thirty miles away.[46]

With one exception, the fourteen people arrested by the police that evening were not campus activists; most were not antiwar or counterculture radicals but just weekend revelers, many of them young people simply caught up in the events. Even Mike Weekley, the sole possible exception, had no activist background. He was arrested in a maladroit attempt to break windows in the campus ROTC building. The crowd terrified and frustrated Kent's decision makers. Filling in for an absent President White, Robert Matson remembered being "completely in the dark as to what caused this thing." The city's police chief, Roy Thompson, also expressed mystification over the trouble, but blamed the turmoil on "agitators" and "subversive groups." An annoyed campus policeman focused on those who eluded the authorities: "You hardly ever grab the hard core." Thompson and others failed to realize the extent to which the "hard core" had broadened.[47]

Unfounded rumors that Weathermen were poised to take over Kent caused the city's new mayor, conservative Democrat LeRoy Satrom, to ask Governor Rhodes to be ready to divert guardsmen to Kent from the deescalating Teamster strike. His more liberal predecessor, John Carson, could not believe what the mayor was contemplating. "I about dropped my teeth," Carson said some years later. "The last thing in the world you would've done is call the Guard. Satrom was a conservative reactionary who didn't know what was going on." With wild reports about out-of-town radicals circulating, the president of the United States fuming about student "bums," and Rhodes looking for an issue to boost his lagging candidacy in the approaching US Senate primary, Satrom announced an 8 p.m. curfew and closed the city's bars, and also set a 1 a.m. curfew on the Kent State campus.[48]

In military terms, the clash in downtown Kent on Friday evening was a bloodless engagement. It was launched opportunistically, when the absence of authority provided an unexpected outlet for antiwar fury. In contrast, the encounter the following evening came precisely where activists expected it would: on the Kent State campus. If there had been any doubt that activists would regroup on campus, the curfew announced by the mayor paradoxically served to concentrate most antiwar radicals in that location—and keep them there. Morning and afternoon passed without incident, but not without tension. Sometime around dusk, purposeful young people began gathering on the Commons near the adjacent ROTC quarters, which, like some of Kent's other buildings, was a former World War II wooden army barracks.[49]

Those seeking to understand the cohort that assembled on the Kent State Commons that night might consider the observations of historians Maurice Isserman and Michael Kazin: "While the war galvanized protestors, it also bred frustration and extremism in their ranks. Vietnam was a particularly volatile issue around which to build a mass movement. . . . [T]he movement would either force the government to end the war, or it would fail."[50]

"Why is ROTC still standing?"

There is no way to divine what, if any, long-term political expectations the militant demonstrators had as they gathered near the ROTC building. Their immediate goals are much easier to determine. Those who attended WHORE's Friday rally encountered a sign asking what many thought was a pertinent question: "Why is ROTC still standing?" Scores went to campus that evening intent on attacking the structure and all that it represented: hatred of Nixon and his expanded war, university complicity and the training of Kent State students to fight in Vietnam and now possibly Cambodia, the military draft, earlier campaigns that failed to remove the institution from campus, and the residual anger at the administration's tactics against SDS.[51]

Some protest veterans came equipped with disguises to better conceal any illegal activity they might commit. The cover of night, along with hats, hoods, sunglasses, and bandanas, hid the identities of the most prepared activists. Although surely ignorant of what Kent's Black & Decker strikers had done to photographers in 1936, and certainly unaware of the same preventive measures used by disorderly Kent State students in May 1962, militants knew that people had gone to jail the year before because of photographic evidence against SDS. There would be no more of that. Photographers on the periphery of the University Commons received blunt warnings from protestors: take pictures at your physical peril. Judging from the scarcity and poor quality of photos taken that evening, most got the message.[52]

When they arrived on the Commons, protestors could see a handful of KSU policemen near the ROTC building, including the SDS's old nemesis, campus police detective Tom Kelly. Not wanting to be recognized, most activists kept several hundred feet away from the building and gathered near the center of the Commons and the Victory Bell. Sensing their inadequate numbers, Rick Felber stood on the bell's brick encasement and called for a march to the dorms, where reinforcements could possibly be found. Hundreds of high-spirited activists and some adolescent risk-takers departed the Commons chanting and whooping; hundreds of additional students left their dorms and joined the throng. After looping around many of the campus residence halls, marchers circled back to the Commons. A few spray-painted antiwar slogans, lit trash can fires, and set off firecrackers. Dozens more collected rocks. Jerry Lewis from the sociology department recognized George Hoffman and Vince Modugno in the crowd and pleaded with them to stop the march. They could do nothing, however, and told Lewis, "We're just following, nobody's organizing this."[53]

As a crowd of as many as fifteen hundred people headed back to the Commons, the advance element made its way towards a rise known as Blanket Hill or Taylor Hill. The apex of the hill featured a newly installed project placed by architectural students, an umbrella-shaped "pagoda" made of concrete and wood that guided pedestrians across the grassy rise and through a passage way between two buildings, Taylor Hall (which housed the university's architecture school) and a dormitory. From the top of the knoll, the ROTC building immediately came into view; as soon as the protestors saw it their voices reached a crescendo, and they charged down the hill, causing what few police stood guard next to the building to retreat. The activist vanguard, astonished that they once again faced no opposition, began stoning the aging one-story structure. KSU's director of safety, needing to justify the lack of police protection around the building, later overstated the strength of the antiwar opposition: "They came at us so swiftly and with such discipline that we could never take the initiative away from them."[54]

That the protestors came on swiftly is not in doubt. The degree of discipline is another matter. More than half the crowd was either new to protest or had participated in only one campus antiwar gathering. Ohio Highway Patrol and FBI investigators later identified hundreds of those present, and relatively few numbered among the radical cohort at the movement's core. A professor described the crowd as being clothed in "fatigue jackets" and "dressed in 'hippie-type' clothing—i.e. bell bottom trousers, vests, head bands etc." Almost all were white; eyewitnesses identified a mere handful of African Americans and described only one man as being of Hispanic origin. A few were high school students and former KSU students.[55]

The size of the crowd testified to the spreading ranks of dissenters and the confluence of political and countercultural radicalism. As many as fifty people attacked the ROTC building, throwing stones that broke many windows on the south and east sides of the building. A few road flares hurled at the structure rolled harmlessly off the roof, while a Molotov cocktail bounced off and exploded on the ground. Several of the most combative participants grabbed a fifty-gallon metal drum and tried to break down the entrance on the east side. The door would not go down. Jerry Rupe wrapped a small flag around a stick and ignited it. Sensing a photo opportunity, and heedless of the large crowd, Nick Haskakis—the conservative resident of nearby Johnson Hall who had protested against BUS during the Oakland police sit-in—snapped Rupe's picture. Instantly, militants surrounded the heavily-built Haskakis and demanded his film. An argument ensued. Another man of nearly equal size settled it quickly by tackling Haskakis to the ground, at which point others began trying to wrestle away the camera. Faculty marshal Glenn Frank, the only authority available, and activist Ruth Gibson pleaded with the attackers to stop. But someone eventually pried the Kodak Instamatic away from Haskakis's grasp. Once the film was exposed, the camera was returned to its owner, who retreated to his dormitory.[56]

A Pyramid of Fire

Many in the crowd believed that their window of opportunity had closed with the failed arson attempt and retreated in anticipation of a police counterattack. When it did not come, a small group advanced to the ROTC building for a second and then a third time in an effort to set it on fire. The most productive attempt came when somebody dipped handkerchiefs into the gas tank of a motorcycle parked next to the building. Lighting the gas-soaked cloth, the individual reached through a broken window and set some curtains on fire. According to one report, a particularly impetuous youngster—possibly a high school student from Canton visiting his brother at Kent that weekend—may have entered the structure to fan the flames, or set additional fires.[57]

Not all were exhilarated by what they saw. Some students considered attacking the militants, but were persuaded by friends to abandon such a risky course. Realizing that the situation called for law enforcement, a professor sprinted to the nearby campus police station to summon officers. But no words from him could motivate the uninterested desk sergeant to act, and he left in frustration. Another faculty marshal felt much the same, telling FBI agents a week later that a police presence would have prevented the burning.[58]

City firemen dispatched to the scene found they lacked police protection. Fire Department logs show a rapid response, as firefighters began unpacking their hoses about nine o'clock. Almost at once they found themselves contending with demonstrators, dozens of whom, including Tom Miller, Doug Cormack, Rick Felber, and Ron Weissenberger, either admitted to dragging hoses away from the firefighters or were believed to have done so. A few radicals who carried knives went to work cutting fire hoses, and the firemen were ordered to withdraw within a half hour of their arrival. Despite the destruction of some fire hoses, the flames seemed to smother. Once more the blaze was reset and again fire trucks arrived at different intervals to extinguish the flames—this time with police protection. Using tear gas, officers skillfully drove the militants back across the darkened Commons.[59]

Fearing that they might be trapped between advancing police and a chain-link fence that bordered the edge of the Commons, militants tore down the barrier. The overexcited crowd then set fire to a small archery shed filled with straw-backed targets. The flames shot upward, threatening to engulf nearby trees and illuminating the previously darkened Commons. After hours of disorderly protest, the crowd now seemed directionless. Authorities feared for the security of the president's house in the near distance. White himself was away at an educational conference in Iowa, but his wife was at home, and campus police ensured they had sufficient numbers of personnel stationed around the house, giving it more protection than they had provided to the ROTC building.[60]

A handful of feverish militants bypassed White's residence altogether and zigzagged to East Main Street, the principal thoroughfare bordering the front of campus. There they began the rampage anew. With few targets on the street, damage proved as inconsequential as it was inexplicable: a glass telephone booth, road signs, and occasional four-legged construction horses were trashed. It did not last long. Rebellious demonstrators suddenly heard, and then saw, a caravan of trucks, jeeps, and armored personnel carriers thundering into Kent from the east. The vehicles carried heavily armed soldiers from Troop G, 107th Armored Cavalry, advance units of the Ohio National Guard who had just finished facing off against striking Teamsters. As had occurred the previous evening, the presence of uniformed authorities quickly dispersed the unruly crowd, breaking students into small groups. Some hurled rocks at the Guard as their vehicles motored through town. Twenty-six-year-old guardsman James E. Pierce, a veteran of Cleveland's 1966 deadly Hough uprising, likened the stoning to "a horizontal hail storm." At least a few guardsmen suffered injuries from rocks and broken glass. Troop G would not forget the battering.[61]

Guard units left their transports and deployed in formation, forcing the scattered ranks of protestors to withdraw from Main Street up the first series of hills on campus. There the troops inflicted a number of injuries with tear gas, rifle butts, and bayonets. Now facing south, the retreating protestors and guardsmen were startled by the sight of the flame-filled sky. Unbeknownst to the protestors, the ROTC building housed between one hundred and two hundred weapons, mostly M-1 rifles but also some of the more lethal M-14s. More important, thousands of rounds of ammunition were stored there. However the fire restarted—whether from poorly extinguished hot embers setting off the ammunition or the work of an arsonist—the wooden structure became a pyramid of fire. For the first time during what would be three nights and one day of encounters, guardsmen surrounded the perimeter of ROTC—now a soaring inferno—and faced thousands of students massed across the Commons. The grounds of Kent State had become a battleground of the expanded Southeast Asian war, and the Commons the most contested terrain on campus. On May 4, it would be once more.[62]

CHAPTER 12

"Right here, get set, point, fire!"

STUDENTS WATCHED the ROTC fire on the night of May 2 with a range of emotions. Many were intoxicated with excitement, including novices who had little involvement in the years of patient and often frustrating organizing against the war. Most of the male-dominated crowd faced the ever-present threat of the military draft, and whatever their degree of familiarity with the campus protest culture and irrespective of gender, many knew of the continuing carnage in Vietnam that had by now included more than 50,000 US soldiers—including some 2,500 Ohioans—killed in action, and hundreds of thousands of Vietnamese casualties. Activists with experience in the antiwar movement expected a strong response to the blaze. Mike Brock—whose brown leather jacket was adorned with a stenciled white panther—understood the dialectic of radicalization and repression: "The more [tear] gas, the more cops, the higher the energy level got."[1]

In their final confrontation late Saturday night, the National Guard used tear gas and bayonets to drive throngs of protestors from the hill overlooking the Commons. Lacking a natural rallying point and with little defense from the gas, the students fled toward the dorms. Some turned to throw rocks at their pursuers, who were led by Major General Sylvester Del Corso. Fifty-seven years old and short in stature, Del Corso had served in the Guard since 1928. Highly decorated, he won the Bronze and Silver Star for action in the Pacific during World War II. He favored a "shoot to maim" policy for looters and believed that "militant, Communist-inspired revolutionaries" were behind the Kent protest. Del Corso could not contain himself during the hot pursuit across campus. He began hurling rocks at the fleeing students and encouraged his men to do the same: "Throw 'em back at those bastards," he urged.[2]

Most students had little trouble outpacing the guardsmen in their retreat. Some lingered just outside the glass-enclosed entryway to the Tri-Towers dorm complex, watching the chaos. A few tried to talk with the soldiers, but Del Corso would have none of it. He was determined to get the students inside the dormitories by any means necessary, and ordered his troops to advance: "Through the glass!" Seeing that the move would pin students between bayonets and the dorm's glass foyer, a deputy sheriff screamed for the troops to stop, sandwiching himself between guardsmen and students. Somehow his intercession worked, as did his pleas to the students to get inside. The overzealous guardsmen even brought members of the press into danger. Reporters at the scene—apparently mistaken for protesters—had .45 caliber handguns put to their heads while they frantically searched for their credentials. Only when Del Corso vouched for the newsmen did the troops holster their weapons. Students who had watched the ROTC fire at a distance, and who managed to keep well ahead of the guardsmen, knew little of these frightening encounters. Those few who experienced the Guard up close recognized that a very dangerous situation existed on campus.[3]

After the Fire

Daybreak brought welcome relief. On Sunday morning most students felt comfortable venturing out, curious to glimpse the ruins of the ROTC building. News of the fire brought former SDSers Jane Boram and Paul Bukosky from Cleveland. They were among the hundreds of people who came from all over northeast Ohio to observe the still-smoking remains, clogging the highways into the city. Many people on campus that day described a cheerful scene that was remarkably at odds with the previous night's events: families picnicked, children played, and a large crowd of curious students fraternized with guardsmen. Others experienced the soldiers' continued antagonism and abuse. One student was called names and poked with a baton by a Guard officer for wearing an army surplus jacket—not unusual garb on college campuses at the time.[4]

If calm generally prevailed at the university, a different mood could be found only blocks away at the city fire station. Governor James A. Rhodes arrived in Kent on Sunday morning for a meeting with Ohio National Guard officers and university administrators filling in for Robert I. White. Always an adroit campaigner, Rhodes saw political opportunity in the tumult at Kent State. As we've seen, Rhodes was seeking the Republican nomination for a US Senate seat. Pre-election polls showed him at a decided disadvantage against his opponent, Robert Taft, a popular congressman with a venerated family name. Only the day before, at a Republican debate in Cleveland, Rhodes and Taft had clashed over the question of who was tougher on protestors. Rhodes could have returned to Columbus after the debate and used the unrest at Ohio State as a photo opportunity, but his proximity to Kent—only thirty-five miles away from Cleveland—made it a short helicopter trip. The ROTC fire provided him with a perfect opportunity to demonstrate his law-and-order stance.[5]

Speaking in a firm tone, Rhodes made it plain to all those present, including KSU board of trustees president Robert C. Dix, that he and the Guard were in charge. He brushed aside the wishes of the Portage County prosecutor, Ronald Kane, who wanted to temporarily close the campus to cool passions. Rhodes vowed to keep the campus open "at all costs." When the press entered, opportunity knocked, and he launched into an inflammatory performance for the scribes and cameras, declaring, "We are going to ask for an injunction . . . equivalent to a state of emergency," and adding, "We're trying to work on it right now."[6]

> The city of Kent is facing is probably the most vicious form of campus-oriented violence yet perpetrated by dissident groups and their allies in the state of Ohio. . . . We have these same groups going from one campus to the other, and they use the universities . . . as a sanctuary. . . . They're the worst type of people that we harbor in America. It's over with in Ohio. I think that we're up against the strongest, well-trained, militant revolutionary group that has ever assembled in America. . . . We are going to eradicate the problem, we're not going to treat the symptoms.[7]

Rhodes's mention of radical "groups going from one campus to the other" echoed the emphasis on "outside agitators" favored by California governor Ronald Reagan, and, more recently, President Nixon. His reference to college campuses being no sanctuary appropriated Nixon's rationale for invading Cambodia, which had frequently been described as an off-limits sanctuary for communist forces in Vietnam. Rhodes's promise to "eradicate the problem" of disorderly dissent merged with Del Corso's careless talk about whether the Guard could resort to firepower. The general, sitting by the governor's side, stated, "We don't want to get into that [the possibility of shooting], but the law says we can if necessary." Rhodes likened students involved in the ROTC burning to Nazi "Brownshirts," directly appropriating the language of Bank of America officials condemning the arson of their Isla Vista branch in California months earlier. Finally, like KSU security director Chester Williams, whose police force initially failed to protect the firemen battling the ROTC fire, Rhodes overstated the strength of the radicals he so despised and exaggerated other facts as well.[8]

Rhodes's incendiary remarks frightened some activists. His threatening tone even convinced a few to leave Kent. Although Vince Modugno and George Hoffman had done nothing deserving of arrest, they, along with Vince's wife (former KCEWV member Carolyn Carson), Ruth Gibson, and former high school SDSer Larry Finn, sought refuge in Linda Bresnahan's apartment in the nearby city of Hudson.[9]

Other activists were among those returning to campus. Mike Alewitz had been in Columbus for a Student Mobilization Committee meeting and came back wondering how he might salvage orderly protest from nights of disorder. Bill Whitaker and Ken Hammond returned to the area after visiting Jim Powrie in Buffalo. With the Teamster strike nearly over, Whitaker had to prepare to go back to work, as well as for Monday's law school classes. Ken and Marilyn Hammond thought of ways in which the spirit of Friday's protest on the Commons might be recaptured, while also contemplating how to spread the national student strike unfolding in New Haven, Connecticut. Such comings and goings were hardly unusual; the university deserved its reputation as a suitcase school. Thousands of students left campus every Friday and returned every Sunday, and May 3 was no exception. This time, however, returning students found the campus occupied by troops. All had heard news of the disorders, ROTC fire, and Guard deployment, but the sight of helmeted, well-armed military troops patrolling the campus was still shocking.[10]

Robert White also returned to Kent that Sunday and briefly encountered Rhodes at the university's small airport, as the governor was preparing to fly back to Columbus. White had spent his entire presidency trying to run the university without interference from the state capital. Rhodes offered his views of the campus radicals to White, but in all likelihood the president did not know the full extent of the tough language spoken by the governor until he learned of it from subordinates.[11]

Nearly two dozen faculty members convened on Sunday and drafted a statement of "Concerned Faculty," which condemned the military occupation of the Kent campus by armed troops, calling it "an appalling sight." They urged authorities to view the students' protests and the burning of the ROTC building within "the larger context of the daily burning of buildings and people by our government in Vietnam, Laos, and now, Cambodia." John Hubbell, Sidney Jackson, and other key initiators of the faculty statement tried to win an audience with White in the hope that he might reassure the university community, but White simply reaffirmed that power had passed to Governor Rhodes. He left communicating with students to vice president Robert Matson.[12]

Matson and student body president Frank Frisina issued a flyer Sunday afternoon detailing how the governor's state of emergency affected the campus. Based on their discussions with Major Harry Jones of the National Guard, they informed the college community that the governor's edict banned all rallies and gave the National Guard the power to make arrests. Major Jones had interpreted the governor's remarks to mean that all campus rallies had been banned, which was untrue—the edict had yet to be signed by Rhodes or made legally explicit. Jones's misunderstanding meant that the National Guard would be prepared to break up all subsequent protests.[13]

Hate in Their Faces

As darkness descended, Sunday evening looked to be a continuation of the previous nights. Yet the mood, the composition of the crowd, and the tactics employed differed significantly from Friday's trashing and Saturday's arson. The issue had shifted: the majority of the students who gathered on the Commons were more concerned with the occupation of their campus than with Cambodia. The Guard presence rallied more students to protest, and the troops' actions would contribute to their radicalization.[14]

Those who gathered on the Commons to protest the Guard presence were initially left undisturbed. Then, at 8:45 p.m., Major Jones—a thin, chain-smoking veteran who had joined the Guard in 1954—decided that the 1 a.m. campus curfew imposed on Saturday morning by Mayor Satrom needed to be moved up four hours, to 9 p.m. Jones ordered the crowd to disperse. Throughout the weekend, such dictates proved to be counterproductive and provocative, and this one was no exception. The crowd marched off toward the president's house, a quarter mile to the northeast, where, near Main Street, they met and were tear-gassed by the 145th Infantry. The students quickly retreated back to the Commons and split into two groups. The smaller segment now headed north to the intersection of Main and Lincoln, where the campus bordered the town, and sat down in classic civil disobedience style in the middle of the street. Like the faculty, the student demonstrators also wanted to see President White, mistakenly believing that he could somehow rid the campus of the National Guard. So they waited calmly for an audience with him, or perhaps with the mayor, who would never come.[15]

Guardsmen quickly flanked the demonstrators blocking the intersection. Most, including freshman Dean Kahler, who grew upon a farm near Canton, were novice protestors. The few exceptions, such as Bill Arthrell (spokesman for the napalm education rally) and 3-C supporters and activists Joe Cullum and Mike Alewitz, had little authority with those occupying the street, most of whom simply wanted the National Guard removed. Their inexperience was reflected in the grab bag of impromptu demands that they put forward, including calls not only for the prompt removal of the Guard but also for the elimination of ROTC on campus, an end to the curfew, amnesty for the ROTC arsonists, acceptance of the BUS demands, and an end to tuition increases.[16]

The standoff ended swiftly when Captain James R. Snyder's company of the 145th Infantry began firing a powdery crowd control agent at the seated protestors. The students, still expecting to hear from either White or Mayor Satrom, felt double-crossed. But they faced further peril. Snyder, a middle-aged Portage County detective nicknamed "Captain Gas" because of his extensive training in the use of noxious agents, halted the chemical barrage and ordered his troops to disperse the students with bayonets. Most, but not all, got away. Reports vary, but between three and seven students were stabbed or slashed. A male student who had been bayoneted in the street made it to a nearby fraternity house that faced Main Street, where he collapsed from blood loss. A military veteran who had previously moved back to the same fraternity house's porch applied pressure to the wound. Angered by what he had seen, the vet next approached a guardsman on the street and asked sarcastically, "Did you find the murderer?" The guardsman replied, "I'd just as soon shoot you as look at you, so get the hell out [of here]." A female student recalled that her small group had their retreat blocked by the wall of the university library, but despite close proximity to the guardsmen felt no apprehension. "Then," she said, "I saw their faces. There was hate [in them]." Still pinned between the library wall and troops advancing with bayonets fixed, yelling, "Get back, get back!," panic began to set in. "Before I knew it, they were on us," she later testified. The student received a puncture wound to her lower abdomen and another to her right leg, while others were struck by rifle butts.[17]

Captain Snyder later described the incident to the FBI, saying that a Specialist 4 in C Company (likely twenty-three-year-old former farm boy Larry Werny) was "required to use his bayonet [on] at least three occasions." Snyder referred to the Browning Automatic Rifle (BAR) man in the unit, who stabbed the female student mentioned earlier (Clevelander Helen Opasker) who became pinned next to Rockwell Hall in her attempt to escape the Guard. Authors of the minority report on campus violence would later use the word "terrorism" in describing the attitude of the students toward the troops' behavior on Sunday evening.[18]

Off campus, individuals who had nothing to do with the disorders were not exempt from Guard transgressions. A sergeant in Troop G of the 107th Armored Cavalry struck an older disabled veteran while the man was in his car, and in a separate incident a company officer in the same outfit jabbed another man through an open car window following a heated argument with the vehicle's driver. In spite of the injuries suffered by these passing motorists and passengers, most of the ugly exchanges occurred between guardsmen and students. An undergraduate seeking to return a library book had a nightstick put to his nose and then cracked against his behind as he tried to obey a guardsman's order to

"Get the hell out of here." Around midnight, guardsmen pitched "two missiles" through the windows of Johnson Hall, a dormitory bordering the Commons. Another resident in the same dorm said that a guardsman pointed weapons at his window, and "rifle butts were swung at students who did not immediately respond to . . . orders to enter Johnson Hall."[19]

BUS leaders warned African American undergraduates to stay away from the soldiers and urged them to avoid the rallies that weekend. Their decision was undoubtedly influenced by experience; some had previously encountered the Guard during disturbances in Cleveland and Akron. According to BUS member Curtis Pittman, black students "felt that if there had been any kind of trouble, that most likely we would be the first ones targeted." Wearing a white armband that identified him as a peace marshal, former BUS president and Humphrey campaign worker Bob Pickett was crossing the campus when he was accosted by several guardsmen. "You better get out of here, nigger," said one, putting a pistol to Pickett's temple. "If you don't turn around and run," said another, "I will put the butt of this gun up your ass." Maintaining eye contact, Pickett slowly backed away with his arms in the air.[20]

By the end of the evening helicopters equipped with searchlights circled the city at rooftop levels. The illumination and the deafening roar of the rotors made the campus and town feel like a war zone, setting both students and local residents on edge. Rob Fox, a student senator at the time, remembered Sunday night as "the night of the helicopters": "It was very frightening. . . . [T]hese helicopters with their searchlights, I felt like I was in Vietnam. . . . Buzzing the Tri-Towers, shouting at us from [their] speakers." The helicopters also stood out in Mary Homer's memory. Homer, who was only ten years old at the time, recalled, "I remember the helicopter searchlights going over our house time and again those frightening nights."[21]

Some city residents, like Richard Foote, took to arming themselves out of apparent fear of protesting students. A lifelong resident who was awarded the Silver Star for gallantry on Okinawa during World War II, he stood guard for several nights at the town's Ohio Edison building with his own twelve-gauge shotgun, loaded with buckshot. Most, however, looked to the Guard for protection. Sergeant Grant of the 145th received plenty of support from neighborhood residents. "Kill those S.O.B.'s if they cause any more trouble," advised some of the enraged citizens. By the time the long night was over, some guardsmen who were previously skeptical of such talk were counted among converts to a get-tough policy. One guardsman said that the students who attacked them "that night were like animals." Still others in Grant's C Company promised that the students were "not going to get away with it." As many nursed bruises, one vowed, "They got us good tonight, but that's the end of it."[22]

Who Were the National Guard?

As daylight spread across the campus on the morning of Monday, May 4, slightly over a hundred of the approximately twelve hundred guardsmen called to duty at Kent State were deployed in the area of the burned ROTC building. According to the only account written by guardsmen, the troops were young men in or barely out of their teens, although the archival record reveals an older subset. Data is available for the members of Troop G, 107th Armored Cavalry, and Company A, 145th Infantry, along with a few men of the 145th's Company C; it shows that most were residents of northeastern Ohio suburbs, small towns, or, in the case of the infantry company, rural areas. Those at the center of conflict on May 4 at Kent State were experienced guardsmen.[23]

In civilian life, those who were not full-time guardsmen or serving in law enforcement had a variety of backgrounds. A number were small businessmen or entrepreneurs: a salesman, several contractors, a life insurance salesman, owners of a linoleum business or a cleaning business. Others who were not self-employed held supervisory positions: an office manager, a manager for Montgomery Ward, the manager of a vending operation, a production supervisor, a construction superintendent, and a material control handler. One was an inspector at the Ravenna Arsenal; another worked for Hagan's Sewer Services, most likely as a plumber. There was one US Postal Service employee. Two or three were self-employed truck drivers, and at least one was a Teamsters member who had faced down both students and his fellow workers. Several worked in automotive shops. At least four or five, and probably more, either attended or graduated from college. One, who worked as a labor relations specialist, had an MBA from Miami of Ohio.[24]

Company A, 145th Infantry, the more culturally homogenous of the two companies, included men with backgrounds similar to those, but—as befits the rural Wayne County area—also contained a number of farmers, an agricultural research specialist, and a saddle builder. No more than four or five of the fifty-member company had ethnic names (including one born in Germany in 1944), with most being of English, German, or Scottish ancestry. Wayne County is predominantly Christian; today, it includes a large number of evangelical denominations, accounting, by one estimate, for as many as half of all worshippers. The Mennonite church as well as several other Anabaptist sects are also represented, as are the mainline Protestant denominations, and Catholics make up about 7 percent of churchgoers. According to the US census, in 1970 the county was a little over 98 percent white. The county reliably votes Republican.[25]

After thirty hours in Kent, some guardsmen thought that students perceived them as "Nazi Storm Troopers," while one Guard officer in his thirties or forties spoke of the students as "hippies and longhairs." Another believed that antiwar protestors were "working for the other side [the communist Vietnamese]." A trooper in the 145th Infantry said that student behavior the second night of his deployment resembled "an attack by wild animals." Not all in his command felt that way, and a number expressed tolerance for or sympathy with the students. Those who had some of the most disturbing encounters with demonstrators at Kent, a somewhat older cohort of guardsmen, found themselves part of the advance against the students on May 4.[26]

Commanders Major General Del Corso and Brigadier General Robert Canterbury already had long military careers, as did Colonel Charles Fassinger and Major Harry Jones, a Tennessee native. Myron Pryor of the 107th grew up in small Ohio communities, including Pomeroy and Mogadore. Pryor joined the Guard at the age of thirty-four and rose to the rank of sergeant.[27]

Texas-born Lieutenant Howard Fallon and Specialist 4 Leon Smith served as policemen in Akron and Beach City, Ohio, respectively. Sergeant Bruce Bragg and Richard Parker belonged to the Wooster police force. Twenty-four-year-old Specialist 4 William E. Perkins, from rural Atwater, had already seen duty at Kent State as a Portage County sheriff's deputy during the SDS disturbances in 1969; Captain Snyder was a detective in the same department. Rodney Biddle's father served as an instructor at a private police academy, from which the younger Biddle would later graduate.[28]

Company A's commander, Captain John Martin—who owned a soybean operation outside Wooster, Ohio—had been drafted in 1955 and served in the 82nd Airborne before enlisting in the Guard ten years later. Of the more than forty guardsmen on whom some information was available, all but a handful were veterans of the disturbances in Hough, Akron, or Youngstown in July 1969. Robert James was among those deployed in Hough and Akron. James W. Farriss and Ronnie Myers, both Specialist 4s, had seen riot duty in Akron during the summer of 1968, and Private First Class Richard Shade had been deployed in Cleveland's Hough section in 1966. These men, and Private First Class Phil Raber, were all farmers in Wayne County.[29]

The mean age of the guardsmen deployed against protestors on Taylor Hill on May 4, and for whom dates of birth were available, was twenty-seven years, five months. Enlisted men were mostly in their mid-twenties; the youngest was nineteen and the oldest thirty-two. The mean age of eight officers, including General Canterbury and Major Jones, was thirty-five. Some of the youngest enlisted men, such as Tennessee-born Billy John Long, probably joined the Guard to avoid Vietnam. Most who enlisted in the Guard after the summer of 1965, such as Lloyd W. Thomas Jr. and Joseph Dale Sholl, who were among a small number of guardsmen with college degrees, were also likely searching for alternatives to Vietnam. Others, such as Roger A. Maas and Russell E. Repp, may have signed up to supplement pay from their day jobs, as their enlistment dates were well before the escalation of the war. Still others—such as Lonnie Hinton, Richard Love, and twenty-nine-year-old Larry Mowrer, had poor vision that might have otherwise kept them out of the service. These guardsmen could see reasonably well with glasses, but could not wear them under gas masks.[30]

One thing that all of these men had in common was an acute lack of sleep during the long week of April 27 through May 4. Aside from thirty-two-year-old Captain James R. Snyder, most did not have the luxury of an hour at home. At the end of April, guardsmen stood with bayonets at the ready as they faced down Teamsters on the Cleveland-Massillon Road. Others watched the overpasses on the extensive network of interstate highways that crisscrosses northeast Ohio, keeping the bridges free of rock-throwing unionists. Some patrolled truck stops to halt the activities of wildcat truckers who were intimidating nonstriking drivers to pull their rigs off the road.[31]

Duty at Kent brought no respite for these exhausted guardsmen. On the morning of May 4, Sergeant Grant's outfit of Company C did not turn in until after 3 a.m., and had been asleep no more than an hour when officers woke them to align their tents. Company A of the 145th did not go into bivouac until 9 a.m. Troop G, 107th Armored Cavalry, slept no more than four hours before replacing A Company that Monday morning.[32]

While an examination of the subset of guardsmen strongly suggests cultural estrangement from the students they were opposing, these differences alone do not account for the outcome of the looming confrontation, as presidential and gubernatorial rhetoric, the stress of battling militant truckers, and the effects of days with little sleep all contributed to the strain. Still, in 1970, with the population divided along so many lines—class, race, partisanship, ideology, urban/ rural tensions, and generational counterculture—Rick Perlstein, one authority on the long Sixties era, was not far of the mark in describing the guardsmen at Kent as having a "put-upon sense of resentment," an attitude that students did very little to rectify.[33]

Morning on the Campus

The weekend of disorderly protest against the Cambodian invasion began spontaneously on Friday when history graduate students buried a copy of the Constitution and asked students to reassemble three days later at noon. That impulse had not diminished by Monday. The cordon of guardsmen surrounding the charred remnants of the ROTC building further heightened the tension on campus. If anything, the weekend's dramatic events only fueled students' awareness of and participation in the rally. Carol Mirman, a senior, had heard about the rally through the student grapevine and decided to attend. She had plenty of company, for the continuing military presence on campus and the profusion of violent incidents over the weekend had convinced many previously uninvolved students to attend the Monday rally. Professors devoted their sessions to discussions about the military occupation in Kent and the violence in Southeast Asia. In some classes, undergraduates stood to broadcast news about a scheduled rally on the Commons, or simply wrote such announcements on blackboards. We've seen that a year earlier, when the 3-C group had called a protest on the Commons to register dissatisfaction with university policy toward SDS, editors of the *Daily Kent Stater* had published a special edition calling on students to avoid the rally. That decision had been extremely controversial, so now, rather than publish another special Monday edition, the paper opted to keep to its regular Tuesday through Friday schedule.[34]

A few organizers met in a hastily arranged session the morning of May 4 to determine what should be done. Mike Alewitz, Ken Hammond, and twenty other activists explored the options. Ultimately, they decided against trying to stop the rally that had been announced three days earlier; perhaps, like the *Stater* editors, they realized that trying to do so was futile.[35]

The authorities were also gearing up for the protest. On Sunday, Governor Rhodes told his senior officers that the Ohio National Guard "should use whatever force necessary to break up a protest on the campus." When somebody asked for a definition of a protest, the governor replied, "Two students walking together." On Monday morning, General Canterbury, President White, Mayor Satrom, and others met at the city's fire station to discuss the governor's orders and the day's rally. Canterbury would later claim that the group decided collectively that the rally "would not be permitted," a claim that White disputed.[36]

Noon on the Commons

It was a bright, largely cloudless day. Students began gathering on the Commons when early classes let out at 10:45. The crowd swelled dramatically an hour later, when the next classes let out at 11:50. By noon thousands of people—students, professors, three hundred active protestors, and curious onlookers—had filled the natural amphitheater. The Commons was the crossroads of the campus, and some were merely passing through on their way to class or lunch. Most, however, had gathered to join the protest or to observe the formation of one hundred guardsmen mobilized to stop them.[37]

At first the assemblage seemed relaxed, if pensive. En route to the Commons, Alan Canfora found himself challenged by a guardsman: "Hey, boy, what's that you're carrying there?" A day earlier, another guardsman had poked him in the chest with a riot baton inside a car in which Canfora was a passenger, so he was not eager to renew any dispute. "Just a couple of flags," he answered. "We're going to make you eat those flags today," the guardsman promised; Canfora shouted back, "Just don't get too close, motherfucker, or I'm going to stick them down your throat."[38]

Those on the Commons eager to decry the Guard and the war clustered near the Victory Bell at the base of Taylor Hill (also known as Blanket Hill), a prominent knoll named for nearby Taylor Hall, a multicolumned building housing the architecture and journalism programs, which dominated the heights. Many gathered around Canfora and his black flags, on one of which he had painted a single word: "Kent." He gave the other flag to his roommate Jim Riggs, who had come to campus with a circle of friends, including Canfora's sister, Roseann (also known as Chic), Frank Zadell, Tom Miller, Marcella Schromen, and John Hartzler.[39]

Approaching the Commons from a class in Bowman Hall, a distance of less than three-tenths of a mile, I remember experiencing a deep feeling of apprehension. From the slight crest in front of my old dorm that overlooks the low-lying Commons, I could see the crowd of students to my right and front. Hearing their antiwar chants and seeing black flags waving in the breeze, I drew closer. When I reached the crowd assembled around the college's Victory Bell, I discovered that the flags were being borne aloft by two of my roommates. Anxiety began to leave me, for the presence of friends and the size of the crowd provided a sense of safety in numbers.

The soldiers aligned in a long skirmish line on the northwest side of the Commons, facing the students one hundred yards away. They began finalizing plans for an advance in the event that the reading of an order to disperse failed to end the growing rally. William Perkins—the Portage County deputy sheriff—got some last-minute instructions from Sergeant Pryor: "Use only as much force as is necessary to defend yourself. When it comes to hand to hand combat, fight force with force." Many of the infantrymen had already covered the breast-pocket area of their uniforms, where their names appeared, to conceal their identity.[40]

Most guardsmen carried .30 caliber ammunition in eight-round magazines. In an apparent mistake, an unknown number of armor-piercing rounds were distributed to those carrying M-1 rifles. NCOs and field officers received .45 caliber shells for their sidearms. Two sergeants, Leon Smith and twenty-five-year-old Matthew McManus, were equipped with twelve-gauge Winchester and Remington shotguns, respectively. Contrary to regulations, some guardsmen brought weapons from home. Proud of what he called his "Dixieland" roots, Major Jones wanted something besides a two-and-a-half-foot riot baton and gladly accepted a .22 caliber Beretta pistol with a distinctive pearl handle, loaned to him by Captain Snyder. Lieutenant Alexander Stevenson carried his own AR-18, a lightweight but heavy-caliber rifle, fitted with a bayonet, the same one he had used to stick a motorist in the left bicep the night before. Together with Snyder, Stevenson had been trained in chemical and biological warfare. As impressive as the guardsmen's armaments were, most students—like President White—seemed unaware that the troops had been issued live ammunition.[41]

Finding Out about Law and Order

Ken Hammond, having realized earlier that the rally could not be stopped, tried instead to give it direction. He stood on the casement of the Victory Bell and, thinking of the rally already under way at Yale that was calling for a national student strike, he bellowed, "Is it the feeling of this group that there should be a strike on this campus?" Jeff Miller, Allison Krause, her companion Barry Levine, and hundreds of other students began to chant, "STRIKE! STRIKE! STRIKE!"[42]

Photos in the 1971 *Chestnut Burr*, the KSU yearbook, show me near a number of my roommates, chanting and with my right fist raised in defiance.

Hammond got no further in his speech before a jeep motored out from the line of guardsmen. General Canterbury, acting on the decision that no rally would be allowed on the campus and eager to confront the protestors, gave the order to disperse the students. He instructed Sergeant Harold Rice of the campus police to order the protestors to leave the area. Rice used a bullhorn to relay the message: "For your own safety, go to your homes and dorms." Rice meant well, and his tone was more plea than command. But the students would have none of it. They felt they *were* at home and that it was the Guard that needed to get off their campus. "Fuck you! Fuck you!" they screamed. "Pigs off campus! Pigs off campus!" shouted longtime activists such as former KCEWV member Rick Lieber and onetime BUS leader Brother Fargo, along with younger rebels like Mike Brock. Someone threw a rock at the jeep, and it bounced off the vehicle. When it became clear that Rice's pleas were futile, Major Jones ran out to the jeep and ordered it to return to the Guard picket line, hitching a ride for the short return trip.[43]

Now it was minutes before the advance. Administrators had already removed themselves from the scene; White and his top officials headed off campus to a popular dining spot for a luncheon meeting. Professors were the only possible mediators left. One, possibly from the psychology department, sensed the enormity of what was about to take place and pleaded with Canterbury to call off the advance. The general, dressed in a dark civilian business suit, brushed him off: "These students are going to have to find out what law and order is all about."[44]

With that, and as if by script, Captain Snyder ordered the grenadiers, including twenty-five-year-old Sergeant Barry Morris, to load canisters into their M-79 launchers and fire when ready. With hundreds of other troops nearby, Canterbury ordered the hundred or so guardsmen to move out against the protesting students. The general knew that although the guardsmen were heavily outnumbered, the students were entirely outgunned. The first canisters began exploding just past noon.[45]

Soon the air was thick with the haze of tear gas. Across a distance of several hundred feet, the soldiers soon lost their ability to distinguish between the thousands of onlookers and three hundred active protestors. Although a soft wind reduced the effectiveness of the gas, most students still scattered. A few, like Canfora, defiantly waved one of the two black flags. Others, like Michael Erwin, who came equipped with his own gas mask, picked up the canisters and hurled them back at the advancing troops. One slow-footed student, who stayed too long to ring the Victory Bell, was clubbed repeatedly by Captain Ron Snyder.[46]

Immediately feeling the effects of the tear gas, I turned and ascended the steep hill that descends sharply from Taylor Hall to the base of the Commons and the Victory Bell, around which the students had rallied. A photo taken from inside the northeast corner of the campus building shows me holding a white handkerchief and yelling to a nearby female student not to rub her eyes.

Three units made up the advance: two from the 145th—Snyder's C Company on the left and Martin's A Company on the right—separated by Captain Raymond Srp's Troop G of the 107th Armored Cavalry. Dividing units can be problematic for command and control purposes, but in this case, either Canterbury or Colonel Fassinger elected to place Troop G in the middle because all the men in the unit, Fassinger later said, had at least "3 1/2 years in the military."[47]

As some students retreated up an incline toward a passageway between Taylor Hall and Prentice Hall (a women's dormitory set next to Taylor on a slight diagonal), Snyder's Company C followed, moving to the left around the back of Taylor Hall, while the main force headed directly up the hill to the right of the building toward the umbrella-shaped Pagoda. Snyder and his thirty men, accompanied by Major Jones and Sergeant Grant, halted at the top of the knoll near the passageway and just beyond a small grove of trees. There, C Company fronted a grassy area crisscrossed by sidewalks between Taylor and Prentice Halls. From this vantage point, Snyder's command could see the ragged ranks of students gathering along the side of Prentice Hall and in the adjoining Prentice Hall parking lot.[48]

Maintaining a perfect Guard alignment without a gap in the line was difficult because of the location of Taylor Hall, but a halt by the main force of Troop G and Company A at the summit of Taylor Hill, near the Pagoda, would have protected both flanks. Instead, General Canterbury and Colonel Fassinger continued to advance, leading the main body over the highest ground on the southwest side of the rise and down the reverse slope of the hill. Students moved aside to maintain what seemed to them to be a safe distance from the troops. Guard reconnaissance had been poor, but as the advance continued, trooper James Pierce, a Kent native and himself a KSU student, took note of the key feature of the familiar terrain: "The area around the Pagoda is the highest point; militarily speaking, high points are advantageous for defense purposes . . . [because they give] a good vantage all around." Canterbury believed that the football practice field, a flat expanse of land beyond the reverse side of Taylor Hill, was the best place for the troops to re-form and "assess the situation," and took the assertive course by pushing forward.[49]

In what Major John Simons, the Guard's chaplain, called a "silly" decision by Canterbury, the general led the men to where the ground flattened to meet a narrow access road and then the slightly lower-lying practice football field. There the two units were hemmed in on one side by a chain-link fence and partially ringed by scattered groups of students on the other three sides, at distances of two hundred feet or more. Soon the main force was joined by Jones, who left the C Company position on the northeast side of Taylor Hill and, without interference, scurried unharmed through hundreds of students to join Canterbury and the other units on the practice field. At that point, the guardsmen fired much of their remaining tear gas.[50]

After climbing Taylor Hill to escape the tear gas, I made my way through the grassy passageway between Taylor and Prentice Halls, unaware that a troop of guardsmen had pursued. I followed students to a twenty-foot-wide area of lawn situated between Prentice Hall and the parking lot. The elongated asphalt parking lot extends the entire 250-foot length of the southwestern face of the dorm. In the first-floor lavatories in the middle of the dormitory wing in Prentice, female students had opened the frosted windows and were passing wet paper towels to students outside who had been overcome by the tear gas. Preoccupied with cleansing my eyes and helping some others affected by the tear gas, I was unaware of the position of the guardsmen, either those eighty yards away on the practice football or those in Company C who had followed but did not advance beyond the eastern side of Taylor Hill. I might have spent five—but no more than ten—minutes next to Prentice Hall.

Students recognized the isolated position of the guardsmen, and many were emboldened by the blunder. Some, including Jeff Miller, Alan Canfora, and Jim Minard, threw stones from the Prentice Hall parking lot to the north of the practice field. Others tossed still-smoking gas canisters back at the troops who had fired them. As their supply of tear gas ran low, guardsmen Okey Flesher and Russell Repp began throwing rocks and canisters back at the students. The stones thrown by both students and guardsmen fell well short. Even so, guardsman James Pierce, carrying an M-I rifle as most of the troops did, compared his unit's position to "Christians in a Roman arena." He might have added that unlike early Christians, guardsmen on the practice field were heavily armed.[51]

At about 12:15, as many as eight guardsmen assumed a firing position, with half of them aiming their rifles at the closest demonstrator, Alan Canfora, who stayed fifty yards from the troops. Though he kept at a distance where he could outrun a pursuing guardsman, Canfora was close enough for one of the riflemen to describe him as a "guy with an Apache headband with a flag." Others pointed their rifles at more distant stone throwers in the Prentice Hall parking lot sixty yards away. Leon Smith, a self-described "old country boy," aimed his weapon at Canfora, whom he found "threatening" because he had "never seen anybody carrying a black flag [before]." James McGee, the Ravenna Arsenal employee, also remembered taking aim at Canfora, whom he described as the "guy waving a black flag." But McGee, who ordinarily wore glasses, found it difficult to get a good look, since guardsmen could not wear glasses under their gas masks.[52]

Around the same time that fellow guardsmen dropped into firing position, Sergeant Barry Morris of Troop G watched Sergeant Pryor fire his .45 in the air, perhaps as a warning shot. If indeed one or more shots were fired, the noise was barely heard and made little impression on the large, raucous crowd. Terrain or atmospheric conditions that day may have further affected the sound carry of the gunfire. Guardsman James Pierce, who had already concluded that the crowd was composed not of "people, but savage animals," heard "an order 'keep your cool and don't shoot unless they try to overrun you.'"[53]

Major Jones, wearing his trademark soft fatigue hat, had just arrived on the practice field with his baton and Beretta. Exhibiting the same take-charge qualities he demonstrated on Sunday when he decided to break up the May 3 rally, he ordered Pryor to put his weapon away and gathered officers and NCOs in a huddle. According to Jones, he observed that the troops were in a vulnerable position and recommended returning to the ROTC building: "You have to get out . . . back to a position where you can secure your forces." Just what else was decided in the huddle has never been fully disclosed, but contingency decisions were likely made. The assertive Canterbury acceded to his field officer. Jones later recalled, "I said, 'Line up, form a wedge, get moving.' I just hollered to anybody that would hear me. The unit commanders, the first sergeant [Pryor], Canterbury and Fassinger issued similar orders."[54]

At approximately 12:18, Pryor heard the order from Jones, while Lieutenant Howard Fallon, the Akron policeman, remembered the same command coming from Canterbury. Evidently ignoring the presence of the higher-ranking colonel, and impressed with the tactical clarity Jones brought to the situation, Canterbury directed the major to "take the rear" during the retrograde movement up the hill. Canterbury, distinctive in his civilian suit, led the wedge-shaped formation back toward the hilltop Pagoda.[55]

The area was now populated by a thoroughly mixed group of protestors, observers, and even oblivious noontime pedestrians. The alacrity of the guardsmen's maneuver left most of those paying attention either perplexed or elated. The sight of her brother, Alan, isolated on the practice field and waving a black flag at the departing guardsmen left Roseann "Chic" Canfora frightened. She and her companion, Jim Riggs, ran to Alan and implored him to return with them to the presumed safety of the Prentice Hall parking lot. Still believing he remained at a safe distance where he could outrun a pursuing guardsman, he told her, "You go. I want to stay a little longer and watch where they are going."[56]

From the first firing of the tear gas, I had lost sight of the group of friends I had encountered on the Commons. Wanting to regain a wider sense of everything taking place around me, I made my way through the Prentice Hall parking area, which brought me closer to the practice field. Along the way I could better observe the position of the guardsmen to my front. Reaching the lower slope of Taylor Hill, where its grassy section connects with the parking lot and a narrow access road, I saw that the guardsmen on the practice field who would soon be in motion. Previously, some had gathered into a huddle before reforming their lines and reversing their original line of march.

From my position on the lower part the reverse slope of Taylor Hill, I could see the guardsmen to my front as they ascended the steeper portion of the hillside. There, from what I now know to be between 210 to 190 feet from the Pagoda, I watched until they reached the summit of the hill. What I recall best is the noise level as people, including me, screamed and cursed the guardsmen who seemed in apparent retreat.

The cacophony of voices fueled tensions. As the guardsmen maintained their orderly withdrawal, Major Jones carefully watched the rear flank. He had seen action in six previous disorders and kept his pistol at the ready. Crossing the service road that divided the practice field from the base of Taylor Hill's reverse slope and then ascending its tree-lined brow, Jones took aim at student activist Jim Minard, who verbally harassed him. "Come on," Jones reportedly replied, "I'll fix you." Minard, a student from working-class Warren, Ohio, watched Jones the rest of the way up the summit. Guardsman James Pierce heard Sergeant Pryor—who like every guardsman but Jones and Canterbury was wearing a gas mask—tell the men within audible range, "If they rush us shoot them."[57]

"It looked like a firing squad"

It was almost 12:25 when guardsmen from Troop G and Company A reached the apex of the hill topped by the Pagoda. Sparse tree growth offered clear sightlines in the direction of the Prentice Hall parking lot. Two dozen students stood on the open-air terrace adjacent to Taylor Hall, observing the action, some about fifty feet from where the two Guard units had stopped abruptly. Student Jim Minard saw Jones signal to the troops by waving his baton in a downward motion. Another nearby student, Harry Montgomery, saw Sergeant Pryor tapping guardsmen on the back just before they halted, while a third student, Charles Deegan, fixed his gaze on the same sergeant tapping people on their helmets and shoulders, putting them in line." Deegan also heard "someone call 'Form up' and then some Guardsmen turned." Twenty-five-year-old guardsman Richard Love—one of two C Company men on the hill—thought as well that he heard Jones yell "Form up!" and "Turn and face the crowd." Following the signals from Pryor and Jones and the verbal orders from an officer (quite possibly Jones), many of the seventy-six troops stopped between the Pagoda and the edge of the Taylor Hall veranda, while others momentarily continued in the direction of the Commons. More than half, among them twenty-seven-year-old Lloyd Thomas of Troop G, responded to the command to "turn around and stand your ground." Most of the active protestors were nearly one hundred yards away, in the Prentice Hall parking lot.[58]

What happened next is still a topic of sharp debate. A Kent State employee who unexpectedly found himself near the guardsmen heard an officer give the command "to turn and fire three rounds." Many of the men in the two units rotated 130 degrees and aimed their rifles at students further down the hill, toward the more distant parking lot at least 260 feet away. Bob Pickett saw Jones, an officer "with a soft hat," make a motion, after which the guardsmen "turned simultaneously . . . and began to fire." From his position on the veranda, Harry Montgomery identified Pryor as "the first one" to turn, aim his pistol, and fire. Freshman Rick Levinger saw the same thing. "One guardsman with a pistol shot first, and then the others opened up," he said. Eyewitnesses' memories of spoken orders soon became garbled, but a long overlooked portion of audiotape leaves little doubt: one or more voices can be heard shouting, "Right here, get set, point, fi—!" It was then, twenty-four minutes into the confrontation, that the first deadly shots rang out.[59]

Many guardsmen responded to the order to shoot. Robert D. James, a twenty-six-year-old from Wayne County, heard a command to fire. Roger Maas, of the same age and also from Wayne County, told the FBI he "heard a bunch of yelling . . . and thought he heard a command to fire." Just feet away, Sergeant McManus temporarily pulled the gas mask from his lower jaw, presumably to be better heard. He later claimed that he ordered the men near him "to fire one volley into the air." Lloyd Thomas heard that order but continued to fire after the initial round, even as students fled down the hillside. But all many of the troops heard was the command to fire. Bill Perkins of Troop G froze momentarily before he too began to fire. "I realized that they [other guardsmen] were shooting at the crowd so I followed suit" he later wrote. After a number of the men opened fire, twenty-five-year-old Sergeant William Case heard somebody yell, "Not at them, over their heads."[60]

"Everything happened so fast," twenty-five-year-old infantryman Paul Naujoks told investigators. "It was like a car wreck." McManus first insisted that "Bill Herschler seemed to fire his weapon into the crowd[,] . . . his whole clip of eight rounds in semi automatic fashion," but later retracted that statement. Dennis L. Breckenridge, a thirty-one-year-old from Hartville, fired multiple times. Larry Mowrer heard no command and, not being able to see well, pointed his weapon in the general direction of the practice field. He fired "on reflex," he later said, when the shooting became a "chain reaction." Mowrer told Highway Patrol investigators: "I was not provoked [into firing]. . . . I didn't have my glasses on[,] . . . really couldn't see. . . . I fired instinctively when I heard the others."[61]

Joe Lewis, an eighteen-year-old freshman from Massillon, was standing like a sentry with his middle finger raised, between sixty and seventy feet from the firing line. Photographs show that of all the students positioned off the veranda, Lewis was closest to the Guard. Troop G member Larry Shafer, a twenty-four-year-old from Ravenna, fired one of his four rounds at Lewis. Shafer saw him go down clutching his stomach while a second round hit him, probably fired from another weapon. That shot likely came from James McGee, who recalled picking out "the closest [student] to me that I noticed." He estimated the student to be sixty feet away. McGee also had vision problems, but saw well enough to put the student in his sights and aim at his left knee. Of all the casualties hit by M-1 or .45 caliber rounds, only Lewis sustained two bullet wounds, one to the abdomen and the other to his left leg. And in all but the case of Shafer and the guardsmen using shotguns, there was insufficient ballistic evidence to determine who shot whom.[62]

Lieutenants Fallon and thirty-two-year-old Dwight G. Cline of Company A both heard an officer on "the flank yell 'fire.'" Cline said, "Some of our people thought this meant them[;] thus a few rounds were fired into the air." James, the Company A man with poor vision, also "clearly heard" the command to "fire." He did so, he said, "to scare the crowd. That's what I thought we were all doing." Troop G men Barry Morris and Ralph Zoller selected targets. Sergeant Morris "dropped to cover and fired two shots" from his .45 automatic "right into the mob where most of the rocks were coming from," while Zoller, a twenty-four-year-old from Mantua, took aim at the leg of a male student who "was by a tree." Investigators could neither confirm nor refute the claims of rock throwing, but days later, Morris's company commander, Captain Raymond Srp, dismissed the need for firing. It was not, he said, "a shooting situation."[63]

The twenty-six-year-old Pierce fired half his clip, striking a fellow student who appeared, he said, "to get hit several more times." His likely target was John Cleary, an architecture student who had simply gone out of his classroom in Taylor Hall to take some photographs. Cleary was about 110 feet from the Guard and fell with a gunshot wound to his chest But Pierce hadn't finished firing. He spotted "a large Negro male shouting and with a rock about to throw it at me." It was Brother Fargo. Pierce pointed his M-1: "I aimed at him and missed." Photographs clearly show Fargo screaming at the Guard—but without a rock.[64]

Watching and listening to television footage taken from behind the Guard position, Secretary of State George Schultz, a former US Marine, was convinced there had been an order to fire and said to a White House speechwriter, "That was a salvo." One witness, a professor of journalism who saw combat during the Korean War, said it all: "It looked like a firing squad."[65]

"Get Down!"

An eerie silence followed the thirteen-second barrage. The quiet was quickly punctured by screams of horror and shouts for help. Doug Vaughan found his friend Jeff Miller beyond help; his lifeless body lay 265 feet from the Guard line, where the access road meets the Prentice Hall parking lot. He had been shot through the mouth and died instantly. Also in the Prentice Hall lot, 343 feet from the Guard position, Alison Krause fell into the arms of her close friend Barry Levine. Blood from her wound soaked her T-shirt, which was emblazoned with the name "Kennedy." Miller's body left Kent in the same ambulance as the dying Krause. Nearer to the Guard line, 225 feet away, Canfora—who had defiantly waved a black flag at guardsmen on the practice field—ducked behind a tree, which shielded his body but not his arm. He took a bullet through his wrist. One of the most experienced activists there that day, Canfora was one of two students formerly associated with SDS to be struck by gunfire. Closer to the firing line than Canfora, Doug Vaughan managed to find a bigger tree.[66]

When the guardsmen reached the hilltop, their movements seemed to blur just before I heard one or two cracks of what sounded like rifle fire. Immediately, I started running away from their position toward the parking lot. I got no more than a few steps when I was knocked to the ground by the force of an M-1 round that had entered my left heel.

I first tried to raise myself to look at my wound. As I was propping myself up by my arms, I heard yelling from nearby: "Stay down! Stay down! It's buckshot!" I looked over; behind a tree some twenty feet from me, was my roommate Alan Canfora, who I had no idea was in the same vicinity. Thanks to his warning I realized we were still under fire, and I lay flat for some seconds longer until the barrage ceased.

At the opposite end of the parking lot, 435 feet from where Jeff Miller fell, Jerry Persky, out on bail from his arrest at the AT&T protest, grabbed YSA activist Jerry Alter and yelled, "Get down!" They survived the hail of bullets. Persky's former girlfriend, Sandy Scheuer, did not. A speech major on her way to class, Scheuer had done no more than observe the protest. Standing nearly 400 feet from the Pagoda, she died within moments from an M-1 round through the neck. Michael Erwin witnessed a student attempting to hold a piece of cloth over her throat. But he was close enough to see that "there wasn't much of a throat left." Roseann Canfora found cover when Jim Riggs pulled her down behind one of about thirty vehicles parked in the half-empty lot. There she heard "bullets zipping" and felt "glass from the windows of the car . . . shatter . . . all over us." They were just feet away from Bill Schroeder—an ROTC cadet with strong doubts about the war—who had been struck in the back. A half hour earlier, some ROTC members had been urging the guardsmen to attack the crowd, unaware that their fellow cadet was an onlooker. When the firing commenced, Schroeder instinctively went to the pavement. As he lay prone, a bullet pierced his back. Looking at Schroeder's motionless body, Roseann Canfora remembered that "his eyes were open, and he was looking up at a very blue sky. He had blood all over his shoulder." Schroeder was the most unlikely of the four fatalities. Second in his ROTC class, he had come from a military science class that ended at just before noon. He fell 382 feet from the soldiers who killed him.[67]

Alan Canfora: "I looked off to my right during the shootings. I could see my roommate, Tom Grace, about ten feet away. The bottom of his foot was blown open. I yelled out to him, 'Keep your head down.' [After the shooting stopped]

I started to get up to help Tom Grace, but I saw there were other people who rushed to his aid. So I thought I'd try to get to the hospital myself. . . . In the hospital, I saw Tom Grace on the table in the hallway. He was just lying there, not being treated by anyone. He was in extreme agony. The bones were protruding out of the bottom of his foot. He was crying and screaming and asking for something to kill the pain. I tried to calm him. . . . They were treating the others who were dying and who were wounded more severely." —From Bud Schultz and Ruth Schultz, *The Price of Dissent: Testimonies to Political Repression in America* (2001), 363–65.

Doug Wrentmore, Donald Scott Mackenzie, and Robby Stamps (the student who had organized the creative protest against napalm two weeks earlier) were all hit in the parking lot at distances of 350, 730, and 550 feet, respectively. Dean Kahler, a twenty-year-old who admitted throwing a rock, had been at KSU for only five weeks. Like Schroeder, he had taken cover as soon as he heard the first rounds. As he lay prone 330 feet from the guardsmen's firing position, partially sheltered by the incline at the edge of the practice field, a round struck him and severed his spinal column. Kahler was permanently paralyzed.[68]

Future journalist Allen Richardson had the good fortune to have been sheltered by a building during the salvo. Kent's senior dissident, Roman Tymchyshyn, had not seen people shot dead since peering out of a basement window in Austria during the closing days of World War II. Paul Cheeks, whose KSU seniority nearly matched Tymchyshyn's, had had a barstool glimpse of the town's first protest of the decade—the October 1960 sit-in to protest racial discrimination at the Corner Bar. On May 4, he had a bird's-eye view of the deadly confrontation from the top floor of Taylor Hall. When the firing began, Cheeks—an instructor in the architecture department—ushered terrified students back from the windows as guardsmen were firing rounds skyward and in two other directions. "It was just inconceivable," he said. "Everybody started to cry."[69]

Uncertainty still clouds the first shot from the hillside, but there is less doubt about one of the last rounds fired that day. Leon Smith, a heavily built part-time policeman and the father of two, discharged five shells from his shotgun; three were of birdshot, two of the more dangerous buckshot. "Just as I pulled the trigger on the 12 gauge . . . I heard the . . . order, 'Cease fire,' and . . . I locked the weapon and turned around," Smith later testified. He was one of just two guardsmen armed with shotguns and closest to twenty-three-year-old Jim Russell, the oldest of the thirteen students shot. Taking wounds to the head and thigh, Russell was the only student hit by shotgun fire.[70]

"I would have regarded it as murder"

Whatever Vietnam veterans experienced after they returned from war, only at Kent State were they shot at by American soldiers. Veterans Pete Winnen, Larry Rose, and Ken Johnson (who had joined SDS while still in the army) once more eluded hostile fire, but this time the shots were from M-1 rifles. Former marines Harry Montgomery (who witnessed Sergeant Pryor giving hand signals and discharging his .45) and Dick Woods also evaded the rounds that had been fired, as did marine reservist Charles Deegan, who was close enough to see Major Jones giving hand signals to the troops. Air force veterans Howard Ruffner and Tim Butz, along with former soldier Frank Zadell, avoided bullets as well, though Zadell said that he came closer to dying at Kent than he did in Vietnam. Navy veteran Bill Heasley went from a student mediator to a student protestor "throwing the tear gas [canisters]" in the span of minutes. Seeing Jeff Miller's awful wound, Heasley "sat down and started to cry." Jon Oplinger, a student, war veteran, and onlooker to the shootings, told a reporter, "Had I witnessed this event in Vietnam, I would have regarded it as murder, and I cannot help but to do so now."[71]

Montgomery, who had been wounded and treated by a corpsman in Vietnam, watched the guardsmen retreat toward the Commons. Knowing that people lay wounded and dying, he "ran after the guardsmen yelling to get their corpsmen up there[,] that they shot some students"; the guardsmen, however, "just kept going." The task of care fell first to students like Brother Fargo and Joe Cullum, who rushed to aid the critically wounded John Cleary. With others helping the fallen, Bob Pickett provided another kind of aid: picking up National Guard shell casings, which he turned over to the FBI.[72]

Captain Snyder—from his position on the northeast side of Taylor Hall—took a few members of C Company into the Prentice Hall parking lot to survey the carnage. He routinely carried two or more pistols, including, according to a fellow guardsman, "a small one in his boot." Snyder verified that one student, Bill Schroeder, was dead. Next, he examined the lifeless Miller. Snyder would later tell the state grand jury that a weapon had been found on Miller's body. Years passed before he admitted to a federal prosecutor that he had made it up. "Everybody was loading up on the Guards with a number of lies," he explained, "and I thought it was time to throw my two cents in and see how they like that." When the crowd began cursing Snyder's men, one guardsman threw a practice grenade in their midst, cutting the lip of a female student. The unit then retreated to the Commons, where they joined the two units that had fired.[73]

"My orders are to move ahead"

The units regrouped at the ruins of the ROTC building and replenished their ammunition supplies. Sergeant Herschler nearly went to pieces, crying that he had shot two teenagers. Breckenridge, who suffered from hypertension, fainted and was carried off by stretcher. Canterbury, seeing that he needed to fortify his men, told McGee and others, "You did what you had to do." Canterbury now reorganized the troops when he realized that the students had regrouped as well, and the units gathered once again on the edge of the Commons. This time, they sat in stunned silence. One of them, Greg Hawthorne, had arrived late for the rally and was behind the firing line at the time of the volley. Seven months earlier, this coal miner's son had attended his first antiwar march, but left apprehensively when somebody threw a rock through the window of Kent's army recruiting station. Now he was one of a thousand students who knowingly risked death rather than end their protest, and among them could be heard cries for vengeance.[74]

Faculty members, most notably Glenn Frank, shuttled between General Canterbury and the immovable crowd of students, begging both sides to end the tense standoff. Canterbury was unmoved, and repeated his words about law and order. He promised that his troops would fire again, this time into a densely packed crowd, if the students failed to disband. Major Jones readied his units, telling Frank, "My orders are to move ahead." Frank refused to back down and promised to stand in his way. An Ohio Highway Patrol officer interceded, buying the professor more time to plead with the students. In the meantime, guardsmen had fanned out and surrounded the students on three sides. Frank, with his voice breaking, convinced the horror-struck students to disperse.[75]

The North Water Street bar scene in downtown Kent, circa 1968–69, where antiwar disorders began on May 1, 1970. The area was home to JB's, where the James Gang played. Also pictured is Orville's Bar. Photo by Gerry Simon.

An antiwar Moratorium march proceeds down Main Street in Kent on October 15, 1969. The march and subsequent rally was Kent's largest protest until the demonstrations against the Cambodian invasion. Courtesy Special Collections and Archives, Kent State University Libraries.

Aerial view of the Kent State campus. The May 4 protest began on the Commons, seen in the upper right. Guardsmen dispersed the protestors there and, in pursuit of them, advanced up the hilltop on which Taylor Hall (center) is situated. Guardsmen next moved between the dorm (top left) and Taylor Hall to the practice football field, the expanse to the left of the parking lot. When guardsmen returned to the upper left-side corner of Taylor Hall, they executed a 130 degree turn and fired down the hill toward the parking lot. Three students were wounded on the grassy area crisscrossed by walkways. Eight others, including the four fatalities, were struck in the parking lot. Photo by Ted Walls, *Akron Beacon Journal*, Aug. 28, 1970.

After students refuse to disperse, three companies of guardsmen advance with tear gas, fixed bayonets, and loaded weapons. Taylor Hall dominates the background. Photo by Jack Davis, KSU News Service.

This photo, which appeared on the cover of *Life* magazine, shows the unconscious John Cleary being aided by bearded Joe Cullum, who also assisted casualty Joe Lewis. Photo by Howard K. Ruffner.

Viewed from Prentice Hall, guardsmen are seen at the umbrella-shaped Pagoda (left of tree) in the upper right of the photo. 1 and 2 mark the positions of fatalities William Schroeder and Sandy Scheuer; 3 and 4 are the positions of Jeff Miller and Allison Krause. Photo by Beverly K. Knowles.

Black United Students leader Erwind Blount, flanked by
Rudy Perry, speaking to a crowd of antiwar students protesting
the invasion of Laos, February 5, 1971. Author's collection.

Vietnam Veterans Against the War leader Ken Johnson
speaking at a campus antiwar rally. By 1971 Vietnam vets
were playing an important role in the antiwar movement.
Courtesy Special Collections and Archives, Kent State
University Libraries.

Protesting students block the principal intersection at Lincoln and Main Streets as demonstrations spill over into town in May 1972. Courtesy Special Collections and Archives, Kent State University Libraries.

An antiwar student and a truck driver, caught in the same protest tie-up, exchange a handshake. Courtesy Special Collections and Archives, Kent State University Libraries.

SDS reunion at Kent State, May 5, 1989. *Front row, from left*: Alan Canfora, Doug Tanner (wearing cowboy hat), Carolyn Pine, Melissa Stephens Whitaker, Howie Emmer, Robin Marks, Rich Hess, Jerry Persky, Tom Grace, Bill Whitaker, Ralph Bevilaqua, George Hoffman. *Second row, from left*: Ed Miller, Bob Lewis; behind Lewis, Joyce Cecora and Candy (Erickson) Knox; Steve Drucker, Mary Ann Jackson, Vince Modugno, Ruth Gibson. *Back row, from left*: George Gibeaut, Jim Powrie, Andy Pyle, Tony Walsh, Matt "Rebel" Flanagan, Lisa Meisel Burlingame, Mark Rudd, Colin Neiburger. Photo by Larry Lamovsky.

CHAPTER 13

Aftermath

INITIAL REPORTS stated that there were dead on both sides. Mayor LeRoy Satrom, who had first requested the presence of the Guard, was leaving city hall when the news of the shootings came across the radio. Ron Weissenberger, a participant in the first three days of protests, learned of the shootings when a friend burst into his apartment to tell him of a radio report that "two students and two guardsmen" had been shot. Hiding out in nearby Hudson, George Hoffman and Vince Modugno heard much the same news. In a banner headline that afternoon, the *Record-Courier* reported that two guardsmen and one student were dead.[1]

Alan Canfora insisted on being released after receiving treatment for his wound at Robinson Memorial Hospital in Ravenna. He knew better than to believe tales of dead guardsmen. He had seen the slain students being wheeled into the emergency room. Returning to his off-campus apartment with a bandaged wrist, he found it crowded with agitated roommates worried about wounded friends and dead telephone lines. All were frantic about what to do. Only Richard "Whitey" Ward was quiet—intensely so. Canfora caught the look in Ward's eyes as the Vietnam veteran opened his buckskin jacket to reveal a World War II German-made Luger pistol in a shoulder holster. Alarmed, Canfora beckoned him aside and asked what his intentions were. Ward, who had not been at the protest, said calmly: "Uncle Sam taught me how to kill. They got four of us and I'm going to get four of them." Canfora convinced Ward to keep his gun holstered, assuring him that the guardsmen had "probably already been arrested."[2]

Ward was not alone in feeling a need for vengeance. Kent State student and former Green Beret lieutenant Ron Arbaugh told a reporter that after the shootings, "I felt like . . . grabbing the first guardsman I could find and beating the guy's head in." Paul "Roby" Bukosky's older brother worried about what Roby might do: "I knew my brother had . . . an almost Old Testament concept of retribution. If there were four dead students there could very well be four dead guardsmen. When we couldn't find him, I was paralyzed with fear." Roby, who had visited Kent and returned to Cleveland the day before the killings, turned up safely.[3]

Persons unknown had already set fire to a shed serving as an airport terminal and damaged six small planes at the KSU landing field, where Governor Rhodes had boarded a plane back to Columbus on the afternoon of May 3. Other acts were more directly retaliatory. Sixteen hours after the killings, at least one unidentified person slipped into a maintenance barn on the southern edge of the campus before dawn and set it afire. Flames silhouetted the escaping arsonist or arsonists, who ignored guardsman Thomas Simmons's order to halt. Simmons took aim and fired twice, but there were to be no more dead or wounded. Simmons discharged the last rounds fired by guardsmen at Kent State.[4]

The guardsmen, meanwhile, regrouped and began constructing a justification for their actions. General Canterbury personally assured James McGee that he had done "what you had to do," while another officer instructed McGee "not to talk about it to the media or to anyone." Within an hour of the shootings, McGee and other soldiers were directed to a campus gymnasium where, according to the US Justice Department, the "claim by the National Guard that their lives were endangered by the students was fabricated subsequent to the event." Erroneous stories quickly made their way into the local media; the *Record-Courier* reported in a corrected edition published later on May 4 that "a search is on for a female sniper who is said to have started the shooting at Kent." Guard commanders, who were probably the source of the false report, embellished the story and began circulating tales of rooftop marksmen.[5]

In the hours following the shooting, guardsmen prepared their handwritten after-action reports. Sergeant William Case's report explained why he had fired in the air: "Only God can take lives and . . . I didn't get the order from him to aim at any human, no matter how hard they threw the rocks. I just couldn't shoot them." Case's convictions were admirable, but he did not have much company. James Pierce, a member of the same unit, was more typical, writing, "After the firing I felt no remorse because it seemed to be the only way to defend myself." An anonymous guardsman from the same unit complained about the stream of profanity they had endured and told a reporter, "It's about time we showed the bastards who's in charge." Another described the mission even more crudely: "I felt like I'd just had an order to clean up a latrine."[6]

Such attitudes were not confined to the units involved in the shooting. Men in the headquarters company of the 107th Armored Cavalry complained to a reporter about "coeds shouting obscenities," and their sergeant, Charles Householder, shook his head over "the caliber of [such] people." A student near troops located elsewhere on the campus testified that "when the firing . . . began," he heard a soldier exclaim loudly, "Shoot the hairy sons-of-bitches!"[7]

The Sternest Repression

Fearing an explosion of such antagonistic sentiments, county prosecutor Ron Kane had wanted to close the university on May 3. He got his wish a day too late. Kane heard a radio report of the shootings on Monday afternoon and successfully petitioned a judge for an injunction to shut the university. Nearly nine thousand students had to evacuate campus within a few hours. Thousands more left their apartments in town.[8]

Passion and loathing gripped the city of Kent. The *Record-Courier* added to it. In later press runs, editors corrected the false headline about the killing of two guardsmen, but they left the same front-page editorial in place, which read in part:

> The Governor stated that the days of the "go easy" policy toward campus law breakers is over, and that they can expect their violence to be met with every law enforcement tool the state has at its disposal.
>
> Amen to that, for Kent in the past three days has had its fill of these violence-prone toughs who use legitimate causes, such as a drive for peace, as vehicles to allow them to riot and disrupt.
>
> The acts of violence in Kent and on campus during the past two days are so serious as to merit the sternest repression.[9]

The influence of this editorial would linger for a long time. For days and weeks after it appeared, letters poured into the paper condemning the students and supporting the lethal actions of the National Guard. Lucius Lyman, owner of a car dealership in Kent and an astute observer of local politics, recalled a decade later that locals "reacted in a very vehement way, damning the students," with feelings running so strong that "the vast majority . . . would have said that the students got what they had coming to them." Lyman, who disagreed with such sentiments, noted when he was interviewed in 1980 that "some of the differences aren't healed today."[10]

In the aftermath of the shootings, schoolchildren were sent home early. Most, like Mary Homer, were frightened. She later recalled that she and her fellow students at Davey Junior High "were herded on buses. A very large man with a baseball bat came on board our bus to protect us, as everyone had the immediate fear of the unknown." Yet if most welcomed protection, at least one student disdained the protectors. With nearly two months remaining of his senior year of high school, Henry Tompkins—whose cousin had died in Vietnam—got kicked off a school bus when he was seen giving National Guardsmen the middle finger. At Cuyahoga Falls High School, alma mater of a number of SDSers, fifty students walked out of their classrooms after declaring that "Rhodes murdered the people by calling out the troops."[11]

College senior Tim DeFrange, a former activist, was student teaching at another local high school when news of the killings reached his classroom. The war that students were protesting had already claimed his brother. Now, as his school was also being closed, he received a call from his mother, who summoned him to Robinson Memorial Hospital to see his dying father for the last time. When DeFrange arrived at the in the intensive care unit his mother told him simply, "He's gone." She also described the flurry of young people being wheeled on gurneys and medical staff crying, and told her son of witnessing a physician holding up an x-ray of a patient (it was Dean Kahler) and saying to a colleague, "Look where this bullet is lodged. He's never going to walk again. In all my years of medicine, this is the most senseless thing I've ever seen."[12]

"Don't Send a Murderer to the Senate!"

Tuesday, May 5, brought state GOP primary, which would decide Rhodes's Senate hopes. In Kent, history professor Ken Calkins put a sign on his lawn that read "Don't Send a Murderer to the Senate!" Calkins got his wish.[13]

Rhodes had been considerably behind prior to the shootings, but he almost overcame the deficit. He lost to Robert Taft by 5,300 votes out of 940,000 cast. But he lost decisively in Portage County, 5,200 to 3,700, despite having the backing of the county's GOP chairman and even though polls showed that the majority of local people sided with the Guard. Voters in Kent State's home county had rejected the messenger, but not his message. Elsewhere in the state, Rhodes's loyalists remained faithful to the governor. He easily won the vote in Ohio's other small towns and rural areas.[14]

The vast majority of students were unable to register their opinions at the polls; as in most states in 1970, the voting age in Ohio was twenty-one. Many, like the students in Cuyahoga Falls, had turned to protest. Rick Felber, who arrived on university grounds just as guardsmen were firing their weapons, headed back to his apartment. There he encountered a terribly shaken Mary Ann Vecchio, a young Florida runaway who had found her way to the campus. The next day, an iconic photograph of her kneeling over Jeff Miller's body appeared in newspapers everywhere in the country.[15]

Like Felber, most students in Kent thought only of fleeing a city where residents openly expressed hatred for them. Kent's citizens represented the sentiments of a substantial proportion of the American public at large, who blamed the students, not the Guard, for what happened at Kent State. Seeking a means out of town on May 4, air force veteran Tim Butz made his way to the city center, where he saw police holding socialist Mike Alewitz—wearing a jacket stenciled with a red fist—and KSU student body president-elect Craig Morgan at gunpoint. Figuring he could do nothing about their plight, Butz tried to walk away. Seeing Butz's short beard and KSU T-shirt was enough for the police, who were soon joined by a quintet of heavily armed men in civilian dress, to apprehend Butz as well. All three were taken to the nearby city jail. There, according to the *Record-Courier*, police arrested them on what was vaguely described as an "open charge"; along with fourteen others, they were held "in connection with the Kent State University violence."[16]

Jailed on this flimsy charge, Alewitz was unable to complete his most pressing task: writing an account of the killings for *The Militant,* the journal of the Socialist Workers Party (SWP). A friend of Sandy Scheuer, Alewitz ached to report what he had witnessed. The job fell to a fellow socialist, Fred Kirsch, a KSU bus driver whose father, Herman, had mentored Kent's earliest antiwar activists. Once released from jail, and with the support of the SWP, Alewitz traveled the country describing the killings he had seen. In Akron, Bill Whitaker was speaking at an antiwar rally with Democratic congressional candidate John F. Seiberling when clearly shaken police approached to tell him what had just happened at Kent. Akron University shut down days later.[17]

Striking the War

Not just in Ohio but across the nation, universities and colleges closed, though in many cases not before experiencing disorders of their own. "Student protest swept like an out-of-control brush fire across the country," one historian notes in a detailed account of the nationwide student strike and antiwar movement. Judy Gollust—who had been part of every dissident group at Kent from CORE to SDS—was in New Haven on the weekend of May 1 for a rally to demand freedom for Black Panther leader Bobby Seale and other party members who were charged with killing a police informer in the city. Thousands of US Marines and National Guard troops were mobilized to contain demonstrations. Gollust went despite a sense of trepidation that she would die there. Then she heard the news from Ohio and later said, "Turned out to be people at Kent who got shot at and not us." Yale's sole loss was the university's ROTC building, which suffered damage in the wake of renewed clashes following the shootings at Kent State.[18]

Elsewhere in New England, Lance Buhl, one of the leaders of civil rights protests in Kent in 1960–61, took time off from his graduate studies at Harvard to attend the campus rally protesting the killings at his alma mater. Roy Inglee—the former KCEWV leader—and his associate, Bob Bresnahan, organized protests for the Student Mobilization Committee (SMC). Bresnahan headed next to Washington, DC, to assist with the most hastily planned national antiwar demonstration ever held in the United States.[19]

Reaction first to Cambodia and then to the Kent killings touched every corner of Ohio, and ultimately the nation. In Oberlin—Bill Arthrell's hometown—students occupied the Oberlin College administration building on the night of Nixon's speech, and then asked the college to open its doors to students forced to leave Kent when the school shut down. Next to Kent, Ohio State came the closest to a fatal confrontation, as twenty students there were wounded by birdshot. Protests affected campuses large and small, including Kenyon College, where Terry Robbins—whose remains had not yet been identified from the March 6 townhouse explosion—had been a student. Kenyon students never took to the message Robbins later preached, and their protests, which involved the vast majority of the campus community, remained peaceful, an oasis of calm in a state where the killings ignited incendiary protests.[20]

Campus or ROTC buildings were damaged or burned at Bowling Green State University—where Terry Robbins's friend, Charlie Tabasko, had years earlier organized an SDS chapter—and even at normally placid John Carroll University in Cleveland. Tabasko did his demonstrating in early May near Case Western Reserve, where Tony Walsh and Danny Thompson—two of Kent's pioneer activists—also were among the thousands marching down Cleveland's Euclid Avenue on the evening of May 4. Not one to socialize, much less join a protest, aspiring cartoonist Harvey Pekar left work at the city's Veteran's Administration Hospital to participate in his first and only demonstration, near Case Western—for, as he later said, the killings were "such a shocking thing." Hunter Havens, in a replay of what he had done in January 1969, when he skipped school to attend the 1969 anti-inaugural in Washington, DC, with the Cleveland and Kent SDS, joined his teenage classmates in the same evening march. John McCann and Barbara Gregorich, a pair of veteran Kent activists associated with the SWP, also worked in Cleveland against the war. ROTC buildings at Case Western and nearby Cleveland State suffered damage, as did others throughout Ohio.[21]

In the southwestern section of the state, a campus building at Miami University experienced a similar fate. At the nearby University of Cincinnati, where Alan Canfora's friend George Caldwell had been a student before entering the Marines, 1,000 students protested the Cambodian invasion by closing off the city's downtown streets, which were reopened only after 145 protestors were arrested. After the shootings, 200 students took over three University of Cincinnati buildings and continued to occupy them once the campus shut down on May 7. The demonstrations persisted into the middle of May, when National Guardsmen were called to southeastern Ohio—the only part of the state still largely untouched by protest—to control disturbances at Ohio University in Athens. The oldest of the state's colleges was the last one to close, after a fire-bomb damaged yet another ROTC building and students broke windows in the city's downtown. At the end of April, Rhodes had defended the forceful use of Guard troops in Columbus, saying there had been "less trouble in Ohio as far as . . . fires than any other state." On May 3, he had vowed not to "knuckle under" to the radicals. By the end of the month, his inflammatory policies caused virtually all of Ohio's state-supported schools to erupt in protest following the National Guard killings.[22]

With so many universities silenced by closure, a hundred thousand protestors responded to an emergency call by the New MOBE to demonstrate in the nation's capital on May 9. Judy Gollust left New Haven to help militants on the political left of the reconstituted New MOBE—the umbrella group that had organized every national antiwar protest since the Pentagon march—build the massive Washington, DC, protest. Bob Bresnahan, representing the more cautious SWP, did the same. National security adviser Henry Kissinger recalled that "Washington took on the character of a besieged city" and that "the Executive Branch was falling apart." Exactly how many former or current KSU students went to the huge march is unknown, but activists like Jerry Persky and Rick Felber were among hundreds who did. They had begun to shake off the fear that enveloped most Kent State students, and they were ready to go into the streets once more. Mike Alewitz, free from his first and only arrest, easily found his way to the speaker's rostrum and told the huge and angry crowd on the mall what the National Guard attack had been like.[23]

The march organizers were bitterly divided on the tactical course of the protest. Many young activists believed that a more forceful approach would have aided in "intensifying the national sense of crisis after Cambodia and Kent State." With SDS now collapsed, the moderate Vietnam Moratorium Committee dissolved, and the heads of the New MOBE at odds, antiwar activists, including tens of thousands of newcomers, lacked credible leadership at the very height of the movement's potential power. Deprived of political guidance, the antiwar young were on their own. Kent students organized an impromptu outdoor session at the rally—"the only 'spread the strike' group discussion held during yesterday's antiwar demonstration," the *Washington Post* noted.[24]

Even without national direction, protest strikes spread. At Washington University in St. Louis, Missouri, a scene played out much like the one at Kent State on the night of May 2. The Army ROTC building had been burned months before, so around midnight on the evening of May 4, protestors chanting "Kent State, Kent State" set fire to an air force ROTC cottage. Former SDS member and Cleveland resident Howard Mechanic participated in the protest, but not, he claimed, in the destruction. That did not prevent his conviction on a federal charge, which netted him a five-year sentence. Having already spent four months in jail on another protest-related charge, he took on a new identity and went into hiding for the next thirty years.[25]

Although he never knew or crossed paths with Howard Mechanic, Jeff Powell, the Stow, Ohio native, also went underground. In the immediate aftermath of the Kent killings, every investigator in town seemed to be asking about Powell and his recently released friends. Surely, state and federal agents reasoned, the discharge from jail of the four Kent SDSers on April 29 and the Kent disorders were linked. Those pressures, combined with a front-page article about Powell in the *Cleveland Press* and threats from the Minutemen, an anti–left wing vigilante group, convinced him that he and his family would be safer if he disappeared. Powell vanished for the next quarter century.[26]

Jackson State—May 15

In Jackson, Mississippi, where Kent State Freedom Rider Danny Thompson had been arrested in June 1961, students at the predominantly African American Jackson State College organized a May 7 protest against the Cambodian invasion and the killings in Ohio. Violent death as a price for civil rights activism was nothing new in the city; the assassination of Medgar Evers in 1963 is the best-known example. The Mississippi state capital was yet another place where Kent State activists had gone to rouse student opposition to the invasion and the subsequent killings. *Daily Kent Stater* photographer Tom Difloure spoke to a hundred students on May 9, protestors who had been called to the rally by the Jackson Peace Coordinating Committee, which had condemned "racism, [and] a senseless war." The rally ended without major incident. Days later, just after midnight on May 15, police unleashed a hail of gunfire at Jackson State students.[27]

As at Kent State, there had been rock throwing, fire and destruction, the calling of the National Guard, and, in the aftermath, false charges of sniper fire. The shooting, though, lasted twice as long—twenty-eight seconds—and police expended more than twice the ammunition fired at Kent, 150 rounds in all. Many of the shots were fired into a women's dormitory, where six coeds were hit. Five African American men were also wounded. Worst of all, two more young people were killed. Proving the lethality of buckshot, twenty-year-old Phillip Gibbs took fatal pellets to the brain, and high school student James Earl Green, eighteen, died when a buckshot slug penetrated three vital organs. For African Americans in Mississippi, such police violence was distressingly familiar, and as usual it would go unpunished.[28]

As a young boy, Gene Young had helped console the mother of James Chaney, one of the three civil rights workers murdered in Philadelphia, Mississippi, in

1964. After the Jackson killings, he helped others, this time using the words of Martin Luther King Jr. and the inspirational lyrics from movement hymns to comfort the grief-stricken students. In front of the same dormitory that had received so much police gunfire, the university president also helped calm the students, but it was Young—a former civil rights activist—and the freedom songs that sustained them.

> Ain' gonna let nobody turn me 'round
> Turn me 'round, turn me 'round
> Ain' gonna let nobody turn me 'round
> I'm gonna keep on walkin', keep on talkin'
> And marchin' up to Freedom Land.[29]

"The most disastrous month"

When word of the Jackson State killings reached the University of North Carolina at Chapel Hill, students tore through the campus breaking windows. But while reaction to the Cambodian invasion and the Kent killings raged in much of the nation, response to the Jackson killings was far more muted. There were no cover stories about Jackson State in *Time* or *Newsweek,* and protests did not widen much beyond the campuses. Even so, strike eruptions reached the Pacific coast. Barbara Brock and Ron Wittmaack were entering the student union building at San Francisco State College, where they were now students, when they heard news of the killings in Kent. Right-wing students had struck Brock during her first antiwar protest on the Kent campus in February 1965; Wittmaack had just finished serving time for his participation in the prolonged Third World Strike at the state college. As they had done many times before, the pair joined in the protests at San Francisco State, where the ROTC building suffered damage. Police also battled youth in nearby Berkeley, where a student had died from police gunfire a year earlier. Fearing larger outbreaks, on May 6 California governor Ronald Reagan closed all twenty-eight state colleges and universities for four days.[30]

Next door in Nevada, a state previously untouched by demonstrations, students disrupted "Governor's Day," which featured an ROTC parade. At Kent State, ROTC cadets had merely encouraged the National Guard, but at the University of Nevada in Reno student soldiers unsheathed their bayonets and faced down their dissenting classmates. Austin, Texas, where Mike Alewitz traveled after speaking in Washington, witnessed a march of twenty thousand people on May 8, the largest antiwar demonstration ever held in the state.[31]

At the top level of US government, Nixon administration officials worried less about the deaths on campus than about the outbursts the killings had generated. Nixon's presidential commission later reported: "The crisis on American campuses has no parallel in the history of the nation. This crisis has roots in American society as deep as any since the Civil War." The president of Columbia University, a campus that had known plenty of protest, called May 1970 "the most disastrous month of May in the history of American higher education."[32]

A Bitter Harvest

Nor was concern over the war entirely limited to campuses. Little noticed by those who have written about the era was the impact in the late 1960s of the Vietnam War on the American economy, which was made more adverse as a result of the tumultuous events of early May 1970. "Our involvement in Cambodia . . . suddenly has become the key to the stock market," one Wall Street broker declared after Kent State. The dive in market value represented the biggest loss since the Kennedy assassination. A week later a Harris poll revealed that four-fifths of businessmen blamed administration policies for the sharp decline. Trying to calm the jitters, defense secretary Melvin Laird, who had opposed the move into Cambodia, announced that all US combat forces would be withdrawn from an active role in Vietnam by June 1971. The brief market surge that resulted lasted less than a day before stock prices dropped again as brokers—borrowing a term used to describe the Johnson presidency—expressed doubts about Nixon's "credibility gap." A business reporter wrote that "some Wall Street analysts have put the tag 'Nixon Bear Market' " on the slump and noted that it was the worst bear market since the Great Depression.[33]

What is remembered about Wall Street is not the decline or investor dread, but rather the attack on hundreds of students by thousands of construction workers in the financial district on May 8. Virtually every general history of the period gives prominent attention to the orchestrated assault, which came to be seen as an emblematic divide between blue-collar workers and middle-class students. In Ohio, however, construction workers were on strike the day of the attack, having walked off their jobs on May 1. Two days after the Kent killings, the United Rubber Workers action expanded to B. F. Goodrich, where Rocco Modugno and other parents of Kent State students worked. The wildcat Teamsters strike, thought to have been settled, erupted again when drivers shut down terminals after companies announced that union members fired during the strike would not be rehired.[34]

Of course, these were economic, not political, strikes. Anger toward anti-war students ran deep in places other than New York City. An Akron Teamster expressed unreserved support for the National Guard yet deserted Nixon's Republican congressional candidate later in the fall election. Still, for some labor leaders the commonality of union and student foes was inescapable. Michigan's labor leaders condemned "the slaughter of four students by the National Guard, who have broken many . . . strikes," while Cleveland's Central Labor Council scorned Nixon's Cambodian policy. At a massive protest in Washington the day after the construction workers' assault, the district head of the Retail Clerks union called for Nixon's impeachment. After the president elicited a supportive statement on the war from AFL-CIO chief George Meany, Abe Feinglass, head of the Amalgamated Meat Cutters union, declared that workers should "tell the students that George Meany does not speak for all of the . . . labor movement." Not long after construction workers ran amok in New York, representatives of twenty-eight unions were part of a crowd of forty thousand protesting the war at the same site in lower Manhattan. In what proved to be his last message, UAW president Walter Reuther condemned the Cambodian invasion in a telegram sent directly to Nixon: "By your action you have driven the wedge of division deeper and you have dangerously alienated millions of young Americans. The bitter fruits of this growing alienation and frustration among America's youth have been harvested on the campus of Kent State University, where the lives of four students were ended by the needless and inexcusable use of military force."[35]

The end?

If most historians have overlooked the part played by labor in the criticism of the war and the Cambodian invasion, virtually all writers agree that after the national strike student dissent largely came to an end. William Rorabaugh, who chronicled Berkeley and its student movement, visited the community as a teenager and attended graduate school at the university there. Nevertheless, he remembered the aftermath of Kent State imperfectly. "It was a quiet, almost ghostly time in Berkeley," he writes in the epilogue to *Berkeley at War*. Seeing four crosses in the city, inscribed with the names of the casualties, convinced him of one certainty: "The sixties, I then knew, were over." Another historian writes that "the 1960s ended with a thirteen-second fusillade in a small Ohio town." Likewise, many townspeople in Kent also believed that lethal gunfire had succeeded in silencing dissent. Some, however, came to know better. Amy Kirkbride, who was six years old on May 4, 1970, remembered that her mother told her, "For everything else we can say about Kent State, at least it put an end to the demonstrations around Vietnam." "But," Kirkbride added, "I don't think she was right."[36]

Now, however, with the university closed, the student exodus complete, and social order kept by a dark-to-dawn curfew enforced by hundreds of National Guard troops, Kent State lay, as one reporter wrote, "motionless and quiet."

On May 8, the guardsmen finally ended their six-day occupation of the town and campus, though students did not return to the university until graduation ceremonies were allowed on June 13.[37]

Alan Canfora, despite a bullet wound that went all the way though his wrist, was out of the hospital. But eight other casualties of Ohio Guard gunfire remained hospitalized for periods ranging from weeks to months. Several, including Joe Lewis and John Cleary, had injuries to their internal organs and spent many weeks recovering from surgery. Paralyzed below the waist by an M-1 bullet to his spine, Dean Kahler was eventually transferred to a rehabilitation center in Canton, where he began the long process of adjustment to life in a wheelchair.[38]

Beatrice Mitchell, a third-shift nurse at Robinson Memorial and mother of a soldier in Vietnam, numbered among those who cared for me until my transfer on May 13 to a hospital in my hometown of Syracuse, NY. Though my own memory of my time there is fragmentary, Mrs. Mitchell recalled in an article published in April 2014 that her patient was "shaken up" and "pretty edgy all night and talking a lot about the incident." One of two antiwar nurses on her floor, she further remembered of the time that "it was so tense and unnerving." —Quoted in Christina Bucciere, "Caring for May 4," *The Burr*, April 2014.

While the wounded convalesced, the parents of Kent State's dead faced the difficult task of burying their children. Three of the families, all with Ohio roots, made private arrangements. The Schroeders laid their nineteen-year-old son, Bill, to rest near the family's home in Lorain, an industrial city where his father, Lou, worked. The plant where he had been employed for fifteen years closed later that summer. The Scheuers had been celebrating their May 4 wedding anniversary when they received news of their daughter Sandy's death. Days later they buried her in Youngstown. The Krauses, who were to emerge as leaders in the fight to win justice for the slain young people, selected for their daughter a small Jewish cemetery in Pittsburgh, where Art Krause—originally from Cleveland—had relocated with his family from suburban Maryland less than a year earlier. Along with Allison's name and the dates of her birth and death, the couple inscribed on their daughter's headstone what she had told a National Guardsman the day before she was killed: "Flowers are better than bullets."[39]

In Plainview, New York, Jeff Miller's Long Island hometown, the community held a candlelight vigil on the evening of May 6 and collected thousands of signatures for a petition to end the war. The following day, grieving family members and friends packed into Riverside Church in Manhattan for a memorial service in Jeff's honor, while another three thousand mourners gathered outside and listened through loudspeakers to eulogies by US senator Charles Goodell and Case Western professor Dr. Benjamin Spock. On an unseasonably cold day, with the wind nipping at their faces, the overwhelmingly young crowd raised their fingers in peace signs or made clenched fists as the coffin containing Miller's body was borne to the hearse. Some wore Black Panther Party buttons. One held a blow-up of the soon-to-be iconic photo of the slain Miller bearing the word "Revenge!" The scene caused Miller's father to observe, "Jeff was a war casualty, the same as if he was shot in Cambodia, or Vietnam, or Laos. And he didn't even have a gun."[40]

In Kent and elsewhere in Portage County, residents wasted no time mobilizing support for those who did have guns: the Ohio National Guard. Kent PTA president and First Christian Church member Doris Amick, whose husband worked as a security guard, cofounded a group called Portage County Citizens for Law Enforcement and launched a petition campaign, one of two such efforts in the area, in support of elected officials for their work in quelling the protests. Her effort caught on, she told the local paper, "like wildfire." The *Record-Courier*—which had erroneously reported the deaths of several guardsmen, called for the severest possible "repression" of the protestors, and baselessly cited reports of snipers having fired on the guardsmen—devoted entire pages to letters from locals venting distaste for activist students. Several letters bore multiple signatures ranging from 45 to 283 names.[41]

Despite widespread local animosity, some students soon returned to the sharply divided town. Jim Riggs, who had participated in three nights of protest against the Cambodian invasion and would later be indicted for his activities on May 4, moved back to his apartment within days of the killings. There he was interviewed by FBI agents who had been dispatched to Kent to collect eyewitness testimony, though in Riggs's case the interviews were brief. Agents quickly determined that he had little to say about his activities or those of his fellow demonstrators. Nor did he reply to telephone messages left that summer from the well-known writer James Michener, whose assistants were conducting research for his book on the shootings.[42]

Riggs remembered that crowds were sparse in downtown bars, as many "people were afraid to come to Kent for a while." Two who did come were Graham Nash and Neil Young, even if the buzz generated by their presence in Orville's Bar shortened their stay. Though marijuana continued to be "a staple of the Kent youth culture," as the rock magazine *Rolling Stone* put it, Riggs recalled that wariness of undercover "narcs" inhibited young people, who now did most of their partying at home.[43]

On June 13, 1970, the Nixon administration announced the establishment of the President's Commission on Campus Unrest. Dubbed the Scranton

Commission after its chair, former Pennsylvania governor William Scranton, the body was charged with investigating the disorders that swept the nation's college campuses in the aftermath of the Cambodian invasion and the killings at Kent State and Jackson State. Made up of a university president, a police chief, a retired air force general, the editor of a national newspaper, three academics, and an attorney, the commission held hearings in Kent during the third week of August 1970. YSA activist Mike Alewitz and May 4 casualty Robby Stamps testified, as did graduate student Steve Sharoff and student leader Bob Pickett. Sharoff and Pickett said essentially the same thing, with Sharoff defiantly telling the nine-member commission that "students on this campus will not allow themselves to be shot at without shooting back."[44]

President White's testimony before the commission was followed by an extemporaneous remark during a question and answer session, which noted the presence of "a great deal of human debris on this campus that should never be here." An assistant to White later conceded in an explanatory letter to a critic that it was "an unfortunate choice of words," but claimed that White was referring not to all students but only to those who "possess little desire or purpose in being here" and might be better off in "vocational and technical training" institutions. Doris Amick of Portage County Citizens for Law Enforcement expressed similar concerns. "Hippies" she told the commission, frightened her. "Their long hair, dirty blue jeans. I just don't like it."[45]

On August 24, just days after the conclusion of the Scranton Commission hearings in Kent, a bomb exploded on the campus of the University of Wisconsin in Madison. On the day of the Kent killings, antiwar activist Karl Armstrong and his younger brother Dwight had resolved to take action in response. Following months of planning, the brothers and several friends parked a van loaded with fuel, fertilizer, and dynamite outside what they believed was an empty Sterling Hall, which housed the Army Mathematics Research Center at the university. Hours before daylight, an enormous blast tore through the building and damaged dozens more, killing a graduate student.[46]

Five days later, violence erupted during a protest march in the large Chicano section of Los Angeles, where antiwar sentiment had been simmering for years. Like other minority communities across the country, Chicanos in LA had borne a heavy burden of the fighting and dying in Vietnam, and as the war dragged on those costs had steadily risen. On August 29, twenty thousand protesters responded to a call issued by the National Chicano Moratorium to march against the war. When police discharged tear gas into the crowd, panicked protestors replied with rocks. As the violence escalated, police began beating demonstrators, then fired into the crowd. Two participants were killed, including the prominent journalist Ruben Salazar, and seventy others sustained bullet wounds.[47]

Kent Police State University

Against the backdrop of the violence in Madison and Los Angeles, on September 26 the Scranton Commission issued its findings. Though it found the behavior of some protesting students at Kent to have been "dangerous, reckless, and irresponsible," the commission concluded that firing on them was "unnecessary, unwarranted, and inexcusable." The report stated: "Even if the guardsmen faced danger, it was not a danger that called for lethal force. The 61 shots by 28 guardsmen certainly cannot be justified. Apparently, no order to fire was given, and there was inadequate fire control discipline on Blanket Hill. The Kent State tragedy must mark the last time that, as a matter of course, loaded rifles are issued to guardsmen confronting student demonstrators."[48]

Two days later, as classes resumed for the new fall semester, Kent State held its first official memorial since the May shootings. Among those to address the crowd of five thousand mourners were Vietnam veteran Tim Butz, who had helped organize Kent's initial protest against the Cambodian invasion; Ralph Abernathy, heir to Martin Luther King Jr. as head of the Southern Christian Leadership Conference; prominent pacifist Ira Sandperl of the California Institute for the Study of Nonviolence; and popular folksinger Phil Ochs. Dean Kahler, paralyzed in the shootings and now confined to a wheelchair, overshadowed them all. Kahler told a capacity crowd that he was glad to be alive. Later, two thousand students held an unplanned candlelight vigil at the site of the killings.[49]

Although the administration lent its tacit support to the memorial service, the university also backed local and state authorities' efforts to ensure that the mass protests of the previous spring did not recur. The Ohio General Assembly adopted legislation making "campus disruption" a new category of crime and made Seabury Ford, Portage County's GOP chairman and an ally of outgoing governor James Rhodes, a hearing officer charged with the enforcing the new law. Local police meanwhile bolstered their ranks with new hires and cracked down on the sale or possession of pot and other drugs, prompting President White to acknowledge that Kent might well "seem like a police state to students."[50]

Meanwhile, scores of observers and antiwar activists, including Roman Tymchyshyn and Ken Hammond, were called to testify before a state grand jury investigating the events preceding May 4. In mid-October the panel returned twenty-five indictments against current or former students and one professor. The majority of indictees hailed from working-class communities; one exception was Craig Morgan, KSU student body president and an ROTC member, who was raised in a solidly middle-class home. A few were prominent activists, such as onetime KCEWV leader Ruth Gibson and the rambunctious

Bill Arthrell, organizer of the napalm education rally. Former SDS leader Ken Hammond and ex-SDS member Alan Canfora, who had made himself conspicuous on May 4 by waving a black flag in front of National Guardsmen, were also charged. Most, however, were students who had no former organizational ties. Probably a third of those indicted, like Canfora's younger sister, Roseann, as well as Joe Cullum, Rick Felber, and Jim Riggs, had participated in antiwar protests prior to May 1970, but a only a handful of those targeted by the grand jury could have been considered leaders. In what many saw as an act of extreme injustice, the grand jury also indicted Joe Lewis but voted not to charge the person known to have critically wounded him, guardsman Lawrence Shafer. Nor were any other guardsmen indicted.[51]

Before the indictments were issued, a *Record-Courier* editorial had offered to jurors "the prayers of the nation . . . as they do their best to arrive at the truth." The grand jury produced a selective truth: a report that did not directly mention the killings. Its authors did, however, devote paragraphs to the language of the protestors, asserting that their words represented "a level of obscenity and vulgarity . . . never before witnessed!" To keep the community free of such protest, Judge Edwin W. Jones issued a court order barring demonstrations at the courthouse and prohibiting grand jury members and witnesses from publicly commenting about the proceedings. Thus juror Dallas Pigott had to wait before freely offering his views. Speaking of the protesting "long hairs" who were not struck by rifle fire on May 4, Pigott later told a reporter, "If they had been killed, [they] would have deserved it." One official pushed the limits of the court order. Assistant grand jury prosecutor Seabury Ford declared in a newspaper interview that the guardsmen "should have shot all troublemakers." Outrage over the remark cost him his job. Yet Ford—a former member of the same 107th Armored Cavalry that killed some of the students—made it clear that he represented popular 'man-in-the-street' opinion. "The point is, it stopped the riot. . . . It just stopped it flat," he argued.[52]

In this uncertain environment, activists regrouped. Some, like Ken Hammond, representing the newly organized Kent Liberation Front (KLF), and Richie Hess, who attached himself to the Yippies, were well-known on campus. Others, including Jim Minard, had ties to the SMC, the national group that helped organize the mass protest a year earlier. But most of the four hundred students who attended the first campus antiwar gathering since the May 4 killings, a week after the campus memorial service, were unaffiliated, and just becoming acquainted.[53]

Kent's antiwar cohort had been without real leadership since the demise of SDS in the spring of 1969, and KLF and the Yippies sought to fill the void. Despite significant differences in beliefs and styles, the loosely Marxist KLF and the theatrical Yippies joined together to boost campus spirits by staging a mock grand jury while the official one met in nearby Ravenna. Expecting the worst, some activists kept toothbrushes with them in the event of a hurried trip to the Portage County Jail in Ravenna, where a sign near the booking station read "If your heart is not in America, you had better get your ass out NOW!"[54]

When attorney William Kunstler, already famous for defending the Chicago 7, came to Kent on October 19 with $2,500 in seed money to help start a defense fund for the indicted students, the KSU administration—backed, of course, by a *Record-Courier* editorial—regressed to its pre–free speech days and refused to let Kunstler appear on campus. Unfazed, he went to one of Kent's North Water Street bars and spoke to a packed house, electrifying all who heard him. Students began selling fund-raising T-shirts for those who had been christened the "Kent 25." The shirts read "Kent Police State University."[55]

Seeking to regain momentum in opposition to the war and win assistance in organizing against the Kent 25 indictments, which were kept secret from most indictees until they were apprehended, Vietnam veterans staged a guerrilla theater in front of Student Union on October 15, while antiwar forces held an outdoor rally of two thousand students on October 16 demanding that the ROTC be abolished on the campus and opposing the indictments. Following the arrest of a prominent indictee, the moderate-to-liberal student body president Craig Morgan, on Monday, October 19, another three thousand people protested the following evening, where Tim Butz, president of KSU Vets Against the War, insisted that students had to organize "to fight repression." At the end of the month, thousands more gathered on the Commons to hear the nationally prominent journalist I. F. Stone ask, "Haven't they heard of the First Amendment in Ohio?"—a jibe directed at both the university's efforts to stop the campus rally and the judge's ban on protests outside the courthouse in Ravenna. An SMC rally against the indictments brought thousands of students to the state capital in Columbus. The month of protests confirmed the movement capable of regrouping, while the size of the rallies and the assistance of Kunstler showed indicted students that they were not alone.[56]

Throughout the fall quarter at Kent tensions mounted, as the familiar cycle of official action and student reaction was renewed. In October, President White blocked plans by Black United Students (BUS) to have a separate homecoming event for African Americans, resurrecting the long-standing issue of racial discrimination. His persistent critic Erwind Blount called the decision part of the "tradition of excluding blacks." Bomb threats emptied university classrooms. One real bomb, planted by unknown perpetrators, damaged the headquarters of BUS, but fortunately caused no injuries and did little damage.[57]

Besides the antiwar left and their sometime allies in BUS, a third group of students now emerged to exert leadership: Vietnam veterans. Former servicemen had long been part of the campus dissident community, first expressing

opposition to the Cold War in the late 1940s and later as part of groups like the
Kent Committee to End the War and SDS, but never as a distinct organization.
Veterans, some of whom came under National Guard gunfire on May 4, were
radicalized along with large numbers of students who had never worn a military
uniform. Indeed, as shocking as it had been for typical students to comprehend
the killings, many veterans were even more outraged.

It is not surprising that servicemen who participated in antiwar dissent in
Vietnam would continue their protest activity when they returned stateside.
In the month before Kent State, Vietnam Veterans Against the War numbered
roughly six hundred members nationwide. Before the year was out, membership more than tripled, and Ohio was one of the states with the largest growth.
Among those who joined the VVAW was former marine John Musgrave. Photos
of soldiers at Kent State "killing our own children," struck him as insane folly.
Another US Marines veteran, W. D. Ehrhart, from a small Pennsylvania community, had a similar reaction. "It isn't enough to turn us loose on Asians," he
thought; "Now you are turning the soldiers loose on your own children." For
Tim Butz the deaths were even more personal. He was present on May 4 and
he knew three of the four people killed; he had also gone to high school with
two of those who did the shooting, Butz threw his energies into VVAW after
the slayings, helping build the local chapter and becoming active at the organization's national level. Scores at Kent State were there to assist him, including
Vietnam veteran Jack Spencer, who had also been a high school classmate of a
guardsman who fired on the students.[58]

Pressed by off-campus hardliners to curb any resumption of protest at KSU,
White began insinuating that the latest wave of dissent might close the university once again. Conservative students responded with a "Keep Kent Open"
campaign. Some moderate and liberal students endorsed a "Power to the Peaceful" theme. To support the "Power to the Peaceful" campaign, Ira Sandperl
was brought back to the campus by student government leaders. He returned
with folksinger Joan Baez, who delivered a powerful performance of "We Shall
Overcome." Yet Sandperl, sporting sandals and a gray beard, urged those irate
over the Kent 25 indictments not to aggravate tensions and seemed to suggest
that it was militant tactics that led to the fatal shootings. Such statements
rankled activists who were convinced that his mission was the same as the
administration's—to enfeeble dissent. White's own use of the formula "commitment to non-violence" represented his search for a middle way between the
right-wing pole of community opinion and the mounting antiwar sentiment
on campus.[59]

White's own distinct middle way came in the form of a letter sent to the
parents of Kent's undergraduates, advising them to tell their children to stay
away from campus antiwar rallies, which featured "undesirable behavior" and

would "no longer be tolerated" at the university. Referring to a recent protest, and echoing the language of the Portage County grand jury report, White noted that "obscenities were prevalent as usual" and accused activist leaders of "deceit." One undergraduate, Thomas Stepp, writing in the *Stater,* conceded that mass mailing had "upset" his mother. But he added, "President White's letter did not intimidate me. . . . I feel disgusted that President White would resort to scaring our parents . . . in order to shut us up, in order to stifle what little voice of dissent we are allowed."[60]

All the while, Kent 25 defendants continued to be apprehended, requiring more attorneys to defend them. Though some, like Stanley Tolliver, a well-known African American civil rights lawyer from Cleveland, were willing to reduce their fees, overall the costs of additional legal counsel necessitated more fund-raising. Neil Young, whose rock anthem "Ohio" had become ubiquitous in the aftermath of May 4, joined other rock performers at a benefit concert in Cleveland for the Kent Legal Defense Fund on November 14. Benjamin Spock donated $1,000 to aid the accused, and David Ifshin, the former president of the National Student Association, raised $2,500 for the defense.[61]

Midterm Surprises: Against the Backlash

If efforts to mount a vigorous legal defense of the Kent 25 lifted spirits on campus, so did the midterm elections, on which the White House also had built high hopes. President Nixon had pursued a hardline campaign, hoping to reinvigorate the conservative backlash that had been triggered by the May protests. As we saw in chapter 12, on the day of the Kent State shootings antiwar Democratic congressional candidate John Seiberling—a grandson of Goodyear founder Frank Seiberling—had been speaking at a peace rally with ex-SDSer Bill Whitaker in Akron. Using a photograph of Seiberling and Whitaker taken at the rally, Seiberling's Republican opponent, Congressman William Ayres, tried to capitalize on anti-student sentiment by running a half-page advertisement with the photo in the *Akron Beacon Journal* a day before the November election. Seiberling refused to disavow his association with Whitaker and, with labor support, scored an upset over the ten-term incumbent.[62]

Gubernatorial candidate John Gilligan, who had proposed the unsuccessful peace plank in the Democratic Party platform at the 1968 convention, likewise had to brave White House efforts to polarize the electorate. The day after Gilligan appeared in Kent to rally his supporters, Nixon sought to nationalize the race by launching a media campaign that portrayed all Democrats "as being on the fringes." Appearing in support of GOP candidates in California, he taunted demonstrators with his trademark V-for-victory sign while standing on his car, eventually provoking some to hurl stones at him. Denouncing the dissidents as "hoodlums," the *Record-Courier* extolled the president's "courage under fire," while Nixon's television commercials asked voters to back candidates who would end "the wave of violence in America." But the message failed to catch on, at least for the time being. In Ohio, Kent and Akron elected a new antiwar congressman, while Gilligan, a dovish Democrat, reclaimed the governor's mansion for his party for the first time since 1958.[63]

CHAPTER 14

Carry On

WITH THE aid of Bill Kunstler and other national figures, activists had recovered from the shock of the killings, the indictments, and the efforts of the university administration to curb their movement against the war. As the grand jury proceedings continued, an increasingly diverse group of antiwar diehards sought to shift culpability for the May 1970 killings from the Kent 25 to former governor James Rhodes and the National Guard. Even as they labored to do so, some activists faced new charges that required them to mount their own defenses. Antiwar adherents counted it a victory when KSU's disciplinary board ruled that former Student Mobilization Committee activists turned Yippie leaders Jerry Persky and Jerry Alter would receive conduct probation, instead of expulsion, for collecting legal defense funds without prior permission. Black United Students (BUS) leaders Erwind Blount and Rudy May had better luck when the board found them not guilty of chalking political messages on campus sidewalks. Kent 25 defendants continued to surrender, as former Kent Committee to End the War in Vietnam leader Ruth Gibson returned from California to face arraignment. Gibson joined her fellow defendants in a press conference to hail a decision by US District Court judge William Thomas at the end of January 1971 to expunge the controversial Portage County grand jury report. The ruling was symbolically important, but the judge did not dismiss the indictments that accompanied the report. Thomas's mixed decision ensured that the proceedings against the Kent 25 would go on.[1]

Now Laos

In the meantime, the attention of antiwar activists at Kent State and elsewhere soon turned back to Southeast Asia, after President Nixon authorized US support for a major incursion into Laos by South Vietnamese troops in early

February 1971. The operation aimed cutting supply lines along the Ho Chi Minh Trail and represented a test of Vietnamization. Proponents of turning the fighting over to the South Vietnamese, who were transported into Laos by US helicopters and backed by American airpower, saw the incursion as an experiment in winning the war by prolonging it.[2]

Recognizing the symbolic value of Kent State, former SDS leader Howie Emmer—still banned from campus as a result of a 1969 injunction, but living in Kent—became one of the first to urge local activists to mount an immediate response to the incursion. Robby Stamps, one of those wounded on May 4, was part of a broad coalition that answered the challenge. Hundreds turned out for a demonstration that would result in three arrests for flag desecration, as protestors had lowered the national colors from the university's flagpole and replaced it with protest banners. Emmer went on to Ann Arbor, Michigan, for a conference of the People's Peace Treaty. There he announced that Kent State had held the first protest in the country against the Laos operation.[3]

Overall, though, response nationwide was far more subdued than it had been to the Cambodian invasion. Like the military operation itself, political protest against it failed to meet expectations. Activists could take solace from opinion polls showing that, unlike the support Nixon had generated for the Cambodian operation, a plurality of respondents opposed the incursion and a solid majority favored a firm date to withdraw American troops from Vietnam. A growing national consensus was emerging that the war needed to be brought to an end.[4]

At Kent, the invasion of Laos sparked another round in the interminable chain reaction of escalation, protest, and police response. If the intent behind bringing armed troops to Kent in May 1970 was to suppress the antiwar movement on campus, the ongoing war did the reverse, succeeding only in enlarging and radicalizing its antiwar base. A huge sampling of opinion taken of the 19,000-member student body in the month following the shootings bore this out, as 7,000 students returned lengthy questionnaires about their beliefs and some 540 reported involvement in the protest as either participants (109) or observers (433). A majority of participants in the May 4 protest described their parents as liberal or moderate. Exactly 50 percent of those who participated in the rally and responded to the questionnaire believed that the violent repression of May 4 justified "violent revolutionary change." Lethal measures gave participants reason to reconsider their future involvement, yet 81 percent of the 109 participant responders felt more committed to their activism as a result of the shootings and only 4 percent less so. Observers at the rally on May 4, 1970, felt similarly to the more active participants, as 43 percent of the 433 respondents indicated that they were more likely to demonstrate against the war, with about half that number (23 percent) being less likely. Most seemed willing to surmount whatever hurdles authorities erected.[5]

Just as Howie Emmer understood that the killings had transformed the image of Kent State from remote backwater to emblematical protest hub, so did more prominent antiwar leaders. Emmer and his companion Nancy Kurshan, the onetime girlfriend of Jerry Rubin, used their connections to bring major movement figures, including acquitted Chicago 7 indictee John Froines and Seattle 7 defendant Mike Abeles (a hometown friend of KSU student Mike Brock), to the campus. Froines visited Kent to mobilize support for a planned May 1971 shutdown of Washington, DC, to protest the ongoing Southeast Asian war.[6]

The wing of the antiwar movement that had favored more confrontational tactics used the momentum of the Ann Arbor People's Peace Treaty convention to launch a new peace group—the People's Coalition for Peace and Justice—that would sponsor another series of demonstrations in the nation's capital. Throughout much of the country, colleges and universities continued to turn out ever larger and more diverse numbers of students for national marches, as they had since the mid-1960s, but without a national, chapter-based organization like SDS many campuses proved less capable of sustained grassroots activities. Still, there were campuses where activity proved more or less continuous, such the University of Kansas, where uniformed authorities killed two young protestors in July 1970. But overall, efforts to repress dissent were fostering it instead. By mid-1971, the antiwar movement may have been less well organized on a national scale and less ideologically driven, but it was wider, deeper, and more diverse than ever. As a result, in the battle of wills between an administration determined to prolong the war as long as possible in order to secure peace on its own terms, and a movement determined to stop it, the movement was winning.[7]

A New President Faces Old Challenges

The protest against the Laotian incursion, which attracted a small number of BUS leaders, also signaled a further renewal of interracial cooperation between African Americans and Kent's largely white antiwar left. When two BUS leaders were arrested for allegedly assaulting a student senator a week after the Laos protest on February 5, a BUS spokesman appealed to campus leftists for assistance, saying "It's now or never." On a snowy night of Lincoln's birthday, several hundred marched in support of BUS to President White's campus home. When the normally sympathetic *Daily Kent Stater* criticized the marchers, activists picketed *Stater* offices. Charles Eberhardt of BUS denounced the paper for racial bias, and the accused pair led a another interracial march to White's house, demanding "Free the BUS Two!" Soon after, a weary Robert White announced his plans to retire.[8]

Most likely, White had made the decision before his home came under siege; by now, he had enough. His presidency, begun in the bleak days following the Kennedy assassination, would end under the lingering cloud of one of the worst calamities ever to befall a college campus. Yet during his tenure he had built Kent State's doctoral programs, attracted a more qualified faculty, and expanded the physical size of the campus, which doubled its student body. The very growth of the campus, during the most tumultuous decade in the history of American higher education, created challenges he could not meet. Caught between voices calling for a crackdown on dissent and a growing movement against the war, White found Kent State's education building, where he returned to teach, far less stressful than his duties running the country's most controversial university.[9]

White's exit elicited little regret from the campus left, although most others felt sympathy. His announcement did not make it any easier for White House speechwriter Patrick Buchanan when he appeared on campus on February 24 at the invitation of the small chapter of Young Americans for Freedom. The event drew a respectable turnout of 175, but the majority came to harass, not to applaud him. The hostile crowd rattled Buchanan, who looked unsure of himself all night. The effort by conservatives—initiated days earlier in a debate with Vietnam Veterans Against the War (VVAW)—to win back some political space on the campus ended in defeat.[10]

White's successor, Glenn Olds, a former US representative to UNESCO who held a doctorate in philosophy from Yale, assumed the presidency in September. With wider-ranging experience than White, Olds used his worldly sophistication to contend with minority groups and the antiwar left in the fight for political supremacy on the campus. Later in life, when he ran for the US Senate in Alaska, Olds—an ordained Methodist minister who had also been a professional boxer in his youth—cast himself as "a tough fighter for troubled times." The Oregon native needed tenacity for his new post at Kent State. But Olds also reached out to students in ways that White did not, hoping to tamp down, or at least redirect, protest. For a time, his approach achieved success with moderate students, yet by 1971 campus politics had become more radical than ever. Indeed, the longer the war went on, the more movement activists at Kent were prepared to escalate their tactics to oppose it. Jerry Persky said as much when he told a group of students in February 1971, "As long as the Vietnam War goes on—and it's going to go on—there's going to be trouble."[11]

Calls made by a range of antiwar coalitions to demonstrate in Washington, DC, were all answered at Kent State, as students participated in a succession of marches from mid-April to early May. A carload of activist feminists from Kent joined the Women's March on the Pentagon. The march, said Beverly Gologorsky, a participant from the South Bronx, caused her to feel "at the

center of a movement that would go . . . beyond that day and beyond the war."
Many more went to the National Peace Action Coalition demonstration on
April 24, a march that surpassed the November 1969 Moratorium in size, if not
in militancy. Marchers congested the length of Pennsylvania Avenue. As usual,
journalist I. F. Stone understood both the accomplishment and the remaining
challenge of stopping the war: "The peace movement has risen from the ashes
of Vietnamization and withdrawal. But it still has a long, hard way to go."
Difficult work lay ahead, yet the dual marches paralleled what was taking place
at Kent State, where, far from contracting, the movement was growing larger
and more diverse.[12]

Dewey Canyon III, a series of highly visible demonstrations organized by
VVAW, followed these mass marches. While it attracted only a tiny fraction of
the enormous throng that demonstrated on April 24, the veterans' protest may
well have been one of the tipping points in a six-year battle for public opinion
against the war. Two dozen former servicemen from northeast Ohio, including
Tim Butz and former SDSer Ken Johnson, spent five days protesting the war
in the nation's capital. One who had planned to be among them was former
Kent student Bob Roshon. Drafted in June 1969, Roshon became a part of the
1st Cavalry Division, which participated in the May 1970 Cambodian invasion.
On May 15 of that year he wrote a friend that after his discharge he intended to
"protest the war," vowing, "I'll be right up there at the front. And when some
short-haired, clean-shaven, right-wing fellow shouts me down, I'll look him in
the eye and say, 'What do you know about it?'" Two weeks later, Roshon was
killed in action in Cambodia.[13]

May Day and May 4

The largest turnout from Kent State was for the most defiant of the protests,
planned by the Mayday Collective, led by Rennie Davis, which functioned as
a countercultural arm of the recently organized People's Coalition for Peace
and Justice and sought to blend counterculture sensibilities with civil disobedience tactics. Along with members of the former Chicago 7, the broad collective included former Kent SDSer Colin Neiburger. Leaders of the Mayday
Collective daringly advanced the slogan "If the government won't stop the war,
we'll stop the government." Organizers hoped to paralyze early morning travel
leading into Washington, DC, by obstructing roads with sit-ins, stalling cars
on bridges, and disabling automobiles. Advised of their plans, President Nixon
fumed, "If they start blocking bridges, we'll throw them right off the culverts."
Police moved preemptively. On May 2, 1971, hundreds of riot-equipped law
enforcement officers, part of a force of 5,000 city police backed by as many as
11,400 federal troops and DC National Guardsmen, forced the removal of tens

of thousands of protestors camping in West Potomac Park near the Tidal Basin, depriving the would-be demonstrators of a base of operation. Many thousands left the city.[14]

Early on Monday, May 3, the remaining protestors, some 25,000 in all, tried in vain to reach the targets, including the Potomac bridges, Pentagon cloverleafs, and key traffic circles, all of which were identified in a tactical manual published by the Mayday Collective. Ohio's contingent never got to its objectives, the Theodore Roosevelt and Arlington bridges. Some of the estimated two hundred from Kent, including Roseann Canfora, Greg Hawthorne, Mike Brock, Steve Lieber, Tom Riddle, and Jim Russell (one of the May 4 wounded), reached Constitution Avenue but were driven off by three-wheeled police motorcycles. A leading pacifist described the tactics of the police: "They were zipping back and forth, gunning their motor scooters. . . . I never saw them in such a nasty mood." At once tactically bold and naive, the May Day organizers had assumed that authorities would not interfere with the planned disruption before Monday's target date, despite knowing that the police had detailed knowledge of their intentions. Seven thousand were taken into custody. Their ranks depleted, the remaining protestors resumed their efforts on Tuesday and Wednesday, resulting in thirteen thousand total arrests—the largest number in American history—including sixty-five from Kent.[15]

One student from KSU landed in the same pen with Dr. Benjamin Spock and said to a reporter of the renowned pediatrician, "This is the guy who brought me up." Many of the real parents were supportive; 40 percent of the jailed dissidents reported that their parents sanctioned their actions, and only 29 percent that their parents were critical. The same survey found that 49 percent of those arrested were self-identified radicals. Slightly more than half were college students, although 33 percent held jobs, the remainder being unemployed. In school or in or out of a job, the antiwar activists often had support from family systems and networks of friends. Even a local reporter who spoke with motorists inconvenienced by the disruption found little enthusiasm for remaining in Vietnam. What he did discover was the dilemma faced by protestors: how best to apply effective pressure to speed the end of the Vietnam conflict without making themselves nearly as unpopular as the war. The reporter wrote that "not a single citizen interviewed expressed approval for continuing the war. They just didn't like having the pattern of their lives—and their livelihoods—interrupted."[16]

The massive number of arrests had an immediate impact on activists who remained behind in Kent to plan for the first anniversary of the May 4 killings. For months a heated struggle had raged over control of the commemoration activities. Authorities fearful of having nonstudents on campus required passes for those not registered at the university. Even so, and despite credible rumors about the deployment to Ravenna of the 107th Armored Cavalry in the days before the anniversary, more than ten thousand people turned out for the memorial events, nearly half of the KSU community. A separate rally organized by the local May Day Coalition drew over three thousand, while a breakaway Yippie faction led some eight hundred students into Rockwell Hall, which was serving as the new ROTC center. Although building occupations had once led administrators to respond with mass arrests, now officials took a different approach. Students were pleased when board of trustees chairman Robert C. Dix entered the building to speak with the sit-in demonstrators demanding an end to ROTC. Whether it was the size, the significance of the day, the attention of the out-of-town press, or the violent boasts several students made to a national reporter that "if they call in the Guard, the kids will kill 'em," the administration took a page from the books of other university executives and simply allowed the sit-in to fade. In so doing, they blunted the edge, at least for a day.[17]

On May 20, Kent's radicals were outraged anew at the conviction of Mike Brock for flag desecration, and the anger spilled out at the annual ROTC review the next day. Even as arrests from the ROTC protest mounted, demonstrations spread into town for the first time since May 1970. A crowd of fifteen hundred roamed the North Water Street section of town, throwing stones at police cars and breaking windows in a number of buildings. Several serious injuries resulted, including one from a particularly brutal police clubbing. In all, over eighty people were arrested, among them Jerry Persky and Howie Emmer. As at the recent May Day protests in Washington, DC, disruptions stretched out over five days. Predictably, the *Record-Courier* condemned "irresponsible hooliganism," but hoped the antiwar "fever has run its course" and would become "a thing of the past." Vietnamization had succeeded in diminishing the number of American casualties. Nevertheless, the war continued with great ferocity, a fact driven home by the intense fighting in April at a fire base in South Vietnam where over a hundred Americans soldiers were killed or wounded, losses called "stunning" by *Newsweek*.[18]

At Kent State protest continued to spread, yet the nature of that protest evolved. At the end of the academic year, a long-simmering debate between Yippies, who had stoked the protests in downtown Kent, and more ideologically oriented radicals caused the latter to reestablish the Students for a Democratic Society chapter as soon as the two-year ban on it expired. Confusion with the SDS rump organization under the national control of the Progressive Labor Party eventually led Kent radicals to shelve the troublesome connection and rename themselves the Joe Hill Collective (JHC). Throughout the course of the war, endemic factionalism undermined the movement to end it, a fact borne out in the collapse of SDS, by the bitter, behind-the-scenes infighting at the hastily called Washington protest in May 1970, and by the split in the national antiwar coalitions that had rival groups—the Trotskyist National Peace Action Coalition and the People's Coalition for Peace and Justice—demonstrating on separate weekends in Washington, DC.[19]

The Kent 25 Trials and Another School Year

By the time school resumed in late September 1971, Glenn Olds was in the second week of his presidency. Olds inherited all of White's challenges along with some new ones. In May, former campus security chief Donald Schwartzmiller, who had been dismissed from his post weeks earlier, had revealed the widespread use of covert agents on campus. Even more sensational was the disclosure that SDS members had been purposefully entrapped during a disruption in April 1969, and that undercover agents had "worked closely with FBI and (G-2) army intelligence" in that operation. Pressure built on Olds to put a stop to such tactics, and in October 1971 the new president announced that police spying would end. Most believed him.[20]

Schwartzmiller's replacement, James Fyke, named before Olds assumed the presidency, looked the part of a tough cop. The heavily built, crew-cut Michigan native had worked with the Cook County sheriff's office in Chicago and had been associated with Kent State's Law Enforcement School since 1969. Administrative representatives who selected Fyke in late 1970 made clear that the new chief would have "closer ties to the President's office," a necessity, officials believed, if the protest movement was to be brought under control.[21]

In addition to the revelations of police agents in their midst, activists also confronted the beginning of the Kent 25 trials just as the new academic year got under way. Parallel to these trials were efforts by moderate students to persuade the US Justice Department to convene a federal grand jury to investigate the May 4 killings. The push for a federal grand jury was sharply criticized by some on the left, who were already faced with the defense of the Kent 25 and wanted no part of a probe by the Nixon administration that might lead to further indictments of protestors. Then, quite unexpectedly, the Kent 25 prosecutors encountered difficulty with their lead case. A onetime protestor and veteran was seated as a juror in the trial of a defendant charged with arson in the May 1970 ROTC fire. Unable to budge holdout jurors and faced with a hung jury, prosecutors had to settle for conviction on a reduced charge. Another arson case was dismissed when prosecutors conceded the likelihood of mistaken identity. Following two weeks of poor results and negative publicity, prosecutors dropped the remaining charges. The *Stater* spoke for most on the campus with a one-word editorial: "Rejoice!"[22]

With attention in Kent diverted by the trials and nationwide antiwar activity at low ebb as a result of ongoing troop withdrawals and lower US casualties, major protests against the war in the fall of 1971 drew only thousands or tens of thousands rather than the huge turnouts of the spring. Nevertheless, dozens from Kent marched in Cleveland along with several thousand others on November 6, in a demonstration jointly sponsored by the National Peace Action Coalition and the People's Coalition for Peace and Justice. Adding yet another layer of complexity, scores of activists to the left of both groups participated as part of the George Jackson Brigade. Met by a group of eight neo-Nazis intent on attacking the antiwar protestors, Kent radicals struck first, routing the fascists, whose regalia included uniforms and swastika armbands. Activities resumed on campus as well, albeit at a diminished pace and intensity. VVAW organized many of the events, working closely with the rechristened JHC. Overall, though, in both Kent and across the country, many felt like Beverly Gologorsky, the militant energized by the Women's March on the Pentagon in April 1971: "I don't think we ever lost hope or determination. But because the war was around for so many years the frustration was high and we ran out of [ideas as to] what to do next."[23]

Returning from a January 1972 trip to China as part of the Progressive Student Delegation, Ken Johnson, the VVAW leader on campus, better recognized the need to expand antiwar activity beyond the mostly internal political study favored by the JHC. As a sergeant in Vietnam, Johnson took on the dangerous responsibility of walking point when on patrol. Now, as a graduate student studying labor history, Johnson's proposal to broaden coalition work—what developed into the May 4th United Front—had an immediate and positive impact on antiwar activity. Johnson contended that student power might well disrupt society, but could never transform it, and his focus on the working class caused a number of Kent's activists to rediscover labor history. Along with Steve Martinot, who had relocated to northeast Ohio in 1971, the pair managed to exert considerable influence on activists in the Kent-Akron area. Martinot, once a prominent Progressive Labor Party theoretician, had come to reject the organization's ideological rigidity and to value independent radical thought. Together, the pair melded existing antiwar passion with a more systematic understanding of the society that had launched and prosecuted the war.[24]

Covert Agents and Transparent War

Though the antiwar cohort at Kent State had steadily expanded since May 1970, not all of those in the activist ranks were what they seemed. Although suspicion of undercover agents had been rife since the organization of the KCEWV in 1965, the activities of Reinhold "Ron" Mohr in the aftermath of the May 4 killings stood out. According to his own later statement, Mohr served "in an undercover capacity in and around the campus" while posing as a student beginning in the fall of 1970. To look the part, Mohr grew his hair long and dressed in the style of many students. For eighteen months, his police superiors were content to have Mohr ingratiate himself with members of the antiwar movement and simply gather information on them. In the early winter of 1972, however, their tactics grew more brazen and provocative in an effort to acquire intelligence on antiwar activity and to lure VVAW and the JHC into illegal activity.[25]

But thanks to Ken Johnson's organizational savvy—and perhaps his military training—he and other radicals were able to keep a step ahead of Mohr. Following an apartment break-in and the theft of records from a residence that housed a number of JHC and VVAW members on February 17, the activists deduced that the forced entry had been committed by somebody familiar with the inside of the dwelling. Almost immediately, suspicion pointed to Mohr, who had befriended the occupants by feigning an interested in antiwar activity and had visited the apartment a number of times. Mohr tipped his hand when he tried to get one campus activist to accept a Chinese-made AK-47 assault rifle—an offer that was immediately declined. The VVAW then tipped off the city police that a student radical was in possession of illegal weapons. Relations between city law enforcement and the KSU police had been strained since May 1970, so the local cops were unaware that Mohr was working undercover when they arrested him in April 1972 while holding an AK-47 and a 40mm rocket launcher.[26]

The furor that followed Mohr's outing coincided with a renewed escalation of the Vietnam War. In the spring of 1972, it involved US aerial bombing and the mining of Haiphong harbor in response to a major North Vietnamese attack known here as the Easter Offensive. For the fourth consecutive spring the university community descended into turmoil. Unprepared for the huge response, which involved a larger number of students than did the demonstrations in 1970, JHC radicals attempted to direct the protests and avoid mass arrests. Even so, the 129 students booked on trespassing charges after occupying an ROTC building represented the largest number (until 1977) taken into custody during a single protest at Kent State.[27]

A substantial turnout—including hundreds of VVAW members—for the second annual May Fourth commemoration remained peaceful, but on May 9 police in town made abundant use of wooden bullets—nonlethal, but terrifying nonetheless—when a huge antiwar demonstration spilled over in the city's streets. Nine days later, a dangerous confrontation occurred at the campus ROTC review, where guns were drawn on protestors for the first time since the fatal shootings. All of this occurred in the midst of bitter recriminations between the new KSU security chief, James Fyke, and antiwar radicals. In addition to the apartment break-in and the related activities by Mohr, tie-rods were cut in an activist's car. His comrades took the fight to Fyke, putting up posters around campus portraying him as a Nazi storm trooper and hitting back with a lawsuit. For Olds, who had declared that police spying would stop, Mohr's arrest and the new round of protests proved a trial by fire. He threatened to declare a state of emergency in order "to sustain a peaceable campus and . . . town."[28]

The end of the 1971–72 academic calendar marked the eighth year of antiwar protest at Kent State. Those who started school in 1968, a time when the fighting in Vietnam reached its peak, graduated with the knowledge that during their college years the war had grown to encompass all of Southeast Asia. As the 1972 presidential election approached and stubborn protest and national disillusionment with the war continued, Nixon further reduced the level of US troops in Vietnam and sharply reduced US casualties. In response to the Easter Offensive in April and May he escalated the use of US air power and perpetuated the fighting. Hence peace activists had to wrestle with the hard reality of ongoing conflict amid a diminished role of American ground forces, just as the White House had to accept that the antiwar movement had not subsided and that the public had generally become disenchanted with US involvement. Public opinion remained ever volatile, however; approval for the war shot up to 59 percent after Nixon's response to the Easter Offensive, but protest soared nationwide as well.[29]

Among local elites as well as concerned citizens who understandably resented the disruptions caused by Kent's antiwar activists, some believed that ways had to be found to spare the community further turmoil. Following a fresh round of protests in April and May 1972 that attracted as many as four thousand demonstrators, back-to-back editorials in the *Record-Courier* sounded a tone of exhaustion, even as national polls gave the president hope that his Vietnamization strategy would ensure his reelection. As one of the paper's editors conceded the day after antiwar students blocked noonday traffic in town, "The truth of the matter is that people are just plain sick of the war."[30]

Trying to pose an alternative to unruly protest, student editors called for the removal of ROTC, while some residents of Kent embraced a KSU professor's plan for a nationwide observance for peace. Billed as the "11th Hour" campaign, the idea involved everyday citizens leaving homes, schools, and workplaces for five minutes at 11 a.m. on Monday, May 15, and standing outside for peace. In comparison to the large and disorderly protests that were engulfing campus and community, the *Stater* found the turnout deficient. All the same, fifteen hundred gathered on the front of campus, with hundreds more outside every classroom building, including four hundred at Bowman Hall, where, seven years earlier, six vulnerable antiwar pickets faced the screams of hundreds of counterprotestors. Even most of the campus buses stopped to let student passengers stand outside, while a hundred townspeople gathered at the main downtown intersection, where protestors in May 1970 had been driven back by police.[31]

"The one chance we have to end this war."

Those hoping to avoid fresh disorders may have taken solace from the peaceful "11th Hour" protest in May, as well as from students embracing electoral politics as a means of ending US involvement in Vietnam. In this regard, SDS's rejection in 1968 of all electoral activity and the August 1972 spray-painting of political slogans on buildings in downtown Kent represented the past more than the future. Throughout the fall, voter registration campaigns and mass rallies replaced confrontational politics.[32]

In the first week of October, Daniel Ellsberg, who had touched off a national firestorm with the release of the Pentagon Papers in June 1971, came to Kent State to talk about the continuing need for antiwar dissent and—more immediately—the candidacy of Democratic presidential nominee George McGovern. Electing McGovern, Ellsberg told a crowd of fifteen hundred Kent students, "is the one chance we have to end this war." *Stater* polls showed students in agreement, with 66 percent favoring McGovern. Later in the month, Tom Hayden and former POW and Green Beret George Smith, campaigning at KSU for McGovern as part of the Indochina Peace Campaign, generated an even larger turnout.[33]

Passage of the Twenty-sixth Amendment in 1971, an effort undertaken by lawmakers in the wake of the student strike in May 1970, lowered the voting age to eighteen and provided young people with an orderly means of affecting Vietnam policy. Many clearly intended to do so, as Portage County registered twenty thousand new voters. On election day, some voters passed political graffiti, still visible from summer months, that read "Nixon Thou Shall Not Win." A younger electorate made the outcome in the county closer than elsewhere, but even the participation of thousands of new voters could not deny Nixon a victory; he carried Portage by 2,600 votes out of 44,000 cast.[34]

Throughout the campaign, the president's supporters had chanted "Four more years" at reelection rallies. Now facing that reality, weary activists doggedly resumed their work. Causes multiplied—women's rights and gay liberation. Still, the war stood out. Jerry Persky, Ken Johnson, and Alan Morris, the latter two of whom had outed undercover agent Ron Mohr, provided the campus movement with continuity. New VVAW president Mike Carmedy, an Akron rubber worker's son, working-class sophomore Mike Pacifico, and blue-collar transfer students Bob Donofrio and Linda Gerard were among those who provided fresh enthusiasm to the work. The steady spread of antiwar sentiment at Kent State was evident in the turnout of some seven thousand students at several showings of the short documentary *Kent State: May, 1970*, produced by independent filmmaker Alva Cox and narrated by veteran actor E. G. Marshall. Weeks later, the campus awoke to chilling headlines of additional campus fatalities: two African Americans had been shot at Southern University in Baton Rouge, Louisiana. Several hundred turned out to protest at Kent State. The slayings, coupled with the reinstatement of Ron Mohr to his campus police position (albeit in a uniformed capacity), reminded activists that challenges remained.[35]

The Christmas Bombings

Winter break at Kent State brought antiwar activists, already dispirited by the November election, news many could hardly bear. In mid-December, the Nixon administration ordered waves of B-52s to bomb North Vietnamese cities in a bid to punish Hanoi for holding firm to its treaty demands at the Paris peace talks. Eight years earlier, aerial sorties code-named "Rolling Thunder" had produced the first public opposition to the war at Kent State. The December raids brought forth one last display, eliciting another spike in antiwar radicalism. An older student who admitted that he had never before "expressed my disgust and opposition" to the war now denounced the bombing escalation, and the war itself, as designed "to protect the interests of the capitalistic and imperialistic masters of the United States."[36]

The massive aerial strikes offered the hawks at home one final display of America military might and convinced a still reluctant South Vietnamese president Nguyen Van Thieu to soften his opposition to the peace process, but they had no significant impact on the unyielding Vietnamese communists. Almost from the beginning of his presidency, Richard Nixon had justified continued involvement in the fighting as a necessary means of forcing North Vietnam to return US prisoners of war. Although such demands were without precedent in the history of American wars—and somewhat illogical, since historically POWs have been exchanged after hostilities cease—it was not until the approaching second inaugural that the Nixon administration, knowing of the war weariness in the nation, agreed to a complete US troop withdrawal in exchange for the POWs' release. As one of Henry Kissinger's aides wryly observed, ultimately the Christmas bombings accomplished nothing more than convincing the North Vietnamese "to accept our concessions." As many historians of the war have concluded, the peace terms that the United States finally accepted to end the Vietnam War were not noticeably different from those they had rejected at the beginning of Nixon's presidency.[37]

A Bitter End to a Bitter War

Fifty Kent SDS members answered the muster call of protest that drew ten thousand hardcore demonstrators to Washington, DC, for Nixon's first inaugural in January 1969. Now, four years later, as many as a hundred thousand, including longtime dissidents like Jerry Persky and Bill Arthrell, along with VVAW leaders Johnson, Morris and Carmedy, turned out to protest what national columnist Joseph Kraft labeled a "bitter inaugural." In a cold, steady wind, a VVAW member played taps in Arlington Cemetery, where 2,500 veterans had gathered to honor the fallen. Given the generally low expectations, few activists were prepared for the news that followed the inaugural protest. Days later, American and North Vietnamese negotiators signed the agreement ending the Vietnam War. Skepticism was justified, yet even skeptics celebrated. But, as Kent's VVAW leader Alan Morris feared, more conflict lay ahead; fighting would continue for another two years, with the last battle not fought until May 1975, off the coast of Cambodia.[38]

Even so, the Paris Peace Agreement represented a generational and historic milestone. Lyndon Johnson, whose presidency was destroyed by the conflict, died prematurely just days before the agreement was signed. Locally, inauguration day also brought word of the resignation of KSU's often-reviled security chief, James Fyke. Glenn Olds attributed to his departure in part to the "problems of directing security operations on a campus restless over the Vietnam conflict and our own tragedy." Peace abroad failed to produce local reconciliation, as intermittent campus conflict, which lingered and then burst anew over the course of six months in 1977, eventually marked the end of Olds's tenure as well. The experienced diplomat and educator, who served four US presidents in a variety of posts, could not, in the end, solve the dispute over how the memory and site of the fatal antiwar confrontation would be preserved.[39]

In 1973, as scores of militants at Kent looked forward to addressing other political issues and economic contradictions—veterans' needs, women's rights, and, most of all, labor issues—many also looked back for a useable past to sustain those future struggles. In the months following the transitory armistice in Vietnam, one member of the Kent community, Mayo Johnson, wrote that May 1970 had left "scars in the minds of people here and around the world." But, Johnson added, it was important not to forget what the "four martyrs" and their fellow demonstrators were protesting: "the illegal and ruthless entry of United States troops into Cambodia."[40]

The 1970 invasion ignited a powder keg built by years of dissent. The killings at Kent State meant to contain the explosion of protest over the Cambodian invasion instead spread embers of dissension to every corner of the country, threatening, in Henry Kissinger's estimation, "the very fabric of government." Thereby, the outcry of opposition against the fatal shootings worked against the Nixon/Kissinger policy and led to an early US withdrawal from Cambodia.[41]

After May 4, radicals believed ongoing direct-action protest to be a necessary measure against the unending war and, consequently, justified acts that disrupted the normal functioning of society. Whatever immoderate means students used to sway the course of the war and, as an unintended consequence, create broader political space for congressional liberals, their methods did little to enhance the popularity of the movement or its participants. Influenced by the disorders they witnessed in Chicago and Washington during and after 1968–69, Kent's antiwar students brought the tactics home. Many, like the Yippies, believed that the enormous countercultural cohort that had grown after Woodstock was certain to consolidate politically. In turn, they supposed their political and cultural modeling would influence upcoming generations and achieve societal transformation. Instead, they learned that changing hairstyles and fashions, while undeniably influencing social mores, did not lead to a transformation of the political culture.[42]

Ideological activists rejected theories of youth culture agency and looked instead to labor for political change. They joined or organized unions, seeking to build up new centers of power, but did not yet realize that unions had already entered a period of decades-long decline, as labor faced deindustrialization, technological innovation, financial deregulation, and globalization of investment. Untiring opponents of the New Deal, exemplified by Ohio's John M. Ashbrook, a founder of the American Conservative Union, were energized anew by funding from business groups and guidance from think tanks. This political-corporate fusion dominated the economic policies of every president after Ford.[43]

Yet in 1973 the resurgence of the American right that culminated in the 1980 election could not be clearly foreseen. All that activists could know then was that as long as the war went on they would persevere in opposing a conflict that had cost them, their families, their communities, and their country too much. Few Kent students may have known of Mario Savio's 1964 extemporaneous lamentation, delivered during the Free Speech crisis in Berkeley, but class commitments, opposition to racial discrimination, and the Vietnam War caused them to carry out its enduring spirit: "There's a time when the operation of the machine becomes so odious, makes you so sick at heart that you can't take part, that you can't even tacitly take part. And you've got to put your bodies upon the gears and upon the wheels, upon the levers, upon all the apparatus and you've got to make it stop." As much as on any university campus during the long 1960s, Kent State students lived and died by these words.[44]

The Death of a Decade?

"The sixties" did not end with the shootings at Kent State and Jackson State, or the bombing in Madison, or the bloodshed of Chicanos in Los Angles. Nor did the peace movement fade away, even in the face of "Vietnamization" and the phased withdrawal of American troops. Far from contracting, the movement only grew larger and more diverse in the years following May 4, making it impossible for the Nixon administration to extend the war indefinitely and ultimately forcing the US to negotiate a settlement on its adversary's terms.

The tendency to use the Kent State killings as an end point, a "death of the decade" thesis, as it were, cannot explain the persistence of activism on the campus where the deaths occurred. Rather than intimidate, the killings intensified feelings on both sides of Kent's political divide, leaving many antiwar activists doggedly resolute. At Kent State, dread battled determination. In the end, determination won.

Cleveland's political culture had been important to the development of activism at Kent State, yet one of its residents, Ellen Glass, a member of Kent's class of 1970, would not be there to see tenacity prevail. Her words, though, painted a picture that others would finish. "Rhodes and Nixon . . . think that you scare kids," Glass said. "But when you kill four students, those things don't happen." Inured to violence rather than cowed by it, radicals like Doug Vaughan—the son of a "hillbilly populist"—became more numerous. Vaughan, who had the survived a slaughter of hundreds of students in Mexico City in early October 1968, insisted on putting the Kent killings in broad context, arguing, "Massacre is nothing new to Browns, Yellows, Reds and Blacks of this world," which he blamed on "American capitalism . . . , racism and imperialism." Going on to what would be a lifetime of activism, Vaughan asserted in the immediate aftermath of the May killings that the students died "trying to stop the war machine."[45]

Wide circulation of the photograph of Jeff Miller's body, an anthem written by Neil Young, and, most of all, the sheer magnitude of the national student strike that involved millions of people, including thousands of workers, ensured that the killings would not be forgotten. Kent State students had little choice but to remember the deaths: thousands of them witnessed the killings or heard the gunfire, many hundreds knew the dead and wounded, Dean Kahler and his wheelchair became a familiar sight on campus, and a bullet hole marked a prominent sculpture near the crest of Taylor Hill. As long as the war lasted, so would the movement to oppose it.

A Battlefield of Memory

THE BATTLE over the meaning and memory of May 4 began almost as soon as the shooting stopped. We've seen that as news of the killings at Kent State University spread in May 1970, outraged students throughout the country went on strike to protest the violent suppression of peaceful dissent, while countless other people expressed the view that Kent's protestors only got what they deserved. In many ways these two reactions framed the subsequent debate: Were the casualties a deliberate act of injustice that must be remembered in order to be rectified? Were these young people unarmed combatants in a war to stop a war? And were the students themselves primarily responsible for what happened—the killings an object lesson in what happens when dissent turns into confrontation? Or was it all just a tragic mistake (like the war itself, as some believed), leaving wounds that could only be healed through acts of reconciliation? How much responsibility lay with Governor Rhodes, who had ordered the National Guard troops to Kent, and how much with the officers who commanded those forces?

On the Kent State campus, the initial phase of the battle pitted those who insisted on highlighting the political significance of May 4 against those who preferred to make it an occasion for personal reflection and collective mourning. Beginning with the observance of the first anniversary of the killings in 1971 and continuing to 1975, antiwar activists clashed with the KSU administration over whether the commemoration should involve a call to further political action or be limited to public rituals of remembrance and shared sorrow. In the immediate aftermath of the shootings, KSU president Robert I. White struggled to come up with a coherent explanation of what had occurred. He established several groups to probe the causes of the turmoil, which reached the unsurprising conclusion that President Nixon's Cambodian gambit had triggered the campus protests. Other administration officials, however, attributed the unrest to "will-o-the-wisp characters who move from campus to campus, from confrontation to confrontation, fomenting unrest and inciting to violence." White himself echoed the idea that outside agitators played a role in the disorders, even though virtually all of the protestors at Kent State either were or had been students there, and all of the casualties on May 4, 1970, were enrolled at the university.[1]

Some of the wounded students who remained enrolled, like Robby Stamps and Dean Kahler, resumed their political activism, and as antiwar protest on campus continued into the new academic year the administration realized that the first anniversary of the shootings could not pass without a public commemoration of some kind. In February 1971, a week after a protest against the invasion of Laos led to arrests for flag desecration, White appointed the student body president, Craig Morgan, graduate student Steve Sharoff, and a mild-mannered KSU administrator and later dean of student affairs, Richard Bredemeier, along with six others, to the President's May 4 Committee. Promoting the view that "It happened to us all," the committee appealed for input from the larger student body. But left-wing students would have none of it. Having battled the university since the spring of 1968, they saw White's administration as complicit in the Vietnam War, if not in the campus killings. Rejecting any notion of a community of suffering, they asserted their right to take charge of the commemoration and formed the alternative, student-led May 4 Coalition for that purpose. Dissent soon spread to the university-sponsored committee, as some faculty members broke away to support the Coalition. Still another allied group, the May Day Coalition, worked at mobilizing students to attend a national protest in Washington, DC, aimed at shutting down the capital during the week of May 3 to dramatize opposition to the continuing war.[2]

In the end, differences between the university and the antiwar left proved insurmountable. Amid published reports of another National Guard deployment to the area and administration threats to bar outsiders from the commemoration by requiring proof of student status, separate observances went on. Drawing from the example of the spontaneous vigil held after the first memorial service in the fall of 1970, sociology professor Jerry Lewis and one of his students, Michelle Klein, organized an unsanctioned candlelight march on the eve of May 4, 1971. The following day, the Victory Bell on the campus Commons, which had called students to the fateful rally a year before, sounded in memory of those killed at Kent and Jackson State. Jesse Jackson spoke at the official ceremony, while Julian Bond was the featured speaker at the gathering organized by the May 4 Coalition. An estimated ten thousand people attended one or both observances; many of them seemed to know or care little about which group sponsored the events. Following the Coalition program, antiwar students took over the ROTC building that replaced the one burned to the ground the previous spring and held it for a number of hours. But there were no arrests. In fact, the only Kent State activists arrested that day were among the hundreds, including May 4 casualty Jim Russell, who left campus for the national protest in Washington, DC.[3]

Over the next four years activist students and May 4th survivors and their families continued to make it explicit that they, and no one else, were guardians of the memories of those killed at Kent State. In April 1975, as Saigon fell to the conquering North Vietnamese Army and its southern allies, the war in Southeast Asia finally ended. In response, and reflecting the radicalization the war had engendered, a number of Kent State students sounded a triumphant note on the occasion of the fifth commemoration of the May 4 killings. Bitter over the dismissal months earlier of a federal conspiracy case against eight guardsmen, and linking the campus killings to the war, crowds of Kent State students heralded what they understood to be a victory in Southeast Asia. "When the actions of our government were condemned," one Ohio daily noted in its coverage of the commemoration, "the overwhelmingly young rally audience responded with enthusiasm rarely seen in this post-demonstration era." Days earlier Michelle Klein, the KSU graduate who had helped organize the 1971 candlelight march, offered a perspective about her obligation to the past. Referring to those like herself who had been students on May 4, she said: "There aren't many of us left [on campus] and we've become a cadre for people to point to." Students like Klein were visible links to a past they would not allow others at Kent State to forget.[4]

KSU officials had a different reaction to the end of the war, seeing it as a time for concluding public commemorations of the May 4 killings. Current and former students Alan Canfora, Dean Kahler, and Robby Stamps, all casualties of the National Guard, sought to preserve the memory of the struggle, believing that, as a national paper put it, "the wounds of Kent State are felt still." Together the three men, whose fates had been randomly joined together by gunfire, took up a proposal made by student government leaders and established the May 4 Task Force to carry on the commemorations. In the years that followed, students who cycled in and out of the Task Force kept the memory of that day alive for successive generations. With annual commemorations and large crowds attracted in major anniversary years, tens of thousands of former and current activists, students, the politically supportive and the historically curious, either took time from classes or returned to campus to participate in the annual remembrance ceremonies. They formed a persistent constituency that saw the killings as synonymous with governmental injustice. By the time of the fortieth anniversary in 2010, two constants remained: the May 4 Task Force candlelight vigil and march honoring the dead and the task force's insistence on linking the vocal antiwar principles of May 1970 to the struggles of the present.[5]

Battling in Court

Despite the conclusions of his own Scranton commission that the shootings were unjustified, President Richard Nixon had determined early on there would be no federal probe of the killings. After his presidency became crippled by the Watergate scandal, however, Nixon's influence in the Justice Department waned. A criminal investigation by the Justice Department then resulted in felony and misdemeanor charges against eight Ohio National Guardsmen in late March 1974 for violating the constitutional rights of the thirteen students shot. Hopes that a trial would disclose new information and result in convictions for the guardsmen were soon dashed. After ten days of testimony, federal judge Frank Battisti granted a directed verdict, dismissing the case before it went to the jury. Battisti ruled that the Justice Department prosecutor had not proved that any of the guardsmen had a specific intent to deprive the students of their constitutional liberties. Leaving the courtroom, one juror told indicted guardsman James McGee, "Now you can get back to a normal life." Four other defendants—James Pierce, William Perkins, Barry Morris, and Matthew McManus—took time to autograph a trial exhibit photograph that showed them firing the fatal salvo at the students. An outraged Arthur Krause, whose daughter had been among the slain, stated, "I still want the truth to come out and it didn't come out here."[6]

Pursuit of answers and legal remedies did not end with the dismissal of the criminal case. Parents of the slain students and families of the survivors filed civil damages suits in Ohio state courts against Governor James Rhodes, KSU's Robert White, and scores of guardsmen and officers. Starting in 1971 and continuing over a four-year period, various levels of Ohio courts all decided that the state had immunity from prosecution under the Eleventh Amendment. Several separate suits filed by families eventually reached the US Supreme Court, with one case—Scheuer v. Rhodes, decided on April 17, 1974—resulting in a reversal of the lower court decisions. In a unanimous ruling, the justices determined that plaintiffs had the right to seek damages against defendants such as Rhodes and the individual guardsmen.[7]

With the way finally cleared, a civil damages trial commenced in Cleveland with jury selection beginning in May 1975, not long after the fifth anniversary of the killings. Following sixteen weeks of testimony, the assault and intimidation of a juror, and repeated telephone threats against the lead counsel for the plaintiffs ("lay off the defendants, or we'll get you"), jurors rendered a 9–3 decision to exonerate all of the defendants. General Sylvester Del Corso of the Ohio National Guard celebrated the verdict as a triumph for "law enforcement in this country." Speaking for the plaintiffs, Arthur Krause, long the mainstay of the thirteen families, denounced the guardsmen as "armed barbarians" and said of the jury, "Thanks to them, murder by the state is correct."[8]

That might well have been the end of legal proceedings had it not been for Sanford Rosen, an appellate attorney with ties to the Mexican-American Legal Defense Fund. Rosen made clear to the plaintiffs that the odds against winning an appeal were steep. But in the midst of a struggle, which had become national news, to stop construction of a gymnasium on part of the site of the Kent State killings, a federal appeals court granted the plaintiffs a new trial. The court found that the presiding judge in the 1975 civil damages case had mishandled the assault and threat to a juror.[9]

That presiding judge stepped down from hearing the case a second time, and after just one day of testimony in late December 1978, the newly assigned federal judge, William K. Thomas, brokered an out-of-court settlement. In return for an end to civil litigation, the agreement stipulated that $600,000 be paid by the state to the families of the plaintiffs and that a statement of responsibility be signed by the sitting governor, two former generals, and twenty-five current and former members of the Ohio National Guard who remained as defendants. Guardsman Larry Mowrer, whose poor distance vision prevented him from seeing where he was firing, was the first to sign; indicted shooter James Pierce was the last. Some called the statement an apology. Others, including one of the signers, General Del Corso, loath to sooth Kent's lingering wounds, maintained that it was nothing of the kind: "There is no apology," he said. "We expressed sorrow and regret just as you would express condolences to the family of someone who died"—a coldly ironic analogy given that four "someones" had been fatally shot at distances ranging from 265 to 390 feet.[10]

Battling on the Landscape of Memory

Jury panels in some of the May 4th trials had been taken by the court to visit the site of the 1970 killings in order to gain a better understanding of the course of the day's events. Some of the very ground they traversed in 1974 had been threatened by the university's plans to expand the school's gymnasium. On May 4, 1977, the seventh annual commemoration of the killings drew a crowd of three thousand (including the mother of slain student Sandy Scheuer, attending her first commemoration); after the ceremony, half that number, chanting "Stop the gym," marched to a building where university trustees were meeting. Hundreds occupied the building to protest the planned gym annex. During the ten-hour sit-in, the protestors fashioned a list of eight demands, most of which concerned justice for the killings and preserving the space where the students had been slain. Drawing on an old name, they styled themselves the May 4th Coalition.[11]

To guard the site, several dozen protestors erected tents on the hilltop from which guardsmen fired the fatal volley. Over the course of the two-month occupation, Glenn Olds—who a year earlier had announced that "the human and public effects of 1970 have been virtually healed"—resigned as Kent State's president. On July 12, police forcefully, but peacefully, arrested 193 people on the "Tent City" site, including Martin and Sarah Scheuer, whose daughter, Sandy, had been slain, all six members of Albert Canfora's family, and Vietnam veteran turned antiwar protestor Ron Kovic. Coalition lawyers, including former KCEWV leader Tony Walsh and Kent 25 defense attorney William Kunstler, sought in vain to stop construction through court action. Several increasingly radical gatherings in September and October, one of which drew three thousand people from other midwestern colleges, defied legal restraining orders and confronted heavily armed police. Even some of the university trustees, including David Dix, son of the former trustee and publisher Robert C. Dix, announced their opposition. "We . . . cannot ignore the worst thing that ever happened to the Kent community," he said. Dix added that plans to efface the site went "against my conscience." A Cleveland newspaper columnist wrote, "I weep for those poor, sorry, stiff-necked Establishment flacks who run Kent State. They are wrong. They are wrong. They indeed are obscene."[12]

The battle to stop the gym, which ironically had begun on May 4, was lost, but the war was won. Over the course of the sixty-two-day occupation, Governor James Rhodes, who had returned to the office in January 1975 and would be elected again in 1978, had been confronted with a Coalition picket during a stop in Portage County and learned that a civil suit against him and the guardsmen had been reinstated. Rhodes's time in office was summarized by a Cleveland newspaper headline at the time of his March 2001 death: "He led Ohio for four terms, but Kent State marred legacy." Of his failure to reveal much about the killings, a newspaper columnist wrote: "James A. Rhodes took a secret to his grave. . . . [Kent State] is still an open wound."[13]

As one century ended and a new one began, students who passed through the May 4 Task Force continued to hold annual candlelight marches and commemoration ceremonies and pressed to have those they never knew be remembered. Through their labors and with support from the families of the fallen, a memorial was dedicated on a site overlooking the Commons in 1990, as well as other commemorative markers and structures that were later installed on the campus. In 1999 memorials were placed where the students were killed in the Prentice Hall parking lot, and in 2007 a historical marker erected by the Ohio Historical Society was unveiled. A new university visitor center at the site, complete with outdoor signage, was dedicated in May 2013. The remainder of the place where guardsmen maneuvered prior to the killings, which had been so encroached upon in 1977, is now part of a larger seventeen-acre area that received a state historical marker in 2007 and was named to the National Register of Historic Places in 2010.[14]

Commemorative activities sometimes played out in a local environment that proved unreceptive. Alan Canfora, frequently maligned for his part in the May 1970 protest and his more central role in the war over its memory, was one of two selected in 2003 to ring a bicentennial bell in Portage County to mark the two hundredth anniversary of Ohio's statehood. The local paper promptly orchestrated a successful campaign to get him disinvited. Getting to the very essence of the long-term political tension between Ohio's urban centers and small-town exemplars, the paper referred to Canfora as a "lightning rod for those with strong feelings about patriotism and the Vietnam War" and emphasized his background, referring to his industrial and once heavily unionized hometown in "bedrock Summit County," which contrasted sharply "to Portage County . . . [whose residents are] happy to celebrate the harvest, the achievements of 4-H youngsters, the nurturing of small business, and the all important work of farming."[15]

Though not the only example of rival visions of how best to remember the campus's history of dissent, such opposition proved, at least thus far in the new century, no longer to dominate Kent State's memory war. Rather, centrally aided by eyewitnesses to the deadly events of May 4th, like Laura Davis and her colleague, the late Carole Teminsky Barbato, also present on campus that day, the university and others have finally, if not entirely, made peace with the past. By determining who would construe the significance of the shootings at Kent State, activists not only kept the memory of the killings from fading from public view, but helped define them as a watershed event in post–World War II American history. Since retributive justice was never won, that must be enough.[16]

APPENDIX

After the War—The Fates of Kent's Activist Generation

MYTHS CONTINUE to shroud the sixties. Conservatives—often people of means—have frequently sought to convince their less prosperous believers that Vietnam-era radical students constituted a social elite. This generalization ignores the fact that the millions of young people enrolled in college during the long 1960s not only attended a wide array of schools, ranging from the highly selective to the noncompetitive, but also came from households of very diverse socioeconomic status.

In the academic continuum of 1960s America, Kent State was located somewhere in the slightly lower end of the broad middle. While admission standards were low, especially for in-state students, scholastic expectations were considerably higher and consistent with comparable state universities within and outside of Ohio. Hence, students who were unprepared or unwilling to do academic work did not graduate. Those who did, including many from its activist cohort, achieved a measure of professional success or made their mark in other ways. A related and enduring myth concerning sixties activists is that the privileged protestors abandoned dissent upon leaving the campus. According to this view, the antiwar cohort discarded activism for financial gain and spent the remainder of their lives seeking material comfort rather than social change. Those intimate with the past know that history is more complicated.

There is considerable scholarship available to refute such notions, but much of it has yet to penetrate popular thinking. In order to better track the assortment of people who figure in the detailed narrative of this book, as well as to address these myths that still surround the sixties, this appendix traces the post-activist years of the dissidents and a few of their professors. While by no means an exhaustive listing of those who people the narrative, it is reasonably comprehensive. Listings also include the organization or organizations with which the activist was associated as well as the years when he or she was most involved. A list of abbreviations used follows the text.

IN THE lonely vanguard of Kent State's long Sixties, the late **Gabriel Kolko** (SLID, 1954) went on to prominence as a historian and the author of thirteen books. **Lance Buhl** (KCHA, 1960–61) eventually followed suit at Harvard, where he obtained a PhD in history. He taught American history there and at Cleveland State University, published in his field, and worked as an educational consultant. He now lives in North Carolina. **Ken Hammond** (SDS, KLDF, Kent 25, 1967–72) also received a doctorate in history from Harvard. A specialist in Chinese history, he teaches at New Mexico State University. His friend **Roman Tymchyshyn** (*TKQ*, KLDF, 1957–77) obtained a number of advanced degrees and taught for years at colleges in Pennsylvania, where he now lives.

Bob Ehrlich, an instructor in the English department when he headed the Kent Committee to End the War in Vietnam (KCEWV, 1965–67), spent his life in academe teaching in the western part of the United States. **Barbara Brock** and her late husband, **Ron Wittmaack** (YSA, KCEWV, 1963–66), worked for years against the war before they returned to Ohio, where Barbara also taught college English. **Carolyn "Candy" (Erickson) Knox** (KCEWV, SDS, 1966–69) remade her life following the upheavals at Kent, and now teaches educational technology at the University of Oregon. As she did at Kent State, Knox continues to nourish activism and activists, now doing so, in part, through an email discussion list. **Larry Simpson** (BUS, 1967–70) became a college administer, serving in a number of posts at schools in Ohio and Massachusetts. **Ollie Fein** and **Charlotte Phillips** (Case Western SDS, ERAP, 1964–67) were never students at Kent, but were among those whose activism influenced the campus movement there. After medical school they continued to support progressive people and causes, such as the Health Policy Advisory Center (Health/PAC).

Among KSU faculty members mentioned in the pages of this book, two appear often: sociologist **Jerry M. Lewis** and historian **Ken Calkins**. Both are now retired. Almost from the start of May 4 commemorative activity, Jerry Lewis taught classes about the killings and continues to be called upon by the national media to comment on the legacy of the fatal shootings. A new and updated edition of his book *Kent State and May 4th* (coauthored with Thomas R. Hensley) was published in 2010. Ken Calkins continues to reside in Kent. Periodically, he contributes his memories about the social movement of the 1960s.

Given the often confrontational nature of Kent State's student movement, it may strike some as odd that a number of former activists chose the law as a profession. **Tony Walsh** (CORE, KCEWV, 1963–66), whose physical size and assertive personality ensured that Kent State had dominant figure in its activist ranks, aided many people and causes during and after law school. He stayed in his native Cleveland, supported Attica and Kent 25 defendants, and was a frequent presence at May 4 observances. He also continued to take stage roles in plays ranging from Shakespeare's Earl of Kent to Steinbeck's Pa Joad, and once acted in a television movie. Walsh died of a heart attack in March 2005. Similarly, **Bill Whitaker** (KCEWV, SDS, 1967–69) worked for the Kent Legal Defense Fund; he now has a legal practice in Akron and, like Walsh, has aided progressive causes and candidates. One of his daughters graduated from Kent State, where she was active in the May 4 Task Force. **Ruth Gibson** (YSA, KCEWV, Kent 25, 1966–72), **Vince Modugno** (KCEWV, SDS, 1966–70), and **Dave Dyer** (YD, 1964–70) all became lawyers in the Akron-Kent area. Dyer became involved in the Portage County Democratic Committee; Gibson, Modugno, and Vince's wife, **Carolyn Carson** (YSA, KCEWV, 1966–70), either maintain a certain visibility in progressive movements or identify with them.

Robert Pickett (BUS, 1968–70) and **Jerry Persky** (SMC, YIP, 1967–73) also became attorneys. Pickett aided the plaintiffs in the *Krause v. Rhodes* civil case by testifying on their behalf. He became part of a successful practice in his native New Jersey. Persky shifted his activism to opposing US involvement in Central America and electoral work. His legal practice is mostly on behalf of people denied Social Security disability claims. He lives with his wife and family in Southern California. **Hunter Havens** (Cleveland SDS, 1969–70) and **Mark Real** (SDS, 1967–70) also pursued careers in the law and retain an interest in civil rights and social advocacy.

Not surprisingly, a few activists turned to writing or journalism. After the collapse of SDS, **Carl Oglesby** spent years as a researcher, speaker, and author. His memoir, *Ravens in the Storm,* published in 2008, was well received and widely reviewed. He died in 2011. Until the early 1970s, **Barbara Gregorich** (YSA, CORE, KCEWV, 1965–67) and **John McCann** (KCHA, YSA, CORE, KCEWV, 1960–68) lived in Cleveland, immersed in left-wing activities. Initially a college professor, Gregorich later became a successful author of both adult nonfiction and children's books. She now lives in Illinois. McCann continued to divide his time between toiling on Lake Erie ore boats and work as a mechanic. He later settled in the Pacific Northwest, where he is believed to have worked in the aircraft industry. He died in the late 1990s before he could be interviewed for this study.

Allen Richardson, who was not affiliated with any antiwar groups, absorbed the literary traditions of his hometown of Elyria, Ohio—once home to Sherwood Anderson—and spent his life as a journalist, much of the time in Europe. Author of several books and an op-ed article about Kent State for the *New York*

Times, Richardson and his wife now live in Connecticut. **Tom Riddle** (MDC, 1970–73) put his computer expertise to work as a member of an NGO in Cambodia during the UN-supervised elections in 1993 and subsequently published *Cambodian Interlude,* a darkly humorous book about that country's humorless situation. The following year he worked in Laos with the Mines Advisory Group, an NGO that instructs Lao people how to safely unearth and destroy unexploded bombs dropped on the country by the US Air Force during the Vietnam War. **Marty Pahls** (SPU, 1962–64) composed the introductions to three collections of salty comic books authored by his former brother-in-law, the writer and illustrator Robert Crumb. He left Cleveland for Chicago and died in the late 1980s.

Paul Cheeks (KCHA, 1960–61; CORE, 1963–64) and **John Cleary**, who was critically wounded on May 4, both became architects. Cheeks became well known in Cleveland's Democratic political circles before moving to Atlanta, where he now resides. Cleary, who did not let his wounding interfere with his career plans, quietly moved on with his life, marrying and settling in Pittsburgh. As years passed, he became more comfortable with his place as a May 4 casualty and appeared on a number of magazine-style television programs and in documentary films about the shootings. **Clarence Rogers Jr.** (KCHA, 1960–61), once denied service in Kent because of his race, completed law school and became a partner in Ohio's first African American firm; he has also served in leading positions on two state and regional transportation commissions and as the head of Ohio's public utilities commission.

Bob Bresnahan (YSA, 1966–70) was one of the few who came from a family of relative means. According to several who knew Bresnahan during his activist days, he is now an executive with a well-known national company.

While many of those who came from working-class or middle-income backgrounds went on to professional careers, many also remained within the labor union milieu for some or all of their lives. Initially, some did so in order to focus their political activities within labor's institutions, but most wanted a socially responsible way to make a living. And, just as life sometimes was on campus, subsequent living was not always easy. Some left Kent because landlords would not rent to them. A number of others continued to be visited and monitored by the FBI. There were those who lost jobs as a result. Some did hard time in prison as a consequence of their confrontational politics or, in rare cases, for drugs.

After completing his jail sentence, **Ric Erickson** (SDS, 1968–69) left his native Ohio for the Pacific Northwest. He worked in food cooperatives and later in the grocery industry, where he held elected positions in the United Food and Commercial Workers Union. **Matt Flanagan** (SDS, 1968–69) stayed in Ohio, where today he is a steward in the International Brotherhood of Electrical

Workers. Like Flanagan, **Jim Powrie** (KCEWV, SDS, 1967–69) participated in a well-attended reunion of the Kent SDS chapter in 1989. Pursuing a variety of jobs, Powrie used his formidable intellect as a grant writer assisting farm workers in California. Later he became an educator in the Pacific Northwest and today lives in New Mexico.

Like his father, **Rick Felber** (Kent 25, 1970–71) found steady blue-collar work and served as a steward in a Teamster local in Minnesota. The career of **Alan Canfora** (YD, SDS, Kent 25, 1968–71) also bears some resemblance to that of his father. Both father and son were drawn to electoral politics, and for over two decades Alan Canfora has served as chairman of Barberton's Democratic Party and as a Summit County elections commissioner. In contrast to his father's UAW activism, however, Alan left industrial employment and union work to devote what free time he has to research and lecturing about Kent State. He heads and maintains an archive for the Kent May 4 Center and works as a law librarian. **Joe Cullum** (3-C, Kent 25, 1969–71) worked at Republic Steel in Canton from the time of the 1977 campaign of reformist Edward Sadlowski for United Steelworkers president until 1992, when he became a high school teacher. A few years later he became the head of his National Education Association local.

Two students not mentioned in the text, **Steve Bauman**, a radical activist, and **Andy Pyle** (SDS, 1968–69), found work in the declining steel industry. Bauman dropped out of Kent to work at Weirton Steel, where he participated in the employee buyout plan that averted closure of the works in the early 1980s. Pyle also managed to secure work in a steel plant that did not close. Active in both his United Steelworkers local and progressive politics, he is now retired. **Mike Brock** (JHC, 1971–72) returned home and went to work at Bethlehem Steel in Lackawanna, New York, not far from the Attica prison, where a 1971 police assault took thirty-nine lives on another Bloody Monday. Later a participant in the reform movement that arose in the steelworkers union, Brock lost his job when Buffalo-area mills shut down in the mid-1970s. Severely injured while working on the Alaska pipeline in late 1977, he recovered to a point, but the injuries took a major toll on his health and contributed to an early death in November 2001. **Paul 'Roby' Bukosky** (SDS, 1968–69) was killed in a workplace accident when he was pinned beneath a tow motor. He was part of a union drive at the time of his death.

Greg Hawthorne (JHC, 1971–72) spent years working in coal mines before moving on to a career in labor journalism at the United Mine Workers and later in labor law. **Steve Lieber** (KCEWV, MDC, 1967–71) became a staff representative for AFSCME and later an election consultant. His friend **Ken Johnson** (SDS, VVAW, JHC, 1968–72) did similar union work with the Ohio Civil Service Employees Association. Johnson moved on to other jobs, but maintained his interest in labor and veterans' affairs. He attended the founding convention of the Labor Party in Cleveland during the mid-1990s.

Fellow veterans and VVAW members **Tim Butz**, **Alan Morris,** and **Mike Carmedy** worked at a variety of jobs. Butz had a short career as an advocacy journalist before heading the Nebraska ACLU. Around 2005, he obtained his long-sought undergraduate degree. Like a number of others named here, neither Morris nor Carmedy completed college. Morris worked in Florida as a commercial fisherman, and Carmedy became a vocal rank-and-file member of the United Rubber Workers while working at the Seiberling Rubber Company. When the plant closed he became a truck driver. Active in a left-wing group, he also testified on behalf of Karl Armstrong in the University of Wisconsin bombing case. Both Morris and Carmedy died of cancer in the 1980s, believed to have been contracted as the result of Agent Orange exposure in Vietnam.

Mark Lencl (SDS, 1968–69) settled in Oakland, California, and worked at an assortment of jobs while devoting himself to performance art based on his searing experiences in Vietnam. **Jerry Alter** (YSA, 1969–72), despite—or perhaps because of—his leftist views, joined the military after leaving Kent. Following a stint in the army, he settled in Cleveland, drove a cab, and became a frequent attendee at May 4 commemorations.

Richie Hess (SDS, YIP, 1968–72), whose father was a printer, moved back to New Jersey after graduation and became a locksmith. **Colin Neiburger** (SDS), who participated in the May 1971 protests in Washington as part of a coalition called the May Day Tribe, did not return home to Baltimore; he moved to the Deep South, marrying and raising a family. There he has raised his voice on behalf of prisoners such as Lori Berenson and Mumia Abu-Jamal. **George Hoffman** (KCEWV, SDS, 1966–70) helped start Kent's first food cooperative, a project characterized more by mutualism than enterprise. He stayed with the effort for many years before using his knack for detail as an accountant for an Akron hospital until his untimely death. **Mary Ann Jackson** (SDS) and her husband, **Larry Lamovsky** (KCEWV), still live in the Kent area, as do **Judy (née Gollust) King** (CORE, KCEWV, SDS, 1964–70) and her husband, **David King**. All of those mentioned in this paragraph returned to the KSU campus for a twenty-year SDS reunion in 1989, an educational affair that nevertheless caused the university enormous consternation.

Mike Alewitz (YSA, SMC, 1968–70) and **Roy Inglee** (YSA, KCEWV, 1963–67), along with **Doug Vaughan** (SDS, 1968–70) and **Corky Benedict** (Cleveland SDS, 1966–70), all continued to devote their lives to socialist or progressive activities. Alewitz went on to become one of the world's foremost radical muralists, publishing a book on the subject with historian Paul Buhle. He worked as a machinist for over a decade, and now teaches art at a state university in Connecticut. Some, like **Dave Edwards** (SPU, YSA, 1964–67), dropped from sight, while others actually went deep underground. As noted in the text, **Jeff Powell** (SDS, 1968–70) disappeared shortly after being released from the Portage County Jail in April 1970. He was not seen again publicly until January 1994, when he surrendered to authorities in Chicago to face charges arising out of the "Days of Rage." At that time he declared himself "proud to have fought for my country against the criminal government of Richard Nixon." Speaking, perhaps, for many other veteran activists, he added that he was "glad not to be at war against my country now." For over a decade he has worked on behalf of children's issues and in opposition to economic globalization. **Don Smith** (YSA, 1963–68), never a student at Kent, nevertheless played a role by recruiting John McCann into the Socialist Workers Party. Smith was living in Chicago when he died a few years ago.

Terry Robbins (Ohio SDS, Weathermen) was killed by his own bomb in March 1970. **Danny Thompson**, who cheated death in the American South as a Freedom Rider in 1961, spoke at a May 4 commemoration in the 1980s. He lived into his sixties, long enough to become the poet laureate of Cleveland as well as an advocate for the homeless. When he died in May 2004 his memorial service drew one thousand mourners. Fittingly, a voter registration meeting was convened in Cleveland that year in his memory. **Sidney Jackson**, a professor of library science who was a member of the Communist Party and one of the first people at Kent State to challenge Cold War orthodoxy, died in 1979. His son **Joe Jackson** (KCEWV, 1966–68) remained in Ohio, became a special education teacher, and continues to sympathize with liberal causes.

Rick Lieber (KCEWV, 1967–68) returned to his native Pennsylvania to teach. **Howie Emmer** (KCEWV, SDS, YIP, 1966–72) relocated to Chicago. One of the keynote speakers at Kent's SDS reunion, he also became a teacher, as did **Roseann Canfora** (Kent 25, 1970–71). Dividing her time between high school and college teaching, Canfora played a significant role in the stop-the-gym protests in 1977, as did the other five members of her family. Like her unionist father, she figured prominently in several strikes. Two of her three children attended Kent State. Following graduation, **Jane Boram** (SDS, 1968–69) worked for many years as a welfare case examiner in Cleveland. Now remarried, she resides in Tennessee, where she continues to practice social work.

Others, like **Charlie Tabasko** (Cleveland SDS, 1966–69) and **Dwayne White** (BUS, 1967–70), lived relatively quiet lives after Kent—Tabasko in the Pacific Northwest and White in his native Louisville. The whereabouts of **Henry Austin** (Deacons for Defense) and **Oscar Hearn** (KCHA, 1961) are unknown. As of this writing, plans are afoot for **Erwind Blount** (BUS, 1970–72) to be interviewed by KSU archivists for the university's May 4 Oral History project.

In addition to Alan Canfora and John Cleary, a number of others who survived their wounds on May 4 became active in commemorative activity at Kent

State, including **Joe Lewis**, **Jim Russell**, **Dean Kahler**, and **Robby Stamps**. Although three of the four found it easier to leave Ohio, all returned occasionally to speak at May 4 commemorations. Lewis and Russell became close friends and neighbors in Oregon, where they found similar jobs: Lewis in a water treatment plant and Russell as a project engineer for a small city government. They were often called upon to speak to school groups about their experiences. Stamps taught sociology and Spanish as well as publishing three nonfiction books unrelated to May 4 topics. In the early 1970s he rendered important work for the Kent-Jackson Medical Fund, which aided those wounded in the two campus shootings. Kahler, perhaps the best known of the nine surviving casualties, was elected commissioner of Ohio's Athens County. Later he taught high school and worked in several of Ohio's Democratic administrations. Russell died in June 2007 and Stamps in June 2008.

IT MAY be instructive to compare the dissidents profiled here with those discussed by the sociologists Jack Whalen and Richard Flacks in their 1989 book, *Beyond the Barricades: The Sixties Generation Grows Up.* They studied a sample of radical activists at the University of California at Santa Barbara indicted for their alleged roles in the 1970 burning of a Bank of America branch in Isla Vista, California (see chapter 11) and followed their post-campus careers. Even with a remarkable similarity of events at the two state universities—a burned building, unruly street demonstrations, mobilization of the National Guard, fatal shootings, a number of protestors wounded by police gunfire, and subsequent indictments of students—there were noteworthy differences between the comparatively well-off radicals who attended UCSB and the less affluent blue-collar and middle-income activists at KSU. Those differences notwithstanding, former students at both universities have mostly lived and worked in ways consistent with the political values they learned while growing up, which came to further maturity as college-age activists. Flacks's individual research showed that, in the main, such students chose "careers that were distanced from or bore a critical relation to the private corporate system."

Of the activists considered here, those who continued to be politically engaged often used the skills they acquired in the student movement to further their electoral, labor union, or activist work. While some entered industry and/or took elected or staff positions in unions hoping to "radicalize" the working class, most did so with more modest political and life goals.[1] The same is true for those who made careers in academia, law, education, and writing. That many would retain a contentious edge, however, was demonstrated in the course of a fierce Internet exchange in the fall of 2000 about the relative merits of Al Gore and the spoiler candidate Ralph Nader. Whatever they did in life, few, if any, betrayed the convictions they formed in the communities of their youth and on the campus of Kent State.

Abbreviations

3-C	Committee of Concerned Citizens of the [Kent State University] Community
BUS	Black United Students
CORE	Congress of Racial Equality
ERAP	Cleveland Economic Research and Action Project, also known as the Cleveland Community Project
JHC	Joe Hill Collective
KCEWV	Kent Committee to End the War in Vietnam
KCHA	Kent Council on Human Affairs
Kent 25	Defendants charged by the Portage County grand jury in 1970
KLDF	Kent Legal Defense Fund
KQ	*The Kent Quarterly* (a literary/political newsletter published by the KSU English Department)
MDC	May Day Coalition
SDS	Students for a Democratic Society
SLID	Student League for Industrial Democracy
SMC	Student Mobilization Committee
SPU	Student Peace Union
VVAW	Vietnam Veterans Against the War
YD	KSU Young Democrats
YSA	Young Socialist Alliance
YIP	Youth International Party (Yippies)

Acknowledgments

WHILE I was preparing these acknowledgments, my friend and fellow historian Norman Caulfield reminded me that the esteemed labor historian David Montgomery used to tell his audiences that history writing was a collective effort. Therefore, just as this study can be read as a collective biography of once youthful activists, the construction of the book itself was also a collective undertaking.

I will begin at the beginning, for in offering my thanks pride of place belongs to Clark Dougan, a now retired senior editor at University of Massachusetts Press. Clark's contributions are seemingly endless. He suggested the study, persisted when I demurred, gave support and encouragement when my confidence flagged, helped shape the argument and sharpen my prose, corrected errors, and introduced me to many others who helped along the way.

At the State of New York's University at Buffalo, Michael Frisch, a leading expert in the field of oral history, not only guided me in the early stages of this project, but also taught some of the most interesting classes that I had in graduate school. He is one of the book's two fathers. Among my other outstanding professors there were Alice Echols, Jesse Lemisch, Mary Shelia McMahon, John Milligan, Gail Radford, Michael Vorenberg, and Jack Larkin. Jack has become a good friend and a lifelong giver of good advice. The university's librarians, especially Jean Dickson and assistant Paul Ryan, were likewise helpful to me throughout the course of my time in graduate school.

At Kent State, I benefited from the instruction of historians John T. Hubbell and the late Frank Byrne. Chances to talk Civil War history with John are opportunities I never miss. I also profited from classes with American literature professor Tom Davis and philosopher Robert Dyal.

There are many others at Kent State who helped and supported me. If not for the university's Special Collections archivists, this book is impossible to imagine.

In the 1990s Nancy Birk began the May 4 Collection, and Cara Gilgenbach helped it grow. Current and retired archivists Amanda Faehnel, Erin Valentine, Lae'l Hughes-Watkins, and Steve Paschen patiently assisted me in countless ways. Former KSU archivist Craig Simpson, now at the University of Indiana, and his coauthor, Greg Wilson, a professor of history at Akron University, have written their own study of Kent State's worst day, and Greg helped hone my analysis of the spring of 1970.

Time spent as a consultant for KSU's May 4 Visitors Center under former director Laura Davis and the late Carole Barbato is among the most rewarding work I have ever done. This public interpretation center and exhibit space is the only facility in the country that interprets the nation's anti–Vietnam War movement. The center is now under the able direction of Mindy Farmer. Thanks also go out to author Jerry Lewis, whose expertise and generosity I value greatly, and to Lori Boes, Kathy Spicer, and Kathy Stafford for their unfailing kindness and support.

Over the many years I spent working on this book, scholars asking who my publisher was would nod knowingly when I mentioned University of Massachusetts Press. The editor of the press's Culture, Politics, and the Cold War series, Chris Appy, is a wonderful historian and, like Clark, an exceptional wordsmith. When an extra pair of eyes was needed, historian Laura Miller provided them. Without Laura's extraordinary developmental editing skills, this book would have been further delayed. At the press, production manager Jack Harrison provided extensive assistance with the illustrations. The exceptional copyediting of Mary Bellino saved me from countless mistakes. Her work immeasurably improved this book. Any remaining errors are entirely my own.

There are so many others to thank. Rusty Leisenheimer is not a librarian, but served me like one with his amazing detective work on the Internet. Roman Tymchyshyn directed my attention to the beginning of Kent State's long Sixties, a past that I otherwise would have overlooked. Norman Caulfield offered sage advice on writing and teaching. Chic Canfora and Alan Canfora both did a great deal, including careful reading and editing and, in Alan's case, fact-checking and furnishing last-minute photos. It is hard to say who is a better editor, although nobody I know has a memory like Alan's. Alan is the founding director of the nonprofit Kent May 4 Center, and made its archives available to me. Allen Richardson is a wonderful writer, editor, and friend, whose words sustained me at a particularly important time on the journey toward the completion of this book. Like so many others listed here, I'll owe him forever.

Alex Bloom, a historian and scholar of the 1960s, has supported this project since the beginning. Carol Wilder, at the New School, has written her own study of the Sixties era and has been very generous to me. Through their scholarship and later their critiques, Van Gosse and Maurice Isserman assisted me in more ways than they might realize. David Blight, from whom I have learned much about historical memory, and his graduate student, Joseph Yannielli, both came through for me in a pinch. I will always be grateful to them. Jeremy Varon, Alan Wald, and Jeffrey Kimball all contributed toward making this a better book.

My current and former colleagues Bob Caputi and Janet Larkin have supported the writing of this book for decades now. Nobody gets by without such friends. Ben Maryniak was not in academe, although few taught me as much or did more. There are few perfect books, but Ben was a perfect friend. Dan Gipple was one of the few to read the entire unedited manuscript, while his wife, Nancy Addie, took the back-cover photograph of me. As is true of most who served in Vietnam, Dan endured. In his own way, he has worked to ensure that others do not have to experience war as he did.

Endless thanks go to Rich and Doug Ensminger for duty above and beyond, and to Rich and all the officers and members of Public Employees Federation Local 167, especially Bob Burke, Dave Chudy, Cathy Curley, Rose Goldstein, Paul Mecca, Bill Philips, Tom Rabent and Don Yetter, who did so much to make the lives of working people better. I am fortunate to have many other friends in the labor movement; among those from whom I learned the most are Shakoor Aljuwani, Roger Benson, Dan Booty, the late W. A. Davis, Kevin Donovan, Jim Duncan, Dan Fetonte, Rich Furlong, and especially Mike Kennan and Dick Lipsitz.

Nate Appy, Kenneth Bindas, Kevin Brady, Lance Buhl, Albert and Anne Canfora, Saul Daniels, Bob and Linda Donofrio, Alex Fraser, Howie Emmer, Barbara Gregorich, Ken Hammond, Joey Hartzler, Marcella Hartzler, Vicky Hartzler, Hunter Havens, Greg Hawthorne, Bruce Hyland, Ken Johnson, Carolyn Knox, Steve Lieber, Tom Michl, Katherine McDonald, Mike and Kendra Pacifico, Jeff Powell, Larry Raines, Jim and Janice Ray, Joel Ray, Jimmy Riggs, Heidi Summerlin, Ronald Tompkins, Jean Tussey, and the late Ken Warren all assisted me. Some shared unique materials; others answered my repeated requests for information. Still others assisted me with research, provided comments on drafts, or graciously put me up in their homes. Some helped in more general ways. Daniel Miller, whose film, *Fire in the Heartland,* should be seen as the documentary version of this book, made available many of his interviews.

John Filo, David and Judy King, Larry Lamovsky, Howard Ruffner, and Gerry Simon are all due my profound thanks for making their photos available for this book.

Linda Franchell kept my computer in operation. In the years before I became acquainted with a keyboard, Joanne Kishel, Ann Schultz, and Marcia Wagner graciously and patiently either turned my note sheets into readable type or reformatted earlier versions of this study.

And for the work of attorneys and legal assistants—Bob Baker, Ellen Goldblatt, William Kunstler, John Lawson, Sandy Rosen, David Scribner, Ben Sheerer, Tony Walsh, and Bill Whitaker, as well as Tom Dietz and Galen Keller—Kent's activist students and Kent State plaintiffs, circa 1969 to 1979, owe a huge debt of thanks.

Kathy Brownjohn, Dr. R. McCormick, and other medical personnel did not contribute directly to this book. Rather, in 1970, their care allowed me to some-day be in a position to write it. Beatrice Mitchell, a nurse at Ravenna's Robinson Memorial Hospital in 1970, contributed her memories and helped me heal.

To students in my American history survey and Civil War courses, who presumably know nothing of their professor's history, I also owe much.

Finally, to my family I owe everything. My mother, Colette, continues to emphasize the importance of "work before you play" discipline, instilled a sense of persistence, and gave me the first history books I ever owned. My late father and namesake taught me how to understand the political world. From him I also learned to value people and their stories. To a more measured degree, my three siblings, Anne, Robert, and Patrick, all share their brother's love of history. My daughter, Alison, and son, TJ, were in their teens when I began researching this study. They have their own careers now in teaching and social work, and I am proud of their accomplishments. My wife, Peggy, has been patient over the years it took to complete this book. She demonstrated that by transforming the room where I worked into a study and by living with a mess of files and books for longer than I thought possible. She accompanied me on my last research trip and discovered late in the process that historical investigation is not boring. To her I dedicate this book.

Notes

An extended version of the notes, which includes additional biographical and historical informa-
tion, is available online at scholarworks.umass.edu/umpress/.

Abbreviations

Archives and Collections

KHS Kent Historical Society, Kent, Ohio
KM4C Kent May 4 Center, Kent, Ohio

Kent State University Libraries

KSUA   Special Collections and Archives
M4C   May 4 Collection, KSUA
White Papers Robert I. White Papers, 1963–1971, KSUA

Yale University Library

ACLU Coll. ACLU of Ohio Kent State Project Records (MS 1800), Manuscripts and
     Archives
KSCY   Kent State Collection (MS 804), Manuscripts and Archives. Unless other-
     wise noted, all boxes and folders cited are in accession no. 1989-M-048, the
     records of David E. Engdahl.

Newspapers

BJ   *Akron Beacon Journal*
CP   *Cleveland Press*
DKS   *Daily Kent Stater*
Guardian *The Guardian* (formerly *The National Guardian*), New York City
NYT   *New York Times*
PD   *Cleveland Plain Dealer*

RC   *Record-Courier* (Ravenna, Ohio, and greater Portage County)
WP   *Washington Post*

Interviews

The following interviews conducted by the author are cited in the notes by last name.

Alewitz, Mike: Nov. 18, 2005
Barber, Cindy: April 7, 2002
Boram, Jane: (telephone) May 19, 2007
Brock, Barbara: Feb. 19, 2000
Brock, Mike: April 16, 1999
Buhl, Lance: (telephone) April 18, 2000
Canfora, Albert, Sr.: April 29, 1998, and
    Feb. 22, 2000
Carson, Carolyn: May 5, 2002.
Cheeks, Paul: (telephone) May 28, 2001
Dyer, Dave: Nov. 18, 1999
Emmer, Howie: March 26, 2006
Emmer, Jack and Ruth: June 10, 2000
Fein, Ollie: (telephone) April 9, 2003
Franklin, Bobby: (telephone) Aug. 11, 2001
Fraser, Alex: (telephone) Feb. 22, 2012
Gregorich, Barbara: (telephone) Sept. 27,
    2001
Hammond, Ken: May 21, 1989
Hawthorne, Greg: Jan. 15, 2005
Hoffman, George: Jan. 22, 2006
Inglee, Roy: (telephone) April 2, 2000
Jackson, Joe: Nov. 11, 2005 (telephone) and
    Dec. 3, 2005
Johnson, Ken: May 4, 1989
Lencl, Mark: May 4 and 6, 2000

Modugno, Vince: May 5, 2002
Nardella, John: (telephone) July 13, 1998
Oglesby, Carl: (telephone) March 10, 2001
Pekar, Harvey: (telephone) April 13, 2009
Persky, Jerry: Aug. 27, 2000
Powrie, James: May 5, 1989
Raines, Larry: April 16, 1999
Richardson, Allen: Nov. 19, 2000
Riggs, Jim: (telephone) April 26, 2014
Rogers, Clarence, Jr.: (telephone) April 11,
    2001
Simpson, Larry: (telephone) April 4, 2006
Smith, Don: Jan. 21 (telephone) and Jan.
    26, 2002
Spencer, Jack: Nov. 1, 2005
Tabasko, Charlie: (telephone) Sept. 8, 2002
Thompson, Danny: (telephone) June 23,
    2001
Tompkins, Henry (pseudonym): Jan. 26,
    2006
Tussey, Jean Y.: (telephone) June 26, 2001
Vaughan, Doug: Aug. 1, 2015
Walsh, Tony: Feb. 19, 2000
Whitaker, William: Nov. 21, 1999, and Jan.
    25, 2006
Wittmaack, Ron: Feb. 19, 2000

Prologue: May 4, 1970

1. Northeast Ohio compared to Germany's industrial region: Phillip R. Shriver, *The Years of Youth: A History of Kent State University, 1910–1960* (Kent: Kent State University Press, 1960), 87. KSU students' communities of origin and the number of out-of-state students during the years cited: Thomas M. Grace, "A Legacy of Dissent: The Culture and Politics of Protest at Kent State University, 1958–1964" (PhD diss., State University of New York at Buffalo, 2003), ix–xix. Influence of class background on political outlooks: Richard Polenberg, *One Nation Divisible: Race, Class, and Ethnicity in the United States since 1938* (1980; New York: Penguin, 1988), 7.

2. Kenneth J. Heineman, *Campus Wars: The Peace Movement at American State Universities in the Vietnam Era* (New York: New York University Press, 1993); Scott L. Bills, ed., *Kent State/May 4: Echoes through a Decade* (1982; Kent: Kent State University Press, 1988).

3. Ohio capped out-of-state enrollment at 20 percent. Joe Eszterhas and Michael D. Roberts, *Thirteen Seconds: Confrontation at Kent State* (New York: Dodd, Mead, 1970), 10.

4. David Halberstam, "US against US," *Boston Globe*, April 30, 2000; see also W. J. Rorabaugh, *Berkeley at War: The 1960s* (New York: Oxford University Press, 1989), 169–70; Bills, introduction to *Kent State/May 4*, 59; and Bills, "The Sixties, Kent State, and Historical Memory," in *Kent and Jackson State, 1970–1990*, ed. Susie Erenrich, special issue, *Vietnam Generation* 2.2 (1990): 169. A more recent study is more nuanced: Mark Hamilton Lytle, *America's Uncivil Wars: The Sixties Era from Elvis to the Fall of Richard Nixon* (New York: Oxford University Press, 2006), 8, 371.

5. On the unseen central part of the country: Nicholas Howe, "Midwest by Midwest," *Dissent* 47.4 (Fall 2000): 95.

6. Faculty member quoted in I. F. Stone, *The Killings at Kent State: How Murder Went Unpunished* (New York: New York Review Books, 1971), 34. The four-class schema: Jack Metzger, *Striking Steel: Solidarity Remembered* (Philadelphia: Temple University Press, 2000), 5–6, 7, 9.

7. James Miller, *"Democracy Is in the Streets": From Port Huron to the Siege of Chicago* (New York: Simon and Schuster, 1987), 320; Bills, "The Sixties, Kent State, and Historical Memory," 170.

8. Peter Novick, *That Noble Dream: The "Objectivity Question" and the American Historical Profession* (1988; Cambridge: Cambridge University Press, 1991), esp. 415–72.

1. The Working Class Goes to College

1. On Kent State: Phillip R. Shriver, *The Years of Youth: A History of Kent State University, 1910–1960* (Kent: Kent State University Press, 1960), 1, 207–8.

2. Oglesby interview.

3. Ibid.; Gabriel Kolko to the author, Feb. 28, 2001; Fraser interview. Kent's early nineteenth-century founding up through the 1940s: Thomas M. Grace, "A Legacy of Dissent: The Culture and Politics of Protest at Kent State University, 1958–1964" (PhD diss., State University of New York at Buffalo, 2003). The Macedonian social/political circle was interracial and almost entirely urban and working class. In addition to those already named, it included Lou Patsouris, Sheldon Wolfe, Kenneth Cooley, and Frank G. Cihlar, all of Cleveland; Ray Metzinger of Youngstown; and Addison Reid of Steubenville, Ohio. The exception to the urban, blue-collar cohort was Joan Flint, the daughter of a Unitarian Universalist minister in Kent. The Macedonians encountered racial discrimination in Kent. When attempting to dine with Ed Gray they were refused service in a Franklin Street tavern. On another occasion, a white member of the group was harassed in a bar for being a "n— lover." The Macedonian, a former Merchant Marine, decked the verbal abuser with one punch. Fraser interview. Carl Oglesby mentions the Macedonians briefly in *Ravens in the Storm: A Personal History of the 1960s Antiwar Movement* (New York: Scribner, 2008), 8–9.

4. In his interview, Fraser recalled that several Macedonians who also lived on campus had copies of the *Daily Worker* slipped under the doors of their dormitory rooms. In the 1955–56 academic year there were 5,717 enrolled students at KSU, and of the first 1,055 (listed alphabetically) in the student directory for that year, 570 were from cities, chiefly Cleveland, Akron, and Canton. For further details, see Grace, "Legacy of Dissent."

5. On the recession: Michael Barone, *Our Country: The Shaping of America from Roosevelt to Reagan* (New York: Free Press, 1990), 301–2. The right-to-work legislation: Melvyn Dubofsky, *The State and Labor in Modern America* (Chapel Hill: University of North Carolina Press, 1994), 202–6; Gilbert J. Gall, *The Politics of Right to Work: The Labor Federations as Special Interests, 1943–1979* (New York: Greenwood Press, 1988), 41–43.

6. The right-to-work battle in Indiana: Gilbert J. Gall, "Thoughts on Defeating Right-to-Work," in *Organized Labor and American Politics, 1894–1994: The Labor–Liberal Alliance,* ed. Kevin Boyle (Albany: SUNY Press, 1998), 195–207. Positions of O'Neill and Lausche: Mike Curtin, "The O'Neill–DiSalle Years, 1957–1963," in *Ohio Politics,* ed. Alexander P. Lamis and Mary Anne Sharkey (Kent: Kent State University Press, 1994), 48–50; and Lausche's statement in an advertisement (sponsored by the RTW Campaign Committee for Issue 2), *BJ,* Nov. 1, 1958. *PD* editorial, Nov. 2, 1958; Robert C. Dix, "Along the Way," *RC,* Nov. 1, 1958.

7. Audio tape supplied by Larry Lamovsky; Lamovsky to the author, April 10, 2009; Modugno, Dyer, and Albert Canfora interviews. Other KSU activists shared memories of the involvement of their parents or extended family members in the campaign against the right-to-work amendment. In addition to Modugno's parents, his uncle Rocco took part in the campaign. In their interviews, Allen Richardson recalled the participation of his father and grandfather; KSU's only Freedom Rider, Danny Thompson, remembered his father's participation; Mark Lencl told of his mother Ruth's activity in her Cleveland industrial shop; and Jack and Ruth Emmer (parents of KSU student Howie Emmer) recalled their participation in the campaign against the bill. Activist Joe Cullum also described the opposition of his parents, Leo and Lucy Cullum, to the bill; Cullum to the author, Dec. 14, 2000.

8. KSU enrollment: Shriver, *Years of Youth,* 208. For and against the right-to-work amendment: *DKS,* Oct. 16 and 22–24, 1958. On William O' Neill: Curtin, "The O'Neill–DiSalle Years," 49. Young Socialist Alliance: Tim Wohlforth, *The Prophet's Children: Travels on the American Left* (Atlantic Highlands, NJ: Humanities Press, 1994), 63.

9. Albert Canfora interview. Vote totals: Gall, "Thoughts on Defeating Right-to-Work," 206–7. Curtin, "The O'Neill–DiSalle Years," 43. On Stephen M. Young: Tom Diemer, "Ohio in Washington: The Congressional Delegation," in Lamis and Sharkey, *Ohio Politics,* 202. O'Neill's charges are contained in his press release of Oct. 23, 1958, box 319, Michael DiSalle Papers, Ohio Historical Society, Columbus (hereafter cited as DiSalle Papers).

10. Richard G. Zimmerman, *Call Me Mike: A Political Biography of Michael V. DiSalle* (Kent: Kent State University Press, 2003), 152–74; Gall, "Thoughts on Defeating Right-to-Work," 202. The impact of Young and the class of 1958 on the Senate: Michael Foley, *The New Senate: Liberal Influence on a Conservative Institution, 1959–1972* (New Haven: Yale University Press, 1980).

11. Tussey interview. See also "Minutes of the Club Executive, No. 18, Oct. 28, 1958," Jean Y. Tussey Papers, Western Reserve Historical Society, Cleveland; and "United Socialist

Parley to Meet in Cleveland," *The Militant,* Nov. 3, 1958, microfilm collection, Tamiment Library and Robert F. Wagner Labor Archives, New York University.

12. *Proceedings, National Conference [of] American Socialists, Tudor Arms Hotel, Cleveland, Ohio, November 28–30, 1958* (Cleveland: Committee of Correspondence, 1959), 1, 42–43, 85, 92, 94–95.

13. Ibid., 13, 86. The author remembers the legal representation Gordon provided to activists at KSU.

14. Grace, "Legacy of Dissent," 41–59, 88–93.

15. Karl H. Grismer, *The History of Kent: Historical and Biographical,* rev. ed. (Kent: Kent Historical Society, 2001), 234–35; Ralph Darrow, ed., *Kent, Ohio: The Dynamic Decades—A History of the Community from the 1930's to the 1990's* (Kent: Kent Historical Society, 1999), 59, 119–20. "Way to treat Communists . . .": quoted in Joseph C. Goulden, *The Best Years: 1945–1950* (New York: Atheneum, 1976), 306–7. Correspondence among the circulation director for *Counterattack,* Davey, and Bowman, dated Aug. 14 and 17, 1950: box 15, George A. Bowman Papers, 1901–1976, KSUA (hereafter cited as Bowman Papers).

16. "Unwelcome Gift," March 16, 1950, and "Sen. McCarthy Accuses 1948 Kent Speaker," March 14, 1950, *Daily Courier-Tribune.* Coverage of the Flag Day rally: *Evening Record/Daily Record-Tribune,* June 14, 1947. "More of an agricultural . . .": Lisle A. Rose, *The Cold War Comes to Main Street: America in 1950* (Lawrence: University Press of Kansas, 1999), 127.

17. Oral histories of John Carson, transcribed Dec. 11, 1992, and Albert Ciccone, transcribed Nov. 11, 1994, KHS. See also Darrow, *Kent, Ohio,* 30–31.

18. Joshua Brown, oral history, transcribed Nov. 10, 1985, KHS. Racial inequity in Lima, Ohio: Perry Bush, *Rust Belt Resistance: How a Small Community Took on Big Oil and Won* (Kent: Kent State University Press, 2012); and in Cleveland: Thomas J. Sugrue, *Sweet Land of Liberty: The Forgotten Struggle for Civil Rights in the North* (New York: Random House, 2008).

19. The *Kent Quarterly* was launched in 1956 and, together with the Macedonians, formed the center of the still largely invisible dissent at Kent in the 1950s. One of the most important figures associated with the publication was Clevelander Roman Tymchyshyn, a roommate of Danny Thompson. Tymchyshyn was also acquainted with the leaders of the Council on Human Affairs. See Kenneth Cooley and Don Thomson, "Blindness We May Forgive," *Kent Quarterly,* Winter 1957.

20. Oglesby and Cheeks interviews; and the following in *DKS:* "SC Supports Southern Lunch-Counter Strikes," April 14, 1960; "Civil Rights War Renewed" (editorial), April 19; "KSU Students Will Continue Sympathy Strikes of Stores," April 26; "Pickets Defy Owner's Warning," April 28; "Human Affairs Council Studies Kent Problems," April 29.

21. Rogers interview.

22. Rogers and Cheeks interviews; Rogers provided the estimate of the number of African Americans at Kent. In 1959–60, according to KSU's student directory for that year, there were 7,554 students enrolled.

23. Buhl, Rogers, and Cheeks interviews. The two other Kent students were Josephine Lavonna Lomba and John Ferrington. See "Human Affairs Council Studies Kent Problems," *DKS,* April 29, 1960. A good source on the conference is James Miller, *"Democracy Is in the Streets": From Port Huron to the Siege of Chicago* (New York: Simon and Schuster, 1987), 33, 36–38.

24. King's experience: Taylor Branch, *Parting the Waters: America in the King Years, 1954–63* (New York: Simon and Schuster, 1988), 351–70. Account of the sit-in: Buhl, Rogers, and Cheeks interviews. The trio also provided details on the late John McCann's involvement; Barbara Gregorich also provided background on him in her interview.

25. "Students in Kent Stage Bar Sit-in Demonstration," *RC*, Oct. 29, 1960; Rogers and Cheeks interviews.

26. "Students in Kent Stage Bar Sit-in Demonstration"; Rogers and Cheeks interviews; Robert C. Dix, "Along the Way," *RC*, Oct. 31, 1960.

27. Lance Buhl, "Outlines Purposes of Kent Sit-In" (letter), *RC*, Nov. 3, 1960; Cheeks interview.

28. "Negro 'Sit-In' Leader Stresses Non-Violence," *DKS*, Feb. 3, 1961. On Lawson: Clayborne Carson, *In Struggle: SNCC and the Black Awakening of the 1960s* (Cambridge: Harvard University Press, 1981), 22–25 and passim. Ritchie's relationship with Lawson: conversation with James Lawson. Thompson's experiences as a Freedom Rider: Thompson interview. On Robert F. Williams and Willie Mae Mallory: Timothy B. Tyson, *Radio Free Dixie: Robert F. Williams and the Roots of Black Power* (Chapel Hill: University of North Carolina Press, 1999). Ritchie had been the choir director for Lawson's father at a church in Massillon, Ohio.

29. The practice of segregating Kent's black students for a six-year period in the 1930s: Shriver, *Years of Youth*, 126. Deed restrictions in Kent in the 1940s: article by Diane Smith, *RC*, circa Aug. 2000. Details of the survey: *BJ*, May 10, 1961. In 1960 there were approximately two hundred foreign and African American students attending KSU.

30. Shriver, *Years of Youth*, 178–80, 236; Buhl interview. Bowman appointed Ritchie in August 1947. "Kent State through the Years," *DKS*, Feb. 1, 2013.

31. Description of student life: *Kent Quarterly*, Fall 1958, Spring 1959, and Spring 1961; "Lowery Lite" (newsletter of Lowery Hall), March 6, 1958, box 33, folder 13, Bowman Papers (issues of the Stopher Hall newsletter, "The Echo," are in the same folder); "Fun at KSU Has Changed over the Years," *DKS*, May 2, 2002.

32. Cheeks interview; John McCann, "Charges Discrimination in Off-Campus Housing," *DKS*, April 14, 1961; "Pres. Bowman Clarifies Housing Policy," *DKS*, April 19. In actuality, there was but one housing list. African American students were directed to apartments that staff in the KSU housing office knew would accept nonwhite tenants. Almost all such landlords were themselves African Americans.

33. "Freedom of Choice" (editorial), and Olsen (letter), *DKS*, April 20, 1961.

34. "Professors Write on Discrimination" (letter), *DKS*, April 28, 1961. Ritchie's KSU personnel file contains a 1947 letter from Ritchie to Bowman accepting his offer of employment. Felver's support for civil rights in 1960: "KSU Discrimination Discussed," *DKS*, May 18, 1960.

35. Bowman's May 2 memorandum could not be found among his voluminous papers; I am grateful to the research librarians at KSU for locating copies among the personal papers of some of the professors he reprimanded. See also "Anti-Bias Bid Backed by 8 Profs," *BJ*, April 28, 1961. The resignation letters are also in the files of the respective faculty members. Although Smith was the first to resign, his planned departure was the last to be announced to the campus community; see "Prof. Smith Resigns Position," *DKS*, May 18, 1961.

36. "Prof. Felver Resigns," *DKS*, May 9, 1961. The fifteen petition sheets and cover letter are in box 18, Bowman Papers.

37. McCann's letter, *DKS*, May 10, 1961; see also "Bowman Non-Committal on Change at Buhl, Hearn Conference," *DKS*, May 11.

38. "Bowman Non-Committal"; "Discrimination Statement Promised," *DKS*, May 11, 1961; "KSU Head Meets with 2 Students on Race Issue," *RC*, May 10, 1961. Hearn told the *RC* that Bowman and the CHA "were at loggerheads throughout the meeting."

39. In addition to the sources cited in the previous note, "Cue to the Public," *DKS*, May 11, 1961; *National Review*, June 3, 1961. Adverse effects of segregation on the American image in Africa: "Freedom of Choice," *DKS*, April 20, 1961.

40. "Pickets Protest Discrimination," *DKS*, May 12, 1961; and *RC*, May 11.

41. "Kent State Students Protest Housing Bias," *Cleveland Call and Post*, May 20, 1961. Comment by Roskens: "35 KSU Students Hit 'Housing Bias,'" *BJ*, May 11, 1961; "Demonstrators Demonstrate against KSU Demonstrators" and "Demonstration Is Harmful to KSU," *RC*, May 11, 1961; Cheeks interview.

42. Fisher to Bowman, May 11, 1961, box 18, folder 2, Bowman Papers. Fisher was the full-time adviser of the *DKS* from 1954 to 1966; see Fred F. Endres, *'Getting the Paper Out': 75 Years of the Kent Stater, 1926–2001* (Kent: School of Journalism and Communication, 2000), 52. The editorial and Greer's statement: "KSU Has Set Excellent Integration Example" and "Demonstration Is Harmful," *RC*, May 10, 1961.

43. "KSU Shuns Picketing Penalties," *BJ*, May 12, 1961; "No Action Planned against Pickets," *RC*, May 12; "Pro and Con," *DKS*, May 12; *Cleveland Call and Post*, May 20; Cheeks interview.

44. "Segregation Still Big Issue" and "No Action Taken against Pickets," *DKS*, May 16, 1961; letters to the *RC*, May 24 and June 8, 1961. Other letters went to the governor; box 77, DiSalle Papers.

45. Buhl and Cheeks interviews; "Neglected American Thanks His Country" (letter by Oscar Hearn), *DKS*, April 25, 1961; "Human Affairs Council Clarifies Position," *DKS*, May 17, 1961.

46. "Movie on Subversion Scheduled," *DKS*, May 18, 1961. Reaction to the film on other campuses: Todd Gitlin, *The Sixties: Years of Hope, Days of Rage* (New York: Bantam, 1987), 82–83; Milton Viorst, *Fire in the Streets: America in the 1960's* (New York: Simon and Schuster, 1979), 172–73, 425. "Thursday evening showing of Operation Abolition" (memo), Glen Nygreen to President Bowman, May 19, 1961, box 13, folder 8, Bowman Papers.

47. "Burnell, Stopher: Two Profs Injured," *DKS*, May 17, 1961; "Prof. Smith Resigns Position," May 18; Burnell et al. to Bowman, May 11, 1961, personnel file; and White to Bowman, May 21, 1961, box 18, folder 2, Bowman Papers.

48. "Time for a Cliché," *DKS*, May 18, 1961; letters of May 11 and May 14, 1961, box 18, folder 2, Bowman Papers; letter, *RC*, May 15, 1961.

49. "Debate Off-Campus Housing Problems," *DKS*, May 23, 1961; "NAACP Meets with KSU Officials," *RC*, May 23; "Ohio NAACP Asks KSU Housing Stand," *BJ*, May 23. Peoples numbered among the first African Americans to teach in Kent's school system; see James F. Caccamo, "African-American History in Kent," in Darrow *Kent, Ohio*, 42–43.

50. "NAACP Head Meets with KSU Officials,' *RC*, May 23, 1961; "NAACP Airs Views with Pres," *DKS*, May 23.

51. "Favors Integration," *DKS*, June 1, 1961. I benefited from Eric Foner, *The Story of American Freedom* (New York: Norton, 1998), 249–306.

52. The meeting between Nixon and Sihanouk occurred in Cambodia during the vice president's 1953 world trip. In a January 1998 letter to the author, Sihanouk recalled meeting Nixon but once, in the provincial capital Siem Reap outside of Phnom Penh. Nixon's campaign stop in Akron: *BJ*, Oct. 1, 1960. The Portage County GOP and Sihanouk's talk in Kent: *RC*, Oct. 3 and 4, 1960. For an account of Sihanouk's trip: Michael Field, *The Prevailing Wind: Witness in Indo-China* (London: Methuen, 1965), 244.

53. "Sihanouk Attacks '*Time*' for Inaccurate Reports" and "Cambodia Supports UN Bid of China," *DKS*, Oct. 4, 1960; "Kent Visit By Prince 'Successful,' " *DKS*, Oct. 18. Editorials: *RC*, Sept. 10 and 21, 1960. Editorial cartoon (by Bill Mauldin): *RC*, Feb. 26, 1964.

54. Jeffrey Kimball, *Nixon's Vietnam War* (Lawrence: University Press of Kansas, 1998), 9–10, 146–230.

55. "Guarding JFK," *BJ*, Oct. 1, 2000. Kennedy quote: John E. Vacha, "Ohio Did That to Me! The 1960 Presidential Election," *Timeline* (magazine of the Ohio Historical Society) 15.1 (Jan.–Feb. 1998): 31. On DiSalle: Zimmerman, *Call Me Mike*, 166–68.

56. Cheeks interview; KSU Young Democrats material, box 344, DiSalle Papers; "Nixon's Experience Gets Faculty Nod," *DKS*, Nov. 4–5, 1960.

57. On the newspapers: Vacha, "Ohio Did That to Me!," 39. "Sweep of Protestant . . .": Theodore C. Sorensen, *Kennedy* (New York: Harper and Row, 1965), 221. Portage County returns: *RC*, Nov. 9, 1960; statewide totals: Theodore H. White, *The Making of the President 1960* (1960; New York: Pocket Books, 1963), 398; county returns: Michael F. Curtin, *The Ohio Politics Almanac* (Kent: Kent State University Press, 1996), 9. "The Democratic Party in Ohio . . .": John H. Fenton, *Midwest Politics* (New York: Holt, Rinehart and Winston, 1966), 132n19.

58. "Nixon, GOP Sweep in Ohio Jolt to DiSalle" and "I'm Scapegoat in Demo Loss, DiSalle Says," *RC*, Nov. 9, 1960.

59. Brian VanDeMark, *Into the Quagmire: Lyndon Johnson and the Escalation of the Vietnam War* (New York: Oxford University Press, 1991), 25, 67, 101, 216–17; Barone, *Our Country*, 337, 399.

60. See comments by William Bundy in Lt. Gen. Harold G. Moore and Joseph L. Galloway, *We Were Soldiers Once . . . and Young: Ia Drang—The Battle That Changed the War in Vietnam* (New York: Random House, 1992), 342; and Sorensen, *Kennedy*, 646.

2. Democracy and Free Speech

1. Growth of SANE at Kent: *DKS*, Feb. 5 and April 2, 3, 11, 1963. The Peace Walk: *DKS*, April 16, 1963. Activities of SANE in Cleveland: "Large Group Makes 'Peace Walk' in Rain," *PD*, April 16, 1961.

2. "Expanding a free world . . .": "We Can Win Cold War" (editorial), *RC*, Nov. 7, 1961. "Their argument would lead . . .": "Build Fallout Shelter?," *RC*, Nov. 16, 1961. See also "Civil Defense Workers Heard by Dandelions [a local women's club]," *RC*, Nov. 9, 1961. On

the 80 percent of Americans supporting the 1963 test ban treaty: Lawrence Wittner, *Rebels against War: The American Peace Movement, 1933–1983* (Philadelphia: Temple University Press, 1984), 280.

3. "Ban the Ban at Ohio State," *The Nation,* May 19, 1962, 436. Bricker's tenure as an OSU trustee: Richard O. Davies, *Defender of the Old Guard: John Bricker and American Politics* (Columbus: Ohio State University Press, 1993), 209.

4. *Communist Activities in the Cleveland, Ohio, Area: Hearings before the Committee on Un-American Activities, House of Representatives,* 87th Cong., 2nd sess., June 5–7, 1962 (Washington, DC: GPO, 1962), 1139–43 (Ruth Emmer's appearance), 1134–39 (the Strausses'); Ruth and Jack Emmer interview. On David Strauss: Jennifer Frost, *"An Interracial Movement of the Poor": Community Organizing and the New Left in the 1960s* (New York: New York University Press, 2001), 50, 52.

5. "Communists Aim at Campus," *DKS,* Oct. 3, 1962; the philosophy professor was Henry Moulds. "We are not helping . . .": quoted in "Bowman Backs Liberal Policy in Political Speaker Choice," *DKS,* May 23, 1962. Bowman's turnaround: "Bowman Opposes Red Speaker," *DKS,* Oct. 23, 1962.

6. Mike Curtin, "The O'Neill–DiSalle Years, 1957–1963," in *Ohio Politics,* ed. Alexander P. Lamis and Mary Anne Sharkey (Kent: Kent State University Press, 1994), 57, 72–73. See also "Need Taxes for Education," *DKS,* Nov. 13, 1962.

7. "House Bill 800," *DKS,* May 2, 1963.

8. *DKS,* May 8–10 and 14–18, 1962. Views of student opponents: " 'Speaker Bill' Draws Student Opinion," *DKS,* May 15, 1963. Kaplan's opposition: "AAUP Opposes Speaker Bill" (letter), *DKS,* May 14, 1963.

9. See the following in *DKS:* "Wylie Pushes Speaker Bill," May 14, 1963; "Bills Touch Off Flurry of Protest by Students," May 10; "Bill Banning Speakers Gets Big OK in House," May 31; "Diluted Speakers Bill Becomes State Law," Oct. 15; and "Nothing New," Oct. 16. Quotes in favor of the bill and its margin of passage: "House OK's Red Speakers Ban," *PD,* May 30, 1963; information about the bill: *PD,* June 28, 1963.

10. Dix to Bowman, April 15, 1964, box 1, folder 12, Bowman Papers; Robert I. White, "The Presidents," in *A Book of Memories: Kent State University, 1910–1992,* ed. William H. Hildebrand, Dean H. Keller, and Anita D. Herington (Kent: Kent State University Press, 1993), 12.

11. "Trustees Approve White as New KSU President," *DKS,* Jan. 18, 1963; "White's All Right," *DKS,* Jan. 22; Hildebrand, Keller, and Herington, *Book of Memories,* 12.

12. Sketch drawn from "Biographical and Historical Note" in the finding aid for the White Papers. Shriver, *Years of Youth,* 192–93, 218, 227–28; James Michener, *Kent State: What Happened and Why* (New York: Random House, 1971), 115.

13. See the following in *DKS:* "Rhodes Seeks Regents," Jan. 17, 1963; "Bowman Nixes Rhodes," Jan. 24; "Presidents Refuse Regent Board OK," Feb. 7; and "Council Backs Group Planning Protest," May 2. See also Richard G. Zimmerman, "Rhodes's First Eight Years," in Lamis and Sharkey, *Ohio Politics,* 72–73.

14. Entries by Paul Le Blanc on the Socialist Workers Party and by Tim Wohlforth on Trotskyism, in *Encyclopedia of the American Left,* ed. Mari Jo Buhle, Paul Buhle, and Dan Georgakas (Urbana: University of Illinois Press, 1992), 727–28 and 782–86, respectively.

See also Barry Sheppard, *The Party: A Political Memoir,* vol. 1 of *The Socialist Workers Party, 1960–1988* (Chicago: Resistance Books, 2005), 18–20; and Paul Jacobs and Saul Landau, *The New Radicals: A Report with Documents* (New York: Vintage, 1966), 54–55.

15. Roy Inglee to the author, March 23, 2000, and Inglee interview.

16. Wittmaack interview. On the situation in Laos: Gordon M. Goldstein, *Lessons in Disaster: McGeorge Bundy and the Path to War in Vietnam* (New York: Times Books / Henry Holt, 2008), 44–48.

17. Information about McCann came from a variety of sources, including Lt. Cooney to Donald Schwartzmiller, March 20, 1964, box 79, folder 3, M4C; Gregorich, Smith, and Wittmaack interviews, and Gregorich to the author, Jan. 7, 2002; and Inglee to the author, April 5, 2000.

18. See the following in *DKS:* "Kent Peace Union Organizes," Oct. 29, 1963; "SPU Hears McCarran Talk," Nov. 5; "SPU Talk Hits McCarran Act" and "No Problems," Nov. 6; and "KSU Official Regrets Taping," Nov. 8. Barbara Brock interview. Background on the demonstration that gave rise to the case of the "Bloomington 3": Mary Ann Wynkoop, *Dissent in the Heartland: The Sixties at Indiana University* (Bloomington: Indiana University Press, 2002), 13–18, 20.

19. Barbara Brock interview. Information about Edwards: Inglee interview, and Inglee to the author, March 23 and Nov. 17, 2000. On Sidney Jackson: Kenneth Heineman, *Campus Wars: The Peace Movement at American State Universities in the Vietnam Era* (New York: New York University Press, 1993), 69–70.

20. Inglee to the author, Nov. 17, 2000; Walsh interview. See also Heineman, *Campus Wars,* 116–17.

21. Dyer interview.

22. Ibid. In my sample of 2,555 names appearing in the 1965–66 student directory, there were four students listed from Coshocton County.

23. Dyer interview; Milton Cantor, *The Divided Left: American Radicalism, 1900–1975* (New York: Hill and Wang, 1978), 183.

24. Population figures: Russell H. Davis, *Black Americans in Cleveland from George Peake to Carl B. Stokes, 1796–1969* (Washington, DC: Associated Publishers, 1972), 270. On the schools: August Meier and Elliott Rudwick, *CORE: A Study in the Civil Rights Movement, 1942–1968* (New York: Oxford University Press, 1973), 242 and passim.

25. Leonard Nathaniel Moore, "The School Desegregation Crisis of Cleveland, Ohio, 1963–1964: The Catalyst for Black Political Power in a Northern City," *Journal of Urban History* 28.2 (Jan. 2002): 139–40.

26. Ibid., 139.

27. Meier and Rudwick, *CORE,* 162. Half-day sessions and details of the arrests: *Cleveland Call and Post,* Dec. 10, 1960, and Feb. 8, 1964, respectively. Leonard N. Moore, *Carl B. Stokes and the Rise of Black Political Power* (Urbana: University of Illinois Press, 2002), 18, 22, 28–34; Fein interview. Charlotte Phillips's participation: Kenneth W. Rose, "The Politics of Social Reform in Cleveland, 1945–1967: Civil Rights, Welfare Rights, and the Response of Civic Leaders" (PhD diss., Case Western Reserve University, 1988), 121.

28. Moore, *Carl B. Stokes,* 36; *Cleveland Call and Post,* April 11 and 18, 1964; Smith interview; Louis H. Masotti and Jerome R. Corsi, *Shoot-Out in Cleveland: Black Militants and the*

Police, July 23, 1968 (Washington, DC: Frederick A. Praeger, 1969), 35. Farmer's statement: *Newsweek*, April 20, 1964, 34. Charlotte Phillips was among those present at the construction site where Klunder was killed. Fein interview.

29. SWP involvement in CORE: Meier and Rudwick, *CORE*, 390. McCann's connection with Cleveland's school integration: Donald Schwartzmiller to Police Lt. Cooney, March 18, 1964, box 79, folder 3, M4C. Schwartzmiller had good connections with both the Cleveland police and the Ohio Highway Patrol, having served with the latter force from 1948 until 1960. For more on his background see "He Gets a Kick Out of Job," *DKS*, Oct. 15, 1963. Don Smith's participation in the protests on the day of Bruce Klunder's death is further indication of the support the SWP gave to the civil rights struggles.

30. "Civil Rights Groups Ask Recognition," *DKS*, Jan. 22, 1964. White's inaugural address and guidelines for campus speakers: "The Second Point" (editorial), *DKS*, Oct. 30, 1963, and "New Committee Forms to Set Speaker Rules," *DKS*, Feb. 5, 1964.

31. "All Possible Steam," *DKS*, Jan. 23, 1964.

32. See the following in *DKS*: "SPU Has Speaker Problems," Jan. 23, 1964; "SPU Attacks Ruling," Jan. 30; "Playing the Game" (editorial) and " 'One Side Is Not Heard in Travel Ban Dispute' " (letter from John McCann), Jan. 31; " 'Don't Tolerate Red Threat,' " Feb. 18.

33. "New Committee Forms to Set Speaker Rules," *DKS*, Feb. 5, 1964.

34. See the following in *DKS:* "Peace Union Hears Morgan," Feb. 12, 1964; "Young Socialist Explains Case," Feb. 14; "CORE's McCann Raps Recognition Hold-Up" and "Rights Leader," Feb. 18.

35. See the following in *DKS:* "Writer Praises CORE, Defends Student Planner" (letter from Robert Cusick), Feb. 4, 1964; "Two-Sided Story" (editorial) and "Rackham, Readers Differ on Procedures," Feb. 18; "Rackham Says Yes to CORE," Feb. 19; and "Implications" (editorial), March 4. Wittmaack and Inglee interviews; Cpl. H. L. McKimmie, Ohio State Highway Patrol, "Report of Investigation," March 9, 1964, box 79, folder 3, M4C.

36. Historically one of Ohio's most conservative areas, Wayne County is home to the *Daily Record,* whose former publisher, Ray Dix, was the twin brother of Kent's Robert C. Dix. Wayne County men were prominent among National Guard members who fired on Kent's students in 1970 (see chapter 12).

37. "Here's Roll Call Vote on Recognition of CORE" and "SC Members Explain Votes," *DKS*, Feb. 21, 1964; Inglee interview.

38. Inglee and Cheeks interviews.

39. Moran quoted in "Moran Resigns SC Post: CORE's 19–18 Win Ignites Fireworks," *DKS*, Feb. 20, 1964. Clark quoted in "Moran to Reconsider if CORE Put on Ballot," *DKS*, Feb. 21. Clark's hometown: "New Spring Editors Change Stater Posts," *DKS*, April 3, 1964. *DKS* criticism of Moran: "Muted Victory" (editorial), Feb. 21, 1964. See also the following in *RC:* "Moran Quits in KSU CORE Protest," Feb. 20, 1964; "CORE Chapter Recognized at Kent State," Feb. 24; and "KSU Men Meet to Consider Action on CORE Recognition," Feb. 25; as well as William O. Walker, "A Student at Kent," *Cleveland Call and Post*, March 7, 1964. The Portage Labor Council: Eugene Fields, " 'Committee for Progress' Is Organized" (letter), *RC*, Feb. 17, 1964. Fields was chair of the Civil Rights Department for the labor council.

40. The critical letters concerning CORE appeared in the Feb. 25, 1964, *DKS;* a negative letter about the SPU appeared the following day's edition. Mike Morrell, head of

the conservative Council on Freedom, authored the letter that disapproved of the *DKS*'s coverage of the SPU. The Carl Braden incident: "'Red Baiting Hampers Rights,'" *DKS*, Feb. 26, 1964.

41. Red-baiting: "Implications" (editorial), *DKS*, March 4, 1964. Walsh's letter: "'University's Fear of CORE Shows a Need for Change,'" *DKS*, Feb. 25, 1964. On campus, red-baiting seemed to be losing steam; see "'Those Bad Guys'" (editorial), *DKS*, March 6, 1964. Off campus reaction: "Colleges Listen to Gus Hall Red Line," *RC*, Jan. 2, 1964.

42. CORE's plans: "CORE Asks President to Announce Deadline," *DKS*, March 3, 1964. On the procedures for choosing the *DKS* editor: Fred F. Endres, *'Getting the Paper Out': 75 Years of the Kent Stater, 1926–2001* (Kent: School of Journalism and Communication, 2000), 29, 33. Perry quoted in Fred F. Endres, *Pathways: An Historical Perspective on 60 Years of Professional Education* (Kent: School of Journalism and Communication 1997), 113. Objections to Slivka being named to the post: "Editors Protest" and "Stater Staffers: Slivka, Krell Fill Top Posts," *DKS*, March 13, 1964. Clark named managing editor: "New Spring Editors Change Stater Posts," *DKS*, April 3, 1964.

43. Ed Glassner, "Roasting Pan," *RC*, Feb. 20, 1964; and "KSU Adopts Rules for Demonstrations of Student Groups," *RC*, Feb. 22, 1964.

44. See the following in *DKS*: "Marchers to Protest New Policy," April 7, 1964; "Officials Ponder Action against Demonstrators," April 8; "Committee Keeps Quiet on Pickets" and "Rights Bring Obligations" (editorial), April 9; "Ad Hoc Group Submits Policy," April 14; "Editorial Bring[s] View from Bowman" and "Officials Place Ad Hoc Picket on Probation," April 15. On the April 7 picket see also Ohio State Highway Patrol, "Report of Investigation," April 8, 1964, box 79, folder 3, M4C. "Academic Freedom Yes! Censorship Board No!" is in the same folder. On the (aborted) plan to bring Lewis Robinson to the campus: *Kent State Free Press and CORE Newsletter* 1.6 (April 13, 1964), box 79, folder 3, M4C. DeBarry won only a single vote in a mock election held later in the fall; students went overwhelming for the Johnson–Humphrey ticket, with 1,029 supporting the Democrats and 590 backing GOP candidate Barry Goldwater. See "Voting Results," *DKS*, Oct. 30, 1964. In the US election, an estimated 2,000 KSU students voted by absentee ballot or by returning to their nearby communities to cast ballots. DeBarry's appearance: "DeBarry Addresses Packed House on Socialist Program, Negro Plight," *DKS*, April 17, 1964; "'Your Fight Part of National Pattern,'" *The Militant*, April 27. On the charges leveled against Slivka and Clark: *Kent State Free Press* 1.7 (April 22, 1964), box 79, folder 3, M4C. See also Slivka, "A Low Punch" (editorial), *DKS*, April 16. Mention of the *BJ* support: April 13 issue of *The Free Press*. Position of the faculty: "AAUP Disputes Demonstration Rules," *DKS*, April 21, 1964.

45. "Revised Policy Cradles Liberties," *DKS*, May 12, 1964; and "Righting Wrong" (editorial), *DKS*, May 13.

46. This version of the YSA/SWP position on Vietnam is from a subsequent statement made by Jack Barnes, national chairman of the YSA, in early 1965: "D.C. March to Protest Vietnam War," *The Militant*, Feb. 15, 1965. See Eric N. Rackham to President White, "Another demonstration" (memo), May 1, 1964, box 79, folder 3, M4C. See also photo story, *DKS*, May 5, 1964. Roy Inglee to the author, April 4, 2000.

47. Tabasko interview; *Investigation of Students for a Democratic Society, Part 2 (Kent State University): Hearings before the Committee on Internal Security, House of Representatives*, 91st Cong., 1st sess., June 24–25, 1969 (Washington, DC: GPO, 1969), 522, 561, and passim.

48. Fein interview; Rose, "Politics of Social Reform in Cleveland," 111–12, 119–22, 130; Frost, *"An Interracial Movement of the Poor,"* 1, 27–47, 52; Kirkpatrick Sale, *SDS* (New York: Vintage, 1973), 29; James Miller, *"Democracy Is in the Streets": From Port Huron to the Siege of Chicago* (New York: Simon and Schuster, 1987), 1, 31–32, 52. The Strausses' appearance before HUAC: "Silence Unwise, Witness Warned," *PD,* June 8, 1962.

49. Tabasko interview. On Gus Hall, see the entry on him in Buhle, Buhle, and Georgakas, *Encyclopedia of the American Left,* 287–88. Arvo Hall and the family's move to New York from Cleveland: Sam Tanenhaus, "Gus Hall, Unreconstructed American Communist of 7 Decades, Dies at 90," *NYT,* Oct. 17, 2000.

50. Tabasko interview. Cleveland Heights was also home to a number of future antiwar activists at Kent State.

51. Ibid.

52. Biographical information about Robbins and his family is from the Kenyon College Library Archives; I am indebted to Nate Appy for his assistance in searching this archive for me. Nathaniel Hawthorne made the observation about Melville in a journal entry dated Nov. 20, 1856.

53. Robbins's interests in high school and his participation in SDS in college: Robbins file, Kenyon College Archives. The file also contains a story about Robbins from the campus newspaper: Rik Kleinfeldt, "Weathermen Leader Was a Product of Kenyon," *Collegian,* Feb. 21, 1985, 3. Dylan's appearance at Kenyon in the fall of 1964: interview by Jay Cocks in *Bob Dylan: The Essential Interviews,* ed. Jonathan Cott (New York: Wenner Books, 2006). Robbins's fervor for Dylan's music: Peter Collier and David Horowitz, "Doing It: The Inside Story of the Rise and Fall of the Weather Underground," *Rolling Stone,* Sept. 30, 1982, 24. "Intense, driven . . . Dylan freak": Kathy Wilkerson, review of *Fugitive Days,* by Bill Ayers, *Z* magazine, Dec. 2001. Charlie Tabasko to the author, Sept. 9, 2002.

54. Gregorich interview; "DeBarry Asks 'Protest Vote,'" *DKS,* Oct. 28, 1964.

55. On the appearances of Barry Goldwater Jr. and Hubert Humphrey (in Ashtabula), see the following in *DKS:* "Goldwater Jr. Outlines Blueprint for Victory," April 16, 1964; "Young Dems Parade With Humphrey," Oct. 7; "Kent Dems Meet HHH," Oct. 9. LBJ's surge of popularity after the Tonkin Resolution: Penny Lewis, *Hardhats, Hippies, and Hawks: The Vietnam Antiwar Movement as Myth and Memory* (Ithaca: Cornell University Press, 2013), 60. Coverage of Johnson's stop in Akron: "LBJ Gives Lowdown to 4,000," *DKS,* Oct. 22, 1964; and Brian VanDeMark, *Into the Quagmire: Lyndon Johnson and the Escalation of the Vietnam War* (New York: Oxford University Press, 1991), 19. Goldwater's swing through the Midwest: Theodore H. White, *The Making of the President 1964* (New York: Atheneum, 1965), 340–42.

56. On the Goldwater campaign at KSU: "GOP'ers Prepare for Meet," *DKS,* April 7, 1964; "GOP Agenda" and "Delegates Protest GOP Poll" (letter by Gerald B. Graham and others), *DKS,* April 9; "Goldwater Too Conservative," *KSU Summer News,* June 30. Bliss quoted in White, *Making of the President,* 351. Vote totals: Curtin, *Ohio Politics Almanac,* 9.

The Young–Taft US Senate race: Tom Diemer, "Ohio in Washington: The Congressional Delegation," in Lamis and Sharkey, *Ohio Politics,* 205. Positive response to Goldwater's statement read at the KSU debate: "Debaters at Forum Extol Goldwaterism," *DKS,* Oct. 16, 1964; "'64—A Conservative Win?" (letter by Graham), *DKS,* Nov. 13. For a similar perspective of the 1964 election, see "Conservatives Take Heart" (by Klaus Bauer, head of the KSU Young Republicans), *DKS,* Nov. 18, 1964.

3. The Beginning of Wartime Dissent

1. See the following in *DKS:* "Folk Trio Concert Is Tomorrow," Sept. 25, 1964, and "These Singers Are Talkers, Too—Back Stage with Peter and Mary," Sept. 30; "Goulet Tops Concert, Singer Closes 'Flashes' Week," Nov. 2, 1965. For what Goulet represented, "Robert Goulet, Actor, Dies at 73," *NYT,* Oct. 30, 2007. A folk concert at the Blind Owl was advertised in the *DKS* on Oct. 2, 1964, and an ad for The Needle's Eye ran in the May 21, 1965, issue. Vince Modugno discussed the Blind Owl and the Needle's Eye in his interview. "Slacks for Classroom?," *DKS,* Jan. 15, 1965.

2. Inglee interview. Roy Inglee had at least one letter appear in the *DKS* in which he identified himself as a member of the YSA; *DKS,* Nov. 6, 1964. Erroneous stories that YSA had already achieved approval of its campus standing ran in the *BJ,* Jan. 8, 1965, and *PD,* Jan. 10.

3. Roscoe R. Creed to Robert I. White, Jan. 8, 1965, and Eric N. Rackham (replying for White) to Creed, Jan. 14; Mrs. Douglas J. Auckland to White, Jan. 9, 1965, and Rackham (replying for White) to Auckland, Jan. 14; all in box 14, folder 41, White Papers. Mrs. John A. Manecke wrote to the governor on Jan. 12, 1965; in addition to hearing from Clifford R. Cloud, deputy assistant to the governor, Manecke received a reply from Rackham on Jan. 22, 1965; box 14, folder 41, White Papers. McCarthy's appearance at KSU: "Seek Truth—McCarthy," *DKS,* Jan. 12, 1965.

4. "Equal Treatment" (editorial, signed with Judie Craig's initials), *DKS,* Jan. 12, 1965.

5. Leon F. Litwack, "Preface," xiii–xvii, and Robert Cohen, "The Many Meanings of the FSM: In Lieu of an Introduction," 1–53, both in *The Free Speech Movement: Reflections on Berkeley in the 1960s,* ed. Robert Cohen and Reginald E. Zelnik (Berkeley: University of California Press, 2002).

6. Transcript (cover dated Jan. 21, 1965), box 14, folder 41, White Papers.

7. Fox to Rackham, Jan. 25, 1965, Rackham to Fox, Jan. 27, 1965, and Rackham to White, same date, box 14, folder 41, White Papers. Inglee's description of YSA's goals: transcript, page 2.

8. White to Rackham, Jan. 31, 1965, and Rackham to Donald H. Desch, Jan. 29, 1965, box 14, folder 41, White Papers.

9. On the Pleiku attack and its aftermath: Fredrik Logevall, *Choosing War: The Lost Chance for Peace and the Escalation of War in Vietnam* (Berkeley: University of California Press, 1999), 323–32, 344, 363.

10. Spock's position at Case Western Reserve: Thomas Maier, *Dr. Spock: An American Life* (New York: Harcourt, Brace, 1998), 211–12, 221, 254–55. Spock's reaction to the air

attacks: Thomas Powers, *Vietnam: The War at Home* (Boston: G. K. Hall, 1984), 54; Maier, *Dr. Spock*, 228–30, 245–48. Inglee interview.

11. See the following in *DKS:* "Socialists Protest over US Vietnam Retaliation," Feb. 9, 1965; "YSA Picketing Draws Jeering Student Crowd," Feb. 10; "Pass the Popcorn" (editorial), Feb. 11; "Writers Consider Counter-Demonstrators' Actions," Feb. 12. See also "Student Protestors Attacked in Ohio," *The Militant*, Feb. 15, 1965; and "Protest Protestors at KSU—Six Young Socialists Demonstrate," *RC*, Feb. 10, 1965. The Stopher Hall dorm became a focal point for counterprotestors for two reasons: it was near the gym and thus housed many athletes, who tended to support the war; and it overlooked both Bowman Hall, site of many of the early antiwar pickets, and the Commons, the open area in the middle of campus that became a protest site.

12. Inglee, Barbara Brock, and Wittmaack interviews. Inglee remembers Brock being kicked, as do several students who referred to the incident in separate letters to the *DKS*, Feb. 12, 1965. Accounts differ, however, and two of the prowar students insisted that the kick "left no ill-effects" and "was an accidental thing that could happen at any type of a gathering, peaceful or otherwise." "Writers Speak Out on YSA" (letter), *DKS*, Feb. 16, 1965.

13. In his interview, Inglee recounted that Cleveland SWP members criticized the YSAers for their rashness. Paul Le Blanc makes much the same point about the influence of the older cadre on YSA members in his entry on the Socialist Workers Party in *Encyclopedia of the American Left*, ed. Mari Jo Buhle, Paul Buhle, and Dan Georgakas (Urbana: University of Illinois Press, 1992), 727–28. Jackson's letters: "Sees No Justification for Vietnam" and "Vietnam Action 'Not Democratic,'" *RC*, Sept. 21 and Nov. 11, 1963. On the SPU/YSA picket see chapter 2.

14. Editorial by Judie Craig (signed with her initials), *DKS*, Feb. 10, 1965; Barbara Brock interview.

15. Nancy Zaroulis and Gerald Sullivan, *Who Spoke Up? American Protest against the War in Vietnam, 1963–1975* (New York: Holt, Rinehart and Winston, 1984), 33–35; Kirkpatrick Sale, *SDS* (New York: Vintage, 1973), 173–74; Rusty L. Monhollon, *"This Is America?": The Sixties in Lawrence, Kansas* (New York: Palgrave, 2004), 77.

16. Inglee interview.

17. On the *Cleveland Press* story: Rackham's reply to William Sullivan of Kent, and the many correspondents who wrote to him about banning YSA, box 14, folder 41, White Papers. Brown to White, March 5, 1965, and White to Betts, [Ronald] Roskens, and Rackham, both dated March 5, 1965, in the same folder.

18. Brown to White, March 15, 1965 (containing Hoover's letter of March 10), and White to Brown, March 18, box 14, folder 41, White Papers.

19. Brown to Betts, March 27, 1965, and Betts to Brown, March 31, 1965, box 14, folder 41, White Papers. White's administration might have taken the unsolicited direction more seriously had it come from Governor James Rhodes.

20. The newspaper coverage is cited in Betts to Brown, March 31, 1965. "White OK's YSA Recognition, Three Other Campus Groups," *DKS*, April 6, 1965. See also Charles V. Riley to Dr. Robert I. White, April 7, 1965, and White to Riley, April 26, box 2, White Papers.

21. Potter's and Davis's involvement in SDS and ERAP: Sale, *SDS*, 28, 93, 107, 114; James Miller, *"Democracy Is in the Streets": From Port Huron to the Siege of Chicago* (New York: Simon and Schuster, 1987), 58–59, 72, 191, 214. Plans for the April 1965 march: Sale, *SDS*, 170–72.

22. John S. Knight, "With Dissenters Mute, Full War Comes Closer," *BJ*, April 4, 1965. For a biographical sketch of Knight, see the finding aid to his papers at the University of Akron, available at www.ohiolink.edu.

23. Tony Walsh, "Writer Airs U.S., Vietnam Policy; Invites Student Walk for Peace" (letter), *DKS*, April 6, 1965.

24. For the preparation of the picket and the protest itself, see the following in *DKS*: "Students Plan Capital March to Protest Viet Nam Fighting," April 8, 1965; "'March on Washington' Group Plans Viet Nam Demonstration," April 14; "Faculty, Students Demonstrate, Prepare for Washington Walk" and "Demonstrate Maturity" (editorial), April 15. Roy Inglee mentioned the teach-in and the SDS representative in his interview. Harassment during the picket: "Students React to Demonstration; Most Think 'Nothing Accomplished,'" *DKS*, April 16, 1965. Antiwar sentiment may have grown after veteran CBS reporter Harry Reasoner spoke on campus at a mock UN assembly program on April 10. Only the six hundred students at the assembly heard Reasoner's ambiguous remarks, but many more read the story's headline. He called for American withdrawal while also stating that "we are there to stay. We will come out all right if we stand firm." "Viet Nam: 'U.S. Get Out,' Says Reasoner," *DKS*, April 13, 1965.

25. Number of campuses involved: Sale, *SDS*, 185; the involvement of students from Kenyon and the leadership of Terry Robbins: Donald L. Rogan, "Revisiting Kenyon in a Time of National Crisis: Vietnam and the Shootings at Kent State," Kenyon College *Alumni Bulletin*, Winter 2004, 48–53; and for Kent: "Students Plan Capital March," *DKS*, April 8, 1965. On transportation to the capital: *DKS*, April 15; Wittmaack and Barbara Brock interviews. On April 20 the *DKS* ran a photo of sociology major Jim Lincoln holding aloft the Kent State sign.

26. Description of the march and comments about Phil Ochs: Todd Gitlin, *The Sixties: Years of Hope, Days of Rage* (New York: Bantam, 1987), 183. On Ochs, and for the quote from Potter's speech, see Sale, *SDS*, 186–87. Miller, *"Democracy Is in the Streets,"* 232–33; Powers, *Vietnam*, 76–77; Tom Hayden, *Reunion: A Memoir* (New York: Random House, 1988), 177.

27. Dix's column: "Along the Way," *RC*, April 19, 1965.

28. The State Department tour and the dilemma LBJ faced as he tried to promote domestic reform while waging an unpopular war: Tom Wells, *The War Within: America's Battle over Vietnam* (Berkeley: University of California Press, 1994), 26–33; see also Powers, *Vietnam*, 59–61. Stearman's appearance, the prowar rally organized by Bufwack and Topp, and Getz's quote: "Soviet Authority Views 'Communist Crossroads'" and "Rally Supports Pres Johnson's Viet Nam Stand," *DKS*, May 12, 1965. In his interview Roy Inglee stated that Topp had organized the counterprotest in February. On the prowar protest see also "Rally to Back Viet Nam War Policy of President Johnson," *DKS*, May 11, 1965.

29. For the action taken by the KSU student senate and Ehrlich's response, see the following in *DKS*: letter from Gary Baker, May 18, 1965; "Ehrlich Criticizes Senate on Defeat

of Selma Bill," May 19; "Rally Supports Pres Johnson's Viet Nam Stand," May 12. Three student senators voted against the resolution favoring the war.

30. "Ohio Regents Will Limit Kent State's Enrollment," *RC,* April 22, 1965.

31. "Biographical and Historical Note" in the finding aid for the White Papers. On the influence Dix exercised in Kent, see James Michener, *Kent State: What Happened and Why* (New York: Random House, 1971), 121.

32. "People resent the university . . .": Harris Dante, oral history, Nov. 19, 1991, KHS. Dante taught education and history at KSU. On Lawrence, Kansas: Monhollon, *"This Is America?,"* chaps. 1 and 2.

33. Marc Kovac, "Former Publisher Dies—Raymond Dix: A Newsman First and Always," *Wooster (OH) Daily Record,* July 21, 2001; interview of David Dix, Sept. 25, 1992, and taped oral history interview of Helen Dix, Dec. 4, 1994, KHS; Michener, *Kent State,* 121. Dix's interest in the hiring process: White to Dix, June 1, 1966, box 2, folder 17, White Papers. Interestingly, Dix had traveled to the Soviet Union in the early 1950s; Helen Dix interview, KHS. Frequency of the board meetings: White to Dix, July 27, 1966, box 2, folder 17, White Papers.

34. "Biographical and Historical Note" in the finding aid for the White Papers; Phillip R. Shriver, *The Years of Youth: Kent State University, 1910–1960* (Kent: Kent State University Press, 1960), 192–93, 218, 227–28; Michener, *Kent State,* 115–16.

35. "Old style college president": interview of Dr. Charles Chandler, April 30, 1996, KHS. The context indicates that Chandler was being descriptive rather than critical. "President White worked harder . . .": interview of Sue Briers-Gambaccini, May 7, 1997, KHS. Briers-Gambaccini worked closely with White from the time he was dean of the education department through his tenure as president.

36. Michener, *Kent State,* 121–22. The information about the men's travel interests is from the Briers-Gambaccini and Helen Dix interviews, KHS; that both liked gray suits is drawn from the author's own memory and period photographs.

37. "Majority Favor U.S. Recent Viet Action," *DKS,* Aug. 5, 1965. Another student, an older upperclassman, quoted in the same story, said: "[I approve of Johnson's policies] because I'm not of the draft age." Poll numbers and the petition campaign at Michigan State: Robert D. Schulzinger, *A Time for War: The United States and Vietnam, 1941–1975* (New York: Oxford University Press, 1997), 233.

38. White's reply of Feb. 16, 1965 to a letter from Senator Gaylord Nelson (D-Wis.) of Jan. 22, box 2, folder 1; White's reply of March 29, 1966 to Barbara Brock, box 2, folder 14; and White's letters to Local Board 138, Selective Service System, Watseka, Illinois, and Samuel Lober, Chairman, Local Board 138, May 12 and May 27, 1965, box 2, folder 16, White Papers.

39. Christian G. Appy, *Working-Class War: American Combat Soldiers and Vietnam* (Chapel Hill: University of North Carolina Press, 1998), 29–30, 33–36; Lawrence M. Baskir and William A. Strauss, *Chance and Circumstance: The Draft, the War, and the Vietnam Generation* (New York: Knopf, 1978), 22–27; George Q. Flynn, *The Draft, 1940–1973* (Lawrence: University Press of Kansas, 1993), 172, 180–81; Michael S. Foley, *Confronting the War Machine: Draft Resistance during the Vietnam War* (Chapel Hill: University of North

Carolina Press, 2003), 38–40, 61; Andrew O. Shapiro and John M. Striker, *Mastering the Draft: A Comprehensive Guide for Solving Draft Problems* (Boston: Little, Brown, 1970), 213–14.

40. Myra MacPherson, *Long Time Passing: Vietnam and the Haunted Generation* (New York: Doubleday, 1984), 110 (Reedy quote); Appy, *Working-Class War*, 15. Industrial employment figures for Barberton: *County and City Data Book, 1962: A Statistical Abstract Supplement* (Washington, DC: GPO, 1963). See also Thomas M. Grace, "A Legacy of Dissent: The Culture and Politics of Protest at Kent State University, 1958–1964 (PhD diss., State University of New York at Buffalo, 2003), xix. Canfora's recollections are from his unpublished memoir. For Mowrer, see his 1975 deposition, box 17, ACLU Coll.

41. On Guard service: Appy, *Working-Class War*, 36–37. Data on Farriss, Lutey, Maas, and Myers: box 16, ACLU Coll. On Herschler, James, and Pierce: Herschler, box 34, folder 439 and box 36, folder 462; James, box 36, folder 462; and Pierce, box 34, folder 439, box 36, folder 470, and box 37, folder 482, all in KSCY; and Spencer interview (Jack Spencer was a high school classmate of Pierce). Composition of Troop G: Joseph Kelner and James Munves, *The Kent State Coverup* (New York: Harper and Row, 1980), 58. The spike in the number of drafted men: Foley, *Confronting the War Machine*, 39.

42. On the small size of the radical movement even in the months after the April 1965 march in Washington: Charles DeBenedetti with Charles Chatfield, *An American Ordeal: The Antiwar Movement of the Vietnam Era* (Syracuse: Syracuse University Press, 1990), 120. Oglesby's election to the SDS presidency, the formation of the Committees to End the War in Vietnam, and new SDS chapters: Sale, *SDS*, 208–9, 219, 122n, 193n, 663; Oglesby interview.

4. The Kent Committee to End the War in Vietnam

1. A sampling of about 17 percent of listings in the 1965–66 KSU student directory shows that 13 percent of students were from out of state, the majority of them from Pennsylvania, chiefly Pittsburgh. New York took second place, with more than half the total coming from the western part of the state, although a good number came from either Long Island or New York City. Most students were from cities, towns, and suburbs located in the Western Reserve, and approximately a third came from the region's industrial urban areas, down from about 50 percent five years earlier. In raw numbers, however, urban students continued to be well represented among Kent's overall student body.

2. Gregorich interview.

3. SDS focus on ERAP rather than the war: Kirkpatrick Sale, *SDS* (New York: Vintage, 1973), 171, 214 (Gitlin quote), 221, 247. Fred Halstead, *Out Now! A Participant's Account of the American Movement against the Vietnam War* (New York: Monad, 1978), 96–97; Tom Wells, *The War Within: America's Battle over Vietnam* (Berkeley: University of California Press, 1994), 51–52, 59–61.

4. Photo stories, *DKS*, Oct. 19, 1965; for more details and the number of counter-protesters, Charles DeBenedetti with Charles Chatfield, *An American Ordeal: The Antiwar Movement of the Vietnam Era* (Syracuse: Syracuse University Press, 1990), 126. Entry for

"Vietnam War" in *The Encyclopedia of Cleveland History,* ed. David D. Van Tassel and John J. Grabowski, 2nd ed. (Bloomington: Indiana University Press, 1996).

5. Material on the KCEWV is in box 79, folder 13, M4C (hereafter cited as KCEWV file); Jackson interview (quotation). Additional information on Ehrlich: Walsh and Howie Emmer interviews; conversation with Ruth Gibson.

6. Halstead, *Out Now!,* 95; "Group Backs US Policy in Hall Demonstration," *DKS,* Oct. 27, 1965.

7. Memo from Sgt. Jack Crawford to Donald Schwartzmiller, Oct. 28, 1965, KCEWV file; Modugno interview; "'Kent Committee to End War' Begins Program of Education," *DKS,* Oct. 29, 1965.

8. "Campus Memo—STUDENT RELIGIOUS Liberals," *DKS,* Oct. 19, 1965; "Organize New Civil Rights Group—SNCC," *DKS,* Oct. 21; Carson interview.

9. "Protest the War in Vietnam" (flyer) and Crawford to Schwartzmiller, Nov. 2, 1965, KCEWV file; "Trio Presents View against Viet War," *DKS,* Nov. 2, 1965; "Guest Speakers Give Separate Viet Views," *DKS,* Nov. 4.

10. Spock's politics and his relationship with Peck: Nancy Zaroulis and Gerald Sullivan, *Who Spoke Up? American Protest against the War in Vietnam, 1963–1975* (New York: Holt, Rinehart and Winston, 1984), 21, 38, 90. Crawford to Schwartzmiller, Nov. 17, 1965, KCEWV file; "Dr. Spock Criticizes Attitudes," *DKS,* Nov. 19, 1965.

11. Jackson interview.

12. "Negroes Show Voting Power in Contest with Racial Issues," *NYT,* Nov. 3, 1965; and "Charges 'Irregularities' after 2,458-Vote Loss," *NYT,* Nov. 4; "Cleveland Negro Almost Upset Machine," *The Militant,* Nov. 22, 1965; Carl B. Stokes, *Promises of Power: A Political Autobiography* (New York: Simon and Schuster, 1973), 91–92 (quotation).

13. Gregorich and Barbara Brock interviews. Tussey's involvement and arrest: "Motion against Evidence Could Clear 30 Arrested—Three from Kent," *DKS,* Feb. 3, 1966. On others arrested, including Lewis Robinson, the mention of communist literature, and the disorderly assembly charges: "Two Instructors Arrested in Raid," *DKS,* Nov. 16, 1965; "Cops in Frame-Up Raid on Cleveland Socialists," *The Militant,* Nov. 29, 1965.

14. Casualties in the Ia Drang: Spencer C. Tucker, ed., *The Encyclopedia of the Vietnam War: A Political, Social, and Military History* (Santa Barbara: ABC-CLIO, 1998), 187; Lt. Gen. Harold G. Moore and Joseph L. Galloway, *We Were Soldiers Once . . . and Young: Ia Drang—The Battle That Changed the War in Vietnam* (New York: Random House, 1992), 346. Deaths of the two pacifists: Wells, *The War Within,* 58.

15. "Students Heckle Anti–Viet Nam Demonstrators," *DKS,* Nov. 23, 1965. Presence of city police and the taking of protestors' names: memo from Rackham to Harold R. Collins, English department, Dec. 8, 1965, KCEWV file. The Nov. 23 KCEWV meeting: Crawford to Schwartzmiller, Nov. 23, 1965, KSU Police Department report, KCEWV file; *The Drummer* 1.1 (Nov. 16, 1965), copy in KCEWV file. The incident involving Ehrlich and Gregorich distributing literature without university authorization: memo from Leroy Peach (Ass't Security Officer) to Dr. James Fox, Nov. 24, 1965, KCEWV file. Involvement and conduct of city police in the picket of Nov. 22: Eric N. Rackham to Dr. Harold R. Collins, department of English, Dec. 8, 1965, KCEWV file.

16. Wells, *The War Within*, 59. Literature YSAers distributed on campus about the NCC gathering indicates that many of them participated in it; see "Attend the National Anti-War Convention, Washington, D.C., November 25–28" and "Call for November Convention of the National Coordination [*sic*] Committee to End the War in Vietnam, November 25–28, 1965," flyers, KCEWV file.

17. Jackson interview.

18. Ibid. Crowd response to Oglesby's speech: Sale, *SDS*, 244; for the text of the speech, see *The New Student Left: An Anthology*, ed. Mitchell Cohen and Dennis Hale, rev. ed. (Boston: Beacon, 1967), 312–21. Coverage of the rally: photo story featuring Ehrlich and Jackson, *DKS*, Nov. 30, 1965.

19. See the following in *DKS:* "Students Heckle Anti–Viet Nam Demonstrators," Nov. 23, 1965 (the petition campaign); Walsh's letter, Nov. 11; nine letters criticizing Walsh, Nov. 17 and 18; letters from Seaman Louis Krbec III, Nov. 3 and 23; "Sign Here" (photo story featuring White), Dec. 1.

20. "College Men Face Prospect of Draft—Hershey," *DKS*, Jan. 7, 1966.

21. Michael S. Foley, *Confronting the War Machine: Draft Resistance during the Vietnam War* (Chapel Hill: University of North Carolina Press, 2003); George Q. Flynn, *The Draft, 1940–1973* (Lawrence: University Press of Kansas, 1993); Christian G. Appy, *Working-Class War: American Combat Soldiers and Vietnam* (Chapel Hill: University of North Carolina Press, 1998); and the following in *DKS:* "Ask Men to Apply for Test," April 5, 1966; " 'Test Can Only Help, Not Hurt'—A Look at New Draft Rulings," April 7; "Insurance for a 2-S" (editorial) and "Profs Discuss 'Draft' Group" (mentions Gregorich), April 8; "Draft Is Discussed," May 11; "Students Make KSU History; No Dismissals Winter Quarter," April 1. Brock's attempt to elicit a statement from White: White to Brock, March 29, 1966, box 2, folder 14, White Papers.

22. Figures on deferments and SSCQT: Flynn, *The Draft*, 199; Foley, *Confronting the War Machine*, 40. SDS opposition to the SSCQT: Michael Useem, *Conscription, Protest, and Social Conflict: The Life and Death of a Draft Resistance Movement* (New York: John Wiley and Sons, 1973), 56–60.

23. Lencl interview. John Conklin is a pseudonym; my conversations with him took place in 2009. Johnson interview. Chris Butler, interview by Daniel Miller, in *Fire in the Heartland: Kent State, May 4th, and Student Protest in America* (documentary; Fire River Productions, 2010).

24. See the following KCEWV flyers (all in KCEWV file): announcement of meeting on Jan. 13, 1966; "Panel Discussion on Vietnam, Stopher Hall"; "Doug Bruce, Civil Rights Worker Just Returned from Mississippi"; "Speakout and March for Peace and Freedom." See also the following in *DKS:* "Protestors Defend U.S. Ideals Says Ehrlich in GCI [Great Contemporary Issues] Speech," Jan. 26, 1966; "Demonstration," Feb. 1; "Demonstration Raps Bombings—30 Take Part," Feb. 2; "Jones Views War" and "What, When, Where . . . ," Feb. 16; "Protesters Elicit Letters," Feb. 18.

25. On Zimmer, and on Pahls's relationship with Crumb: Thomas M. Grace, "A Legacy of Dissent: The Culture and Politics of Protest at Kent State University, 1958–1964" (PhD diss., State University of New York at Buffalo, 2003) 125–26; on their connection to Pekar, Pekar interview. The art scene in Van Deusen Hall: letters in the *DKS*, Feb. 1, 6, and 13, 1962.

26. Popularity of the Erie Café: Wittmack and Barbara Brock interviews. Carolyn Knox and Chris Butler, interviews by Daniel Miller, *Fire in the Heartland* (documentary). Formal dress for dorm meals: "Student Criticizes Cafeteria Dress; Says Heels Cause 'Undue Strain,' " *DKS,* Oct. 5. 1965. White quoted in "Protestors: 'Involved Students,' " *DKS,* May 13, 1966.

27. Modugno to the author, Jan. 12, 2006. Material on the Student Religious Liberals is in box 79, folder 43, M4C. Characterization of the SRL: Kenneth J. Heineman, *Campus Wars: The Peace Movement at American State Universities in the Vietnam Era* (New York: New York University Press, 1993), 220. Father Zinn is listed as an antiwar speaker on the Kent campus in the spring of 1968 on a flyer titled "Why We Are Striking," which lists the endorsers and speakers; copy in KCEWV file.

28. Modugno and Hoffman interviews.

29. Hoffman interview; "Kent Committee to End the War in Vietnam" (with photo of Dave Edwards carrying the sign), *DKS,* April 14, 1966; LeRoy Peach to Donald L. Schwartz-miller, " 'Demonstration' of Kent Commitee [*sic*] to End war in Viet Nam," April 14, 1966, KCEWV file.

30. Conversation with Dave Dyer; Modugno interview.

31. Aptheker's journey to North Vietnam: Tom Hayden, *Reunion: A Memoir* (New York: Random House, 1988), 195–97. The controversy at UNC: William J. Billingsley, *Communists on Campus: Race, Politics, and the Public University in Sixties North Carolina* (Athens: University of Georgia Press, 1999), 180–82 and passim. Aptheker's Kent visit: "Aptheker, Communist, Gives Views on Vietnam," *DKS,* May 18, 1966; and "Prof Commends Kent's Policy," *DKS,* May 26; Jackson interview; Heineman, *Campus Wars,* 69; "A Few Jeer Red's Speech at KSU," *BJ,* May 20, 1966; J. R. (Jack) Crawford to D. L. (Donald) Schwartzmiller, May 20, 1966, KCEWV file.

32. American losses in the first three weeks of March 1966: William M. Hammond, *Reporting Vietnam: Media and Military at War* (Lawrence: University Press of Kansas, 1998), 81; killed-in-action figure for 1966: James S. Olson and Randy Roberts, *Where the Domino Fell: America and Vietnam, 1945 to 1990* (New York: St. Martin's, 1991), 164, 301. Draft calls: Clark Dougan and Samuel Lipsman, *A Nation Divided* (Boston: Boston Publishing, 1984), 72.

5. Fire in the City, Vigils on the Campus

1. Immediate causes of the riot: Philip W. Porter, *Cleveland: Confused City on a Seesaw* (Columbus: Ohio State University Press, 1976), 225–27, 232–33; "The Hough Riots," in *The Encyclopedia of Cleveland History,* ed. David D. Van Tassel and John J. Grabowski, 2nd ed. (Bloomington: Indiana University Press, 1996), 526. "This is just like Vietnam": quoted in Daniel R. Kerr, *Derelict Paradise: Homelessness and Urban Development in Cleveland, Ohio* (Amherst: University of Massachusetts Press, 2011), 160.

2. Porter, *Cleveland;* "The Hough Riots"; Ed Grant and Mike Hill, *I Was There: What Really Went On at Kent State* (Lima, OH: C.S.S. Publishing, 1974), 23 (quotation). Casualty figure and number of fires: "The Hough Riots," 526.

3. Details about the dinner gathering: Walsh interview. Relative success of the Cleveland Projects: James Miller, *"Democracy Is in the Streets": From Port Huron to the Siege of*

Chicago (New York: Simon and Schuster, 1987), 211–12. On Ayers and Witherspoon: Bill Ayers, *Fugitive Days: A Memoir* (Boston: Beacon Press, 2001), 82, 89. According to Ayers, Alex Witherspoon was a pseudonym.

4. Blount's address: "Black Recounts Kent 'Struggle,'" *PD,* July 4, 1970. Simpson lived on East 186th Street, approximately seven miles from the center of the upheavals. While his family strongly supported the civil rights movement, they did not experience any of it firsthand. Simpson interview; "Wants to Liberate His People," *BJ,* Dec. 15, 1969. Another future leader of the KSU Black United Students, Rudy Perry, also lived in Cleveland near where the 1966 disturbances occurred.

5. Charles DeBenedetti with Charles Chatfield, *An American Ordeal: The Antiwar Movement of the Vietnam Era* (Syracuse: Syracuse University Press, 1990), 155, 158. Aug. 6 protest in Cleveland and size of the turnout: "Antiwar Rally Due Today," *PD,* Aug. 6, 1966; "Negroes Seeking Freedom, Rally Here," *PD,* Aug. 7. Carmichael and the other speakers scheduled for the demonstration: "Support Day of Protest on Aug. 6th" and "The Killing in Vietnam Must Stop!," box 79, folder 13, M4C (hereafter cited as KCEWV file). Casualty rates for black soldiers: Christian G. Appy, *Working-Class War: American Combat Soldiers and Vietnam* (Chapel Hill: University of North Carolina Press, 1998), 19–21; Wallace Terry, *Bloods: An Oral History of the Vietnam War by Black Veterans* (New York: Random House, 1984), xiv. Participation of Thompson and Campbell: Thompson interview; conversation with Emity Campbell.

6. Polls on the hardening of racial attitudes: William H. Chafe, *The Unfinished Journey: America since World War II* (New York: Oxford University Press, 1991), 337; G. Calvin Mackenzie and Robert Weisbrot, *The Liberal Hour: Washington and the Politics of Change in the 1960s* (New York: Penguin, 2008), 327, 331. Polls on the Vietnam War: DeBenedetti and Chatfield, *An American Ordeal,* 162; Robert D. Schulzinger, *A Time for War: The United States and Vietnam, 1941–1975* (New York: Oxford University Press, 1997), 234–35. Congressional election returns In Ohio: *Statistics of the Congressional Election of November 8, 1966* (Washington, DC: GPO, 1967), 33–34. Weakening of Democratic strength in rural Ohio: Kevin P. Phillips, *The Emerging Republican Majority* (New Rochelle, NY: Arlington House, 1969), 322 (chart 93). State and county counts for Rhodes: Richard Zimmerman, "Rhodes's First Eight Years, 1963–1971," in *Ohio Politics,* ed. Alexander P. Lamis and Mary Anne Sharkey (Kent: Kent State University Press, 1994), 73; Michael F. Curtin, *The Ohio Politics Almanac* (Kent: Kent State University Press, 1996), 57.

7. "Hough Violence," *DKS,* Oct. 28, 1966.

8. Tom Wells, *The War Within: America's Battle over Vietnam* (Berkeley: University of California Press, 1994), 95; Nancy Zaroulis and Gerald Sullivan, *Who Spoke Up? American Protest against the War in Vietnam, 1963–1975* (New York: Holt, Rinehart and Winston, 1984), 94; Fred Halstead, *Out Now! A Participant's Account of the American Movement against the Vietnam War* (New York: Monad, 1978), 202. Fort Hood resisters: "Joint Statement by Fort Hood Three," in *"Takin' It to the Streets": A Sixties Reader,* ed Alexander Bloom and Wini Breines (New York: Oxford University Press, 1995), 255–57. SWP's promotion of the Fort Hood Three case: DeBenedetti and Chatfield, *An American Ordeal,* 155; "What Can You Do?" and "Sick of the War in Vietnam?" (flyers), KCEWV file.

9. Nov. 26 meeting and the need to find ways to broaden antiwar activities: Wells, *The War Within*, 113. Ehrlich quoted in "Anti-war Advocates Speak-Out," *DKS*, Oct. 12, 1966. Political theater used by the KCEWV: Kenneth J. Heineman, *Campus Wars: The Peace Movement at American State Universities in the Vietnam Era* (New York: New York University Press, 1993), 177–78. Television appearance: "3 Discuss 'New Left' on TV 49," *DKS*, Nov. 15, 1966.

10. Modugno, Carson, and Hoffmann interviews. There may have been an additional component to the rock-throwing incident, as Modugno recognized his assailant as somebody from high school with whom he had once had a dispute. See also "A Veteran's View," *DKS*, Feb. 16, 1967; and "Vietnam Protesters Try New Approach," *DKS*, Feb. 28.

11. See the following in *DKS*: "Students to Vote on Vietnam Issue" and "22 Profs Back Viet Statement—'Citizens for a Free Vietnam,'" Feb. 28, 1967; "Pro or Con" (editorial), March 1; "Students Favor War Escalation," March 3. Several prominent members of the history department, including its chairman, Henry N. Whitney, signed the statement. The sophomore's recollection: Robin Marks-Fife, remarks made at an SDS reunion at Kent State, May 6, 1989.

12. Hoffman interview.

13. Jackson interview. Howie Emmer, in his interview, gave a similar assessment about the value of the vigils.

14. Whitaker interview.

15. Ibid.

16. Conversation with Ric Erickson. He started college at Ohio State in 1962, transferred to Akron University, and moved on to Kent State. On his father, Edward O. Erickson, see "United Dem Pull Puts Erickson in Mayor Seat" and "The Erickson Victory" (editorial), *BJ*, Nov. 8, 1961.

17. "26 English Professors Sign 'Peace' Statement," *DKS*, March 2, 1967; the full-page ad ran in the *DKS* on June 2. Among the prominent faculty signers were Harris L. Dante and William H. Kenney from the history department; Sidney Jackson, library science; Richard Myers, art; Jerry Lewis, sociology; and Byron Lander, Murray Fishel, and Peter Crossland, political science.

18. See the following in *DKS*: "KCEWVN Sponsors Concert—Student Jazz Quintet," April 6, 1967; "KCEWV Marches to New York," April 12; "NYC March Ends 'Vietnam Week,'" April 18. Whitaker, Carson, and Hoffman interviews, as well as Daniel Miller's interview with Judy Gollust in *Fire in the Heartland: Kent State, May 4th, and Student Protest in America* (documentary; Fire River Productions, 2010). See also Wells, *The War Within*, 132–35.

19. Wells, *The War Within*, 150–56, McNamara quoted on 155–56; Simon Hall, *Peace and Freedom: The Civil Rights and Antiwar Movements in the 1960s* (Philadelphia: University of. Pennsylvania Press, 2005), 108–9.

20. Criticism of the UN march and the quote "unspeakable malignance": "Student against Subversives, for American Way of Life," *DKS*, April 19, 1967; "'Protestors: Ask Yourselves Why,'" *DKS*, April 21. On Wayne Morse see "Morse: 'US Influence in UN Eroding,'" *DKS*, May 2, 1967; for the give-and-take over Morse's appearance, see *DKS*, May 5, May 10, and May 16.

21. The position taken in the May 25 *DKS* letter was moderate in tone and freely quoted Democratic senator Wayne Morse, yet it also indicated that due to the "American troop build-up" it would be "necessary that we show the Johnson Administration the more they escalate the more sustained will be our response."

22. Michael Rossman, *The Wedding within the War* (Garden City, NY: Doubleday, 1971), 9. For a critique of Rossman's narrative, see John Downton Hazlett, *My Generation: Collective Autobiography and Identity Politics* (Madison: University of Wisconsin Press, 1998), 72–82.

23. "Drug Scene—'Much More Subtle Here': Explore KSU In-World Habits," *DKS,* Jan. 26, 1967; "Kent's Artistic In-Crowd— 'Avoid Pseudo-Hippies in Drug Activity,'" *DKS,* Jan. 27.

24. "Downtown Kent—Where the Action Is!," *DKS,* Jan. 24, 1967.

25. "Building Rapidly Alters Campus," "Franklin Gets DuPont Fund [Grant]," and "Timesman Salisbury Lectures Here," *KSU Summer News,* Aug. 17, 1967. Coverage of the lecture and Getz's observation: "Warns on Bombs Near China," *KSU Summer News,* Aug. 31, 1967.

26. See the following in *DKS:* "11 Poli Sci Profs Urge LBJ to De-escalate War," Nov. 29, 1967; "Faculty Committee to Work for De-escalation of Viet War," Oct. 17; Peter Crossland, "Faculty Urged to Take Stand on Viet War" (opinion), Oct. 20; "KCEWV School to Probe War," Nov. 3; "U.S. Withdrawal Wouldn't Hurt Economy—Cochran," Nov. 9; "'Modern Man Is Trigger Happy'—Dr. Hildebrant," Nov. 8, and his letter of clarification, "Prof Criticizes Report of Viet School Speech," Nov. 15; and "Negro's Commitment in Vietnam Questioned" (about a presentation by J. Ashley Higginbotham that was critical of the role African Americans were forced to play in Vietnam), Nov. 16.

27. "KSU Graduate Keynotes Visiting Lecture Series," *DKS,* Nov. 14, 1967; "Campus Chatter," *DKS,* Oct. 5 (quoting a review by Jack Newfield, *NYT Book Review,* Sept. 24). Kolko's relationship with Oglesby: conversation with Oglesby.

28. Franklin interview.

29. On Calkins: Maurice Isserman, *If I Had a Hammer: The Death of the Old Left and the Birth of the New Left* (New York: Basic Books, 1987), 158, 167, and passim; Kenneth R. Calkins, "Frustrations of a Former Activist," in *Kent State/May 4: Echoes through a Decade,* ed. Scott L. Bills (1982; Kent: Kent State University Press, 1988), 101. For his work on the de-escalation committee, see "Profs Aid Anti-War Movement," *DKS,* Dec. 6, 1967.

30. Inglee interview. Letters and coverage in *DKS* on YSA positions: David Edwards, "Students Urged to Vote Socialist in '68," Oct. 5, 1967; Ronald Wittmaack, "Socialist Explains Ideology," Oct. 24, and "'Un-American' Termed an Obsolete Label," Oct. 31; and Roy Inglee, "Viet from '54 Scanned," Nov. 14. For the reorganization, see "Young Socialist Alliance Seeks Recognition Anew," *DKS,* Nov. 17, 1967.

31. The SWP's advocacy of black power: Paul Le Blanc, "Trotskyism in the United States: The First Fifty Years," in *Trotskyism in the United States: Historical Essays and Reconsiderations,* ed. George Breitman, Paul Le Blanc, and Alan Wald (Atlantic Highlands, NJ: Humanities Press, 1996), 42. On Williams: Timothy Tyson, *Radio Free Dixie: Robert F. Williams and the Roots of Black Power* (Chapel Hill: University of North Carolina Press, 1999). On the Panthers: Gene Marine, *The Black Panthers* (New York: Signet, 1969). On the

Deacons: Lance Hill, *The Deacons for Defense: Armed Resistance and the Civil Rights Movement* (Chapel Hill: University of North Carolina Press, 2004). Appearance by Henry Austin and the YSA sponsorship: Milton E. Wilson, "Involvement / 2 Years Later: A Report on Programming in the Area of Black Student Concerns at Kent State University, 1968–1970," box 1, Milton E. Wilson, Jr., Papers, KSUA, 253, 277.

32. Quotations are from the Hoffman and Wittmaack interviews. Carson interview; she discussed her own involvement as well as Gibson's. Gibson is also covered in Heineman, *Campus Wars,* 178. Modugno provided additional background on the internal life of the committee. The KSU administration took interest in the divisions inside the committee, as Dean Eric Rackham phoned White on Oct. 27, 1967, to report that "a power struggle exists within the Kent Comte [*sic*]"; box 22, folder 48, White Papers.

33. Jackson and Franklin interviews.

34. For more on YSA, see Sale, *SDS,* 621; and Paul Jacobs and Saul Landau, *The New Radicals: A Report with Documents* (New York: Vintage, 1966), 54–58.

35. Quotations: Robert M. Fogelson, *Violence as Protest: A Study of Riots and Ghettos* (Garden City, NY: Doubleday, 1971), 105, 118. The convergence of the two movements would be brief. A good many white leftists advocated equality in word and deed, but between the years 1965 and 1970, most African Americans on the campus preferred that the struggles not intersect.

6. Moving toward Resistance

1. "No end in sight": Westmoreland quoted in Edward Doyle and Samuel Lipsman, *America Takes Over: 1965–67* (Boston: Boston Publishing, 1982), 175. R. W. Apple, "Vietnam: The Signs of Stalemate," *NYT,* Aug. 7, 1967. Humphrey quoted in Robert D. Schulzinger, *A Time for War: The United States and Vietnam, 1941–1975* (New York: Oxford University Press,, 1997), 256. "The enemy . . . is certainly losing": quoted in Clark Dougan and Samuel Lipsman, *A Nation Divided* (Boston: Boston Publishing, 1984), 127; also includes mention of Humphrey, Bunker, and other officials.

2. Doyle and Lipsman, *America Takes Over,* 175; Apple, "Vietnam." On McCarthy: Charles DeBenedetti with Charles Chatfield, *An American Ordeal: The Antiwar Movement of the Vietnam Era* (Syracuse: Syracuse University Press, 1990), 201–2.

3. Norman Mailer, *The Armies of the Night: History as a Novel, the Novel as History* (New York: New American Library, 1968), 105–35; Nancy Zaroulis and Gerald Sullivan, *Who Spoke Up? American Protest against the War in Vietnam, 1963–1975* (New York: Holt, Rinehart and Winston, 1984), 140; Kirkpatrick Sale, *SDS* (New York: Vintage, 1973), 383–86; Fred Halstead, *Out Now! A Participant's Account of the American Movement against the Vietnam War* (New York: Monad, 1978), 333–40; Tom Wells, *The War Within: America's Battle over Vietnam* (Berkeley: University of California Press, 1994), 174–75, 195–203. Howie Emmer interview.

4. Hoffman and Barbara Brock interviews; Hoffman to the author, April 15, 2006. Emmer's speech and remarks at the SDS reunion, May 5–6, 1989, tape in the author's possession. Powrie interview. See also the following in *DKS:* "KCEWV in D.C. Rally," Oct. 20, 1967; "Marcher Finds No Peace" (photo story), Oct. 24; "Pentagon Rally 'Modern Morality Play'" (letter), Oct. 25.

5. Kenneth J. Heineman, *Campus Wars: The Peace Movement at American State Universities in the Vietnam Era* (New York: New York University Press, 1993), 165; Powrie interview; conversations with Speed Powrie; *Fire in the Heartland: Kent State, May 4th, and Student Protest in America,* dir. Daniel Miller (documentary; Fire River Productions, 2010).

6. Mailer, *Armies of the Night,* 160–61, 181, and passim. Differences among MOBE leaders: Wells, *The War Within,* 174–79; Howie Emmer, "Pentagon Rally Provokes Commitment," *DKS,* Nov. 2, 1967.

7. Emmer, "Pentagon Rally"; Powrie interview; Sale, *SDS,* 385; Powrie's speech at SDS reunion, May 5, 1989; Howie Emmer interview.

8. Emmer, "Pentagon Rally."

9. Sale, *SDS,* 369–74, 387.

10. For details of the protest, see the following in *DKS:* "Kent Police Photograph Protestors," Oct. 27, 1967; "Protest Photos Debated Today," Oct. 31; "KCEWV Protests Dow-Napalm Producers" and "He Seeks Enlightenment for Dow Chemical Co." (letter by Irwin Loibman), Nov. 1; "Dow, KCEWV Trade Statements" and "Campus Group Urges Disposal of Vigil Pix," Nov. 2. See also see Betty R. Hovencamp, Director of Student Activities, to Robert E. Matson, Dean of Students (memo), Nov. 3, 1967, and KCEWV flyer about the Dow protest, KCEWV file. For a photo of Professor Lough and the hecklers showing signs from Stopher Hall, see *Chestnut Burr '68* (KSU yearbook), 44–45.

11. For a description of the tensions, see Hovencamp to Matson, Nov. 3, 1967. Background on YSA's participation in campus antiwar activity: Tim Wohlforth, *The Prophet's Children: Travels on the American Left* Atlantic Highlands, NJ: Humanities Press, 1994), 154–56.

12. Jackson and Hoffman interviews; conversation with Steve Lieber. On the Stokes campaign see the following in *DKS:* "Stokes Rep. to Recruit for Election Day Help," Nov. 2, 1967; Ken Hammond, "Students Urged to Help Stokes Campaign," Nov. 3. See also "Stokes Is Elected Mayor—Victory Margin Less Than 2,500 Votes," *PD,* Nov. 7, 1967.

13. See the following in *DKS:* "Faculty Presents Anti-War Panel" (the forum also featured Howie Emmer), Nov. 28, 1967; "KCEWV to Protest at Induction Center," Dec. 6; "KCEWV Rally Attracts 200" and "Viet Opinions Surveyed," Dec. 7. On the swings of public opinion in the fall of 1967: Melvin Small, *Covering Dissent: The Media and the Anti–Vietnam War Movement* (New Brunswick, NJ: Rutgers University Press, 1994), 84; James S. Olson and Randy Roberts, *Where the Domino Fell: America and Vietnam, 1945 to 1990* (New York: St. Martin's, 1991), 173; Neil Sheehan, *A Bright Shining Lie: John Paul Vann and America in Vietnam* (New York: Random House, 1988), 695.

14. See the following in *DKS:* Robert I. White, "More 'Ups' in View," Sept. 26, 1967; editorial (critical of Matson's decision to cancel use of a university bus for travel to the Cleveland protest), Dec. 8; Frank Frisina, " 'Retreat from Vietnam Wouldn't End War,' " Nov. 9.

15. Westmoreland quoted in David F. Schmitz, *The Tet Offensive: Politics, War, and Public Opinion* (Lanham, MD: Rowman and Littlefield, 2005), 69; Komer quoted in Olson and Roberts, *Where the Domino Fell,* 181. Battle of Khe Sanh and the extent of the Tet Offensive: Jonathan Randal, "U.S. Marines Seize 3D Hill in Vietnam," *NYT,* May 6,

1967; Charles Mohr, "Khe Sanh Shelled under Fog Cover," *NYT,* Jan. 26, 1968; James H. Willbanks, "Winning the Battle, Losing the War," *NYT,* March 5, 2008.

16. Consequences of the Tet Offensive: Bruce Palmer Jr., *The 25-Year War: America's Military Role in Vietnam* (Lexington: University Press of Kentucky, 1984), 79–81. The *Wall Street Journal* quoted in Clark Dougan and Stephen Weiss, *The Vietnam Experience: Nineteen Sixty-Eight* (Boston: Boston Publishing, 1983), 68. For Cronkite's assessment: Mark Kurlansky, *1968: The Year That Rocked the World* (New York: Ballantine, 2004), 61.

17. Proposed troop increase: William M. Hammond, *Reporting Vietnam: Media and Military at War* (Lawrence: University Press of Kansas, 1998), 122–25. Inglee's position: " 'Peace Candidate Is Not New Phenomenon,' " *DKS,* Dec. 8, 1967.

18. The registration form, completed on Feb. 26, 1968, is in the Hoffman file in box 77, M4C. Hoffman is listed as SDS president, Modugno as vice president, Abby Schindler as secretary, and Dan Stratton as treasurer. Weisberger's apprehension and Hoffman's readiness for SDS: Hoffman interview. Description of SDS: "The Draft: Hell No We Won't Go!" (interview of Hoffman and Modugno), *DKS,* Jan. 17, 1968. For a mention of SDS activities and anti-draft positions in NLN, see Sale, *SDS,* 374–77.

19. Quote from militant Henry Austin and the description of the initial BUS meetings: Milton E. Wilson, "Involvement / 2 Years Later: A Report on Programming in the Area of Black Student Concerns at Kent State University, 1968–1970," box 1, Milton E. Wilson, Jr., Papers, KSUA, 277–78. Initially, BUS had two co-chairs, but when they went to a more conventional structure to satisfy Student Affairs Council requirements they began using the more typical titles of president, vice-president, etc. Baldwin quoted in Jonathan Yardley, "James Baldwin Strikes a Spark," *WP,* Feb. 16, 2004.

20. Austin's first appearance in Kent and its sponsorship by YSA: Wilson, "Involvement," 253, 277. For Austin's background, see Lance Hill, *The Deacons for Defense: Armed Resistance and the Civil Rights Movement* (Chapel Hill: University of North Carolina Press, 2004), 140–43 and passim. Austin's activities in Cleveland: Lance H. Hill, "The Deacons for Defense and Justice: Armed Self-Defense and the Civil Rights Movement" (PhD diss., Tulane University, 1997), 360–62.

21. KSU Police Sgt. J. R. Crawford to D[onald] L. Schwartzmiller, Feb. 16, 1968; the memo concerned a report by Lawrence W. O'Brien, identified as a KSU freshman, who provided details of Austin's participation in radical meetings to the campus police. Cleveland police chief Michael J. Blackwell called attention to O'Brien's willingness to provide information in a letter to Kent City Police, who passed along the tip to Schwartzmiller. The Crawford memo and Blackwell's letter are in the Dwayne White file, box 78, M4C. Austin's activities in Cleveland: Hill, "The Deacons for Defense and Justice," 360–62, quotation on 362.

22. Austin's appearance at Kent State and the press release: "Militant Spokesman Lectures," *DKS,* Jan. 18, 1968. Austin and Tuck's talks on campus in February and the involvement of SDS: "KCEWV Sets Dow Protest," *DKS,* Feb. 21, 1968; Ronald Weisberger and George Hoffman, "Dow Won't Debate," *DKS,* Feb. 22; "Demonstrators Protest Napalm," *DKS,* Feb. 23. On Halstead and the SWP: "Reason for War Economic—Halstead," *DKS,* Feb. 22, 1968. Marine losses suffered at Khe Sanh: Stanley Karnow, *Vietnam: A History* (New York: Viking, 1983), 553.

23. "Poll Rates Nixon Best at Handling War," *NYT,* Aug. 25, 1968. In April 1968 a Gallup poll asked: "Do you think the U.S. made a mistake sending troops to fight in Vietnam?" Forty-eight percent said yes, 40 percent said no, and 12 percent had no opinion. The March polling was virtually identical, with 49 percent saying yes; 41 percent saying no, and 10 percent with no opinion.

24. Conversations with Carole Teminsky Barbato.

25. Dyer interview.

26. "Hill Backs McCarthy for Pres.," *DKS,* Jan. 16, 1968. Date of the primary and Kennedy's announcement: Lewis Chester, Godfrey Hodgson, and Bruce Page, *An American Melodrama: The Presidential Campaign of 1968* (New York: Viking, 1969), 119, 132.

27. "Johnson Will Not Run Again—Students Jubilant," *DKS,* April 2, 1968; "Students to Aid McCarthy Dive," *DKS,* April 3; Judy Gollust King to the author, Feb. 20, 2006; and conversations with David King and Joe Sima. Interview of Harriet Begala, April 30, 1991, KHS. See also "McCarthy for President Campaign Opens in Kent," *RC,* March 27, 1968.

28. "Thousands Leave Washington as Bands of Negroes Loot Stores," *NYT,* April 6, 1968; "Washington Turmoil Subsides" and "U.S. Troops Sent to Baltimore; Death Toll Grows," *NYT,* April 8. Louis H. Masotti and Jerome R. Corsi, *Shoot-Out in Cleveland: Black Militants and the Police, July 23, 1968* (Washington, DC: Frederick A. Praeger, 1969), 39–40. On Cincinnati: Ed Grant and Mike Hill, *I Was There: What Really Went On at Kent State* (Lima, OH: C.S.S. Publishing, 1974), 137; "Cincinnati Clam after Rioting," *NYT,* April 6, 1968. James T. Patterson, *Grand Expectations: The United States, 1945–1974* (New York: Oxford University Press, 1996), 686.

29. See the following in *NYT:* "Port Work Suspended as Tribute," April 6, 1968; "Hanoi Sends Condolences to Group Led by Dr. King," April 9; "Rioting Disquiets G.I.'s in Vietnam," April 8; "Maddox Is Upset, but Atlanta Flags Fly at Half-Staff," April 9; "Gallup Poll Finds Nixon Leads 3 Chief Democratic Contenders," April 20; "Wallace Insists He's Not a Bigot—Stresses on Texas Tour His 'Compassion' for Negro" and "Petition Drive in South," April 28.

30. See the following in *DKS,* April 9, 1968: "No Violence Forecast Here" (Fargo quote); "America's Dream" (editorial); and "Local Tribute to a Slain Leader" (Pickett's remarks). Carmichael quoted in Jules Witcover, *The Year the Dream Died: Revisiting 1968 in America* (New York: Warner Books, 1997), 156. See also "YSA Supports Carmichael View on King's Murder" (letter by Roy Inglee and David Edwards), *RC,* April 10, 1968; and White to William VanderWyden, KSU Student Body President, and Robert Pickett, Vice President, April 17, 1968, box 4, folder 23, White Papers.

31. "Students March in Memory of King," "Local Tribute to a Slain Leader," and "Kent Shocked," *DKS,* April 9, 1968; and "500 March in Kent in Memory of King," *RC,* April 9. Tompkins interview.

32. Genesis of the nationally sponsored, locally arranged protests: Sale, *SDS,* 399–403, 406, 428–30. For details of the week-long series of meetings and protests, see the following in *DKS:* "Class Strike Planned," April 11, 1968; "SDS Holds Vigil to Back Spock," April 16; "Socialist to Discuss Black Nationalism" (mentions Austin's appearance) and "Speak at Newman" (details of Watson's talk at the Needle's Eye and Cornell's talk at the Newman Center), April 18; "Students Boycott Friday for Peace," April 25. See also "Peace Calendar—Kent State

University" (flyer outlining the events), KCEWV file. The rally in Cleveland, chaired by Rev. Robert Bonthius of the city's Peace Action Council, drew a large, racially mixed crowd. Speakers included Rev. Philip Berrigan, Willie Ricks of SNCC, Jim Harvey of the National Black Student Anti-Draft Union, and Mike Spiegel of SDS. See "2,000 Protest War, Racism in Mall Rally," *PD*, April 27, 1968.

33. "Heckler's Barbs Turn to Bullets" and "Voices of Dissent, Officials Collide," *DKS*, April 30, 1968. Difficulties between the administration and the organizations and individuals backing the strike: "Attention!" (flyer), KCEWV file; see also Betty R. Hovencamp to Ruth Gibson, April 25, 1968, box 28, folder 48, White Papers. The sharp tone of the letter represented a significant change from the kind words Hovencamp had about Gibson months earlier during the first protest rally against Dow.

34. Modugno's complaint to campus police, Gibson's arrest, and the charges by the Kent Committee against the administration: "Voices of Dissent, Officials Collide" and "Hecklers' Barbs Turn to Bullets," *DKS*, April 30, 1968. Although campus police found no evidence that a rifle was used to fire the BBs or pellets, this was widely thought to be the case. For details of the incident see the memo from White to the Faculty Senate, May 2, 1968, box 28, folder 48, White Papers. One alarming detail in the same memo concerned a police radio log from 1:09 p.m. about a call reporting that a "male subject 6' 2" parked car on south side of Prentice Hall and proceeded on foot toward the Commons with a shotgun"; according to the log, officers were dispatched to the scene. This was the only reference I could locate pertaining to the alleged sighting of an armed man.

35. "HHH Here on May 3," *DKS*, April 24, 1968. Humphrey's announcement as a candidate (on April 27): Witcover, *The Year the Dream Died*, 182. Humphrey had the misfortune of making his announcement on a day when tens of thousands of people throughout the country were demonstrating against the war; it also came only ten days before Ohio's primary.

36. See Hubert H. Humphrey, *The Education of a Public Man: My Life and Politics* (Minneapolis: University of Minnesota Press, 1991), 322. Changes in Humphrey's position on Vietnam between 1965 and 1968, including his later break with Johnson in the last weeks of his 1968 campaign: Lloyd C. Gardner, *Pay Any Price: Lyndon Johnson and the Wars for Vietnam* (Chicago: Ivan R. Dee, 1995), 165, 294–95, 320, 470–83, 488–92. "Nation-wide Coverage with Humphrey Visit," *DKS*, May 1, 1968; for Pitts's role in initiating the walkout, "Wins Bible Belt Seal of Approval," *DKS*, May 7 (the headline writer apparently considered Kent part of the Bible Belt).

37. The resignations were from Eric Rackham, dean of student services, and John Kamerick, vice-president and provost; see "Two Resignations," *DKS*, May 9, 1968. "Welcome and present": White to Humphrey, April 25, 1968, box 4, folder 24, White Papers.

38. "Wins Bible Belt Seal of Approval"; Simpson interview. For more of the content of Humphrey's talk and the identity of those joining the walkout, see *Chestnut Burr '69* (KSU yearbook), 42–43. Humphrey's 1948 speech: Robert A. Caro, *Master of the Senate: The Years of Lyndon Johnson* (New York: Alfred Knopf, 2002), 439–45.

39. "Wins Bible Belt Seal of Approval"; Simpson interview. The *RC* coverage mentioned the walkout but focused on the mainly positive reception Humphrey received in Kent. See, among others, "Reception 'Magnificent'—HHH Says of KSU, Kent" and "It Was Day

of Sidelights, Highlights with No. 2 Man," *RC,* May 4, 1968. Pickettt quoted in "Ohio Students Acclaim HHH," *WP,* May 4, 1968. See also R. C. Dix's column, "Along the Way," May 6, 1968; Dix, who met with Humphrey, discussed the exchange between Pickett and Humphrey and how the encounter with the vice president had impressed Pickett.

40. Campus poll: "KSU Students Dovish—According to DKS Poll," *DKS,* May 1, 1968. The poll, which had run in the *DKS* the previous week, gave only two options, hawk or dove (a somewhat elastic term); 177 students responded, with 71 percent choosing "dove." In response to a question on US military presence in Vietnam, 58 percent favored a gradual reduction of American forces, while just 12 percent backed the antiwar demand of immediate withdrawal. Austin's letter: "Peace a Little Extreme," *DKS,* May 14, 1968.

41. Powrie, Simpson, and Jackson interviews. The most sensational headline of the out-of-town papers examined was "Humphrey Challenged by Negro," in the *Chicago Sun Times;* more typical was "HHH Emotionally States Hopes after Negroes Stage Walk Out," in the *Boston Globe* (both on May 4, 1968). Locally, the story was reported under the favorable banner "HHH at Kent State Shows His Style," in the *CP* of the same date. None of these stories appeared on the front page, although all were carried in the first section. Television coverage: *Chestnut Burr '69,* 43. The author also recalls watching the report on the *CBS News.*

42. Charles Kaiser, *1968 in America: Music, Politics, Chaos, Counterculture, and the Shaping of a Generation* (New York: Grove, 1988), xv. Ohio's awarding of party convention delegates in 1968: Michael Barone, *Our Country: The Shaping of America from Roosevelt to Reagan* (New York: Free Press, 1990), 439; number of delegates won by the respective candidates: Richard G. Zimmerman, *Call Me Mike: A Political Biography of Michael V. DiSalle* (Kent: Kent State University Press, 2003), 261–62. On Columbia University and the general strike in Paris: Kurlansky, *1968,* 178–208 and 209–237.

43. For the differing approaches of Westmoreland and Abrams, see George C. Herring, *America's Longest War: The United States and Vietnam, 1950–1975,* 2nd ed. (Philadelphia: Temple University Press, 1986), 153, 197, 209, 212–13.

44. Protest by African American students: "BUS Stages Sit-in," *DKS,* May 29, 1968; BUS sought a full-time teaching position for Pitts as well as his appointment as "the black co-ordinator and head of minority affairs." For the nature of the dispute, see White to Dr. Lawrence Litwack, EEOC, May 15, 1968, and White to Robert Pitts, May 17, box 4, folder 26; White to Robert Pitts, May 23, 1968, and White to Dr. Morin, May 28, box 4, folder 27, White Papers. Pitts had been active in the formation of the KSU CORE chapter in 1964; see box 79, folder 3, M4C. "Wash-Out '68" (editorial), *DKS,* May 14, 1968.

7. Election 1968

1. Joe Sima to the author, Dec. 30, 2010. Kennedy's remarks: Arthur M. Schlesinger Jr., *Robert Kennedy and His Times,* vol. 2 (Boston: Houghton Mifflin, 1978), 916. RFK's broad appeal and photos of his funeral train: Jefferson Cowie, *Stayin' Alive: The 1970s and the Last Days of the Working Class* (New York: New Press, 2010), 75–77, 81; Peter Jennings and Todd Brewster, *The Century* (New York: Doubleday, 1998), 369.

2. Theodore H. White, *The Making of the President 1968: A Narrative History of American Politics in Action* (New York: Atheneum, 1969), 285. Wallace quoted ibid., 403–4, from an interview with columnist James Kilpatrick.

3. Stephan Lesher, *George Wallace: American Populist* (Reading, MA: Addison-Wesley, 1994), 379–80, 391, 405–6, 408–9, 434–35; Rick Perlstein, *Nixonland: The Rise of a President and the Fracturing of America* (New York: Scribner, 2008), 265–66, 277, 283–85, 299–300, 306; Jonathan Rieder, "The Rise of the 'Silent Majority,'" in *The Rise and Fall of the New Deal Order, 1930–1980,* ed. Steve Fraser and Gary Gerstle (Princeton: Princeton University Press, 1989), 259.

4. "Report of the Akron Commission on Civil Disorders," April 1969, 8–9, available at http://sc.akronlibrary.org/local-history/online-books; "Curfew Cools Akron Down," "Fear Grips Integrated Akron District," and "Mixed Atmosphere Marks Riot Scene," *PD,* July 20, 1968.

5. Ed Grant and Mike Hill, *I Was There: What Really Went On at Kent State* (Lima, OH: C.S.S. Publishing, 1974), 32, 137.

6. "Akron Negroes Picket, Boycott Home Area Stores," *PD,* July 23, 1968; "Akron Curfew Draws Challenge by Negro," *PD,* July 24. Ballard quoted in Grant and Hill, *I Was There,* 33. "Report of the Akron Commission," 13–24, quotations on 19.

7. Wallace campaign advertisement: "Today Is Ohio Wallace Day," *PD,* July 20, 1968; see also "Wallace Drumbeaters Pound at Shopping Centers in Area," *PD,* July 21. One petition signer told a reporter, "You hear nothing but Wallace on the [Murray] Hill," an area that had been the site of violence directed toward black picketers during a school integration effort in 1964.

8. For sociological explanations of such violence, see Joe R. Feagin and Harlan Hahn, *Ghetto Revolts: The Politics of Violence in American Cities* (New York: Macmillan, 1973), especially chap. 1. Cleveland's African American residents had experienced years of unpunished brutality from vigilantes who operated with tacit police support. See Louis H. Masotti and Jerome R. Corsi, *Shoot-Out in Cleveland: Black Militants and the Police, July 23, 1968* (Washington, DC: Frederick A. Praeger, 1969), 36–41, which includes background information on the dismal social conditions in the city and on Evans's experience in the service, including his injury during the Korean War and subsequent psychomotor epilepsy, which caused "aggressive behavior . . . under stress" (40–41).

9. Masotti and Corsi, *Shoot-Out in Cleveland,* 33–57; and "3 Police, 3 Civilians Killed on East Side; Guard Called," *PD,* July 24, 1968.

10. The slain marine was AWOL from his unit. See Masotti and Corsi, *Shoot-Out in Cleveland,* 61–63; and "Man, Sons Held in Murder of Negro at Bus Stop," *PD,* July 26, 1968.

11. Del Corso's denunciation of Stokes: Masotti and Corsi, *Shoot-Out in Cleveland,* 66, 75. Stokes's decision to deploy African American officers and community residents and the reaction to the decision by some police: Leonard N. Moore, *Carl B. Stokes and the Rise of Black Political Power* (Urbana: University of Illinois Press, 2002), 88; "Cleveland Police Enraged, Score Delay in Troop Call" and "'Battle Part of Black Power Plot,'" *RC,* July 24, 1968.

12. Milton E. Wilson, "Involvement / 2 Years Later: A Report on Programming in the Area of Black Student Concerns at Kent State University, 1968–1970," box 1, Milton E.

Wilson, Jr., Papers, KSUA, 64. On Blount: James Michener, *Kent State: What Happened and Why* (New York: Random House, 1971), 28.

13. Jeffrey Powell to the author, Feb. 14, 2000; I also drew heavily on his unpublished memoir, "The Storm." For more on the campaign, see Irwin Unger and Debi Unger, *Turning Point: 1968* (New York: Charles Scribner's Sons, 1988), 205–11; and " 'Let No One Be Denied'—But in Resurrection City, 'Someday' Is Not at Hand,' " *Newsweek*, July 1, 1968. King's intentions: Milton Viorst, *Fire in the Streets: America in the 1960's* (New York: Simon and Schuster, 1979), 432–33.

14. Boram interview. Others were indifferent to books and topical literature. KCEWV member Joe Jackson found himself increasingly alienated from the newly formed SDS chapter and the premium its members seemed to place on confrontation over education. KCEWV member Ruth Gibson felt that activists like George Hoffman had betrayed the committee by organizing SDS. For his part, Hoffman never saw the value of debating Trotskyism with Gibson or Roy Inglee. For Hoffman and many others, marijuana, long hair, and psychedelic rock were taking the place of coffee houses, Ivy League hairstyles, and Marxist study.

15. See "Democratic Convention 1968" and "Democratic Convention 1968" (flyers), box 107, folder 2, M4C. SDS member Charlie Tabasko persisted with his efforts to organize for the convention protest despite being badly beaten "in a black neighborhood" while trying to do some political work. Tabasko interview. For the atmosphere immediately prior to the convention: Drew Pearson and Jack Anderson, "Report Chicago a Powder Keg on Convention Eve," *RC*, Aug. 24, 1968. On the fear factor and Mayor Daley's controversial order: "Lots of Law, Little Order," *Newsweek*, Sept. 9, 1968; "Area Doves Wanted on Trip to Chicago," *PD*, Aug. 25, 1968; David Farber, *Chicago '68* (Chicago: University of Chicago Press, 1988), 171–72.

16. Powell, "The Storm"; Hoffman and Powrie interviews; conversation with Erickson. For another version of the trip Erickson took south, see Michener, *Kent State*, 83. Size of the Akron–Kent SDS contingent: "Area War Protestors Head to Chi," *RC*, Aug. 24, 1968. Erickson and Zamaria quoted in "Summer in the City, Chicago '68," *DKS*, Sept. 24, 1968.

17. Howie Emmer and Ruth and Jack Emmer interviews. Involvement of Sid Peck and the Peace Council: "Prof Says Violence Will Rock Chicago" and "Area Doves Wanted on Trip to Chicago," *PD*, Aug. 25, 1968. Involvement of Tony Walsh, Corky and Jennifer Benedict, Carol McEldowney, Terry Robbins, and Charlie Tabasko: "Chicago, Cleveland, Chicago, Cleveland," *The Big Us* (Cleveland SDS newsletter) 1.2 (Oct. 11, 1968); Tabasko interview.

18. A teenager was shot to death just before the convention opened. See Jules Witcover, *The Year the Dream Died: Revisiting 1968 in America* (New York: Warner Books, 1997), 320. Hoffman's and Powell's participation: Hoffman interview; and Powell, "The Storm," which includes a graphic account of the threats made to his personal safety by as many as four officers who picked him up for a curfew violation. Being under eighteen, he was taken to a police station for being out after 9 p.m. without adult supervision; Real won Powell's release that night by posing as a priest and convincing the officers to discharge the youth into his custody. Police conduct on Sunday evening: Farber, *Chicago '68*, 180–83.

19. Hayden's arrest: Viorst, *Fire in the Streets*, 454; Farber, *Chicago '68*, 183–84; Powell, "The Storm."

20. Powell, "The Storm"; Farber, *Chicago '68*, 186–91. See also "Chicago Police Beat Medics, Clevelander Says" and "Clevelanders Tell of Beatings by Police at Chicago Rally," *PD*, Aug. 30, 1968.

21. Witcover, *The Year the Dream Died*, 322; Powell, "The Storm"; Powrie and Hoffman interviews. The Peace Plank was defeated by a vote of 1,500 to 1,000. See also "Ohio's Vote Is 67–48 against Peace Plank," *PD*, Aug. 29, 1968; and Lewis Chester, Godfrey Hodgson, and Bruce Page, *An American Melodrama: The Presidential Campaign of 1968* (New York: Viking, 1969), 524–37. According to one estimate, for every six demonstrators there was one agent, but even if this number is highly inflated, there were plenty in the crowd; see Farber, *Chicago '68*, 169–70.

22. Farber, *Chicago '68*, 196–98; "Dr. Peck Beaten—Tells of Fascist Behavior," *PD*, Aug. 30, 1968; Tabasko and Hoffman interviews.

23. Powell, "The Storm"; Farber, *Chicago '68*, includes photos that provide a good sense of the mayhem (gallery following 207). The beatings inside McCarthy's fifteenth-floor headquarters room: Witcover, *The Year the Dream Died*, 343; "Lots of Law, Little Order," *Newsweek*, Sept. 9, 1968.

24. White, *The Making of the President 1968*, 352, 354; "Polls: Confusing and Exaggerated," *Time*, Aug. 9, 1968, 19. The Harris poll, however, showed Humphrey ahead by five points.

25. "Nearly 10,000 Attend Randolph Fair," *RC*, Aug. 23, 1968; "Nixon Leads Portage County, Wallace Has Narrow Edge Over HHH," *RC*, Oct. 5, 1968.

26. See the following in *RC*: "Dix Newsman Is Clubbed in Riot, Deplores Police Action," Aug. 29, 1968; "Battle of Chicago" (editorial) and "DiPaolo Defends Daley's Handling of Chi Riots," Aug. 30; "Chicago: What Alternatives?" (letter), Sept. 3; "Urges Support for the Police" and "Must Look at Themselves" (letters), Sept. 6.

27. Whitaker, Tabasko, and Powrie interviews. Television coverage: Maurice Isserman and Michael Kazin, *America Divided: The Civil War of the 1960s* (New York: Oxford University Press, 2000), 233–34.

28. On the formation of SDS and its broader educational arm, see "University of SDS," *DKS*, Oct. 8, 1968. The notice for the Sept. 28 meeting featured a Dylan quote, "20 Years of Schooling and They Put You on the Day Shift." Of the issues mentioned on the flyer, the first five dealt with student concerns; the others were "racism, the Vietnamese war, the draft, [and] the coming election," in that order. Copy in the author's possession. Terry Anderson, *The Movement and the Sixties: Protest in America from Greensboro to Wounded Knee* (New York: Oxford University Press, 1995), 239–410. Canfora's background: Albert Canfora interview and conversations with the younger Canfora in 1968. Flanagan's background: box 77, M4C, and from the author's own knowledge of him. Bukosky's background: Leonard "Buk" Bukosky (Paul's brother) to the author, June 25, 2002, and Barber interview; Barber (who was Bukosky's high school girlfriend) described his time in a seminary as being his political "spark."

29. Lencl and Johnson interviews. Hudson's background: box 107, folder 10, M4C, and from a friend, David King. Gorup's background: Boram interview (Boram is Gorup's former wife).

30. Persky and Alewitz interviews. Hess completed a KCEWV/SDS activist survey for the author in May 2000. Another student, Colin Neiburger, from suburban Baltimore, was

in the same Jewish fraternity and, like Hess, became an important leader in SDS. Neiburger's background: box 78, M4C; and US House Committee on Internal Security, *Investigation of Students for a Democratic Society, Part 2 (Kent State University): Hearings before the Committee on Internal Security, House of Representatives,* 91st Cong., 1st sess., June 24–25, 1969 (Washington, DC: GPO, 1969), 546 (hereafter cited as HCIS, *Investigation, Part 2*). The register of suspected members of SDS compiled by the Kent State police, although it is not entirely accurate and some of the addresses are faulty, lists eight with out-of-state addresses, a percentage in line with the figure of approximately 20 percent for the student body as a whole.

31. Of fifty-nine SDS leaders/members either listed in the KSU police files or cited in the HCIS report, twenty-three were women; see box 107, folder 10, M4C, and the index to HCIS, *Investigation, Part 2*, i–iv. Carolyn Knox tells her story of having transferred to Kent State from Vassar in the documentary *Fire in the Heartland: Kent State, May 4th, and Student Protest in America,* dir. Daniel Miller (Fire River Productions, 2010). Schindler grew up in New York City and is listed as being from Scarsdale. See HCIS, *Investigation, Part 2*, 547; and box 107, folder 10, M4C. Boram interview.

32. David D. Van Tassel and John J. Grabowski, eds., *The Encyclopedia of Cleveland History,* 2nd ed. (Bloomington: Indiana University Press, 1996), 837, 1019–20; conversations with Alan Canfora; Tabasko interview; Charles Kaiser, *1968 in America: Music, Politics, Chaos, Counterculture, and the Shaping of a Generation* (New York: Grove, 1988), 213 and passim. On WMMS, see Ron Rollins, "Rock On," *Ohio Magazine,* May 2007, 21–22.

33. Here the author relied on his own specific memories of Kent in the fall of 1968. The Joplin album was *Cheap Thrills* (1968). On Crumb's five years in Cleveland, see the introduction by former KSU activist Marty Pahls (Crumb's brother-in-law), "The First Girl That Came Along," in Robert Crumb, *The Complete Crumb Comics,* vol. 3 (Seattle: Fantagraphics Books, 1997), vii–xii. *Rolling Stone* first appeared in Nov. 1967; see Abe Peck, *Uncovering the Sixties: The Life and Times of the Underground Press* (1985; New York: Citadel Press, 1991), 53; and Michener, *Kent State,* 71. On marijuana use (and police response) in the Kent area, see the following in *RC:* "Hold Ravennan on Marijuana Charge—KSU Police Make Arrest," Oct. 18, 1968; "KSU Student Arrested on 'Pot' Charge," Oct. 23; "Nab 3 in Portage Raids—More Arrests," Oct. 29.

34. See the following in *DKS:* "Ohio Campaign—HHH Boosts Youth," Sept. 24, 1968; "HHH Rally Tonight," Oct. 2; "Student Asks Support for Humphrey" (letter from Christopher Kobrak), Oct. 3, 1968. In addition to the Oct. 2 article on McWilliams, see also "Hold Rally," *BJ,* Oct. 2, 1968, which mentions the appearance by the *Nation's* editor.

35. The appearance by McWilliams was publicized but not reported; the author relied on his own memory of the talk. The lecture is covered in "Sorensen," *DKS,* Oct. 22, 1968; Erickson quoted in "Sorensen: Don't Sit Out Election—Heckled at KSU," *RC,* Oct. 19. In a conversation with the author, Robert Smedley, a supporter of SDS, remembered Erickson as being well versed and persuasive during his exchange with Sorensen that October evening.

36. George Markell, "Free University," and the lengthy criticism by Steven L. Shotsberger, "University of SDS," *DKS,* Oct. 8, 1968. For retorts, see "Free U. Comment" (letters from Jane Boram and professors Arif Kazmi and Thomas Lough), *DKS,* Oct. 11.

37. "Newsgirl Punched by Wallace Aide," *DKS,* Oct. 4, 1968; "250 Protesters Jeer Wallace

in Canton," *BJ*, Oct. 2; "Wallace Backer Slugs Collegian," *BJ*, Oct. 3. Photo caption to "I'm Not a Racist, Wallace Declares" and "George Wallace Rally an 'Experience' for Newsman," *RC*, Oct. 3, 1968.

38. Mark Real was among those pictured in the photo accompanying the news story "Law and Order Candidate Causes Disturbances at Akron AIP Rally," *DKS*, Oct. 4, 1968. Real quoted in "Wallace Rally Attracts Mock 'Klansmen,'" *BJ*, Oct. 2, 1968. See also "Wallace's Stock Speech Cheered," *BJ*, Oct. 2; "How the Akron Area Reacted to Wallace" and "Psst, Pal, Wanna Meet a Real Klansman?," *BJ*, Oct. 3. "The worst since Wallace . . .": quoted in "Wallace Uses Hecklers to Promote His Candidacy," *RC*, Oct. 3.

39. Wallace support among Akron police: "Law and Order Candidate Causes Disturbances," *DKS*, Oct. 4, 1968. Confederate uniform: "'He's for God and Country,'" *BJ*, Oct. 2, 1968. On Rex Humbard: "Work for Big Wallace Turnout in Akron Area," *BJ*, Oct. 1; and "I'm Not a Racist," *RC*, Oct. 3.

40. Wallace quote on Vietnam: "Law and Order Candidate Causes Disturbances," *DKS*. Support for Wallace among Appalachian whites and former Goldwater voters: "Work for Big Wallace Turnout in Akron Area," *BJ*, Oct. 1, 1968; "'He's for God and Country,'" *BJ*, Oct. 2.

41. "'Whippies Jeer Wallace,'" *DKS*, Oct. 8, 1968; "Cleveland Violence in Wallace's Campaign" and "10 Hurt, Demonstrators Blocked Exit," *BJ*, Oct. 6; and "Chicago, Cleveland," *The Big Us* 1.2 (Oct. 11, 1968). SDSer Corky Benedict explained that Whippies stood for (W)allace-Hippies.

42. The *Plain Dealer* characterized the speech as "inaudible," while the Akron paper reported that the clamor of protestors made LeMay's talk almost impossible to hear. "Scuffles Mar Wallace Rally, Six Injured," *PD*, Oct. 6, 1968; and "Cleveland Violence Is First in Wallace Campaign," *BJ*, Oct. 6. The African American militant is identified in the SDS paper, *The Big Us*.

43. "Confront Nixon" (SDS flyer), box 77, folder 2, M4C; "Nixon's 2 1/2 Problems," *Time*, Oct. 18, 1968, 22; "Nixon Gets Akron's Mixed Blessing" and "'Orders from Washington' Mustered Heckler Brigade?," *BJ*, Oct. 11, 1968; Dyer interview; Timothy DeFrange, interview by Helene Cooley, April 30, 1990, Kent State Shootings Oral Histories Collection, M4C. Alan Canfora's account, which corroborates DeFrange, is in Viorst, *Fire in the Streets*, 512. Not all from KSU opposed Nixon; the Akron audience included 150 student supporters. See "KSU Delegation Is Orderly" and "Nixon Tells Large Akron Crowd He'll Carry Ohio." *RC*, Oct. 11, 1968.

44. "Warn Against Violence at the Polls," *BJ*, Oct. 9, 1968.

45. Gallup poll and efforts to mobilize union voters: "UAW Organizing" and "Wallace Scores with UAW," *BJ*, Oct. 2, 1968; "Ohio Labor Maps War on Wallace," *BJ*, Oct. 38. Albert Canfora interview. "In precinct after precinct . . .": Hubert H. Humphrey, *The Education of a Public Man: My Life and Politics* (Minneapolis: University of Minnesota Press, 1991), 284.

46. Nardella interview. Nardella, who was known for his gentlemanly manner, recalled that Greene's coarse language startled him. Greene's support of Humphrey in 1972: Perlstein, *Nixonland*, 635 and passim.

47. Chester, Hodgson, and Page, *American Melodrama*, 708, 717; Humphrey, *Education of a Public Man*, 284.

48. "Abel Blasts Demonstrators—At Chicago Convention," *RC,* Sept. 7, 1968.

49. *DKS* editorial and the canvass in Akron: "Humphrey for President." *DKS,* Oct. 22, 1968; and "Open Dem HQ," *DKS,* Oct. 29; the author remembers Colton's pitch to the students. R. C. Dix, "Along the Way," *RC,* Nov. 4, 1968.

50. " 'I'm a Man You Can Trust' " and "Cold Wind Whistles as Crowd Sings—Warmup for Humphrey," *BJ,* Oct. 28, 1968; and "HHH in Ohio," *BJ,* Nov. 3. "Those brave men . . .": quoted in Witcover, *The Year the Dream Died,* 426–27. McCarthy's last-minute endorsement: White, *The Making of the President 1968,* 449. Final polls: Chester, Hodgson, and Page, *American Melodrama,* 749; "The Ohio Vote" (chart), *BJ,* Nov. 3, 1968.

51. SDS protests: photo story and "SDS and Rights" (editorial), *DKS* Nov. 5, 1968; and "Students Jeer Voting Protest," *RC,* Nov. 6. The author, who was a student in the political science class, was one of those befuddled. SDS flyer promoting the rally: box 107, folder 2, M4C.

52. "9 out of 10 Registered to Vote Do," *BJ,* Nov. 6, 1968; and "The War, 'Social Unrest' Bothering Voters in Ohio," *BJ,* Nov. 2.

53. Chester, Hodgson, and Page, *American Melodrama,* 759. Statewide voting total: Curtin, *Ohio Politics Almanac,* 9. *Beacon Journal* poll: "The Ohio Vote," *BJ,* Nov. 3, 1968. Portage County results: "Portage Vote at-a-Glance," *RC,* Nov. 6. Portage County totals were Humphrey, 16,340; Nixon, 15,061; and Wallace, 5,089. Union in lessening the Wallace votes: "Believe HHH Won Back Some of Labor's Votes," *BJ,* Nov. 6, 1968.

8. Black and White (Alone) Together

1. Jeffrey Powell, "The Storm" (unpublished memoir). The borrowed Rambler: Ric Erickson to the author and Carolyn Harper Knox to the author, March 1, 2011. For the number and new locations of SDS chapters, see Kirkpatrick Sale, *SDS* (New York: Vintage, 1973), 479.

2. Sale, *SDS,* 64, 121–22, 461–65.

3. Powell, "The Storm"; the name "Donovan" was bestowed on him by fellow SDSer Terry Robbins. Gibeaut's home state is given in US House Committee on Internal Security, *Investigation of Students for a Democratic Society, Part 2 (Kent State University): Hearings before the Committee on Internal Security, House of Representatives,* 91st Cong., 1st sess., June 24–25, 1969 (Washington, DC: GPO, 1969), 545 (hereafter cited as HCIS, *Investigation, Part 2*).

4. Number of delegates attending the National Council in Boulder and the votes taken: Sale, *SDS,* 483–86. For more on PL, see David Barber, *A Hard Rain Fell: SDS and Why It Failed* (Jackson: University Press of Mississippi, 2008), 145–48.

5. The list of contacts at Cleveland area high schools appears in *The Big Us* 1.2 (Oct. 11, 1968). Havens's high school: conversation with Havens. Powell's experience at Stow High School in early Sept. 1968 and Carson's meeting with student organizers: "Appeal to Kent, Stow Students to Form Own Union," *RC,* Sept. 23, 1968; the editorial appeared on Sept. 25.

6. Powell, "The Storm."

7. For notice of Rudd's speech, see "SDS Brings Rudd" and "Columbia U . . . It Could Happen Here?" (letter by Art Fine), *DKS,* Oct. 24, 1968. Rudd's chairmanship of the Co-

lumbia SDS chapter: Mark Rudd, *Underground: My Life with SDS and the Weathermen* (New York: HarperCollins, 2009), 43. Number of urban residents driven from their dwellings by Columbia's policies and the criticism leveled by the *NYT:* Mark Kurlansky, *1968: The Year That Rocked the World* (New York: Ballantine, 2004), 195, 203; for more on the Columbia uprising, see Sale, *SDS*, 430–41.

8. "The WKSU Incident," box 107, folder 12, M4C. Murvay's involvement and her role in the incident: HCIS, *Investigation, Part 2*, 502–4.

9. On Rudd's appearance see the following in *DKS:* "Rudd Explains Student Movement, Chairman of Columbia SDS" and "Rudd Rips U.S. Policies to DKS," Oct. 29, 1968; "Student Denounces SDS 'Swear-in' as Disgraceful" (letter), Nov. 1. See also "Rudd Gets Rude Awakening—Audience Not Captivated," *RC,* Oct. 26; and Randy Wallick, "Roasting Pan" (opinion), *RC,* Oct. 28. Rudd's difficulties subsequent to the speech: Sale, *SDS,* 483; James Michener, *Kent State: What Happened and Why* (New York: Random House, 1971), 99–100. Rudd does not discuss the incident in his memoir. Ayers editorial cartoon: *DKS,* Nov. 5, 1968. A copy of the eye-catching flyer SDS used to publicize Rudd's talk, "Columbia Is Coming, Up Against the Wall!," is in the author's possession.

10. "The WKSU Incident"; HCIS, *Investigation, Part 2,* 502–4.

11. Davis quoted in "Campus Rebels: Who, Why, What," *Newsweek,* Sept. 30, 1968, 64. Davis's speech at KSU: "Rennie Davis Talks on sds [*sic*]," *DKS,* Oct. 31, 1968; "Davis Addresses SDS," *DKS,* Nov. 5. SDS ROTC protest: *DKS* photo story, Nov. 1, 1968. A copy of the flyer about Davis's talk, "Chicago, the Elections, and Beyond," is in the author's possession.

12. *Newsweek,* Sept. 30, 1968, 68.

13. Kurlansky, *1968,* 354–55.

14. See White's remarks of July 19 (prepared for an unstated presentation) and his letters of thanks to several of his German counterparts, also dated July 19, box 4, folder 31; White to Dr. Logan Wilson, July 22, 1968, box 4, folder 32, White Papers.

15. Box 4, folder 30, and box 4, folder 32, White Papers; HCIS, *Investigation, Part 2,* 475–76.

16. "Student Affairs: A Tough Job," *RC,* June 26, 1969; White to Matson, June 21, box 4, folder 30, White Papers. Matson's temperament: "Black Students Tell of Tensions behind Kent Walkout," *CP,* Nov. 20, 1968; and Barclay D. McMillen and William J. Armstrong, "Kent State, May 4, 1970: Who Really Was Responsible for the Shootings?," unpublished memoir, 1999, box 131, folder 14, M4C. KSU had three vice presidents, for student affairs, academic affairs, and business and finance.

17. For a biographical sketch of McMillen see the finding aid to his papers, M4C; and "Prof Steps beyond Classroom," *DKS,* Jan. 22, 1969. See also White to McMillen, July 5, 1967, box 3, folder 35, and White to McMillen, Aug. 9, 1968, box 4, folder 33, White Papers; and McMillen and Armstrong, "Kent State, May 4, 1970."

18. Rumors of the boycott: White to Vice President Ronald Roskens, Aug. 6, 1968, box 4, folder 33; White's contacts with Dix: White to Dix, Oct. 4, 1968, box 4, folder 38, White Papers. Article placed by Dix: "C. of C. in Kent Greets Freshmen," *RC,* Sept. 17, 1968. The author recalls the long reception lines in which White stood patiently.

19. "KSU Sets Ground Rules for Keeping the Peace," *RC*, Sept. 3, 1968; White to Matson, Sept. 9, 1968, box 4, folder 36, White Papers. Within the month, Thigpen was appointed as a part-time coordinator of the Human Relations Center; see "KSU to Assist Negro Students through New Center," *BJ*, Sept. 26, 1968.

20. Background on Pickett: "VanderWyden Is Student Head," *RC*, Nov. 17, 1968. Fargo's views: "Whites Get Black View of KSU, Kent," *RC*, Oct. 11, 1968.

21. For the role played by Roberts as well as the names of the two Oakland Police recruiters, see an undated document titled "Analysis" (probably written by Barclay McMillen and Akron attorney and KSU trustee Robert Blakemore), box 33, folder 42, White Papers. On the situation in Oakland, see Gene Marine, *The Black Panthers* (New York: Signet, 1969), 156–73, 183–84; David Hilliard and Lewis Cole, *This Side of Glory: The Autobiography of David Hilliard and the Story of the Black Panther Party* (Boston: Little, Brown, 1993), 187–208; and Henry Hampton and Steve Fayer, *Voices of Freedom: An Oral History of the Civil Rights Movement from the 1950s through the 1980s* (New York: Bantam, 1990), 514–19, which includes the testimony of the police officers involved in the shoot-out in which Hutton was slain.

22. The section heading (as well as the chapter title) is borrowed from the 1970 album *Alone Together* by Dave Mason. For the details of the start of the sit-in, see the "Analysis" document cited in the previous note. See also HCIS, *Investigation, Part 2*, 505–8, 569 (photo); Marti Bledsoe and Kathryn Spearman, "The First BUS Trip," *Kent Alumni Magazine* 7.54 (1999): 6–8; and "Black Students Tell of Tensions behind Walkout," *CP*, Nov. 20, 1968. Although White had already named Donald Thigpen to a minor post in the administration, he participated in the sit-in. It is unclear whether he did so with the tacit approval of the administration. Whatever understanding may have existed, Thigpen served as a go-between throughout the week-long crisis.

23. Pickett's participation: Milton E. Wilson, "Involvement/2 Years Later: A Report on Programming in the Area of Black Student Concerns at Kent State University, 1968–1970," box 1, Milton E. Wilson, Jr., Papers, KSUA, 280 (includes photo). Simpson interview. Nelson Stevens, a graduate student, was the first BUS member to be identified as facing charges; see "Kent Charges 9 in Oakland Fray," *Painesville (OH) Telegraph*, Nov. 15, 1968. For Ghe's participation, see "250 Negroes Leave KSU, Protest Administration," *PD*, Nov. 19. It is very likely that Fargo was involved in the sit-in, but given the understandable reluctance of people to identify themselves unnecessarily, his name did not appear in any of the press coverage of the event. Additional information drawn from Whitaker, Boram, and Hoffman interviews; Powell, "The Storm," also offers considerable detail.

24. The author, then a resident of Johnson Hall, witnessed Haskasis strike the mock pose outside the main entrance to the dormitory. The description of Haskasis is based on the author's recollection and on Michener, *Kent State*, 205. Disturbances during the march: notice to students by Dean David Ambler (director of residence halls), dated Nov. 14, 1968, and Special Bulletin (issued under White's signature), Nov. 18, box 33, folder 42, White Papers. On the march that followed the sit-in see also "Matson's Manner Questioned" (letter) and "Twin Towers Reacts to BUS, SDS Protest," *DKS*, Nov. 19, 1968. Nov. 12 planning meeting between BUS and SDS: see HCIS, *Investigation, Part 2*, 506–7. Real's prediction: Whitaker interview.

25. SDS meeting: "Protestors Talk in KSU Student Group Sessions" and "Student Charged in Sit-In at KSU," *RC*, Nov. 15, 1968. Stevens's connection to BUS: Wilson, "Involvement," 290. Separate meetings held by Matson: Special Bulletin to Faculty from Robert I. White, Nov. 18, 1968, copy in the author's possession. Description of Matson and his approach in the meeting with the African American students and their families: McMillen's account in McMillen and Armstrong, "Kent State, May 4, 1970"; and "Matson's Manner Questioned," *DKS*.

26. On Matson, see "Black Students Tell of Tensions," *CP*, Nov. 20, 1968. According to McMillen, Matson and Roskens were unyielding and White followed their lead; see McMillen and Armstrong, "Kent State, May 4, 1970." White's absence from campus (he had been at a meeting with the trustees at a nearby country club): "Analysis," box 33, folder 42, White Papers. "An impossible alternative": quoted in Wilson, "Involvement," 283.

27. Growth of conservative opposition on the campus and the possibility of Panther leaders coming to Kent State: "BUS Sifting Strategy in KSU Amnesty Fight," *RC*, Nov. 17, 1968; for a sampling of newspaper coverage supporting a crackdown, see "Negroes Fail to Sway Kent's Get Tough Plan," *Dayton Journal Herald*, Nov. 18, 1968. Powell's meetings with Catholic clergy who were estranged from the church: Powell, "The Storm." Support for BUS by KSU faculty, including Jerry Lewis: "KSU Professor Won't Teach until Black Students Return—3 Others Support Militants," *BJ*, Nov. 19, 1968. "On the fringe of large-scale disorder": HCIS, *Investigation, Part 2*, 478. In his interview, Simpson provided details of how BUS won support for the walkout. The most reliable approximation of the number of African American students who left the campus was provided by Donald Thigpen, who figured that "at least 400" did so. See "Walkout by Negroes Threatened at Kent," *CP*, Nov. 18, 1968. "Never seen a quieter . . .": "BUS Stages Mass Walkout to Akron," *DKS*, Nov. 19, 1968. "Most dramatic event . . .": Persky interview.

28. White's firm stance and the shock generated by the walkout: "Kent Stunned by Walkout but Predicts Early Return," *CP*, Nov. 19, 1968. Letters and telegrams supporting White: box 33, folder 42, White Papers. Support for BUS on other Ohio campuses: "Leaders Vow to Continue Kent Walkout, Sympathy Protests Also Scheduled at Central, Wooster," *Canton (OH) Repository*, Nov. 20, 1968. The SDS teach-in was held on the day of the walkout and featured a number of professors, including sociologists Jerry Lewis and Thomas Lough, as well as political scientist Peter Crossland; see "Profs, Students Air Views on BUS Boycott," *DKS*, Nov. 19, 1968. "None of the administrators . . .": quoted in "KSU Professor Won't Teach," *BJ*, Nov. 19.

29. On McMillen's differences with Matson over the handling of the crisis and for the extended quote: McMillen and Armstrong, "Kent State, May 4, 1970."

30. McMillen and Armstrong, "Kent State, May 4, 1970," makes clear McMillen's heightened involvement. For some of what BUS gained, see "Key KSU Posts for Negroes May Ease Campus Racial Tension," *CP*, Nov. 22, 1968. For more on the turnabout with BUS, see Matson's comments in HCIS, *Investigation, Part 2*, 496–97.

31. See "Black United Students Return from Self-Exile" and "Homecoming" (editorial), *DKS*, Nov. 22, 1968. The first public reaction from an unnamed BUS spokesman was: "We are coming home with pride and dignity. We're black and we're proud." Quoted in

"KSU Administration's Evidence Insufficient to Charge BUS, SDS," *DKS,* Nov. 21. For the complete text of the BUS proclamation, see "Statement Made by Black United Students at the Administration Building upon Their Return to the Kent State University Campus on Thursday, Nov. 21, 1968, at 5:15 P.M.," box 33, folder 42, White Papers.

32. Real quoted in "KSU Administration's Evidence Insufficient to Charge BUS, SDS," *DKS,* Nov. 21, 1968.

33. "1968 was not a year . . .": Kurlansky, *1968,* 200. Real's illness: Powell, "The Storm." Mark Real, "Kent Liberation, Round One," *The Big Us* 1.6 (Dec. 6, 1968).

34. Real, "Kent Liberation, Round One." The mention of "police infiltration" may refer to a campus policeman who had attended several of SDS's initial meetings in the fall and whose identity was revealed.

35. Hiring of Paul Cheeks: Wilson, "Involvement," 58. Cheeks also discussed his return to KSU in his interview. "They shoot and kill . . .": "Black Students Tell of Tensions," *CP,* Nov. 22, 1968.

36. SDS flyer in the author's possession.

37. Rudd quoted in Todd Gitlin, *The Sixties: Years of Hope, Days of Rage* (New York: Bantam, 1987), 337. Authorship of "Who Rules Kent?" (copy in the author's possession): Powrie and Hammond interviews. The book that may have stimulated the pamphlet is G. William Domhoff, *Who Rules America?* (Englewood Cliffs, NJ: Prentice-Hall, 1967). "The global profit-making machine . . .": quoted in HCIS, *Investigation, Part 2,* 573. Rudd's line of reasoning on behalf of the "action faction" position: "Columbia: Notes on the Spring Rebellion," in *The New Left Reader,* ed. Carl Oglesby (New York: Grove, 1969), 290–312.

38. On Hutton's killing, see Joshua Bloom and Waldo E. Martin, *Black against the Empire: The History and Politics of the Black Panther Party* (Berkeley: University of California Press, 2013), 119–24 and passim.

39. White to Chiaramonte, Nov. 23, 1968, box 5, folder 3, White Papers.

40. White to Ashbrook, Dec. 11, 1968, box 5, folder 5, White Papers. On Ashbrook, see Rick Perlstein, *Before the Storm: Barry Goldwater and the Unmaking of the American Consensus* (New York: Hill and Wang, 2001), 176–79.

41. SDS chapter at North Texas State: Sale, *SDS,* 122. White to Kamerick, Dec. 3, 1968, box 5, folder 4, White Papers.

42. McMillen and Armstrong, "Kent State, May 4, 1970." Robbins quoted in Barber, *A Hard Rain Fell,* 149.

43. "Repression of black people": "Capsule Comments by White, SDS, on BUS Walk-out," *DKS,* Nov. 19, 1968.

44. Real, "Kent Liberation, Round One." See also Lance Morrow, "1968: The Year That Shaped a Generation," *Time,* Jan. 11, 1988, 27.

9. SDS Spring Offensive

1. Whitaker interview. Whitaker was insistent that no shoving had occurred during his argument with the conservatives. For the particulars of the dispute see Whitaker file in box 78, M4C. The full Hitler quote is in Nancy Zaroulis and Gerald Sullivan, *Who Spoke*

Up? American Protest against the War in Vietnam, 1963–1975 (New York: Holt, Rinehart and Winston, 1984), 241.

2. Failure of the vote over supporting the protest: Jeffrey Powell, "The Storm" (unpublished memoir). Debate within the MOBE: Tom Wells, *The War Within: America's Battle over Vietnam* (Berkeley: University of California Press, 1994), 292. For military and police preparation for the inauguration, see *Rights in Concord: The Response to the Counter-Inaugural Protest Activities in Washington, D.C. A Special Staff Study Submitted by the Task Force on Law and Law Enforcement to the National Commission on the Causes and Prevention of Violence* (Washington, DC: GPO, 1969), 88–93 (commonly known as the Walker Report).

3. James Michener, *Kent State: What Happened and Why* (New York: Random House, 1971), 84–87; Milton Viorst, *Fire in the Streets: America in the 1960's* (New York: Simon and Schuster, 1979), 512.

4. KSU Police Department records identify Post, Cecora, and Boram as being among those going to Washington. Powell's role in arranging the transportation for the group: Powell, "The Storm." Boram provided further details in her interview. Hunter Havens's participation in the Washington protest: conversation with the author. Influence Kent's SDS coffee house had on local high school youth, including Finn: Hoffman interview. For a photo of some of the participants in the protest, including Finn, Mary Ann Jackson, Powrie, Whitaker, Emmer, Erickson, Hess, and Marilyn Davis Hammond, see *DKS,* Jan. 24, 1969.

5. Hammond, "New Left Notes," *DKS,* Jan. 10, 1969. Powrie and the offset press: Powrie, speech at the SDS reunion at Kent State, May 5, 1989, tape in the author's possession. Nixon quoted in Frank van der Linden, *Nixon's Quest for Peace* (Washington: R. B. Luce, 1972), 13.

6. Powell, "The Storm." Participation limited by the "bitter cold": *Rights in Concord,* 86. "Small, hard core . . .": "Young Demonstrators at Parade Throw Smoke Bombs and Stones at Nixon's Car," *NYT,* Jan. 20, 1969, quoted in Zaroulis and Sullivan, *Who Spoke Up?,* 209–10.

7. Powell, "The Storm." "Numbers to Know," a MOBE/SDS flyer (copy in the author's possession), lists the location of eleven important protest sites for the counter-inaugural, including inaugural receptions.

8. Powell, "The Storm"; he devotes four pages to the encounter. While he does not specify the location, it appears to have been the Washington Hilton. See "Youth Unites at Capitol," *DKS,* Jan. 21, 1969.

9. Arrests: "Hecklers Mar Nixon's Day, *DKS,* Jan. 21, 1969. Protest at the Smithsonian: *Rights in Concord,* 99–103; "Clashes Erupt after March," *WP,* Jan. 20, 1969. Boram interview; Powell, "The Storm," and conversation with the author.

10. Muddy conditions: Zaroulis and Sullivan, *Who Spoke Up?,* 210; for other details, see *Rights in Concord,* 104–5; "Counter-Inaugural Opens in Bubbling Bedlam," *WP,* Jan. 19, 1969. The ball took place in a circus tent, whose thin walls offered meager shelter from the cold winter night.

11. Debate at the Brightwood Church: Viorst, *Fire in the Streets,* 514; for more details, including the participation in the protest by African American youth, see *Rights in Concord,* 105–13. For additional specifics, see "250,000 Applaud Parade; Protesters Clash with Police"

and "Nixon Hailed, Receives Uneven Welcome," *WP,* Jan. 21, 1969; Bobbi Smith, "PS on DC," *The Big Us* 1.8 (Jan. 25, 1969); Powell, "The Storm."

12. Powell, "The Storm." Canfora quoted in Viorst, *Fire in the Streets,* 513–14. "Washington: People, Police, Protestors," *DKS,* Jan. 22, 1969. Reaction of MOBE's leaders, including Rennie Davis and Sid Peck: Wells, *The War Within,* 293; Zaroulis and Sullivan, *Who Spoke Up?,* 209–11; Charles DeBenedetti with Charles Chatfield, *An American Ordeal: The Antiwar Movement of the Vietnam Era* (Syracuse: Syracuse University Press, 1990), 243–44. "Voices from another era . . .": Jonathan Schell, *The Time of Illusion* (1975; New York: Vintage, 1976), 25. Nixon's reaction: Robert Dallek, *Nixon and Kissinger: Partners in Power* (New York: HarperCollins, 2007), 95.

13. The bombings were first made public by William Beecher, in "Raids in Cambodia by U.S. Unprotested," *NYT,* May 9, 1969. The story failed to gain much traction, although the leak infuriated the White House. William Shawcross, *Sideshow: Kissinger, Nixon and the Destruction of Cambodia* (New York: Simon and Schuster, 1979), chap. 1 and especially 28, 33–35, 105; Jeffrey Kimball, *Nixon's Vietnam War* (Lawrence: University Press of Kansas, 1998), chaps. 7 and 8. "The dormant beast . . .": Kissinger quoted in Kimball, *Nixon's Vietnam War,* 133. For SDS programs, see the following in *DKS:* "Exiles Report on Guatemalan Situation," Jan. 30, 1969; " 'Protest-Priests' Talk Here Today" (the priests spoke on the Vietnam War), Feb. 19; "Bringing It On Home" (column by Ken Hammond that mentions the Dominican Republic), Feb. 14.

14. On SDS programs and the crashing of the dance, see the following in *DKS:* "Exiles Report on Guatemalan Situation" (a Jan. 24 talk by Maryknoll missionaries), Jan. 30, 1969; " 'Protest-Priests' Talk Today" (Fathers Begin and Mayer), Feb. 19; "Not a Protest" (editorial) and "The President's Ball" (photo story), Feb. 4; M. J. Kukla, "SDS Image Change Starts at Tri-Towers" (column), Feb. 7; Ken Hammond, "Bringing It On Home" (column), Feb. 14. See also "Party Talk" and "Why Try to Make Something Out of Nothing?" (SDS flyers), box 80, folder 5, M4C. Another SDS flyer, "Why Washington?" (copy in the author's possession) explained the chapter's participation in the protest and advertised a Jan. 30, 1969, teach-in.

15. David Barber, *A Hard Rain Fell: SDS and Why It Failed* (Jackson: University of Mississippi Press, 2008), 146–58; Max Elbaum, *Revolution in the Air: Sixties Radicals Turn to Lenin, Mao, and Che* (New York: Verso, 2002), 69–70. It should be noted that the Kent SDSers named in this paragraph represented a softer ideological version of the Revolutionary Youth Movement II activists mentioned in the two studies. For Vaughan: KCEWV/SDS activist survey conducted by the author in 2000; Vaughan to the author, July 24, 2015.

16. Barber, *A Hard Rain Fell,* 146–58; Elbaum, *Revolution in the Air,* 69–70; Todd Gitlin, *The Sixties: Years of Hope, Days of Rage* (New York: Bantam, 1987), 246–47, quotation on 257. On Dohrn and Robbins, see Kirkpatrick Sale, *SDS* (New York: Vintage, 1973), 469, 478, 481, 483–84, 490, 510.

17. Details of the Flanagan incident: Flanagan file in box 77, M4C. Criticism of Flanagan's arrest by the Lutheran campus minister (Cordelia Mullikin) and others: box 43, folder 2, White Papers; see also US House Committee on Internal Security, *Investigation of Students for a Democratic Society, Part 2 (Kent State University): Hearings before the Committee on Internal Security, House of Representatives,* 91st Cong., 1st sess., June 24–25, 1969

(Washington, DC: GPO, 1969), 509–10 (hereafter cited as HCIS, *Investigation, Part 2*). McMillen's account: Barclay D. McMillen and William J. Armstrong, "Kent State, May 4, 1970: Who Really Was Responsible for the Shootings?," unpublished memoir, 1999, box 131, folder 14, M4C. See also "'Immoral' Leaflets Lead to Freshman's Arrest," *DKS*, Feb. 28, 1969; and "Senators Defy 'Obscenity' Arrest," *DKS*, March 10. Charges against Flanagan were later dropped.

18. See the following in *DKS:* "200 Art Students Plan Walkout," March 6, 1969; "1,200 Call for Art Changes," March 7; "Repair West Hall by Spring," March 10.

19. The SDS circular "Now is the time of the furnaces . . . ," mentioning the demands and the regional conference: HCIS, *Investigation, Part 2*, 602–12.

20. Ibid., 602–12.

21. "Study Credit Elimination for Kent State ROTC Cadets," *RC*, April 3, 1969; "Pressure at KSU?" (editorial), *RC*, April 4; "Kent Legion Post Opposes Any Move against ROTC," *RC*, April 5. George P. Manos, Young Republicans, to Governor James Rhodes, April 5, 1969, box 33, folder 10, White Papers. White, who received a copy of Manos's letter to Rhodes, was infuriated by it; see White to Manos, May 15, 1969, box 43, folder 17.

22. White to Chester A. Williams (KSU public safety director), Jan. 24, 1969, box 5, folder 11, and Williams to White, Jan. 29, box 35, folder 22, White Papers. "The university had no advance information . . .": Richard Edwards, university spokesman and assistant to White, quoted in "Revolutionaries Probed at KSU," *RC*, April 2, 1969; in his denial, Edwards seemed to be protesting a bit too much. McMillen, in McMillen and Armstrong, "Kent State, May 4, 1970," cryptically mentions "other areas . . . [in which] we were gearing up for S.D.S."

23. "To announce too much . . .": French diplomat Charles-Maurice de Talleyrand, quoted in Garry Wills, *Henry Adams and the Making of America* (Boston: Houghton Mifflin, 2005), 152.

24. "Rally at Union, April 8, 1969," box 80, folder 2, M4C. This file contains a transcript of the rally, made from a tape recording by Margaret Ann Murvay. SDS publicized the rally in a flyer, "Dare to Struggle, Dare to Win!," box 21, series 2 (Hammond Papers), folder 12, M4C. "Arrest 5, Suspend 7, End SDS Charter" and "SDS Bumps Heads with Campus Police," *DKS*, April 9, 1969.

25. "Rally at Union"; McMillen and Armstrong, "Kent State, May 4, 1970"; HCIS, *Investigation, Part 2*, 510–13; "KSU's SDS Opens Spring Offensive," *RC*, April 8, 1969. Powell, in "The Storm," disputes the police version of the seriousness of the pushing and shoving at the Administration Building. Allen Richardson, a *DKS* reporter present at the rally, recalled the scene years later: "I remember there was some pushing and shoving . . . though by any standard, it was incredibly minor. . . . Hardly the sort of thing that should result in arrests, . . . and certainly not in arrests with charges as serious as assault and battery." Richardson to the author, Feb. 8, 2007.

26. McMillen and Armstrong, "Kent State, May 4, 1970." Caris's age: Loris C. Troyer, *Portage Pathways* (Kent: Kent State University Press, 1998), 99–101.

27. McMillen and Armstrong, "Kent State, May 4, 1970." The arrests: HCIS, *Investigation, Part 2*, 510–13. Other campuses where the organization was banned: Sale, *SDS*, 551. "Arrest 5, Suspend 7, End SDS Charter," *DKS*, April 9, 1969.

28. Conversation with Powell; and Powell, "The Storm," which also recounts the scene when he and the others were arrested and taken to the Portage County lockup, as well as their surprise when the injunctions were unexpectedly handed to them in jail. See also "Arrest Sixth Student," *DKS*, April 11, 1969; and "Charges and Suspensions Filed against SDS at KSU," *RC*, April 9.

29. Ken Hammond recalls that Fairbanks's article was titled "Old Wine in New Bottles"; Hammond to the author, Jan. 23, 2013. That was also the title of Fairbanks's talk; see "Asian Conference Brings Noted Speakers," *DKS*, April 15, 1969. SDS flyer with the Dylan "weather man" quote: box 21, series 2 (Hammond Papers), folder 12, M4C.

30. Turmoil at the conference: "SDS Arrests Total 5; KSU Is Tense" and "KSU Firm but Fair" (editorial), *RC*, April 10, 1969; "350 Greeks March In Opposition to SDS," *DKS*, April 10. Ross quoted in "'Unified Greeks' Ward Off SDS at Asian Affairs Conference," *DKS*, April 11. Ross's major: KSU student directory, 1968–69. Speakers featured at the conference: "Asian Conference Brings Noted Speakers," *DKS*, April 15, 1969. The SDS response appeared in a flyer with a recycled title, "Now Is the Time of the Furnace" (copy in the author's possession).

31. McMillen, in McMillen and Armstrong, "Kent State, May 4, 1970," states that he was critical of the decision to hold the hearings on campus. Identities of the two SDSers: "Arrest 60 at Hearing Break-up—Charge 7 with 'Riot,'" *DKS*, April 16, 1969.

32. Flyer quoted in HCIS, *Investigation, Part 2*, 578.

33. Transcript made from a tape of the rally, box 80, folder, 3, M4C.

34. For a profile of Mellen (then in Ohio to attend an SDS conference) and what he called "the best speech of his life," see Viorst, *Fire in the Streets*, chap. 13, quotation on 516. Lencl interview; conversation with Dyer. Among several descriptions of the day's events, see "Charge 7 with 'Riot,'" *DKS*, and "Press Writer Tells about Kent Melee," *CP*, both April 17, 1969.

35. "Charge 7 with 'Riot.'" Lencl's activities: HCIS, *Investigation, Part 2*, 533; McMillen and Armstrong, "Kent State, May 4, 1970"; Lencl interview. In a conversation with the author, Alan Canfora, who witnessed the struggle at the third-floor doorway, recalled that Lencl and a few others disassembled a freestanding coat rack situated next to the door in order to obtain the metal rail.

36. Role of Moore and Calkins: Ohio State Highway Patrol, "Report of Investigation," subject: "Subversive Activities," box 80, folder 3, M4C, 15. Local coverage: "SDS Backers Storm KSU Music, Speech Center, Get Arrested" (photo story), "58 Arrested in KSU Outbreak," "Agitators Force Police to Work around Clock," and "Almost All Able to Post Bond," *RC*, April 17, 1969.

37. Kelley's quote (made in a taped private interview) and details of the events and arrests: KSU Detective Tom Kelley to Corporal D. D. Sumrok, Ohio Highway Patrol, April 28, 1969, box 80, folder 3, M4C. Number of African American students inside the building: tape transcript of the Fred Fuller Park rally on April 17, 1969, box 80, folder 5, M4C.

38. McMillen and Armstrong, "Kent State, May 4, 1970." While sections of McMillen's highly useful account smack of self-importance, he is, at times, rueful. Unless Robert Matson elects to tell his version of events, McMillen's description likely will remain the best available.

39. Transcript of the 3-C rally on April 22, 1969, box 79, folder 1, M4C. KSU administration's stance: "'Issue Is Survival'—White," *DKS*, April 18, 1969. Rally at Fred Fuller Park: "SDS Pep Rally Gathers 250," *DKS*, April 18, and tape transcript of the rally, box 80, folder 5, M4C.

40. 3-C leadership and the resulting activity: "31 to Steer 3-C," "Since Thursday," and "Ohio Region of SDS Moves Forces to Kent," *DKS*, April 21, 1969. Hoffman and Modugno gave their opinions about the "action-faction" in their interviews. The armed protest: Donald Downs, *Cornell '69: Liberalism and the Crisis of the American University* (Ithaca: Cornell University Press, 1999).

41. Spying by the Ohio Highway Patrol: Highway Patrol, "Intelligence Unit Report," April 20, 1969, box 80, folder 3, M4C. Efforts to discredit Sharoff: interview with Sharoff in Stephen Weiss, Clark Dougan, David Fulghum, et al., *The Vietnam Experience: A War Remembered* (Boston: Boston Publishing, 1986), 106–12. See also Heidi Summerlin, "A Value Added Analysis of the Emergence and Demise of the Concerned Citizens of Kent Group in April 1969," unpublished paper, May 2007, box 84, folder 19, M4C.

42. 3-C members: "31 to Steer 3-C." Gollust, interview by Daniel Miller, in *Fire in the Heartland: Kent State, May 4th, and Student Protest in America* (documentary; Fire River Productions, 2010); Hoffman and Alewitz interviews; Joe Cullum to the author, Dec. 12, 2000; conversations with Carole Teminsky Barbato.

43. Conversations with Carole Teminsky Barbato.

44. Howie Emmer, Lencl, Alewitz, Albert Canfora, Modugno, Persky, Powrie, and Hoffman interviews.

45. Conversations with Carole Teminsky Barbato.

46. "Faculty-Student Unit Opposes Student Rally," *RC*, April 21, 1969; and Randy Hines (guest column), "Roasting Pan," *RC*, April 24. SDSers who came to the campus from the conference: Alice McPeak, "Kent, Kent, Kent, Kent!," *The Big Us* 2.3 (April 26, 1969).

47. All of the articles mentioned ran in the *DKS* special issue of Monday, April 21, 1969; at this time the paper's regular editions appeared only from Tuesday to Friday. A sidebar to the story headlined "VanderWyden Renounces" includes a criticism of Sharoff by Frisina. The spoof SDS poster (copy in the author's possession) used headlines from area papers such as the *RC* and *BJ*, but especially from the *DKS* extra, which were superimposed on stock-market page quotes. The reverse side featured a lengthy article titled "Lies!!" Smarting from the criticism, the *DKS* ran an editorial defending itself on May 8.

48. Pickett's statement: photo and caption, *DKS*, April 22, 1969. See the following in *RC*: "White Rejects '3-C Demands,'" April 21, 1969; "Student Vote to Be Taken," April 22; and "KSU Election Nixes Proposed Boycott," April 24. Transcript of a tape of the meeting, box 79, folder 1, M4C. Referendum results and White's opinion on the *DKS*: "Correct Vote Released—8,615 Votes Cast" and "White's Testimony Lauds DKS Extra," *DKS*, April 29, 1969.

49. Bail bond costs: Terry Robbins and Lisa Meisel, "War at Kent State," *New Left Notes*, April 29, reprinted in HCIS, *Investigation, Part 2*, 636. SDS members had able representation, and attorneys from Cleveland charged only for their legal expenses.

50. Appearances by Mallory and Mayfield at the May 9–11 rally at Case Western Reserve: *The Big Us* 2.4 (May 9, 1969). Memorandum from Tom Kelley to Don Schwartzmiller, May

1, 1969, box 80, folder 5, M4C. Benedict's and Dohrn's remarks and the flyer advertising the meeting program: HCIS, *Investigation, Part 2,* 559–61, 630. "Carried to the limit . . .": Robert C. Dix, "Along the Way," *RC,* April 24, 1969.

51. Activists like Joe Jackson stayed away from antiwar protest rather than associate with those they saw as promoting ultra-radicalism. Jackson interview. In his interview, Alewitz said of SDS: "We initiated a defense, which SDS immediately attacked. This was very typical [of them]." "A liberal . . . coalition . . .": Robbins and Meisel, "War at Kent State." "Liberal group [that] didn't . . .": McPeak, "Kent, Kent, Kent, Kent!" Suspicion of 3-C leader Sharoff by SDS: Sharoff interview in Weiss et al., *A War Remembered,* 107. Boram and Powrie interviews. On Oglesby see Sale, *SDS,* 522; and his interview in Joan Morrison and Robert K. Morrison, *From Camelot to Kent State: The Sixties Experience in the Words of Those Who Lived It* (New York: Times Books, 1987), 297–307.

52. Ohio State Highway Patrol, "Report of Investigation," May 28, 1969, box 80, folder 5, M4C. A transcript of a tape of the affair is in the same folder. In the wake of the Music and Speech protest, many SDS members who spoke at rallies, like Candy Erickson and Mark Lencl, were charged with inciting to riot. "Liquid Crystals Chained Shut!" leaflet: copy in the author's possession. Opposition to the arrests: "Here We Go Again" (editorial), *DKS,* May 27, 1969.

53. Fates of SDS members: boxes 77 and 78, M4C. Campus mood in the aftermath of the SDS protests and the 3-C's efforts to ensure fair treatment of the students: Sharoff interview in Weiss et al., *A War Remembered;* Alan Canfora's recollections in Viorst, *Fire in the Streets,* 518; Kenneth Calkins, "Escalating Tensions Explode into Tragedy at Kent State," *BJ,* April 27, 2000. Allen Richardson to the author, Feb. 8, 2007.

54. Resignation of the religious coordinator: "Second Calm Day on KSU Campus," *RC,* April 11, 1969. "SDS doesn't radicalize people . . .": transcript of a tape of the 3-C meeting, May 7, 1969, box 79, folder 1, M4C.

55. The *DKS's* backing of Frisina: "DKS for Frisina," *DKS,* April 18, 1969. Examples of the cordiality between Frisina and White include White to Frisina, July 28, 1969, box 5, folder 27, White Papers. Frisina's background: "Frisina Elected at KSU," *RC,* April 23, 1969; Joe Eszterhas and Michael D. Roberts, *Thirteen Seconds: Confrontation at Kent State* (New York: Dodd, Mead, 1970), 26. On Satrom: Michener, *Kent State,* 122–24; interview with Lucius Lyman Jr. in *Kent State/May 4: Echoes through a Decade,* ed. Scott L. Bills (1982; Kent: Kent State University Press, 1988), 72; Ralph Darrow, ed., *Kent, Ohio: The Dynamic Decades—A History of the Community from the 1930's to the 1990's* (Kent: Kent Historical Society, 1999), 23.

56. Dix, "Along the Way," *RC,* April 24, 1969; White to Louis K. Harris (the university's provost), March 15, 1969, box 5, folder 16, White Papers. Campus protest activity nationwide, including the campus killings: Sale, *SDS,* 511–12, 641.

10. Months of Protest, Days of Rage

1. James Miller, *"Democracy Is in the Streets": From Port Huron to the Siege of Chicago* (New York: Simon and Schuster, 1987), 13–14, 119, 200, 202–3, 223, 233, 311.

2. Kirkpatrick Sale, *SDS* (New York: Vintage, 1973), 64, 121–22, 135–36, 176, 211, 218–19, 465, 493–94. PLP's union work: Leigh David Benin, *The New Labor Radicalism and New York City's Garment Industry: Progressive Labor Insurgents in the 1960s* (New York: Garland, 2000).

3. Robert Pardun, *Prairie Radical: A Journey through the Sixties* (Los Gatos, CA: Shire Press, 2001), 173–74. RYM: Mike Klonsky, "Toward a Revolutionary Youth Movement," in *Revolutionary Youth and the New Working Class: The Praxis Papers, the Port Authority Statement, the RYM Documents and Other Lost Writings of SDS,* ed. Carl Davidson (Pittsburgh: Changemaker Publications, 2011), 134–39. Sale, *SDS,* 306, 310–11, 332–34, 410–11, 470–71, 511–56.

4. Sale, *SDS,* 456. The author recalls some Kent SDSers adopting a "greaser" look that had not been uncommon a few years earlier in his own neighborhood in Syracuse, NY.

5. Jeffrey Powell, "The Storm" (unpublished memoir); Jim Powrie, remarks at Kent SDS reunion, May 5, 1989, tape in the author's possession; Boram interview. Flanagan can be seen at the convention in the documentary *The Sixties: The Years That Shaped a Generation,* dir. David Davis and Stephen Talbot (Oregon Public Broadcasting, 2005). Sale, *SDS,* 564; Pardun, *Prairie Radical,* 279.

6. Sale, *SDS,* 557–64. In the documentary *Fire in the Heartland,* Carolyn Knox tells of being in Kent with Robbins when he decided on the title of the position paper; see also Thai Jones, *A Radical Line: From the Labor Movement to the Weather Underground, One Family's Century of Conscience* (New York: Free Press, 2004), 174.

7. Boram interview. Among the many sources on the SDS convention, Sale continues to be the most thorough: *SDS,* 563–74. More recent sources include Jones, *A Radical Line,* 194–98. Powrie's description: remarks at Kent SDS reunion, May 1989.

8. Andrew Kopkind, "The Real SDS Stands Up," in *Weatherman,* ed. Harold Jacobs (Berkeley: Ramparts Press, 1970), 15–50. Klonsky and the position of RYM II: David Barber, *A Hard Rain Fell: SDS and Why it Failed* (Jackson: University of Mississippi Press, 2008) 149–50, 157.

9. Powell, "The Storm." July 4 event: Lorraine Rosal, "Who Do They Think Could Bury You?," in Jacobs, *Weatherman,* 150. "Retain a sense of struggle . . .": Bill Ayers and Jim Mellen, "Hot Town: Summer in the City, or, I Ain't Gonna Work on Maggie's Farm No More," in Jacobs, *Weatherman,* 34. Elsewhere in Ohio, members of the Akron Collective marched through Garfield High School in late July 1969, disrupting summer classes and allegedly "shouting obscenities." The protest resulted in ten arrests. See "Tells of SDS Invasion of Akron School," *RC,* Oct. 29, 1969.

10. Powell, "The Storm." For a sampling of the condemnation of Weatherman, see the following in Jacobs, *Weatherman:* Jack Weinberg and Jack Gerson, "Weatherman," 111–18; Tom Hayden, "Justice in the Streets," 296–300; and Michael P. Lerner, "Weatherman: The Politics of Despair," 400–420.

11. Characterization of life in the collectives: Jeremy Varon, *Bringing the War Home: The Weather Underground, the Red Army Faction, and Revolutionary Violence in the Sixties and Seventies* (Berkeley: University of California Press, 2004), 60; see also Kenneth J. Heineman, *Campus Wars: The Peace Movement at American State Universities in the Vietnam Era* (New

York: New York University Press, 1993), 230–31. Powell, "The Storm," provides rich detail about the internal strains and external threats. Weatherman recruiting efforts: Milton Viorst, *Fire in the Streets: America in the 1960's* (New York: Simon and Schuster, 1979), 518–19.

12. As Canfora's roommate in 1969–70, I came to know many of his Barberton friends.

13. Conversation with Alan Canfora. Others from Kent who attended Woodstock and discussed the event with the author include Jerry Persky, Richie Hess, and Jeff Hartzler. For a summary of the festival, see Mark Hamilton Lytle, *America's Uncivil Wars: The Sixties Era from Elvis to the Fall of Richard Nixon* (New York: Oxford University Press, 2006), 334–38.

14. Surveys on marijuana use: Anderson, *The Movement and the Sixties,* 260. For more on its consumption, see David Farber and Beth Bailey, *The Columbia Guide to America in the 1960s* (New York: Columbia University Press, 2001), 389; Maurice Isserman and Michael Kazin, *America Divided: The Civil War of the 1960s* (New York: Oxford University Press, 2000), 150, 155, 158. Pardun, *Prairie Radical,* 103. Paul Krehbiel, *Shades of Justice: A Memoir* (Altadena, CA: Autumn Leaf Press, 2008), 222–27. McDonald's Old Left background and antiwar activism: W. J. Rorabaugh, *Berkeley at War: The 1960s* (New York: Oxford University Press, 1989), 97.

15. Krehbiel, *Shades of Justice,* 225; Michael Frisch, "Woodstock and Altamont," in *True Stories from the American Past,* vol. 2, ed. William Graebner (New York: McGraw-Hill, 1993), 217–39, quotations on 225, 229, and 230; Abe Peck, *Uncovering the Sixties: The Life and Times of the Underground Press* (New York: Pantheon, 1985), 180. Jacob Brackman, "My Generation" (1968), in *Smiling through the Apocalypse: Esquire's History of the Sixties,* ed. Harold Hayes (New York: Crown, 1987), 366.

16. "KSU Student Horde Descends Next Week," *RC,* Sept. 19, 1969; and "Kent Rock Festival Scene," *RC,* Sept. 29. Advertisement for the opening of Hallelujah Leathers and Halcyon Days, *DKS,* Oct. 28, 1969. Thompson's quote and the listing of other shops: "Downtown Has New Spirit," *DKS,* Feb. 20, 1970. The photo of the flag-bearing concert-goers was taken by Judy Gollust. 1969 casualty figure: http://www.archives.gov/research/military/vietnam-war/casualty-statistics.html; Stanley Karnow (*Vietnam,* 616) gives a slightly lower figure of 10,000.

17. US House Committee on Internal Security, *Investigation of Students for a Democratic Society, Part 2 (Kent State University): Hearings before the Committee on Internal Security, House of Representatives,* 91st Cong., 1st sess., June 24–25, 1969 (Washington, DC: GPO, 1969), 487–90, 500–501, quotation on 500; "Dr. White Testifies on SDS," *KSU Summer News,* June 26, 1969; "White to Probers: SDS Is Enemy," *KSU Summer News,* July 3. White's satisfaction with the congratulatory letters: Barclay D. McMillen and William J. Armstrong, "Kent State, May 4, 1970: Who Really Was Responsible for the Shootings?," unpublished memoir, 1999, box 131, folder 14, M4C.

18. "Spring Offensive Gets Fall Showing," *DKS,* Sept. 30, 1969; "Erickson Refused New Trial," *RC,* Oct. 2; Powell, "The Storm"; Boram interview.

19. Gollust and King interviews with Daniel Miller in *Fire in the Heartland: Kent State, May 4th, and Student Protest in America* (documentary; Fire River Productions, 2010); Powrie, Wittmaack, Barbara Brock, Gregorich, and Inglee interviews. Other SDSers who had avoided arrest included Ken Johnson, Andy Pyle, and Doug Vaughan.

20. Alewitz interview. On the SMC: Tom Wells, *The War Within: America's Battle over Vietnam* (Berkeley: University of California Press, 1994), 274–76, 292, 332.

21. Alewitz interview. YSA participation in the Moratorium, the origins of the VMC, and the reorganization of the New MOBE: Fred Halstead, *Out Now! A Participant's Account of the American Movement against the Vietnam War* (New York: Monad, 1978), 467–90. Also valuable is William H. Chafe, *Never Stop Running: Allard Lowenstein and the Struggle to Save American Liberalism* (New York: Basic Books, 1993), 328–35.

22. Mike Alewitz, "Anti-Viet Action, Time Is Now" (column), *DKS*, Sept. 30, 1969; and "Moratorium Gains Faculty Support," *DKS*, Oct. 9. The ongoing divide over the actions of the administration: "Praise, Criticism Aimed at KSU Handling of Disruption," *RC*, Oct. 8, 1969. Alewitz and Boram interviews.

23. For the number of student military veterans and their comments, list of fraternities supporting the moratorium, a photo of a modish Rob Ross (leader of the anti-SDS protests in April 1969), and the antiwar editorial, see the following in *DKS:* "Bitter, Proud—KSU Vets View Vietnam," Oct. 15, 1969; "Peace Hike Stays Just That—Peaceful," Oct. 16; "Highlights of Greek Week 1969" and "No Fancy Prose" (editorial), Oct. 7. Mike Brock interview. DeFrange's death: "Mark's Name Will Live at Viet Orphanage," *RC*, Oct. 14, 1969. DeFrange's participation in the Moratorium march: interview of Harriet Begala, April 30, 1991, KHS. Canfora's recollections are from his unpublished memoir. By the fall of 1969, his hometown of Barberton, a city of 30,000, had lost fifteen soldiers; two more would die in 1970. Belmont County casualties: Hawthorne interview. In general, the county suffered disproportionately high losses.

24. "Gilligan Heads List of Kent Moratorium Rally Speakers," *RC*, Oct. 13, 1969; "Kent March for Peace Was Peaceful," *RC*, Oct. 16; "Survey Favors Gradual Withdrawal" and "Today's Events," *DKS*, Oct. 15. Alewitz interview; Allen Richardson to the author, Feb. 16, 2007.

25. Campus opinion: "Survey Favors Gradual Withdrawal," *DKS*, Oct. 15, 1969. Number of combat deaths and Begala's role, "40,000th American Dies in Vietnam," *RC*, Jan. 8, 1970; "Asks Support for Moratorium" (Begala letter), *RC*, Oct. 14, 1969. For Pierson, see "Kent, Ravenna Reactions Mixed on KSU Moratorium," *RC*, Oct. 16, 1969.

26. "Kent, Ravenna Reactions Mixed on KSU Moratorium"; "Satrom Wins in Kent Sweep," *RC*, Nov. 5, 1969.

27. "SDS Readies for Chicago," *Guardian* (New York City), Oct. 4, 1969. Police preparation: Tom Thomas, "The Second Battle of Chicago," in Jacobs, *Weatherman*, 196–97; Wells, *The War Within*, 338, 366–67; and Barber, *A Hard Rain Fell*, 184. Origin of the term "Days of Rage": Dan Berger, *Outlaws of America: The Weather Underground and the Politics of Solidarity* (Oakland, CA: AK Press, 2006), 107.

28. For the explosion and the police quote: Sale, *SDS*, 606. Powell's account: "The Storm." Van Veenendaal's injuries: Thomas, "The Second Battle of Chicago," 203; Berger, *Outlaws of America*, 111. While the mayhem generated the most publicity, a RYM II rally produced the largest turnout, with 10,000 former SDSers, Black Panthers, and members of the Young Lords (a Puerto Rican organization) marching. Davidson, *Revolutionary Youth and the New Working Class*, v–vi.

29. "Look at this scum . . ." and subsequent quotes: Powell, "The Storm."

30. Charges from the Chicago protests: "Jury Indicts Three Ex-KSUers," *DKS*, Dec. 3, 1969. In addition to Powell, the grand jury indicted Lencl and Flanagan for mob action; for indicted co-conspirators see Sale, *SDS*, 648. Pleas and sentencing, as well as the *RC* editorial: "63 to Plead Guilty in KSU Demonstrations," *RC*, Oct. 29, 1969; "Sentence 38 in KSU Demonstrations" and "SDS' Erickson: Glad to Get It Over With," *RC*, Oct. 30; "KSU Decisions Fair, Just," *RC*, Oct. 13. On the rally led by Real and Rudd's appearance, see the following in *DKS*: "Weekend Vandals Smear Buildings with Posters," Oct. 28, 1969; "Hit Dow, Discuss Demands," Oct. 30; "With Protest Weathermen View ROTC," Nov. 6. Spock's comments: "U.S. a 'Police State,'" *RC*, Oct. 28, 1969.

31. Real's warning and his exchange with the hecklers: "Kent State SDS Vows New Action," *RC*, Oct. 30, 1969. SMC rally: "Rallies: Hit Dow, Discuss Demands," *DKS*, Oct. 30, 1969.

32. Those planning the protest at Kent State: "Slate Peace Activities," *DKS*, Nov. 14, 1969, and the cover note from Sue Gambaccini-Briers (White's secretary) to White, Nov. 11, 1969, box 46, folder 27, White Papers. Conversation with Rick Felber. For an account of the author's involvement, the participation of his roommates, and the makeup of the coalition that sponsored the protest, see Viorst, *Fire in the Streets*, 519–20. Canfora provided additional details in a conversation with the author. Pepper-spray tear gas used by DC police: "Police Clear 'The Circle,'" *DKS*, Nov. 18, 1969. "Something of the fighting spirit . . .": Varon, *Bringing the War Home*, 126.

33. Charles DeBenedetti with Charles Chatfield, *An American Ordeal: The Antiwar Movement of the Vietnam Era* (Syracuse: Syracuse University Press, 1990), 263; "Police Clear 'The Circle,'" *DKS*. For a description of the scene, see Wells, *The War Within*, 392. Halstead, *Out Now!*, 516 (quotation).

34. Canfora's encounter with the pole-wielding man: Canfora to the author, May 7, 1999. Dellinger quoted in "Leaders Speak Out on March, America," *DKS*, Nov. 18, 1969. The author remembers Riggs's involvement in the protest at the Justice Department. See also Wells, *The War Within*, 395.

35. DeBenedetti and Chatfield, *An American Ordeal*, 263–65. Speeches and comments by Nixon and Agnew: Wells, *The War Within*, 382–87, Agnew quoted on 382. "Peace Now!," *DKS*, Nov. 18, 1969.

36. On the YSA/SMC: Sale, *SDS*, 621; Alewitz interview. "Had not accepted the fact . . .": Sam Brown (VMC coordinator), quoted in Wells, *The War Within*, 400. On militants' below-the-radar activity and the draft board fires in Akron, Lorain, Painesville, and Norwalk, see "FBI Suspect May Be in Kent Area," *RC*, Oct. 13, 1969; "May Deploy Armed Guards at Draft Boards," *RC*, Oct. 23; "Ohio Draft Raid," *Guardian*, Jan. 24, 1970.

37. New Selective Service System lottery system: "Men Born Sept. 14 Are First in Draft Lottery," *RC*, Dec. 2, 1969; Flynn, *The Draft*, 246–48. Nixon quoted in Wells, *The War Within*, 396.

38. Allen Richardson to the author, Feb. 16, 2007; Hawthorne interview. The author, a roommate of Riggs, also made the trip. Vietnamization: Kimball, *Nixon's Vietnam War*, 137–39. Reduced enrollment: "KSU Enrollment Drops 2,156 Winter Quarter," *DKS*, Jan. 8, 1970.

39. The authoritative (although somewhat subjective) account of Hampton's killing, and

that of fellow Panther Mark Clark, is Jeffrey Haas, *The Assassination of Fred Hampton: How the FBI and the Chicago Police Murdered a Black Panther* (Chicago: Lawrence Hill Books, 2010). Student reaction in Illinois: Brian K. Clardy, *The Management of Dissent: Responses to the Post Kent State Protests at Seven Public Universities in Illinois* (Lanham, MD: University Press of America, 2002), 64. Abernathy quoted in the *Guardian*, Dec. 20, 1969. Pickett quote: "Repression U.S.'s Dominant Theme" (column), *DKS*, Jan. 7, 1970. Willmott's conversion: Berger, *Outlaws of America*, 121. Wilkerson quoted in Varon, *Bringing the War Home*, 156. Powell, "The Storm."

40. "An all-but-forgotten movement": Wells, *The War Within*, 403; DeBenedetti makes much the same point about the seeming inactivity (*An American Ordeal*, 267, 271, 278). Boram interview; Powell, "The Storm."

41. See the following *Black Watch* articles reproduced in Milton E. Wilson, "Involvement / 2 Years Later: A Report on Programming in the Area of Black Student Concerns at Kent State University, 1968–1970," box 1, Milton E. Wilson, Jr., Papers, KSUA, 298–306: "1970—A New Emphasis" and "The New Era of BUS: Right On!" (Blount's editorship and election as BUS president; issue of March 30, 1970); "A Need for Revolution" (on the Hampton killing; March 30, 1970); "Hero of the Month" (Dec. 10, 1969 issue; the original version includes the Panther graphics). Increasing number of working-class African American students in the late 1960s: Martha Biondi, *The Black Revolution on Campus* (Berkeley: University of California Press, 2012), 4, 29. Conference in defense of the Black Panther Party: "BUS Members Chicago Bound to Defend the Rights of Panthers," *DKS*, March 5, 1970.

42. Neither Simpson nor Pickett entirely departed from the spirit of the times. The BUS rally in support of Fred "Ahmed" Evans (who was sentenced to death after the shootings described in chapter 7) provided evidence of that. See "100 Rally in Evans' Support," *DKS*, May 29, 1969. With SDS banned and with BUS having made little effort to attract an audience beyond their own membership, African Americans made up most of the crowd at the rally for Evans.

43. On commonalities with antiwar whites, see the following articles from *Black Watch* reproduced in Wilson, "Involvement": Fargo, " 'Hell No We Won't Go' " (issue of Nov. 25, 1969); Darlene Clark, "First the Vietnamese, Then the Blacks" (Dec. 10, 1969); "Believe It or Leave It Alone" (unsigned, but likely by Blount; March 30, 1970).

44. "The Day After" protests and the belligerent response to the verdicts: "Conspiracy Trial Ends, Five Convicted" and "Nationwide Demonstrations Support Chicago 8," *Guardian*, Feb. 28, 1970. The bombing in New York City: Varon, *Bringing the War Home*, 174.

45. "The hard core . . .": Sale, *SDS*, 625. Powell, "The Storm." For his affidavit, see Terry Robbins file in box 78, M4C. See also Peter Collier and David Horowitz, "Doing It: The Inside Story of the Rise and Fall of the Weather Underground," *Rolling Stone*, Sept. 30, 1982.

46. Veterans' participation in antiwar protest: Andrew E. Hunt, *The Turning: A History of Vietnam Veterans Against the War* (New York: New York University Press, 1999), 33–39. Opposition to the war among blue-collar Americans: Christian G. Appy, *Working-Class War: American Combat Soldiers and Vietnam* (Chapel Hill: University of North Carolina Press, 1998), 38–42. Polls on working-class attitudes toward the war: Penny Lewis, *Hardhats, Hippies, and Hawks: The Vietnam Antiwar Movement as Myth and Memory* (Ithaca: Cornell University Press, 2013), 50–52, 109.

11. Cambodia—A Match to the Last Straw

1. Overthrow of Prince Sihanouk: Milton Osborne, *Sihanouk: Prince of Light, Prince of Darkness* (Honolulu: University of Hawaii Press, 1994), 202–16; William Shawcross, *Sideshow: Kissinger, Nixon and the Destruction of Cambodia* (New York: Simon and Schuster, 1979), 112–27.

2. White House reaction to Sihanouk's overthrow: Henry Kissinger, *White House Years* (Boston: Little, Brown, 1979), 463–65, 488; "U.S. Now Declares Forces May Cross Cambodian Border; U.S. Policy Shifts in Cambodia Issue," *NYT,* March 29, 1970.

3. Nixon's pessimism: H. R. Haldeman, *The Haldeman Diaries: Inside the Nixon White House* (New York: G. P. Putnam's Sons, 1994), 118.

4. Tom Wells, *The War Within: America's Battle over Vietnam* (Berkeley: University of California Press, 1994), 403.

5. Cathy Wilkerson, *Flying Close to the Sun: My Life and Times as a Weatherman* (New York: Seven Stories Press, 2007), 1, 322–48, quotation on 326.

6. Ibid., 341–42; Mark Rudd, *Underground: My Life with SDS and the Weathermen* (New York: William Morrow, 2009), 192–98; Bill Ayers, *Fugitive Days: A Memoir* (Boston: Beacon Press, 2001), 183–85; Thomas Powers, *Diana: The Making of a Terrorist* (New York: Bantam, 1971), 135–42. Robbins's use of the name "Adam": Jeffrey Powell, "The Storm" (unpublished memoir). Robbins's activism had been guided by signposts: the controversy over the execution of Caryl Chessman; King's 1963 March on Washington; and the assassination of John Kennedy, which the high school senior interpreted as evidence of extremism run amok. Within seven years, Robbins—inspired by Melville's *Moby Dick* and Howard Fast's *Spartacus*—had been driven by experience with poverty, racial bigotry, and the Vietnam War to the extremes he once deplored. This capsule portrait was prepared from Robbins's admission application to Kenyon College, and Rik Kleinfeldt, "Weathermen Leader Was a Product of Kenyon," Kenyon *Collegian,* Feb. 21, 1985, Kenyon College Library Archives, Gambier, Ohio.

7. "A House on Eleventh Street," *Newsweek,* March 23, 1970; see also "The Seeds of Terror," *NYT,* Nov. 22, 1981.

8. Powell, "The Storm."

9. Conversation with Bill Ayers. "It had always been a question . . .": quoted in Peter Collier and David Horowitz, "Doing It: The Inside Story of the Rise and Fall of the Weather Underground," *Rolling Stone,* Sept. 30, 1982, 35.

10. Deaths of the two SNCC members: for the most recent account see Akinyele Omowale Umoja, *We Will Shoot Back: Armed Resistance in the Mississippi Freedom Movement* (New York: New York University Press, 2013), 179–80.

11. Bank burning in Isla Vista: Jack Whalen and Richard Flacks, *Beyond the Barricades: The Sixties Generation Grows Up* (Philadelphia: Temple University Press, 1989), 31–32; see also "Stand at Isla Vista," *Time,* March 23, 1970.

12. "If it's to be a blood-bath . . .": quoted in *Los Angles Times,* April 8, 1970; a better-known version appeared in the *San Francisco Chronicle* on the same date: "If it takes a blood-bath, let's get it over with." See Gitlin, *The Sixties,* 414–15, 481n414.

13. Meany quoted in Philip S. Foner, *U.S. Labor and the Vietnam War* (New York: International Publishers, 1989), 20–21. Penny Lewis, a sociologist specializing in labor studies, has shown that by late 1967 opposition to the war was more prevalent among the working class than among more affluent sectors. Penny Lewis, *Hardhats, Hippies, and Hawks: The Vietnam Antiwar Movement as Myth and Memory* (Ithaca: Cornell University Press, 2013), 50–52.

14. Alliance for Labor Action and role of the SWP: Edmund F. Wehrle, *Between a River and a Mountain: The AFL-CIO and the Vietnam War* (Ann Arbor: University of Michigan Press, 2005), 139–40, 159, 262n34. Foner, *U.S. Labor,* 92; Lewis, *Hardhats, Hippies, and Hawks,* 113. Inflationary effects of the 1960s economy: Robert Brenner, *The Boom and the Bubble: The US in the World Economy* (New York: Verso, 2002), 102.

15. Mail strike: "Postal Strike—The Effect," *U.S. News & World Report,* April 6, 1970; and "The Strike That Stunned the Country," *Time,* March 30, 1970.

16. Many historians neglect the strike wave in the spring of 1970; exceptions include Peter B. Levy, *The New Left and Labor in the 1960s* (Urbana: University of Illinois Press, 1994), 151–53; and George Katsiaficas, *The Imagination of the New Left: A Global Analysis of 1968* (Boston: South End Press, 1987), 135–36. Teamsters strike: the most recent treatments are three essays in *Rebel Rank and File: Labor Militancy and Revolt from Below during the Long 1970s,* ed. Aaron Brenner, Robert Brenner, and Cal Winslow (New York: Verso, 2010): Cal Winslow, "Overview: The Rebellion from Below, 1965–81," 1–18; Kim Moody, "Understanding the Rank-and-File Rebellion in the Long 1970s," 134–38; and Dan La Botz, "The Tumultuous Teamsters of the 1970s," 210–21. Local coverage of the truck strike appeared in the *RC* almost daily during April 1970, and in the *BJ* on April 2, 7, and 27.

17. Among the many sources on the Teamsters, the GOP, and the union hierarchy's feud with Democrats John and Robert Kennedy, see Arthur M. Schlesinger Jr., *Robert Kennedy and His Times,* vol. 1 (Boston: Houghton Mifflin Harcourt, 1978), 141–47; and Robert Dallek, *An Unfinished Life: John F. Kennedy, 1917–1963* (Boston: Little, Brown, 2003), 219–20, 282. Between 1965 and 1970 Rhodes deployed the Guard over two dozen times to subdue civil disturbances; see Ed Grant and Mike Hill, *I Was There: What Really Went On at Kent State* (Lima, OH: C.S.S. Publishing, 1974), appendix B, 137–38. The gubernatorial primary fight: Rowland Evans and Robert Novak, "Rhodes Is Running Scared," *BJ,* April 14, 1970; Richard L. Maher, "Rhodes Took Gamble in Alerting Guard [to Teamster Strike]," *CP,* May 2, 1970.

18. Whitaker interview; the proclamation is quoted in Bill Whitaker, "The Big Chill: The Stifling Effect of the Official Response to the Kent State Killings," in *Kent and Jackson State, 1970–1990,* ed. Susie Erenrich, special issue, *Vietnam Generation* 2.2 (1990): 142. Paul Probius, the composite character in James Michener's *Kent State,* is based largely on a sketch of Whitaker. His difficulty with his fellow workers because of the length of his hair, while but one example, reinforces the point made by Peter Levy that "the counterculture probably antagonized workers more than the New Left's politics." Levy, *The New Left and Labor,* 86.

19. Whitaker interview.

20. Ibid.

21. Face-off between guardsmen and truckers: front-page photo story, *BJ,* April 27, 1970; "Trucks Roll under Guard Protection," *BJ,* April 29; "Tense, but Quiet as Guardsmen Move

the Trucks," *BJ*, May 2. Gen. Sylvester T. Del Corso, state commander of the Guard, told the *BJ* (April 29) that the troops were under orders to fire at the strikers if fired upon. Background on Grant: Grant and Hill, *I Was There*, back cover. On Love: box 36, folder 470, KSCY. On Lutey: box 16, ACLU Coll.

22. United Rubber Workers strike: "7,600 Idle in Akron—URW Strikes Goodyear, Other 3 Still Working," *BJ*, April 21, 1970; "Next URW Target: Goodrich?," *BJ*, May 2. Construction workers' strike: "3600 Strike in Building Trades," *CP*, May 1, 1970. As we have seen, Alan Canfora, Vince Modugno, and Rick Felber, along with Tim Butz, were among the students attending Kent State in 1970 whose fathers worked for Goodyear, Goodrich, or other rubber companies. On Leo Cullum and his son's service in Vietnam: Joe Cullum to the author, Dec. 14, 2000. On John Felber and his son's service: conversation with Rick Felber; and Felber to the author, June 12, 2009. Declining rate of profit: Brenner, *The Boom and the Bubble*, 119–20.

23. Alewitz interview; "April Moratorium" (editorial), *DKS*, April 8, 1970; "Withdrawal Favored, SMC Poll Shows," *DKS*, April 14; Modugno interview. The April 14 protest: "Weather Keeps Some Away, KSU Students March," *DKS*, April 15, 1970; "KSU's Anti-War Front Dampened," *BJ*, April 15. Rubin's appearance: "Rubin to Speak Here Today," *DKS*, April 10, 1970; "Jerry Rubin: 'We are a generation of obscenities,'" *DKS*, April 14; "Rubin Speaks at KSU," *RC*, April 2; "Rubin a Sad Case" (editorial), *RC*, April 13.

24. The Cleveland protest: "Antiwar Offensive This Month," *Guardian*, April 4, 1970; and "Antiwar Actions across U.S.," *Guardian*, April 25. Involvement of students from Kent: Milton Viorst, *Fire in the Streets: America in the 1960's* (New York: Simon and Schuster, 1979), 524–25; George Caldwell to the author, Aug. 8, 2013. Combat deaths since March 1: www.americanwarlibrary.com/vietnam/vwc24.htm.

25. "Antiwar Actions across U.S.," *Guardian*, April 25, 1970; "Making War against the War Makers," *Burning River Oracle* (Cleveland) 1.5 (May 1–13, 1970); "Police, Marchers Clash at AT&T," *DKS*, April 16, 1970; "Rally, Jeers, Greet A T & T," *PD*, April 16. Viorst, *Fire in the Streets*, 524; conversation with Alan Canfora; Persky, Franklin, Mike Brock, and Alewitz interviews. See also the author's own testimony in Christian G. Appy, *Patriots: The Vietnam War Remembered from All Sides* (New York: Viking, 2003), 386.

26. "Making War against the War Makers," *Burning River Oracle* 1.5 (May 1–13, 1970); Thomas Powers, *Vietnam: The War at Home* (1973; Boston: G. K. Hall, 1984), 200.

27. Robert Stamps, "Save the Pooch," in Erenrich, *Kent and Jackson State*, 114.

28. Ibid.; "Crowd Rallies to Stop Napalming of Dog," *DKS*, April 23, 1970; conversation with Bill Arthrell. The names of the organizers were handwritten on the flyer (photocopy in the author's possession) as contact people. A photo in the *DKS* identifies the speaker as Bill Arthrell, although Stamps identifies him as Lars Christensen.

29. Stamps, "Save the Pooch." Conversation with Dean Kahler (a KSU freshman present in the crowd).

30. See the following in Milton E. Wilson, "Involvement / 2 Years Later: A Report on Programming in the Area of Black Student Concerns at Kent State University, 1968–1970," box 1, Milton E. Wilson, Jr., Papers, KSUA: "250 Negroes Leave KSU," *PD*, Nov. 19, 1968 (280); "Black Student Protest KSU's Big Problem in Fall," *BJ*, Aug. 9, 1970 (321–22); "Blacks

for Colleges in Great Demand, But . . . ," *BJ,* June 28, 1970 (346–51); and Wilson's commentary (354).

31. Election of Blount and his fellow officers: "The New Era of BUS: Right On!," *Black Watch,* March 30, 1970, in Wilson, "Involvement," 298; see also E. Timothy Moore, interview by Craig Simpson, May 14, 2009, and Curtis Pittman, interview by Sandra Perlman Halem, May 4, 2000, Kent State Shootings Oral Histories Collection, M4C.

32. "Goal of BUS," March 30, 1970, and Wilson's chronicle of events, in Wilson, "Involvement," 301, 322.

33. "Why Aren't They Playing?," *Black Watch,* Dec. 10, 1969, in Wilson, "Involvement," 389; and the following in *DKS:* Robert Pickett, "KSU Needs More Black Athletes," Jan. 14, 1970; Richard Zitrin, "Pickett 'Misses the Boat,'" Jan. 16; Robert Pickett, "The Black Athlete Continued," Jan. 21; Lafe Tolliver and Bob Pickett, "Blacks Speak Out," Jan. 30; Richard Zitrin, "Blacks Are 'Sickening' in KSU Loss," Feb. 6. For an unpublished response to the article, see letter from Mike Bailey, Feb. 9, 1970, reproduced, along with letters and columns published in the *DKS,* in Wilson, "Involvement," 267–69, 389–90, 392, 396.

34. Wilson, "Involvement," 322 (Wilson's account of events) and White to Blount, April 17, 1970, 323–26; "BUS Answers Pres. White's Letter," *DKS,* April 24, 1970.

35. Cloud's arrival and the BUS action: "BUS 'Greets' Candidate" and "Black Marchers Stage Silent Demonstration," *DKS,* April 28, 1970. Demonstrations at Ohio State: Lauren Hallow, "1970 Protests Erupted across Ohio, Tear Gas at OSU," *The Lantern* (OSU student newspaper), May 4, 2010; and Martha Biondi, *The Black Revolution on Campus* (Berkeley: University of California Press, 2012), 160–61.

36. Powell, "The Storm"; see also "SDS Leaders in KSU Melee Are Released," *RC,* April 30, 1970; "'Kent Four' End Sojourn in County Jail," *DKS,* April 30.

37. Pessimism in the ranks of the antiwar opposition: Terry Anderson, *The Movement and the Sixties: Protest in America from Greensboro to Wounded Knee* (New York: Oxford University Press, 1995), 349. Nixon and the situation in Cambodia: Jeffrey Kimball, *Nixon's Vietnam War* (Lawrence: University Press of Kansas, 1998), 193–210. Turn of the New Left toward Marxism: David Barber, *A Hard Rain Fell: SDS and Why it Failed* (Jackson: University of Mississippi Press, 2008), 219–21.

38. "Could reveal . . . the accumulated impact . . .": Kissinger, *White House Years,* 483. Nixon's strategic thinking: Kimball, *Nixon's Vietnam War,* 209. The April 30 presidential address is quoted in Malcolm Caldwell and Lek Tan, *Cambodia in the Southeast Asian War* (New York: Monthly Review Press, 1973), 437–40.

39. Coverage of US operations in Cambodia includes the following in *NYT:* Henry Kamm, "Cambodia Hints at Shift toward Joint Troop Use," April 2, 1970; Terence Smith, "Cambodian Events Worry Key U.S. Aides in Saigon," April 20; Henry Kamm, "Cambodia Calls for Military Aid in Note to Nixon," April 22; and Max Frankel, "Nixon Aides Split on Cambodian Issue," April 24. Hoffman interview; Powell, "The Storm"; Raines interview.

40. James Michener, *Kent State: What Happened and Why* (New York: Random House, 1971), 13–15, 19–22, 48; Hoffman, Modugno, and Mike Brock interviews; conversation with Tim Butz. On Butz see Michener, *Kent State,* 12–15, 20–22; Andrew E. Hunt, *The Turning: A History of Vietnam Veterans Against the War* (New York: New York University Press, 1999),

41–42. May 1 WHORE rally: Sharoff, interview by Clark Dougan in Weiss et al., *A War Remembered*, 108; and Bill Warren, ed., *The Middle of the Country: The Events of May 4th as Seen by Students and Faculty at Kent State University* (New York: Avon, 1970), 38–46. Plant's involvement: "Speech of May 3 [*sic*], 1970," in Warren, *Middle of the Country*, 43–46. Hammond's role: Joe Eszterhas and Michael D. Roberts, *Thirteen Seconds: Confrontation at Kent State* (New York: Dodd, Mead, 1970), 31.

41. BUS rally: Michener, *Kent State*, 26–33; "'Through Talking,' BUS Head Declares," *RC*, May 2, 1970; Mike Brock interview. Protests at OSU: "Demonstrations at Ohio State," *Guardian*, May 9, 1970.

42. Mike Brock, Hoffman, and Modugno interviews; Sharoff interview in Weiss et al., *A War Remembered*. For Erickson's own account of his chance meeting with Hoffman and Modugno (who are not named in the story), see "The Meaning of People Pulled Apart," *Detroit Free Press*, May 24, 1970. In "The Storm," Powell tells of Neiburger being taken to a farm house well outside of town and his own stay at his parents' house in nearby Stow. Emmer spent that weekend in Cleveland.

43. Mike Brock, Hoffman, and Modugno interviews; Sharoff interview in Weiss et al., *A War Remembered*; "'Down with Nixon,' Scream 500 Rioting Kent Students," *BJ*, May 2, 1970. Tymchyshyn quoted in "The Crucial Hours at Kent State," *Detroit Free Press*, May 24, 1970. Appearance of the motorcycle gang: Eszterhas and Roberts, *Thirteen Seconds*, 36.

44. Conversations with John Hartzler and Marcella Hartzler; Mike Brock interview. For Alan Canfora's account of the evening, see Viorst, *Fire in the Streets*, 528–30.

45. Michener, *Kent State*, 48–65; Mike Brock and Raines interviews. See also "7 Injured, Police Arrest 14," *RC*, May 2, 1970. In one major irony, the Kent police chief had just commended Kent's students for being "well-behaved": "Thompson Praises Students at KSU," *RC*, May 1, 1970.

46. Dyer interview. Satrom and Law Day: Eszterhas and Roberts, *Thirteen Seconds*, 27; Michener, *Kent State*, 122–23; and Satrom's own account in his testimony during the 1975 civil damages trial: *Krause v. Rhodes* (trial transcripts), vol. 42, pp. 10,686ff., M4C. Rick Felber to the author, July 16 and Nov. 16, 2000, and conversation with Felber.

47. "Charged in Kent," *RC*, May 2, 1970. Most listed out-of-town addresses; the Water Street bars attracted young people from throughout northeast Ohio. Weekley, a Kent State student and friend of Kent 25 defendant Thomas Miller, knew radical activists, but is not known to have participated previously in antiwar protests. Matson quoted in "City of Kent, KSU Officials in Conference," and Thompson quoted in "7 Injured," both in *RC*, May 2, 1970. KSU policeman quoted in Michener, *Kent State*, 57–58.

48. For the events of May 1 and of subsequent days and nights, see *Report of the President's Commission on Campus Unrest* (Washington, DC: GPO, 1970), 239–82. The city's police chief, Roy Thompson, believed there were "strangers in town." Interview of Thompson, Nov. 27, 1991, KHS. John Carson, oral history, transcribed Dec. 11, 1992, KHS. Nixon's characterization of students: "Nixon Puts 'Bums' Label on Some College Radicals," *NYT*, May 2, 1970. Conflicting signs that the Teamster strike might be waning: "Akron Truckers Okay New Contract; Resume Hauling" and "Rhodes May Call More Guardsmen," *RC*, May 2, 1970. Crackdown by Satrom: "Kent Curfew Ordered Tonight; Bars Closed," *RC*, May 2.

49. *Report of the President's Commission,* 243–47; Hoffman and Mike Brock interviews. See also James J. Best, "The Tragic Weekend of May 1–4, 1970," in *Kent State and May 4th: A Social Science Perspective,* ed. Thomas R. Hensley and Jerry M. Lewis, 3rd ed. (Kent: Kent State University Press, 2010), 4–31.

50. Maurice Isserman and Michael Kazin, "The Failure and Success of the New Radicalism," in *The Rise and Fall of the New Deal Order, 1930–1980,* ed. Steve Fraser and Gary Gerstle (Princeton: Princeton University Press, 1989), 223.

51. For mention of the anti-ROTC sign, see *Report of the President's Commission,* 240. For some of the motivations of the students, see Stuart Taylor, Richard Shuntich, Patrick McGovern, and Robert Genther, *Violence at Kent State, May 1 to 4, 1970: The Students' Perspective* (New York: College Notes and Texts, 1971), 29–30.

52. FBI file no. 98-46479, "Kent State Shooting—Part 1 of 8," available at https://vault.fbi.gov/Kent%20State (hereafter cited as FBI, "Kent State Shooting"). Except for individual interview statements, most names in the FBI file are redacted. For additional mention of the warnings given to the photographers, see Barclay D. McMillen and William J. Armstrong; "Kent State, May 4, 1970: Who Really Was Responsible for the Shootings?," unpublished memoir, 1999, box 131, folder 14, M4C.

53. Kelley's presence: Eszterhas and Roberts, *Thirteen Seconds,* 78; and McMillen and Armstrong, "Kent State, May 4, 1970." The FBI reported that 8,500 students (approximately 40 percent of the student body) lived on campus in the spring of 1970; FBI, "Kent State Shooting." Hoffman interview; Rick Felber to the author, April 28, 2007.

54. KSU's director of safety and public services (Chester Williams) quoted in Michener, *Kent State,* 211. McMillen recounts his chance encounter with KSU security officer Don Schwartzmiller and detective Tom Kelley, and how he advised the pair that the crowd could not be contained, in McMillen and Armstrong, "Kent State, May 4, 1970."

55. FBI, "Kent State Shooting." In his FBI statement, one KSU student, nineteen-year-old Phil Haas, told of being present at every demonstration over the four-day period, although he appears to have been an exception. A few, such as Dale Smiley, were high school students, while an unknown number, including Tom Foglesong, were former KSU students.

56. Identification of Rupe and the brawl over the camera: FBI, "Kent State Shooting." The confrontation with Haskakis is also covered in Michener, *Kent State,* 193–94, 205–6; and Eszterhas and Roberts, *Thirteen Seconds,* 79.

57. The title of this section is borrowed from a watercolor depicting a barn inferno by the Ohio naturalist painter Charles Burchfield. FBI, "Kent State Shooting"; see also Eszterhas and Roberts, *Thirteen Seconds,* 80–81; "KSU Rioters Put Torch to ROTC Building," *BJ,* May 3, 1970; "ROTC Building Gets Torch; Firemen Pelted," *RC,* May 4. See also James Renner, "The Kent State Conspiracies—What Really Happened on May 4, 1970?," *Cleveland Free Times,* May 3–9, 2006.

58. Interviews with a student and professors in FBI, "Kent State Shooting." Tension and resentment between city and university police may well have played a role in the failure to defend the building, as campus officers had not come to the aid of city police on May 1. On the following evening campus police were left to their own devices until Portage County sheriff's deputies arrived. They were later reinforced by units of the State Highway Patrol and

Ohio National Guard. See James and Paula Banks, "Kent State: How the War in Vietnam Became a War at Home," in *Vietnam and the Antiwar Movement: An International Perspective*, ed. John Dumbrell (Aldershot, UK: Avebury, 1989), 68–81; Roy Thompson, in his KHS interview, also hints at these strains.

59. FBI, "Kent State Shooting"; Ron Weissenberger to the author, Feb. 6, 2003. Miller, Cormack, Felber, and Weissenberger are identified in the FBI report. They were part of a group of twenty-five defendants indicted in the aftermath of the disorders, known as the Kent 25. For interviews with two of the firemen, see Grant and Hill, *I Was There*, 42–47.

60. FBI, "Kent State Shooting." The Whites' whereabouts: Thomas R. Hensley, *The Kent State Incident: Impact of Judicial Process on Public Attitudes* (Westport, CT: Greenwood Press, 1981), 34; McMillen and Armstrong, "Kent State, May 4, 1970." In their thorough account of the evening of May 2, Eszterhas and Roberts slightly confuse the timing of the shed fire (*Thirteen Seconds*, 34).

61. The destruction on Main Street was described by a faculty marshal in his interview in FBI, "Kent State Shooting"; see also "ROTC Building Gets Torched," and Saul Daniels, "4 Killed—11 [*sic*] Wounded," in Warren, *Middle of the Country*, 65–96. Rock-throwing incident: Grant and Hill, *I Was There*, 50. "A horizontal hail storm": after-action report by SP4 James E. Pierce, May 4, 1970, KSCY. For Pierce, see box 37, folder 482, KSCY. The after-action reports cited here from the Kent State Collection at Yale were examined in the Kent May 4 Center archive.

62. Weapons and ammunition destroyed, and the Guard movements around the building: FBI, "Kent State Shooting." Debate on the cause of the fire: Renner, "The Kent State Conspiracies." Rick Felber, who doubts that the fire was planned, recalls that when he returned to the Commons, "The building was smoldering, not in open flame and the fire appeared to be going out. We [Jerry Rupe and I] could only see two sides [of the building] so it is possible someone was on the other side. . . . I do not recall any sound of explosion[,] just the fire suddenly coming back to life and the building breaking out in open flame." Felber to the author, April 28, 2007. On May 1, 2015, video footage of the fire was posted to YouTube by Robert Elan, a Kent State student in May 1970, who recorded the footage on Super 8 film. What is significant about the video is that it shows that the fire reignited in the very portion of the southeast corner of the building where radicals set the fire some forty-five minutes beforehand. www.youtube.com/watch?v=90pCEynlrpc.

12. "Right here, get set, point, fire!"

1. Vince Modugno, George Hoffman, and Carolyn Carson, experienced activists all, recalled in their interviews that they left Kent on May 3, believing that retribution might be in store. For more on the effort to hold Hoffman and others accountable for the disorders, see "Here's What Happened at Kent State, Part 1," *CP*, May 15, 1970. Year-by-year US losses in the war, as well as losses by town and state, can be viewed at www.archives.gov/research /military/vietnam-war/. Mike Brock interview.

2. Del Corso quoted in "Shoot-to-Kill View Challenged," *PD*, June 2, 1968; and "Del Corso Raps Militant Dissidents," *Columbus (OH) Citizen-Journal*, March 31, 1970. Del

Corso's background: Joe Eszterhas and Michael D. Roberts, *Thirteen Seconds: Confrontation at Kent State* (New York: Dodd, Mead, 1970), 89–103.

3. Eszterhas and Roberts, *Thirteen Seconds*, 86–87.

4. *Report of the President's Commission on Campus Unrest* (Washington, DC: GPO, 1970), 256. "Commission on KSU Violence Report" (1972), 4 vols., box 201, M4C, 4:133–34. Boram traveled with Bukosky, who was still on probation. After going to campus and checking on friends in town, they returned to Cleveland. James Michener, *Kent State: What Happened and Why* (New York: Random House, 1971), 255.

5. Richard C. Zimmerman, "Rhodes's First Eight Years, 1963–1971," in *Ohio Politics,* ed. Alexander P. Lamis and Mary Anne Sharkey (Kent: Kent State University Press, 1994), 80–81; Eszterhas and Roberts, *Thirteen Seconds,* 110–13, 134–44.

6. Zimmerman, "Rhodes's First Eight Years"; Michener, *Kent State,* 245–53 ("at all costs" quoted on 250); *Report of the President's Commission,* 253–55 ("We are going to ask for an injunction . . ." quoted on 255).

7. Quoted in Peter Davies, *The Truth about Kent State: A Challenge to the American Conscience* (New York: Farrar, Straus and Giroux, 1973), 21–22.

8. Ibid., 21–22; *Report of the President's Commission,* 253–54.

9. Modugno, Carson, and Hoffman interviews.

10. Alewitz and Whitaker interviews; conversation with Jim Powrie; Heineman, *Campus Wars,* 246.

11. *Report of the President's Commission,* 255.

12. For the "Statement of 23 Concerned Faculty" and an explanation of it, see John Hubbell, "A Point of Clarification," *Kent State: Ten Years After,* special issue, *Left Review* 4.2 (Spring 1980): 32. Michener, *Kent State,* 260.

13. Hubbell, "A Point of Clarification"; Eszterhas and Roberts, *Thirteen Seconds,* 114. Ban on rallies: Davies, *The Truth about Kent State,* 24–25; James and Paula Banks, "Kent State," in *Vietnam and the Antiwar Movement: An International Perspective,* ed. John Dumbrell (Aldershot, UK: Avebury, 1989), 75; *Report of the President's Commission,* 255–56; Thomas R. Hensley, *The Kent State Incident: Impact of Judicial Process on Public Attitudes* (Westport, CT: Greenwood Press, 1981), 51; Joseph Kelner and James Munves, *The Kent State Coverup* (New York: Harper and Row, 1980), 149–56. Frisina's credibility among antiwar students had been comprised by his pro-administration activities in the spring of 1969; see *Report of the President's Commission,* 256; and Kenneth J. Heineman, *Campus Wars: The Peace Movement at American State Universities in the Vietnam Era* (New York: New York University Press, 1993), 232.

14. Eszterhas and Roberts, *Thirteen Seconds,* 118–19; *Report of the President's Commission,* 256; Stuart Taylor, Richard Shuntich, Patrick McGovern, and Robert Genther, *Violence at Kent State, May 1 to 4, 1970: The Students' Perspective* (New York: College Notes and Texts, 1971), 47–48.

15. Jones's activities and the movements of the crowd: Michener, *Kent State,* 267–70; see also his photograph in Eszterhas and Roberts, *Thirteen Seconds* (fourth page of the gallery); for his testimony, see *Krause v. Rhodes* (trial transcripts), vol. 20, pp. 4927ff., M4C. On the 145th Infantry see Ed Grant and Mike Hill, *I Was There: What Really Went On at Kent State*

(Lima, OH: C.S.S. Publishing, 1974), 53. The curfew: *Report of the President's Commission*, 245.

16. Kahler's participation: Kelner and Munves, *Kent State Coverup*, 47–49. Alewitz interview. The six demands are listed in Michener, *Kent State*, 272, and the photos of Cullum and Arthrell appear on 270 and 275, respectively.

17. Alewitz interview. For more on Sunday evening and Capt. Snyder, see Michener, *Kent State*, 273–77. Snyder's nickname: his testimony in *Krause v. Rhodes*, vol. 20, pp. 4717ff.; for his background, see his statement to the FBI, May 10, 1970, his statement to the Ohio State Highway Patrol (OSHP), June 22, 1970, and his civil trial deposition, Feb. 28, 1975, all in box 37, folder 489, KSCY. The students' testimony: "Commission on KSU Violence Report," 4:125–26. The veteran who aided the bayoneted student: FBI file no. 98-46479, "Kent State Shooting—Part 1 of 8," section 6C, 43. On the student bayoneted near the library (Helen Opasker), see Michener, *Kent State*, 280.

18. Snyder's FBI statement, May 10, 1970, box 37, folder 489, KSCY. For his activities on May 3, and the identity of the BAR man mentioned in the text, see William Barry Furlong, "The Guardsmen's View of the Tragedy at Kent State," *NYT Sunday Magazine*, June 21, 1970. The students' testimony: "Commission on KSU Violence Report," 4:125–26.

19. Testimony of Sgt. Lawrence Shafer, *Krause v. Rhodes*, vol. 7, pp. 1275ff.; and testimony of Lt. Alexander Stevenson, vols. 25 and 26, pp. 6346ff. "Commission on KSU Violence Report," 4:131, 135–36.

20. Warnings given to members of BUS: Simpson interview; oral history by Curtis Pittman, May 4, 2000, Kent State Shootings Oral Histories Collection, M4C. Pickett threatened by guardsmen: testimony of Robert Pickett, *Krause v. Rhodes*, vol. 13, pp. 2951ff. In Eszterhas and Roberts, *Thirteen Seconds*, 125–26, Erwind Blount, one of the principal organizers of the BUS rally on May 1, told of being fired on by police late in the evening of May 3; there is no other record of the claim. For an angry verbal exchange with guardsmen and an account of guns being pointed at Blount and Rudy Perry, see Michener, *Kent State*, 279–80.

21. Oral histories by Rob Fox, May 4, 2000, and Mary Homer, May 2, 1990, Kent State Shootings Oral Histories Collection, M4C. Helicopters buzzing Greg Hawthorne's apartment: Hawthorne interview.

22. Richard Foot, interview, Dec. 13, 1991, KHS; and his obituary, *BJ*, Aug. 19, 2009. Grant and Hill, *I Was There*, 57. Grant added that he did not believe the bellicose statements implied that his fellow guardsmen were prepared to kill. "Were like animals": quoted in Eszterhas and Roberts, *Thirteen Seconds*, 124.

23. Number of guardsmen at Kent State: Kelner and Munves, *Kent State Coverup*, 143. Information on the guardsmen and their backgrounds was drawn from that source and from Furlong, "The Guardsmen's View"; *Krause v. Rhodes* depositions and testimony; Grant and Hill, *I Was There*; Michener, *Kent State*; Scott L. Bills, ed., *Kent State/May 4: Echoes through a Decade* (1982; Kent: Kent State University Press, 1988); FBI statements; and OSHP interviews.

24. FBI statements and OSHP interviews. For civil trial depositions, 1975, see box 16, ACLU Coll.; *Krause v. Rhodes*, vol. 44 and depositions.

25. For a listing of Company A troops, see Davies, *The Truth about Kent State*, 227–28. The German-born soldier was Paul R. Naujoks: FBI statement, May 10, 1970, KM4C; unless otherwise noted, all FBI statements cited hereafter are also from the Kent May 4 Center. For the racial composition of the area and its political loyalties, see Michael F. Curtin, *The Ohio Politics Almanac* (1996; Kent: Kent State University Press, 2006), 8–11, 151. Wayne County religious life: statistics for the county at www.sharefaith.com/guide/church-directory/ohio/index.html, and church advertisements in the *Wooster Daily Record*, 2014.

26. Grant and Hill, *I Was There*, 52–55; Furlong, "The Guardsmen's View"; "Guardsmen Kill 4 Students, *WP*, May 5, 1970; interview with guardsman Robert Gabriel in Bills, *Kent State/May 4*, 118.

27. On Del Corso, see Eszterhas and Roberts, *Thirteen Seconds*, 89–103. On Canterbury, who at fifty-five was a twenty-three-year veteran of the Ohio National Guard as well as a construction superintendent, see box 35, folder 446, KSCY, which contains information from his 1975 deposition and testimony at the civil damages trial. On Fassinger, who was thirty-nine, see *Krause v. Rhodes*, vol. 28, pp. 7107ff. On Jones, see Kelner and Munves, *Kent State Coverup*, 129; and box 36, folder 465, KSCY. On Pryor, see *Krause v. Rhodes*, vol. 14, pp. 3126ff., and box 28, folder 33, KSCY.

28. On Fallon: his FBI statement, May 8, 1970, KM4C. On Smith, *Krause v. Rhodes*, vol. 23, pp. 5837ff. On Bragg: FBI statement, May 10, 1970. On Parker: Eszterhas and Roberts, *Thirteen Seconds*, 171. On Perkins: "'Doing Their Job,' Says Guardsman's Father," *CP*, March 30, 1974 (this source lists his age at that time as twenty-eight); see also his OSHP interview, June 9, 1970, box 36, folder 480, KSCY. On Snyder: box 37, folder 489, KSCY, which includes information from his OSHP statement (June 22, 1970), FBI statement (May 10, 1970), and civil deposition (Feb. 28, 1975). On Biddle: his deposition, box 12, ACLU Coll.

29. On Martin: *Krause v. Rhodes*, vol. 27, pp. 6673ff.; he also appears to be the unnamed officer described in Furlong, "The Guardsmen's View," as "the one officer in the outfit who had combat experience in Vietnam." On James: box 36, folder 462, KSCY. On Farriss: box 35, folder 457, KSCY. On Myers (also listed as Robby Brooks Myers): box 16, ACLU Coll. On Shade and Raber: box 64B, folder 17, M4C. Myers was the guardsman in the brief conversational exchange with Allison Krause.

30. On Long: his FBI statement, May 12, 1970, KM4C. On Thomas, Sholl, Maas, and Repp: box 16, ACLU Coll. On Hinton: *Krause v. Rhodes*, vol. 44, pp. 11,003ff. On Love and Mowrer: box 36, folders 470 and 479, respectively, KSCY. In his deposition, Mowrer said that "half the company wore glasses," and added that "a lot of people couldn't see [well]." In general, although they have often been characterized as "scared kids" or "not much older than the students," determining the exact age of individual guardsmen is difficult. The KSU Commission on Violence attempted to obtain more detailed information about the ages of the troops from officials, but reported that they got little cooperation from the Ohio National Guard. Gen. Del Corso told the commission in August 1970 that the average age of guardsmen was twenty-three ("Commission on KSU Violence Report," 4:135–36). The median age of enlisted men and officers I drew from a subset of approximately forty guardsmen who were on the hill at the time of the firing. The median age of eight guardsmen indicted by a Federal grand jury in 1974 was then about twenty-eight, the oldest of whom

were James Pierce and Barry Morris. One source listed indicted guardsman Ralph Zoller as having eleven years of Guard service, but this is almost certainly incorrect. If the ages given for the eight indictees in the *CP* article " 'Doing Their Job' " are correct, Zoller could have been no older than twenty-five at the time of the shootings.

31. Grant and Hill, *I Was There*, 57–58, 62–63; *Report of the President's Commission*, 259.

32. Grant and Hill, *I Was There*, 57–58, 62–63; *Report of the President's Commission*, 259.

33. Rick Perlstein, *Nixonland: The Rise of a President and the Fracturing of America* (New York: Scribner, 2008), 484. It should be noted that while the cultural conflict did not cause the guardsmen to pull the triggers of their weapons, the antipathies made it easier to do so.

34. Carol Mirman, interview by Sandra Perlman Halem, April 1, 2000, Kent State Shootings Oral Histories Collection, M4C. For classroom discussions on May 4, see Michener, *Kent State*, 327, 346–47; and *Report of the President's Commission*, 260. As I noted in the prologue, the political science class I attended that morning, which met from 11:00 to 11:50, was devoted to a discussion of the war. At the conclusion of the class, a young woman, whom I recognized as a supporter of the SMC, stood and announced the noon rally.

35. Alewitz interview; Sharoff interview in Clark Dougan, David Fulghum, and Denis Kennedy, *A War Remembered* (Boston: Time Life Education, 1986), 110.

36. Rhodes's remark, overheard at the Kent fire station, was reported by Michael Delaney, the Guard's public information officer, who was one of a small number of guardsmen appalled by what happened at Kent State. See "Rhodes Okayed Force, Kent Grand Jury Told," *CP*, Jan. 7, 1974; Hensley, *Kent State Incident*, 55–57; Eszterhas and Roberts, *Thirteen Seconds*, 147–48. See also Carole A. Barbato, Laura L. Davis, and Mark Seeman, "This We Know: Chronology of the Shootings at Kent State," in *Democratic Narrative, History, and Memory*, ed. Carole A. Barbato and Laura L. Davis (Kent: Kent State University Press, 2012), 206.

37. For the timing of events, see *Report of the President's Commission*, 261–63; for the crowd size, Bills, introduction to *Kent State/May 4*, 16.

38. Milton Viorst, *Fire in the Streets: America in the 1960's* (New York: Simon and Schuster, 1979), 507; conversation with Alan Canfora. In his interview with Viorst, Canfora readily conceded that his remark was "arrogant."

39. The author relied on his own recollection of those assembled. All can be seen in photographs taken that day.

40. Pryor's instructions: box 28, folder 333, KSCY. Covering of the name tags: see the depositions and interview with the OSHP of James McGee, box 36, folder 472, KSCY, and Barry Morris, box 14, ACLU Coll. McGee stated, "It seems like all the Guardsmen I saw—let's say 50 percent of them—had their name tags removed from sight whether they were from the 145th or the 107th." Magnifying photographs taken on May 4 often reveals guardsmen's nametags either absent or covered; see, for example, fig. 7 in Davies, *The Truth about Kent State*, 67.

41. The confusion over the distribution of ammunition is in the deposition of Harry Jones; for this and information on Jones, Smith, McManus, and Snyder, see the following boxes and folders in KSCY: Jones, box 36, folder 465; Smith, box 37, folder 488; McManus, box 28, folder 325, and box 36, folder 473; Snyder, box 37, folder 489. On Stevenson: *Krause v. Rhodes*, vol. 26, pp. 6346ff. On whether students were aware of loaded weapons, see Hensley, *Kent State Incident*, 59. On White's claims, see "Kent Prexy Says He Didn't Know

Guns Were Loaded," *CP,* May 6, 1970. It is not easy to determine the veracity of his claims; when he returned to Kent on the afternoon of May 3, vice president Robert Matson, who had been at the earlier meeting when Del Corso and Rhodes discussed the option of firing on students, presumably have briefed him about what was said there.

42. For a photo of Hammond atop the casement, see Michener, *Kent State,* 326. For photos of Jeff Miller (no relation to Tom), Krause, and Levine, see Davies, *The Truth about Kent State,* figs. 5 and 16.

43. Canterbury's testimony: box 35, folder 446, KSCY. The account of Rice's pleading, the chanting, and the rock thrown at the jeep is from personal observation and from listening to audio recordings of the day. For the crowd: Eszterhas and Roberts, *Thirteen Seconds,* 150. Rick Lieber's presence: conversation with Steve Lieber (Rick's cousin). Brother Fargo and Maj. Jones can be seen in photos 7 and 9 in *Report of the President's Commission,* 306–7 and 310–11. Mike Brock interview; Michener, *Kent State,* 329.

44. Hensley (*Kent State Incident,* 55–57) characterizes White's noontime gathering as a working lunch. For the entreaties of the professor, see the testimony of Maj. Harry Jones, *Krause v. Rhodes,* vol. 20, pp. 4927ff. "These students are going to have to find out . . .": quoted in Michener, *Kent State,* 331. See also "Gen. Canterbury to Testify before KSU Jury," *PD,* Feb. 28, 1974.

45. Firing of tear gas and the number of guardsmen in the advance: Michener, *Kent State,* 331–32. Morris's age is given in "'Doing Their Job,'" *CP,* March 30, 1974. In his deposition, Col. Fassinger admitted that there were four hundred additional troops available in the area and that the one hundred who made up the attacking force was an inadequate number; box 9, ACLU Coll.

46. Michener, *Kent State,* 331; Eszterhas and Roberts, *Thirteen Seconds,* 153–54. On Erwin, who was later indicted by the Portage County grand jury, see the account he gave to the FBI, box 34, folder 438, KSCY. See also Michael Erwin, interview by Sandra Perlman Halem, April 4, 2000, Kent State Shootings Oral Histories Collection, M4C. For photos of Snyder striking the student, see Davies, *The Truth about Kent State,* 78–79.

47. Hensley, *Kent State Incident,* 60. For the best map of the National Guard advance, see Davies, *The Truth about Kent State,* 35. Srp would turn thirty-five in June 1970; see his deposition, box 9, ACLU Coll. Capt. Snyder, the head of Company C, believed, however, that his men had the most crowd control experience of all the Guard units sent to Kent State; see his deposition and interview with the OSHP, June 22, 1970, box 37, folder 489, KSCY.

48. Grant and Hill, *I Was There,* 77–78.

49. The original plan called for a halt at the crest of Taylor Hill; Canterbury made an unexpected decision to pursue the students beyond that point. See *Report of the President's Commission,* 266; and Michener, *Kent State,* 337. Canterbury later testified: "We needed to move down to the practice field to reform. . . . [M]y judgment was [that it] was the best place to turn around and assess the situation." Canterbury's 1975 trial deposition, box 35, folder 446, KSCY. Maj. Jones, who seemed to know the field best and showed the most initiative, if not always the most judgment, later said under questioning, "I do not have any understanding as to why they continued beyond the crest and went down into the practice field." Jones's testimony, box 36, folder 465, KSCY. Pierce's trial testimony: *Krause v. Rhodes,* vol. 18, pp. 4315ff.

50. Simons's comment: "Summary of Depositions, Engdahl Memo," box 1, folder 35, James Munves Papers, KSCY. For more on Simons's opinions: Kelner and Munves, *Kent State Coverup*, 153. Contrary to widely disseminated reports, the guardsmen had not exhausted their tear gas supply; guardsman Russell Repp had eight unused canisters. See Michener, *Kent State*, 339.

51. Activities of Miller (photo) and Minard: *Report of the President's Commission*, 340–41; Eszterhas and Roberts, *Thirteen Seconds*, 158. For Flesher and Repp: *Krause v. Rhodes*, vol. 23, pp. 5769ff.; Eszterhas and Roberts, *Thirteen Seconds*, 158. "Christians in a Roman arena": Pierce's 1970 testimony to the county grand jury, box 37, folder 482, KSCY.

52. "Guy with an Apache headband . . .": quoted in Eszterhas and Roberts, *Thirteen Seconds*, 156. Smith's account: box 37, folder 488, KSCY. McGee's account: his 1975 deposition, box 36, folder 472, KSCY.

53. Morris initially recounted that he saw Sgt. Pryor—also a member of the 107th Armored Cavalry—fire one shot in the air while the two units were on the practice field; box 14, ACLU Coll. In civil court in 1975, however, Morris kept quiet about what he had seen, as he had been instructed by his attorney not to answer questions about Pryor. Pryor always claimed his weapon was not even loaded. See "Conflicts Come to the Surface in Kent Civil Trial Testimony," *CP*, June 13, 1975. There may also have been a .22 fired on the practice field; see *Report of the President's Commission*, 268. For mention of a shell casing being picked up on the practice field, see Michener, *Kent State*, 359. One guardsman, James W. Farriss, told FBI agents that while on the practice field, "he noted that one shot was fired by an officer from the 107th Armored Cavalry," explaining that "this shot was from a .45 caliber automatic pistol which is normally carried by officers." If Farriss counted NCOs among the officers, he was correct. Farriss FBI statement, May 8, 1970, KM4C. Richard Schreiber, a professor of journalism watching through field glasses from the veranda of Taylor Hall, said he witnessed a guardsman fire a .45 pistol. See *Report of the President's Commission*, 268; and "The Crucial Hours at Kent State," *Detroit Free Press*, May 24, 1970. For the effect of terrain and atmospheric conditions on sound, sometimes called "acoustic shadow," see John B. De Motte, "The Cause of a Silent Battle," in *Battles and Leaders of the Civil War*, ed. Robert U. Johnson and Clarence C. Buel, vol. 2 (1887; repr., New York: Thomas Yoseloff, 1956), 365. Pierce's statement to the OSHP: box 37, folder 482, KSCY.

54. Jones's statements: his 1975 deposition, box 36, folder 465, KSCY; his full deposition is in box 9, ACLU Coll.

55. Pryor's trial testimony, *Krause v. Rhodes*, vol. 14, pp. 3126ff.; Fallon's FBI statement of May 8, 1970; Jones, box 36, folder 465, KSCY. For Canterbury's attire, see the Howard E. Ruffner photo of him (fig. 50) in Davies, *The Truth about Kent State*. Canterbury is to the right of a light pole, back row, fourth from left.

56. See Davies, *The Truth about Kent State*, for photos (by John P. Filo) of Roseann Canfora next to her brother (fig. 40) and Alan Canfora and Riggs (on Alan's left; fig. 39). Canfora's conversation with his sister: Alan Canfora to the author, Feb. 19, 2007.

57. Minard's encounter with Jones: Eszterhas and Roberts, *Thirteen Seconds*, 160; "Kent State: Martyrdom That Shook the Country," *Time*, May 18, 1970; and Capt. Srp's description of the encounter, box 29, folder 342, KSCY. See also Kelner and Munves, *Kent State Coverup*, 129. For Pierce's account, see box 36, folder 482, KSCY. Guardsmen giving orders

may have pulled their gas masks away from their mouths so their commands could be heard by those nearby. On the level of sound, Jones said: "The intensity of the noise was very high. You couldn't get anybody's attention . . . I could holler at the top of my voice." *Krause v. Rhodes*, vol. 20, pp. 4927ff.

58. Montgomery's testimony: *Krause v. Rhodes*, vol. 5, pp. 926ff. Deegan's testimony: "Sergeant Fired First Shots at Students, Witness Says," *PD*, June 24, 1975. Minard quoted in "Kent State," *Time*, May 18; his account of the events is in "Commission on KSU Violence Report," 4:243–44. In the KSU commission report, Minard recounts that Jones "was wearing a soft cap, not a helmet, and was armed with a .45-caliber pistol in a hip holster," an accurate description except that Jones carried a .22 pistol. Love's account: box 36, folder 470, KSCY. Thomas's account: box 37, folder 493, KSCY. See also "Commission on KSU Violence Report," 4:244, for the account of student James G. Woodring, who, the commission wrote, believed he saw Jones "turn toward the men, say something, turn back, and then fire into the ground."

59. The KSU employee, Jack Albright, was loyal to the Guard. He conveyed his story to four neighbors, including Kent professor Robert Fernie, within hours of the shootings. Months later, Michener found it much more difficult to get Albright to talk, but did get him to answer the following question: "Did you hear an officer say, 'Turn around and fire three rounds?' 'Well, I heard . . . well, yes. I heard it.'" Michener, *Kent State*, 363–64. Pickett's testimony: *Krause v. Rhodes*, vol. 13, pp. 2951; Pickett was the fourth witness to indicate that he either heard or saw Jones give a command or signal to fire. Montgomery's *Krause v. Rhodes* testimony. On Levinger: Eszterhas and Roberts, *Thirteen Seconds*, 62. The summary of Levinger's account in the KSU Commission report (244) seems to indicate that he identified Jones as the officer "who had a .45 pistol, [and the one to] shoot first; afterward the other guardsmen opened up. He [Levinger] identifies this officer as one who earlier was taunting students, saying, 'Come on.'" (Thus Levinger, like Minard, misidentified the type of pistol Jones carried.) Levinger does not indicate if Jones was pointing his sidearm. If the major did aim, there is no known photograph of him doing so. While eyewitness testimony and photographic evidence supports Pryor's role in the shootings, the sound analysis does not. According to a report provided to the Justice Department by the firm of Bolt, Beranek and Newman, the first shot fired was from an M-1 rifle. "Analysis of Recorded Sounds from the 1970 Episode at Kent State University," Feb. 28, 1974, 22, available at http://media .cleveland.com. On the recording, see "Kent State Tragedy Echoes on Audiotape," *BJ*, March 8, 2001; "Kent State Tape Is Said to Reveal Orders," *NYT*, May 2, 2007; and John Mangels, "Activists Press Government for Action on Kent State Shooting Review," *PD*, May 8, 2011. For the controversy over what it reveals, see the following in *BJ*: William A. Gordon, "Was There an Order to Fire?," May 4, 2007; Alan Canfora, "What's the Harm in Probing May 4?," May 9; and Thomas M. Grace, "The Evidence of an Order to Shoot," May 14.

60. Robert D. James, statement to the OSHP, June 9, 1970, box 36, folder 464, KSCY; Roger Maas, FBI statement, May 7, 1970; Sgt. Matthew McManus, OSHP statement, box 36, folder 473, KSCY, and testimony, *Krause v. Rhodes*, vol. 22, pp. 5307ff.; Lloyd Thomas's account, box 37, folder 493, KSCY, and Kelner and Munves, *Kent State Coverup*, 244. For Perkins and Case: their respective statements to the FBI, May 9; and after-action report of May 4, box 64B, folder 17, M4C.

61. On Naujoks: his FBI statement, May 10, 1970, KM4C; and Eszterhas and Roberts, *Thirteen Seconds*, 162. On McManus: his OSHP statement, June 13, 1970, box 36, folder 473, KSCY, and *Krause v. Rhodes*, vol. 22, pp. 5307ff. Herschler later stated, "I never told Sgt. McManus that I fired my entire clip"; box 36, folder 462, KSCY. On Breckenridge: *Krause v. Rhodes*, vol. 45, pp. 11,226ff. On Mowrer: his OSHP statement, June 8, 1970, and 1975 deposition, box 36, folder 479, KSCY.

62. Kelner and Munves, *Kent State Coverup*, 86–93. For the definitive photograph of Lewis, see Davies, *The Truth about Kent State*, fig. 53. On Lewis, see also Allen F. Richardson, "Kent Recalled," *NYT*, Aug. 7, 1975. In speaking of a student later determined to be Joe Lewis, Shafer told the FBI on May 7, 1970: "I did not observe anything in his hands, but I felt I was about to be attacked by this individual and I fired at this person. I can approximate that this individual was twenty-five feet from me when I fired." (Lewis was between 60 and 70 feet away.) Box 34, folder 439, and box 37, folder 487, KSCY. McGee told the OSHP investigator that he fired three times; box 36, folder 472, KSCY.

63. After-action reports of Fallon, Cline, and Morris, box 64B, folder 17, M4C. James's testimony, *Krause v. Rhodes*, vol. 24, pp. 5944ff., and box 36, folder 464, KSCY. Zoller's account: box 37, folder 495, KSCY; and box 14, ACLU Coll. His age is given in " 'Doing Their Job,' " *CP*. For the rock-throwing claim, see *Report of the President's Commission*, 271–72. Srp's FBI statement: Kelner and Munves, *Kent State Coverup*, 122.

64. On Pierce: his FBI statement, May 7, 1970, box 34, folder 439, and 1975 trial testimony, box 37, folder 482, KSCY. Pierce told the agents, "I looked to my left, towards Taylor hall and observed a male about ten feet away [the closest student wounded was between 60 and 70 feet from the Guard] on the steps with a rock in his hand and his arm drawn back. . . . I had my rifle at hip level. I turned toward this person and fired. The male fell and as he fell he appeared to get hit several more times. I then turned back to the right and fired into the crowd." The physicians who treated John Cleary believed he was hit only once, but that the bullet made several apparent entry/exit wounds.

65. For Shultz's reaction, see William Safire, "One Blow for Truth," *NYT*, Oct. 9, 1986. Safire writes: "From the sound, he [Shultz] knew an order had been given to fire at the students, and—a good administration soldier, but not one to march over cliffs—he would not accept explanations that the shooting had been sporadic." Gen. Canterbury insisted just the opposite. At his press conference the day after the shootings, the general said, in response to the first question he was asked: "I was there. There was no order to fire." When asked about warning shots, he replied, "They were not ordered to fire at all." And still later: "Under normal conditions a [*sic*] order to fire is given. However, under these conditions there was no normalcy." Transcript of press conference of Brig. Robert Canterbury, May 5, 1970, photocopy, KM4C. "It looked like a firing squad": Charles Brill, quoted in "Kent State," *Time*, May 18, 1970.

66. On Canfora: Bud Schultz and Ruth Schultz, *The Price of Dissent: Testimonies to Political Repression in America* (Berkeley: University of California Press, 2001), 361–65. The author was the other former SDS member to be wounded. Vaughan's recollection: Doug Vaughan to the author, 16, 2003. On Miller and Krause: Davies, *The Truth about Kent State*, 52–53; on Krause see also Eszterhas and Roberts, *Thirteen Seconds*, 207; and Jeff Kisseloff,

Generation on Fire: Voices of Protest from the 1960s, An Oral History (Lexington: University of Kentucky Press, 2007), 254–65.

67. Persky interview. The author walked the area of the shooting with Jerry Alter on May 4, 2007. Erwin's statement: box 34, folder 438, KSCY. On Roseann Canfora, see Schultz and Schultz, *The Price of Dissent*, 364. Schroeder had been prone when shot, but by the time Roseann Canfora saw his body other students had turned him over to try to aid him; Alan Canfora to the author, Sept. 17, 2014. Canfora has hundreds of photos taken the day of the killings. On Schroeder and his fellow ROTC cadets: Bureau of Criminal Identification and Investigation files, box 30, folder 364, KSCY; Michener, *Kent State*, 351, 393–94; Barbato, Davis, and Seeman, "This We Know," 216, 218. Schroeder is reported to have told his ROTC commander, Don Peters, that he opposed Vietnam War and would go to Canada after college. Donald Peters, FBI interview, KM4C.

68. Barbato, Davis, and Seeman, "This We Know," 217; Kelner and Munves, *Kent State Coverup*, 51.

69. Richardson interview. For Tymchyshyn, see OHSP, "Report of Investigation," Aug. 14, 1970, box 77, folder 26, M4C. On his background in wartime Europe, Tymchyshyn to the author, various dates. Cheeks interview.

70. On Leon Smith: his testimony in *Krause v. Rhodes*, vol. 24, pp. 5893ff. When asked by the OSHP if he "hit the student," Smith replied, "Possibly, I saw him grab his right shoulder[,] then run down over the hill out of sight." Box 37, folder 488, KSCY. At the Portage County grand jury sessions in 1970, McManus was asked about shooting Russell. "You don't think you hit him?" He replied, "It has since been found apparently that I did." Box 36, folder 473, KSCY. Russell's wounds and his distance from the firing line: Kelner and Munves, *Kent State Coverup*, 55, 115–16. According to the Bolt, Beranek and Newman report, "Analysis of Recorded Sounds," the last shot fired was also from an M-1 rifle (23).

71. On Winnen, Rose, and Ruffner: Michener, *Kent State*, 366, 368, 377; "At War with War," *Time*, May 18, 1970. On Butz and Johnson: conversation with Butz; Johnson interview. See also Larry L. Rose, "Kent State Shootings Shocked Viet Vet," *Corpus Christi Caller-Times*, May 4, 2000. On Deegan: box 34, folder 438, KSCY; "Ex-student Says Pryor Fired Gun," *BJ*, June 24, 1975. On Montgomery: *Krause v. Rhodes*, vol. 5, pp. 926ff. On Dick Woods: Eszterhas and Roberts, *Thirteen Seconds*, 270. On Zadell: conversation with Alan Canfora. Heasley's account: William Derry Heasley, interview by John Burnell, May 4, 1990, Kent State Shootings Oral Histories Collection, M4C. On Jon Oplinger: "Guard Chief, Senator Feud over Shooting," *St. Petersburg Times*, May 8, 1970; and his book *Quang Tri Cadence: Memoir of a Rifle Platoon Leader in the Mountains of Vietnam* (1993; Jefferson, NC: McFarland, 2014). J. Michael Orange, a Vietnam veteran and former and future Kent State student, had witnessed the protests on May 1 and 2 but had returned to work along the Lake Erie shoreline when the killings occurred. See J. Michael Orange, *Fire in the Hole: A Mortarman in Vietnam* (Lincoln, NE: Writers Club Press, 2001). For the reactions of three others who were Vietnam veterans, see "KSU Moderates Angry, Frightened," *CP*, May 7, 1970.

72. On Montgomery: *Krause v. Rhodes*, vol. 5, pp. 926ff.; "'It Was Murder,' Former Marine Who Saw It States," *RC*, May 8, 1970. Cullum and Fargo are shown aiding Cleary

in a photo on the cover of *Life* magazine, May 15, 1970. On Pickett: *Krause v. Rhodes,* vol. 13, pp. 2951ff.

73. On Snyder: his 1975 deposition, box 37, folder 489, KSCY; and Kelner and Munves, *Kent State Coverup,* 123–25. Snyder carrying extra weapons: testimony of guardsman Michael Delaney, box 35, folder 451, KSCY. The cursing and the thrown practice grenade: Michener, *Kent State,* 380.

74. On Herschler: Kelner and Munves, *Kent State Coverup,* 101. An examination by the Justice Department showed Herschler's rifle to have been fired, but he maintained that he had made no less than three switches of weapons with fellow guardsmen. On Breckenridge: Kelner and Munves, *Kent State Coverup,* 201. Canterbury's comments to McGee: his 1975 trial deposition, box 36, folder 472, KSCY. For a photo of the seated crowd, see Michener, *Kent State,* 401. Hawthorne interview.

75. While a number of accounts of this final showdown have been written, I relied on Michener, *Kent State,* 400–408, and Carole Barbato and Laura Davis, "Ordinary Lives: Kent State, May 4, 1970," in *Time It Was: American Stories from the Sixties,* ed. Karen Manners Smith and Tim Koster (Upper Saddle River, NJ: Pearson / Prentice Hall, 2008), 369–70. History graduate student Steve Sharoff, who had helped organize the 3-C civil liberties coalition and the May 1 rally where the Constitution was buried, also played an important, if underappreciated, role as a go-between.

13. Aftermath

1. Satrom's deposition, box 12, ACLU Coll. On Weissenberger: "Kent Twenty-Five: The Accused," *The Burr* (KSU student magazine), May 4, 2000; and Weissenberger to the author, Feb. 6, 2003. Hoffman and Modugno believed they would be blamed for the protests. They were right: the very afternoon they heard the false reports about the guardsmen, city police entered Modugno and Carson's North Water Street apartment looking for evidence of their supposed leadership. Incorrect *RC* headline: Scott L. Bills, introduction to *Kent State/May 4: Echoes through a Decade,* ed. Bills (1982; Kent: Kent State University Press, 1988), 20; Thomas M. Grace, "A Legacy of Dissent: The Culture and Politics of Protest at Kent State University, 1958–1964" (PhD diss., State University of New York at Buffalo, 2003), 325–28.

2. Conversation with Alan Canfora. Ward was not involved in the protest but went to Canfora's apartment after getting news of the casualties. Jammed and overloaded telephone lines: James Michener, *Kent State: What Happened and Why* (New York: Random House, 1971) 420.

3. Arbaugh quoted in "The View from Kent State: 11 Speak Out," *NYT,* May 11, 1970. On Paul Bukosky: Leonard "Buk" Bukosky (Paul's brother) to the author, Sept. 11, 2002. Roby's whereabouts: Boram interview.

4. Destruction at the airport: "Vandals Damage 6 Planes at Portage County Airport," *RC,* May 4, 1970. The article indicates that the arson might have been the work of environmental radicals. Burning of the university-owned maintenance barn: Michener, *Kent State,* 422. The shots were fired by guardsman Thomas A. Simmons. Simmons FBI statement, KM4C. The Daily Staff Journal, 1BN, 145 Inf., 29 April–5 May 1970, indicates that one

round was fired, although Simmons's own report states two. The log indicates that "one shot at a arson suspect after refusing to halt. Sheriffs Depart. reported an armed man in a car in the area." 1970 Ohio National Guard Logs, 1970 May 2 and May 5, box 91, ACLU Coll. Simmons was the last guardsman to discharge his weapon, but Portage County deputy sheriffs reportedly fired on a car on the southern edge of campus Sunday, May 10. When the vehicle failed to stop for a roadblock, deputies opened up, but apparently missed the occupants. See "Shots Are Fired Sunday Night," *Wooster (OH) Daily Record,* May 11, 1970.

5. McGee's statement, box 36, folder 472, KSCY. Capt. Srp and Sgt. Pryor gave Barry Morris the same directive; see Morris's deposition, box 14, ACLU Coll. Troops directed not to speak to the media: "Guards Heed Silence Order," *Wooster Daily Record,* May 8, 1970. For the self-preservation justification, see Peter Davies, *The Truth about Kent State: A Challenge to the American Conscience* (New York: Farrar, Straus and Giroux, 1973), 223; and "Colonel: Guard Has Right to Self-Defense," *RC,* May 5, 1970. For the sniper theory promoted by Guard officers (and later some enlisted men), see "Del Corso Says Sniper Fired before Guard," *RC,* May 5, 1970. There has long been controversy over the role of plainclothes agent Terry Norman, from whom a .38 revolver was taken shortly after the shootings. For a summary, see Tom Hayden, "Closure at Kent State?," *The Nation* (online edition), May 15, 2013; and Janis Froelich, "Kent State—A New Look," *Tampa Tribune,* April 30, 2006.

6. William Case's after-action report, box 64B, folder 17, M4C; Pierce's after-action report, box 37, folder 482, KSCY. Richard Harwood and Haynes Johnson, "The Tragedy at Kent: A Generation in Conflict," *WP,* May 7, 1970. "I felt like I'd just had an order . . .": quoted in "Kent State," *Time,* May 18, 1970.

7. "Bitter Ohio Guardsmen," *CP,* May 5, 1970; and "Commission on KSU Violence Report" (1972), 4 vols., box 201, M4C, 4:136–37. Householder speculated that a cherry bomb triggered the shooting. "We are all trained not to fire until fired upon," he told the paper.

8. Thomas R. Hensley, *The Kent State Incident: Impact of Judicial Process on Public Attitudes* (Westport, CT: Greenwood Press, 1981), 68; James J. Best, "The Tragic Weekend of May 1–4, 1970," in *Kent State and May 4th: A Social Science Perspective,* ed. Thomas R. Hensley and Jerry M. Lewis, 3rd ed. (Kent: Kent State University Press, 2010), 24.

9. "University Must Oust Hooligans," *RC,* May 4, 1970.

10. Interview of Lucius Lyman Jr., in Bills, *Kent State/May 4,* 72–74.

11. Mary Homer, oral history, May 2, 1990, Kent State Shootings Oral Histories Collection, M4C; Tompkins interview; "Falls High Students Protest KSU Deaths," *BJ,* May 6, 1970.

12. Timothy DeFrange, interview by Helene Cooley, April 30, 1990, Kent State Shootings Oral Histories Collection, M4C. See also Sarah E. Tascone, "Behind Closed Doors," *The Burr,* Spring 1995, 46–47.

13. Kenneth R. Calkins, "Escalating Tensions Explode into Tragedy at Kent State," *BJ,* April 27, 2000.

14. The primary vote and its interpretation: Richard G. Zimmerman, "Rhodes's First Eight Years, in *Ohio Politics,* ed. Alexander P. Lamis and Mary Anne Sharkey (Kent: Kent State University Press, 1994), 80–83; and "'70 Election Trends—The First Clues," *U.S. News & World Report,* May 18, 1970. While Zimmerman feels the shootings may have helped Rhodes, some news outlets speculated that Rhodes "may have been hurt by the killing[s]." See "Primaries," *Time,* May 18, 1970.

15. Conversation with Rick Felber.

16. Alewitz interview; Michener, *Kent State,* 420–21; "Here Are Latest Arrests at KSU," *RC,* May 5, 1970. Alewitz had been wearing a sport jacket at the time of the shootings, but to better portray his outrage he exchanged it for a protest jacket. All three men were later charged with breaking the 8 p.m. curfew, although they were arrested at 4 p.m. See Butz's "Arrest/Booking Report," Kent, Ohio, City Police, in the Butz file in box 77, M4C.

17. Alewitz interview. Kirsch and Mike York wrote a front-page article for May 15, 1970 issue of *The Militant,* copy in box 172A, M4C. See also Fred Halstead, *Out Now! A Participant's Account of the American Movement against the Vietnam War* (New York: Monad, 1978), 538. Whitaker interview.

18. "Student protest swept . . .": Tom Wells, *The War Within: America's Battle over Vietnam* (Berkeley: University of California Press, 1994), 425. Judy Gollust King to the author, Feb. 20, 2006; George Katsiaficas, *The Imagination of the New Left: A Global Analysis of 1968* (Boston: South End Press, 1987), 118–19; Kirkpatrick Sale, *SDS* (New York: Vintage, 1973), 637.

19. Buhl and Inglee interviews. Judy Gollust King provided the information about Bresnahan's involvement in the planning for the May 9 protest in Washington.

20. Protest at Oberlin and the housing of KSU students there: "Campuses Here Are Shut for Anti-War Activities," *CP,* May 6, 1970; "200 Students Plan 'Kent State in Exile' at Oberlin College," *WP,* May 10, 1970. Protest at Ohio State: "Violence Level Reduced as OSU Is Calmed," *RC,* May 1, 1970; "Demonstrations at Ohio State," *Guardian,* May 16. Protest meetings at Kenyon: Donald L. Rogan, "Revisiting Kenyon in a Time of National Crisis: Vietnam and the Shootings at Kent State," (Kenyon) *Collegian,* Winter 2004, 48–53.

21. On Bowling Green, John Carroll, Cleveland State, and Case Western: Sale, *SDS,* 637; and Katsiaficas, *Imagination of the New Left,* 123. Arson at John Carroll and Case Western: "2 ROTC Fires Reported Here," *CP,* May 7, 1970. Cleveland march: "4,000 at CWRU Honor Dead at Kent," *CP,* May 5, Tabasko, Walsh, Thompson, Gregorich, and Pekar interviews; conversation with Havens.

22. Events at Miami University: Sale, *SDS,* 637. On Ohio University: "Millions Protest against Cambodia Invasion throughout U.S.," *Guardian,* May 23, 1970. On Cincinnati: "Cincy Students Block Traffic; 145 Arrested," *CP,* May 2, 1970; and "Ohio College Students Protest in Columbus," *CP,* May 8. On Rhodes: Joe Eszterhas and Michael D. Roberts, *Thirteen Seconds: Confrontation at Kent State* (New York: Dodd, Mead, 1970), 141 (first quotation); Michener, *Kent State,* 253.

23. Judy Gollust King to the author, Feb. 20, 2006. Kissinger quoted in Wells, *The War Within,* 430. Persky and Alewitz interviews; conversation with Rick Felber. KSU students at the protest: "200 Students Plan 'Kent State in Exile.'"

24. For the tensions, which led to a split in the New MOBE and the end of the VMC, see Wells, *The War Within,* 409, 437–46. "200 Students Plan 'Kent State in Exile.'"

25. Events at Washington University and Mechanic's involvement and time underground: "Many Campuses Display Anger," *CP,* May 5, 1970; "ROTC Hut Burned at Turbulent Time in History," *St. Louis Post-Dispatch,* Feb. 12, 2000; Lisa Belkin, "Doesn't Anybody Know How to Be a Fugitive Anymore?," *NYT Sunday Magazine,* April 30, 2000; "Howard's End?," *Phoenix New Times,* Feb. 24, 2000. Mechanic was convicted of throwing a cherry bomb, although there were no witnesses.

26. Jeffrey Powell, "The Storm" (unpublished memoir). For one example of the interest in Powell and the SDS leaders, see the report by Sgt. D. D. Sumrok, Ohio Highway Patrol, June 5, 1970, box 107, folder 27, M4C.

27. Tim Spofford, *Lynch Street: The May 1970 Slayings at Jackson State College* (Kent: Kent State University Press, 1988), 18–32, quotation on 31.

28. Ibid, 53–79.

29. Ibid., 78–79. A photo of Young with Mrs. Fannie Chaney and CORE leader Dave Dennis, taken a CORE meeting in Kansas City, MO, appeared in *Muhammad Speaks,* July 31, 1964, not long before the bodies of Chaney and his two companions were found buried in an earthen dam in Mississippi.

30. Barbara Brock and Wittmaack interviews; Sale, *SDS,* 637. For UNC and the California campuses, see "Millions Protest against Cambodia," *Guardian,* May 23, 1970; and the photos that accompany "The Rebellion of the Campus," *Newsweek,* May 18, 1970. On the issue of race and the responses to the Kent and Jackson State shootings, see Tom Grace, "Address Delivered at Kent State, May 4, 1987," in *Kent and Jackson State, 1970–1990,* ed. Susie Erenrich, special issue, *Vietnam Generation* 2.2 (1990): 26–31. Closing of California campuses: "Here Are Colleges Facing Protests," *CP,* May 7, 1970.

31. University of Nevada protests: Brad E. Lucas, *Radicals, Rhetoric, and the War: The University of Nevada in the Wake of Kent State* (New York: Palgrave Macmillan, 2006), 106–9. University of Texas: Doug Rossinow, *The Politics of Authenticity: Liberalism, Christianity, and the New Left in America* (New York: Columbia University Press, 1998), 238; Alewitz interview.

32. *Report of the President's Commission on Campus Unrest* (Washington, DC: GPO, 1970), 1. Columbia University president William McGill quoted in William Leuchtenburg, *A Troubled Feast: American Society since 1945* (1979; Glenview, IL: Addison-Wesley, 1983), 245.

33. See the following in *NYT*: "Analysts: Tough Year at the Plate," Sept. 7, 1969; "Bear Market Hits August '63 Level," May 6, 1970; "Nixon Policy Found Tied to Stock Drop," May 11; "Big Board Prices Drop Once More" (quotation) and "AMEX Prices Slip," May 13. Stocks recovered from the sharp downturn later in the year.

34. Among the many sources on the construction workers' riot, see Penny Lewis, *Hardhats, Hippies, and Hawks: The Vietnam Antiwar Movement as Myth and Memory* (Ithaca, NY: ILR Press, 2013), 159–85; Jefferson Cowie, *Stayin' Alive: The 1970s and the Last Days of the Working Class* (New York: New Press, 2012), 135–36; James T. Patterson, *Grand Expectations: The United States, 1945–1974* (New York: Oxford University Press, 1996), 755–56; and William H. Chafe, *The Unfinished Journey: America since World War II* (1991; New York: Oxford University Press, 2010), 414. The organizer of the melee, construction union head Peter Brennan, was rewarded with a White House luncheon and was later named Nixon's Secretary of Labor. See Wells, *The War Within,* 447; and Peter Levy, *The New Left and Labor in the 1960s* (Urbana: University of Illinois Press, 1994), 1–3. The Ohio construction strike: *RC,* May 1. Extended Teamster wildcat strike and the expansion of the rubber strike: "Teamsters Shut Six Terminals," *BJ,* May 5, 1970; "BFG Struck; 4,520 Idled in Akron," *BJ,* May 7.

35. On the Akron Teamster, see "Concern about Economy Grows among Workers," *NYT,* Oct. 29, 1970. When his fellow miners learned that Greg Hawthorne was a Kent State

student later that spring, he found the issue of Guard deployment against the Teamsters the best way to create an understanding of the campus antiwar position. "The slaughter of four students . . .": James Watt, CAP Director of Michigan's UAW, quoted in "Labor," *Burning River News* 1.6 (May 13–27, 1970); the same article also includes criticism of the war by Gus Scholle, president of the state's AFL-CIO. On the Cleveland AFL-CIO and labor participation in the New York antiwar protest, see "Labor Movement Begins to Act on Indochina War" and "N.Y. Workers, Students Demand Peace," *Guardian,* May 30, 1970. David Livingston of the Retail Clerks quoted in "Speakers Denounce Rhetoric," *WP,* May 10. On Meany's well-known backing of the war, see Nancy Zaroulis and Gerald Sullivan, *Who Spoke Up? American Protest against the War in Vietnam, 1963–1975* (New York: Holt, Rinehart and Winston, 1984), 333. Feinglass quoted in "Unions Differ on Indochina War," *NYT,* May 13, 1970. For the complete text of Reuther's telegram to Nixon, see *America in the Sixties—Right, Left, and Center: A Documentary History,* ed. Peter B. Levy (Westport, Ct: Greenwood Press, 1998), 166.

36. W. J. Rorabaugh, *Berkeley at War: The 1960s* (New York: Oxford University Press, 1989), 169–70; Milton Viorst, *Fire in the Streets: America in the 1960's* (New York: Simon and Schuster, 1979), 543. For a more nuanced view, see Maurice Isserman and Michael Kazin, *America Divided: The Civil War of the 1960s* (New York: Oxford University Press, 2000), 261–71. Amey Kirkbride, oral history, May 1, 1990, Kent State Shootings Oral Histories Collection, M4C.

37. Closing and eventual reopening of KSU: James J. Best, "The Tragic Weekend of May 1–4, 1970," in Hensley and Lewis, *Kent State and May 4th,* 24, 28. "Motionless and quiet": "Hum of Jeeps Breaks Eerie Silence," *RC,* May 7, 1970; see also "Curfew in Kent Begins at 11p.m.," in the same issue. Guard pullout: Hensley, *Kent State Incident,* 74.

38. For brief descriptions of Lewis's and Cleary's wounds, see Joseph Kelner and James Munves, *The Kent State Coverup* (New York: Harper and Row, 1980), 92–94, 116.

39. Louis Schroeder's job loss: Kelner and Munves, *Kent State Coverup,* 195. On Sandy Scheuer, author's conversations with the family. On Krause: Doris Krause and Barry Levine, "Allison's Story," in Jeff Kisseloff, *Generation on Fire: Voices of Protest from the 1960s, An Oral History* (Lexington: University Press of Kentucky, 2007), 244–65.

40. "L.I. Town Mourns a Kent State Victim," *NYT,* May 7, 1970; Eszterhas and Roberts, *Thirteen Seconds* (New York: Dodd, Mead, 1970), 272–75. For a photo of mourners at Miller's funeral, see Mitchell Goodman, *The Movement toward a New America: The Beginnings of a Long Revolution* (Philadelphia: Pilgrim Press, 1970), 524.

41. Amick and the petition campaign: "Petitions of Citizens Laud Guard, Police," *RC,* May 8, 1970; "Kent State Has Quiet Autumn, but Trouble Possible," *WP,* Feb. 21, 1971. The letters in the *RC* ran in the issues of May 7–9, 1970.

42. Riggs interview.

43. Ibid. John Lombardi, "A Lot of People Were Crying, and the Guard Walked Away," *Rolling Stone,* June 11, 1970, 6–8.

44. Pickett and Sharoff quoted in "Rhodes Shuns Hearing at KSU," *PD,* Aug. 20, 1970. For a list of the witnesses and commission members, see box 127A, folder 48, KSU Administrative Offices, Papers, 1968–77, KSUA.

45. White's remark had been quoted in an article in the *Cincinnati Enquirer,* Aug. 20, 1970; Mrs. Carol Sedgwick, a Cincinnati resident, wrote to White on Aug. 29 criticizing the statement. White's assistant Ronald Beer replied on his behalf on Sept. 10; the remaining quotations are from his letter. Box 127A, folder 49, KSU Administrative Offices Papers. Amick's testimony: "Rhodes Shuns Hearing," *PD,* Aug. 20, 1970.

46. "Dwight Armstrong, Who Bombed a College Building in 1970, Dies at 58," *NYT,* June 26, 2010.

47. Terry H. Anderson, *The Movement and the Sixties: Protest in America from Greensboro to Wounded Knee* (New York: Oxford University Press, 1995), 364–65.

48. *Report of the President's Commission,* 289–90.

49. "A Time to Remember May 4," *RC,* Sept. 29, 1970; see also "The Fifth Victim of Kent State," *Life,* Oct. 16, 1970, 42–43. The author also spoke at the service, held in KSU's Memorial Gym.

50. For the legislation, known as House Bill 1219, see "Bill 1219 Hits Hard, Disruptions Now a Crime," *DKS,* Oct. 1, 1970. Ford's role: Michener, *Kent State,* 527. Drug crackdown: "Kane Asks Record 135 Indictments," *RC,* Sept. 11, 1970. Police hires: "Beef-up of Kent Police Force Due" and "University to Get Tough, Kent City Officials Told" (White quotation), *RC,* Sept. 17, 1970.

51. Although this panel is commonly referred to as a Portage County grand jury, it was technically a state grand jury convened in the county. For a list of those testifying, see "Jurors Tour May 4 Shooting Scene," *RC,* Sept. 14, 1970. Indictees are listed in "Kent Twenty-five," *The Burr,* May 4, 2000, 37–46. Morgan's background: "Craig's Father Says Son, Students Are Persecuted," *RC,* Oct. 20, 1970. For the guardsmen, see Thomas R. Hensley, "The May 4th Trials," in Hensley and Lewis, *Kent State and May 4th,* 69–70; and "25 Indicted; Guardsmen Absolved," *RC,* Oct. 16, 1970.

52. *RC* editorial: "Jury's Awesome Task," Oct. 9, 1970. For the text of the Portage County grand jury report, see I. F. Stone, *The Killings at Kent State: How Murder Went Unpunished* (New York: New York Review Books, 1971), 145–58. Pigott quoted in Diane K. Shah, "A Year Later at Kent State . . . People Are Still Running Scared," *National Observer,* April 26, 1971. Prohibition of protest and comment: "Jones Bans Courthouse Protest," *RC,* Oct. 14, 1970. For the reaction to Ford's remarks, see the following in *RC:* "Bar Wants Ford and Frank Charged," "Ford's Resignation Asked—By KSU Faculty Senate President Nurmi," and "Ford Off Track" (editorial), Oct. 26, 1970; and "Say Ford Ousted as Grand Jury Counsel," Oct. 28.

53. "Yippies, KLF: 'Come Together,'" *DKS,* Oct. 8, 1970.

54. Yippie Jerry Persky was one of those carrying a toothbrush. For the sign, see "Arthrell: 'Pawns'—In a Tranquil Place," *DKS,* Oct. 28, 1970.

55. See the following in *RC:* "Kunstler to Students—'Stand United or Fall One-by-One,'" Oct. 20, 1970; "Needs Judges' Permission," Oct. 23; "KSU Cases Should Be Argued in the Courts" (editorial), Oct. 22. For *DKS* coverage, see "Morgan: Kunstler Coming," Oct. 19, 1970; "Kunstler: 'Cling Together, Unite,'" Oct. 20; and (on the fundraising) "Student Defense Fund Collects $200 for Students' Legal Fees," Oct. 22. Sale of T-shirts: "Defense Fund Plans Benefit Concert," *DKS,* Oct. 23. The author has one in his possession.

56. See the following in *DKS:* "KSU Veterans Against the War Held Guerrilla Theater to Dramatize 'the Horrors of War'" (photo story), Oct. 16, 1970; "Yippies' Rally Friday" (first rally) and "Morgan: Kunstler Coming," Oct. 19; "Doctor White Rejects Yippie Demands," Oct. 20; "Morgan Calls for National Moratorium," Oct. 21 (second rally and Butz quote); "I. F. Stone Asks: 'No First Amendment Here?,'" Oct. 27; "4,000 Students" (photo story), Nov. 3 (Columbus rally). Alewitz interview.

57. See the following in *DKS:* "White Cancels Black Homecoming," Oct. 14, 1970; "Bomb Shatters Black Calm," Oct. 27; "BUS Leader Asks—Who Did It?," Oct. 29; "Bomb Scares Increase," Nov. 10.

58. Dissent among servicemen in Vietnam: H. Bruce Franklin, *Vietnam and Other American Fantasies* (Amherst: University of Massachusetts Press, 2000), 59–70. Growth of VVAW and Musgrave's involvement: Gerald Nicosia, *Home to War: A History of the Vietnam Veterans' Movement* (New York: Crown, 2001), 52–53 (Ehrhart quote), 292 (Musgrave quote), 542. For more on how Kent State affected Vietnam veterans, see W. D. Ehrhart, *Passing Time: Memoir of a Vietnam Veteran Against the War* (Amherst: University of Massachusetts Press, 1986), 85–97. On the growth of VVAW and on Butz, see Andrew E. Hunt, *The Turning: A History of Vietnam Veterans Against the War* (New York: New York University Press, 1999), 32, 41–45, 54. Spencer interview; see also Spencer's letter, "Does History Repeat Itself?," *RC,* Oct. 3, 1970; and "Veterans Against War Speak Out," *DKS,* Oct. 15, 1970.

59. The Keep Kent Open campaign and pressure from conservatives: "Petitions Start Campus Tour Again," *DKS,* Oct. 28, 1970; and "Dr. White's Mail Is 'Frightening,'" *DKS,* Nov. 5. The Power to the Peaceful campaign: *The Phoenix: Newsletter of Non-Violent Revolution* (published by a group of KSU students), Sept. 28, 1970, box 82, folder 10, M4C; "Baez, Sandperl Plan Lectures," *DKS,* Oct. 28, 1970; "Two Extend 'Think Week' Nonviolence Theme," *DKS,* Nov. 10.

60. Original copies of White's letter, "Dear Parents," Oct. 20, 1970, and memo, "Restatement of University Policy," Oct. 19, in the author's possession. Stepp's response appeared in the *DKS,* Oct. 27, 1970. See also "White: KSU Situation Volatile," *RC,* Oct. 15, 1970.

61. See the following in *DKS:* "Dragnet Total: 18; Arrests Continue," Oct. 27, 1970; "Tolliver's 'Save America in Spite of Itself,'" Nov. 10; "Blood, Sweat & Tears Remembers Kent State, Do You?" (advertisement), Nov. 11; "Performs Cleveland Concert for LDF," Nov. 17; David Ifshin is mentioned in "Dubis Explains Legal Defense Fund," Nov. 17, and "Syracuse Donates $2,546 to Defense," Nov. 20. The author served on the KLDF board of trustees and recalls opening the envelope containing Spock's check.

62. Whitaker interview; "Ayres' Attack Reflects Tight Race," *BJ,* Nov. 1, 1970; advertisement, *BJ,* Nov. 2. For more on Ayres, see Tom Diemer, "Ohio in Washington: The Congressional Delegation," in Lamis and Sharkey, *Ohio Politics,* 209.

63. On Gilligan: Christian G. Appy, *Patriots: The Vietnam War Remembered from All Sides* (New York: Viking, 2003), 309–13. The law and order campaign: Clark Dougan and Samuel Lipsman, *The Vietnam Experience: A Nation Divided* (Boston: Boston Publishing, 1984), 158–59. Gilligan's time in Kent, Nixon's campaign incident, and the critical editorial: "Warns of Dem Overconfidence, Gilligan Speaks in Kent," *RC,* Oct. 29, 1970; "Nixon Hits 'Radicals' Who Attacked Car," *RC,* Oct. 30; "Worst in America," *RC,* Oct. 31. On Nixon's

commercials, see Rick Perlstein, *Nixonland: The Rise of a President and the Fracturing of America* (New York: Scribner, 2008), 534–35.

14. Carry On

1. See the following in *DKS*: "Persky, Alter Appeal Sentences," Jan. 12, 1971; "No Plea Date Set for Ruth Gibson," Jan. 19; "Blount, May Found Innocent," Jan. 20; "Judge Rules Jury Report Invalid," Jan. 29. The judge, William K. Thomas, ordered the report to be destroyed. Thomas R. Hensley, *The Kent State Incident: Impact of Judicial Process on Public Attitudes* (Westport, CT: Greenwood Press, 1981), 98.

2. On Laos, see Bruce Palmer Jr., *The 25-Year War: America's Military Role in Vietnam* (Lexington: University Press of Kentucky, 1984), 106–15.

3. "Protesting Laotian Attack, Coalition Calls for Noon Rally," *DKS*, Feb. 5, 1971; "Teach-in Committee Sponsors Peace Week," *DKS*, Feb. 9. The author accompanied Emmer to Ann Arbor. The People's Peace Treaty and the size of the Laotian protests: Nancy Zaroulis and Gerald Sullivan, *Who Spoke Up? American Protest against the War in Vietnam, 1963–1975* (New York: Holt, Rinehart and Winston, 1984), 344–47.

4. Internal debate over Laos, press coverage of the invasion, and its generally dismal results: Palmer, *The 25-Year War*, 105–14; William M. Hammond, *Reporting Vietnam: Media and Military at War* (Lawrence: University Press of Kansas, 1998), 235–48. National polling: Charles DeBenedetti with Charles Chatfield, *An American Ordeal: The Antiwar Movement of the Vietnam Era* (Syracuse: Syracuse University Press, 1990), 298–99.

5. Stuart Taylor, Richard Shuntich, Patrick McGovern, and Robert Genther, *Violence at Kent State, May 1 to 4, 1970: The Students' Perspective* (New York: College Notes and Texts, 1971), 103, 141, 153.

6. "Froines Urges D.C. Close-down" and "Ask Support for People's Peace Treaty— Seattle 8 Members Discuss Their Trial," *DKS*, Feb. 11, 1971. For a sketch of Nancy Kurshan, see "May Day Coalition Activist," *DKS*, April 22, 1971.

7. The People's Coalition for Peace and Justice arose from the New Mobilization Committee to End the War in Vietnam, which had collapsed after the May 1970 protest in Washington, DC. The PCPJ won the allegiance of most of the radical antiwar leaders not associated with the Trotskyist National Peace Action Coalition. See Tom Wells, *The War Within: America's Battle over Vietnam* (Berkeley: University of California Press, 1994), 471–73. University of Kansas killings: Rusty L. Monhollon, *"This Is America?": The Sixties in Lawrence, Kansas* (New York: Palgrave, 2004), 1–2, 213.

8. See the following in *DKS*: "Police Charge Two BUS members," Feb. 5, 1971; "Blount Blasts 'Repression,'" Feb. 11; "200 Students March in Snow to White's House" (photo story), Feb. 12; "Demonstrators Protest Stater Editorial," Feb. 16; "Stater Follows 'Racist' Policy in Black Coverage" (letter), Feb. 18; "Pres. White Retires" (photo story), Feb. 19; "BUS Defense Fund Raising More Money," Feb. 25.

9. William H. Hildebrand, Dean H. Keller, and Anita D. Herington, *A Book of Memories: Kent State University, 1910–1992* (Kent: Kent State University Press, 1993), 12, 186.

10. "War Debate Ends in Disagreement," *DKS*, Feb. 23, 1971; "Audience Mocks Presidential Aide," *DKS*, Feb. 25. The author was present for Buchanan's talk.

11. On Olds, see Scott L. Bills, ed., *Kent State/May 4: Echoes through a Decade* (1982; Kent: Kent State University Press, 1988), 48–49, 191–93; the campaign slogan as well as some of the biographical information is taken from Olds's 1986 US Senate campaign brochure, copy in the author's possession. Persky quoted in "Kent State Escapes Violence," *WP,* Feb. 16, 1971.

12. "Women March on Pentagon," *DKS,* April 16, 1971; "Spring Sprouts Antiwar Activities" and "May Day Coalition Plans Announced," *DKS,* April 20. Gologorsky quoted in Christian G. Appy, *Patriots: The Vietnam War Remembered from All Sides* (New York: Viking, 2003), 413–17. Size of the crowd and I. F. Stone's observation: Zaroulis and Sullivan, *Who Spoke Up?,* 358–59. The author participated in the April 24 march and had friends who attended the Women's March.

13. See the following in *DKS:* "Butz, Vets Group Offer Spring Plans," April 14, 1971; "Anti-War Vets Plan D.C. Rally" and "Spring Sprouts Antiwar Activities," April 20; "GI Planned to Lead Protests, but Lost Life in Cambodia," April 27.

14. "Mayday! 1971: The Government's Worst Nightmare," *Guardian,* May 22, 1991. Nixon quoted in Rick Perlstein, *Nixonland: The Rise of a President and the Fracturing of America* (New York: Scribner, 2008), 565 The author coordinated work on the Kent campus with that of the volunteer staff of the Mayday Collective.

15. "7,000 Arrested," *WP,* May 4, 1971; "Traffic Normal, Jails Full," *Washington (DC) Evening Star,* May 4, 1971. I relied on my own recollection for Kent's participants. Steve Lieber, in a conversation with the author, recalled his participation as well as Jim Russell's. All of the targets are listed in the Mayday manual, copy in the author's possession. See also "Student Views Washington May Day," *DKS,* May 12, 1971. "They were zipping back and forth . . .": David McReynolds quoted in Wells, *The War Within,* 500.

16. The student jailed with Spock and the survey: "May Day Protestors—Who Were They?," *BJ,* May 23, 1971. The paper interviewed 168 of those taken into custody. Motorists inconvenienced by the protest: Haynes Johnson, "Protestors Irk Citizens," *WP,* May 4, 1971.

17. See the following in *DKS:* "Coalition Protests May 4 Plans," April 2, 1971; "Makes Third Change—Gov. Cancels Guard," April 23; "Coalition Rally Develops into Sit-in," May 5; see also Robert C. Dix, "Along the Way," *RC,* May 3, 1971. "If they call in the Guard . . .": quoted in Diane K. Shah, "A Year Later at Kent State . . . People Are Still Running Scared," *National Observer,* April 26, 1971; the same student added, "I've seen half a dozen guns in students' rooms."

18. *RC* coverage of the protest includes: "Police, Rain End Kent Disturbance" and "Brock Found Guilty," May 20, 1971; "64 Arrested in Police Sweep of Kent," May 21; "Police Disperse Kent Crowd" and "Howie Emmer Arrested," May 22; "A Dangerous Game" (editorial), May 24. *DKS* coverage: "Police Sweep" and "Questions" (editorial), May 25, 1971. *DKS* editors questioned both the rationale for the disorders and the police beating of a KSU professor. The Vietnam battle: "The Bloody Attack on Fire Base Mary Ann," *Newsweek,* April 12, 1971, 45.

19. "SDS Schedules March," *DKS,* May 26, 1971; Johnson interview; Joe Hill Collective flyers, in the author's possession.

20. "Former Chief Reveals Agents Were at KSU—Undercover Work Began in 1966," *DKS*, May 14, 1971. Schwartzmiller's reasons for disclosing the information are not known, but he was unhappy with his dismissal. Olds and the undercover police issue in October 1971: D. Ray Heisey, "Sensitivity to an Image," in Bills, *Kent State / May 4*, 192.

21. "Fyke New KSU Security Chief," *RC*, Dec. 31, 1970. Fyke had been associated with KSU's Law Enforcement School since 1969. Quotations are from the report of the hiring subcommittee (part of the larger Kegley Commission), box 11, M4C.

22. Among the extensive coverage of the Kent 25 trials, see *DKS*, Sept. 27–Dec. 7, 1971, and *RC*, Nov. 23–Dec. 8, 1971. "Rejoice!" (editorial), *DKS*, Dec. 8, 1971. The author recalls the opposition to the federal grand jury.

23. "Antiwar Rally Set for Saturday," *DKS*, Nov. 5, 1971; coverage of the protest: "Hecklers, Weather Combine to Put Blemish on Peace Rally," *PD*, Nov. 7. See also Zaroulis and Sullivan, *Who Spoke Up?*, 371–72; and Wells, *The War Within*, 528–29. The author participated in the Cleveland march. Gologorsky quoted in Appy, *Patriots*, 415.

24. Johnson interview. Beginning in Feb. 1972, Johnson authored a five-part series in the campus newspaper about his trip; see, for example, "Nixon's China Visit Major Feat?," *DKS*, Feb. 8, 1972. JHC position statement, copy in the author's possession. On Martinot see Leigh David Benin, *The New Labor Radicalism and New York City's Garment Industry: Progressive Labor Insurgents in the 1960s* (New York: Garland, 2000), 102–6, 126–30.

25. Campus undercover agents: "Former Chief Reveals Agents Were at KSU," *DKS*, May 14, 1971; "Police 'Saturated' '71 Demonstrations," *DKS*, April 7, 1972. "In an undercover capacity . . .": Mohr's statement, April 28, 1972, box 80, folder 32, M4C (in the statement he mistakenly gives his date of hire as Aug. 18, 1972).

26. Extensive coverage of Mohr's arrest ran in both *DKS* and *RC*, April 25–Oct. 17, 1972. See in particular "Fyke Slams Weapons Exposure," *RC*, April 26, 1972; and "Olds: No Further Police Surveillance," *DKS*, May 2. For a detailed account, see Ted Joy, "Espionage at Kent State: 'Quite Legal, Quite Ethical,'" *The Nation*, Jan. 29, 1973, 144–48. For Mohr's version, see "Ron Mohr's Roommate Explains," *DKS*, June 1, 1972. According to Mohr's own statement, he advised his "supervisor, Commander [Robert] Winkler, [that] . . . I had purchased the weapons. He instructed me to retain them pending further orders."

27. "Nixon at War," *Time* (cover story), May 1, 1972; "1,500 Protest Vietnam Step-up," *DKS*, April 27, 1972; "Police Move 800 Back onto Campus—Protesters Block Traffic," *DKS*, April 28; "Court Bans Further Disruption at KSU," *RC*, April 27; "129 Arrested at Kent State," *BJ*, April 27. JHC radicals were caught off guard by the some of the Yippies' impulsive actions, which included the occupation of the ROTC building; see Steve Martinot, "Some Questions Concerning Party Organization," *New Marxist Forum: A Journal of Debate and Theory for Marxist-Leninists*, no. 1 (Jan. 1973), copy in the author's possession.

28. See the following in *RC*: "3,000 March in KSU Vigil," May 4, 1972; "Police Disperse KSU Demonstrators," May 10 (describing the wooden bullets as "more than an inch around and a half-inch thick"); "Olds Says He'll Use Riot Bill," May 11 (Olds quote) and "Police Disperse Protesters in Kent," May 12; "13 Arraigned after ROTC Disruptions," May 19. "Memorial March" (photo story), *BJ*, May 5, 1972; "Students, Police Clash at KSU," *BJ*, May 10. The author relied on his own memory of the perilous situation during the ROTC

review and the attempted sabotage of the activist's car. Posters depicting Fyke as a storm trooper, in the author's possession See also Kenneth J. Heineman, *Campus Wars: The Peace Movement at American State Universities in the Vietnam Era* (New York: New York University Press, 1993), 255. The surveillance resulted in an ACLU suit, *VVAW v. Fyke.*

29. Opinion polls: Jeffrey Kimball, *Nixon's Vietnam War* (Lawrence: University Press of Kansas, 1998), 316.

30. "KSU Danger Point" (editorial), *RC,* April 27, 1972; "He's Not Ending War" (editorial), *RC,* April 28.

31. See the following in *DKS:* "Move ROTC Facilities," May 2, 1972; "5 Min. for Peace" (editorial) and "11th hour Campaign Evolves from Rally," May 11; "11th Hour Plan Draws Wide Eyes," "From Townspeople: 11th Hour Drive Gets Weak Reply," and "'11th Hour' Goes Door-to-Door," May 12; "11th Hour Vigil Gets Mixed Support," May 16. See also "National Involvement in '11th hour' Is Urged," *RC,* May 11.

32. "Vandals Spraypaint KSU, City," *KSU Summer News,* Aug. 10, 1972; "Estimate 2,600 to Register Tues.," *DKS,* Oct. 5, 1972.

33. See the following in *DKS:* "Ellsberg: U.S. Too Used to Lies," Oct. 5, 1972; "McGovern Wins in DKS Poll," Oct. 11; "Calls Nixon 'War Criminal,'" Oct. 25. A later poll of students showed 75 percent for McGovern and just 15 percent for Nixon.

34. "54,000 Registered in Portage Co.," *DKS,* Oct. 11, 1972; and "Final Tallies of Election Listed," *DKS,* Nov. 9. McGovern carried only two of the state's eighty-eight counties, the worst Democratic showing since 1956.

35. Coverage of the array of political issues ran in the *DKS,* Aug. 10–Sept. 28, 1972; for mention of those named, *DKS,* Oct. 18 and 19. On Cox's film: "Lack of Administrators at Film Appalling—[Paul] Keane," *DKS,* Oct. 31, 1972. Southern University killings: "KSU Reaction to S.U. Shooting," *DKS,* Nov. 21, 1972. On Mohr: "Mohr Reinstated; Olds Criticized," *DKS,* Oct. 17, 1972.

36. The Christmas bombings: Kimball, *Nixon's Vietnam War,* 364–66. "Human Life Supreme" (letter by Harvey Chase), *DKS,* Jan. 5, 1973.

37. On the POW issue, see H. Bruce Franklin, *M.I.A. or Mythmaking in America: How and Why Belief in Live POWs Has Possessed a Nation* (New Brunswick: Rutgers University Press, 1992), 48–75. Thieu's reaction: Kimball, *Nixon's Vietnam War,* 366–68. "To accept our concessions": Daniel Davidson interview in Appy, *Patriots,* 463–65. For the judgment of one historian, see George Herring, *America's Longest War: The United States and Vietnam, 1950–1975,* 2nd ed. (Philadelphia: Temple University Press, 1986), 255.

38. Kraft's syndicated column, titled "Bitter Inaugural," ran locally in the *RC* on Jan. 21, 1973. The Jan. 20 protest: "Kent State Students Join Demonstration." *DKS,* Jan. 23, 1973. Morris's reaction to the peace accords: "Area Joyous over Viet War End," *RC,* Jan. 24, 1973. For the May 15, 1975, rescue, see Ralph Wetterhahn, *The Last Battle: The Mayaguez Incident and the End of the Vietnam War* (New York: Da Capo, 2001).

39. "Fyke Resigns as Police Head,'" *RC,* Jan. 20, 1973; Olds quoted in "Fyke Resigns; New Security Director Sought," *DKS,* Jan. 24. Departure of Olds: Bills, *Kent State/May 4,* 133, 193, 210.

40. "Remember Why They Protested" (letter), *DKS,* April 18, 1973.

41. Kissinger quoted in Maurice Isserman and Michael Kazin, *America Divided: The Civil War of the 1960s* (New York: Oxford University Press, 2000), 270.

42. The antiwar movement's effect on the conduct of the war will likely remain controversial. For all the attention to this, too little has been given to the staying power of the Vietnamese. On the debate over the use of force, Wilson Carey McWilliams contended that "violence has always troubled the liberal. . . . Violence is nothing new for the American poor; it is new for the intellectual and middle classes . . . because of . . . [the] violence which reaches the campus, penetrating 'our' [liberal] space in unexpected ways." McWilliams, "Has Liberalism Come Apart at the Seams?," *NYT,* June 22, 1969. On the thinking of the Yippies: letter from Jerry Persky, circa Oct. 1975, copy in the author's possession.

43. On Ashbrook, see Mary C. Brennan, *Turning Right in the Sixties: The Conservative Capture of the GOP* (Chapel Hill: University of North Carolina Press, 1995), 2, 37, 162n17, and passim. For links between the Old Right and the conservative ascendancy beyond the 1970s, see Kim Phillips-Fein, *Invisible Hands: The Making of the Conservative Movement from the New Deal to Reagan* (New York: Norton, 2009)

44. Savio quoted in *"Takin' It to the Streets": A Sixties Reader,* ed. Alexander Bloom and Wini Breines (New York: Oxford University Press, 1995), 111–12.

45. "The View from Kent State," *NYT,* May 11, 1970 (Glass quote) and Doug Vaughan, "The Ends of Repression," both in *The Middle of the Country: The Events of May 4th as Seen by Students and Faculty at Kent State University,* ed. Bill Warren (New York: Avon, 1970), 144, 147, 151."Hillbilly populist": Doug Vaughan to the author, Jan. 16, 2003; on Mexico City, Vaughan interview and subsequent conversation.

Epilogue: A Battlefield of Memory

1. "Struggle to Recovery," *Kent* magazine (KSU Office of Alumni Relations) 3.6 (June 1970): 4 (quotation), 13, 18, 22. For a fuller treatment of Kent State's memory wars, see Thomas M. Grace, "Kent State and Historical Memory," in *Democratic Narrative, History, and Memory,* ed. Carole A. Barbato and Laura L. Davis (Kent: Kent State University Press, 2012), 8–29.

2. "White Picks May 4 Committee" and "Police Nab Three 'for Flag Desecration,'" *DKS,* Feb. 11, 1971; "It happened to us all," ad signed by the President's May 4 Committee, *DKS,* March 5; Kenneth J. Heineman, *Campus Wars: The Peace Movement at American State Universities in the Vietnam Era* (New York: New York University Press, 1993), 37–39, 179, 248, and passim; "May 4 Subcommittee Seek Approval," *DKS,* April 9, 1971; and "Coalition Implementing Plans," *DKS,* April 16. White would also face suits by the families of those killed and wounded on May 4, 1970; see Joseph Kelner and James Munves, *The Kent State Coverup* (New York: Harper and Row, 1980), 15, 35, 62.

3. "The Candlelight Vigil," in *Kent State/May 4: Echoes through a Decade,* ed. Scott L. Bills (1982; Kent: Kent State University Press, 1988), 172–73; "Coalition Rally Develops into Sit-in," *DKS,* May 5, 1971; "Student Views Washington Mayday," *DKS,* May 12; "May Day Protestors—Who Were They?," *BJ,* May 23; conversations with Steve Lieber and Jim Russell.

4. "Days of Sorrow, Five Years Later," *Painesville (OH) Telegraph*, May 5, 1975; "Generation Ruined for Antiwar Beliefs," *BJ*, May 1, 1975 (second quotation).

5. Bills, introduction to *Kent State/May 4*, 34; Daniel St. Albin Greene, "When a World Collapsed—Kent State Wounded Tell Their Grim Story," *National Observer*, May 3, 1975 (quotation); "A Moment Kent State Won't Forget," *NYT*, May 3, 2010.

6. Thomas R. Hensley, "The May 4th Trials," in *Kent State and May 4th: A Social Science Perspective,* ed. Hensley and Jerry M. Lewis, 3rd ed. (Kent: Kent State University Press, 2010), 67, 71–76; "Judge Acquits Guardsmen in Slayings at Kent State," *NYT*, Nov. 9, 1974; for the author's response to the verdict see Thomas M. Grace, "The Kent State Ruling: Unanswered Questions" (letter), *NYT*, Nov. 17, 1974. For a shot of the guardsmen signing the photo see William A. Gordon, *The Fourth of May: Killings and Coverups at Kent State* (Buffalo, NY: Prometheus Books, 1990), photo gallery following 144.

7. Kelner and Munves, *Kent State Coverup*, 34–35; Hensley, "The May 4th Trials," 76–77.

8. Kelner and Munves, *Kent State Coverup*, 228–29; Hensley, "The May 4th Trials," 77–78.

9. The author relied on his personal collection of Rosen's remarks during a plaintiffs' meeting in Cleveland and the oral arguments for the appeal in the Sixth Circuit in Cincinnati, Ohio, on June 21, 1977. Months later, on Sept. 12, the court issued its decision in favor of a new trial.

10. For the text of the statement see Thomas R. Hensley, *The Kent State Incident: Impact of Judicial Process on Public Attitudes* (Westport, CT: Greenwood Press, 1981), 122–23; the signers are listed on a copy of the original in the author's possession. "A Late Apology," *Time*, Jan. 15, 1979.

11. For a photo of the jury standing next to the National Guard firing position at the Pagoda, see Hensley, "The Legal Aftermath," in Hensley and Lewis, *Kent State and May 4th*, 61; see also Hensley, "Kent State 1977: The Struggle to Move the Gym," in the same volume, 144–67.

12. Miriam R. Jackson, "Brothers and Sisters on the Land: Tent City, 1977," in *Kent and Jackson State, 1970–1990*, ed. Susie Erenrich, special issue, *Vietnam Generation* 2.2 (1990): 95–112; for the Cleveland newspaper quote, Alan Canfora, "The May 4 Memorial at Kent State University," in the same volume, 86. David Dix quoted in Hensley, "Kent State 1977," 151–52.

13. Hensley, "Kent State 1977," 150; for the headline, *PD*, March 5, 2001. "James A. Rhodes took a secret . . .": David Giffels, "A Talkative Man Seals a Three-Decade Silence," *BJ*, March 5, 2001. See also Keith McKnight, "James Rhodes Dies—Former Governor Was Loved and Hated," *BJ*, March 5, 2001; and Wolfgang Saxon, "James Rhodes, Ohio Governor Who Sent the National Guard to Kent State, Dies at 91" *NYT*, March 6.

14. "Kent State Protest Scene Nominated as Historic Site," *Columbus (OH) Dispatch*, Dec. 2, 2009; "A New Day Dawns: May 4 Visitors Center to Offer Diverse Perspectives," *Kent State Magazine* 9.2 (Spring 2010): 20–21; May 4 Visitors Center, National Historic Site Tour, May 4 Memorial brochure, May 4, 2010; "Four Decades Later, Kent State Turns a Page: New Center Memorializes 1970 Student Shootings," *Wall Street Journal*, Nov. 23, 2012; "May 4 Events at Kent State Remain Heavy with Emotion," *BJ*, May 5, 2014.

15. "A Curious Choice: What Criteria Did State Unit Use to Select Canfora for Bell Role?," *RC*, Aug. 11, 2003; "Canfora Out as Bicentennial Bell Ringer—Public Outcry Takes Toll on State Commission, Fair Board," *RC*, Aug. 12; "Canfora Won't Ring Bell—1970 KSU Protester Withdraws from Portage Bicentennial Ceremony," *BJ*, Aug. 14.

16. For a comprehensive summary of commemorative work, attempts to prove a Ohio National Guard order to fire, and the critics of these efforts, see Tom Hayden, "Closure at Kent State?," *The Nation*, online edition, May 15, 2013, www.thenation.com.

Appendix

1. Suzanne Gordon used the word "radicalize" to characterize goals of some young Marxists who moved "from campus to factory" in the 1970s, seeking to transform unions and workplaces. See her review of Kim Moody's *An Injury to All: The Decline of American Unionism*, in the *Guardian*, May 3, 1989.

Index